PROFESSIONAL PRACTICE FOR
INTERIOR DESIGNERS
IN THE GLOBAL MARKETPLACE

FAIRCHILD
BOOKS

PROFESSIONAL PRACTICE FOR
INTERIOR DESIGNERS
IN THE GLOBAL MARKETPLACE

Susan M. Winchip

PhD, LEED AP, IDEC, MIES

Professor Emerita
Illinois State University

Fairchild Books

New York

Also by the Author

Sustainable Design for Interior Environments, 2nd Edition © 2011

Fundamentals of Lighting, 2nd Edition © 2011

Visual Culture in the Built Environment: A Global Perspective,
1st Edition © 2010 (2010 ASID Joel Polsky Prize Award)

Designing a Quality Lighting Environment, 1st Edition © 2005

Executive Director & General Manager: Michael Schluter
Executive Editor: Olga T. Kontzias
Assistant Acquisitions Editor: Amanda Breccia
Senior Development Editor: Joseph Miranda
Assistant Development Editor: Laurie Gibson
Assistant Art Director: Sarah Silberg
Production Director: Ginger Hillman
Production Editor: Jessica Katz
Assistant Production Editor: Lauren Vlassenko
Ancillaries Editor: Amy Butler
Associate Director of Sales: Melanie Sankel
Copyeditor: Joanne Slike
Cover Design: Michael Miranda
Cover Art: © Nic Lehoux
Text Design: Tronvig Group
Page Layout: Precision Graphics
Photo Research: Kenneth Cavanagh

Illustrations: Vanessa Han

Library of Congress Catalog Card Number: 2012930178
ISBN: 978-1-60901-138-3
GST R 133004424

TP09 CH16

Contents

Part III

Part IV

Appendices

Extended Contents

Preface

*Today, interior designers working across the globe are focused on a diversity of design values for clients: addressing needs, designing for operational payback, and creating a new and evolving sustainable aesthetic. We are resetting our profession with interior design actions that engage culture, values, experiences, metrics, functional disciplines, and more. We are establishing a **new** interior design profession to meet the desires and needs of our future. This crossroads in the profession's development requires truth-searching! We must expand our design response to be ahead of the game, to lead and respond to future demands, to be technically sophisticated, to create the experiences that our clients need for success, and to be the design consultant that the client and the world's societies respect for the value we bring.*

Eva L. Maddox, FIIDA, Assoc. AIA, LEED AP
Design Principal, Perkins + Will / Eva Maddox *Branded Environments*
Cofounder *Archworks*

Eva Maddox eloquently summarizes expectations of interior designers in today's global context and calls attention to the profession's "crossroads": "We are establishing a new interior design profession to meet the desires and needs of our future."

The essence of Ms. Maddox's declaration—originally written for the Foreword in *The State of the Interior Design Profession*—is reflected in this *new* book on the topic of professional practice for interior designers. A "new interior design profession" requires understanding the *new* approach to professional practice:

* An approach that addresses "interior designers working across the globe"

* An approach that focuses on "values for clients," "operational payback," and "sustainable aesthetics"

* An approach that "engages culture, values, experiences, metrics, and functional disciplines"

* An approach that demonstrates how to "lead and respond to future demands"

* An approach that explains how to "create the experiences that our clients need for success"

* An approach that explores how to "be the design consultant that the client and the world's societies respect for the value we bring"

Professional Practice for Interior Designers in a Global Marketplace is the *new* book for understanding the *new* approach to professional practice for interior designers by incorporating content that reflects profound changes in the profession over the past 30 to 40 years as well as addressing the unique learning expectations of students born in the Millennial Generation (1981–2000).

A major *new* approach in the book that is reflective of the practices of the Millennial Generation is the sequence of the learning process. The book begins by reviewing what students and entry-level professionals need to know to launch their careers as practicing interior designers (Figure P.1) rather than using the traditional approach that begins with starting an interior design business.

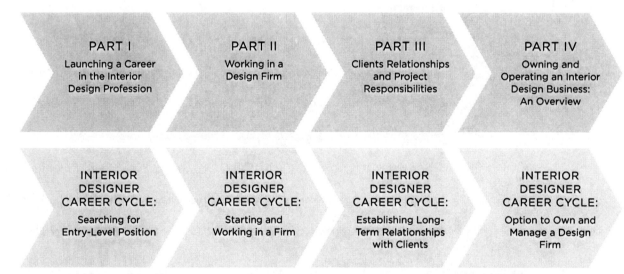

PART I
Launching a Career in the Interior Design Profession

PART II
Working in a Design Firm

PART III
Clients Relationships and Project Responsibilities

PART IV
Owning and Operating an Interior Design Business: An Overview

INTERIOR DESIGNER CAREER CYCLE:
Searching for Entry-Level Position

INTERIOR DESIGNER CAREER CYCLE:
Starting and Working in a Firm

INTERIOR DESIGNER CAREER CYCLE:
Establishing Long-Term Relationships with Clients

INTERIOR DESIGNER CAREER CYCLE:
Option to Own and Manage a Design Firm

Figure P.1. The graphics illustrate the sequence of topics in the book and how the order reflects the typical career cycle of an interior designer. The topical sequence graphic also demonstrates the cumulative effect of the book's organizational structure—Part I is the background for Part II. Parts I and II are the foundation for Part III and the first three Parts serve as the base for Part IV.

Thus, the reader first understands how to launch a career in the interior design profession followed by information that is important to know when working in a design firm, including building long-term client relationships and project management responsibilities. The last Part in the book provides the overview of essential topics related to owning and operating an interior design business.

Most of the content in the book focuses on professional practice material that is important to know when you are working as an interior designer. Less emphasis is devoted to professional practice information related to owning a small business. Why?

The primary reason for this *new* approach to a professional practice book is to help students and entry-level professionals to first become amazingly successful interior designers. Once a designer is successful, then it is relatively easy to start his or her own design firm. Therefore, *Part IV Owning and Operating an Interior Design Business: An Overview* can be used as a thinking platform for determining whether or not to start a new business—information that is useful for exploratory discussions with various professionals, including attorneys and accountants.

Outlining professional practice in a natural order of a career life cycle is just one of the book's approaches to understanding the *new* interior design profession. As illustrated in Box P.1, the book reviews contemporary topics that are critical to the work of today's interior designer, such as globalization, value-added premises, sustainability, multidisciplinary collaboration, consensus building, workplace etiquette, multiple generations, and social responsibilities.

However, within the context of current issues the book still explains traditional topics associated with professional practice, including types of design firms, job searches, project compensation/fees, business formations, and human resources (Box P.1).

Yet the book has a *new* approach to even the traditional topics by explaining the material within the context of contemporary business practices, such as using social media in the workplace, charrettes, virtual teamwork, and intercultural business communication styles/protocols, and seeking LEED (Leadership in Energy and Environmental Design) certification.

Contemporary and traditional topics merge to emphasize the major theme of the book—*building client relationships*. As noted by Ms. Maddox, interior designers "create the experiences that our clients need for success, and to be the design consultant that the client and the world's societies respect for the value we bring."

Throughout the book there are examples of how designers can "create the experiences that our clients need for success." Explanations begin with *Part II Working in a Design Firm* and continue to the end of the book. Highlights include understanding intercultural relationships (Chapter 5), building long-term client relationships (Chapter 7), client and project management strategies for the phases of the design process (Chapters 8 and 9), operating and managing a green interior design business (Chapter 11), strategic planning (Chapter12), marketing (Chapter 13) and human resources (Chapter 14).

The premise for this theme is that building long-term client relationships is imperative to the success of an interior designer. A successful designer can hire attorneys, accountants, insurance brokers, and managers to assist with business and legal responsibilities. However, a designer cannot hire someone to take care of client relationships. Thus, to be successful, the designer absolutely must build long-term client relationships while maintaining sound business practices.

The ability to build long-term relationships is a skill that, obviously, can be adapted to a variety of professions. Understanding how to develop adaptable professional skills is another *new* approach that is incorporated in the book. There was a time when interior designers fundamentally had one a career option: *Own your own business*. Naturally, the option still exists, but today there are many more opportunities for interior designers as well as design firms.

Overview of Contemporary and Traditional Professional Practice Topics Covered in Book

Contemporary Professional Practice Topics	Traditional Professional Practice Topics
Globalization	Fundamentals of the Interior Design Profession
Value to Clients, End Users, Businesses, and Society	Ethics
Collaboration	Licensing
Sustainable Design	Professional Organizations
Integrating LEED Certification with Project Management	Professional Preparation
Owning and Operating a Green Interior Design Business	Career Opportunities
Professional Networking	Attaining an Entry-Level Position
Client Relationship Cycle	Interviewing
Client Relations/Interpersonal Skills	Entrepreneurship
Public and Community Service	Business Plans
Social Responsibilities	Professional Resources
Detailed Analysis of the Integrated Design Process (IDP) and Project Management/Client Relationships/Value Added/LEED Certification (see Tables 9.1–9.3)	Business Structures
	Legal Requirements
	Financial Data and Management
Humanitarian Design	Professional Business Responsibilities
Risk Management	Professional Compensation and Fees
Information/Knowledge Management	Design Contracts
Recessions/Economic Downturns	Pricing and Trade Sources
401(k) plans	Contract Administration
Global Economy	General Accounting and Administrative Practices
Design-Build Services	Strategic Planning
International Practice/Business Cultural Dimensions	Project Management
International Business Communication Styles/Business Protocols	Marketing and Public Relations
	Presentations
Technology and its Impact on the Profession	Employment Laws
Search Engines	Human Resources
Corporate Blogs	U.S. Laws and Professional Practice
Social Networks: Facebook, LinkedIn, and Twitter	Business Policies and Operations
Interdisciplinary Teams	
Virtual Teamwork	
Charrettes	
Workplace/Business Communication Etiquette	
Effects of Changing Demographics	
Working for/with Four Generations	
Global Influences Affecting Practice	
Evidence-Based Design (EBD) Solutions	
Project Management and Client Relationships	
Life-Cycle Costing	
Enterprising Marketing	
Benchmarking	
Continuous Improvement Strategies	

The book expands on topics that are important for professional practice *and* can open doors for new job opportunities, such as international practice, project management, marketing/visual communications/branding, and strategic management. Understanding how to maximize adaptable professional skills is especially important during fluctuating economic times.

Art Program

The book's *new* approach to professional practice for interior designers also applies to its art program. Why can't a professional practice for interior designer's book have color, graphics, and photographs of the built environment? Knowing that people in artistic professions are inclined to be disinterested in business practices, I have incorporated features that typically appeal to visually oriented individuals and are aligned to intriguing aspects associated with the built environment.

The art program was created to illustrate complex topics, reduce quantity of text, and support the text with graphics and photographs of interiors. Illustrations as well as case studies, tables, and boxed features are positioned in the text to provide "visual breaks" and to summarize facts and details.

Pedagogical Features

Every interior design educator knows the importance of teaching students that being a successful interior designer requires sound business practices. Unfortunately, without meaningful engagement with the topics in professional practice books, the message is lost and students merely do what is required to pass a course.

In addition to *new* approaches to the profession, the book has *new* approaches to pedagogical features. Engaging the Millennial student requires a textbook that attracts their attention in the first chapter by discussing topics that address their immediate needs, and proceeds through information they will need for an entry-level position. Topics related to owning and operating a business are presented at the end of the book.

The book has been written to address the unique expectations of students born in the Millennial Generation. For example, to support how current students are learning, the content is presented from a global as well as an interdisciplinary perspective. An example of this emphasis on globalization and how designers should become accustomed to the world's extensive variety of languages is that each chapter in the book begins by translating the word "chapter" into several languages. By the end of the book the reader will have seen "chapter" in 56 languages.

From an interdisciplinary perspective, the content includes materials from various professionals, such as architects, human behaviorists, psychologists, sociologists, economists, project managers, strategic planners, and marketing/branding/communications specialists.

To address the ideological and pedagogical preferences of the Millennial Generation, the book emphasizes teamwork, technological applications, knowledge prompts embedded in the text ("Checking for Comprehension"), approaches for diverse learners, and world-changing initiatives, such as serving communities. Web addresses that tend to be permanent are included with the text to enable readers to use their mobile devices to quickly and easily access the referenced information.

To appeal to Millennial students as well as visual learners, business topics typically perceived as "boring" are succinct and accompanied by a photos, illustrations, case studies, boxed inserts, reading breaks, and thought-provoking projects.

The book is written using short paragraphs, simple language, and summaries of key skills and knowledge. To expand an understanding of professional terms, every chapter has key terms that are described in the text as well as defined in the glossary.

Comprehensive Supplements

Professional Practice for Interior Designers in a Global Marketplace is the first professional practice textbook written for the Millennial Generation within the context of the expanding responsibilities of interior designers in the twenty-first century as well as their interests in technology, globalization, sustainability, collaboration, and humanitarian design.

The book is primarily intended for upper-level interior design professional practice courses, but can also be used as an upper-level supplementary text in studio courses.

To support the study of professional practice, the text is accompanied with the following supplements for the instructor:

- Instructor's Guide
  - Chapter outlines with suggestions for lectures, discussions, and projects
  - Teaching tips for mobile devices, collaborative activities, experiential exercises, case studies, and maximizing student learning
  - Sample course outlines
  - Test bank with multiple choice, true/false, and essay questions
- PowerPoint Presentation Slides
  - Presentation slides are organized by chapters
- Presentation slides include lecture outlines, discussion questions, embedded web links, and text images

References

Allwork, R., ed. 1961. *Interior Design and Decoration: Manual of Professional Practice*. New York: American Institute of Interior Designers.

Martin, C. S., and D. A. Guerin. 2010 (page xviii). *The State of the Interior Design Profession*. New York: Fairchild Books.

Acknowledgments

Writing this book has been an amazing journey, and I am very grateful to all of the professionals who have contributed to the process. First and foremost I am very grateful to Olga Kontzias, Executive Editor—this book would not be possible without her extraordinary vision and dedication to the profession.

I extend my sincere gratitude to the reviewers: Michelle R. Brown, Baylor University; Beth Stokes, The Art Institute of Portland; Grace F. Baker, Cazenovia College; Jennifer Blanchard Belk, Winthrop University; Renée Hearn, IADT Nashville; and LuAnn Nissen, University of Nevada-Reno. The reviewers' expertise helped to strengthen and improve my work.

I also thank the fabulous staff at Fairchild Books, including Joe Miranda, Senior Development Editor; Laurie Gibson, Assistant Development Editor; Ginger Hillman, Production Director; Jessica Katz, Associate Production Editor; Lauren Vlassenko, Assistant Production Editor; Sarah Silberg, Assistant Art Director; Kenneth Cavanaugh, Photo Researcher; and Amy Butler, Ancillaries Editor.

As always, I am very grateful for the love and support of my husband, Galen, and for my new joys in my life—Christian and Sebastian.

List of Acronyms

Chapter 1

American Academy Healthcare Interior Designers (AAHID)

American Institute of Interior Designers (AID)

American Lighting Association (ALA)

American Psychological Association (APA)

American Society of Heating, Refrigerating and Air-Conditioning Engineers (ASHRAE)

American Society for Interior Designers (ASID)

Architects Without Frontiers (AWF)

Architecture for Humanity (AFH)

Building Design & Construction (BD+C)

California Council for Interior Design Certification (CCIDC)

Canada Green Building Council (CaGBC)

Certified Aging-in-Place Specialist (CAPS)

Council for Interior Design Accreditation (CIDA)

Environmental Design Research Association (EDRA)

Green Building Certification Institute (GBCI)

Habitat for Humanity Canada (HCH)

Habitat for Humanity International (HFHI)

Heating, Ventilating, Air-Conditioning, and Refrigeration (HVAC&R)

Homes (HOMES)

Interior Design & Construction (ID+C)

Interior Design Educators Council (IDEC)

Interior Design Experience Program (IDEP)

Interior Designers of Canada (IDC)

International Federation of Interior Architects/ Designers (IFI)

International Furnishings and Design Association (IFDA)

International Interior Design Association (IIDA)

Leadership in Energy and Environmental Design (LEED)

Leadership in Energy and Environmental Design Professional Accreditation (LEED AP)

Lighting Certified (LC)

National Association of Home Builders (NAHB)

National Council for Interior Design Qualifications (NCIDQ)

National Council on Qualifications for the Lighting Professions (NCQLP)

National Fire Protection Association (NFPA)

National Kitchen and Bath Association (NKBA)

Neighborhood Development (ND)

Operations & Maintenance (O+M)

United Nations High Commissioner for Refugees (UNHCR)

United States Green Building Council (USGBC)

World Interiors for the New Generation (WING)

Chapter 2

American Society for Interior Designers (ASID)

Brazil, Russia, India, and China (BRIC)

Building Design Partnership (BDP)

Building Information Modeling (BIM)

Computer-Aided Design (CAD)

Consumer Price Index (CPI)

Council for Interior Design Accreditation (CIDA)

Design Research News (DRN)

General Services Administration (GSA)

Individual Retirement Account (IRA)

Indoor Air Quality (IAQ)

Indoor Environmental Quality (IEQ)

Integrated Project Delivery (IPD)

Kohn Pederson Fox (KPF)

Leadership in Energy and Environmental Design (LEED)

Occupational Employment Statistics (OES)

Post-Occupancy Evaluation (POE)

United States Green Building Council (USGBC)

Chapter 3

American Society for Interior Designers (ASID)

Council for Interior Design Accreditation (CIDA)

Grade Point Average (GPA)

Hellmuth, Obata, Kassabaum (HOK)

Interior Designers of Canada (IDC)

International Interior Design Association (IIDA)

National Council for Interior Design Qualifications (NCIDQ)

Occupational Outlook Handbook (OOH)

Letter Of Agreement (LOA)

Questions And Answers (Q&A)

Request For Information (RFI)

Request For Proposal (RFP)

Request For Qualifications (RFQ)

Uniform Commercial Code (UCC)

Chapter 8

Actual Cost (AC)

American Institute of Architects (AIA)

American National Standards Institute/Project
Management Institute (ANSI/PMI)

Association for Project Management (APM)

Building Information Modeling (BIM)

Client Relationship Cycle (CRC)

Construction Industry Council (CIC)

Construction Management at-Risk (CMaR)

Cost Benefit Analysis (CBA)

Design-Bid-Build (DBB)

Design-Build (DB)

Design Quality Indicator (DQI)

Earned Value (EV)

Earned Value Management System (EVMS)

Furniture, Furnishings, and Equipment
(FF&E)

Information Technology (IT)

Integrated Project Delivery (IPD)

International Organization for Standardization
(ISO)

International Project Management Association
(IPMA)

Mechanical, Electrical, Plumbing/Fire
Protection (MEP/FP)

Plan-Do-Check-Act (PDCA)

Planned Value (PV)

Process Decision Program Chart (PDPC)

Program Evaluation Review Technique (PERT)

Project Life Cycle (PLC)

Project Management Institute (PMI)

Project Management Plan (PMP)

Responsible, Accountable, Consult, Inform
(RACI)

Strengths, Weaknesses, Opportunities, Threats
(SWOT)

Time And Materials (T&M)

Total Quality Management (TQM)

Work Breakdown Schedule (WBS)

Chapter 9

American Institute of Architects (AIA)

American Society for Interior Designers (ASID)

Canada Green Building Council (CaGBC)

Cash On Delivery (COD)

Computer Assisted Qualitative Data Analysis
Software (CAQDAS)

Continuing Education Units (CEUs)

Cost Benefit Analyses (CBA)

Council for Interior Design Accreditation
(CIDA)

Design-Bid-Build (DBD)

Earned Value Management System (EVMS)

Environmental Design Research Association
(EDRA)

Evidence-Based Design (EBD)

Fire Protection (FP)

Furniture, Furnishings, and Equipment
(FF&E)

General Contractor (GC)

General Services Administration (GSA)

Heating, Ventilating, and Air-conditioning (HVAC)

Integrated Design Process (IDP)

Interior Designers of Canada (IDC)

International Furnishings and Design Association (IFDA)

International Interior Design Association (IIDA)

Leadership in Energy and Environmental Design (LEED)

Life-Cycle Cost Analysis (LCCA)

Mechanical, Electrical, and Plumbing (MEP)

National Institute of Building Sciences (NIBS)

Post-Occupancy Evaluation (POE)

Project Life Cycle (PLC)

Project Management Plan (PMP)

Request For Comments (RFCs)

Request For Information (RFI)

Statistical Package for Social Sciences (SPSS)

Strengths, Weaknesses, Opportunities, Threats (SWOT)

United States Green Building Council (USGBC)

Whole Building Design Guide (WBDG)

Chapter 10
American Marketing Association (AMA)

American Society for Interior Designers (ASID)

Anticybersquatting Consumer Protection Act (ACPA)

Attitudes, Interests, and Opinions (AIO)

Bureau of Labor Statistics (BLS)

Business Owner's Policy (BOP)

Certified Public Accountant (CPA)

Client Relationship Cycle (CRC)

Commercial General Liability (CGL)

Community Development Financial Institution (CDFI)

Doing Business As (DBA)

Dun & Bradstreet (D&B)

Economics and Statistics Administration (ESA)

Employer Identification Number (EIN)

Equal Employment Opportunity Commission (EEOC)

Federal Employer Identification Number (FEIN)

Federal Trade Commission (FTC)

Federal Unemployment Tax Act (FUTA)

Haines, Lundberg, and Waehler (HLW)

Interior Designers of Canada (IDC)

Internal Revenue Service (IRS)

International Council for Small Business (ICSB)

Internet Corporation for Assigned Names and Numbers (ICANN)

Leadership in Energy and Environmental Design (LEED)

Limited Liability Company (LLC)

National Small Business Association (NSBA)

Procurement Technical Centers (PTACs)

Profit and Loss (P&L)

Rogers, Taliaferro, Kostritsky and Lamb (RTKL)

Self-Employment (SE)

Service Corps of Retired Executives (SCORE)

Small Business Administration (SBA)

Small Business Development Centers (SBDCs)

Small Business and Entrepreneurship Council (SBE Council)

United States Association for Small Business and Entrepreneurship (USASBE)

United States Patent and Trademark Office (USPTO)

Chapter 11
Carpet and Rug Institute (CRI)

Chain of Custody (CC)

Environmental Protection Agency (EPA)

Federal Trade Commission (FTC)

Forest Management (FM)

Forest Stewardship Council (FSC)

Greenhouse Gas (GHG)

Indoor Air Quality (IAQ)

Indoor Environmental Quality (IEQ)

Interior Design + Construction (ID+C)

International Organization for Standardization (ISO)

Polychlorinated Biphenyls (PCBs)

Processed Chlorine Free (PCF)

Resource Conservation and Recovery Act (RCRA)

Universal Waste Rule (UWR)

Volatile Organic Compound (VOC)

Chapter 12
Allied Board of Trade (ABT)

Dun & Bradstreet (D&B)

Hellmuth, Obata, Kassabaum (HOK)

Plan-Do-Check-Act (PDCA)

Profit and Loss (P&L) statement

Strengths, Weaknesses, Opportunities, and Threats (SWOT)

Chapter 13
American Marketing Association (AMA)

Building Information Modeling (BIM)

Chartered Institute of Public Relations (CIPR)

Client Life Cycle (CLC)

Illinois Institute of Technology (IIT)

Indoor Air Quality (IAQ)

Internet Corporation for Assigned Names and Numbers (ICANN)

Chapter 14
Age Discrimination in Employment Act of 1967 (ADEA)

Americans with Disabilities Act of 1990 (ADA)

Consumer Credit Protection Act (CCPA)

Davis-Bacon and Related Acts (DBRA)

Department of Labor (DOL)

Employee Retirement Income Security Act (ERISA)

Employer Identification Number (EIN)

Equal Employment Opportunity Commission (EEOC)

Equal Pay Act of 1963 (EPA)

Fair Credit Reporting Act (FCRA)

Fair Labor Standards Act (FLSA)

Family and Medical Leave Act (FMLA)

Federal Trade Commission (FTC)

Federal Unemployment Tax Act (FUTA)

Genetic Information Nondiscrimination Act of 2008 (GINA)

Health and Human Services (HHS)

Immigration and Nationality Act (INA)

Internal Revenue Service (IRS)

Occupational Safety and Health Act (OSHAct)

Occupational Safety and Health Administration (OSHA)

McNamara-O'Hara Service Contract Act (SCA)

Patient Protection and Affordable Care Act (PPACA)

Personal Responsibility and Work Opportunity Reconciliation Act (PRWORA)

Plan Do Check Act (PDCA)

Savings Incentive Match Plan for Employees of Small Employers (SIMPLE)

Simplified Employee Pensions (SEPs)

Small Business Administration (SBA)

Social Security Administration (SSA)

Uniform Commercial Code (UCC)

United States Green Building Council (USGBC)

PART

LAUNCHING A CAREER IN THE
INTERIOR DESIGN PROFESSION

Part I Launching a Career in the Interior Design Profession begins the exploration of professional practice by reviewing the fundamentals of being an interior designer in the globally oriented twenty-first century. In reflecting the theme of this book, Part I emphasizes contemporary expectations of the profession, including designing sustainable built environments, participating in international collaborations, grooming adaptable professional skills, and optimizing social media.

To emphasize globalization and how designers need to become accustomed to the world's extensive variety of languages, Chapter 1 begins the translation of the word "chapter" into several languages. As noted in the Preface, by the end of the book you will have seen the word "chapter" in 56 languages.

The first chapter in Part I provides an overview of important aspects of the interior design profession that a person should be aware of before searching for his or her first job. In Chapter 2, career opportunities are explored, including types of design firms, areas of specialization, earnings, compensation plans, and benefits. The last chapter in Part I, Chapter 3, examines how to prepare, search, and interview for entry-level positions.

CHAPTER 1

Fundamentals of the Interior Design Profession

Hoofstuk 1(Afrikaans)
Kapitulli 1 (Albanian)
الفصل 1 (Arabic)
Գլուխ 1 (Armenian)
1-ci fəsil (Azerbaijani)

After learning the content in Chapter 1, you will be able to answer the following questions:

- How does the interior design profession provide value to individuals and society, including contributions to socially conscious initiatives and projects?

- How are professional organizations representing multiple disciplines beneficial to the work of an interior designer and provide valuable contributions to society?

- How are licensing, registration, and professional examinations important to the interior design profession and society?

- How are public and community service critical to interior designers who are working in a global era with social responsibilities?

Chapter 1 begins the exploration of launching your career by posing the question, "Why do you want to be an interior designer?" The section proceeds with information that focuses on defining the multifaceted profession and describing international projects that illustrate the design profession's contributions to humanity. The next section in this chapter introduces various professional organizations from the perspective that designers working in the future must collaborate with individuals from multiple disciplines throughout the world. Hence, there are extensive benefits associated with joining design-related organizations as well as affiliated professional organizations, manufacturing/industry organizations, and academic associations.

An important function of professional design organizations is to advocate for legislation that requires licensing and registration—important for protecting interior designers' ability to practice. These topics are explored by examining legislation in the United States and Canada with a specific emphasis on reviewing the National Council for Interior Design Qualifications' (NCIDQ) examination. The section concludes by summarizing professional credentials related to specialized market certificates.

Content explored in the *Public and Community Service* section is very important for interior designers working in an era of **globalization** that concentrates on **social responsibilities**. Interior designers can provide service to their local community and the profession, as well as international volunteer projects. The first step to volunteering is to understand how the design profession is engaged in service activities and to connect with national organizations that specialize in community projects. Participation in philanthropic activities can assist you with formulating a career plan and can extend your personal and professional networks.

Value of the Interior Design Profession

As you begin your professional career, people might ask, "Why do you want to be an interior designer?" The question might be posed in an interview or during casual conversations with friends and family. The question can become more profound during economic downturns because people can have the impression that hiring an interior designer is a luxury. Therefore, in addition to explaining why you want to be an interior designer, your response might require educating people about the interior design profession and its value. Your task is especially complex because you might have to explain the profession to people of four different generations, each with their own attitudes, expectations, and experiences. The generations are the Silent Generation (born 1925–1945), Baby Boomer Generation (born 1946–1964), Generation X (born 1965–1980), and the Millennial Generation (born 1981–2000).

Defining the Interior Design Profession

There are several reasons why we often have to educate the public about our profession. First, interior design is a relatively new profession—even though people have been designing the built interior environment since the beginning of civilization. Therefore, many people have never worked with an interior designer and do not understand how the responsibilities and challenges of the profession have dramatically changed in the past 50 years.

For the most part the general public has been exposed to the work of interior designers via popular magazines that primarily profile high-end residences, television programs, media buzz, and websites. A cartoon published in *The New Yorker* magazine in 1965 provides an example of impressions some people had of work associated with our profession (Figure 1.1).

Even though the cartoon is several decades old, its message might still resonate in the minds of people, most notable with those of the Silent and Boomer Generations. Another example of how the interior design profession was conceptualized in the 1960s is evident in the definition of an interior designer provided by the American Institute of Interior Designers (AID):

"Good grief, Marge! Not my pajamas, too!"

Figure 1.1 A cartoon published in The New Yorker magazine in 1965 provides an example of impressions some people had of work associated with the interior design profession. *(Robert Day/The New Yorker Magazine)*

The Interior Designer is a person qualified, by training and experience, to plan and supervise the design and execution of interiors and their furnishings, and to organize the various arts and crafts essential to their completion (Allwork 1961).

A comparison of AID's definition of an interior designer and NCIDQ's current definition of interior design provides an excellent analysis of how the profession has been transformed in the past 50 years:

Interior design is a multifaceted profession in which creative and technical solutions are applied within a structure to achieve a built interior environment. These solutions are functional, enhance the quality of life and culture of the occupants and are aesthetically attractive. Designs are created in response to and coordinated with the building shell and acknowledge the physical location and social context of the project. Designs must adhere to code and regulatory requirements, and encourage the principles of environmental sustainability. The interior design process follows a systematic and co-ordinated methodology, including research, analysis and integration of knowledge into the creative process, whereby the needs and resources of the client are satisfied to produce an interior space that fulfills the project goals (NCIDQ 2012).

Providing Value to Individuals and Society

As you develop an answer that explains to people why you want to be an interior designer, it is important to reflect on how the profession has developed and to communicate the differences to your audience. As illustrated in Table 1.1, the interior design profession progressed dramatically in the twentieth century. Some of the most significant accomplishments focused on

Table 1.1 Overview of the History of Professional Practice for Interior Designers (20th Century to the Present)

Decade/ Topics	Professional Organizations/ Professional Services	Legislation/ Management Theories	Education	Publications	Research/ Testing	Affiliated Professional Organizations
1900–1909	Wiener Werkstätte, 1903 Deutscher Werkbund, 1907		In 1904, Frank A. Parsons joined the Chase School of New York (founded in 1896) and created the interior decoration program	*House and Garden Magazine*, 1901 *The Craftsmen Magazine*, 1901 Edith Wharton and Ogden Codman, *The Decoration of Houses* (1907, c 1897) A. Munsell's *A Color Notation*, 1905	American Society for Testing and Materials (ASTM), 1902	50th anniversary of The American Institute of Architects (AIA), 1907 National Association of Building Owners and Managers (NABOM), 1907
1910–1919	The Decorators Club, New York, 1914 Design and Industries Association (DIA), 1915	F. W. Taylor's Principles of Scientific Management, 1911	New York School of Interior Design founded by Sherrill Whiton, 1916 Bauhaus School, 1919	*Arts and Decoration Magazine*, 1910 Elsie de Wolfe, *The House in Good Taste* (1913) *Progressive Architecture*, 1919	Metal Office Furniture Co. (Steelcase), 1912 eventually industry research	American Institute of Graphic Arts, 1914
1920–1929	McMillen, Inc., 1924	Mary Parker Follett's Creative Enterprise, 1924	New York School of Interior Design chartered, 1924	*L'Esprit Nouveau*, 1920–1925 Le Corbusier's *Vers une Architecture*, 1924 *Better Homes and Gardens*, 1924 *Architectural Digest Magazine*, 1925	Herman Miller, 1923 eventually industry research	
1930–1939	The National Furniture Designers' Council, 1933 Society of Interior Decorators of Ontario (SIDO), 1934 American Institute for Interior Decorators (AIID), 1931 became American Institute of Decorators (AID), 1936 Designers' Institute of the American Furniture Mart, 1936 became American Designers Institute (ADI), 1938 SOM, 1936	Federal Home Loan Bank System, 1932 Housing Act of 1934 and the Federal Housing Agency (FHA) Elton Mayo's Human Problems of an Industrial Civilization, 1933 C. I. Barnard's Functions of the Executive, 1938	The Cranbrook Academy of Art, 1932 Bauhaus School closes, 1933	*Interior Design*, 1931 *Interior Design and Decoration*, 1937		

		Table 1.1 *(continued)*				
Decade/ Topics	**Professional Organizations/ Professional Services**	**Legislation/ Management Theories**	**Education**	**Publications**	**Research/ Testing**	**Affiliated Professional Organizations**
1940– 1949	Society of Industrial Designers (SID), 1944 Knoll Planning Unit, 1946 International Furnishings and Design Association (IFDA), 1948	Housing Act of 1949 and the Urban Redevelopment Agency	The Chase School renamed in honor of F.A. Parsons, 1941	E. Noyes' *Organic Design Home Furnishings*, 1941 F. Schroeder's *Anatomy for Interior Designers, and How to Talk to a Client*, 1948		National Association of Home Builders (NAHB), 1942
1950– 1959	Industrial Designers Institute (IDI), 1951 National Society for Interior Designers (NSID), 1957 formed from an AID group	Housing Act of 1954 Peter Drucker's *Practice of Management*, 1954	Industrial Design Education Association (IDEA), 1957	R. Faulkner's *Inside Today's Home*, 1954	Steelcase Corporate Development Center Workplace Studies	100th anniversary of The American Institute of Architects (AIA), 1957 American Society of Heating, Refrigerating and Air-Conditioning Engineers (ASHRAE), 1959
1960– 1969	AID became American Institute of Interior Designers (AIID), 1961 Institute of Store Planners (ISP), 1961 Retail Design Institute, 1961 American Institute of Kitchen Dealers (AIKD), 1963 International Federation of Interior Architects/ Interior Designers (IFI), 1963 National Office Furnishings Association (NOFA), 1963 Industrial Designers Society of American (IDSA) after merging several organizations, 1965 Institute of Business Designers (IBD), 1969 Gensler, 1965	Demonstration Cities and Metropolitan Development Act of 1966 Architectural Barriers Act of 1968	Interior Design Educators Council, 1963	*Contract* Magazine, 1960 H. Dreyfuss' *The Measure of Man: Human Factors in Design*, 1960 J. Itten's *The Art of Color: The Subjective Experience and Objective Rationale of Color*, 1961 J. Panero's *Anatomy for Interior Designers*, 1962	American Society for Testing Materials, 1961 Color Marketing Group, 1962	NABOM became Building Owners and Managers Association (BOMA) International, 1968

Table 1.1 (continued)

Decade/ Topics	Professional Organizations/ Professional Services	Legislation/ Management Theories	Education	Publications	Research/ Testing	Affiliated Professional Organizations
1970–1979	Interior Designers of Canada (IDC), 1972 Interior Design Society (IDS), 1973 NSID and AID became the American Society of Interior Designers, 1975 International Society of Interior Designers (ISID), 1979	Consumer Products Safety Act, 1972 Community Reinvestment Act of 1977	Foundation for Interior Design Education Research (FIDER), 1970 National Council for Interior Design Qualification (NCIDQ), 1974	V. Papanek's *Design for the Real World, Human Ecology and Social Change*, 1971 *The Journal of Interior Design Education and Research*, 1975 J. Nuckoll's *Interior Lighting for Interior Designers*, 1976	H. Siegel's *Guide to Business Practices: A Practical Checklist*, 1976	
1980–1989	International Facility Management Association (IFMA), 1980 AIKD becomes National Kitchen & Bath Association (NKBA), 1983 SIDO became the Association of Registered Interior Designers of Ontario (ARIDO), 1984 Council of Federal Interior Designers (CFID), 1986	Alabama first state with legislation to regulate interior designers, 1982 Total Quality Management (TQM)		*Metropolitan Home*, 1981 V. Papanek's *Design for Human Scale*, 1983 S. Reznikoff's *Interior Graphic and Design Standards*, 1986 S. Rossbach's *Interior Design with Feng Shui*, 1987	Center for Inclusive Design and Environmental Access (IDeA), 1984 Center for Universal Design, 1989	
1990–1999	IBD, ISID, and CFID formed the International Interior Design Association (IIDA), 1994	American with Disabilities Act (ADA), 1992 International Code Council (ICC), 1994 Homesteading and Neighborhood Restoration Act of 1995		J. Pile's *Dictionary of 20th Century Design*, 1990 J. Banham's *Encyclopedia of Interior Design*, 1997	Universal Design Learning Lab, 1990 National Council on Qualifications for the Lighting Professions (NCQLP), 1991 Carnegie Mellon Green Design Institute, 1992 Intypes (Interior Archetypes), 1997 The Center for Real Life Kitchen Design, 1998	U.S. Green Building Council (USGBC), 1993 National Association of Home Builders (NAHB)
2000–Present			FIDER becomes Council for Interior Design Accreditation (CIDA), 2006		GREENGUARD Environmental Institute (GEI), 2001 InformeDesign website, 2003 ASID Research Design Connections website IIDA Knowledge Center research website, 2007	

the development of professional organizations, educational programs, legislation, research centers, and socially responsible designs. These initiatives as well as users' satisfaction with interior environments contributed to improving the credibility of the design profession.

Even though it has become more commonplace for people with diverse socioeconomic statuses to work with an interior designer, the design profession must still explain to people how our work provides value to clients, end users, and society. Explanations are especially important during recessions or other difficult times, such as war.

An effective approach to educating people about the profession is to describe projects that have made contributions to individuals and society. Examples could include one of your designs or projects completed by professionals. Explanations should focus on how the design provides value to a client, individuals, and society.

To provide value to a client, the design must reflect the client's philosophy and accomplish the goals of the project. Providing value to society includes designs that are environmentally, economically, ethically, and socially responsible. The case study described in Box 1.1 is an example of how the design profession provided value to a client, users of the facilities, and society.

Big Brothers Big Sisters in St. Louis, Missouri*

Project Profile: New headquarters for the Big Brothers Big Sisters of Eastern Missouri, in St. Louis, Missouri, designed by Trivers Associates, Inc. Adaptive reuse project in the former Woolworth department store; 24,000 square feet (2,230 square meters). The headquarters needed space for employees, volunteers, children, and families.

Client Profile: Founded in 1902, Big Brothers Big Sisters is a national one-to-one mentoring organization with several local agencies. Big Brothers Big Sisters of Eastern Missouri operates with the following philosophy:

Mission: "To provide a mentor for every child who wants and needs one."

Values: "We have just one core value: **to be accountable**. We are accountable for ensuring the safety, well-being and satisfaction of our Little Brothers, Little Sisters, volunteers and employees; building mentoring friendships that make a difference; and creating an organizational culture of quality, respect, integrity, high performance and fun."

Design Solutions and Value:

* To have value to the organization, design solutions had to support the philosophical perspectives of Big Brothers Big Sisters of Eastern Missouri:

  * Focus on a built environment that helped to ensure the "safety, well-being and satisfaction" of the users of the facilities as well as fostering the formation of friendships.

  * Reflect a "culture of quality" and encourage "respect, integrity, high performance and fun."

* The CEO of the organization, Becky James-Hatter, provides an assessment of the completed facilities:

  "We are absolutely thrilled with the way the new building turned out. The building maintains its historical significance while the new design energizes our staff and members of the community that come through our doors."

(Box 1.1 continued on page 10)

Box 1.1

Big Brothers Big Sisters in St. Louis, Missouri* (continued)

In addition to comments from the client, another way to evaluate the design's success is to study photographs of activities at their headquarters, which were posted on their website. Photos included events such as graduation, a spring break party, a Christmas party, and clothing drives to help the people of Haiti recover after their devastating 2010 earthquake.

These photographs depict the value of a well-designed built environment:

- Rooms are filled with people; especially important to a volunteer organization.

- People are happy while engaged in a variety of activities; essential to an organization that emphasizes building relationships.

The matrix below portrays one approach to analyzing how the design solutions provided value to the organization, children, families, volunteers, staff, and society.

Design Solutions/Organizational Values	Ensuring safety, well-being, and satisfaction	Building friendships	Fostering quality, respect, high performance, and fun	Sustainability
Adaptive reuse building with historical connections to the community.		✓	✓	✓
A welcoming entrance and reception area that also presents a professional appearance.	✓	✓	✓	
Space planning with flexibility for various activities and diversity of users.	✓	✓	✓	✓
Space planning for conversation and dining.	✓	✓	✓	
Light-colored walls and "cheerful" sunburst patterns in bright colors for upholstery.	✓	✓	✓	
Textiles and furniture are durable and easy to maintain.	✓		✓	✓
Comfortable furniture for conversation groupings and supportive designs for task chairs.	✓	✓	✓	✓
An abundance of daylighting and views in collaborative spaces.	✓		✓	✓
Electrical light sources aligned to tasks, such as reading, writing, and conversation.	✓	✓		✓
Signage and space planning enables easy egress in an emergency.	✓			✓

*Adapted from: Big Brothers Big Sisters. 2010. *Big Brothers Big Sisters of Eastern Missouri.* (http://www.bbbsemo.org/). Retrieved July 2010.

Socially Conscious Organizations

To illustrate new expectations of the design profession, excellent sources for projects are socially conscious organizations, such as Architecture for Humanity, Habitat for Humanity International, UN-HABITAT, International Crisis Group, United Nations High Commissioner for Refugees (UNHCR), and Architects Without Frontiers (AWF). Interior designers, students, and other design professionals are actively involved with these projects. Thus, the activities and accomplishments of these organizations not only illustrate the value of our design profession; they reflect many of the responsibilities associated with our "multifaceted profession" in the twenty-first century.

Architecture for Humanity (AFH) is a commendable example of how design professionals and students throughout the world are working together to make contributions to society. AFH demonstrates how an organization, as well as 40,000 professionals living in 28 countries, is dedicated to serving humanity. Most importantly, AFH's success would not be possible without the thousands of interior designers, architects, students, and volunteers who have been willing to commit their time and expertise to helping people in need.

An excellent example of the work of AFH is the organization's project, the Haiti School Initiative. The project was developed to help the people of Haiti rebuild their communities after the devastating earthquake that occurred there on January 12, 2010. The earthquake resulted in the deaths of over 200,000 people, and more than a million were left homeless. One Haitian project is the reconstruction of the Institut Foyer du Savoir (Home of Knowledge Institute), Port-au-Prince. Designers working on the project include Heidi Arnold, Rachel Litherland, and Lisa Smyth. The Institut Foyer du Savoir accommodates 400 students from kindergarten to 6th grade (ages 3–20 years old) and includes classrooms, administration office, multipurpose room, kitchen, and a water collection cistern (Worldchanging 2012). Construction of the institute began in August 2011. (see Figure 1.2.)

Figure 1.2 An excellent example of the work of AFH is the organization's project the Haiti School Initiative. The project was developed to help the people of Haiti rebuild their communities after the devastating 2010 earthquake.

One project is the reconstruction of the Institut Foyer du Savoir (Home of the Knowledge Institute), Port-au-Prince. The institute accommodates 400 students from kindergarten to 6th grade and includes classrooms, administration office, multipurpose room, kitchen, and a water collection cistern. *(Architecture for Humanity/Designer: Alison McCabe)*

Checking for Comprehension

- What three key topics stand out in your mind from NCIDQ's definition of the interior design profession?

- How would you explain the value of the interior design profession during a job interview?

Professional Organizations

Architecture for Humanity is just one example of an organization that you might be involved with as a student and continue with during your first professional position. In pursuing your first job, another question you might be asked in an interview is, "What professional organizations have you been involved with?"

In the initial years of our profession most people would have responded by identifying an organization specifically established for the profession, such as ASID (American Society for Interior Designers; a consolidation of two earlier organizations—NSID, for National Society of Interior Designers, and AID). To respond to the profession's new expectations, many designers are joining organizations with various missions.

Professional Design Organizations

Designers as well as students continue to select membership in a professional organization specifically for interior design, such as ASID, the International Interior Design Association (IIDA), or the Interior Designers of Canada (IDC). But the new challenges and multifaceted responsibilities of the profession are now leading designers to join a variety of professional organizations, including AFH, the United States Green Building Council (USGBC), Canada Green Building Council (CaGBC), the Environmental Design Research Association (EDRA), or the International Furnishings and Design Association (IFDA). (see Figure 1.3.)

Generally, when designers join an organization that is not directly affiliated with interior design, the decision is based on an area of specialization. For example, an interior designer interested in sustainable design might choose to join USGBC or CaGBC. If a designer's work often involves flammability standards, membership in the National Fire Protection Association (NFPA) could be beneficial. A designer might want to join the American Psychological Association (APA) because of that person's interest in exploring how the built environment affects the behavior of people.

An overview of the variety of professional organizations and their profiles is presented in Table 1.2 (see Appendix A for a comprehensive list of professional organizations and interior design blogs). Examples in Appendix A include at least one interior design organization from five continents. Especially noteworthy information is the list of benefits of an organization to you as well as to society. For example, the

INTERIOR DESIGN ORGANIZATIONS
American Society of Interior Designers (ASID)
Interior Designers of Canada (IDC)
International Federation of Interior Designers/Architects (IF)
International Interior Design Association (IIDA)

AFFILIATED PROFESSIONAL ORGANIZATIONS
American Institute of Architects (AIA)
American Society of Heating, Refrigerating, and Air-Conditioning Engineers (ASHRAE)
International Association of Lighting Designers (IALD)
United States Green Building Council (USGBC)

PROFESSIONAL ORGANIZATIONS

MANUFACTURING AND INDUSTRY ORGANIZATIONS
American Lighting Association (ALA)
Business and Institutional Furniture Manufacturer's Association (BIFMA)
Carpet and Rug Institute (CRI)
National Fire Protection Association (NFPA)

ACADEMIC ORGANIZATIONS
American Psychological Association (APA)
American Sociological Association (ASA)
Environmental Design Research Association (EDRA)
National Art Education Association (NAEA)

Figure 1.3 Due to the new challenges and multifaceted responsibilities of the profession, designers are electing to join a variety of professional organizations.

Table 1.2 Profiles of Professional Organizations	
Organization (URL)	**American Society of Interior Designers (http://www.asid.org/)**
Vision/Mission	ASID is a community of people driven by a common love for design and committed to the belief that interior design, as a service to people, is a powerful, multi-faceted profession that can positively change people's lives. Through education, knowledge sharing, advocacy, community building and outreach, the Society strives to advance the interior design profession and, in the process, to demonstrate and celebrate the power of design to positively change people's lives (ASID, 2010).
Membership Categories	Professional, Allied, Educator, Student, Student Advancement, Industry Partner
Benefits to Students/ Professionals	**Students:** "Student Lounge" updates and articles related to the needs of students: (1) How to Become an Interior Designer, (2) Developing Your Career, (3) Student Awards & Competitions, (4) Interested in ASID Student Chapters, (5) Current News & Events, (6) Committees, and (7) Publications Center. **Professionals:** Programs, resources, and initiatives that are designed to promote professional growth, build networks, and enhance knowledge.
Online Resources	Events, Education, Practice & Business, Knowledge Center, Awards & Competitions, Chapter Resources, Advocacy, News Room, and Membership Information
Organization (URL)	**Interior Designers of Canada (IDC) (http://www.interiordesigncanada.org/about.html)**
Vision/Mission	Interior Designers of Canada, with the support of its seven provincial association members, provides a forum for the unified voice of Canadian interior designers, so that the profession continues to grow and receive recognition and respect, locally, nationally and internationally, from government, industry and the public sector (IDC, 2010).
Membership Categories	Professional, Industry Alliance
Benefits to Professionals	Education, Professional Qualifications, Continuing Education, Liaisons (activities and services), Liability Insurance
Online Resources	News & Events, Education, Employment, Directory & Links
Organization (URL)	**International Federation of Interior Architects/Designers (IFI) (http://www.ifiworld.org/#Homepage)**
Vision/Mission	To expand internationally the contribution of the Interior Architecture/Interior Design profession to society through exchange and development of knowledge and experience in education, practice and fellowship (IFI, 2010).
Membership Categories	Full, Associate, Educational, Corporate, Affiliate, Correspondent, Promotional
Benefits to Professionals	IFI is a member of the International Design Alliance (IDA), a strategic venture between three leading international design organizations, including The International Council of Societies of Industrial Design (ICSID) and The International Council of Graphic Design Associations (ICOGRADA). The alliance focuses on opportunities to further the design discipline based on multidisciplinary collaboration.
Online Resources	Programs & Events, Advocacy Platforms (Environmental Stewardship/Socially Responsible Design/ Universal Design/Intellectual Property Rights/Education), Publications
Organization (URL)	**International Interior Design Association (IIDA) (http://www.iida.org/)**
Vision/Mission	IIDA, with respect for past accomplishments of Interior Design leaders, strives to create a strong niche for the most talented and visionary Interior Design professionals, to elevate the profession to the level it warrants, and to lead the way for the next generation of Interior Design innovators. The Association provides a forum to demonstrate design professionals' impact on the health, safety, well being and virtual soul of the public, balancing passion for good design and strategy for best business practices. IIDA stands at the intersection of passion and strategy where designers create extraordinary interiors and experiences (IIDA, 2010).
Membership Categories	Professional Interior Designer, Professional Architect, Associate, Educator, Student, Affiliate, International, Industry
Benefits to Students/ Professionals	**Students:** *Student Central*—Student Blog/Campus Centers/Career Center/Student Task Force; *Student Mentoring Week*; *Social Media*—Facebook/Twitter/LinkedIn; *Student Groups* **Professionals:** Subscriptions to leading magazines, tuition reimbursement opportunities, Chance to reach Forum colleagues around the world, Chapter initiatives, International events
Online Resources	Chapters, Forums, Professional Development, Achievements, Articles, Event Calendar, Competitions, Advocacy, Foundation, Careers

mission of the International Federation of Interior Architects/Designers (IFI) is "To expand, internationally and across all levels of society, the contribution of the Interior Architecture/Design profession through the exchange and development of knowledge and experience, in education, practice and fellowship" (IFI 2011).

Benefits to society provided by the activities of the IFI are very comprehensive. Through multiple initiatives IFI focuses on advancing the principles associated universal design, environmental stewardship, and socially responsible design. IFI is involved with World Interiors Day, WING (World Interiors for the New Generation) workshops, IFI's Design for All Award, and Pro-Vitae, a program for collaborative philanthropic-design projects.

Affiliated Professional Organizations

Affiliated professional organizations, such as the ASHRAE (American Society of Heating, Refrigerating and Air-Conditioning Engineers), provide members with the benefits of having access to the most current and emerging technologies associated with heating, ventilating, air-conditioning, and refrigeration (HVAC&R). Members also have the ability to provide input into the development of HVAC&R technology and standards. By developing state-of-the-art technologies and standards, society benefits from improved indoor air quality, efficient building designs, energy savings, and optimum building performance.

Interior designers can benefit from membership in manufacturing and industry professional organizations. Organizations such as the American Lighting Association (ALA) produce materials and sponsor educational seminars and online education courses on current and emerging topics related to lighting. ALA is also involved with legislative action and sponsoring network forums that enable a designer to share information with lighting manufacturers, showrooms, and other industry leaders. Society benefits from ALA initiatives by having more energy-efficient lighting, effective labeling, safe practices, and reliable e-commerce procedures.

Affiliated Academic Professional Organizations

Some academic professional organizations, such as APA, have degree requirements that a designer might not have; however, interior designers can benefit from information available to nonmembers, such as publications and online information.

EDRA is an excellent example of an academic organization that can be very beneficial to interior designers as well as society. Because EDRA is an international, interdisciplinary organization, its members benefit from membership by being able to share information related to the built environment with a variety of disciplines, including architecture, landscape architecture, social science, facility management, and education.

The organization's purpose, as posted on EDRA's website, is "... the advancement and dissemination of environmental design research, thereby improving understanding of the interrelationships between people, their built and natural surroundings, and helping to create environments responsive to human needs" (EDRA 2011). EDRA's advancement of **evidence-based design** solutions provides valuable information that designers can apply to practice. Society benefits by having built environments that improve the quality of life, such as age-friendly community designs, intergenerational interactions, collaborative work environments, barrier-free settings, and environmentally conscious designs. For nonmembers, EDRA has a Facebook group and is on LinkedIn.

The Interior Design Educators Council (IDEC) is another academic organization that engages in research related to the built environment as well as being involved with advancing the profession and promoting principles associated with effective education. IDEC is an excellent resource for learning about current research results and teaching opportunities in colleges and universities.

IDEC as well as other organizations, such as ASID, IDC, and IIDA, collaborates with the Council for Interior Design Accreditation

(CIDA). CIDA is the leading organization for accrediting interior design education programs at colleges and universities in the United States and Canada. In 2010, ASID reported that there were approximately 350 and 20 interior design public and private education programs in the United States and Canada, respectively. Within these programs in the United States 155 were accredited by CIDA and Canada had 14.

To achieve CIDA accreditation, programs must successfully complete a rigorous self-evaluation and peer review. Consequently, "CIDA-accredited programs assure the public that interior design education prepares students to be responsible, well-informed, skilled professionals who make beautiful, safe, and comfortable spaces that also respect the earth and its resources" (CIDA 2010).

CIDA's standards are very important to your career because they focus on preparing you for an entry-level position and your "future professional growth" (see Appendix B). Furthermore, CIDA's standards provide an overview of the skills, knowledge, and abilities that future employers expect an employee to possess. This information can be valuable as you are developing your résumé and preparing for job interviews (see Chapter 3).

Checking for Comprehension
- Given your interests, which professional organization do you think provides society with the most benefits? Explain why.

- How do you think academic professional organizations assist the design profession?

Licensure, Registration, and Professional Credentials

Licensing and **registration** are also examples of initiatives that can provide benefits to society. Professional organizations such as ASID, IIDA, and IDC are actively involved with providing financial resources, supporting coalitions, and advocating legislation that requires professionals to be licensed or registered by a state licensing board.

Licensing and registration qualifications include the NCIDQ certificate. In addition to the NCIDQ credential, an interior designer can demonstrate professional expertise in a specific market by obtaining certifications in areas such as sustainable design, healthcare, lighting, and kitchen design.

Licensure and Registration

Licensing and registration are legal permissions that enable an individual with the appropriate credentials to practice a profession (Figure 1.4). Generally, licensing is the term used in a state or province when legislation is used to determine who can practice a profession. Registration is associated with legislation that stipulates who may use a specific title.

The importance of licensing and registration likely drives this question during a job interview: "What are your plans to become licensed?" A satisfying response to this inquiry requires an understanding of why it is important to be licensed or registered, familiarity with state laws, and knowledge of how you can meet the legal requirements.

Licensing and registration are critically important to our profession and society because the legislation validates that a licensed or registered interior designer is *qualified* to practice activities legally prescribed for the profession. Qualifications are education, experience, and examination. Legislation is necessary to control and regulate the profession because jurisdictions have determined that the work of interior designers affects the public health, safety, and welfare.

To understand state and province laws requires knowledge of terminology associated with licensing. The major types of legislation related to licensing and registration are licensing, **title acts**, **practice acts**, **self-certification**, and **permitting**. As of 2012 there are 27 states, the District of Columbia, Puerto Rico, and 8 Canadian

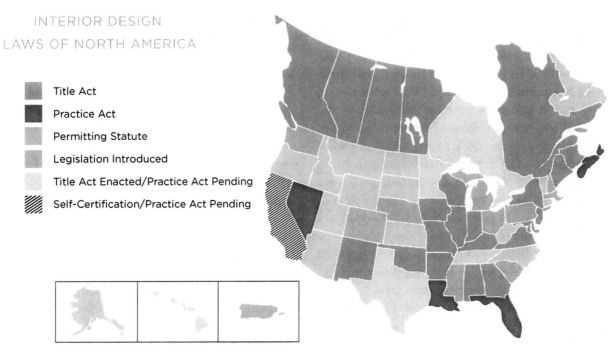

■ Title Act

■ Practice Act

■ Permitting Statute

■ Legislation Introduced

□ Title Act Enacted/Practice Act Pending

▨ Self-Certification/Practice Act Pending

Figure 1.4 Map of the United States and Canada illustrating registration laws.

provinces that have title or practice legislation. At a minimum the laws specify the number of years of education and experience required to legally practice interior design. A listing and contact information for state/province boards and agencies that regulate the interior design profession are in Appendix C.

Title and Practice Acts

Title acts specify requirements for using a professional title, such as "Licensed Interior Designer," "Certified Interior Designer," or "Registered Interior Designer." Title acts are the most frequent type of legislation. As an example, the title act in Illinois specifies that only qualified persons are permitted to use the title of Registered Interior Designer. The act also stipulates that the profession of interior design refers to:

Persons qualified by education, experience, and examination, who administer contracts for fabrication, procurement, or installation in the implementation of designs, drawings, and specifications for any interior design

project and offer or furnish professional services, such as consultations, studies, drawings, and specifications in connection with the location of lighting fixtures, lamps and specifications of ceiling finishes as shown in reflected ceiling plans, space planning, furnishings, or the fabrication of non-loadbearing structural elements within and surrounding interior spaces of buildings but specifically excluding mechanical and electrical systems, except for specifications of fixtures and their location within interior spaces (Illinois General Assembly 2011).

Practice acts prescribe what an interior designer may or may not do as well as delineate the requirements for being able to work as a professional interior designer. An individual must be licensed to work as an interior designer. For example, Nevada's Practice Act defines the "practice as a Registered Interior Designer" and stipulates: "No person may practice: (c) As a registered interior designer or use the title of registered interior designer, in this State without having a certificate of registration issued to him pursuant to the provisions of this chapter" (Nevada State License 2011). The term "registered interior designer" includes:

1. An analysis of:

   (a) A client's needs and goals for an interior area of a structure designed for human habitation or occupancy; and

   (b) The requirements for safety relating to that area;

2. The formulation of preliminary designs for an interior area designed for human habitation or occupancy that are appropriate, functional and esthetic;

3. The development and presentation of final designs that are appropriate for the alteration or construction of an interior area of a structure designed for human habitation or occupancy;

4. The preparation of contract documents for the alteration or construction of an interior area of a structure designed for human habitation or occupancy, including specifications for partitions, materials, finishes, furniture, fixtures and equipment;

5. The collaboration in the completion of a project for the alteration or construction of an interior area of a structure designed for human habitation or occupancy with professional engineers or architects who are registered pursuant to the provisions of title 54 of NRS;

6. The preparation and administration of bids or contracts as the agent of a client; and

7. The review and evaluation of problems relating to the design of a project for the alteration or construction of an area designed for human habitation or occupancy during the alteration or construction and upon completion of the alteration or construction (Nevada State License 2011).

Self-Certification and Permitting

As of 2012, the only state or province that has self-certification legislation is California. Self-certification is similar to a title act except that an organization rather than a jurisdiction is responsible for administering the requirements of the law. Beginning in January 1992, the California Council for Interior Design Certification (CCIDC) has been responsible for administering the requirements of California's Certified Interior Designers law. Therefore in administering California's law, "Only the CCIDC can determine eligibility to be a Certified Interior Designer in the State of California. Designers who meet the education, experience and examination criteria of the CCIDC Board are allowed to use the "Certified Interior Designer" title and are recognized in the State of California" (California Council for Interior Design Certification 2011).

Permitting is legislation that requires an interior designer to obtain a permit for prescribed services. To date, Colorado is the only state or province that has a permitting statute; currently, professional organizations are involved in trying to pass state registration legislation.

Professional Credentials: NCIDQ Examination

To meet the qualifications for licensure or registration requires education, experience, and the NCIDQ examination. In 1972, AID and NSID determined that NCIDQ should be created to test minimum competencies of interior designers. NCIDQ was formally incorporated in 1974, and the first exam was in April 1974.

Over the years, the first exam has evolved into the current process that is illustrated in Figure 1.5. To help you prepare for the NCIDQ examination, ASID developed the STEP program, which is a workshop conducted over several days. During the sessions, participants are able

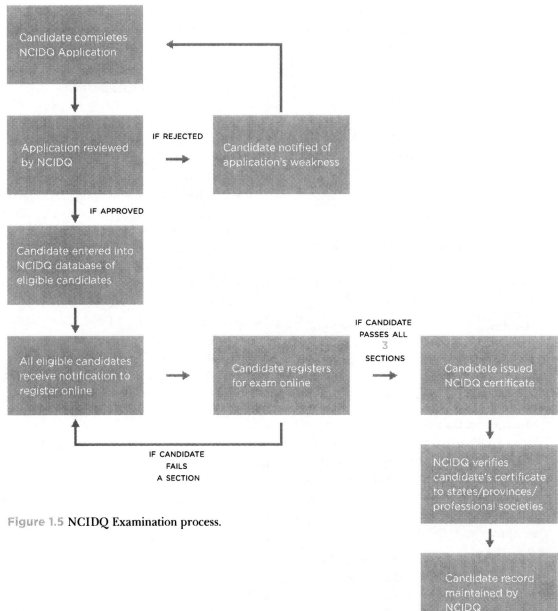

Figure 1.5 NCIDQ Examination process.

to work with instructors on the various components of the examination.

To take the interior design examination, NCIDQ requires "at least six years of combined college-level interior design education and interior design work experience" (NCIDQ 2011). NCIDQ education requirements stipulate that candidates "must complete most or all of your education before you can begin accruing qualified interior design work experience. All coursework used to satisfy the eligibility requirements must be taken for college credit" (NCIDQ 2011). NCIDQ has different eligibility requirements for CIDA degrees and non-CIDA interior design degrees.

Requirements for work experience specify, "All *qualified* work experience used to satisfy the eligibility requirements must be interior design related. Work experience can be full-time or part-time. NCIDQ recommends that you work under the direct supervision of an NCIDQ Certificate holder, a registered interior designer or an architect who offers interior design services" (NCIDQ 2011).

There is an important component to NCIDQ's "*qualified* work experience" that affects individuals who begin accruing interior design work experience after January 1, 2008.

> When your direct supervisor is an NCIDQ Certificate holder, a licensed/registered interior designer or an architect who offers interior design services, your qualified hours are counted at 100 percent. When you work in other supervisory relationships, your hours accrue at lower values. How much qualified work experience is needed depends on a number of factors, including your education and what type of qualified work experience you received (NCIDQ 2011).

IDEP and NCIDQ Sections

One way to complete NCIDQ's supervised work experience requirement is to complete NCIDQ's Interior Design Experience Program (IDEP). IDEP provides a "structure for transitioning between formal education and professional practice" (NCIDQ 2011). For bachelor's or master's degrees, NCIDQ recommends applying for IDEP after completing three years (96 semester/144 quarters credits) of formal education in an interior design program. For an associate's degree NCIDQ suggests applying for the IDEP at the completion of the degree (no less than 60 semester/90 quarter credits of interior design coursework).

The NCIDQ examination has two comprehensive multiple-choice sections that test content areas, and a practicum section. Content areas for Section I are codes, building systems, construction standards, and contract administration. Section II involves design application, project coordination, and professional practice. Areas in the practicum section are space planning, lighting design, egress, life safety, restroom, systems integration, and millwork. For complete information regarding the examination and IDEP refer to NCIDQ's website: www.ncidq.org.

Professional Credentials: Specialization Certificates

To demonstrate additional professional expertise, many interior designers elect to earn certificates in a specialized area. Credentials beyond the NCIDQ certificate can be important to clients and can be especially helpful if you are searching for a job during challenging economic times. Many disciplines have credentialing certificates, but some of the areas that are most common in the design profession include sustainable designs, lighting, healthcare, remodeling, and kitchen/bath designs.

The most common credential for demonstrating expertise in sustainable designs is the Leadership in Energy and Environmental Design Professional Accreditation (LEED AP, LEED Green Associate). In coordination with the USGBC, the Green Building Certification Institute (GBCI) is responsible for administrating LEED's credentialing process. According to GBCI, "LEED Professional Credentials demonstrate current knowledge of green building technologies, best practices, and the rapidly evolving LEED Rating Systems. They show differentiation in a growing and competitive industry, and they allow for varied levels of specialization" (2010).

The areas of AP specialization are Building Design & Construction (BD+C); Homes (HOMES), Interior Design & Construction (ID+C); Operations & Maintenance (O+M); and Neighborhood Development (ND). Eligibility requirements, exam information, fees, and credential maintenance requirements are available at http://www.gbci.org.

The National Council on Qualifications for the Lighting Professions (NCQLP) is a nonprofit organization that "establishes the education, experience and examination requirements for baseline certification across the lighting profession" (2010). LC (Lighting Certified) is the designation granted after successfully passing NCQLP's examination.

The LC Candidate Handbook and information regarding a student internship LC program are at http://www.ncqlp.org/. According to NCQLP, the Intern LC Program is available to undergraduate and graduate students who are within one year of graduation from accredited schools. The Intern LC Program is designed to accelerate the LC certification process.

The National Kitchen and Bath Association (NKBA) also has a student internship program, but NKBA's program has a different purpose. NKBA's Intern Program is structured to provide a link between students from NKBA-accredited programs who are looking for work experience through an internship and employers who are interested in sponsoring an intern. As the name of the organization designates, NKBA is an organization for professionals specializing in designing kitchens and bathrooms. NKBA also sponsors a certification program; information is available at http://www.nkba.org.

Two certificates related to health and well-being are the Certified Aging-in-Place Specialist (CAPS) sponsored by the National Association of Home Builders (NAHB; see http://www.nahb.org/) and a certificate associated with the American Academy Healthcare Interior Designers (AAHID; see http://www.aahid.org/).

The CAPS designation program was developed to "teach the technical, business management, and customer service skills essential to competing in the fastest growing segment of the residential remodeling industry: home modifications for the aging-in-place" (NAHB 2010).

AAHID's vision is "to be recognized by the healthcare industry as the certification board of choice in assessing and qualifying the knowledge, skills, and abilities of healthcare interior designers" (AAHID January 2010). Qualifications for a Board Certified Healthcare Interior Design are education, examination, and work experience. An overview of a person who has the AAHID certificate and demonstrates how

her work as an interior designer provides value to patients, family, caregivers, staff, hospitals, and other professionals is provided in Box 1.2.

> ### Checking for Comprehension
>
> * What are the differences between licensing and registration?
>
> * What are the key steps involved with the NCIDQ examination?

Public and Community Service

As mentioned in Box 1.2, volunteering with professional organizations is one way designers can provide value as well as advance our profession. Working as a volunteer with a professional organization can also involve legislative activities, such as contacting state officials, monitoring upcoming bills, and reviewing drafts of state building codes. In addition to professional organizations, many international, national, state, and local agencies welcome volunteers.

Volunteer Programs

Volunteering and civic engagement gained national attention in 2009 when President Barack Obama signed the Edward M. Kennedy Serve America Act on April 21 of that year. The Act "reauthorizes and expands national service programs administered by the Corporation for National and Community Service, a federal agency created in 1993." The Corporation reported that "A total of 63.4 million volunteers contributed 8.1 billion hours of service in 2009. Equaling an estimated dollar value of approximately $169 billion for their services" (Corporation for National and Community Service 2010). Signing the Serve America Act also established September 11 as the National Day of Service and Remembrance. On this day people are asked to provide service to their communities.

Given the importance of public and community service, it is very likely that you will be asked in an interview a question related to the

Board Certified Healthcare Interior Designer*

Professional Profile

Linda Gabel, AAHID

Professional Experience: Over 26 years and the last 21 years dedicated to pediatric and adult acute healthcare facilities design.

Professional Practices:
- Collaboration

  - Hands-on collaboration with patients, families, staff, and artists.

  - Collaborations with entire design team.

- Evidence-based design methodologies

Value to Individuals and Society:
- Interior environments that are "true family-centered care."

- Interior environments that meet the needs of people with diverse socio-economic backgrounds, cultures, and age groups.

- Interior environments that enhance the healing process.

- Interior environments that reduce stress for patients, families, caregivers, and staff.

- Value to society by volunteering as the 2005–2009 IIDA Healthcare Forum Advisor and founding member of AAHID.

- Value to society by presenting successful healthcare designs at professional conferences and universities.

*Adapted from: American Academy Healthcare Interior Designers (AAHID). 2010. *AAHIDArticles*. http://www.aahid.org/. Retrieved July 2010.

---

topic, such as "What lessons did you learn from your service activities?" Simultaneously during the interview it is important for you to ask how the firm has been involved in community service and what support is given to employees who are engaged in volunteer activities.

Generally, answers to these questions from an individual and employer's perspective tend to focus on the benefits received from participation, most notably making a difference in the lives of others. Additionally, a person can benefit by developing problem-solving skills, acquiring new knowledge, improving collaboration strategies, networking, learning tolerance, practicing public speaking, and gaining respect for diverse cultures, ethnicities, and economic classes.

Benefits to a business can include building relationships with the community, enhanced reputation through sponsorships, and improving the quality of life. Research also indicates

health benefits associated with volunteering: Compared to individuals who do not volunteer, people who provide service have lower mortality rates, function more effectively, and have lower rates of depression as they age (Corporation for National and Community Service, 2010).

There are a variety of ways that a professional and a business can be involved with service activities at the local, national, and international levels. For example, as discussed previously in this chapter, many architects, designers, planners, and firms are involved with AFH. Nonprofit organizations such as Habitat for Humanity International (HFHI) offer volunteer opportunities throughout the world as well as in local communities.

As of 2011, globally HFHI has been responsible for building more than 500,000 houses and "providing more than 2.5 million people worldwide" (HFHI 2011). (see Figures 1.6a–b.)

Figure 1.6 a–b HFHI builds in more than 25 countries in the regions of the Middle East and Africa. The Habitat homes illustrated in 1.6a were recently built in Malawi—a country with 18 Habitat affiliates.

Homes in Indonesia were destroyed by the tsunami in 2004. HFHI responded to the crisis by helping to rebuild their homes (b). *(Habitat for Humanity)*

HFHI has affiliates in 80 countries, all 50 states, the District of Columbia, Guam, and Puerto Rico. Established in 1985 Habitat for Humanity Canada (HCH) was the first national Habitat organization outside the United States and currently has 72 active affiliates.

Corporation Volunteer Initiatives and Resources

Many corporations and architectural/design firms have contributed to their communities through financial donations, in-kind products, providing training to volunteers, and encouraging their employees to become involved with service. For example, Home Depot has a comprehensive community relations program that includes "volunteerism, do-it-yourself expertise, product donations and monetary grants to meet critical needs and build affordable communities" (Home Depot 2011).

In partnership with several corporations and nonprofit organizations, the Home Depot Foundation and the company's employees were extensively involved with rebuilding homes and communities impacted by Hurricane Katrina in 2005 as well as rebuilding in Joplin, Missouri, after the devastation caused by tornadoes in 2011.

Herman Miller, Inc., a major furniture manufacturer with net sales over $2 billion in fiscal year 2008, contributes to global communities through environmental advocacy as well as volunteerism. For example, employees of Herman Miller have adopted a highway and improve the site by cleaning up the roadsides. Celebrity Bette Midler has also become involved with this effort through the New York City's Adopt-A-Highway program.

A statement provided by Herman Miller explains the company's service ethos: "We reach for a better world by giving time and money to our communities and causes outside the company; through becoming a good corporate citizen worldwide; and even in the (not so) simple act of adding beauty to the world. By participating in the effort, we lift our spirits and the spirits of those around us" (Herman Miller 2011).

Another corporation in the design profession that has a commitment to sustainability is Gensler—a global interior design, architecture, sustainability, and planning firm with an industry ranking of number one in *Interior Design*'s "Top 100 Giants" in 2011. Gensler works on approximately 3,000 projects every year involving more than 3,000 professionals in 41 locations. The company emphasized service in its Annual Reports, "At Gensler, our people give their time and expertise year-round to causes they feel passionate about. That inspires us as a firm to consistently go beyond business as usual to support the cities where we work and live" (Gensler

2010). This statement is supported by volunteering time and expertise to 300-plus causes, including a "Junior Achievement Shadow Day," "Volume: New Libraries for Chicago Schools," and a design for the "Botswana Innovation Hub."

The third firm listed on *Interior Design*'s "Top 100 Giants" in 2011, HOK, also provided examples of community service. HOK is a global planning and architectural design firm that has more than 2,000 people in 24 offices throughout the world. An example of its associates' volunteering activities is posted on YouTube. Associates from HOK's Singapore office rode a ferry to Batam, Indonesia, in 2008 to be involved with a home building project sponsored by Habitat for Humanity, "Batam Build." HOK associates helped with construction by digging holes, hauling building materials, and laying bricks.

Nonprofit Organizations

To learn how to become involved with public and community service, you can contact local, national, or international nonprofit organizations by going to their website, or the Points of Light/HandsOn Network can provide ideas for opportunities related to the built environment. Points of Light Foundation is an independent, nonprofit organization established in 1990 to "encourage and empower the spirit of service."

In 2005, 29 corporate leaders (currently more than 60 companies) of Fortune 500 companies founded HandsOn Network Corporate Council. HandsOn Network merged with the Points of Light Foundation to become the Points of Light Institute in 2007. The merger created the "largest volunteer management and civic engagement organization in the nation" (Points of Light Institute 2007).

To volunteer for a project or program in your community, you might contact one of the HandsOn Action Centers at http://www.handsonnetwork.org/. HandsOn Action Centers are located in more than 240 communities throughout the United States; there are also 11 international locations. HandsOn Network collaborates with more than 70,000 nonprofit organizations. Some of their "impact projects" include wheelchair ramp construction, watershed protection projects, and reducing the "carbon footprint through neighborhood-based conservation and restoration projects" (HandsOn Network 2011).

Another online resource for finding volunteer opportunities in your community is http://serve.gov/ (Figure 1.7). In addition to identifying volunteer projects, Serve.gov's website includes a "Stories of Service" blog, toolkits for creating your own volunteer project, and a project registration function that enables you to recruit volunteers for your project. Serve.gov and HandsOn Network provide you with the ability to stay connected to volunteer opportunities by signing up on Facebook, YouTube, and Twitter.

Volunteer Canada is a program for volunteerism that was founded in 1977. The program has more than 86 centers in all of the Canadian provinces including the Yukon Territory. Over 12 million Canadians volunteer every year through community service activities, such as promoting Canadian culture and the arts, maintaining green spaces, and supervising events. Videos of Volunteer Canada and Volunteering

Figure 1.7 Over 5,000 volunteers worked to clean up the environment after the disastrous Deepwater Horizon BP oil spill in the Gulf of Mexico in 2010. (© *Zhang Jun/Xinhua Press/Corbis*)

in America, a similar program in the United States, are available on YouTube.

Checking for Comprehension

* What are the first concepts that come to mind when you think about volunteering?

* What kinds of design-related volunteer activities would you enjoy?

Service is an important activity for your professional development and should become a highlight of your career. Service as well as the other topics discussed in this chapter, including the value of the design profession, professional organizations, licensure, and professional credentials, are essential to an interior designer working in the twenty-first century.

In continuing to prepare you for an entry-level position, information presented in this chapter should be integrated with the content presented in the next chapter. Chapter 2 reviews different types of design firms, design practice specialties, as well as nontraditional opportunities. You will learn how globalization affects the design profession as well as advantages and cautions related to international practice. An overview of global economics is presented, and a profile of what you might expect with regard to salaries and benefits.

Knowledge and Skills Summary

Highlights

* A comparison of AID's definition of an interior designer in the 1960s and the current definition of the profession provided by NCIDQ succinctly illustrates changes in the profession.

* Architecture for Humanity (AFH) is an excellent example of how design professionals throughout the world are working together to make contributions to society.

* Designers are members of professional organizations specifically for interior design, such as ASID, the International Interior Design Association (IIDA), or the Interior Designers of Canada (IDC). Designers are also joining affiliated professional organizations, such as the National Kitchen and Bath Association (NKBA).

* Licensing and registration are legal permissions that enable a person with the appropriate credentials to practice a profession.

* The major types of legislation related to licensing and registration are licensing, title acts, practice acts, self-certification, and permitting.

* Experience is required for licensing, registration, and eligibility for NCIDQ's examination.

* The Edward M. Kennedy Serve America Act reauthorizes and expands national service programs.

* Many architecture/interior/planning firms, design-related manufacturing corporations, and retailers are involved with community service projects.

* Points of Light/HandsOn Network is the largest volunteer management and civic engagement organization in the nation.

Key Terms

evidence-based design

globalization

licensing

permitting

practice acts

registration

self-certification

social responsibilities

title acts

Projects

Philosophy and Design Project

An important element to advancing the profession of interior design is to educate people about the profession's contributions to society. Conduct an online review of service projects performed by professional organizations, architecture/design/planning firms, and nonprofit organizations related to design. The review should include at least three examples in each category and should include any postings on social networks, such as Facebook or LinkedIn.

Develop a summary of your review in a table. Based on the results as well as any other considerations, develop a statement that reflects your philosophy regarding the profession's contributions to society. Prepare an oral presentation (approximately 10 minutes) of your review and philosophical statement. The presentation should be made to a group of people who have the opportunity to interact with you and can provide feedback on your philosophical statement.

Research Project

Identify a team of three to five members. Your team's assignment is to first identify three states that have not finalized licensing/registration legislation. Team members should develop a plan to contact representatives from each of the three states and individuals associated with ASID or IIDA who are involved with legislation advocacy. The team should gather information on the status of legislation in the three states as well as nationally. Research methods should include reviewing documents, online postings, and interviews.

The team should prepare a one-page summary of its findings, including recommendations for passing legislation. If possible, the team should present its findings to state legislatures and/or representatives of professional organizations. For the presentation the team should develop graphics that illustrate the findings.

Human Factors Research Project

Identify an interdisciplinary team of five to seven people. Your team should identify a local service project and then volunteer their collective time, labor, and expertise. While engaged with the service project, each team member should create a journal of the experience. The journal should include observations of human behavior and reactions about the strengths and weaknesses of how the project was organized and facilitated.

Team members should review each journal and develop a written summary that delineates reactions to human behavior and recommendations for how to engage people in volunteering and strategies to maintain a volunteer's involvement with service projects. Your recommendations might be presented to a service organization and could be posted on an appropriate social network site for feedback. The team should create a report (approximately three pages) that summarizes the project and includes the journals.

References

Allwork, R. 1961. *AID Interior Design and Decoration Manual of Professional Practice.* 2nd ed. New York: American Institute of Interior Designers.

American Academy Healthcare Interior Designers (AAHID). January 2010. *AAHID Candidate Handbook*. http://www.aahid.org/ pdf/Handbook_for_2010.pdf. Accessed July 24, 2010.

———. 2010. *Credentialing*. (http://www.aahid. org/). Accessed July 24, 2010.

American Society of Interior Designers (ASID). 2010. *About ASID*. http://www.asid.org. Accessed July 29, 2010.

California Council for Interior Design Certification (CCIDC). 2011. *About CCIDC*. http:// www.ccidc.org/about_ccidc.html. Accessed May 28, 2011.

Corporation for National and Community Service. 2010. *Volunteering in America 2010.* Washington, DC: Corporation for National and Community Service. http://www.volunteeringinamerica.gov/assets/resources/FactSheetFinal.pdf. Accessed June 24, 2010.

Council for Interior Design Accreditation (CIDA). 2011. *Professional Standards 2011.* http://www.accredit-id.org/. Accessed February 10, 2012.

Council for Interior Design Accreditation (CIDA). 2010. *Professional Standards.* http://www.accredit-id.org/. Accessed July 24, 2010.

Environmental Design Research Association (EDRA). 2011. *About EDRA.* http://www.edra.org/. Accessed May 31, 2011.

Gensler. 2010. *2010 Annual Report.* http://www.gensler.com/uploads/documents/AR_2010_02_18_2011.pdf. Accessed September 4, 2011.

Green Building Certification Institute (GBCI). 2010. *LEED Professional Credentials.* http://www.gbci.org/main-nav/professional-credentials/credentials.aspx. Accessed July 24, 2010.

Habitat for Humanity International (HFHI). 2011. *Habitat for Humanity International Fact Sheet.* http://www.habitat.org/. Accessed May 28, 2011.

HandsOn Network. 2011. *Reduce the Carbon Footprint Though Neighborhood-based Conservation and Restoration Projects.* http://www.handsonnetwork.org/impact/environment. Accessed September 4, 2011.

Herman Miller. 2011. *What We Believe.* http://www.hermanmiller.com/About-Us/What-We-Believe. Accessed May 28, 2011.

Home Depot. 2011. *The Home Depot Foundation.* http://www.homedepot.com/. Accessed May 28, 2011.

Illinois General Assembly. 2011. *Senate Bills.* http://ilga.gov/legislation. Accessed May 28, 2011.

Interior Designers of Canada (IDC). 2010. *About IDC.* http://www.interiordesigncanada.org/about.html. Accessed July 29, 2010.

International Federation of Interior Architects/Designers (IFI). 2011. *Mission and Core Values.* http://www.ifiworld.org/#Homepage. Accessed May 31, 2011.

International Interior Design Association (IIDA). 2010. *Vision and Mission.* http://www.iida.org/. Accessed July 29, 2010.

National Association of Home Builders (NAHB). 2010. *What Is a Certified Aging-in-Place Specialist (CAPS)?* http://www.nahb.org/. Accessed July 24, 2010.

National Council for Interior Design Qualification (NCIDQ). 2012. *Definition of Interior Design.* http://www.ncidq.org. Accessed February 20, 2012.

———. 2011. *NCIDQ Exam Eligibility Requirements.* http://www.ncidq.org. Accessed May 28, 2011.

———. *Interior Design Experience Program (IDEP).* http://www.ncidq.org. Accessed May 28, 2011.

National Council on Qualifications for the Lighting Professions (NCQLP). 2010. *About NCQLP.* http://www.ncqlp.org/. Accessed July 24, 2010.

Nevada State License. 2011. *Chapter 623—Architecture, Interior Design and Residential Design.* (http://www.leg.state.nv.us/NRS/NRS-623.html). Accessed May 28, 2011.

Points of Light Institute. 2007. *Our History.* http://www.pointsoflight.org/faq. Accessed September 4, 2011.

Worldchanging. 2012. Institut Foyer du Savior (Home of Knowledge Institute). http://openarchitecturenetwork.org/projects/institutdufoyer. Accessed April 2, 2012.

CHAPTER 2

Career Opportunities in Interior Design

Kapituloa 2 (Basque)
Кіраўнік 2 (Belarusian)
Глава 2 (Bulgarian)
Capítol 2 (Catalan)
第2章 (Chinese)

After learning the content in Chapter 2, you will be able to answer the following questions:

* What are the various types of design firms?

* What are the design practice specialties and nontraditional career opportunities?

* What are interior design compensation policies and employee benefits?

* How does globalization affect the interior design profession?

* How does global economics and finance affect the built environment and the design profession?

Chapter 1 provided you with an awareness of how the design profession provides value to individuals and society. The chapter also included an overview of professional organizations, licensure, and service opportunities. Ideally, volunteering should first occur while you are a student. Involvement with professional organizations can strengthen your understanding of interior design and demonstrates to prospective employers that you are committed to the profession. Service to socially conscious agencies reveals that you are willing to contribute to important causes.

Volunteering can also assist you with the further development of your career plan, as can networking—an important strategy for identifying career opportunities discussed in this chapter. Thus, volunteering and involvement with professional organizations are related to this chapter's review of different types of design firms, design practice specialties, in addition to nontraditional opportunities.

Other topics in this chapter include interior designer earnings, compensation plans, and various types of employee benefits. The chapter also provides an overview of globalization and its impact on the design profession, including international practice. Chapter 2 concludes by focusing on how global economics and finance affect the work of interior designers and career opportunities.

Types of Design Firms

A question you will be frequently asked is "Where do you want to work?" Fortunately, the interior design profession has numerous career opportunities throughout the world. Many of the reasons why designers have multiple options is because of the wide range of skills and knowledge that are required for the profession as well as the extensive number of businesses that work with designers, such as manufacturers of furniture, lighting, textiles, and equipment.

Each contact is a chance to pursue a career. These opportunities are multiplied and enhanced by globalization. Thus, to respond to the previous question, you have the ability to select from various options; the challenge is to know what is available and how a position aligns with your career goals (see Chapter 3).

General Characteristics of Design Firms

The two major design categories are **residential** and **commercial**, also referred to as **contract design**. Fundamentally, residential work involves designing someone's home, and commercial design focuses on public spaces. Generally, a firm specializes in residential or commercial design, but often has experience designing interiors in both categories.

In exploring career options one of the first issues is to determine your comfort level with the size of a firm. A business can be organized as a **sole proprietor**, whereby an individual owns the firm, or a **corporation** with multiple owners (for detailed information see Chapter 10). Moreover, design positions are available in firms with only a few employees as well as large firms that employ hundreds or thousands of people (Figure 2.1). Typically, responsibilities in a larger firm are more specialized; in a small firm a designer can be involved with every aspect of a project beginning with conceptualization through **post-occupancy evaluations (POE)**.

According to ASID (2010) in 2009 there were 13,388 interior design firms in the United States and approximately 80 percent of these firms had fewer than five employees. Fifteen percent had a staff that numbered between 6 and 20, and only 5 percent had more than 20 employees. From a different perspective, according to *Interior Design*'s "Top 100 Giants," approximately 25 percent of the 2010 "giants" had more than 100 people on their design staff; 50 percent of the firms had between 30 and 100 employees; and 25 percent had fewer than 30 employees. The highest number of design staff was 820 and the lowest was 6.

Generally, services provided by the "giants" include architecture, interior design, sustainable

Figure 2.1 Gensler works on approximately 3,000 projects every year involving more than 3,000 professionals in 41 locations. One of the company's projects is this corporate campus for the Johnson Controls company in Wisconsin.

Gensler developed the master plan, historic preservation of a conference center, renovation of two buildings, and two building additions (2010). The campus illustrates the highest concentration of LEED Platinum certified buildings in the world (Gensler 2010). (*Johnson Controls*)

design, urban planning, lighting, and product design. Their markets focus on corporate, education, government, hospitality, residential, commercial office buildings, cultural, healthcare, and retail.

Location is another factor associated with both the number of employees and the demand for design services. ASID reported in 2010 that of the 13,388 interior design firms in the United States, 42 percent were located in major metropolitan regions, including Chicago, Los Angeles/Long Beach, New York, Atlanta, and Dallas.

In Canada the highest number of design firms was in Ontario and British Columbia. Nearly all of the firms on the "giants" list have headquarters in major cities. Many of these firms have several offices in regions categorized as North America, Central and South America, Asia/Pacific, Europe, and Africa and the Middle East.

These statistics are important to your career plan. Most of your potentially future employers are located in major metropolitan regions.

If you are interested in designing large public spaces, then for the most part, the best opportunities exist in larger firms located in major cities. If you do not intend to live in a large city, or do not want to work for a large firm, then your options for designing large public spaces are more limited.

It is also important to remember that entry-level positions in large firms, such as those listed on the "Top 100 Giants," are uncommon. *Professional experience is essential.* How you acquire experience is explored in Chapter 3. An example of what a large firm expects when hiring an interior designer at the intermediate level (among others) is provided in the list of qualifications in Box 2.1 (Gensler 2010).

Opportunities in Retail, Manufacturers, Government, and Corporations

In addition to positions in an interior design or architectural firm, other opportunities for designers include working for retailers, manufacturers, the government, and corporations.

Box 2.1

Qualifications Posted for Interior Design Positions

Positions	Qualifications
An Interior Designer at the Intermediate Level (Gensler, 2010)	5–7 years' professional experience including proven track record of leading the design of commercial interiors projects. Bachelor's degree from an accredited school of design. Strong planning abilities and the ability to mentor team members, offer guidance and leadership. Knowledge of the total project process including fee and team management, schedules and budgets. Self-starters with good verbal and written communication skills both in Chinese [for position in Beijing] and English. Proficiency in the use of AutoCAD and other 3D computer design programs. Understanding of Revit is a plus. Strong skills in client relationship management and presentation.
Sales Professional Position in Ralph Lauren's *Home Department* (IIDA, 2010)	Ideal candidates will have previous sales experience and/or a background in interior design and a passion for the Ralph Lauren brand. The ability to build long-term relationships with customers, excellent communication, interpersonal and customer service skills, and strong time management/project skills are critical.
Project Manager with a Furniture Manufacturer (Herman Miller, 2010)	Associate degree or equivalent experience in business and design. Extensive product knowledge. Strong interpersonal skills. Detail oriented. Basic knowledge of computer operations and administrative applications. Ability to work irregular hours and extended shifts. Strong customer service orientation. Associate degree or equivalent experience in business. Minimum of five years' experience in contract furniture.
Space Planner at an Athletic Shoe Manufacturer (IIDA, 2010)	Bachelor's degree in Interior Design, Architecture, Facilities Management, or a related field. Minimum of 3 years' professional experience in a corporate environment responsible for space planning and managing move processes and resources. Ability to read, understand, and direct CAD work on floor plans, schematics, shop drawings, and blueprints. Proficiency with AutoCAD applications and systems. Knowledge of office space design, building codes, local compliance requirements to the federal fire code, city, state, and federal regulations and ADA (Americans with Disabilities Act), OSHA (Occupational Safety & Health Administration) regulations. Intermediate-level computer skills, including Microsoft Word, Excel, PowerPoint, and MS Project. Strong customer service orientation with a sincere desire to satisfy client requirements. Ability to communicate with tact and diplomacy to all levels of management. Must be able to safely move around sites under different phases of construction. This may include maneuvering through, around, and over construction supplies, debris, etc.; climbing stairs if building elevators inaccessible and/or inoperable during construction phase. Ability to work extended hours and/or weekends during peak times with little or no advanced notice.

Retail positions center on furniture stores, office furnishings dealers, home furnishings stores, and building materials and supplies dealers. Retail positions enable you to gain experience in specific aspects of interior design, and often provide the opportunity to acquire skills in sales, presentations, and perhaps business operations. Qualifications for a sales professional position in a retail store are listed in Box 2.1.

Working for a manufacturer of products used in interiors, such as textiles or furniture, also provides experience in the profession and

Box 2.1

Qualifications Posted for Interior Design Positions *(continued)*

Positions	Qualifications
Government-Sponsored LEED Certification Reviewer at the USGBC (IIDA, 2010) (abbreviated list)	Bachelor's degree (Master's degree preferred) in a field of study related to one or more of the following specialties: Architecture (architecture, landscape architecture, interior design). Currently licensed professional in specialty area preferred. Other professional certifications as relevant to area of expertise. LEED AP required; with specialty preferred. LEED Certification Reviewer certificate preferred (required after hire for Reviewer II and above). Experience with a variety of high-performance building projects, including LEED projects. Specialization in a high-performance building attribute such as energy efficiency, water efficiency, materials efficiency, indoor environmental quality, etc. Ability to read, understand, and interpret building floor plans, sections, site plans, zoning maps, interior furniture and finish plans, construction specifications and operational policies. Detailed technical understanding of and experience with one or more of the following design and building topics: common construction methods, materials specification, fenestration, HVAC systems, plumbing systems, electrical systems, landscape design and management, master planning, land use, zoning, urban development. Detailed technical understanding of and experience with common environmental building codes and standards relevant to specialty. Excellent judgment, analytical thinking, and problem-solving skills. Energetic, detail-oriented, and able to prioritize. Experience serving in technical consultative role. Excellent written and verbal communication skills, including technical writing. Strong interpersonal and customer service skills. Ability to work well both independently and on teams.
Non-Tenure Temporary Faculty Member Position Announcement (IIDA, 2010)	**Responsibilities** Teach studio and lecture courses in one or more of the following areas: social and behavioral aspects of the near environment; construction, systems and materials for interior environments; lighting and environmental systems; AutoCAD and BIM software; materials and products; history, theory, and context of design; business practices; and sustainable theories and application in design. Participate in curriculum development and marketing for Interior Design program including distance delivery. Be actively involved with industry and relevant professional associations. **Qualifications** Master's degree in Interior Design or related field required; Ph.D. preferred. The candidate accepted for this position must be able to meet eligibility requirements for work in the United States at the time appointment is scheduled to begin and continue working legally for the proposed term of the appointment. The selected candidate must be able to communicate effectively in English. Strongly Preferred: NCIDQ certification, LEED Associate status. Desired: Previous experience in teaching, including distance education; professional practice.

enables you to build relationships with design firms. The possibilities are extensive, as reflected in the increasing number of products that interior designers specify every year. In 2005 and 2009 interior designers specified products and services worth $57 billion and $75 billion products and services, respectively (ASID 2010). These numbers should escalate due to the growing number of sustainable products on the market.

As a manufacturer's representative, one of your responsibilities is to service design firms that are specifying your product. Servicing the firm includes providing product updates in a timely manner and resolving problems associated with a product's quality, delivery, or performance. An example of qualifications for a project manager position with a furniture manufacturer is provided in Box 2.1.

Large corporations have **in-house designers** who work in a variety of departments, such as facility planning, facilities management, and architectural services. Working as an in-house designer involves planning facilities for the company's internal customers as well as any external clients. For example, working as an interior designer for an insurance company could entail designing offices for managers as well as facilities owned by agents in various locations. Box 2.1 includes a list of qualifications for a design position with a major manufacturer.

Interior design career opportunities also exist in the government. Federal, state, and local governments are responsible for thousands of buildings throughout the United States. The U.S. General Services Administration (GSA) alone is responsible for 8,600 buildings and 425 historic properties. State-supported universities and colleges also have facility planning departments that employ interior designers. Box 2.1 provides a list of qualifications required for a government-sponsored design-relation position (LEED certification reviewer at the USGBC).

Checking for Comprehension

* Describe at least three characteristics of design firms.

* How would you prepare to interview for a job as an in-house designer for a corporation?

Design Practice Specializations and Nontraditional Opportunities

The preceding section provided an overview of the major types of design firms. These categories have areas of specialization that include markets with substantial opportunities, such as commercial offices, as well as positions with less demand, such as museums and transportation.

In addition to the fundamentally traditional interior design career opportunities, there are other options related to the design profession, such as photography and marketing. For the purpose of the discussion in this section, "nontraditional" options are considered opportunities that normally exist in professions other than interior design and architecture.

An awareness of all the options available to an interior designer are especially important when the economy is weak or when a person is interested in pursuing a new challenge. By constantly monitoring global events, designers can identify new ways to use their skills and abilities. For example, developments in the area of nanotechnology have the potential to create a multitude of new products for the built environment. Keeping abreast of this technology requires a survey of several disciplines, such as medicine, electronics, and textile science.

Updates should be acquired from a variety of sources, such as newspapers, books, journals, and websites of credible organizations and agencies. To obtain reliable and credible Internet information, you should research an organization's background and assess its qualifications.

Design Practice Specializations
Throughout the years interior designers have been involved with designing every type of built environment. Within the categories of residential and commercial design, there are numerous areas of specialization. Contrary to present categorizations, the author contends that "sustainable design" should *not* be considered one of these unique areas. Listing sustainable design in a separate category implies that buildings might or might not be designed to be sustainable. Given the importance of sustaining our planet for current and future generations, it is imperative that the design profession applies the principles of sustainable design and development to *all* built environments. Therefore, in echoing the book's approach to discussing the design profession within the context of the twenty-first century, the discussions that follow assume it is not necessary

to have a "sustainable design" category because hopefully in the near future most buildings will be designed to be sustainable. However, the author proposes that within the topic of sustainable design there are several practice areas of specialization; these are reviewed in this section.

Residential specializations can be classified by single- or multi-dwelling units as well as by rooms or functions. Therefore, a residential interior designer might specialize in kitchens, bathrooms, home theaters, lighting, or accessories. For an overview of a residential project, please refer to the case study described in Box 2.2. The case study and the details provided were selected to illustrate the value of the design profession.

Box 2.2
Residential Case Study*

Project Profile: An affordable 12-story residential high-rise for working families in San Diego designed by Joseph Wong Design Associates. The high-rise has 136 apartments with private balconies, laundry facilities, community rooms, an affordable new and used clothing store, and a 12th floor deck. On the second floor there is a playground, basketball court, and barbecue grills. "Seven units are reserved for households with one or more special needs adults (HIV positive, AIDS, mental illness, homeless, or at-risk of becoming homeless)." Units have one, two, and three bedrooms, and range from 553–1,300 square feet (51–121 square meters).

Client Profile: Father Joe's Villages began in 1950 with a lunch line and thrift store for the homeless. Today the organization has seven large villages in the Southwest and has the following vision and purpose:

"We envision communities where everyone is able to obtain food, housing, healthcare, and education; and achieve his or her full potential."

"Our Mission is to help our neighbors in need break the cycle of homelessness and poverty by promoting self-sufficiency through an innovative continuum of care, multi-disciplinary programs, and partnerships that come together in the spirit of our CREED [compassion, respect, empathy, empowerment, dignity] to teach, learn from, and challenge our neighbors and one another" (*Village News*, 2009).

Design Solutions and Value:

- To have value to the organization, design solutions had to support the philosophical perspectives of Father Joe's Villages. The design had to focus on having a built environment that accommodated multi-disciplinary programs and fostered compassion, respect, empowerment, and dignity.

- One way to evaluate the design's success is to understand the perceptions of the families who live in the facilities:

A woman in a one-bedroom apartment notes, "Absolutely the best thing is I can enjoy the sunlight that comes through my apartment. I have a view of the sunrise every day; whereas my old apartment was on the first floor and DARK. It is gorgeous, modern, clean, and safe. I have onsite parking and a laundry room. It is centrally located, easy access to City College, Balboa Park, and I can easily visit family and friends. Great freeway access too."

(Box 2.2 continued on page 34)

Box 2.2
Residential Case Study* *(continued)*

- Another resident appreciates "the balcony with a view of the Coronado Bay Bridge," the "well-appointed kitchen," and his "contemporary furnishings, much of which he purchased at Father Joe's Village auctions."

- An eight-year-old girl enjoys the "playground in the 'backyard' on the second floor."

Remarks from the residents and the accompanying photographs depict the value of a well-designed built environment and demonstrate how designers can help to address a societal need by designing affordable facilities. The matrix below portrays one approach to analyzing how the design solutions provided value to the organization, residents, staff, and society.

Design Solutions/Organizational Values	Ensuring safety, well-being, and satisfaction	Promoting self-sufficiency through an innovative continuum of care	Fostering involvement with multi-disciplinary programs	Sustainability
Cost-effective construction methods and materials.	✓	✓		✓
Aesthetically designed architecture and interiors.	✓	✓	✓	
Access to outdoors via balconies, second floor "backyard," and the deck on the 12th floor.	✓	✓	✓	✓
Multi-purpose community rooms.	✓	✓	✓	✓
Exercise room, children's play area, and basketball court located on the second floor.	✓	✓	✓	
Laundry rooms with closed-circuit monitors of play area.	✓	✓		
Durable, aesthetically pleasing, and easy to maintain materials/equipment: granite countertops, custom cabinetry, and stainless steel appliances	✓	✓		✓
An abundance of daylighting and views in every unit.	✓	✓		✓
Location close to amenities, recreation, and public transportation.	✓	✓		✓

*Adapted from: *Village News*. 2009. Volume 19, Issue 1. www.neighbor.org.

The variety of commercial buildings is extensive, but the most frequently designed built environments include offices, healthcare, education, hospitality, retail, and the increasingly popular **mixed-use buildings**. A mixed-use building is designed to accommodate several different functions. For example, a mixed-use building might have offices, condominiums, restaurants, and retail stores.

Designers might also be involved with designing the interiors for transportation facilities, cultural, justice, and entertainment. Box 2.3 has a case study focusing on commercial design, and how the work of an interior designer can add value to a client, users of the space, and society.

In addition to designing for a specific market, such as healthcare, there are career opportunities based on the unique skills of an interior designer, such as **CAD (computer-aided design), BIM (building information modeling), Revit,** **integrated project delivery (IPD),** historic preservation, lighting, ergonomics, rendering, and models (Box 2.4). Because of globalization, in the near future some of these opportunities might become more limiting. To reduce production costs, some firms have been outsourcing services, such as drafting, to foreign companies; it appears this practice is on the rise.

Box 2.3
Commercial Case Study*

Project Profile: A children's psychiatric ward at Evangelisches Königin Elisabeth Herzberge Hospital in Berlin designed by Dan Pearlman. The ward is 15,070 square feet (1,400 square meters).

Client Profile: The hospital's goal is "your health" from a holistic treatment perspective and is supported with the following information (modifications made in the translation from German to English):

"You are important to us as human beings, not just as a patient with specific symptoms. We are here for you to listen and assist you in healing. Undoubtedly contributing to the healing process is a pleasant atmosphere. Our hospital is located in a beautiful, sprawling park, which invites you to linger or walk. All areas of the hospital, including the historic buildings, are constructed around 1900, completely modernized. The rooms and common rooms are bright, friendly and modern."

The hospital's Department of Psychiatry and Psychotherapy for Children and Young Adults was developed to provide treatment to (Evangelisches Königin Elisabeth Herzberge Hospital, 2010) "children and young people who have lost their emotional or mental physical balance, their everyday life can no longer cope alone and the need for a defined period of time on a protected environment and require support."

Design Solutions and Value:

- To have value to the client, design solutions had to support the philosophical perspectives of the hospital as well as the children's psychiatric ward. The design had to focus on having a built environment that reflected a holistic perspective to healing, demonstrated that patients were important to them as human beings, had a pleasant atmosphere, and provided a protected and supportive environment for children and young adults.

- One way to evaluate the design's success is to study the perceptions of the professionals who work with the children. Doctors have noted that the "adolescents seem less aggressive and the younger children mellower." Another physician commented, "In this open, friendly atmosphere, parents and relatives of the children and adolescents can engage more easily in the therapeutic process." The matrix below portrays how the design solutions provided value to the patients, family members, staff, and society.

(Box 2.3 continued on page 36)

Box 2.3

Commercial Case Study* *(continued)*

Design Solutions/ Organizational Values	Holistic treatment of patients	Promoting the perspective that patients were important as human beings	Fostering a protected and supportive environment for children and young adults	Pleasant atmosphere	Sustainability
Spaces in a renovated historic building that specifically accommodate psychiatric therapies: colors—orange (healing), green (motivation), and blue (relieving stress); Elise's Island theme; and age-appropriate designs (see below).	✓	✓	✓	✓	✓
Designs based on a tale of the hospital's guardian angel, Elise. Told to all patients, the tale is about how Elise dreamed up her own island and when she left the hospital she gave them the island to help other children feel safe.	✓	✓	✓	✓	
Island and age-appropriate space planning: three zones for different age groups (Dune Beach for the youngest; Palm Cove for preteens; Rock Haven for the oldest).	✓	✓	✓		
Island and age-appropriate graphics: Dune Beach—bird nests with mother's feeding; Palm Cove—parrots, trees, and rope ladders; Rock Haven—clipper ship to "set sail from their elders."	✓	✓	✓	✓	
Island and age-appropriate furniture, materials, and accessories: Dune Beach—nooks, fuzzy carpeting, and drapes; Palm Cove—hammock, climbable surfaces and furniture; Rock Haven—bean bag chairs and lounge seating.	✓	✓	✓	✓	✓
An abundance of daylighting and views to the park.	✓	✓	✓	✓	✓
Durable and easy to maintain materials and surfaces.	✓			✓	✓

*Adapted from: http://www.keh-berlin.de. 2010 and LaBarre, S. 2010. Fantasy Island. *Metropolis Magazine*, Volume 29 no. 11.

Interior Design Career Options

Residential

Single-dwelling, multi-dwelling, condominiums, apartments, model homes, retail furniture, retail department stores, retail specialty stores.

Commercial

Offices (private/corporate), hospitality (restaurants/hotels/motels), healthcare (hospitals/clinics/out-patient surgery centers/nursing homes), retail, education (pre-K–12/higher education), government (local/state/regional/national), institutional design, office furnishings store, corporate in-house design, facility and planning management.

Specialized Buildings

Mixed-use buildings, adaptive reuse, entertainment (spas/resorts/country clubs/casinos), religious, museums, libraries, funeral homes, transportation, elderly care centers, assisted living centers, transportation, children's hospitals, birthing centers.

Specialized Spaces

Medical/dental offices, set design, retail visual merchandiser, sets for theater/television programs/films/commercials, television home shows, designer showrooms, childcare centers, home staging, storage/closets, music rooms, game rooms, media rooms, conference rooms.

Specialized Products

Artwork, antiques, floor coverings, office furniture, upholstery, wall/ceiling treatments and coverings, light fixtures, accessories, craftwork, window/door products, cabinetry, plumbing hardware, appliances.

Specialized Skills

CAD (computer-aided design), BIM (building information modeling), Revit, integrated project delivery (IPD), computer modeling and visualization, historic preservation, renovation, restoration, conservation, adaptive reuse, lighting, universal design, aging-in-place, codes, ergonomics, rendering, models, graphic design, photography, marketing, journalism (magazines/newspapers), urban planning, project management, lifestyle designs, e-commerce, nanotechnology applications, design management, brand building, research/development, acoustics, feng shui, exhibit design, wayfinding, behavioral factors, specification writer, sales, media specialist, real estate, color consultant, public relations, artist, space planner, LEED certification, indoor environmental quality (IEQ), indoor air quality (IAQ), renewable resources, daylighting, energy-efficient lighting, bioclimatic designs, building footprint conservation, refurbishment, reclamation dealer, water management, carbon-neutral/zero-energy designs.

As sustainable designs become more mainstream, a designer might elect an area of expertise. Some of the potential specializations include adaptive reuse, LEED certification, indoor environmental quality (IEQ), indoor air quality (IAQ), renewable resources, daylighting, energy-efficient lighting, bioclimatic designs, building footprint conservation, refurbishment, reclamation dealer, water management, and carbon-neutral and zero-energy designs.

Nontraditional Career Opportunities

In pursing career opportunities an interior designer might be interested in connecting his or her interest in design with other disciplines that have been found to be interesting, perhaps while taking a course or as a hobby (Box 2.4). Some of these areas include graphics, photography, journalism, merchandise displays, television, film, theater, urban planning, and product design. For example, someone interested in photography and design might want to pursue a career working as a photographer for an interior design magazine. The performing arts present opportunities to design the sets for stages.

To create merchandise displays, retailers require people who understand how to apply the elements and principles of design for a specialized purpose. These skills and knowledge are also important for a product designer. In addition, as illustrated in the case study described in

---

Box 2.5
Product Designer Case Study*

Studio:

Antenna Design, Partners, Sigi Moeslinger and Masamichi Udagawa; Founded in 1997 in New York

Projects

- User interface for New York's Metropolitan Transportation Authority's (MTA) MetroCard vending machines (serves 5 million riders each day)

- Interior of MTA's subway cars

- PDAs for Palm, wireless devices for Fujitsu

- Bloomberg computer terminals and peripherals

- Interactive art installations (*Firefly*, 2001; *Blowing Gently*, 2002)

- Knoll's Antenna Workspaces (post-panel, post-cubicle office system; designed to be flexible, affordable, and attractive)

Design Solutions Based on Observations and Listening

MTA Subway Cars
- Create the illusion of greater space: Cars have light-colored walls and ceilings.

- Conceal dirt: Dark-patterned floors.

- Ease cleaning: Cantilevered seats.

- Vandalism solution: Replaceable layers on windows.

Client Reactions to the MTA Designs
"Of course their design is excellent, but what made my mouth drop open was how well they accommodated all our user groups: riders, maintenance staff, our other designers. The things they made weren't foreign objects. They suited our needs perfectly."

"Vandalism is always a possibility. And of course, it does upset us. It's sort of like messing up your own living room. But it was also very exciting to ride the subway and hear people talk to each other about our cars. I think good design encourages people to take a sense of ownership and pride in the system."

*Adapted from: Shulman, K. 2010. "Intense Listeners." *Metropolis Magazine* 29(11), 102–107; 125; 127.

Figure 2.2 Antenna Design, Partners, Sigi Moeslinger and Masamichi Udagawa in their New York studio. The projects of these two successful product designers reflect the art of research, observation, and listening to the needs of their clients. (© Adam Krause)

Box 2.5, other skills essential for designers are the art of observation and listening to the needs of a client and end users (Figure 2.2).

Excellent listening skills are also helpful for **branding** consultants—an emerging career area in marketing. Branding consultants are responsible for managing a company's brand by identifying marketing strategies that reinforce the brand through a variety of activities, such as public events, advertisements, and communication.

Another nontraditional career opportunity exists in education. In the United States and Canada there are 350 and 20 interior design programs, respectively (ASID 2010). Approximately 35 percent of the programs are accredited by CIDA and more than 62 percent of the faculty members have experience as designers (ASID 2010). Faculty positions are either tenure or non-tenure lines. Essentially, a tenure line position provides a faculty member with the opportunity to have continuous employment; a non-tenured position is renewed on an annual basis. To see a list of teaching responsibilities as well as qualifications, please refer to a university's position announcement in Box 2.1.

Compensation and Benefits

Having an awareness of career opportunities helps to provide an overview of where your next project might be located in the future as well as what you might be earning in the future. For example, international design firms have already experienced that fees charged to clients can vary considerably between cities, regions, countries, and type of project. Fees charged to a client in India can be significantly different than a client in London. Moreover, there are wide variances in what constitutes billable services, such as travel expenses. Understanding local practices, including fees, is essential to these situations. How do fees affect your career? Fees affect job opportunities, your salary, as well as your future income.

Salaries
What salary would you like to receive as an entry-level interior designer? In addition to

international fee variances, global economies and financial circumstances affect your compensation rates and benefits that an employer can extend to employees. Within this context you should have an awareness of salary ranges as well as what could be included in employee benefits.

Fortunately, there are many resources available online that can provide an overview of salaries. One of the most reliable is the U.S. Department of Labor's Bureau of Labor Statistics (see http://www.bls.gov/home.htm). The Bureau publishes semiannual occupational employment statistics (OES) for more than 800 occupations. OES include national employment estimates as well as industry, state, and metropolitan profiles for interior designers, not including self-employed workers.

As illustrated in Table 2.1 in 2010 the national mean hourly wage and the mean annual wage for interior designers was $25.05 and $52,100, respectively. Most of the jobs were in the specialized design services industry (15,810), and the highest annual mean wage was working in the architectural, engineering, and related services.

The state and metropolitan profiles provided in the OES report demonstrate that the states with the highest concentration of interior designers were California, Texas, New York, Florida, and Illinois. The top metropolitan areas that had the highest concentration of interior designers were in New York/New Jersey; Los Angeles; Washington, DC/Virginia; Dallas; and Chicago.

Table 2.1 also provides hourly and annual mean wages for the top-paying states and

Table 2.1 National Mean Hourly and Annual Wages for Interior Designers		
Industry/Related Industry	**Mean Hourly Wage**	**Mean Annual Wage**
National	$25.05	$52,100
Specialized Design Services	$25.21	$52,430
Architectural, Engineering, and Related Services	$27.17	$56,520
Furniture Stores	$23.49	$48,870
Building Material and Supplies Dealers	$22.22	$42,060
Residential Building Construction	$23.23	$48,320
Newspaper, Periodical, Book, and Directory Publishers	$34.97	$72,750
Federal Executive Branch (OES Designation)	$34.45	$71,660
Management, Scientific, and Technical Consulting Services	$31.44	$65,400
Management of Companies and Enterprises	$29.06	$60,440
Department Stores	$28.06	$58,360
Top Paying States/Metropolitan Areas		
California	$27.04	$56,240
Texas	$24.74	$51,470
New York	$30.96	$64,400
Florida	$23.45	$48,770
Illinois	$23.95	$49,810
New York-White Plains-Wayne, NY-NJ Metropolitan Division	$32.62	$67,840
Los Angeles-Long Beach-Glendale, CA Metropolitan Division	$27.25	$56,670
Washington-Arlington-Alexandria, DC-VA-MD-WV Metropolitan Division	$30.64	$63,740
Dallas-Plano-Irving, TX Metropolitan Division	$27.65	$57,510
Chicago-Naperville-Joliet, IL Metropolitan Division	$25.72	$53,490

Source: U.S. Department of Labor, May 2010, *Bureau of Labor Statistics*, http://www.bls.gov/oes/20010/may/oes271025.htm. Retrieved May 28, 2011.

metropolitan areas. Note that the highest pay is often a reflection of a location's cost of living. As you are researching job opportunities, examine a city's cost of living figures, which include state taxes and the regional Consumer Price Index (CPI) for goods and services. There are many free online sources for this information, such as realtor's services and the banking industry. For example, CNN Money has a cost of living calculator that enables you to compare salaries in different cities. For example, to maintain the same standard of living, a person with a $30,000 annual wage living in Des Moines, Iowa, would need an estimated $71,920 to live in Manhattan. Compared to Des Moines, groceries, utilities, transportation, and healthcare are more expensive in Manhattan, but the largest difference is for housing—an estimated 360 percent higher.

Benefits

Salary and a city's cost of living are just two of the factors that you have to examine while considering career options. Employee benefits are also very important factors, and their dollar value should be considered a boost to a base salary. Without benefits, such as health insurance, you would have to pay the expenses yourself. The dollar value of benefits can equate to many thousands of dollars per year. Benefits might or might not be advertised on a company's website. Therefore, as you are researching firms online, if they do not list benefits do not assume that the company does not offer benefits. You can request benefits information by contacting the company.

Fundamentally, employee benefits can be divided into traditional and nontraditional. Traditional benefits include healthcare insurance (medical, dental, vision), company-sponsored pension plans, **401(k) retirement plans**, Social Security matching contributions, holidays, and paid vacation and sick days. With the exception of retirement plans, most of these benefits are fairly easy to understand.

Most retirement plans require shared contributions from the employer and employee. A company or government-sponsored pension plan basically pays a retired employee until the person dies, and then frequently a percentage of the pension is paid to any survivors. The amount of the pension is usually determined by a person's most recent salary. Under this arrangement the company retains control of the investment. Company-sponsored pension plans still exist, but in the twenty-first century more businesses are shifting their retirement plans to 401(k)s, or defined contribution plans.

401(k)'s

As a student you should have a fundamental awareness of 401(k)'s and how they can affect your future. Chances are very good that when you interview for positions, employers will mention 401(k)'s and explain their **vesting** requirements. If you obtain a position with a company that has a 401(k) retirement plan, soon after starting the job you might have to determine the investment strategy for your 401(k).

Your investment strategy will affect the amount of money you will have when you retire and for how long. As resources available in the Social Security program diminish, establishing a retirement plan early in your career is becoming essential.

401(k)'s are basically a retirement savings account that you manage and control. Corporations are shifting the responsibility and any risks associated with investments to their employees. This is an excellent example of why it is important to have a basic understanding of global economics and finance. You are responsible for determining how much you want to contribute through payroll deductions as well as how the money will be invested.

Employers can match your contribution, but the amount is based on company policies. Contributions are deducted from your salary before taxes, which reduces your taxable income. In addition, investments and profits are not taxed until the money is withdrawn, which is generally during retirement years when your income is lower. For these reasons as well as having an income stream in retirement, financial planners highly recommend that when given the opportunity, an employee should participate in a 401(k) plan as early as possible and contribute at the maximum level allowable.

In establishing a 401(k) plan, one of the initial steps is to review your employer's investment options. An employer has a plan administrator that has several investment alternatives, including **profit sharing** and **mutual funds**.

Profit sharing refers to owning stock in your employer's company. Because your salary will always be dependent on the success of the company, financial advisors suggest that, if anything, only a small percentage of your salary should be invested in company stock. The key is to diversify your assets.

Mutual funds have thousands of investors and have a diversified composition of investments, such as stocks, bonds, Treasury bills, and/or cash. Financial planners recommend that when selecting a mutual fund you should invest for the long term and choose funds that have demonstrated steady growth and that perform well over time.

Other recommendations provided by financial planners related to 401(k)s include understanding your employer's vesting rules, portability arrangements, investment rebalancing strategies, and lump-sum payments. Vesting is associated with when you are eligible to participate and when your employer's contributions become your assets. The amount and the time can vary according to your employer's rules. Some employers allow you to be immediately eligible and immediately vested; other companies have time restrictions.

The 401(k)'s portability feature enables you to take your 401(k) plan with you when you change jobs. You can **rollover** your 401(k) into your new employer's program or an **IRA** (individual retirement account). Financial advisors do not recommend that you spend the cash or that you take out loans from the 401(k), unless there is an emergency. Any withdraws should be repaid as quickly as possible.

Research has indicated that people rarely change their investment portfolio. As your 401(k) progresses, financial advisors suggest that periodically you should reevaluate your investments and when necessary rebalance the portfolio by making sure you have a diversified composition.

When you retire you can receive the money that is invested in your 401(k) in a one lump-sum payment. To help ensure an income for the rest of your life, financial planners stress that you should develop a plan that distributes the money over a long period of time.

Nontraditional Benefits

In contrast to traditional benefit programs that can last throughout your lifetime, most often, nontraditional benefits are available only while you are employed with a company. Generally, nontraditional benefit programs focus on helping employees balance their work and life responsibilities, and some are available only at large corporations.

A variety of programs can be included in the nontraditional benefit category, including performance bonuses, parental leave, adoption assistance, tuition reimbursement, travel concierge services, wellness programs, product discounts, and financial planning advice.

Nontraditional benefits can also include on-site facilities, such as child daycare, gyms, health services, massage therapy, dry cleaners, postal services, and car washes.

Checking for Comprehension

- Identify at least five different career opportunities for interior designers.

- Describe three different ways an interior designer can provide value to society.

Globalization and International Business Practices

Globalization and multiculturalism has expanded career opportunities for the design profession. This section explains globalization within the context of how the phenomenon has impacted professional practice. The global marketplace has enabled a designer to work for a firm with offices in several regions of the world or design facilities for a client who has buildings all over the globe. In either situation you must be aware of the opportunities, issues, and challenges associated with international business practices.

Globalization: Impact on the Design Profession

As you are searching for a position, or soon after accepting a job as an interior designer, someone might ask you a question related to working on a project in a foreign country. Imagine if the person asked you to identify important factors to consider when working on a project in Bosnia-Herzegovina. How would you respond? To help you prepare for such questions, this section reviews important considerations related to globalization and explains how they affect working on an international project (Box 2.6 and Figure 2.3). An excellent starting point is to understand the concept of globalization as well as some of the key controversies that surround the topic.

Box 2.6

International Case Study: Bosnia-Herzegovina (Bosnia)*

Examples of Characteristics of a Foreign City Useful for Business Practices Bosnia-Herzegovina (Bosnia)	Applicability to the Business Practices of Interior Designers
Country Profile **Area:** 51,129 sq. km **Location:** Southeastern Europe on the Balkan Peninsula; Sarajevo is the capital **Time zone:** Eastern Standard Time (EST) + 6 hours **Currency:** Marka (BAM) **Country Codes:** International Country Code (U.S. 011) + 387 **Climate:** With a combination of Alpine and Mediterranean climates, the country has cold winters, hot summers, and heavy rain in the early summer months.	Important basic knowledge for building client relationships and for business travel. An awareness of the country's profile and culture demonstrates interest in the community and can help you to engage in meaningful conversations with your client as well as other local professionals, contractors, and suppliers.
Culture People enjoy coffee visits, walks in parks, movies, literature, leisurely meals, music, winter sports, hiking, basketball, and soccer. Crafts include woodcarving, book arts, textiles, embroidery, painting, carpet weaving, and metalwork. Colors and patterns used in carpets and embroidery are unique to each town. A mixed heritage of architecture is reflected in various types, such as Muslim mosques, and Orthodox and Catholic churches as well as numerous styles, including Roman, Early Christian, Byzantine, Islamic, Early Medieval, Romanesque, Gothic, Renaissance, and Baroque. Examples of important representative buildings and structures include Roman baths in Banja Luka, the reconstructed Old Bridge (Stari most) in Mostar, mosques and fortresses in Travnik, and Turkish coffee cafés (kafanas). (see Figure 2.3.) In Sarajevo: the Vijecnica National Theater, National Library, National Museum, Central Bank, Gazi Husrev-Bey Masque, Sarajevo Cathedral, and Bascarsija (Old Town).	Understanding characteristics of people, religion, and history provides insight regarding attitudes, values, beliefs, personal conflicts, and foreign influences. Cultural information is important to know when developing client relationships, engaging in collaborative initiatives, following business protocols and customs, and negotiating contracts (see Chapter 5).
People and Religion Several ethnic groups from the Slavic tribes, but the three major groups in descending order of population are the Bosnian Muslims (Bosniaks), Serbs, and the Croats. Each group has a different religion: (1) Bosniaks—Islam, (2) Serbs—Orthodox, and (3) Croats—Catholic. Approximately 60 and 40 percent of the people live in rural and urban settings, respectively.	Understanding characteristics of people and religion provides insight regarding attitudes, values, beliefs, personal conflicts, and foreign influences. This information is important to know when developing client relationships, engaging in collaborative initiatives, following business protocols and customs, and negotiating contracts (see Chapter 5). In addition, demographic data can be useful for marketing purposes.

(Box 2.6 continued on page 44)

Box 2.6

International Case Study: Bosnia-Herzegovina (Bosnia)* (continued)

Examples of Characteristics of a Foreign City Useful for Business Practices Bosnia-Herzegovina (Bosnia)	Applicability to the Business Practices of Interior Designers
History Started approximately 3,000 years ago with the settlement of Illyrians. First century A.D. a Roman province followed by the South Slavs beginning in the 500s. Hungarian Empire's rule began in the 12th century until the mid-15th century; but with a short period of independence when the viceroys, or bans, ruled the country. The Ottoman Empire introduced Islam and conquered Bosnia in 1463 followed by Herzegovina in the 1480s. After Russia declared war in 1877 and defeated the Ottoman Empire in 1878, the Congress of Berlin determined that Austria-Hungary should have temporary control of Bosnia. Austria-Hungary gained formal control of Bosnia in 1908. A Bosnian Serb assassinated Archduke Franz Ferdinand, heir to the throne, which prompted the start of World War I. After the war Bosnia became part of Yugoslavia. During World War II Germany controlled Yugoslavia and after the war the country was under the power of the Communists until 1990. Bosnia declared independence from Yugoslavia in 1992; however, many Serbs were opposed to the declaration and began a three-year war (1992–1995) with the non-Serbs, which involved ethnic cleansing. The war resulted in the deaths of more than 250,000 people and the destruction of many buildings, factories, and bridges. The 1995 Dayton Peace Agreement created a nearly equal division of the country into the Muslim-Croat federation and the Bosnian Serb republic.	Understanding characteristics of people, religion, and history provides insight regarding attitudes, values, beliefs, personal conflicts, and foreign influences. Historical information is important to know when developing client relationships, engaging in collaborative initiatives, following business protocols and customs, and negotiating contracts (see Chapter 5). Historical events can affect business relationships and transactions. Countries with long histories are especially challenging due to influences from numerous cultures for centuries.
Government Parliamentary democracy. The Dayton Peace Agreement instituted that Entities control taxation and business development. Nationwide value-added tax (VAT). Customs collected by a customs service. President coordinates international and nongovernmental organizations. Council of Ministers is responsible for foreign trade policies, custom policies, and monetary policies. Federation Government contacts: Development, Entrepreneurship and Crafts—Velimir Kunic; Trade—Desnica Radivojevic; Environment and Tourism—Nevenko Herceg. Embassy in United States: 2109 E. Street NW, Washington, DC.	Government information is important to know when developing client relationships, engaging in collaborative initiatives, following business protocols and customs, and negotiating contracts (see Chapter 5). This knowledge is also important for understanding taxation policies, business development policies, customs regulations, environmental requirements, trade policies, and the legal system.
Economy Nominal GDP (2009 est.): $16.5 billion (U.S. $1=1.45KM) GDP real growth rate (2009 est.): 3.2% Inflation rate (2009 est.): 0.6% Average monthly net salary (2009): $544 Natural resources: hydropower, coal, iron ore, bauxite, forests, copper, lead, zinc, cobalt, and prime farmland Industry: Steel, aluminum, minerals, vehicle assembly, textiles, wooden furniture, domestic appliances, oil refining	Economic information is important to know when developing client relationships, engaging in collaborative initiatives, following business protocols and customs, and negotiating contracts (see Chapter 5). Knowledge about the economy is important for determining fees, predicting building costs, and identifying businesses that may be profitable. Generally, the most successful businesses are associated with a country's natural resources as well as its primary industries.

Adapted from: http://www.state.gov/r/pa/ei/bgn/index.htm; *The World Book Encyclopedia*, 2004; *Bosnia-Herzegovina* (Chicago: World Book, Inc. and Bosnia-Herzegovina, 2010).

Figure 2.3 The reconstructed Old Bridge (Stari most) in Mostar, Bosnia-Herzegovina. (© *John Miles/Getty*)

Many people have developed definitions for globalization, most of which center on economics, politics, culture, and finance. The culturally related definition that appears to connect with the interior design profession is the one provided by Anthony Giddens: "Globalization can thus be defined as the intensification of worldwide social relations which link distant localities in such a way that local happenings are shaped by events occurring many miles away and vice versa" (1990). This broad definition of globalization could be applied to the earliest civilizations through to the present day. However, the concept of globalization was not acknowledged until the 1970s. Why? The explanation that follows helps to provide an understanding of the evolution of the concept.

Some form of trade between nations has occurred for thousands of years, but as communication, technology, and transportation progressed, the world theoretically became smaller. New World discoveries and colonization required financial resources, technological developments, and reliable means of travel. Interactions between countries accelerated during the nineteenth and early twentieth century when many technologies, such as the steam engine, electrical power, the airplane, automobile, and telephone, were invented.

Beginning in the 1970s the world appeared to be becoming increasingly small due to the ease by which people could fly around the globe, see each other on television, talk with each other, acquire international goods quickly, and then, finally, instantly interact with each other by using the Internet and mobile devices. Therefore, the concept of globalization required a series of developments and events that enabled people worldwide to have immediate "social relations" and impact each other's lives.

What does this mean to the work of an interior designer? By thinking about globalization as a means to conceptualize a *small planet*, a designer must have an excellent working knowledge of current events as well as various cultures, politics, religions, economies, histories, customs, environmental conditions, and geographical features. Other important issues related to business aspects of the profession, such as contracts, consultants, and currencies, are discussed in the next section. A *small planet* can cause a designer who is working in New York City to be instantaneously impacted by the collapse of the stock market in Tokyo. A *small planet* can cause global warming and worldwide fear of nuclear weapons and contracting certain diseases. A *small planet* requires peace, social justice, respect for diversity, environmental conservation, collaborative solutions, and international agreements.

The design profession is also impacted by some of the arguments regarding the value of globalization. Some economists contend that globalization has advanced society by the exchange of international products and services. Other individuals have claimed that globalization has imposed Western values and lifestyles on other cultures, especially people living in developing countries. Western influences are mostly associated with the "Americanization" of the planet as illustrated by the worldwide distribution of Coke products, McDonald's restaurants, and Nike shoes and apparel. The dire consequence is cultural homogenization, which can easily happen in the built environment, as evidenced by the proliferation of suburban developments and hundreds of franchise restaurants, hotels, and retail stores. Generally, the same design is used for these buildings regardless of their location.

Globalization should not result in the loss of local artisans, indigenous materials, or vernacular architecture—traditional building style for a location. In contrast, an interior designer is in the formidable position to integrate best practices with the unique facts and attributes of a given locality. These same principals apply to professional business practices. When you are working on a project in a foreign country, you must understand the local business culture, protocols, and legal requirements (Box 2.6 and Chapter 5).

International Practice: Opportunities and Challenges

As you are pursuing an entry-level position, you will most likely discover a firm that has an international practice. Some design firms have a national office with projects in foreign countries, and others have a headquarters in a major city along with offices in several national and international locations. Does this appeal to you? Determining your level of interest in working for these firms requires a fundamental understanding of international practice, including multinational challenges, how they are established, how they are organized, and operational procedures.

There are many ways that a firm begins an international practice. Most are the result of networking; few have been the result of strategic planning. For example, common ways for a firm to obtain its first foreign project is through referrals from a client, property developer, other professional, or another design firm either nationally or internationally. Some projects are initiated by the government, a firm seeking a partnership, or a client interested in having a building designed in a foreign location.

A firm with a desirable specialization can be recruited by a foreign client or another practice. Winning an international competition is another way that a firm begins an international practice. To bolster revenues during economic downturns, some firms pursue international opportunities, but generally success depends on

thorough research, effective networking, and many other considerations.

Many factors that contribute to a successful international as well as national practice are based on engaging in a thorough analysis of the location, the needs of the client, and familiarity with local codes and standards (Box 2.6). Some of the items that are critical to research for international projects include taxes for foreign companies, liability insurance policies, currency conversions, **intellectual property rights**, local labor situation, and the legal system.

To develop a true understanding of how to operate and manage professional services in a foreign location, design firms hire local people, such as consultants, translators, law firms, and perhaps accountants. Prevailing construction methods and materials need to be identified as well as suppliers and sources. Business etiquette and protocols must be researched as well as local fee structures, scope of services practices, contractual arrangements, billing policies, ethical standards, quality determinants, dispute resolution procedures, technological capabilities, and support staff.

All of these factors must be analyzed within the context of potentially great distances, and multiple languages, communication protocols, time zones, and systems of weights and measures. Literal translations are not always appropriate; thus the need for translators who understand the profession as well as written and verbal customs in perhaps multiple countries. Images are often considered an effective means to communicate universally.

International Design Firms

Generally, the most successful international practices require a large staff with diverse expertise and considerable large project experience, such as Gensler, HOK, Perkins + Will, Nikken Sekkei, Building Design Partnership (BDP), Kohn Pederson Fox (KPF), RTKL, and RMJM. Aedas, the firm that was named the 2010 International Practice of the Year, had more than 2,000 staff members in 39 offices worldwide. The chairman of Aedas noted that Revit BIM software and a focus on sustainability contributed to the company's success. A description of the firm illustrates the importance of understanding local cultures as well as current issues associated with professional practice:

> We provide international expertise with innate knowledge and understanding of local cultures. Our designers are committed to contribute and lead in the societies we design for. We have a holistic approach to sustainability which shows our care not only for the built environment but also for the people we work with and the societies we live and work within. We draw upon a global network of expertise, employing people from around the world and embracing the diverse influences and ideas throughout our multi-cultural organisation (Aedas 2010).

Foster + Partners is another example of a successful international practice; the firm illustrates an approach to multinational organizational structures and operational procedures. Foster + Partners has offices in 22 countries and more than 1,000 employees representing over 50 countries. The firm contends that "creativity and personal service are best nurtured by the compact group where 'small is beautiful'" (Foster + Partners 2010). The firm's organizational structure provides insight regarding how to maximize the diverse talents and expertise of a large firm for the benefit of a client (Box 2.7 and Figure 2.4).

Foster + Partners Design Groups*

Foster + Partners Teams of Professionals

Provide input to all phases of the design process (Figure 2.4).

I. Executive Board

* Norman Foster, as Chief Executive
* Two-Joint Heads of Design
* Financial Officer
* Two Senior Executives

II. Design Groups (six)

* Led by a Senior Partner.
* Other members are based on creating a team with a variety of expertise and experiences (e.g., working on small and large projects in a variety of locations).

Responsibilities of the Design Groups

* Developing and communicating the design concept through specialist disciplines:

  * Materials and Environmental Research, Product Design, Space Planning, Interior Design, Communications, Graphics, Visualisations, Model Making, and 3D Computer Modelling.

* Some members travel to the location of the project and work in a local office through the duration of the project.

(Box 2.7 continued on page 48)

Box 2.7

Foster + Partners Design Groups* *(continued)*

III. Design Board

* Foster (Chair)
* Chief Executive
* Two-Joint Heads of Design
* Another permanent position
* Three Advisors with three unique areas of expertise:
  * Ecology and sustainability
  * Interface with clients and user groups and the social agenda
  * Graphic visualizations

Responsibilities of the Design Board
* Review the design of new projects.
* Composition can be altered when appropriate.

IV. Project and Specialist Teams

* With the support of multiple in-house disciplines, project teams are responsible for the project beginning with the appointment through to its completion.
* The specialist teams' areas of expertise are information technology, contract management, construction, and a modelling group for advanced 3D computer modelling technologies as well as traditional model making.

* Information centre is responsible for researching materials and products with an emphasis on sustainable buildings: "We believe that we have a responsibility to try to persuade clients to adopt sustainable strategies—even small steps in the right direction are better than none at all."

  * Promote "a strong sustainable design ethic."
  * Establish a sustainability profile for every project with targets, technologies, and methods.
  * Sustainability profiles are accessed by the staff for future projects.
  * Sustainability forum with members from the six design groups, the information centre, and representatives from the departments responsible for communications, training, and research.
  * Continuous training and apply the results of internal and external research to projects.

*Adapted from: Foster + Partners, 2010, *The Way We Work*, http://www.fosterandpartners.com/. Retrieved July 2010.

Checking for Comprehension

* Identify two ways that demonstrate how the world has conceptually become small.
* Describe three different topics that are important for an international practice.

Global Economics and the Design Profession

Foster + Partners is an example of an international practice that has developed a strategy for success in a global economy. A fundamental understanding of global economics and finance can provide you with background information

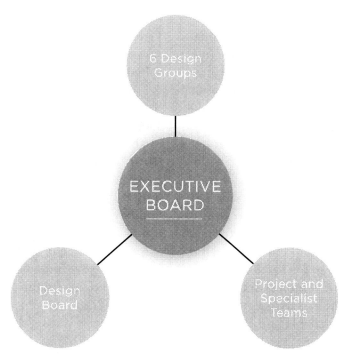

Figure 2.4 Foster + Partners has several teams of professionals that provide input to all phases of the design process, including the executive board, six design groups that are led by a senior partner, a design board, and project and specialists teams.

you can use while searching and interviewing for positions, and will help you understand how you might be compensated in the future. Knowledge of global economics and finance is especially important during times of recession and fluctuations in the marketplace.

Global Economics and Finance

Anthony Giddens, the individual whose definition of globalization was cited earlier in this chapter, also discussed the economic and financial consequences in the age of "modernity": "whoever studies cities today, in any part of the world, is aware that what happens in a local neighborhood is likely to be influenced by factors—such as world money and commodity markets—operating at an indefinite distance away from that neighborhood itself" (Giddens 1990). Naturally, Giddens' statement is true for the work of an interior designer regardless of that person's involvement with international clients or work in foreign offices.

At this point you might be wondering, why does a student majoring in interior design need to study "world money and commodity markets"? From a basic perspective, your work, your pay, your future retirement, your future clients, and your future employer's business are all impacted by worldwide economic conditions as well as the global financial markets. From a consumer perspective, every time you purchase a product made in a foreign country, you are participating in global economics and are affecting international economies. The ability to instantly access your money from an ATM in Tokyo is an example of the efficiency and immediacy of global financial transactions.

One approach to understanding how global economics and finance affect you and the design profession is to reanalyze the previous explanations related to globalization; most noteworthy is the perspective of the world as a *small planet*. The same improvements in communication, technology, and transportation that affected business opportunities and international design teams have simultaneously impacted global economies and financial markets. In fact, the worldwide opportunities that the design profession enjoys today would not be possible without international monetary agreements and regulations (see Chapter 5).

The most recent financial crisis—beginning with the collapse of the credit markets in the summer of 2007 until 2009—provides an excellent example of how monetary conditions can instantly affect markets throughout the world, including the design profession. For example, on a smaller scale the financial crisis affected the previously discussed design for Knoll's Antenna Workspaces (Box 2.5). In response to the crisis, Antenna Design was required to design a furniture system that was affordable and had a reasonable shipping weight.

On a large scale, the total dollar value of residential and nonresidential construction declined by 15 percent between 2008 and 2009, and there was a 12 percent reduction from mid-years 2009

and 2010 (U.S. Bureau of Census 2010). (see Figure 2.5). This obviously impacted the profession—less construction and fewer home sales resulted in less work for interior designers.

To contend with the financial crisis, design firms had to reconsider their opportunities, such as pursuing international construction jobs in the emerging markets, for example, **BRIC (Brazil, Russia, India, and China)**. The BRICs have been identified as countries that could have a dramatic role in world markets by 2025 and beyond. The basic premise for this projection is that these four countries combined constitute 40 percent of the world's population, and their governments have been developing policies and institutions that stimulate economic growth (Wilson and Purushothaman 2003).

To survive during the crisis, design firms reconnected with past clients to find new business and developed new services, such as sustainable design, strategic planning, and branding. In addition, to conserve resources, design firms were forced to reduce their staffs. Thus, as you search

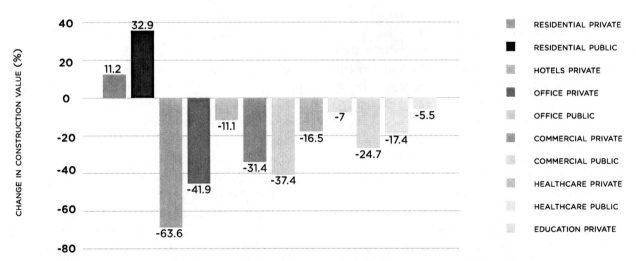

VALUE OF PRIVATE AND PUBLIC
CONSTRUCTION IN THE U.S. (MILLIONS OF DOLLARS)
MID-YEAR 2009-2010

Figure 2.5 The total value of residential and nonresidential construction declined by 15 percent between 2008 and 2009, and there was a 12 percent reduction from midyears 2009 and 2010 (U.S. Bureau of Census 2010).

for career opportunities, it is important to keep in mind the impact that global economics can have on a design firm and make certain that you are fully aware of current news and world conditions.

In addition to networking with professional organizations, as discussed in Chapter 1, you should read local, national, and international newspapers and news magazines. The *Wall Street Journal* is an excellent example of a publication that focuses on global issues as well as finances. Publications of affiliated professional organizations, such as EDRA's *Design Research News (DRN)*, are also good sources of information associated with the work of designers. Being informed will also be beneficial when you must respond to questions related to global issues during job interviews—a topic discussed in the next chapter.

Checking for Comprehension

- Identify ways an interior designer can stay busy when there is a slowdown of new construction projects.

- Why do you think it is important for interior designers to keep abreast of global conditions and events?

Having an awareness of global economics and how it affects the design profession is an important step as you prepare to search for an entry-level position. This chapter reviewed other elements that are important to know as you pursue career opportunities, such as types of design firms, design practice specializations, and nontraditional opportunities. Compensation and benefits were examined to offer an awareness of what you can expect in an entry-level position. The discussion about where you can search for a job included examining the impact of globalization on the design profession as well as international practice.

The global financial crisis and recession affected the design profession and is a tremendous lesson for designers, especially those who are searching for jobs: We must keep abreast of national and global events (and other topics we traditionally view as uninteresting).

To help you with the job search process, information presented in this chapter and the content reviewed in Chapter 1 should be integrated with the material discussed in the next chapter. Chapter 3 examines career planning, networking strategies, résumés, and design portfolios. The chapter also explains how to create a job search plan and ways to strategize the search process. The last section in Chapter 3 explores interviewing techniques as well as approaches to negotiating a job offer.

Knowledge and Skills Summary

Highlights

- The two major design categories are residential and commercial.

- In addition to positions in an interior design or architectural firm, other opportunities for designers include working for retailers, manufacturers, the government, and corporations.

- Within the categories of residential and commercial design, there are numerous areas of specialization.

- In pursing career opportunities, an interior designer might be interested in connecting his or her design interests with other disciplines found to be interesting.

- Traditional job benefits include healthcare insurance (medical, dental, vision), company-sponsored pension plans, 401(k) retirement plans, and vacation time.

- Globalization has enabled a designer to work for a firm with offices in several regions of the world or to design facilities for a client with buildings all over the globe.

- Many factors that contribute to a successful international practice are based on engaging in a thorough analysis of the location and being familiar with global business practices.

- A fundamental understanding of global economics and finance can provide background information you can use searching for jobs.

Key Terms

401(k) retirement plan

branding

BRICs (Brazil, Russia, India, China)

building information modeling (BIM)

commercial design

computer-aided design (CAD)

contract design

corporation

in-house designer

individual retirement account (IRA)

integrated project delivery (IPD)

intellectual property rights

mixed-use building

mutual fund

post-occupancy evaluations (POE)

profit sharing

residential design

Revit

rollover

sole proprietor

vesting

Projects

Philosophy and Design Project

There are numerous career opportunities for interior designers. An important element in having a job that you will enjoy is working for a company that shares your philosophical perspectives and values. Use the Internet to find design firms and other employers related to the design profession, such as manufacturers of interior products. Review their websites to obtain the following information: (1) philosophical and value statements and (2) examples of projects or products that reflect the firm's philosophical beliefs.

In a table, provide a summary of your findings and discuss which firms and/or corporations share your beliefs and values. This exercise will be very useful as you develop your career plan, search for positions, and interview with potential employers (see Chapter 3).

Research Project

Employers and employees in the twenty-first century have been involved with establishing 401(k) retirement plans. Put together a team of three to five members. Your team's assignment is to learn more about stocks by researching individual companies. Resources are available at the library and online. Identify five companies that appear to be good long-term investments. Share your results with at least two other teams and discuss the various options.

Based on your team's research and discussions with other teams, develop an oral presentation (approximately 10 minutes) of your team's recommendations for stocks. Your team's report should include a profile of the five companies, your assessment of the research process, and recommendations for how to identify stocks for a 401(k) retirement plan.

Human Factors Research Project

To design the built environment in a foreign country requires considerable research and an understanding of local geographical features, history, lifestyles, and cultures. Identify an interdisciplinary team of five to seven people. Your team should select a foreign city located in the BRICs.

Your assignment is to research the city and identify important professional practice characteristics of the city that would be important to know when designing a local project. Your team should prepare a video of your results that includes illustrations and a summary of how globalization affected the city and the design profession.

References

Aedas. 2010. *About Aedas*. http://www.aedas. com/. Accessed July 9, 2010.

American Society of Interior Designers (ASID). 2010. *The Interior Design Profession: Facts and Figures*. Washington, DC: American Society of Interior Designers.

Association of Southeast Asian Nations (ASEAN). 2010. *Overview*. http://www. aseansec.org. Accessed November 19, 2010.

Baker, K. 2009. *Consensus Construction Forecast*. http://www.aia.org/practicing/economics/ AIAS076259. Accessed July 17, 2010.

Bosnia-Herzegovina. 2010. *Bosnia-Herzegovina Tourism*. http://www.bhtourism.ba/eng/ default.wbsp. Accessed July 9, 2010.

Fairtrade Labelling Organizations International (FLO). *What We Do*. http://www. fairtrade.net. Accessed November 19, 2010.

Foster + Partners. 2010. *Data*. http://www. fosterandpartners.com/. Accessed July 27, 2010.

Gensler. 2010. Careers. http://www.gensler. com/. Accessed July 27, 2010.

Gensler. 2010. *Johnson Controls*. http://www. gensler.com/#projects/207. Accessed July 27, 2010.

Giddens, A. *The Consequences of Modernity*. Stanford, CA: Stanford University Press, 1990.

Herman Miller. 2010. *How You Can Join Us*. http://www.hermanmiller.com/. Accessed July 29, 2010.

International Interior Design Association (IIDA). 2010. *Career Center*. http://www. jobtarget.com/c/search_results.cfm?site_ id=251. Accessed July 29, 2010.

International Monetary Fund (IMF). 2010. *About the IMF*. http://www.imf.org/external/. Accessed July 14, 2010.

North American Fair Trade Organization (NAFTA). 2010). *North American Fair Trade Organization (NAFTA)*. http://www.ustr.gov/ trade-agreements/free-trade-agreements/ north-american-free-trade-agreement-naf-ta. Accessed July 29, 2010.

Shulman, K. 2010. "Intense Listeners." *Metropolis Magazine* 29(11), 102–107; 125; 127.

Statistics Canada. 2010. *Housing Starts, by Province*. http://www40.statcan.ca/l01/cst01/ manuf05-eng.htm. Accessed July 30, 2010.

The World Bank. 2010. *About Us*. http://www. worldbank.org/. Accessed July 28, 2010.

The World Book Encyclopedia. 2004. s.v. "Bosnia-Herzegovina." Chicago: World Book, Inc.

U.S. Bureau of Census. 2010. Housing Starts. http://www.census.gov/const/www/ quarterly_starts_completions.pdf. Accessed July 1, 2010.

———. 2010. *May 2010 Construction at $841.9 Billion Annual Rate*. http://www.census.gov/ const/C30/release.pdf. Accessed July 1, 2010.

U.S. Department of Labor. (Updated May 2010). *Bureau of Labor Statistics*. http:// www.bls.gov/oes/2009/may/oes271025.htm. Accessed July 29, 2010.

Wilson, D., and R. Purushothaman. 2003. *Dreaming with BRICs: The Path to 2050*. http://www2.goldmansachs.com/ideas/brics/ book/99-dreaming.pdf. Accessed July 17, 2010.

World Economic Forum. 2010. *Our Organization*. http://www.weforum.org/en/index.htm. Accessed July 28, 2010.

World Trade Organization (WTO). 2010. *About the WTO—A Statement by the Director-General*. http://www.wto.org/. Accessed July 28, 2010.

CHAPTER

3

Attaining an Entry-Level Position

Poglavlje 3 (Croatian)
Kapitola 3 (Czech)
Kapitel 3 (Danish)
Hoofdstuk 3 (Dutch)
Peatükk 3 (Estonian)

After learning the content in Chapter 3, you will be able to answer the following questions:

* How do you develop a career portfolio and networking strategies?

* What are the best strategies for developing résumés, cover letters, and design portfolios?

* How do you create a job search plan and implement search strategies?

* What are important interviewing considerations and job offer negotiation strategies?

Chapters 1 and 2 started the process of reviewing topics that are important to know when you are seeking an entry-level position as an interior designer. Chapter 1 reviewed how the interior design profession provides value to individuals as well as society. The chapter continued by explaining the importance of professional organizations, licensing, registration, and public and community service.

Chapter 2 introduced the various types of design firms, areas of design specialties, nontraditional opportunities, compensation policies, and employee benefits. In order for you to be competitive in the twenty-first century, Chapter 2 provided an overview of globalization, global economics, and finance with a focus on how international policies impact the design profession.

As you read Chapter 3, you should refer to the information presented in Chapters 1 and 2, and integrate the content with the various topics and materials that are presented in this chapter (Figure 3.1). For example, it will be important for you to incorporate topics covered in the first two chapters as you develop a **career portfolio** and **networking** strategies.

Content integration should continue as you study the next sections in this chapter, which emphasize how to find a job that is best for you. The second section of this chapter reviews how to create your search materials, including **résumés**, **cover letters**, business cards, and **traditional/digital design portfolios**. This section is followed by suggestions for developing your job search plan and ways that you can effectively search for positions. The chapter concludes by reviewing the best approaches to interviewing and what you should do after interviews, including negotiation strategies.

Career Portfolios and Networking Strategies

In an age of global opportunities, economic fluctuations, evolving technologies, as well as changes in market demands, a **career plan** for an interior designer should account for these conditions by including **career management** strategies. Planning and managing a career becomes even more important when one realizes that a person has an average of five *different* careers in a lifetime. Critical components to career management are establishing **networks** and engaging in effective networking practices. Networks are invaluable to multifaceted careers that can entail numerous specialties within a global marketplace.

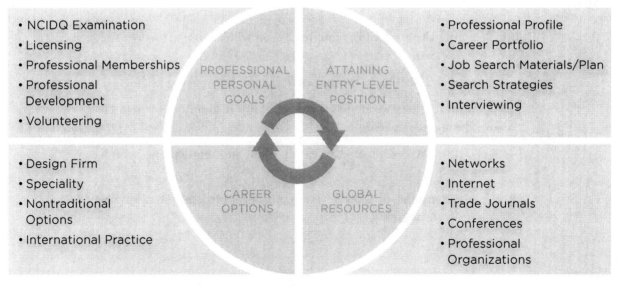

• NCIDQ Examination
• Licensing
• Professional Memberships
• Professional Development
• Volunteering

PROFESSIONAL PERSONAL GOALS

ATTAINING ENTRY-LEVEL POSITION

• Professional Profile
• Career Portfolio
• Job Search Materials/Plan
• Search Strategies
• Interviewing

• Design Firm
• Speciality
• Nontraditional Options
• International Practice

CAREER OPTIONS

GLOBAL RESOURCES

• Networks
• Internet
• Trade Journals
• Conferences
• Professional Organizations

Figure 3.1 Integration of content in Chapters 1, 2, and 3.

Preliminary Tasks: Self-Assessment and Professional Profile

How can you demonstrate to an employer that you are perfect for the job? The first step is to engage in **self-assessment**, or a process that can identify what you can offer an employer. It might appear to be unnecessary; people tend to believe that they know themselves very well. The challenge is succinctly identifying and articulating your abilities, skills, and values as you develop your career plan, résumé, and interview presentations. Thus, conducting a self-assessment is excellent for collecting details about yourself that you can use throughout the job search process as well as career management. Information gathered during the self-assessment process can also be used to assess how your characteristics match the needs of a potential employer.

There are a variety of approaches to the self-assessment process. The goal is to engage in a process that provides you with a framework for knowing your skills, interests, abilities, attitudes, values, strengths, weaknesses, work styles, and motivators. In addition, the self-assessment process should result in an understanding of your **transferrable skills**, a very important element to finding a job during a recession or when you are seeking a career change. The activity can be performed by using standardized career assessments, such as the Myers-Briggs Type Indicator (http://www.myersbriggs.org/), Birkman (http://www.birkman.com/#), Strong Interest Inventory (https://www.cpp.com/), or SkillScan (http://www.skillscan.com/). The self-assessment process also can be done through journaling or writing bulleted summaries.

Self-assessment journaling involves documenting your activities and reactions to events for several weeks—ideally a semester in school. The primary focus is to record tasks that required you to solve problems. As you record your activities, identify which skills and abilities you used for the task. Documenting your reactions should include (1) how much you enjoyed or disliked the task, (2) the degree of success, and (3) any elements you perceived were problems in completing the task. At the conclusion of your journaling process you should be able to develop a self-assessment profile.

Another approach to the self-assessment process is to write a bulleted summary that describes your previous successful activities. Summaries could be based on a recent project you completed for an interior design course or an inspiring volunteer experience (Box 3.1). Excellent resources for identifying skills and knowledge required for the interior design profession are CIDA, NCIDQ, and position descriptions as presented in Chapter 2. Key to the process is identifying how you solved a problem by using skills, abilities, strengths, and knowledge as well as determining your weaknesses, motivators, and work style.

After you have developed the self-assessment lists, you should prioritize the items according to level of ability and interest (Table 3.1). For example, if you listed drawing two-dimensional plans as a skill, you should determine your level of proficiency as well as your extent of interest in drawing floor plans. In addition, you should determine an item's ability to be transferred to a different occupation and how an item addresses the demands of employers.

The results of your self-assessment process can be used to develop a brief **professional profile**, or a summary of your interests and most important skills. The purpose of the profile is to have a coherent and organized summary of your professional characteristics that you can easily recite during interviews as well as casual conversations. In approximately one paragraph, a professional profile should identify (1) what type of work you desire, (2) your skills and abilities related to solving design problems, and (3) an example of how you used your skills to solve a problem (Box 3.2).

A professional profile should be memorized and developed to be adaptable to various audiences. For example, when attending a professional conference, you might meet someone who could be a potential employer. In this situation your professional profile would be discussed from a general perspective. During an interview your professional profile should reflect the specific interests of the employer.

Box 3.1

Self-Assessment Summary of an Interdisciplinary Team Project

Project Overview and Parameters

An adaptive reuse of a historic industrial building (1890) in Seattle, Washington. Project site is on the National Register of Historic Places. Building types for the project include a restaurant and commercial office. Square footage: 10,000 square feet (929 square meters). The two-story mixed-use project requires a new interior for the multi-tenant building. The restaurant and bar are on the first floor and the second floor is leased to an environmental conservation organization. Both tenants are seeking LEED-CI Platinum certification.

The owner is interested in a bioclimatic design that includes solar energy harvesting, green roof, natural ventilation/passive cooling, extensive daylighting, views to the outdoors, and energy-efficient lighting systems. The design should have extensive adaptive reuse, salvaged materials, FSC wood, rapidly renewable materials, and low-VOC adhesives, sealants, paints, coatings, and carpeting.

Completed Project and Reactions

I was one of six members of an interdisciplinary team. Each bullet includes a summary of a task that was required to complete the project and summary statements in brackets. Bracketed notes identify the skills, abilities, and knowledge that was required to complete the task and personal reactions regarding interest in performing the task as well as ability as assessed by fellow team members and the professor's feedback. The bulleted information can be used to create my self-assessment summary.

Assessment of Overall Work Environments

* Team work was done in a design studio.

   [I enjoyed working with a team in the design studio because of the daylight, but as noted below, I did not like some of the tasks I was assigned and I did not want to manage the team.]

* Working alone was in my apartment.

   [My apartment was convenient, but there were a lot of distractions. Overall a hard place to work because I couldn't concentrate.]

Assessment of Project Tasks

* Developed an outline of the project's requirements, schedule, and budget.

   [Required knowledge of creating schedules, budgets, and used writing skills. I enjoyed helping to develop the preliminary budget.]

* Developed a research program that included surveys, interviews, and observations.

Box 3.1

Self-Assessment Summary of an Interdisciplinary Team Project (continued)

[Required knowledge of research methodologies, human behavior, historical preservation, universal design, globalization, and interdisciplinary collaboration. Used verbal and written communication skills. I enjoyed helping to develop the research items related to human behavior, historical preservation, and globalization. Our professor commended our research methodologies and understanding of historic preservation, but noted the lack of attention to universal design.]

· Developed preliminary design concept statements, sketches, plans, and overlays.

[Required knowledge of problem solving, space planning, codes, LEED standards, sustainable design, universal design, human behavior, historic preservation, restaurant requirements, office space needs, and interdisciplinary collaboration. Used verbal and written skills as well as sketching. Used research skills to understand important characteristics of Seattle, Washington, bioclimatic design, solar energy harvesting, green roof designs, natural ventilation, daylighting, rapidly renewable materials, VOCs, FSC wood, and energy-efficient lighting systems. Used AutoCAD to draw two- and three-dimensional plans, elevations, and sections.]

[I enjoyed helping to solve problems related to restaurant space planning, achieving LEED certification, historic preservation, bioclimatic design, and accommodating cultural diversity.]

[I did not enjoy sketching or aspects related to energy conservation. Fellow team members noted my lack of skills in sketching and interest in energy conservation; thus, other individuals were assigned the tasks.]

> Gives you a summary of what you don't enjoy doing.

· Developed construction drawings, lighting/electrical plan, specifications, budget, and selected materials, furniture, colors, and finishes. Presented design to the class.

[Required knowledge of problem solving, space planning, codes, LEED standards, sustainable design, sustainable products, universal design, human behavior, historic preservation, restaurant requirements, office space needs, and interdisciplinary collaboration. Used verbal and written skills and executed hand-drawn renderings. Used AutoCAD to draw two- and three-dimensional plans, reflected ceiling plan, elevations, and sections.]

[I enjoyed specifying sustainable products and any items that were required for the restaurant. I also liked preparing the presentation boards. Our professor commended our design for its creativity and how well we addressed the needs of the client.]

[Negative comments focused on the development of our specifications and details that were missing in our oral presentation.]

Table 3.1 Sample Chart for Conducting a Self-Assessment				
Self Assessment Items	**My Level of Interest***	**My Level of Ability***	**Transferable***	**Level of Employer Interest***
Resolving Problems	5	4	5	5
Being Accountable	5	4	5	5
Making Decisions	4	4	5	5
Listening	5	4	5	5
Work Ethic	5	5	5	5
Social Responsibilities	5	4	5	4
Self-Motivation	5	5	5	5
Critical Thinking	4	4	5	4
Lifelong Learning	5	5	5	4
Leadership	3	3	5	4
Diversity	5	5	5	4
Reliability	5	5	5	5
Hard Work	5	5	5	5
Enthusiasm	5	4	5	5
Integrity	5	5	5	5
Initiative	5	5	5	5
Ambitious	4	4	5	4
Willingness to Learn	5	5	5	5
Conducting Research	5	5	5	4
Writing	4	4	5	5
Oral Communication	4	4	5	5
Using Technology	3	4	5	5
Creativity	5	4	4	4
Teamwork	4	4	5	4
Independent Work	5	5	5	4
Size of an Employer's Organization	4	N/A	N/A	4
International Practice	5	4	5	4
Geographical Location	5	N/A	N/A	4
Volunteering	5	4	5	4
Self-Assessment of Specific Design Skills/Knowledge/Abilities				
Understanding of and ability to apply sustainability theories to design solutions.	5	5	5	5
Understanding of and ability to apply universal design theories to design solutions.	5	5	4	5
Understanding of and ability to apply human behavior theories to design solutions.	5	5	5	5
Understanding the effects of globalization on the design profession.	5	5	3	5
Understanding of and ability to apply color theories to design solutions.	5	5	3	4
Understanding of and ability to apply space planning concepts to design solutions.	4	4	2	4

Table 3.1 Sample Chart for Conducting a Self-Assessment (*continued*)				
Self Assessment Items	My Level of Interest*	My Level of Ability*	Transferable*	Level of Employer Interest*
Understanding of and ability to apply illumination theories to design solutions.	5	5	1	4
Understanding of and ability to execute all phases of the design process.	5	5	2	5
Drawing sketches.	4	4	3	4
Producing contract documents.	3	4	1	5
Producing presentation boards.	3	4	2	4
Producing models.	3	4	2	3
Understanding of business practices.	5	5	5	5
Understanding of movements, traditions, and periods in interior design, architecture, and furniture.	5	5	2	4
Understanding of spatial concepts and 2- and 3-dimensional design.	5	4	2	5
Knowledge of how to specify furniture.	4	5	2	5
Knowledge of how to specify finish materials.	4	5	2	5
Knowledge of how to specify lighting and equipment.	5	5	2	4
Knowledge of energy conservation.	5	5	3	5
Knowledge of building systems.	3	4	1	4
Knowledge of interior construction.	3	4	1	4
Knowledge of regulations.	3	5	2	5
Knowledge of environmental indoor quality (EIQ) and indoor air quality (IAQ).	5	5	2	5

*Scale: 1–5 (5—Very high; 4—High; 3—Neutral; 2—Low; 1—Very low or not applicable)

Developing a Career Portfolio

Your values, interests, skills, and abilities that you identified in the self-assessment process are critical to the development of your career portfolio. This portfolio should include your career plan, résumé, cover letters, business card, promotional materials, and design portfolio. In addition, a career portfolio should have a collection of documents, professional projects, photographs, drawings, and illustrations that reflect your future aspirations. For example, if your career goal is to eventually work in London for a large design firm that specialized in sustainable designs, your career portfolio could have a collection of sustainable projects designed by firms with at least one office in London. Your career portfolio could include documents concerning London as well as initiatives associated with sustainable designs, such as new products, materials, legislation, credentials, and research studies.

To develop a profile of potential employers, your portfolio could also include a collection of projects completed by the firms as well as specific designers. If you are interested in eventually owning your own business, your career portfolio might include documents and illustrations associated with real estate, business laws, insurance policies, and marketing.

Career Plan and Career Management

An important element of your career portfolio is a career plan that specifies a strategy to manage your career. Your career plan should include items that are important to you professionally as well as personally. The plan should include responses identified in the self-assessment

Box 3.2

Example of a Professional Profile

Gives your current status.

Indicates type of work you desire.

I am a senior at ABC University who is majoring in interior design. I am planning to graduate in May of 2012. I would like to find an interior design position in a firm that specializes in healthcare and is located in a major city. Specifically, I would like to work on projects that require developing solutions for people with special needs. This is interesting to me because I am proud of my creativity, my ability to solve complex design problems, and my ability to apply theories of human behavior and universal design. I used these skills during an internship at the XYZ Children's Hospital and the results were very positive. Family members of patients reported that my design for the children's play area helped to reduce anxieties and gave their child an opportunity to forget about their illness and just have some fun.

Indicates your skills related to solving design problems.

Example of how you used your skills to solve a problem.

---

process as well as other items. For example, a career plan could include where you would like to live at various stages of your career, what type of design firm you want to work for, which areas of specialization, and the type of working conditions. The plan could describe the types of people you want to work for as well as who you want to work with. Your career plan could also identify your credential goals, education interests, position aspirations, and salary and benefit expectations.

To begin developing your career plan, you might want to partner with another person who also is searching for his or her first position. Your partner might or might not be an interior design major. The important factor is having someone who is reliable, is earnest about having a career, and is willing to be thoughtfully engaged in the process.

The purpose of the career partner is to have one person who is familiar with your aspiration, and who can respond to your career plan, career portfolio, job search initiatives, résumé, design portfolio, interviews, and offers. You reciprocate by providing your partner with feedback and advice, and by keeping the person on task.

Working with a career partner is especially helpful today because of the extensive global job opportunities available online and the frequency of their updates. One of the most important elements to developing and maintaining a career plan is having current information. Up-to-date information from a variety of design-related as well as non-design-related sources can help you understand your current and future choices. Innovative design firms continuously apply this concept to their practice. For example, during the recent recession when design firms were having difficulty attracting new clients, professionals scanned federal government documents to identify new government projects that were sponsored by the economic stimulus package.

Your career plan should include projections for what you think you might want to do at various time intervals and what you will have to accomplish to reach your goals. Some career planning experts suggest that you should develop your plan by starting with the end—ultimately, what do you want to accomplish with your life? You might be wondering, "How is it possible to decide what I want to do with my life when I am just starting my career?"

One approach to answering this question is to study the life of a successful interior designer and review the following items: (1) professional employment positions from the beginning of their career until their death or the present situation, (2) their professional responsibilities and length of time, and (3) individuals and events important to their career.

In Figures 3.2a–b note how interior designer and architect Benjamin Baldwin's career ended as a Charter Member of *Interior Design* magazine's Hall of Fame for Interior Designers in 1985, but began in graduate school by drawing, painting, and working in sculpture. Notice how often Baldwin changed jobs and moved to different locations, and the importance that travel had to his career.

Baldwin highlighted his worldwide travel experiences in his autobiography beginning with traveling in the United States and Canada when he was 12 years old with his grandparents. He also noted his work with Eliel Saarinen, Harry Weese, Marcel Breuer, Edgar Kaufmann Jr., Frank Parrish, and others. Baldwin had approximately 10 years of professional experience before opening his own firm. Also observe various skills valuable to his career that were acquired doing activities in non-design places of employment, such as staff writer for *The LIT*.

Your career plan should include your current situation and career projections for 5 to 7 years, 15 years, and 30 to 40 years. These are suggested time intervals and represent typical career patterns for interior designers. For example, after completing an entry-level position you will find there are many positions available for designers with 5 to 7 years of experience. At this stage of your career you should have successfully completed the NCIDQ examination and applied for licensing or registration.

As noted previously, passing the NCIDQ examination provides you with the requirements for licensure. Furthermore, the NCIDQ examination is used as a requirement for professional membership in interior design organizations. During the early stages of your career you might want to acquire special certifications, such as LEED-AP,

NCQLP, and NKBA. With 15 years of experience you might be interested in owning your own business, and after 30 to 40 years you will most likely be looking toward your retirement.

Managing a career is absolutely essential in the twenty-first century. Career management entails an acknowledgment that jobs do not last forever, and that you intend to be prepared for ever-changing economic conditions, industry setbacks, evolving technologies, tough competition, job dissatisfaction, and new opportunities. Career management involves constantly scanning global events to determine their impact on the profession as well as potential options they might create (see Chapter 2).

Acquiring current information requires being involved with professional organizations, networking, volunteering, attending conferences, and reading a variety of materials, such as newspapers, journals, research reports, government documents, and financial summaries. New information should be integrated with your career portfolio and perhaps might prompt you to revise your career plan.

Networks and Networking Strategies

Networks and networking strategies are key elements to career management and should be included in your career portfolio. The assistant secretary of the U.S. Department of Labor reported that because 80 to 90 percent of jobs are not advertised, networking can be an effective means to find positions (Grizzard 2005). Fundamentally, networking is building relationships in person or through virtual online experiences.

In addition to helping you find a job, networks can assist you with professional activities, such as locating new projects, suppliers, installers, products, materials, professional courses, and volunteer opportunities. Networking strategies involve developing a plan that includes various types of networks, identifying new contacts, and a process to maintain connections.

The two general types of networks are personal and professional. Networks can include individuals in your current life as well as in the past. Personal networks include friends, family

1913	**Born Montgomery, Alabama**
1928–1931	Staff Writer for *The LIT* at Lawrence Preparatory School in New Jersey
1931–1935	Princeton University, Department of Architecture: Drawing, painting, drama/movie critic, and set design
1936–1938	Princeton University, Graduate School: Architecture, drawing, painting, sculpture, designs for fountains/fireworks for 1939 New York World's Fair, and thesis on housing
1938–1939	Cranbrook Academy of Art, Bloomfield Hills, MI: Architecture/town planning with Eliel Saarinen, re-planning Buffalo, NY's waterfront, photography, ceramics, textiles, metal, and painting
1939–1940	Office of Eliel and Eero Saarinen, Bloomfield Hills, MI: Model for Smithsonian Art Gallery project, exhibited textiles at NY World's Fair, designed samples for the Work Projects Administration weaving project; and exhibited paintings at Princeton University and Museum of Fine Arts in Montgomery, AL
1940–1941	Office of Harry Weese in Kenilworth, IL (Chicago suburb): Designer and contractor of small residences; award recipient for designing contemporary furnishings (outdoor, living room non-seating, bedroom)
1941–1945	U.S. Navy: Photo interpretation and publications officer
1945–1947	Interior Designer for Skidmore, Owings, and Merrill, New York **Specialization:** interiors, furniture, and all furnishings for Terrace Plaza Hotel in Cincinnati; and editorial representative for *Arts and Architecture*
1948–1950	Established own firm, Design Unit New York in New York City Designed residences, interiors, furniture, products, tea cart, and line of printed fabrics.
1951–1954	Moved firm to Montgomery, AL (hometown) and added a contemporary furniture/furnishings retail store **Specialization:** architecture and interior design.
1955–1963	Moved firm to Chicago (Weese experience) **Specialization:** interiors, display rooms, and products.
1963–1973	Moved practice back to New York **Specialization:** interior design.
1973–1979	East Hampton and Sarasota Residences Wrote book about design work and designed Ben Baldwin Collection of furniture.
1981–1991	Work Exhibited in Museums and Designated Charter Member of *Interior Design* magazine's Hall of Fame for Interior Designers, 1985 **Died April 1993**

TRAVEL

1925–1928	USA and Canada
1928–1931	Bermuda and first trip to Europe
1934	Germany and France
1939–1940	Car trip to West Coast
1952	Europe, primarily Venice
1956	Tangier, Portugal, Spain, and Venice
1957	London
1960–1961	Spain, Greek Islands, Italy
1964	Europe
1969–1970	Around the world
1968–1969	Three trips to St. Maarten
1978	Hawaii to research gardens and plants
1981	Milan Furniture Show and Switzerland
1982	Los Angeles
1984	France, Italy, Germany, Yugoslavia, London, and English gardens
1987	Scandinavia, Leningrad, Vienna, Venice, and London
1991	Caribbean (Antigua, Grenada, Barbados)

(a)   (b)

Figure 3.2a–b Professional timeline of Benjamin Baldwin (1913–1993)* (a). *House & Garden* magazine, April 1, 1965 cover, showing the sunporch of the Hallmark House by architect, Edward Larrabee Barnes, interiors by Benjamin Baldwin (b). *(© Condé Nast)* *Source: Baldwin, B. (1995—Copyright Elizabeth H. Baldwin). *Benjamin Baldwin: An Autobiography in Design.* New York: W. W. Norton & Company.

members, and neighbors. Professional networks include professors, academic advisors, coworkers, fellow volunteers, and people connected to your job, such as interior designers, architects, contractors, manufacturers, educators, and members of professional organizations.

Your professional network could include people you have met while involved with a collaborative project, attending a conference, taking courses, traveling, or participating in activities sponsored by professional organizations. Online sites, such as Facebook, Twitter, and LinkedIn, enable you to connect and share information with people in various disciplines throughout the world.

There are many ways you can add new people to your networks when you are online, and when you are involved with social and professional activities. The basic approach is to mention your area of interest to people and then ask them if they know someone who can provide you with job information. Their response could include names of individuals as well as new networks.

Reading and responding to online posts is a way to add people to your networks. For the sake of your reputation, post only professional responses. The important element is to *always* record names, contact information, and affiliation. Without a conscious effort to record this information, it is very easy to forget and lose potentially valuable contacts. What should you do with this information?

After you have identified people in your networks, your plan should include how you will routinely connect with these individuals. Your goal should be to touch base with someone at least once a year. Online is a convenient means to maintain connections, but for more meaningful discussions try to have face-to-face contacts whenever possible.

In-person and online conversations should have a professional tone and follow business etiquette practices (discussed later in this chapter). Written materials should be grammatically perfect and have no spelling errors. Abbreviated

words and sentences (e.g., those used in texting) are not appropriate for any business communication medium.

A key component to success with your networks is developing a reciprocity mindset. Thus, as you accept information and help from people, you should also be asking yourself, "How can I help people in my network?"

Résumés and Traditional/ Digital Design Portfolios

Networks and networking strategies are key elements of your career portfolio and can assist you with developing and evaluating your job search materials, including résumés, cover letters, design portfolio, business card, and promotional pieces. Please note that most of the items are pluralized because you should tailor your search materials to the individualized needs of each employer.

Searching for a job as well as managing a career in the twenty-first century requires customized résumés, cover letters, and promotional pieces. However, within the customization, all of your search materials should have a unified visual appearance or a **visual identity system**. In addition, your professional materials might need to be prepared in a variety of formats, such as print, CDs, DVDs, PDF files, and websites.

Note that this section's discussion of portfolios is presented as a topic within the context of preparing your search materials and is not intended to be an overview of the important elements associated with preparing a portfolio. Developing a design portfolio is a complex process that requires considerable time, and can be an entire course.

Résumés

To be competitive in a global workplace, your materials must be professional and reflect the cutting edge. In addition, be sure to use appropriate intercultural business communication styles that are reviewed in Chapter 5. Contrary to some practices, your résumés should *not* be your historical personal summary and they should *not* be perceived as the means to get a job. You should *not* assume that after you have given your résumé to an organization, you have completed the application process.

Contemporary résumés should present a progressive attitude that includes a summary of *how* your skills, knowledge, and strengths can provide value to a specific organization; hence, the major reason why you should develop several résumés. Your résumé should prompt a prospective employer to enthusiastically contact you for an interview. If you do not receive a response, follow up. Persistence shows employers you are serious.

Professional Visual Appearance

What is required to create a résumé that will entice an organization to contact you for an interview? First and foremost, your résumé must have a professional appearance—an exceptionally important quality when applying for a position in the design profession. An employer's first glance of your résumé can cause the person to immediately reject your application, or it can encourage him or her to read the document.

Color and font choices can be important factors. Avoid bright colors and unconventional fonts. Some people also have an immediate tactile reaction to the paper texture; your résumé should therefore be printed on high-quality paper. Moreover, ink saturation is more effective on fine-quality paper, which results in precisely printed letters and words.

Readability is a crucial element of your résumé's professional appearance. An easily readable document requires appropriate paper, colors, typeface, font size, page borders, and spaces (Box 3.3). High-quality paper should have a blank background and a neutral color, such as white, off-white, buff, or light gray. These colors contrast well with black ink.

The typeface should be easy to read, such as Times New Roman, Garamond, Courier, or

---

Box 3.3

Sample Résumé Prepared for a Specific Job Posting

TAC International Job Description

See A on résumé and cover letter (Boxes 3.3–3.4).

See B on résumé and cover letter (Boxes 3.3–3.4).

See C on résumé and cover letter (Boxes 3.3–3.4).

See D on résumé and cover letter (Boxes 3.3–3.4).

See E on résumé and cover letter (Boxes 3.3–3.4).

See F on résumé and cover letter (Boxes 3.3–3.4).

See G on résumé and cover letter (Boxes 3.3–3.4).

See H on résumé and cover letter (Boxes 3.3–3.4).

See I on résumé and cover letter (Boxes 3.3–3.4).

- 2–3 years' professional experience including a proven track record of multidisciplinary collaboration.
- Strong planning abilities and understanding of sustainability and globalization.
- Knowledge of the design process including objectives, evidence-based design, team management, and budgets.
- Self-motivated with good oral and written communication skills.
- Strong skills in design research, problem solving, presentations, and creative thinking.
- Proficiency in use of AutoCAD and other 3D computer design programs. Understanding Revit is desirable.
- Degree from a CIDA-accredited school.

Box 3.3

Sample Résumé Prepared for a Specific Job Posting *(continued)*

John J. Smyth

P. O. Box 1234 Denver, CO 12345
(555) 555.5555
johnjsmyth@name.com
LinkedIn: https://www.linkedin.com/xxx

OBJECTIVE (optional): Position as an interior designer for an international firm.

HIGHLIGHTS OF QUALIFICATIONS

- Experienced team worker on multidisciplinary projects. **B**
- Proven effectiveness in planning and designing sustainable interiors. **C and D**
- Demonstrated ability to implement the design process. **E**
- Highly motivated and proficient communication skills, design research, and problem solving. **F and G**

EXPERIENCE & SPECIAL SKILLS   A - total number of years from 3 experiences.

AAA Interior Design, Boulder, CO   2011–present
Intern   **B**

- Actively participated in multidisciplinary projects that involved LEED certification and knowledge of globalization. **D**
- Gathered, analyzed, and synthesized research data, worked closely with project managers to apply results to design solutions. **G**
- Assisted with projects that resulted in over $100,000 in revenues.

ABC University, Facilities Management, Boulder, CO   2009–2011
Assistant Designer   **H**

- Rendered drawings for presentations through CET technology.
- Assisted with the review of construction plans, office layout designs, and furniture.
- Created space planning and coordinated the moving of office employees by the deadline date. **G**

Habitat for Humanity, Boulder, CO   2009–2011
Volunteer   **D**

- Researched sustainable products and conducted educational workshops in energy conservation, rapidly renewable products, and indoor air quality. **D**
- Assisted with the development of achieving zero energy usage for residences in Boulder.
- Participated in the selection of furniture, finishes, and equipment for collaborative projects. **B**

SPECIAL SKILLS: AutoCAD, AGi32 version 2.1, Revit, and fluent in Spanish and French.   **H**

EDUCATION & PROFESSIONAL MEMBERSHIPS   **I**

ABC University, Boulder CO
Bachelor of Science, CIDA Accredited Program; Major: Interior Design   2008–2012

International Interior Design Association (IIDA)   2010–Present
Environmental Design Research Association (EDRA)   2010–Present
American Psychological Association (APA)   2009–Present

References Available on Request

Arial, and the preferred font size for most of the document is 11 or 12 points. A larger font size might be used for headings, but it is important to be consistent when varying font size as well as any boldface, line thicknesses, or indents. Page borders should be 1 inch with single or 1.5 line spacing. Line spacing between sections should be at least double.

You might want to design a personal **logo** that can be used for all your search materials. The design should have a sophisticated appearance and a subdued color. It should be a size that is appropriate for an 8 1/2″ × 11″ (21.6 × 27.9 cm) sheet and that can be scaled for smaller as well as larger formats.

Résumés for entry-level positions should be limited to one page. Subsequently, résumés could be expanded to two pages. Résumé sheets should be flat, never folded.

As you select varying attributes of your résumé, be sure to experiment with what happens to its appearance after being transmitted over the Internet. Electronic transmissions and scanners can alter some formats, such as tables, centering, or line spacing. Many large corporations automatically scan résumés; therefore, for these employers, all of the information in your résumé should be left-justified and the document should be saved as a text-only file. In addition, after a résumé is scanned, the information is processed with software designed to search for key words that usually appear in job descriptions, such as AutoCAD or oral and written communication skills. To attract attention to your résumé, it must include these words (Box 3.3).

Résumé Content

Your résumé *must* be grammatically perfect, with appropriate punctuation, excellent sentence structure, flawless spelling, and no typos. Do *not* rely on your computer's spelling and grammar function. Be sure to proofread your document several times and ask at least two other people to check it for accuracy. Employers have rejected résumés for just one spelling error.

The three major types of résumés are **functional**, **chronological**, and a combination of the two. A functional résumé is written to highlight skills, abilities, and strengths, and is generally used by people who do not have significant relevant work experience (Box 3.3).

Chronological résumés are arranged to feature someone's work experience and are often used by people with a history of relevant professional experience. Some résumés are written to combine the features of the functional and chronological résumés by blending a job applicant's strengths with that person's work experiences.

An essential element to any format is to specifically identify and highlight skills, abilities, and experiences that match a job description. For example, earlier in the book, Box 2.1 listed a job description for an interior designer at the intermediate level. The firm was looking for someone with a "proven track record of leading the design of commercial interiors projects," "strong planning abilities," "ability to mentor team members," and ability to "offer guidance and leadership" (IIDA 2010). Therefore, the résumé of the person applying for this position should highlight these specific requirements as well as the other items listed in the description and examples that support the skill or ability (Box 3.3). As discussed in the next section, these highlights should also be included in the cover letter.

Regardless of the type of résumé, the basic content should include contact information, qualifications summary (highlights), education, experience, honors (Figure 3.3), activities, professional memberships, special skills, and references (Box 3.3). An "objective" is optional; some employers view this as an outdated item on a résumé.

As illustrated in Box 3.3 action phrases are essential and should be quantified whenever possible. For example, rather than identify your

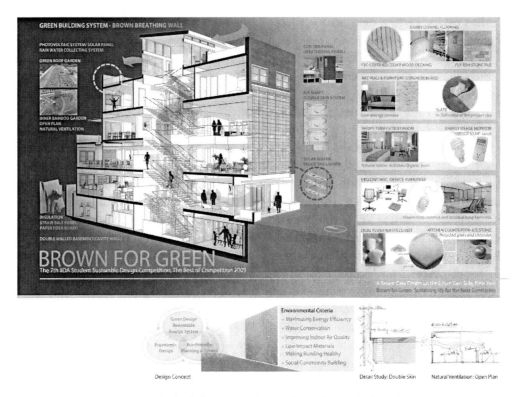

Figure 3.3 Résumés often include honors and awards, such as winning the IIDA Student Sustainable Design competition. In 2010, Joung-youn Park of the New York School of Interior Design won for *Brown for Green*—"a community center that cares for the elderly and strives to educate children on the upper east side of New York." *(© Joung-youn Park)*

responsibilities associated with a position (i.e., "Worked with customers") you should provide an action phrase that states the quantifiable results that were accomplished, such as "Researched and contacted new clients, resulting in an increase in new design projects of more than 35%." As another example, rather than state that you are proficient in AutoCAD, provide examples of projects using AutoCAD.

Contact information should be displayed in the heading of your résumé; include your name in a highly visible font size and list your current/permanent address, cell phone number, e-mail address, web page (if applicable), and perhaps your Facebook, Twitter, and/or LinkedIn contacts. Provide the telephone number you answer on a frequent basis and be sure to have a professional recording on the phone. If included,

your objective should be specific to the job you are seeking, but you could include an additional objective that describes your career ambition.

Highlights of your qualifications should succinctly state the skills, knowledge, experience, and abilities you possess that match the requirements for a position. As with all of your search materials, your résumé should use the terms that are used in the design profession and avoid slang as well as trendy jargon. Good sources for these terms are job descriptions, CIDA's professional standards, and NCIDQ documents.

Education information should include the name of a school, location, degree earned, years, major(s), minor(s), honors, and perhaps relevant courses. You could include your grade point average (GPA) if it is at least a 3.0 in your major. Your most recent education should be listed first, followed by earlier institutions, but generally college graduates should not list their high school. Students working toward graduation should state the expected date of graduation.

How can you include examples of work experience when you are searching for an entry-level position? Generally, the "experience" category is for work, but often people searching for entry-level positions do not have relevant work experience. In these situations, the list could include a variety of experiences that are relevant to the position, such as internships, volunteer work, campus activities, clubs, professional organizations, and class projects. Many of these experiences demonstrate skills, such as critical thinking, communications, or social responsibility, which are easily transferrable to various positions.

As is the case with your education section, your most recent experience should be listed first, followed in descending chronological order. For each experience you should include the name of the employer or organization, location, title, and at least three action phrases/verbs that demonstrate your skills, abilities, and knowledge.

Whenever possible items listed under the headings "Activities, Interests, and Special Skills" should also attempt to match information provided in the job description. For example, a job description in Box 2.1 included Chinese as a requirement for a position in Beijing. To apply for this position, the job seeker's résumé should list speaking Chinese as a special skill.

Another job description in Box 2.1 stated, "Must be able to safely move around sites under different phases of construction. This might include maneuvering through, around, and over construction supplies, debris, etc.; climbing stairs if building elevators inaccessible and/or inoperable during construction phase" (IIDA 2010). A résumé for this position might list under the "Activities" or "Interests" category mountain climbing or another physically active sport. Make certain that the information is true and is verifiable for specific work-related statements.

Generally, for the reference section résumés state, "References available upon request," rather than listing names and contact information. However, you should prepare a separate page that lists the names of at least three references and each person's title, organization, location, phone number, and e-mail address. Your reference sheet should have your contact information at the top of the page in the same format as your résumé and should be printed on the same paper as your résumé. Before sharing the list to a potential employer, you must receive permission from the reference and provide him or her with your résumé and the job description.

Cover Letters and Business Cards

All résumés, including e-résumés, should have a cover letter. A cover letter is especially important for applicants with minimum relevant experience because the document enables you to demonstrate your enthusiasm for the position, highlight your skills, and explain how your unrelated experiences can still provide value to your employer. Like the résumé, the cover letter must be grammatically perfect as well as having appropriate punctuation, excellent sentence structure, flawless spelling, and no typos.

The cover letter should share the visual appearance of your résumé, such as using the same paper, typeface, color system, and personal logo. Generally, cover letters should have a font size of 12, have single or 1.5 line spacing, and be left-justified. If you are sending your résumé via e-mail, the cover letter should be in the message section of the e-mail.

A cover letter should conform to standard business practices by including your contact information, date, and the employer's name and address (Box 3.4; see Chapter 5, especially Box 5.4, for international formats). The letter should begin with "Dear" followed by the person's proper title, such as Mr., Mrs., Ms., or Dr., and then the specific individual's name (refer to Chapter 5 for the format of international business letters). Be sure to check the correct spelling of the organization and the individual's name. Techniques for identifying the name of an individual are reviewed later in this chapter (see "Search Strategies" section).

The letter should have at least three paragraphs, including an introduction, body, and closing. The letter should conclude with a formal closing, such as "Sincerely," followed by your signature, typed name, and "Enclosure: Résumé" as well as the names of any other documents included with your résumé.

The first paragraph in a cover letter should indicate which position you are applying for and where you found the job posting, such as the classifieds section of a newspaper or the company's website. If a position was not advertised, you should explain your interest in trying to secure employment with that organization. In both situations you should provide highlights that demonstrate your familiarity with the organization and how you can provide value to the company. These highlights can be used as the transition to the second paragraph or body of the letter.

The second paragraph should summarize your key skills, abilities, and knowledge and provide specific examples that support your statements. Upon receiving permission, you might want to include a brief quote (testimonial) from an employer or professor that reflects well on your abilities. Ideally, you should match the items with words and phrases in the job description (Boxes 3.3 and 3.4).

The body of the letter can also be used to explain any atypical situations in your résumé, such as frequent job changes or long periods of unemployment. Keep in mind that employers usually evaluate the employment record of an entry-level person with a softer lens than when considering a candidate with years of professional work experience. Generally, information in the body of the letter can be presented in approximately two paragraphs, but a person with considerable relevant experience might need additional paragraphs.

The last paragraph of a cover letter should provide a summary statement regarding your qualifications and suggest future actions, such as scheduling an interview. As illustrated in Box 3.4, your letter should specifically state what you would like to happen, who should initiate the contact, the means of communication, and a timetable. To provide another example of your enthusiasm for the position, you might elect to be the one who will call or e-mail the employer to initiate a possible date for a phone call or interview.

As you are preparing your résumé and cover letter, you might also create your business card. By working on these three materials at the same time, you ensure that all will have the same visual appearance, including the same typeface, color system, and personal logo. Information that should be printed on your business card includes your name, job title (if applicable), address, cell phone number, e-mail address and your Web page (if applicable), and perhaps your Facebook, Twitter, and/or LinkedIn contacts.

Your business card should be aesthetically pleasing and limited to essential contact information. The back of the card can be used to highlight your skills, expertise, and areas of design specialties (refer to Chapter 5 for international business protocols).

Design Portfolios
The development of your visual identity system continues with the design of your portfolio. Your résumé, cover letter, business card, portfolio, and any other promotional materials should present a unified appearance. This becomes especially important when the materials are examined at the same time. Thus, the typeface, color system, and personal logo you selected for your printed materials should also be used for your design portfolio.

It is very important to remember that your visual identity system communicates an underlying message to prospective employers: Your job search materials are a reflection of your design skills as well as your creativity. This becomes especially significant when you create your design portfolio.

Box 3.4

Cover Letter Prepared for a Specific Job Posting (see Box 3.3)

John J. Smyth

P. O. Box 1234 Denver, CO 12345
(555) 555.5555
johnjsmyth@name.com
LinkedIn: https://www.linkedin.com/xxx

Your contact information.

August 20, 2012

Marie Truman
Human Resources Office
TAC International
1233 State St.
Denver, CO 34523

Employer's name and address.

Proper title.

Dear Ms. Truman:

I am writing in response to TAC International's advertisement in the *Boulder Times*. I have been extremely impressed by your firm's emphasis on sustainability and energy optimization, and your commitment to social responsibilities. I have experience with sustainable designs, including energy conservation methods. I am very enthusiastic about the possibility of interviewing with your firm.

Introduction with source and interest in the firm.

As a recent graduate of ABC University in interior design, I am seeking a position with an international design firm. My CIDA-accredited program provided me the opportunity to study key concepts and practices related to planning, sustainability, evidence-based design, and budgets. My excellent grades demonstrate my knowledge of the design process and my skills in AutoCAD, AGi32, and Revit. Moreover, my fluency in French and Spanish can make a positive contribution to your international projects.

Body of the letter with details that match job description (see Box 3.3).

I

C, D, and E

H

Other highlights of my achievements that relate to your requirements include my three years of related work experience. Most recently, as an intern at AAA Interior Design, I gained experience with multidisciplinary projects, LEED certification initiatives, globalization, and projects that resulted in over $100,000 in revenues. As an assistant designer in the University's Facilities Management department, I was able use computer design programs as well as my personable communication skills to resolve problems associated team management and moving employees to new facilities by deadlines. As a volunteer with Habitat for Humanity, I was able to fulfill my interest in social responsibilities and gain experience with sustainability, planning, energy conservation, and collaborative projects.

A

B

H

F

I would greatly appreciate the opportunity to meet with you to discuss my qualifications. I believe my education and work experience enable me to make a very positive contribution to your organization. I look forward to receiving a phone call or e-mail from you soon. Thank you for your kind consideration.

Closing with follow-up information.

Sincerely,

Complimentary closing.

John J. Smyth

Enclosures: Résumé and DVD

Enclosures with letter.

You should see your portfolio as an extension of your design skills, creativity, and your ability to solve problems (Figure 3.4). Impressive portfolios are well designed, present a unified appearance, and are easy for the viewer to both handle and read. How is this accomplished?

The first step is to collect all the materials that *could be* appropriate for the portfolio. These should support the skills, knowledge, and abilities you are claiming on your résumés and cover letters. As stated previously, you must be prepared to tailor your search materials for the specific needs of an employer. Therefore, by collecting a variety of materials, you should be able to select specific items for each interview.

If you have gaps in your portfolio, do not hesitate to develop examples that demonstrate your most recent skills and knowledge. You do not have to limit your portfolio to projects created for classes, internships, or jobs. Depending on where you are interviewing, you might also include other items related to the design profession, such as photography, drawings, paintings, or ceramics. Furthermore, do not hesitate to rework previous projects. Your portfolio should demonstrate your best work, which might involve redrawing plans developed in introductory courses or adding new drawings to a previous project.

What you select and how you present the materials in your portfolio communicates to a potential employer your skills, abilities, and experiences as well as how well you understand the requirements of a position. Therefore, your portfolio should be prepared for *every* interview. The items in the portfolio should reflect the needs of the employer and should be sequenced in a manner that attracts attention from the beginning and culminates in an example of your best work. A portfolio should generally have between 10 and 20 items. However, quality and relevance is always preferred over quantity or projects that are irrelevant to the interviewer.

When presenting your portfolio, pay attention to the reactions of the interviewer. Spend more time on projects that appear to be

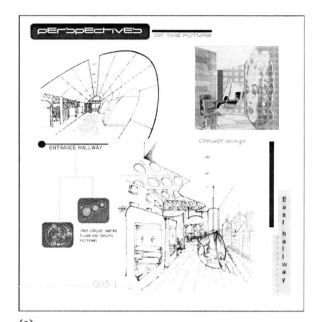

(a)

(b)

Figure 3.4a-b Examples from Iraissa Marrero's portfolio: "Prospectives of the Future" (a) and a commercial project for an advertising agency (b). (© *Iraissa Marrero*)

interesting to him or her and only briefly describe items that seem to lose that person's attention. There are occasions when people will review your portfolio without your being present. In these situations people pace themselves, but without your input your portfolio must be easily understood and communicate well to the viewer. Therefore, as you design your portfolio you must consider both situations. More details regarding interviews and interviewing are discussed later in this chapter.

Design Portfolio Presentation Types

To have a design portfolio that can be prepared for each interview requires a flexible presentation unit. For print portfolios the options include lightweight cardboard, bookcase portfolios with multi-ring mechanisms, screw post portfolios, presentation cases, boxes, photo albums, and ring binders with removable vinyl sleeves. Portfolios are available in a variety of materials, including metal, canvas, linen, leather, plastic, and imitation leather.

Digital portfolios, such as CDs and DVDs, can be presented in a case or package with a cover that reflects your visual identity system. Digitally based portfolios, including PDF files, slideshow presentations, and interactive websites, are especially flexible because you can easily delete, add, and rearrange the items depending on your audience. In addition, digital portfolios enable you to demonstrate computer animation skills.

Your selection of the presentation unit (as well as other factors) plays an important role in having a portfolio that has a unified appearance. Even though your portfolio might have a variety of materials in different sizes, your portfolio itself should be viewed as one project with unifying elements that reflect your visual identity system. As previously mentioned, items that can unify your portfolio include using the same paper, colors, typeface, logo, positioning on pages, borders, headings, and consistency with varying font sizes.

All materials must be clean and neat, and must present a professional appearance. Rework or remount any items that are wrinkled, torn, or have frayed edges. Sketches are an exception and should be included in your portfolio. They are very important for helping someone to understand your problem-solving process—an especially important trait for people who lack professional experience.

To resolve the dilemma of including "messy" sketches in a professionally designed portfolio, you might want to create a separate folder for the sketches that you can present upon request. Your design portfolio as well as your résumés, cover letters, and business cards become important elements in your career portfolio and are critical to your job search plan.

Checking for Comprehension

- What are the basic types of résumés?

- Identify three important characteristics of a design portfolio that has a professional appearance.

Job Search Plan and Strategizing Opportunities

Thus far in this chapter, we have reviewed career portfolios, networking strategies, résumés, and design portfolios. These items and ideas set the stage for your job search. Competing in a global marketplace requires a well-thought-out job search plan that includes several methods. A job search plan should become part of your career portfolio and should be updated even after you have a job.

As stated earlier, people average five different careers in their lifetime, but the variety of positions becomes even greater when you examine the number of jobs within each career. In your lifetime you might have 15 to 20 different jobs. Hence, a job search plan that always has the most current information will let you quickly access contacts in order to pursue career opportunities.

Elements of a Job Search Plan

A job search plan is a structured and purposeful approach to looking for a job. The job search plan should be written—not some ideas that exist only in your mind. Why do you need to write a job search plan? In the same way you would plan a wedding, a job search plan helps you stay on task, remember critical details, and identify important items, contacts, and deadlines. A job search plan is critical for making sure your search process is organized and efficient.

A basic job search plan should have (1) a list of where you can identify openings, (2) multiple search strategies, (3) a dedicated space for the task, (4) a job search partner, and (5) a schedule with weekly goals. A starting point in developing career opportunities is to reexamine topics reviewed in Chapter 2, such as types of design firms, design practice specializations, *Interior Design*'s "Top 100 Giants," nontraditional opportunities, and international practice.

Your list of where to search for job openings should begin with your networks, such as friends, family members, neighbors, professors, coworkers, social media contacts, and previous employers. Be prepared to provide these people with your résumé and your electronic portfolio, if available. You might be able to identify opportunities by connecting and working with people associated with professional associations, design centers, campus career services, alumni associations, internship and/or job shadowing programs, and design conferences.

Other sources to learn about job openings are trade journals, state workforce/economic development agencies, local chambers of commerce, and newspaper employment classifieds. You can also search for job opportunities published by the United States Department of Labor: O*NET OnLine (http://online.onetcenter.org/) and the Occupational Outlook Handbook (OOH; (http://www.bls.gov/OCO/).

You might want to begin developing your list of resources by reviewing the information posted on O*NET OnLine and OOH. O*NET OnLine has a summary report for the interior design profession that includes a description of tasks, tools and technology, knowledge, skills, abilities, work activities, work context, job zone, interests, work styles, work values, related occupations, and wages/employment. In 2011 O*NET OnLine projected that the growth for the interior

design profession was faster than average (14 percent to 19 percent) and the projected need was for 35,900 additional employees by 2018. O*NET OnLine's data includes national figures as well as information for each state.

The OOH has information about a specific occupation or topic as well as job search tips and data on the job market in each state. Information related to interior designers includes the nature of the work, training, other qualifications, advancements, employment, job outlook, projections data, earnings, wages, and related occupations. Significant points identified for interior designers in the 2010–11 Edition are as follows:

* Keen competition is expected for jobs because many talented individuals are attracted to this occupation.

* Self-employment is common; many interior designers work in small firms or on a contract basis.

* Post-secondary education—either an associate's or a bachelor's degree—is necessary for entry-level positions; some states license interior designers (Bureau of Labor Statistics 2011).

As you develop your search strategies it is very important to remember OOH's second bullet item as well as the statistics discussed in Chapter 2. According to a 2010 report by ASID, in 2009 there were 13,388 interior design firms in the United States; approximately 80 percent of these firms had fewer than five employees. Fifteen percent had a staff between 6 and 20, and only 5 percent had more than 20 employees (ASID 2010). (see Figure 3.5.) How does this affect your search?

Generally, it is not practical for small firms to advertise for one position, nor do they have **human resources** personnel to screen applicants and process candidates. Therefore, you should not interpret the lack of an advertisement as a reflection of a firm not being interested in hiring a new employee. You might contact that company on a day when one of its employees

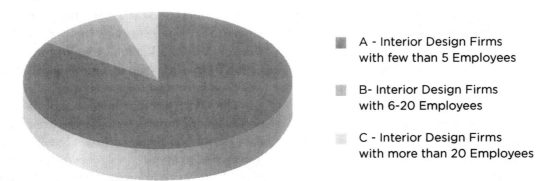

A - Interior Design Firms with few than 5 Employees

B- Interior Design Firms with 6-20 Employees

C - Interior Design Firms with more than 20 Employees

Figure 3.5 According to ASID (2010), in 2009 there were 13,388 interior design firms in the United States. Most of the firms had fewer than five employees.

just requested medical leave, or when the firm receives news that it won a contract for a very large project. The next section discusses topics such as how to introduce yourself to people at these firms—and possibly obtain an interview.

Search Strategies

The best approach to attaining a job is to use multiple search strategies. Your list of strategies might change as you progress through the search process, but the critical element is to use several methods to search for your job. Remember: There are advertised and *many* unadvertised job opportunities.

Some of your search strategies can include personal contacts, working with career placement offices, **informational interviews**, and researching the Internet. Other strategies include internships, **job shadowing, experience-seeking proposals**, and volunteering.

Generally, it is *not* effective to mail or e-mail an unsolicited résumé because it is typically not read. The U.S. Department of Labor has indicated that the methods discussed below are considered some of the most effective techniques in the twenty-first-century global marketplace.

In-person or virtual personal contacts are viewed as very effective methods for finding a job. Discuss your job search with people in your networks and ask if they know of any openings. If the response is "no," ask if they know someone who might have the information. Inquire if

it is acceptable for you to contact the person and if you can mention your contact as the source of the referral. These same questions should be used when communicating with new contacts after establishing a relationship with the individuals.

Some excellent activities for enhancing your job search include internships, job shadowing, attending professional conferences, visiting design centers, and working as a volunteer. While engaged in these activities, you can also discuss your job search ideas and efforts with your fellow participants.

Personal contact can also include meeting with an advisor at a career placement center. Advisors might be aware of openings and can provide assistance in developing your résumé, cover letter, and interviewing skills (see the section "Professional Materials and Job Interview Etiquette" later in this chapter).

Another personal contact method is to ask a potential employer for an informational interview. The purpose of the informational interview is to learn more about an organization and to have personal contact with people who work for the organization, preferably with people involved with hiring decisions. Keep in mind an informational interview does not have any immediate prospect of employment. To arrange for an informational interview, call a firm and request the name of the person responsible for hiring.

Large organizations often have a human resources department for screening applicants. When applicable, try to circumvent this unit and instead ask for the name of the person who hires interior designers. Even if the firm does not have any openings, try to arrange a meeting with the hiring manager for the purpose of learning more about both the firm and the design profession.

To develop your information interviewing skills prior to talking with your dream employers, schedule your first appointments with firms near the bottom of your potential employers' list.

Social Networks and Company Websites

In-person contacts can be very effective for finding a job, and one approach to creating an opportunity for a face-to-face meeting is **social networks**. Used appropriately, social media can be a means to finding a job. LinkedIn is considered to be the most professional networking site, but people have also been able to find jobs using Facebook, Twitter, or MySpace. Online social networks enable you to create your personal profile, connect with people around the world, and build networks.

When using social networks for business purposes, your personal profile must have a professional appearance, should feature current information, and should include a recent and appropriate photograph of yourself. Online protocols include politely responding to inquiries, sharing expertise, participating in discussions, being respectful, and a mindset that people should "give more than they take."

LinkedIn's focus on professionalism can help during your job search by connecting you with leads, employers, and working professionals. When you have a job, professional connections via LinkedIn can provide assistance with numerous job-related responsibilities, such as locating products, resolving installation problems, substituting discontinued items, and identifying someone with specialized expertise.

As noted with social media, when used properly the Internet can be an efficient job search method. Many organizations and corporations advertise job openings on their websites, and you might find postings on job search portals, such as Monster (http://www.monster.com/), Careerbuilder (http://www.careerbuilder.com/), and Salary (http://www.salary.com/).

Job search portals might not include many interior design postings, but they are useful for obtaining data about salaries based on your education, geographical location, and work experience. Some of the best online sources for interior designers are employers, professional organizations, government agencies, newspapers, and trade journals. Moreover, you might want to post your résumé on sites dedicated to the design profession, such as those for trade journals or associations (for example, ASID, IDC, and IIDA).

The Internet is also a very important resource for researching information about an organization. For example, HOK's website has a comprehensive overview of what it is like to work at HOK by posting blogs, videos on YouTube, photos on Flicker, bookmarks on Delicious, and pages on Facebook, VisualCV, LinkedIn, and Twitter. According to the company's website, "Life at HOK is a group blog that showcases the perspectives and personalities of HOK people around the world. On this blog a group of 30 emerging voices are sharing their thoughts, experiences and sources of inspiration" (http://hoklife.com/).

Job Search Plan: Schedules and Activities

Searching for a job requires discipline, considerable time, perseverance, multiple search methods, and some degree of openness to new ideas and opportunities. Searching for a position should be considered a full-time job. Therefore, one of the first steps is to identify a specific place that you will use for your search process.

The location should be designated for this purpose and any distractions, such as a television, should not be there. The space should be studious, yet comfortable, because if you are jobless you should spend between 40 and 60 hours per week searching for a job.

As with planning your career, you should also identify a job search partner. This person might or might not be familiar with the design profession. The important element is that your partner will help you to stay on task and is willing to brainstorm ideas with you as well as discuss your results at various stages of the search process.

Job Search Schedule and Research

A job search schedule is basically a summary of your search plan with personal activities. The schedule should include weekly goals, days of the week, hours of each day, activities, completion dates, outcomes, reactions, and follow-up actions. The schedule should allow time for current employment responsibilities, personal time, and activities that can improve your professional skills, abilities, knowledge, and credentials (Table 3.2).

Enhancing your qualifications as you are searching for a job can strengthen your career portfolio while demonstrating to prospective employers that you have initiative and a strong

Table 3.2 Sample Job Search Schedule and Log of Activities						
Week 1 **Goals for Week 1: Contact potential employers to schedule 5 interviews, read 5 current design-related articles, and research the websites of 5 prospective employers and 10 design-related manufacturers.**						
	Monday	**Tuesday**	**Wednesday**	**Thursday**	**Friday**	**Saturday**
8:00	Exercise	Job	Exercise	Job	Exercise	Volunteer work
9:00	Contact employers for interviews.		Contact employers for interviews.		Contact employers for interviews.	
10:00						
11:00						
12:00	Lunch	Lunch	Lunch	Lunch	Lunch	
1:00	Research employers.	Internship	Research manufacturers.	Internship	Research employers.	
2:00						
3:00						
4:00						
5:00						Assessed success in completing weekly goals: All goals were accomplished and I had one additional interview. Next week I could read more articles/books.
6:00						
7:00	Read articles.		Read articles.			
8:00						
Completed Tasks	Contacted 8 employers; identified 5 employers' websites; and read 2 articles.	Job and intern responsibilities.	Contacted 10 employers; researched 10 manufacturers' websites; and read 3 articles.	Job and intern responsibilities.	Contacted 7 employers; and researched 5 employers' websites.	Volunteer responsibilities.
Results	2 interviews and learned about energy technologies.	Gained experience with creating budgets.	2 interviews and learned about manufacturers of residential energy technologies.	Gained experience with charrettes.	2 interviews and learned about projects completed by 5 firms.	Participated in building the interior walls at a Habitat for Humanity house.

Table 3.2 (continued)

Week 1

Goals for Week 1: Contact potential employers to schedule 5 interviews, read 5 current design-related articles, and research the websites of 5 prospective employers and 10 design-related manufacturers.

	Monday	Tuesday	Wednesday	Thursday	Friday	Saturday
Follow-up Actions	Send résumé and cover letters; find more articles on energy technologies.	Need to understand more about budgets and project management.	Send résumé and cover letters; find more articles on sustainability.	Need to understand more about collaborative projects.	Send résume and cover letters; try to find more information about the projects by researching USGBC and trade journals.	Contact two of the volunteers who have professional experience and ask them to review sustainable building methods.
Reactions to Activities	Excited about the 2 interviews; concerned about finding employers' websites; enjoyed reading about new energy technologies.	Budgets are not interesting, but I understand the importance of being accurate and thorough.	Excited about 2 more interviews; concerned about being able to learn about all of the advances in energy products; enjoyed reading about wind energy.	I enjoyed being part of a charrette; but noted difficulties associated with building consensus.	Excited about the 2 interviews and the projects completed by the firms.	Really enjoyed working on the site and learned a great deal about construction methods.
Activities to Improve Qualifications	Internship, design-related volunteer activities, and reading articles about energy technologies and sustainability.					
Developments in the Profession	The impact of energy technologies on residential design.					
Developments in Related Industries	New energy technologies and their impact on sustainable designs.					
Global Current Events Affecting Profession	The decline in interest rates is anticipated to improve the residential and commercial building markets. The high cost of oil will impact heating bills, which will increase the demand for energy-efficient buildings. Terrorist attacks in India could affect the construction of new buildings.					

work ethic—personal qualities that are especially noteworthy when someone has minimal relevant work experience.

Your job search schedule should also include time that is dedicated to staying current with developments in the profession, related industries, and world affairs. Knowledge of these occurrences can be helpful during interviewing and can provide you with ideas for new career opportunities.

Your schedule should allocate time for researching information posted on a potential employer's website. To effectively research a website, you should create a strategy that enables you to uncover issues both related to your self-assessment and important to your career goals. For example, your strategy should include a plan to thoroughly read every page on an organization's website and to pay particular attention to important portals, such as "About Us," "Careers," "Projects," "Services," "Clients," "News," and "Markets." Your strategy could entail consistently considering (and responding to) specific questions, such as the examples in Box 3.5.

Box 3.5

Examples of Questions Used to Evaluate Design Firms' Websites

- Does the website provide you with an overview of their clients and their projects? If yes, are these the clients you want to work with? Are their projects interesting to you? Does the number of projects correspond with the size of the organization you want to work for?

- Does the website provide you with an overview of what it would be like to work at the organization? If yes, is the work environment appealing? Are there current employees you can contact for further information?

- Does the organization list international locations? Are the locations interesting to you?

- Does the website include a list of their leaders and a biographical profile? If yes, do you agree with their philosophy? If no, are you concerned that you may not be able to acquire information about the organization's leaders?

- Does the website include corporate information, such as mission statements, goals, and annual reports? Are the statements and goals aligned with your career aspirations?

- Does the organization invest in research studies, videos, publications, and current issue reports? If yes, do you support the issues that are addressed? If it does not appear that the organization invests in educational and research initiatives, is this troublesome to you?

- Does the website include information related to sustainability, social responsibilities, diversity, teamwork, advancement opportunities, continuing education, and benefits? If yes, do you agree with the philosophy presented? If no, are you concerned that the information is missing?

- Does the firm have internships and/or scholarships that could help you acquire work experience?

- Does the website have a "News" portal? If yes, what is being reported on this page? Awards? Articles in major trade magazines? Announcements of new projects? Are these important to you?

- Has the company received awards? Are the awards for teamwork or for an individual's accomplishment? Has the firm won an award for service or for being an excellent company to work for?

- Is the information current? Is the website attractive to you and reflect an image you can relate to? Does it include blogs and social media contacts? If yes, what is your opinion of the information?

Acquiring Work Experience

Researching an organization's website is also important for trying to obtain work experience—another activity that should be included on your job search schedule. As mentioned in Chapter 2, work experience is *very* important to employers.

Some organizations will only hire people with several years of experience. Why? A major reason is because of the high cost of projects.

An interior designer can be responsible for specifying *millions of dollars* of products and services. Mistakes can be enormously expensive and can result in the loss of the client, related future projects, and potential referrals. Considerable experience helps to reduce the likelihood of costly mistakes. In addition, designers with experience have a clientele base that often can be relied on for repeat business.

How can you get experience when people want to hire those who already have experience? An answer for this "chicken or the egg" question is to try several approaches that generally revolve around the willingness to work for free or modest pay. Internships and job shadowing are excellent means to gain experience because an employer has a minimum investment in time and resources. There are paid and unpaid internships.

Excellent work performance during an internship often results in a job opportunity because the organization has become accustomed to having you work with them, and people realize that you provide value. Keep in mind that global opportunities also exist; if this is of interest to you, study a country's immigration policies (which you can find online).

Another way to obtain experience is to volunteer for a community organization related to the design profession, such as Habitat for Humanity (Figure 3.6). Or you could become involved with an organization that allows you to engage in design-related tasks. For example, local historical societies often need volunteers to be docents for historical properties or to assist with research, displays, and educational programs.

Some people have been very creative in acquiring work experience by approaching organizations with new ideas for internships. The fundamental idea is to match your interests with work experience. For example, if you had a personal interest in photography, you might contact a local photographer and ask for an internship that would involve designing the backgrounds for portraits or perhaps arranging the interiors for people who need photographs of their home for a real estate agent.

You might also want to contact a potential employer by submitting a proposal that outlines

Figure 3.6 Another way to obtain experience is to volunteer for a community organization related to the design profession, such as Habitat for Humanity. Habitat has student-led Campus Chapter programs that partner with local Habitat affiliates. *(Habitat for Humanity)*

(1) what type of work you are willing to do, (2) a specified period of time for your service, and (3) whether or not you would like compensation for your service. The work could involve helping with installations, researching new products, building models, renderings, and organizing and updating the organization's product literature and sample library. The goal is to gain experience. A perfect time to get experience (either paid or unpaid) is while you are in school—as well as when you are searching for a job.

Checking for Comprehension

* Identify three important elements that should be included in a job search plan.

* Identify two methods you could use to get professional work experience.

Interviews and Negotiating a Position

A comprehensive job search plan and rigorous implementation can result in invitations for job interviews. Numerous activities should precede an interview, including conducting further research on the organization, preparing answers to possible questions, and sharpening presentation skills. When presented with a job offer, you need to be aware of the conditions of employment and know how to negotiate the offer.

U.S. Interview Preparations

Receiving an invitation for an interview is an indication that the employer is interested in your skills, abilities, and experiences. Your résumé opened the door for an interview; the interview provides you with the opportunity to receive a job offer. Therefore, you should devote considerable time to preparing for the interview. Getting ready for an international interview requires knowing intercultural business communication styles and protocols as discussed in Chapter 5. An interview can be especially important for interior designers because the meeting allows an employer to study how you might interact with clients and the quality of your presentation techniques—another important skill when working with a client.

What needs to be done? You should plan to further research the organization and relevant current, and if possible, previous employees. Your networks, as well as the organization's website and other Internet sites (such as those for trade journals), might help you obtain this information.

Organizational information can assist you in responding to the interviewer's questions and can help to prepare your own questions for the interview. Knowing some details about people you will meet could ease any anxieties associated with introductions; this can help you to remember names. In addition, people will be impressed that you had the interest and the initiative to research information about the organization.

You should be cognizant of the organization's projects, clients, markets, annual reports, future initiatives, and news. Try to memorize specific details related to the position and your interests, such as Mary XYZ's humanitarian award or the company's most recent LEED certification project.

To align your search materials with the organization's needs, your preparations should include updating your résumé, references, and personal profile, as necessary. Your design portfolio should be reexamined, and perhaps projects should be added or removed according to the needs of the employer.

Do *not* assume that you do not have to study your search materials because you recently developed the documents and projects. Take the time to study and remember items on your résumé and details in your design portfolio, such as how you developed your design concepts, problem statements, budgets, and how your solutions addressed the needs of the clients. Revisiting the information before an interview will help you to appropriately respond to questions, and helps to reinforce the connection between the employer's needs and your skills, abilities, and knowledge.

Professional Materials and Job Interview Etiquette

Make sure that you have business cards and fresh copies of your résumé and reference sheet. Your paper portfolio should be clean and without any frayed, bent, or torn edges. CDs and DVDs should be in an appropriate package; plan to bring copies for the employer's use after the interview. As you are preparing your search materials, rehearse both your responses to questions and your portfolio presentation.

Presenting a portfolio during a job interview can be challenging because of the variety of conditions and situations. Therefore, review a variety of scenarios and identify ways you could overcome any obstacles. For example, how would you handle having to present your portfolio on your lap in a small office filled with material swatches, product samples, papers, and drawings? In another setting, how would you present in a formal conference room with ten or more people in the room? In some interviews you might not have immediate access to a computer, or a computer screen might be too small for people to see the details in your drawings.

As noted previously, another circumstance to consider is that people might review your portfolio without your being there. Thus, to be prepared for various situations, you should rehearse your presentation while standing, sitting, with technology, without technology, and in small and large spaces. In situations when you are not present, your portfolio should be easy to understand, be logically organized, and include projects related to both the position and the organization.

Take considerable time in preparing answers to potential questions, and develop an initial list of questions you might ask during an interview. Your list of questions might be revised as you proceed through the interview. Examples of interviewer questions, things to consider before responding, and questions you might ask are listed in Box 3.6. Try to ask open-ended questions and avoid questions that can only generate a "yes" or "no" answer. Generally, open-ended

Box 3.6

Sample Interview Questions and Response Considerations

Sample Interviewers' Questions and Response Considerations

> Note behavioral item.

> Suggestions for answering questions.

- Tell me about yourself. [An example of a behavioral item. Hint: Response could be derived from your professional profile.]

- Describe a situation that required you to solve a problem. [An example of a behavioral item. Hint: Response could take the form of a story and should refer to one of the design-related skills required for the position.]

- Describe a time when you had to deal with a difficult person and how you resolved the situation. [An example of a behavioral item. Hint: Response could take the form of a story and should demonstrate that you are able to work with a variety of personalities and are willing to compromise for the good of an organization.]

- Why are you interested in working for this organization? [Hints: Response should reflect your research of the organization. Your response could identify projects completed by the firm that you found interesting and/or specific skills that were listed in the job description.]

- Why are you interested in this position? [Hint: Response should demonstrate your enthusiasm for the job and project confidence that you could be successful in the position.]

- Tell me about your favorite class project. [Hint: Response should emphasize the skills you have that align with the job description.]

- Tell me about a favorite project designed by our firm. [An example of a research question intended to discover your level of interest in the organization. Hint: The assumption is that if you are truly interested in the position, you would be well prepared for the interview, including learning as much about the firm as possible. Be prepared by thoroughly researching the firm, and remember their projects and perhaps their clients.]

(Box 3.6 continued on page 84)

Box 3.6

Sample Interview Questions and Response Considerations *(continued)*

- If you were working with a team of designers on a project, which task would you request? [Hints: Response should focus on the skills you have that align with the job description. In addition, your answer could focus on your willingness to engage in teamwork.]

- What are your greatest strengths? [Hint: Response should focus on the needs of the organization and the skills you have that align with the job description.] Weaknesses? [Hint: Response should focus on areas of improvement, not on skills listed as requirements for the position.]

- What would you like to do five and ten years from now? [Hint: Response should demonstrate your goal-setting skills and your commitment to the profession.]

- Why did you include these items in your design portfolio? [Hint: Response should focus on the skills you have that align with the job description.]

- Which courses did you enjoy the most at school? [Hint: Response should focus on the skills you have that align with the job description.] The least? [Hint: Response should focus on courses unrelated to the needs of the organization.]

- Why did you study interior design? [Hint: Response should demonstrate your enthusiasm for design, working with people, and your goal-setting skills.]

- What are some of the most important issues facing interior designers today? [Hint: An example of a research question intended to discover your knowledge of current events and developments in the design profession. Prior to the interview

be sure to read current newspapers and trade journals.]

Your Sample Questions

Hint: Avoid asking questions regarding salary and information that is posted on an organization's website or in its other publicly accessible documents (e.g., trade magazines, annual reports, newspaper articles). Asking these questions can give the interviewer the impression you may not be very interested in the organization because you did not try to find that information before the interview. In addition, the interviewer might conclude that you did not adequately prepare for the interview. As illustrated below, questions you may want to ask the hiring manager can focus on the organization's role in the design profession, as well as items that can provide you with more information about the organization, the position, your potential future boss, coworkers, and the next steps in the interview process.

- Would you please tell me about some of your collaborative organizations?

- What do you think are your firm's most significant contributions to the design profession?

- What do you think are your firm's strengths and weaknesses?

- How would you describe your firm's organizational culture?

- Generally, when do new employees begin to work with their own clients?

- What are my opportunities for advancement?

Box 3.6

Sample Interview Questions and Response Considerations *(continued)*

- Are there opportunities for entry-level designers to be assigned international work?

- How do you measure performance and how is the information communicated to me?

- How do you make decisions?

- What are your biggest challenges?

- How would you describe the people I would work with?

- After this interview when will I hear from you?

- Is there any information about me that I can clarify?

questions can provide more meaningful information and usually encourage conversation.

Note that some of the items in Box 3.6 deal with your possible behavior in the future. Behavioral questions during interviews could also include design case studies that require you to provide solutions to problems, such as accommodating people who are physically challenged, resolving personality conflicts between project team members, or improving the sustainable features of a design. For positions that require specific technical skills, such as AutoCAD or Photoshop, be prepared to create a drawing or illustration.

Carefully listen to each question as well as any information the interviewer is presenting to you, such as the number of employees, the history of the firm, or a list of the company's newest projects. You might begin to feel overwhelmed or tired during the interview, but always appear to be positive and eager to learn. Your responses should connect to the job requirements, demonstrate your knowledge of the organization, and highlight your qualifications.

Your responses should also demonstrate knowledge of current global events, trends, and terms used in the design profession. Avoid negative comments about past or current co-workers, employers, professors, institutions, and classmates. Do not enquire about salary

information. If an interviewer raises the topic, try to avoid responding with specific information; instead indicate that you are willing to work for prevailing compensation rates. Salary discussions should be reserved for job offers and subsequent negotiations.

Dress and Grooming Expectations

As you prepare your search materials, plan your attire, shoes, grooming, and hairstyle. You might want to consider a unified appearance by coordinating what you wear to the interview with the design of your portfolio, notepad, writing instrument, and briefcase. The total package reflects your branding identity and communicates your design skills to an employer.

Be cautious with visible tattoos and body piercing. Your appearance and attire should be professional and, as discussed in Chapter 7, should be acceptable to several generations. Apparel should be well-fitted, without wrinkles, and in an appropriate color, such as black, gray, brown, or blue. Designers often wear black. Skirts should be mid-length.

To subtly suggest your sense of design, you might want to add a small, but creative accessory, such as a silk scarf or piece of handcrafted jewelry. Generally, sandals are not acceptable; closed-toe shoes are preferred. To avoid being distracted during an interview, your shoes as well as garments should be comfortable. Neat hairstyles and grooming must be professional, such as clean and trimmed fingernails. Use perfume and after-shave colognes sparingly, and avoid any heavy scents.

Interviewing and Negotiations

An employer might want to conduct a telephone screening interview before asking you to visit the organization. In this situation you can easily refer to your written list of answers, questions, and professional profile. Telephone interviews are generally more effective when you dress professionally and stand rather than sit during the conversation. Standing tends to help keep you alert and creates a greater sense of formality.

Your responses should be concise and articulate—try to avoid long pauses, a monotone speech, or rambling statements. Your voice should be an appropriate volume and reveal enthusiasm as well as professionalism.

Your contact will inform you when there is more than one person involved with the interview and is listening on a speaker phone. In these circumstances, during the interview you should acknowledge these people, and at the end of the interview all of the people should be thanked for their time and consideration.

When you have the opportunity to interview in person, plan your trip and perhaps travel to the business before the day of the appointment. A trial run will let you to know exactly where the business is located, the best means of travel, and the amount of time you will need to arrive at the site approximately 10 minutes early.

The first impression people have of you is very important. When you arrive for the interview you should greet *everyone* you meet with a smile, direct eye contact, a firm handshake from a standing position, and a friendly introduction. Being friendly to everyone is especially important in small firms—the most common type of business in the design field. Frequently, small organizations will ask every person who works for the firm to comment on job applicants.

In addition to being personable to *everyone* you meet, you should be polite, thank people, stand straight, and project confidence without arrogance. Your attitude should reveal your strong interest in seeking to learn as much as possible, an especially important quality for a person searching for an entry-level position.

You might encounter several different types of interviews, even while interviewing at the same organization. Types of interviews include one-on-one, group, **teleconferencing**, and **videoconferencing**. Interviews can also be conducted during a meal. The fundamental difference between the different types of interviews is responding to questions from one person or several people.

When interviewing in a group, try to remember the names of the individuals and their area of expertise. Referencing their competencies in a conversation can demonstrate your people skills, ability to both listen and remember, and knowledge of professional responsibilities.

An excellent approach to introducing yourself to people is to refer to your professional profile. A polished and prepared statement can help reduce your anxieties, and provides people with a starting point for a conversation. As with a telephone interview, your responses should be polite and articulate, and have an enthusiastic overtone. However, in-person meetings tend to be more conversational with fewer recitations of questions and answers.

These interviews also provide both you and the interviewers with the opportunity to study body language. By observing the interviewers' physical reactions, you might have an indication of their interest or agreement with your statements and can adjust your responses accordingly. The interviewers will be noticing your posture, eye contact, and your reactions to people, statements, and questions. Employers might also take note of your awareness of design features in their facilities.

During an interview you should never smoke, use your cell phone, chew gum, use foul language, groom your hair, or apply lipstick. To avoid the temptation to text, read a text, or call someone, put your cell phone on silent or vibrate mode while you are at the organization.

Social skills—including those related to dining—are especially important for a position that requires interacting with clients. Interviewing during a meal can present special challenges, as people notice dining etiquette, and food or beverage spills. Ordering food that is easy to eat, and requires utensils rather than fingers, can help reduce the possibility for embarrassing situations. Generally, you should not order alcoholic beverages.

Use proper table manners (see *Emily Post's Etiquette* by Peggy/Emily Post), including placing your napkin on your lap, waiting until everyone has received their food before you begin eating, not talking while eating, and using the proper utensil, bread plate (left side), and water glass (right side). When in doubt follow the lead of your interviewer, and when dining in a foreign country make the effort to learn the proper cultural customs before the meeting (see Chapter 5).

At the end of any type of interview, prepare a statement that allows you to comfortably close the conversation. You might want to reiterate your interest in the position and the organization, and indicate your hopefulness that the interviewer will get back to you as quickly as possible. If the interviewer does not offer a time frame, request this information.

Always conclude by thanking people for the opportunity, and within one or two days after the interview, send a written thank you note, preferably using the U.S. mail service. Your note should have your contact information at the top of the page in the same format as your résumé and should be printed on the same paper as your résumé. The note might be handwritten or typed, or if you have been communicating with the interviewer via e-mail, the thank you message could perhaps be sent using the Internet. If possible, send a thank you note to every person who interviewed you.

Post-Interview Activities

In addition to the very important task of promptly writing a thank you note to your interviewers to demonstrate your knowledge of business protocols, immediately after your interview you should record several items that should become part of your career portfolio. This information can help you to assess job offers, and it provides you with ways to improve your search materials and future interviewing. Items that you could record are as follows:

- Names, titles, and contact information for each person you met during the interview

- List of questions you were asked and your responses

- List of questions you asked and their responses

- List of items in the job requirements that the interviewers seemed to focus on

- List of your skills, abilities, knowledge, and experiences interviewers appeared to be interested in, or were ignored

- Your reactions to (1) people you met, (2) information they gave you, (3) how you were treated, (4) the overall work environment and facilities, and (5) the firm's location, surrounding amenities, and the ease in commuting to the site

- A summary of how the organization relates to your self-assessment profile

After conducting a thorough analysis of your interviewing experience, you might want to reconnect with people in your network who might know people you met at the organization. These connections might be able to provide you with additional information about the organization, such as salary ranges.

Your analysis of questions and responses might prompt you to redraft your original lists. Based on the interview experience and your impressions of interviewers' interests and dislikes, you might want to revise your résumé, cover letter, business card, or design portfolio.

The last two items in the bulleted list above are especially important if the organization presents you with a job offer. When contemplating a job offer, some people tend to focus on salary and benefits. Although these are obviously critical elements of the position, other important considerations include your compatibility with the people you would work with, the type of tasks you would be expected to perform, how the job affects your personal life, opportunities for advancement, and the overall culture of the organization. Thus, when receiving an offer you should perform an assessment of the proposal and the other considerations that are critical to having a successful **life/work balance**.

Your self-assessment profile is an excellent tool for analyzing how well an organization addresses your needs and interests in addition to how well you would be able to provide value to the organization. If you are not selected for the position, you should promptly send a written thank you letter to the hiring manager. If applicable, the note could mention your interest in having the person contact you if new opportunities arise in the near future.

Job Negotiations

Terms in a job offer generally include a salary, list of benefits, vacation days, 401(k) stipulations, medical/dental/vision insurance, and a starting date. After thanking the hiring manager for the job offer, you should indicate that you would like a short amount of time to evaluate the proposal. Generally, you should return the call within 24 to 48 hours. This period should be adequate for reviewing the offer and lets you to respond in a timely manner. If you did not receive the offer in writing, request a copy; you should not provide an answer until you have been able to study the written document.

Thoroughly read each detail of the job offer, and create a list of items that are unclear and any missing information. To evaluate the salary offer, you can conduct an online search of your fair market value. There are several websites, such as bls.gov, that can provide salary ranges for a job in a specific geographic location.

Salary ranges can also be determined based on your education and experience. You can also ask people in your network for salary information. Before discussing the offer with the employer, you might want to create a list of your minimum salary requirements and other items that are important to you and your career, such as benefits, days of vacation, and your tasks and responsibilities on projects.

After you have conducted a thorough analysis of the job offer, and how the position fulfills your needs and aspirations, schedule an in-person meeting with the hiring manager. An in-person meeting is the appropriate setting for discussing and negotiating your job offer. Most employers expect a job candidate to negotiate an offer; thus, you should not hesitate to do this.

Successful negotiations depend on reasonable requests and compromises from both parties. Your researched fair market value provides a credible rationale for asking for a higher salary than the job offer. In negotiating a salary, you might want to accept a lower amount in order to improve other aspects of the offer, such as terms for advancement, tuition reimbursement, or **compensatory** or **comp time** for volunteer activities. Regardless of the outcome at the conclusion of negotiations, you should thank the person for the offer and his or her time, followed by a written thank you note immediately after the meeting.

> Checking for Comprehension
> * Describe three tasks that should be completed before an interview.
>
> * What would be important for you in a job offer?

Chapter 3 concludes Part I by reviewing the last stages of attaining an entry-level position as an interior designer. This chapter examined career portfolios, networking strategies, and the development of résumés, cover letters, and design portfolios. These elements were important for the discussions related to job search plans, schedules, interviews, and job negotiations.

The information covered in Chapter 3 combined with content in Chapters 1 and 2 provides you with some of the fundamentals of the interior design profession. As a whole, the three chapters are the foundation for the book's next part and chapter.

The purpose of Part II is to examine the critical information you should know when working in a design firm. Professional business responsibilities are essential for your first job as well as any other experience that is important for your career, such as internships or job shadowing. Chapter 4 specifically addresses professional business responsibilities, including planning, ethics, multidisciplinary collaboration, virtual teamwork, and business etiquette.

In Chapter 5, global business environments are analyzed with an emphasis and examination on how globalization affects the business of interior design. Chapter 6 provides an understanding of how to charge for your professional services, and suggestions for writing contracts that are appropriate for your clients and can help to ensure that you will be properly compensated for your time and expertise.

Knowledge and Skills Summary

Highlights

* A critical element to a career plan is engaging in self-assessment, or identifying what you can offer an employer.

* The results of your self-assessment process can be used to develop a professional profile or a summary of your interests and most important skills.

* A career portfolio should include search materials, and a collection of documents, professional projects, photographs, drawings, and illustrations that reflect your aspirations.

* A career plan includes projections for what someone might like to do at various time intervals and what is required to accomplish those goals.

* The two general types of networks are personal and professional.

* Networking strategies involve developing a plan that includes various types of networks, identifying new contacts, and a process to maintain connections.

* Résumés, cover letters, business cards, and promotional pieces must have a professional appearance.

* The three major types of résumés are functional, chronological, and a combination of both.

* A design portfolio should be viewed as an extension of a person's design skills, creativity, and ability to solve problems.

* A basic job search plan should have (1) a list of where to find openings, (2) multiple search strategies, (3) a dedicated space for the task, (4) a job search partner, and (5) a schedule with weekly goals.

* A résumé can open the door for an interview; the interview provides an applicant with the opportunity to receive a job offer.

* Types of interviews include telephone, one-on-one, group, and videoconferencing.

* Negotiating a job offer should be done in person.

Key Terms

career management

career plan

career portfolio

chronological résumé

comp time (compensatory time)

compensatory time (comp time)

cover letter

digital design portfolio

experience-seeking proposal

functional résumé

human resources

informational interview

job shadowing

life/work balance

logo

network

networking

professional profile

résumé

self-assessment

social networks

teleconferencing

traditional design portfolio

transferrable skill

videoconferencing

visual identity system

Projects

Philosophy and Design Project

The chapter reviewed several techniques you can use to conduct a self-assessment. The purpose of this project is to complete a self-assessment that you can use throughout your job search process as well as career management. The information gathered during the self-assessment process can also be used to assess how your characteristics match the needs of a potential employer.

For this project you are to use two self-assessment techniques: (1) as illustrated in Box 3.1, write a bulleted summary that includes a description of a class project, an assessment of the overall work environment, and an assessment of the project tasks; and (2) as in Table 3.1, create a list of self-assessment items and determine your level of interest and ability, as well as the item's transferability and your view of the level of employers' interest.

Based on the two self-assessment processes, write a report (approximately three pages) summarizing the results and a list of the items you believe are important for your career and how they can match the needs of a potential employer. Submit a copy of both self-assessment exercises in addition to the report.

Research Project

Use the Internet to research jobs, contacts, and salaries in cities that are potential locations for your first position as an interior designer. Identify five positions you think are interesting, and create a summary of each job that includes the (1) job requirements, (2) best approach for applying for the job, (3) advantages and disadvantages of each position, (4) details about the firm that you learned by additional research, and (5) strategies for writing cover letters for each position. Submit your summary in a table and include any images that support your interest in the position.

Human Factors Research Project

Put together a team of five members. The team should discuss their views on business etiquette and develop ten recommendations for interview etiquette. Each person on the team should prepare for an interview that includes presenting his or her portfolio. Practice interviews should be conducted using the following formats: (1) one-to-one with the rest of the team critiquing the interview and (2) one-to-two with the rest of the team critiquing the interview.

Every member of the team should practice being interviewed using each format. Each person should submit a written report (approximately three pages) that includes (1) the team's recommendations for interview etiquette, (2) a summary of the team critiques, (3) that person's own reactions to being interviewed one-to-one and one-to-two, and (4) his or her own reactions to observing other individuals being interviewed.

References

American Society of Interior Designers (ASID). 2010. *The Interior Design Profession: Facts and Figures*. Washington, DC: American Society of Interior Designers.

Baldwin, B. 1995. (Copyright Elizabeth H. Baldwin). *Benjamin Baldwin: An Autobiography in Design*. New York: W. W. Norton & Company.

Birkman, R. W. 2010. *The Birkman Method*. http://www.birkman.com/#. Accessed November 22, 2010.

Bureau of Labor Statistics. 2011. *Occupational Outlook Handbook*. 2010–11 ed. http://www.bls.gov/OCO/. Accessed September 5, 2011.

Careerbuilder. 2010. *Jobs*. http://www.careerbuilder.com/. Accessed November 22, 2010.

Council for Interior Design Accreditation (CIDA). 2011. *Professional Standards 2011*. http://www.accredit-id.org/. Accessed February 10, 2012.

Grizzard, W. R. 2005. "Vital Signs: How to Be Taken Seriously When Networking with Professionals." Washington, DC: 2005. National Youth Leadership Network Conference. http://www.dol.gov/odep/archives/media/speeches/vital.htm. Accessed November 22, 2010.

HOK. 2010. *Life at HOK*. http://hoklife.com/. Accessed November 22, 2010.

International Interior Design Association (IIDA). 2010. *Career Center*. http://www.iida.org/. Accessed September 10, 2010.

Monster. 2010. *Jobs*. http://www.monster.com/. Accessed November 22, 2010.

Myers-Briggs Type Indicator. 2010. *My MBTI Personality Type*. http://www.myersbriggs.org/. Accessed November 22, 2010.

National Council for Interior Design Qualification's (NCIDQ). 2010. *NCIDQ*. http://www.ncidq.org. Accessed June 19, 2010.

O*NET OnLine. 2011. *Find Occupations*. http://online.onetcenter.org/. Accessed September 5, 2011.

Post, P. 2004. *Emily Post's Etiquette*. New York: HarperCollins Publishers.

Salary. 2010. *Personal Job Search*. http://www.salary.com/. Accessed November 22, 2010.

SkillScan. 2010. *Skillscan*. http://www.skillscan.com/. Accessed November 22, 2010.

Strong Interest Inventory. 2010. *CPP: The People Development People*. https://www.cpp.com/. Accessed November 22, 2010.

U.S. Department of Labor. 2010. *Occupational Outlook Handbook (OOH)*. http://www.bls.gov/OCO/. Accessed September 10, 2010.

WORKING IN A DESIGN FIRM

Part I reviewed important topics associated with getting an entry-level position as an interior designer. The purpose of Part II is to provide you with the business-related information that you must know when you attain your first job as an interior designer and can also be used for internships. Part II has three chapters. Chapter 4 initiates the discussion by examining professional business responsibilities, including personal management strategies, ethics, multidisciplinary collaboration, and various categories associated with business etiquette.

In Chapter 5, global business environments are analyzed by expanding on content related to globalization that was presented in Chapter 2. Chapter 5 reviews how globalization affects the business of interior design by discussing international practice, cultural dimensions, and intercultural communication styles. The chapter concludes by examining intercultural business protocols associated with meetings, negotiations, and socializing.

The last chapter in Part II examines several ways to be compensated for your professional services and delineates how to determine fees and compensation. Chapter 6 also reviews important general accounting and administrative practices that are used by designers on a daily basis. The chapter ends by reviewing U.S. laws associated with the work of an interior designer, such as liability, contracts, and intellectual property.

CHAPTER 4

Professional Business Responsibilities

Chapter 4 (Filipino)
4 luku (Finnish)
Chapitre 4 (French)
Capítulo 4 (Galician)
თავი **4** (Georgian)

After learning the content in Chapter 4, you will be able to answer the following questions:

* What are professional goals, ethics, and strategies for productivity?

* What are the best methods for collaboration and multidisciplinary teamwork?

* What are important workplace practices, including appropriate etiquette concerning office space, meetings, and dealing with office gossip?

* What is verbal and written communication etiquette?

* How should I practice proper netiquette?

Chapter 4 begins the part in the book that focuses on what is important to know when working in a design firm. The chapter initiates the topic by examining professional business responsibilities. When you begin an entry-level position, you will be working with many professionals who have a wide range of expertise, experience, and age. Some colleagues might have over *40 years* of design experience. Therefore, to feel comfortable working with experienced professionals you must have a working knowledge of business fundamentals—many of which you can begin to practice while you are still a student.

The chapter starts by discussing personal management strategies, including how to establish goals as well as managing time, information, and knowledge. The next topic is ethics and how an interior designer must be knowledgeable about the profession's standards as well as ethics associated with business.

Chapter 4 proceeds by reviewing strategies for effective multidisciplinary collaboration, including how to be a valuable team member, team building, conflict resolution, charrettes, and virtual teamwork. The concluding section examines appropriate workplace and business etiquette, such as proper office space behavior, verbal and written communication etiquette, and a newer etiquette category: **netiquette**.

Personal Management Strategies and Professional Ethics

Your career as an interior designer should begin with professional behaviors that become admirable habits. Professional behavior involves being productive, self-motivated, courteous, honest, and ethical. Your new employer expects professional behavior. To prepare for these expectations, you can work on some tasks before beginning employment, such as developing drafts of your professional goals and practicing strategies that can help you to manage time, information, and knowledge.

Following ethical standards can also prepare you for your professional obligations. As an interior designer your behavior will revolve around the profession's ethics, which focus on responsibilities to the public, the client, colleagues, the design profession, and your employer.

Professional Planning and Efficiency: Goals, Time, Information, and Knowledge

How should you begin your first professional job? An entry-level position is especially challenging because of the lack of knowledge about day-to-day operations of a design firm. In addition, your first job might be at a firm with seasoned professionals who might not have the time to explain tasks and responsibilities.

One approach to this dilemma is to work on professional tasks before arriving the first day, such as writing drafts of your goals and establishing personal management strategies. Goal setting might not be an exciting activity to some people, but goals will help you to identify the most productive tasks and will enable you to be more efficient with your time—key elements in your future performance reviews.

The content for the draft of your goals can be derived from the job description for your position and by reviewing the notes that you recorded after your interview (see Chapter 3). Your post-interview notes should include comments by your boss as well as other colleagues about expectations of the position. Thus, the job description and interview notes, as well as your personal aspirations, can form the foundation for your professional goals.

Goals appear to be simplistic statements, but they are not easy to write. Goals should *not* be a list of activities. Your goals must reflect the needs of the organization, your boss, and your clients. For example, if your new employer's goals are to create designs that are good for the environment, then most likely your boss will want your goals to reflect the principles of sustainability. Personal goals should also be measurable and reasonable to achieve. Thus, you might develop a goal that states you will "identify 25 rapidly renewable products within 5 days."

To accommodate various tasks and professional responsibilities, develop prioritized goals that address daily, weekly, monthly, quarterly, and annual responsibilities. Generally, the longest time spans provide the basis for developing shorter schedules. Thus, your daily goals should be based on your weekly goals and your weekly goals are derived from monthly and then annual achievements. Following is an example of how an annual goal is used as an umbrella for shorter-term goals:

Annual goal: I will have 20 new clients in 2012 by networking, attending community events, and working with my mentor.

Quarterly goals: I will have 5 new clients each quarter as a result of networking, attending community events, and working with my mentor.

Monthly goals: I will meet with 3 potential clients each month by networking, attending community events, and working with my mentor.

Weekly goals: I will contact 5 potential clients each week by networking, attending community events, or working with my mentor.

Daily goals: I will contact 1 potential client each day by networking, attending community events, or working with my mentor.

You should discuss drafts of your goals with your boss and others involved with helping you to accomplish your goals. These people can help you to prioritize activities and should be able to assess the accuracy of your deadlines. Furthermore, as you discuss your goals with your boss, clarify how your goals affect your performance reviews.

Prioritized goals must be accompanied by a plan. In the same manner as developing the search plan described in Chapter 3 (Table 3.2), you should create a plan that outlines how you will accomplish your goals. Your plan should include a list of the activities that need to occur in order for you to achieve each goal as well as the sequence of events, timeline, required resources, and the names of people involved with the activities.

Your plan could be summarized in a table or a graphic illustration (Figure 4.1). As you did

when developing your goals, review a draft of your plan with your boss and other appropriate individuals. In addition, at the end of each day and week you should review how well you accomplished your goals and revise your schedule accordingly.

After several weeks if you have not been able to achieve what seems to be reasonable goals, you might want to closely examine how you are spending your time. A big problem could be unexpected events or various other interruptions,

Figure 4.1 Prioritized professional goals must be accompanied by using a plan. Your plan should include a list of activities that need to occur in order to achieve each goal; these can be summarized graphically.

such as people stopping by your desk, unanticipated phone calls, surfing the Web, texting, or frequently checking your e-mail or cell phone.

To determine exactly how you are spending your time, create a detailed log of your activities. Remember to include *every* unexpected event, *every* interruption, and the duration of each. Thus, if you stopped writing to read a text message, this should be recorded on your log. Based on an analysis of the activities, you should be able to identify unproductive interruptions and inefficient tasks. How you can manage these situations is discussed in the next section.

U.S. Time Management Practices

Establishing goals and developing plans to achieve your goals can save time because your schedule and efforts can be directed toward the tasks that are most important for your job. Saving time is important to organizations; however, as discussed in Chapter 5, cultures have different perceptions of time, which is important to know when you are working in a global marketplace. Generally, time in the United States equates to profits and is particularly important for organizations that operate on billable hours, as design firms do.

Time is an especially sensitive topic when a firm hires entry-level employees. Learning a new job takes time, but learning a new profession takes considerable time. Thus, when an organization hires someone with minimal or no professional experience, it can take years before that person can generate more revenue than the costs associated with his or her employment (for example, salary, benefits, and the consumption of other resources). Therefore, it is imperative that you rapidly become an expert at **time management**. Mastering this skill will help you as you begin your career and will be invaluable in the future when deadlines require you to work on several projects simultaneously.

One of the first steps of time management is selecting an organizational format, such as apps for mobile devices, a cell phone calendar, ringbound daily planner, or a software program. Choose the format that is the easiest for you to check and update. In addition, your employer might have a networked software program for scheduling employee meetings. Your organizational format should allow you to schedule appointments and activities by the hour, and perhaps have an area for recording prioritized tasks and reminders. You might also want a system that allows you to look at one week at a time as well as a monthly calendar.

As described in the previous section, understanding how you are using your time can help to make better use of it. Every interruption, including checking your cell phone, affects your concentration and increases the amount of time required to complete a task.

Some of the most common situations that can affect time management include unexpected responsibilities, interruptions, and procrastination. However, some unexpected responsibilities are required for your job, such as attending an unscheduled meeting or having to complete a project earlier than its scheduled due date. Consequently, a considerable amount of your time is used for unexpected job-related activities. You should therefore allocate additional time in your daily or weekly schedule to accommodate these responsibilities. By planning for the unanticipated task, your schedule should not be significantly affected by the interruption. If the unexpected does not occur, then you simply have more time to complete other assignments.

Another way to reduce interruptions is to schedule specific times for routine tasks, such as reading e-mail, answering phone messages, or reading correspondence and documents. Planning a specific time for routine activities allows you to concentrate on other tasks and helps ensure that you complete other tasks. Key to this strategy is an understanding that multitasking itself can be an interruption.

In contrast to a prevailing idea that multitasking is efficient, neuroscientists have actually determined that the brain can *proficiently* perform only one task at a time (Moran 2007). For example, writing an e-mail and talking on the phone at the same time can be accomplished, but each task can be completed more efficiently if done independently. In addition, multitasking can cause more errors. Therefore, to conserve time and to make your best effort, plan to work on only *one* work-related task during a specific time period.

To help eliminate procrastination, try to identify why you are not working on a task and then attempt to resolve the issue. For example, procrastination can happen when the amount of work is overwhelming or when someone does not have the appropriate expertise.

One way to complete large assignments is to divide the project into several manageable activities ("chunking"). Consider creating a checklist or other visual aid to help you see your progress toward the goal. And when you receive an assignment that is beyond your level of expertise, make an immediate effort to enlist the help of coworkers or people in your networks, or perhaps acquire additional education.

Information Management

In addition to demonstrating efficiency, you should also demonstrate an ability to effectively remember new information, such as products, vendors, manufacturers, clients, and business procedures. You will be exposed to thousands of new pieces of information on the job. How can you remember the information when you need it? Creating an **information management** strategy will help you retain and retrieve information.

The first step to managing information is to create a system for organizing all of the items you need to do your job, such as paper documents, web pages, drawings, photographs, products, vendors, professionals, e-mail messages, and electronic files. Organizing software programs, such as FranklinCovey and Google Desktop, have been developed for many of these purposes.

Traditional file cabinets with labeled folders might be appropriate for organizing some information, but keep in mind that to support sustainability practices, organizations are instituting paperless offices. In selecting an appropriate organizing tool, the goal should be to identify a method that enables you to efficiently create files and then easily access, share, and discard information.

There are many strategies for organizing information, such as color coding, directories/subdirectories, tickler files, and using the traditional "inbox," "pending," and "outbox." Try to handle a document only once instead of setting the task aside and then returning to it several times before completing the work. This simple tactic will save time.

What type of information needs to be managed? In addition to managing project information, interior designers must have a system for organizing hundreds of products and manufacturers. The system can be organized by types of products, manufacturers, and price points.

As a student you can begin to create these professional files by reading advertisements in trade journals and noting sources cited in architectural/interior design articles. Creating manufacturers' files before starting your first job saves time and helps you manage substantial amounts of information and knowledge.

Suggestions for files include the following categories: appliances, building materials, ceilings, custom design environments, doors, flooring (hard), flooring (resilient), furniture (residential), furniture (commercial), glass, hardware, kitchen/bath, lighting, signage/wayfinding, surfacing materials, technology, textiles, wall surfaces (coverings/paints/stains), and windows. Files should have manufacturers' contact information and brief descriptions of their product lines, including price ranges.

For sustainability purposes, files could be categorized by the location of manufacturers—a way to help conserve transportation fuel by identifying manufacturers closest to a project—as well as other green criteria. Professional files could also include the most current information on codes, regulations, standards, professional organizations, trade shows, continuing education opportunities, and volunteering.

Knowledge Management

As people learn information as well as processes and personalities, they gain knowledge. When you begin your first job, you will be working with professionals whose experiences and expertise have resulted in **tacit knowledge**. Fundamentally, tacit knowledge is in someone's mind and is contrasted to **explicit knowledge**, which is readily available to people via several means, such as written documents, drawings, or photographs.

Knowledge management techniques can help to build tacit knowledge and maximize the potential of explicit knowledge. A top-rated definition posted online described knowledge management as "a systematic approach of set guidelines in which data is collected, accumulated, and made easily available to all seeking knowledge and experiences to excel themselves in order to achieve a communal growth in an organisation" (PD 2010). Managing knowledge becomes especially important when people are not able to attend project meetings or if they are no longer working with the organization.

Knowledge management requires strategies that enable you to tap into tacit knowledge and identify materials that can provide explicit knowledge. Acquiring tacit knowledge can be done by using a variety of techniques, such as listening intently at meetings, networking, asking appropriate questions, and engaging in discussions with people who have considerable experience with job-related activities. Ideally, you should try to learn aspects of a project that were never recorded in documents, drawings, or photographs. Often questions that begin with "How" or "Why" can reveal tacit knowledge.

An excellent time to acquire tacit knowledge is soon after a project is completed. At this time people can readily identify information that typically is not recorded, such as problem-solving strategies, unrealized solutions, decision-making processes, effective means of communication, causes of delays, unnecessary expenses, problems with suppliers, personality traits, budget overruns, defective materials, delivery issues, and the pros and cons of various installation methods.

Information gleaned from the discussions should be recorded and retained in files for future use. By using knowledge management strategies, you will build your tacit knowledge and be able to share information with clients and coworkers.

Managing tacit as well as explicit knowledge becomes critical to teamwork because the team's composition can change during the course of a project, and team members might not be able to attend every meeting. Thus, the team should utilize strategies that convert tacit knowledge into explicit knowledge. Techniques that can be effective include (1) videotaping meetings, (2) using a blog to record the team's progress, (3) providing online access to all project-related documents and drawings, and (4) creating detailed written minutes of meetings that highlight key decisions.

In addition, to help ensure a project's "memory," a team should have members who are assigned to the project from the very beginning and are required to attend every meeting. These people are able to respond to questions about the project's history and can help to update new members as they join the team.

Western Professional and Business Ethics

Knowledge can become an ethical issue when a person refuses to share his or her tacit knowledge with fellow team members. In addition, as explored in this section, many other issues are considered to be subtopics of ethics. Because interior design is a business, this discussion examines ethics and standards of practice associated with the design *profession*—as well as **business ethics**.

Why should we study ethics? The philosophical nature of the topic might appear uninteresting to you, but it is essential that you understand recognized standards of the profession and business so that you can apply the principles to your behavior and future practice. As evidenced recently by some celebrities, professional athletes, businesspeople, journalists, and politicians, ethical misconduct can destroy careers—it can also result in prison time when laws are violated. The topic is so important to the profession that NCIDQ developed two monographs on the topic: *Ethics and the Design Profession* (2000) and *Ethical Decision Making for Designers* (2008).

What exactly is ethics? According to Merriam-Webster's Dictionary (2010), **ethics** is "the discipline dealing with what is good and bad and with moral duty and obligation" and **professional ethics** is "the principles of conduct governing an individual or a group." Thus, ethics is basically about doing the right thing: lessons you learned as a child.

Ethics translates to being honest, truthful, kind, fair, and a law-abiding citizen. People who behave in an ethical manner are respected and establish a reputation for having good judgment, integrity, trustworthiness, and a sense of responsibility.

The definition of ethics sounds reasonable; however, a disconnect can occur when people have different values and view good and bad from dissimilar perspectives. Diverging personal values becomes even more complex with globalization due to the influences of cultural norms or shared behavioral expectations as well as other factors, such as local laws and construction practices. This is why the word "Western" appears in the title of this section. The views presented here reflect a Western perspective.

Thus, when you engage in international practice, you must genuinely understand the prevailing customs and keep in mind that some practices might not agree with your personal ethics or the standards of professional practice in Western countries (see Chapter 5). These are circumstances that require a critically important faculty: using good judgment because you have to determine the course that aligns with your moral compass while accommodating the needs of the client. Good judgment is also an element of ethicality.

Western Professional Ethics

Behaving in an ethical manner is especially important in a profession that affects the life, safety, and welfare of the public, and relies on reputation for repeat business and referrals. ASID, IIDA, and professional Canadian organizations have all acknowledged that interior designers' ethical responsibilities are to the public, their clients, other professionals, the design profession, and their employer (Box 4.1). In recognizing these responsibilities, organizations have created codes of conduct that are specific to an interior designer's expertise and services.

Professional organizations also include enforcement policies and have procedures for filing ethics-related claims against a member if that person has violated the code. In addition, violations of an organization's code of ethics can result in termination of membership.

Obviously, you will not be interested in trying to memorize a professional code of ethics; thus, to understand how to behave in an ethical manner, consider studying the lives of people who have reputations for being ethical. Professionals that are considered the most ethical include the clergy, physicians, and teachers.

From a design perspective, the book *Towards an Ethical Architecture* includes several examples of projects by Gregory Henriquez that were designed within the context of social justice—a perspective focused on the principles of equality for all people (Figure 4.2).

Ethical behavior can also be studied by reviewing projects associated with some of the socially conscious organizations described in Chapter 1, such as Architecture for Humanity (AFH), Habitat for Humanity International (HFHI), UN-HABITAT, or Architects Without Frontiers (AWF).

An excellent way to think about ethical behavior is to engage in discussions or debates with colleagues. Fictitious or real-world case studies can be used; the goal is to review how situations can create ethical dilemmas and to practice a decision-making process that leads to using good judgment.

Newspapers can be a source for case studies, particularly stories that report a tragedy that occurred because of building code violations

Box 4.1

International Interior Design Association (IIDA) Code of Ethics*

Preamble

Professional and Associate Members of the International Interior Design Association shall conduct their interior design practice in a manner that will encourage the respect of clients, fellow interior designers, the interior design industry and the general public. It is the individual responsibility of every Professional and Associate Member of IIDA to abide by the Code of Professional Ethics and Conduct, Bylaws, Policies and Position Statements of the Association.

Definitions

The terms used in this Code shall be defined in the same manner in which they are defined in the Bylaws, Policies and Position Statements of the Association.

Responsibility to the Public

In performing professional services, Professional and Associate Members shall exercise reasonable care and competence, and shall conform to existing laws, regulations and codes governing the profession of interior design as established by the state or other jurisdiction in which they conduct business.

In performing professional services, Professional and Associate Members shall at all times consider the health, safety, and welfare of the public.

In performing professional services, Professional and Associate Members shall not knowingly violate the law, or counsel or assist clients in conduct they know, or reasonably should know, is illegal.

Professional and Associate Members shall not permit their name or signature to be used in conjunction with a design or project for which interior design services are not to be, or were not, performed under their immediate direction and control.

Professional and Associate Members shall not engage in any form of false or misleading advertising or promotional activities and shall not imply, through advertising or other means, that staff members or employees of their firms are Professional or Associate Member unless such is the fact.

Professional and Associate Members shall not make misleading, deceptive or false statements or claims about their professional qualifications, experience, or performance.

Professional and Associate Members shall not, by affirmative act or failure to act, engage in any conduct involving fraud, deceit, misrepresentation or dishonesty in professional or business activity.

In performing professional services, Professional and Associate Members shall refuse to consent to any decision by their clients or employers that violate any applicable law or regulation, and which, in the Professional and Associates Members' judgment, will create a significant risk to public health and safety.

Professional and Associate Members shall not attempt to obtain a contract to provide interior design services through any unlawful means. Professional and Associate Members shall not assist any person seeking to obtain a contract to provide interior design services through any unlawful means.

Responsibility to the Client

Professional and Associate Members shall undertake to perform professional services only when they, together with their consultants, are qualified by education, training or experience to perform the services required.

Before accepting an assignment, Professional and Associate Members shall reasonably inform the client of the scope and nature of the project involved, the interior design services to be performed, and the method of remuneration for those services. Professional and Associate Members shall not materially change the scope of a project without the client's consent.

Box 4.1

International Interior Design Association (IIDA) Code of Ethics* *(continued)*

Prior to an engagement, Professional and Associate Members shall disclose, in writing, to an employer or client, any direct or indirect financial interest that they may have that could affect their impartiality in specifying project-related goods or services, and shall not knowingly assume or accept any position in which their personal interests conflict with their professional duty. If the employer or client objects to such financial or other interest, Professional and Associate Members shall either terminate such interest, or withdraw from such engagement.

Professional and Associate Members shall not reveal any information about a client, a client's intention (s), or a client's production method(s) which they have been asked to maintain in confidence, or which they should reasonably recognize as likely, if disclosed, to affect the interests of their client adversely. Notwithstanding the above, however, Professional and Associate Members may reveal such information to the extent they reasonably believe is necessary (1) to stop any act which creates a significant risk to public health and safety and which the Professional or Associate Member is unable to prevent in any other manner; or (2) to prevent any violation of applicable law.

Responsibility to Other Interior Designers and Colleagues

Professional and Associate Members shall pursue their professional activities with honesty, integrity and fairness, and with respect for other designers' or colleagues' contractual and professional relationships.

Professional and Associate Members shall not accept instruction from their clients that knowingly involves plagiarism, nor shall they consciously plagiarize another's work.

Professional and Associate Members shall not endorse the application for membership in the Association of an individual known to be unqualified with respect to education, training or experience; nor shall they knowingly misrepresent the experience, professional expertise, or moral character of that individual.

Professional and Associate Members shall only take credit for work that has actually been created by the Member or the Member's firm or under the Member's immediate direction and control.

Responsibility to the Association and Interior Design Profession

Professional and Associate Members agree to maintain standards of professional and personal conduct that will reflect in a responsible manner on the profession.

Professional and Associate Members shall seek to continually upgrade their professional knowledge and competency with respect to the interior design profession.

Professional and Associate Members shall, wherever possible, encourage and contribute to the sharing of knowledge and information among interior designers, the interior design industry, and the general public.

Professional and Associate Members shall offer support, encouragement, and information to students of interior design.

Professional and Associate Members shall, when representing the interior design profession, act in a manner that is in the best interest of the profession.

Professional and Associate Members may only use the IIDA appellation in accordance with current Association policy.

Professional and Associate Members shall not knowingly make false statements or fail to disclose any material fact requested in connection with their applications for membership in the Association.

*Source: IIDA, 2011, *International Interior Design Association Code of Ethics*, http://70.32.66.49/pdfs/IIDA_SoCalChapter_CodeofEthics.pdf. Retrieved September 6, 2011.

Figure 4.2 Ethical behavior can be studied by reviewing socially conscious projects. Bella Bella Community School in Waglisla, Campbell Island, British Columbia, by Gregory Henriquez, is a community development project for the Heiltsuk people, one of Canada's First Nations communities. Henriquez focused on reclaiming Heiltsuk's culture and traditional heritage: "In our architectural practice we encounter many different cultures, community groups and individuals. Our role as consultants is to, on one level, simply provide design services to our clients, yet we also feel a moral obligation to participate in these important discussions to help provide resolution" (Weir 2006, p. 53). (© Christopher Grabowski)

(Box 4.2). Often these violations are tied to unethical behavior, such as bribing building inspectors, switching quality materials with substandard components to save money, or not recommending optimum safety standards in order to be the lowest bidder and win business.

A process that can be used to engage in ethical discussions or debates includes the following activities: (1) identify ethical issues by comparing actions with the basic definition of ethics as well as ethical codes developed by a professional organization, such as IIDA, (2) identify potential decisions, (3) explore the ramifications of each decision, and (4) determine the appropriate course of action.

As an example of how you can apply these steps to a case study, see Box 4.3. Obviously, there are many other approaches to the situation described in Box 4.3—as well as consequences and other ramifications. You can also practice ethical judgment exercises by completing the *Philosophy and Design* project at the end of the chapter.

Western Business Ethics

In addition to ethics associated with the design profession, interior designers should be aware of Western business ethics. Why is it necessary to study ethics beyond our profession's standards? Codes of ethics and standards of professional conduct prescribed by interior design professional organizations are central to the work of an interior designer; however, you will also be actively involved with numerous other businesses with ethical issues that are beyond the scope of our profession. These businesses include (1) manufacturers of all the products that designers specify, (2) corporations owned by clients, (3) construction companies, and (4) installers and suppliers.

Therefore, behaving in an ethical manner requires an understanding of the ethical issues that confront businesses in general. In addition, as reviewed in Part IV of this book, if you are interested in owning your own firm, you must be current with ethical issues in the world of business.

Some ethical issues overlap both professional ethics and business ethics, such as obeying laws, being honest, and upholding responsibilities to the public, customers, and one's industry. In addition to ethics shared with the interior design profession, business ethics encompass areas such global markets, multinational corporations, downsizing/layoffs, working conditions, employee rights, marketing, accounting,

Box 4.2

Ethical Considerations:
Beverly Hills Supper Club Fire, Southgate, Kentucky*

"...I looked over my shoulder, and I heard a big whoosh sound... There was flame and smoke and it just rolled into the room and it was the blackest smoke I'd ever seen... I wasn't thinking about anything but getting out of there, because the smoke was right on us...I got up to the double door, which did not lead to the outside; it led into another bar and I jumped back into the crowd...I grabbed ahold a man's collar. He pulled me on through and I turned around to look because the smoke and the flames were coming, the smoke was coming out the double doors out of the Cabaret with me, right at the back of my head. There must have been flame, because my blouse was burnt. As I came out, I turned to look and the people weren't screaming anymore. The smoke had covered them all up." (NFPA, 1978, p. 44)

This quote is from a waitress who worked at the Beverly Hills Supper Club in Southgate, Kentucky, the evening of the disastrous fire on May 28, 1977. As a result of the fire 164 customers and employees died, and more than 70 people were injured. The National Fire Protection Association (NFPA) conducted an investigation and determined the cause of the fire and contributing factors:

- Fire began in the Zebra Room, which had "the presence of concealed, combustible ceiling tile and wood materials used for supports provided a fuel supply for continued spread of the fire through the original ceiling and other concealed spaces."

- The number of people in the Cabaret Room far exceeded the number of occupants that the room could safely accommodate according to codes and standards in effect at the time.

- The capacity of the means of egress for the Club, and especially for the Cabaret Room, was not adequate for the occupant load or for the actual number of occupants that were in the building at the time of the fire.

- "The interior finish in the main north-south corridor exceeded the flame spread allowed for places of assembly in the *Life Safety Code*, and contributed to the rapid spread of fire from the Zebra Room to the Cabaret Room."

- "The Beverly Hills Supper Club was not provided with automatic sprinkler protection as required by codes in effect in Kentucky at the time of the fire" (NFPA 1978).

In addition to the many deviations from national consensus fire codes and standards, the NFPA investigative team found the following:

- No permits were issued for an area under construction.
- The [exit] door from the Viennese Room was reportedly camouflaged by drapes to look like a window and hide an exit sign.

Review the descriptions above and consider the ethics of several people involved with the tragedy, such as the owner, employees, customers, architects, interior designer, contractors, building inspectors, and fire marshals.

Note problem with materials.

Note code violation.

Note code violation.

Note code violation and problem with finish.

Note code violation.

Note code violation.

Note code violation and problem with materials.

Note suggestion to consider ethical violations

*Source: National Fire Protection Association (NFPA), 1978, *Beverly Hills Supper Club Fire Southgate, Kentucky May 28, 1977*, http://www.nfpa.org/assets/files/pdf/fisouthgate.pdf. Retrieved November 24, 2010.

A Process for Engaging in Ethical Discussions: XYZ Interiors

XYZ Interiors Background

A local government was soliciting bids for the renovation of its historical courthouse. The courthouse was located in the heart of the city and was used by some of the most prominent community members. The project was very appealing to design firms because of the substantial profits that could be realized as well as the potential for new clients due to the visibility of the courthouse and the people who worked in the building. XYZ Interiors was very interested in bidding for the project, but the organization did not have experience with historical structures. How should XYZ Interiors handle the situation?

Note question to answer.

Process for Ethical Discussion

(1) Identify the ethical issues. First step.
Based on IIDA's Code of Ethics, "Professional and Associate Members shall undertake to perform professional services only when they, together with their consultants, are qualified by education, training or experience to perform the services required." The ethical issue is with the result of XYZ Interior's lack of experience in designing historical buildings.

(2) Identify potential decisions: Second step.
   (A) XYZ does not submit a bid for the project.
   (B) XYZ submits a bid and plans to research historical renovations.
   (C) XYZ contacts a firm with historical renovation experience and asks that company to submit a joint bid.

(3) Potential ramifications of each decision:
   (A) By not submitting a bid for the project, XYZ upholds IIDA's code of ethics, but the firm has lost the opportunity to design a fabulous project and potentially secure new clients. First potential ramification to consider.
   (B) By submitting a bid, XYZ might win the competition: Second potential ramification to consider.

> • Even with research the firm's lack of experience could result in a design that does not adequately address the standards for a historical structure. XYZ Interior's reputation could be seriously affected, and some of its current clients might decide to switch to another firm.

> • The firm's historical research results in an excellent project, but the time and resources needed for the research process resulted in financial losses and the firm's regular clients being ignored for months.

Box 4.3

A Process for Engaging in Ethical Discussions: XYZ Interiors *(continued)*

(C) XYZ contacts a firm with historical renovation experience and asks that company to submit a joint bid:

Third potential ramification to consider.

- XYZ upholds IIDA's code of ethics by involving people with historical renovation experience.

- The firm with historical renovation experience could decide to submit a bid without XYZ Interiors.

- XYZ Interiors and the firm with historical experience jointly submit a bid, but XYZ Interior's lack of experience with the firm resulted in an unacceptable design and a poorly executed design process.

- XYZ Interiors and the firm with historical experience jointly submit a bid and the design was sensational.

(4) Which decision would you make? List the reasons supporting your decision.

Your ethical decision?

---

information technology (IT), and consumer safety and product liability.

Some businesses have ethical responsibilities to the government and also to a concept referred to as "corporate citizenship" (see Part IV). The critical element in this discussion is for you to be aware of business ethics and how business situations might affect your personal value system and our professions' code of ethics.

To understand how business ethics can affect your work as an entry-level designer, revisit the topics related to business ethics identified in the previous paragraph and consider your views regarding an issue in the context of working with businesses. For example, a tremendous amount of attention has focused on global working conditions. What are your views on working conditions? Would you be interested in specifying a product for a client if the manufacturer was found to be in violation of child labor laws? Similarly, would you consider recommending

an electrician who works for a company that was convicted of accounting fraud?

Globalization has escalated the development of multinational corporations. Business ethics related to this area can involve national allegiances. Thus, when a business has offices throughout the world, the organization must decide whose interest is most important—and that decision could result in an ethical dilemma for you. For example, ABC Luminaires, a manufacturer of lighting fixtures, has factories in the United States, China, and India. To the detriment of people working in the United States, the lighting corporation decided to reduce the number of U.S. workers and increase the number of employees in India. This cost-saving decision resulted in an extraordinary light fixture at an incredible reasonable price. If you had to specify 1,000 light fixtures for a client with a limited budget, would you send the order to ABC Luminaires?

These situations are examples of how you can be involved with business ethics even though you might not own a business. As is the case with professional ethics, the key is to: (1) identify the ethical issues, (2) understand strengths and weaknesses of various decisions, (3) explore the consequences and ramifications of each decision, and (4) determine the appropriate course of action.

Because business ethics is related to your area of expertise, you must be aware of the whole spectrum of business ethics and, when appropriate, conduct the research needed to make ethically sound decisions. As you will discover in Chapter 7, ethical behavior is absolutely essential to the ability to build long-term client relationships—the lifeblood of the design profession.

> ### Checking for Comprehension
> * Identify two ways you can manage knowledge.
>
> * Why is it important to understand and practice professional and business ethics?

Multidisciplinary Collaboration and Virtual Teamwork

Ethics can affect the effectiveness of teams—an essential way of working in the twenty-first century. When team members are not respectful or do not communicate honestly with each other, the team can fail.

Ethical behavior is a cornerstone for effective teamwork, and as explored in this section, many other considerations must also be met for success. As you will learn, effective teamwork has become even more challenging because of the broad diversity in the composition of team members and the growing use of virtual teamwork.

Multidisciplinary Collaboration

As you review job descriptions, note the increasingly cited requirement that reads, "proven track record of **multidisciplinary collaboration**." The importance of this skill becomes even more apparent when an employer includes this requirement on a list with only a few other items. As an entry-level candidate for a position, how do you respond to this expectation?

To have a "proven track record," you must demonstrate how you have been a member of several teams that were able to successfully complete their goals. As a student, teamwork experiences could include classroom projects, internships, and student clubs. Another excellent opportunity to gain teaming experience is through community volunteer activities.

There are several ways to gain multidisciplinary collaboration experience before your first professional job. For example, as you are involved with teams as a student, prioritize activities that involve people from a variety of disciplines. In particular, community volunteering can be excellent for this purpose because it often involves people from a range of occupations and interests. Moreover, community volunteering can provide the experience of serving as a leader of a subgroup—another important skill for your "proven track record."

Why "multidisciplinary collaboration"? There are various reasons why multidisciplinary collaboration is important, many of which are discussed throughout this book. However, the overarching fact is that twenty-first-century professional practices include teaming, the participation of **stakeholders**, and globalization.

Using teams in every stage of the design process has become so expected and pervasive that building certification documents, such as LEED Rating Systems, refer to "project teams," "design teams," "construction teams," and "commissioning teams." Typically, each of these teams is composed of experts from a variety of disciplines, including interior design, architecture, lighting design, geotechnical engineering, civil engineering, structural engineering, mechanical engineering, and landscape architecture.

Numerous disciplines are needed to fulfill the requirements of certification standards as well as to provide the expertise required to build the technologically complex buildings of the twenty-first century. Moreover, many of the green building certification initiatives involve input from a variety of people who have an interest in the project. Stakeholders can include developers, neighbors, government officials, community leaders, and local businesses.

Stakeholders can also include people and organizations from numerous countries. As discussed in Chapter 2, international projects involve the host country as well as local people from a variety of professions, such as translators, lawyers, accountants, commissioning agents, developers, and contractors. Involving stakeholders in the design process helps ensure that people who will occupy the structure are satisfied with the building's design.

Input from stakeholders is often obtained through **charrettes**. A French word for *cart*, the origin of the term is derived from the nineteenth-century practice of requiring architectural students studying at the École des Beaux Arts in Paris to hurriedly deposit their final projects in a cart.

In contemporary practice a charrette is "an intensive, multi-disciplinary week-long design workshop designed to facilitate an open discussion between stakeholders of a development project. A team of design experts meets with community groups, developers, and neighbors over a period of 3–4 days to 2 weeks long, gathering information on the issues that face the community. The charrette team then works together to find design solutions that will result in a clear, detailed, realistic vision for future development" (Schommer 2010).

Effective Teams and Team Members

To build your "proven track record of multidisciplinary collaboration" requires an understanding of what is required to have effective teams that are composed of people from different disciplines as well as diverse interests, values, experiences, conflicts, problem-solving skills, ages, ethnicities, races, genders, educational achievements, and socioeconomic status.

This long list of characteristics and variables helps explain why employers want people with *multidisciplinary* collaboration experience, not just a collaboration record. You must demonstrate your ability to collaborate with people who have a variety of characteristics and backgrounds.

Collaboration requires an understanding of the difference between groups and **teamwork**. Groups do not have a unified set of goals; each person tends to view his or her interests as most important. Therefore, groups often work independently and might or might not cooperate on initiatives. Successful collaboration requires teamwork.

What are the important elements of an effective team, and how can you be a good team member? Some of the components of an effective team are beyond your responsibility as an employee and are the responsibility of the organization, such as creating a culture that encourages open communication and prescribing reasonable deadlines for the team's work. An organization is also responsible for providing a team with essential resources, for example, hiring consultants, purchasing technology, and having an efficiently planned work space.

Assuming that your organization provides the appropriate elements for effective teams, other critical components focus on team composition and policies that support knowledge management. A team should be as small as possible, while including all of the people needed to complete the task. When the number of team members becomes unmanageable, people should be divided into subgroups.

Every person on a team should have a specific reason for his or her involvement, such as that individual's expertise, background, or professional experience. As mentioned previously, a team should have members who are assigned to the project from the very beginning and participate in every meeting.

Teams should have a purpose, goals, outcomes, deadlines, budgets, and evaluation policies and procedures. Teams should also promote a culture that encourages excellence, innovation, optimism, freedom of expression, and blameless attitudes. Team meetings should occur only when necessary and when they happen they should have (1) a facilitator, (2) a scribe, (3) an appropriate location, (4) an agenda with tasks that can be accomplished within a prescribed time limit, (5) specific roles and tasks for each member, and (6) a process for evaluating the effectiveness of the meeting.

To be an outstanding team member requires exceptional behavior in meetings as well as at other times. A good way to gain a better understanding of how to be effective in a meeting is to notice the behavior of people during meetings you attend while in school. You will see behavior that encourages productive outcomes; you will also see behavior that wastes time and is disrespectful.

Effective team members arrive at meetings a few minutes early, appropriately prepared, and with their cell phones silenced. During the meeting team members should (1) have a positive attitude, (2) respect diverse opinions, (3) provide substantive suggestions, (4) listen intently, (5) actively participate, (6) ask appropriate questions, (7) stay attentive to the team's tasks, and (8) volunteer for jobs.

The responsibilities of a team member extend beyond meetings. Team members are responsible for implementing tasks identified in meetings and should maintain a commitment to the team's decisions. Assignments must be completed accurately, thoroughly, and in a timely manner.

When someone in a collaborative arrangement fails to fulfill his or her obligations, the entire project might be affected with serious consequences, such as losing a design competition because of a late entry or causing workers to be laid off because of construction delays. Furthermore, team members should discuss the project only with appropriate people determined by the team—and they should always maintain confidentiality. Ideally, the team should determine how the outcomes of the project will be communicated, including who will deliver the results to whom and when.

Teaming Processes and Conflict Resolution

A "proven track record of multidisciplinary collaboration" necessitates membership on several teams that have successfully achieved their goals (Figure 4.3). Successful teams institute a **teaming process** that includes an agreed-upon method for making decisions and solving problems.

Soon after a team is assembled, members should develop a process for making decisions. The team should identify what decisions should be determined by the entire team, a subgroup, or an individual. The team should also determine protocols for people who are unable to attend decision-making meetings. For example, are they able to vote? If yes, when is his or her vote counted? Before or after discussions?

Teaming processes should also include an agreed-upon method for solving problems. Problem-solving strategies begin by creating a *clear* definition of the problems. A problem statement should be succinct and address only *one* issue. To encourage a full exploration of solutions to a problem, the statement should *not* include a method for solving the problem. Each team

Figure 4.3 Designed by Perkins + Will, *One Haworth Center* is an example of a project that involved an interdisciplinary approach. According to the firm, "Interdisciplinary means many talents brought together in a coordinated and powerfully appointed way" (Perkins + Will, 2010, p. 1). *(Steve Hall © Hedrich Blessing)*

member should be involved with developing the statement and should agree with its final version.

The next step for the team is to thoroughly analyze and discuss each problem. Based on the analysis, the team should identify important criteria for proposed solutions (Table 4.1). The team should brainstorm several solutions and then discuss the respective strengths and weaknesses of each one. As illustrated in Table 4.1, to prioritize solutions, each team member should designate a value for each solution and the criteria.

Using this process or a similar method is very effective because *all* team members contribute to developing the criteria used to evaluate options, and the resultant prioritized list reflects the opinion of *all* members. Consequently, the process—rather than an individual—determined the outcomes. People are more inclined to agree with these objectively based solutions and are more likely to support the tasks required to implement the decisions. Once consensus has been reached, the team can focus on what is required to carry out the solution, such as identifying tasks, responsibilities, individuals, timelines, budgets, and resources.

Unfortunately, even when using structured prioritization matrices to help formulate decisions, some teams are not productive. Conflicts can stall progress, cause personnel problems, and eventually prevent the successful completion of the project. Conflicts can arise from a variety of reasons, such as interpersonal dislikes, stereotypical assumptions, misunderstandings, and varying needs and interests.

How can you try to prevent conflict, and what is your role in conflict management? Following the guidelines for being an effective team member, as described above, is an excellent approach to trying to prevent and manage conflict between you and other team members. However, if you become involved with conflict, you should be aware of resolution methods.

Conflict mediation experts recommend that if you have a conflict with another individual, you should attempt to have a discussion with the person in a mutually agreed-upon setting. Prior to the meeting you should reexamine your views on the issue and consider alternatives. The goal of the meeting is to listen to each other's perspectives and try to understand the

Table 4.1 Case Study Prioritization Matrix

Problem Statement: The light fixtures we have been specifying for our clients' conference rooms are consuming too much electricity.

One proposed solution is to identify energy-efficient light fixtures. The team identified five potential manufacturers of conference light fixtures (A–F) and criteria for the fixtures. As shown below each team member designates a value for each potential light fixture manufacturer and the criteria. A summation of the values provides the team with a prioritized list of the proposed solutions.

Options/Criteria	A	B	C	D	E	F
Meets ENERGY STAR Qualifications	10	10	10	1	1	10
Meets International Energy Conservation Code 2009 High Efficacy Requirements	10	10	10	1	1	10
High efficacy	10	10	10	1	1	10
Long operational life	10	10	10	1	1	10
Even distribution of light	5	10	1	10	5	10
Low maintenance	1	1	5	5	5	1
Dimmable	10	10	10	1	1	1
3-year warranty	1	10	5	10	1	10
Totals	57	71	61	30	16	62

Lighting manufacturers.

Criteria in column determined by team.

Values used to evaluate criteria.

Values: 1—Unsatisfactory; 5—Moderately satisfactory; 10—Very satisfactory other person's views within the context of their background and experiences.

Often it is important to review each person's assumptions about an issue. For example, you might have a conflict with a team member you thought was more interested in profits than designing an energy-efficient building. To determine the validity of this assumption, you should discuss it during your meeting. Perhaps the person is very committed to energy-efficient buildings and assumed you were aware of that position.

Discussions should focus on resolutions that are the good for the project, the client, and the organization. When one-to-one meetings are unsuccessful you might want to request that a neutral third party be involved. Unresolved conflicts not only affect a project but ultimately might negatively impact future teaming initiatives as well as other career opportunities.

Charrettes and Virtual Teamwork

Achieving a "proven track record of multi-disciplinary collaboration" can also include charrettes and **virtual teamwork**. As you will note in reading this section, both of these approaches require you to possess unique teaming skills. Charrettes have become important for community projects that require the participation of stakeholders and are used for sustainability projects.

Charrettes and the Integrated Design Process (IDP)

Charrettes are conducted to solicit feedback from a variety of stakeholders in a project and charrettes have become very useful for projects that affect the public, such as government buildings, urban planning, environmentally sustainable designs, zoning ordinances, and community development. Charrettes, or intense working sessions, are conducted with a team of designers and the project's stakeholders.

Key elements to the **integrated design process** (IDP) are to (1) involve all willing stakeholders, (2) conduct the sessions onsite, if possible,

(3) encourage full participation, (4) develop holistic designs that address multiple interests, (5) provide **feedback loops**, and (6) utilize effective time management.

The last item is one of the defining characteristics of a charrette. To be successful, charrettes must have a precisely planned timeline of events. Note in the aforementioned definition of a charrette that the meetings should occur "over a period of 3–4 days to 2 weeks long." Frequently, charrettes occur in 4 consecutive days, but the number of days might be increased for larger projects that involve a large number of participants.

Consecutive days are necessary in order to keep the group on task and avoid losing participants. Continuously working on a design also helps to manage knowledge (a topic previously addressed in this chapter). Furthermore, a compressed timeline helps to sustain enthusiasm for the project by providing prompt feedback to the stakeholders, such as quickly showing them revised drawings of the project (Figure 4.4).

To illustrate how a charrette works, read the case study in Box 4.4. Even though most charrettes require several days, depending on the goals of the project, a charrette can be done in one day, as demonstrated in Box 4.4.

Figure 4.4 During a charrette, participants develop a conceptual design for the Southface Eco Office. *(Southface)*

Box 4.4
Southface Energy Institute Charrette Case Study*

Southface Energy Institute Background

Since 1978, the Southface Energy Institute has "worked with the construction and development industry, government agencies and communities to promote sustainable homes, workplaces, and communities" (Southface, 2010, p. 1). In 2002, during Southface's annual Greenprints Conference, the organization conducted a one-day "High Performance Buildings Charrette" for the new addition to the Institute's building.

Charrette Process

Goals of the Charrette: To collect viable high-performance building ideas and strategies for the new addition. Each team was asked to "design a 'net zero' energy addition to Southface and brainstorm ideas and strategies to meet a LEED Platinum level for the addition."

> Clear and concise goal of the charrette.

Charrette Facilitators: Experts in integrated design, LEED, and energy efficiency. Representatives from Southface provided the teams with information regarding the project program, site, and goals.

> Charrette facilitators should be experts in the topic.

Charrette Participants and Teams: 55 participants from a wide variety of backgrounds and fields: "Southface employees, architects, engineers, government employees, green building consultants, university staff members, builders, and public and private company representatives." Participants were assigned to one of six teams. Each team had various levels of expertise and areas of disciplines.

> Ideally participants in a charrette should have diverse backgrounds and professions.

Charrette Schedule

Thursday Evening
- One-hour gathering to meet each other and listen to three presentations: (1) description of the project program, site, and goals, (2) to initiate brainstorming—the value of high-performance buildings, and (3) logistical instructions for the teams.

> Background activity.

Friday
- Presentation: In-depth analysis of the existing Southface Institute building and the need for the addition. Energy and environmental goals and targets were reviewed, including net-zero energy consumption.

> Background activities.

- Introductions and logistical arrangements were described.

(Box 4.4 continued on page 114)

Southface Energy Institute Charrette Case Study* *(continued)*

- Video viewing of the first LEED Platinum building—The Chesapeake Bay Foundation Merrill Center, followed by a presentation that focused on high performance. — Background activity.

- Six breakout working groups were formed to discuss the LEED rating system checklist and determine which credits may be applicable to the Southface project. Teams were given one hour for the discussion and concluded that Southface should be able to get at least 52 points out of the possible 69 points needed for LEED Platinum. — Team discussion time.

- All working groups reconvened to brainstorm strategies for attaining the LEED points. Teams were given the rest of the morning and most of the afternoon (Figure 4.4). — Discussion with all participants. / Team discussion time.

- Late afternoon, each group delivered a presentation. — Discussion with all participants.

- Closing comments by participants, facilitators, and Southface employees. The charrette drawings/boards were displayed at a conference reception.

Outcomes of the Charrette

Many of the ideas and strategies developed during the charrette focused on "environmental excellence and high performance concepts found in the LEED Green Building Rating System." Ultimately, Southface wanted the charrette to: (1) inform and educate the participants about energy and environmental considerations associated with buildings, (2) establish a database of outside contacts, (3) document the charrette as a training tool, and (4) use the addition as a benchmark for environmental excellence in design and construction (Design Harmony, 2002).

*Adapted from: Design Harmony in cooperation with NREL and BuildingGreen, 2002, *Greenprints Charrette: Southface Energy Institute New Building*, http://www.wbdg.org/pdfs/charrette_southface.pdf. Retrieved November 23, 2010.

Virtual Teamwork

Charrettes are an example of a basically no-tech approach to multidisciplinary collaboration, but increasingly organizations are using several types of technology for virtual teamwork. Technological developments have provided professionals with the ability to successfully implement virtual teamwork. Consequently, organizations are increasingly using virtual methods to facilitate interactions and to save time and money. These outcomes are important for nationally based initiatives, but they become essential for international projects. Virtual teamwork enables an organization to involve professionals throughout the world, and to do so with minimum costs, and regardless of the time and location.

You are already familiar with various design technologies and tools that can be used by a virtual team, such as AutoCAD, Adobe Photoshop, Rhino, and other 3D computer design programs (Figure 4.5). While drawing, sketching, and modeling tools are important to virtual teamwork, because of the purposes of this book, this section will not review these tools but will instead focus on technologies and tools that can be used for business practices. Thus, this section describes important considerations for (1) structuring virtual teams, (2) available technologies, and (3) successful operations.

Fundamentally, virtual teamwork involves team members who are collaborating to perform a task in an artificial space. Note that in this description of virtual teamwork, it is not necessary for the team members to be dispersed geographically. Thus, virtual collaboration can occur within an organization as well as with people in various regions of the world.

Many of the same teaming considerations discussed earlier in this chapter can apply to virtual teamwork, such as appropriate compositions, policies, and procedures. However, collaborating in virtual space, most notably when

Figure 4.5 Rendy Himawan designed the Diavolo chair using a combination of Rhino and T-Splines. (© rendyhimawan.com)

there is never any face-to-face interaction, does present unique challenges that must be addressed in order to have successful outcomes.

Advantages and Disadvantages of Virtual Teamwork

Formulating effective virtual teams requires an understanding of the advantages and disadvantages of the practice. An important advantage of virtual teamwork is the ability to have a team of people with the expertise and experience that is essential to a project regardless of their geographic location.

Virtual teamwork enables an organization to involve individuals with unique specializations as well as people who have an understanding of the local culture, codes, regulations, and materials. Interacting virtually allows for the conservation of resources such as time, travel expenses, office space, and print materials.

The technologies and tools used to connect people and conserve resources also become important for managing information and knowledge. As discussed in this section, technology becomes an excellent means to document the integrated design process. Technology can be the tool to record conversations, decisions, design ideas, budgets, resources, contracts, and processes. Access to this information is important for team members, and documentation is required for green building certification programs. Documented details of a project can also be helpful for conducting project evaluations and subsequent recommendations for future practice.

But without proper planning and processes, some of the advantages of virtual teams can become disadvantages. For example, involving people with specific expertise in worldwide locations can create basic logistical problems. **Synchronous** interactions can be very difficult when some team members have to work at 2:00 a.m. The off-hours time period can become even more problematic when the person does not have access to the required facilities (e.g., the organization's office or the project location).

And some organizations might not have the appropriate hardware, software, equipment, or support staff. Moreover, some regions in the world experience frequent blackouts or might not have continuous broadband connectivity.

In addition to potential logistical problems, which can be resolved fairly easily with proper planning and resource allocations, virtual teams can encounter interpersonal conflicts that can be caused by working in virtual space. Misunderstandings are compounded when it is necessary to translate languages, and team members have diverse cultures with unique business protocols (see Chapter 5). As is the case with traditional teaming arrangements, interpersonal conflicts can be caused by ineffective communication. However, communication problems in virtual teams are generally attributed to the lack of face-to-face contact.

Interacting in virtual space can alter the effectiveness of nonverbal communication cues, such as not being able to see someone folding their arms as a sign of opposition or hear someone tapping a foot because of boredom or impatience. Moreover, the absence of a shared physical environment prohibits spontaneous contacts that can allow the chance to discuss and resolve an issue. Some of these simple interactions can happen while two people are walking down the same hallway or after work at a local restaurant.

Lack of face-to-face interactions can also make it more difficult to feel a connection with other team members, which can result in mediocre work, unresponsiveness, feelings of isolation, unconcern, and uninhibited communication usage, such as being rude or using swear words.

Disconnected feelings can become more pronounced when virtual team members speak different languages and have diverse cultures with unique customs. For example, if English was your second language, you might feel uncomfortable if you couldn't understand a design solution or a joke because of the unfamiliar terms. Consequently, team cohesiveness can be affected, and reaching consensus might require intense negotiations and extra time.

To help resolve problems associated with virtual interactions, it is extremely important for people to have very detailed instructions, prescribed responsibilities, frequent project updates, and ample opportunities for questions and answers.

Virtual Teamwork Technologies and Tools

Technologies and tools can help to overcome some communication problems. The key is matching technology with the needs of the team. A virtual team needs a means to communicate in a variety of ways, including one-to-one, one-to-many, and many-to-many.

Team members need technology for (1) making decisions, (2) sharing information, (3) providing input on designs and documents, (4) discussing ideas and solutions, and (5) adhering to schedules. Another consideration is whether the communication must be done at different times or at the same time, referred to as **asynchronously** and synchronously, respectively.

Therefore, virtual teams can determine the appropriate **communication channels** by analyzing their choices using the following criteria: (1) number of communicators, (2) required tasks, and (3) asynchronous or synchronous interactions. Some of the major types of communication channels include the telephone, **instant messaging (IM)**, **text messaging**, **e-mail**, blogs, social networking technology, **podcasts**, teleconferencing, videoconferencing, **web-based meeting systems**, discussion forums, and **wikis**. Communication methods with visual components are especially useful to designers.

Telephones are obviously an example of synchronous communication and are effective for one-to-one conversations that require discussions. IM, texting, and e-mail can be used to communicate with one person, a subgroup, or the entire team, and are especially useful for situations when people need immediate information. E-mail can additionally be used for documentation purposes.

Blogging, social networks, and podcasts are also effective for quick messages, but are used to distribute information to many people. Podcasts are audio or video files that can be downloaded to a personal computer or a portable device, such as an iPod or MP3 player.

Teleconferencing, videoconferencing, **telepresence**, and interactive webinars are useful collaboration tools when the team has to communicate with each other to make decisions, solve problems, and hold discussions. Teleconferencing uses a telephone to conduct a meeting; videoconferencing has audio and video capabilities. Both technologies are live and people are able to interact with each other at numerous locations.

Telepresence is a type of technology that improves videoconferencing by giving people the impression that others are actually at the meeting (Figure 4.6). Web-based meeting systems use the Internet as the means to connect people. Team members can participate in meetings, training sessions, or panel discussions in real time.

Virtual teams require collaboration technology and tools. These are the tools that enable virtual teams to have a central location for real-time editing of documents, accessing information, sharing work spaces, as well as communicating through electronic media.

Following the same concept as Wikipedia, wikis are used for the collaborative editing of online content. Wikis can also be used for

storing documents, communication, and personal pages. A useful tool for virtual meetings is an electronic interactive whiteboard. Electronic whiteboards capture and retain words and drawings that have been created on the board. The information can then be stored, printed, or electronically distributed.

Although technology is constantly changing, sources for the most current applications are reputable organizations, such as Google and Microsoft. For example, Google Docs is a free, online tool for virtual collaborative tasks. Features include real-time development of documents, spreadsheets, presentations, drawings, and forms (http://www.google.com/google-d-s/). Virtual team members can access documents from their computer, cell phone, or tablet and publish materials online.

Microsoft's Project Professional 2010 has components that allow for the central location of (1) documents, (2) standard templates, (3) team calendars, (4) announcements, and (5) enhanced communication with wikis, blogs, and discussion forums (http://www.microsoft.com). All of these technology tools still require appropriate business communication etiquette, a topic reviewed at the end of this chapter.

Figure 4.6 Telepresence improves videoconferencing by giving the impression that people are in actual physical attendance at a meeting. (© *HO Market Wire Photos/Newscom*)

Checking for Comprehension

* Identify three important characteristics of an effective team member.

* Based on your personal experience, identify two advantages and two disadvantages of virtual teamwork that were *not* discussed in this chapter.

Western Business Etiquette

Thus far in this chapter, we have reviewed various strategies you can use when you begin your first professional position, such as managing time, information, knowledge, and working in an ethical manner. Also explored were approaches to multidisciplinary collaboration, including how to be an effective team member in a variety of formats, such as charrettes and virtual space.

All of these important topics must be understood within the context of your professional behavior. Emily Post, an expert on etiquette, noted "to make a pleasant and friendly impression is not only good manners but equally good business" (Post and Post 2005). Proper etiquette serves as the guide for your interactions with your boss, coworkers, colleagues, clients, contractors, vendors, and stakeholders. Business etiquette guides how you should communicate with people, when discussions should occur, and where they should take place.

Western Workplace Etiquette

Chapter 3 started an exploration of business etiquette by examining expected protocols for job interviews, such as appropriate appearance and behavior. In this section, other aspects of business etiquette are reviewed, but this does not complete the discussion. As you will read in future chapters, etiquette—being polite—affects numerous aspects of your professional life, including international interactions, travel, and client relationships.

You might think that etiquette is a dated concept and has no or little bearing on your professional career; after all, Emily Post's book on *Etiquette in Society, Business, Politics and at Home* was first published in 1922. But the reality is that proper etiquette is not only essential to the work of an interior designer today, it is essential to success in the twenty-first century workplace. Why?

In addition to traditional reasons for understanding and demonstrating business etiquette, such as displaying strong interpersonal skills, many of the topics we discuss in this book are tied to proper etiquette. For example, collaborating with multi-disciplinary teams requires proper etiquette. Working in a global market requires proper etiquette. Outstanding interpersonal skills require proper etiquette. Appropriate use of electronic media requires proper etiquette. Excellent negotiation and communication skills

require proper etiquette. Developing lifelong relationships with clients requires proper etiquette. Promotions and advancements are connected to proper etiquette.

Many of these items are very often part of job requirements (see Chapter 2). For example, "Strong interpersonal skills," "The ability to build long-term relationships with clients," "Excellent verbal and written communication skills," and "Proven track record of multidisciplinary collaboration."

Proper business etiquette is important in any work environment, but it becomes even more critical to the work of an interior designer because of the social skills required to successfully serve clients (see Chapter 7). An interior designer must have also excellent interpersonal and communication skills as well as proper manners while dining, entertaining, meeting, presenting proposals, and socializing.

Work Environment Etiquette

Workplace etiquette focuses on issues specific to a work environment, such as personal offices, common equipment and spaces, as well as communication etiquette. A pleasant and productive work environment requires that people are considerate, respectful, and adaptable—especially when they must share the same space.

In the office environment you should use proper etiquette whenever you are interacting with others. For example, if you want to talk with someone who has a private office, you should acknowledge that a closed door indicates the person wants privacy and return at another time. If your issue is critically important, knock on the door and ask the person for a few moments of time. If the person cannot meet with you, ask how he or she would like you to follow up. Even when a door is open, you should knock first and ask if it is a good time to talk. And if you have a private office, do not abuse the situation by keeping your door closed on a regular basis.

Generally, etiquette issues are not frequent concerns when people have private offices, but problems escalate in shared spaces, such as cubicles, sample libraries, conference rooms, break rooms, and office supply spaces. If you are working in a cubicle, be sensitive to any activity or condition that can distract or interrupt your coworkers. For example, monitor loud sounds, such as talking on the phone, using a speaker phone, or listening to the radio or computer audio.

Because voices can be heard easily in cubicle areas, be cautious of people who might overhear your conversations and do your best to ignore what others are discussing in their space. To help block conversations and other types of distracting noises, you can use a **white noise system**. Smells can also travel to other cubicles; thus, be sensitive about introducing odor-producing items in your space, such as food and fragrances.

Do not assume you can interrupt a coworker in a cubicle at any time—or that it is acceptable to talk to someone by leaning over a shared partition. As mentioned previously, respect the privacy of others by requesting a convenient time to meet.

To ensure your own privacy, you might want to develop a visual cue that lets people know when they can enter your space, such as a raised or lowered flag. In addition, when you have an appointment with colleagues, you might want to hold the meeting in a conference room or another space away from the cubicle area.

In any office, you should be sensitive to what is on your walls and desk, but the items become very noticeable in open cubicles. Messy desks can be disturbing to coworkers; at minimum, your desk should be tidy by the end of each day.

Cleanliness also becomes an important etiquette concern in common spaces, such as sample libraries, conference rooms, break rooms, and office supply rooms. The room should be left in perfect condition by cleaning up spills, discarding or recycling unwanted items, straightening chairs, and turning off any lights and equipment.

A sample library can be especially problematic because of the large number of items that are often looked through quickly in advance of an approaching deadline. So that they can be promptly located, samples should be kept in their proper place. As a courtesy to coworkers, in addition to returning your samples to their appropriate location, take time to file materials that were left in the room by other designers. If someone has left something in a room, such as client files, do not read the documents—instead, return the materials to the person as soon as possible. This same policy should be used for documents left in other spaces or equipment, such as a shared copier.

Tidiness and sounds can also become an issue if you have a home office and you are required to participate in some type of videoconference. To avoid distractions during the meeting, you should be seated in a workplace setting and wear professional apparel. Make sure coworkers are not able to hear sounds or noise generated by sources such as children, pets, kitchen appliances, washers, dryers, radios, computers, and televisions.

Western Business Communication Etiquette

There are various reasons why employers list "Excellent verbal and written communication skills" as a requirement for positions, including their desire to have an office environment that functions efficiently and effectively. Every activity in a workplace requires verbal or written communication skills, or both.

Excellent communication skills help to facilitate negotiations, reduce errors, enhance client relations by establishing a sense of connection and rapport, and can save time by preventing the need for clarification or additional information. Effective communication is becoming even more important in the culturally diverse workplace and global collaborations because of multiple languages and customs (see Chapter 5).

In regard to language, always follow standard rules of grammar and use proper business communication etiquette. In both verbal and written communication, avoid jargon, texting abbreviations, slang, buzzwords, and coarse language. Generally, to prevent offending someone, humor should be used with caution.

If you need to apologize to someone, the most effective way to do it is face-to-face. If this is not possible, call the person. E-mail apologies might be acceptable in situations when the offense is very minor or you have not been able to reach the person for an extended period.

Confidential information is especially important in the workplace. Be sure to ask your boss what information can be shared with whom, by whom, and at what time. Confidentiality includes your personal life; separate personal and business communication.

Verbal Business Communication Etiquette

Verbal communication etiquette begins with employing a pleasant tone as well as proper grammar, pronunciation, and word usage. In addition, do not speak in a monotone, too quickly, or too loudly, especially when you are talking on a cell phone. Avoid bad habits, such as repeatedly saying, "you know," "uh," or "like."

Verbal communication etiquette requires the mindset that you are talking *with* someone rather talking *to* someone. To talk *with* someone necessitates effective listening skills and appropriate body language (see Chapters 7 and 5, respectively). The listening process involves receiving information, interpreting its content, and then letting the person know you are participating in the conversation by providing polite feedback, such as a verbal acknowledgement, questions, or simply nodding.

To genuinely process information, you must have an open mind and give the person your complete attention. During face-to-face and telephone conversations, you should not be engaged in distracting activities, such as answering your cell phone, texting, reading documents, or using your computer. The only writing that should occur is note-taking, which should be done only after receiving permission from the other person.

Telephone etiquette involves having an appropriate voice mail recording that clearly states your name and organization followed by a request for the caller's name, phone number, and a convenient time to return the call. Return calls within 24 hours.

When you answer the phone, pleasantly state your name and the name of your organization, and then ask how you can help the caller. When leaving a message on a recorder, state your name, organization, phone number, a very brief reason for your call, and when you will be available for the returned call. Providing the information needed to return a call saves time and can help to prevent misunderstandings and inaccurate information.

Verbal communication etiquette also becomes important during meetings, brainstorming sessions, office small talk, and social settings. Be careful when engaging in office small talk, as these conversations can merge into an undesirable situation—office gossip.

In addition to protocols regarding language, listening, and other issues previously discussed, during meetings you should listen carefully to each person's views and ask only pertinent questions that are succinctly composed at the appropriate time. People have embarrassed themselves in meetings by asking about something previously discussed and resolved.

Actively listening also becomes important when you are asked a question. By paying attention to the discussion, you might be able to anticipate a question and perhaps have time to craft a response that demonstrates your expertise as well as your effective communication skills. To develop your best answers, you might want to write down the key points. Note-taking on paper or laptop are generally acceptable in meetings. However, using a cell phone is not appropriate unless the device is needed for some application during the meeting, such as retrieving data or delivering a presentation.

Brainstorming sessions, a common technique in today's workplace, require special etiquette considerations. The informal nature of the process can give the impression that people can talk at any time and say what they want to anyone. Thus, there may be several conversations underway simultaneously, people might shout, have private side conversations, or work on an unrelated task. In contrast to these behaviors, brainstorming sessions can be productive only when people are cordial to each other, listen to everyone's perspectives, and are willing to recognize that all ideas are important and should be thoughtfully analyzed by the entire group.

Verbal communication etiquette also becomes important when you are dealing with office gossip, engaged in small talk, working with vendors/suppliers, and speaking with clients and coworkers in a social setting. To maintain excellent interoffice relationships, you should not participate in the spread of office gossip by either listening to rumors or sharing inappropriate information.

A gossip-free policy is very useful when you are engaged in small talk. Impromptu conversations should focus on inoffensive topics, such as the weather, your vacation plans, or new movies. Business-related topics can be discussed as long as people who should be involved with the conversation are present and the discussion does not evolve into inappropriate office issues.

Effective verbal communication is very important when working with vendors, contractors, and suppliers. Verbal skills are essential for ensuring accurate orders, instructions, and information (as well as presenting a professional image). Even though contracts are used for business transactions, there are many times when an interior designer verbally communicates some aspect of a project, such as telling an installer where to mount a light fixture or describing a particular color to a paint specialist. Concise and complete instructions will help to ensure a project is completed as planned, on time, and according to the contracted budget.

The work of an interior designer often involves social engagements (see Chapter 5), such as the grand opening of a building, a dinner event to honor project donors, showroom receptions at conferences, or clients' private parties. Even though these are social events, you must still use professional protocols and proper communication etiquette, beginning with introductions.

Generally, your clients should always be introduced first. Thus, if you are talking with a client and another person joins the conversation, you should pause and introduce your client to the other person. This introduction should be followed by introducing the person to your client. If you do not know a person's name, politely ask. After handshakes, the conversation should proceed by discussing a topic of interest to everyone.

Eating can be challenging at these events because it is difficult to eat and talk at the same time, and frequently you will also have to hold your plate and a drink. Select food items that are easy to eat, and in a professionally based setting, alcoholic beverages are generally either avoided or very moderately consumed. Always have clean and dent-free business cards with you, and offer your card to a person at an appropriate time.

Generally, the best time to present your card to a person is after they have offered their card to you. If the person does not offer their card to you and you believe the person needs the information, then toward the end of the event present your card to him or her. For meetings abroad follow the business card protocols used in each country (see Chapter 5). If name tags are used, place the tag below your right shoulder, allowing others to easily read your name while you are shaking hands.

Written Business Communication Etiquette

Proper name tag etiquette continues with what is written on the paper. The tag should have your full name and can also include the name of your firm. Generally, "Dr.," "Mr.," or "Ms." are not included with the name. If you need to write a tag for yourself, use a bold marker and print your name in large, legible letters.

Other written communication etiquette applies to business letters, thank you notes, **memorandums**, e-mail, IM, text messaging, blogs, and social media.

Regardless of the informality of a situation, such as texting a coworker, all business correspondence must have correct spelling, grammar, and punctuation. In addition, *all* forms of messages should be proofread before they are sent. Business letters follow a format similar to the one used for your cover letter (see Chapter 3), with the inclusion of a reference line.

Correspondence printed on company letterhead should have a date, reference line, recipient's name (spelled correctly) and title/position, full address, salutation beginning with "Dear," body of the letter, complimentary close (for example, "Sincerely," "Very truly yours," or "Sincerely yours"), signature, and the name/title of sender. A reference line is used to highlight the purpose of the letter, for example, "RE: Proposal for designing the new office for ABC Corporation."

Successful corporations require efficient business correspondence. All of the required information should be included in the first correspondence, thus eliminating the need to ask for clarification or missing details. To ensure that information is concise, accurate, and comprehensive, begin the letter-writing process with an outline.

The body of the letter begins by explaining the purpose of the letter, followed by a brief description. The last paragraph should state concluding remarks and when appropriate, follow-up activities. As always, the letter must have accurate spelling, grammar, and punctuation.

It is important that you write the letter using language and content that is appropriate for the recipient. For example, do not use trade words in letters written to people who are not familiar with the profession. Moreover, non-design professions might need an explanation for terms such as "rapidly renewable materials" or "VOCs."

Another form of business correspondence is thank you notes—an important gesture for showing your gratitude to clients, professionals, vendors, coworkers, or your boss. A handwritten thank you note for business purposes often uses correspondence cards that are approximately 4″ × 6″ (10 cm × 15 cm) with your name printed at the top. The message should be brief, generally three to four sentences in length.

A stamp, rather than metered mail, should be used on the hand-addressed envelope. For some informal situations, such as a thank you to a coworker, e-mail is acceptable; however, a thoughtfully composed, handwritten note will always present the most favorable impression.

Memorandums, or memos, are brief correspondences often used for interoffice communication. As illustrated in Box 4.5, addresses, salutations, and complimentary closures are not included in a memo. Initials next to the sender's name generally substitute for a signature. The message should be brief, often just one paragraph.

Business Netiquette

Written etiquette also applies to business communication via the Internet, such as e-mail, IM, text messaging, blogs, and social media. Etiquette associated with these electronic media is referred to as "netiquette," or protocols for communicating online. Business e-mail messages follow many of the same elements of memos, such as succinctness. However, some inappropriate e-mail use has prompted the need for e-mail communication netiquette focused on creating effective messages.

E-mail netiquette includes proper sender/recipient protocols as well as parameters concerning content, such as avoiding complaints and personal remarks. The sender's signature feature should include only his or her name, relevant title, and contact information (including organizational web address and office/cell phone numbers).

When sending a message to several recipients, respect people's privacy by not disclosing the entire list in the "To" section. The "Subject" or "RE" line should not be a general statement but instead provide a brief description of the purpose of the e-mail. Thus, the subject line should encourage someone to open the message. For example, rather than "Project Update," the subject line could read, "Team completed design concept for ABC building."

As with memos, the content of e-mails should briefly summarize the purpose of the message

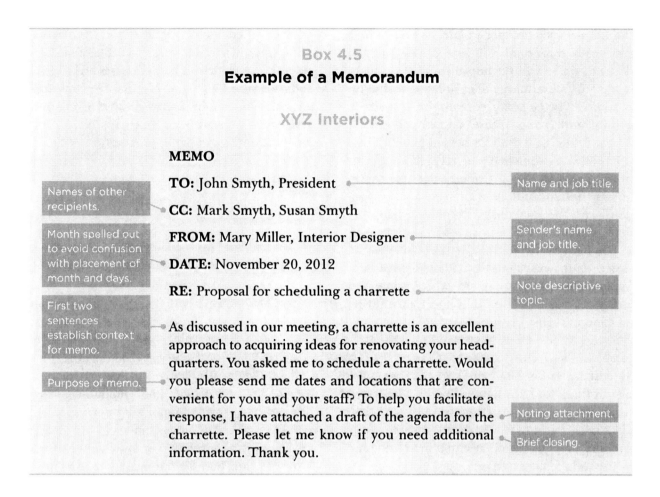

Box 4.5
Example of a Memorandum

XYZ Interiors

MEMO

TO: John Smyth, President — *Name and job title.*

CC: Mark Smyth, Susan Smyth — *Names of other recipients.*

FROM: Mary Miller, Interior Designer — *Sender's name and job title.*

DATE: November 20, 2012 — *Month spelled out to avoid confusion with placement of month and days.*

RE: Proposal for scheduling a charrette — *Note descriptive topic.*

As discussed in our meeting, a charrette is an excellent approach to acquiring ideas for renovating your headquarters. You asked me to schedule a charrette. Would you please send me dates and locations that are convenient for you and your staff? To help you facilitate a response, I have attached a draft of the agenda for the charrette. Please let me know if you need additional information. Thank you.

First two sentences establish context for memo.

Purpose of memo.

Noting attachment.

Brief closing.

and expectations of the recipient, if any. When necessary, include deadlines and any other information associated with your request. Bulleted or numbered lists can help to provide an easy-to-read summary, but e-mails should not have an assortment of emoticons, colors, backgrounds, or numerous abbreviations and acronyms. Moreover, do not use all capital letters; this sends a "shouting" message to your recipients.

Remember: E-mail messages are *not* private. Employers can access your messages, people can forward e-mails to unexpected recipients, and original messages can be modified with false or misleading information. Therefore, e-mail should not be used to convey confidential information, criticism, complaints, anger, coarse language, offensive humor, or office gossip. In other words, realize that every e-mail message could be read by everyone in an office—as well as anyone else around the world.

Many of the principles associated with e-mail netiquette, as well as other business correspondence, also apply to texting, IM, blogs, and social media. Communication can be shared globally; thus, messages and other items—such as photos—should present a professional image. Messages should be concise, accurate, and appropriate for a business environment.

People tend to overlook writing rules when using texting and IM because messages and responses are quick and brief—hallmarks of their popularity and effectiveness. But the rules of grammar, spelling, and punctuation still apply when writing business-related messages, including texting and IM. An informal writing style can be acceptable with friends, but for the most part is inappropriate in the business environment.

Business netiquette considerations associated with these electronic media are fundamentally based on the same customs and manners that should be used in face-to-face conversations, a critically important skill in a profession that depends on strong relationships. Using a technology to communicate does not negate the importance of being polite, considerate, respectful, helpful, and saying "please" and "thank you."

As is the case with in-person interactions, when meeting someone new via technology, introduce yourself and provide a brief description of your background. As with in-person interactions, give the relationship time to develop before asking for referrals or assistance. As with in-person interactions in a private office with a closed door, you should ask if it is convenient for someone to engage in IM (when the person indicates "busy," respect that and wait until he or she is available for your message).

As with in-person interactions in a workplace, be respectful of people's time; do not overuse IM or send long messages (or keep people on the phone for longer than is necessary). As with in-person interactions in a diverse workplace, when using IM you should consider your audience, and be careful not to offend someone or use unfamiliar acronyms.

Netiquette considerations unique to blogs include (1) using your real name, (2) posting your own comments, (3) not repeating comments, (4) posting useful and relevant information, (5) thoughtfully responding to other bloggers' comments, and (6) being respectful of varying opinions—especially when someone criticizes your comments.

Social networks also have netiquette guidelines that are based on their distinctive characteristics. As discussed in Chapter 3, two of the most popular social networks are Facebook and LinkedIn. Both of these are focused on building worldwide relationships. However, because Facebook was developed to "keep up with friends, upload an unlimited number of photos, share links and videos, and learn more about the people they meet" (Facebook 2010), the site is more appropriate for personal use and, if possible, should be used exclusively for this purpose. How can you defriend your boss?

Even when you restrict Facebook to personal use, you still should present a professional appearance; current and future bosses and clients might see your pages and postings. For business purposes you might want to join LinkedIn, a service provider with an emphasis on professional networks and job opportunities.

As stated previously, regardless of whether you are using no technology or the newest technology, always practice verbal and written communication etiquette. This knowledge as well as the other topics discussed in this chapter, including personal management strategies and multidisciplinary collaboration, provides important information for your career as an interior designer.

The content presented in this chapter serves as a basis for material discussed in the next chapter, *International Business Practices*. Topics in Chapter 5 focus on international professional practice and the customs and resources required to work in a global marketplace.

Knowledge and Skills Summary

Highlights
* Personal management strategies involve developing professional goals and managing time, information, and knowledge.

* An interior designer's behavior revolves around the profession's ethics, which focus on responsibilities to the public, clients, colleagues, the design profession, and the designer's employer.

* Multidisciplinary collaboration requires knowing how to work with people from different disciplines as well as diverse interests, values, and experiences.

- Technological developments have provided professionals with the ability to successfully implement virtual teamwork.

- Collaborating with multidisciplinary teams requires proper business etiquette.

- Excellent communication skills help to reduce errors, facilitate negotiations, enhance client relations by establishing a sense of connection and rapport, and can save time by preventing the need for clarification or additional information.

- Effective communication is becoming even more important in the culturally diverse workplace and in global collaborations because of multiple languages and customs.

- Netiquette applies to business communication via the Internet, such as e-mail, instant messaging (IM), text messaging, blogs, and social media.

Key Terms

asynchronous

business ethics

charrette

communication channel

e-mail

ethics

explicit knowledge

feedback loop

information management

instant messaging (IM)

integrated design process (IDP)

knowledge management

memorandum

multi-disciplinary collaboration

netiquette

podcast

professional ethics

stakeholder

synchronous

tacit knowledge

teaming process

teamwork

telepresence

text messaging

time management

web-based meeting system

virtual teamwork

white noise system

wikis

Projects

Philosophy and Design Project

The purpose of this project is to give you experience in developing good judgment. Based on the tragedy at Beverly Hills Supper Club in Southgate, Kentucky (Box 4.2), you are to work in a team of three to five members and complete the following: (1) identify the ethical issues, (2) provide a rationale for the ethical issues, and (3) determine how this case study informs your professional practice.

To identify an ethical issue, you should compare each activity with the basic definition of ethics as well as ethical codes developed by a professional organization, such as IIDA. Develop a brief summary of your response and prepare an informal presentation (approximately 10 minutes) to the class that includes images.

Research Project

The first step to managing information is creating a system for organizing all the items you need to do your job, such as paper documents, web pages, drawings, photographs, products, vendors, professionals, e-mail messages, and electronic files.

Develop a scheme for an information management plan. You can select the type of format as well as an organizational system. The information management plan should include a system for organizing products and manufacturers as well as two examples of manufacturers' information in each file.

Human Factors Research Project

A "proven track record of multidisciplinary collaboration" necessitates membership on several teams that have successfully achieved their goals. Successful teams institute a teaming process that includes an agreed-upon method for making decisions and solving problems.

Identify a team of three to five members. The team has the following assignment: (1) develop policies and procedures for collaborative problem solving and decision making, (2) be sure to include virtual teaming in the policies and procedures, and (3) provide a rationale for your problem-solving and decision-making policies and procedures. Develop a summary of the policies and procedures for collaborative problem solving and decision making, and post on a project blog.

References

American Society of Interior Designers (ASID). 2010. ASID Code of Ethics & Professional Conduct. http://www.asid.org/about/ethics/. Accessed September 24, 2010.

Design Harmony in Cooperation with NREL and BuildingGreen. 2002. *Greenprints Charrette: Southface Energy Institute New Building*. http://www.wbdg.org/pdfs/charrette_southface.pdf. Accessed November 23, 2010.

Facebook. 2010. *Company Overview*. http://www.facebook.com/facebook?v=info. Accessed September 24, 2010.

Long, D. H. 2008. *Ethical Decision Making for Designers*. Washington, DC: National Council for Interior Design Qualification (NCIDQ).

Long, D. H. 2000. *Ethics and the Design Profession*. Washington, DC: National Council for Interior Design Qualification (NCIDQ).

Merriam-Webster's Dictionary. 2010. *Ethic*. http://www.merriam-webster.com/dictionary/ethic. Accessed September 5, 2010.

Moran, M. January 2007. Researchers Find Neural Bottleneck Thwarts Multitasking. *Vanderbilt Register*. http://www.vanderbilt.edu/register/articles?id=31525 Accessed September 4, 2010.

National Council for Interior Design Qualification (NCIDQ). 2008. *Ethical Decision Making for Designers*. Washington, DC: National Council for Interior Design Qualification.

National Council for Interior Design Qualification (NCIDQ). 2000. *Ethics and the Design Profession*. Washington, DC: National Council for Interior Design Qualification.

National Fire Protection Association (NFPA). 1978. *Beverly Hills Supper Club Fire Southgate, Kentucky May 28, 1977*. http://www.nfpa.org/assets/files/pdf/fisouthgate.pdf. Accessed November 24, 2010.

PD. 2010. *Knowledge Management*. http://www.knowledge-management-online.com/knowledge-management16.html. Accessed September 4, 2010.

Post, E. 1922. *Etiquette in Society, Business, Politics, and at Home*. New York: Funk & Wagnalls.

Post, P., and P. Post. 2005. *Emily Post's The Etiquette Advantage in Business*. New York: HarperResource.

Schommer, J. 2010. *Charrettes Defined*. http://www.charrettecenter.net/charrettecenter.asp?a=spf&pfk=7&gk=261. Accessed September 17, 2010.

Southface. 2010. *Welcome to Southface!* http://www.southface.org/about/letter/. Accessed November 24, 2010.

Weir, D., ed. 2006. *Towards an Ethical Architecture: Issues within the Work of Gregory Henriquez*. Vancouver: BLUEIMPRINT.

CHAPTER 5

International Business Practices

Kapitel 5 (German)
Κεφάλαιο 5 (Greek)
Chapter 5 (Haitian Creole)
קרפ 5 (Hebrew)
अध्याय 5 (Hindi)

After learning the content in Chapter 5, you will be able to answer the following questions:

- What are key considerations to providing design services in a global marketplace?

- How can interior designers establish meaningful intercultural relationships?

- How do cultural variances in attitudes, values, and beliefs affect intercultural business practices?

- How does a culture's communication style affect intercultural business practices?

- What are intercultural business protocols with respect to appointments, meetings, negotiations, decision making, socializing, and gift giving?

As reviewed in Part I, success in business today requires an understanding of global events, economics, and financial systems. Chapter 2 introduced how globalization has impacted the design profession and reviewed some of the opportunities and challenges associated with international practice.

Chapters 3 and 4 continued to examine how globalization is affecting career opportunities for interior designers as well as professional business responsibilities. This chapter expands on these topics by specifically examining international business customs and protocols. Information related to opening and managing an international business is reviewed in Part IV.

The purpose of this chapter is to prepare you for working as a global interior designer by analyzing various approaches to international practice and reviewing the role of culture in intercultural business relationships. The latter topic is obviously important when you are working on international projects, but it has become equally critical to the day-to-day activities in local offices because of the diversity of today's workforce as well as multicultural clients. Therefore, even if you are not interested in working for a global interior design firm, the chapter's content will help you understand how to work in a world of intercultural interactions.

Globalization guarantees that you will be working with people with diverse heritages, cultures, backgrounds, customs, values, manners, ages, and physical abilities. As discussed in the previous chapter, this probability is enhanced by the rapid advancements in the technologies used to support virtual teams. Thus, having excellent relationships with people you work with as well as your clients requires an understanding of intercultural relationships.

Chapter 5 begins the exploration of international business practices by analyzing various collaborative arrangements and logistical considerations. Intercultural attitudes, values, and beliefs are reviewed within the context of how they affect decisions, information requirements, and schedules.

To further expand on intercultural business communication styles, the next section analyzes languages, nonverbal communication, greeting protocols, and appropriate topics for casual conversations. The last section in the chapter reviews intercultural business protocols associated with conducting meetings, negotiating, and decision making. And because socialization and gift giving are important elements of business for many cultures, these customs are discussed and recommendations provided.

As a caveat to the chapter, cultural information introduced here is not intended to be comprehensive and is not proposed to present a stereotype of the people in any country. Obviously, every person you meet has attitudes, likes, dislikes, and mannerisms. In fact, an interior designer must understand these attributes in order to address the needs of a client.

The descriptions in the following pages are simply an overview of cultural differences and are based on the expertise of various research studies and international sources, including data collected by the U.S. government. Recognizing that there are differences is one of the first steps to developing successful multicultural relationships—absolutely essential to international business practices.

International Practice, Collaboration, Ventures, and Logistics

A major theme that permeates this book is the impact of globalization on the design profession. In support of this approach is CIDA's *Standard 2. Global Perspective for Design*, which states, "Entry-level interior designers have a global view and weigh design decisions within the parameters of ecological, socio-economic, and cultural contexts" (CIDA 2011).

Interior designers are working with clients, professionals, vendors, suppliers, contractors, and coworkers from regions throughout the world. Success requires an understanding of international collaboration practices as well as logistical requirements that are critical to business operations. A sign of cultural fluency is being open-minded, respectful, polite, and nonjudgmental. This perspective will benefit the person conducting business across the globe. **Ethnocentrism** or feelings of ethnicity superiority should be replaced with **polycentrism**—a mindset that respects the values, attitudes, behavior, and customs of people throughout the world.

International Practice and Collaboration

An interior designer might realistically work in one of the following scenarios:

1. Lives in the United States and works for a firm with one U.S. office but has clients who are building facilities throughout the world. Some of the firm's clients are Japanese corporations that are renovating office space in the United States.

2. Lives in Canada and works for a firm whose only office is in London.

3. U.S. citizen living in Hong Kong and working for a firm with headquarters in Abu Dhabi and multiple offices throughout the world.

4. Lives in the United States and owns a firm with headquarters in New York City and offices in Shanghai, Mumbai, and Dubai.

5. Lives in New York City and works for a firm that has ten offices in the United States and international offices in London and in Shanghai. In addition, the firm has 30 partners—creating global alliances in Latin America, Asia-Pacific, Australia, Europe, the Middle East, and Africa.

When you are reviewing the above scenarios, several issues should be evident. First, as discussed in the previous chapter, technology has enabled people to live in one location and virtually collaborate with others throughout the world. Another practice that the scenarios reveal is that design firms are maintaining a headquarters while establishing offices in locations that are driven by regional market demands. The cities identified above are some of the locations commonly used for branch facilities. Other popular international cities are Beijing, Singapore, Tokyo, Mexico City, Delhi, and Moscow.

Where a firm invests in regional facilities is determined by new construction opportunities as well as conditions and incentives offered by the host country. Design firms seek states with favorable tax laws, encourage foreign investments, and accommodate international travel.

Scenario 5 describes how firms are able to concurrently design facilities in regions throughout the world, known as "intercultural collaboration." Therefore, if a U.S. firm wants to compete for its first project in Kuala Lumpur and lacks local associates, one solution is to collaborate with organizations with experience working in the city. Collaboration can be with design/architectural firms or companies/individuals that specialize in other areas, such as engineering, property development, urban planning, landscaping, or graphic design.

Key to the collaboration is connecting with native people who understand local codes, laws, materials, and building practices. Thus, companies that have successfully worked on projects in a foreign location have established relationships with local citizens. These global alliances reduce the cost of owning and operating a foreign office, such as rent, utilities, furniture, equipment, and salaries.

International Ventures

Global alliances are driven by market demands as well as the accommodations provided by the host country. When a firm is exploring international ventures, there are additional important issues, including ease of doing business, communication technologies, security issues, socioeconomic conditions, environmental standards, and international monetary and trade programs (Box 5.1). How can a designer acquire this information?

Box 5.1

International Monetary and Trade Programs

The Bretton Woods Agreement and System

In July 1944 representatives from 45 countries convened in Bretton Woods, New Hampshire, to create an economic cooperation agreement. The purpose of the agreement was to avoid the global economic consequences associated with the Great Depression by regulating international economic relations.

At the meeting representatives established the International Monetary Fund (IMF), the International Bank for Reconstruction and Development (current World Bank), and the International Trade Organization (ITO) or the General Agreement on Tariffs and Trade (GATT; current World Trade Organization or WTO). The Bretton Woods agreement lasted until the early 1970s.

International Monetary Fund (IMF)

The Bretton Woods agreement established the IMF in 1944. Currently, the IMF is "an organization of 187 countries, working to foster global monetary cooperation, secure financial stability, facilitate international trade, promote high employment and sustainable economic growth, and reduce poverty around the world" (IMF 2010).

IMF activities include the following:

- Policy advice to governments and central banks based on analysis of economic trends and cross-country experiences

- Research, statistics, forecasts, and analysis based on tracking of global, regional, and individual economies and markets

- Loans to help countries overcome economic difficulties

- Concessional loans to help fight poverty in developing countries

- Technical assistance and training to help countries improve the management of their economies (IMF 2010)

The World Bank

The World Bank was established as the International Bank for Reconstruction and Development at the Bretton Woods conference in 1944. Currently the World Bank "is a vital source of financial and technical assistance to developing countries around the world. Our mission is to fight poverty with passion and professionalism for lasting results and to help people help themselves and their environment by providing resources, sharing knowledge, building capacity and forging partnerships in the public and private sectors" (The World Bank 2010).

Key activities at The World Bank are the following:

- Poverty reduction and the sustainable growth in the poorest countries, especially in Africa

- Solutions to the special challenges of post-conflict countries and fragile states

- Development solutions with customized services as well as financing for middle-income countries

- Regional and global issues that cross national borders—climate change, infectious diseases, and trade

- Greater development and opportunities in the Arab world

- Pulling together the best global knowledge to support development (The World Bank 2010)

World Trade Organization (WTO)

The 1948 GATT rules formed the basis for the establishment of the WTO in 1995. Today, the WTO's mission is to "provide a forum for negotiating agreements aimed at reducing obstacles to international trade and ensuring a level playing field for all, thus contributing to economic growth and development. The WTO also provides a legal and institutional

Box 5.1

International Monetary and Trade Programs (continued)

framework for the implementation and monitoring of these agreements, as well as for settling disputes arising from their interpretation and application" (WTO 2010). Following are some of the activities of the WTO:

- Negotiating the reduction or elimination of obstacles to trade (import tariffs, other barriers to trade) and agreeing on rules governing the conduct of international trade (e.g., antidumping, subsidies, product standards, etc.)

- Administering and monitoring the application of the WTO's agreed rules for trade in goods, trade in services, and trade-related intellectual property rights

- Monitoring and reviewing the trade policies of our members, as well as ensuring transparency of regional and bilateral trade agreements

- Settling disputes among our members regarding the interpretation and application of the agreements

- Building capacity of developing country government officials in international trade matters (WTO 2010)

World Economic Forum

The World Economic Forum (http://www.weforum.org/en/index.htm) began as the European Management Forum in 1971. The name was changed in 1987 in order to include provisions related to resolving international conflicts.

The World Economic Forum is a not-for-profit organization that is "striving towards a world-class corporate governance system where values are as important a basis as rules. Our motto is 'entrepreneurship in the global public interest.' We believe that economic progress without social development is not sustainable, while social development without

economic progress is not feasible" (World Economic Forum 2010).

The vision for the World Economic Forum is that it aims to be (World Economic Forum 2010):

- The foremost organization which builds and energizes leading global communities.

- The creative force shaping global, regional and industry strategies

- The catalyst of choice for its communities when undertaking global initiatives to improve the state of the world

Association of Southeast Asian Nations (ASEAN)

ASEAN is an organization that was founded in 1967 by Indonesia, Malaysia, Philippines, Singapore, and Thailand. Current members include the founding states and Viet Nam, Myanmar, Lao PDR, Cambodia, and Brunei Darussalam.

The aims and purposes of ASEAN are the following (ASEAN 2010):

- To accelerate the economic growth, social progress and cultural development in the region through joint endeavours in the spirit of equality and partnership in order to strengthen the foundation for a prosperous and peaceful community of Southeast Asian Nations

- To promote regional peace and stability through abiding respect for justice and the rule of law in the relationship among countries of the region and adherence to the principles of the United Nations Charter

- To promote active collaboration and mutual assistance on matters of common interest in the economic, social, cultural, technical, scientific and administrative fields

(Box 5.1 continued on page 132)

Box 5.1

International Monetary and Trade Programs (continued)

- To provide assistance to each other in the form of training and research facilities in the educational, professional, technical and administrative spheres

- To collaborate more effectively for the greater utilization of their agriculture and industries, the expansion of their trade, including the study of the problems of international commodity trade, the improvement of their transportation and communications facilities and the raising of the living standards of their peoples

- To promote Southeast Asian studies

- To maintain close and beneficial cooperation with existing international and regional organizations with similar aims and purposes, and explore all avenues for even closer cooperation among themselves

North American Fair Trade Organization (NAFTA)

NAFTA is a free trade agreement between the United States, Canada, and Mexico. The agreement was effective in 1994. The agreement provided the elimination of any remaining duties and quantitative restrictions on January 1, 2008 (NAFTA 2010).

According to NAFTA (2010) as of 2010 the North American free trade area involved 444 million people that were producing $17 trillion worth of goods and services.

Fairtrade Labeling Organizations International (FLO)

FLO is several organizations that are committed to securing fair practices and policies for producers. FLO's main tasks are to (FLO 2010):

- Set international Fairtrade standards

- Organize support for producers around the world

- Develop global Fairtrade strategy

- Promote trade justice internationally

The World Bank provides data—based on the regulatory environment—regarding ease of doing business (World Bank 2010). For example, according to the World Bank's report in 2010, Singapore was ranked first for ease of doing business, followed by New Zealand, Hong Kong, the United States, the United Kingdom (UK), Denmark, Ireland, Canada, Australia, and Norway. The report also provides other business-related rankings, including ease of starting a business, obtaining construction permits, employing workers, paying taxes, and protecting investors.

As an important agency for promoting business activities, the World Bank also has data regarding expenditures for information and communication technologies as well as the number of Internet users. For instance, in 2009 regional rankings for Internet users (per 100 people) were United States (78.1 percent), Euro Area (67 percent), European Union (67.1 percent), Latin America and the Caribbean (31.5 percent), Europe and Central Asia (36.6 percent), East Asia and Pacific (24.1 percent), the Middle East and North Africa (21.5 percent), Arab World (18.4 percent), Sub-Saharan Africa (8.8 percent), and South Asia (5.5 percent) (World Bank 2010).

The United Nations Office on Drugs and Crime (UNODC) has information on crime as well as corruption (UNODC 2010). The World Bank and the United Nations have socioeconomic data that includes income distributions as well as urban and rural poverty rates. For a sustainability perspective, both organizations also have environmental data and programs.

The World Bank globally monitors fresh water, clean air, forest areas, grasslands, marine resources, and agricultural ecosystems. Water pollution is reported as well as emissions of CO_2, methane, and nitrous oxide, which are gases associated with climate changes. For instance, in 2007, CO_2 emissions (metric tons per capita) of the world's various regions were North America (19.1 percent), Europe and Central Asia (7.2 percent), East Asia and Pacific (4.0 percent), the Middle East and North Africa (3.7 percent), Latin America and the Caribbean (2.7 percent), South Asia (1.2 percent), and Sub-Saharan Africa (0.8 percent) (World Bank 2010).

The United Nations Environment Programme (UNEP) sponsors programs and initiatives focused on protecting the environment for future generations, including B4E (Business for the Environment), an "international conference for dialogue and business-driven action for the environment" (UNEP 2010).

As with any partnership, along with the advantages there are some disadvantages. Contractual agreements with global alliances must concisely prescribe each party's responsibilities within the context of mutually understandable design and business practices. What does this mean?

Obviously, contracts should specify exactly what work will be performed, by whom, for what amount, and the completion date (see Chapter 7). However, when a contract with global business cultures is entered, different views can exist regarding tasks, requirements, and deliverables. For example, most U.S. firms expect to execute a project beginning with the first phase of the design process through to the post-occupancy evaluations. But a collaborative international partner might want the U.S. firm to work on the project only up to the schematic design phase. Moreover, each firm might have very different approaches to teamwork, sustainable designs, and compensation fees. Naturally, many of these issues can occur in any partnership, but the differences are more pronounced when the business agreement involves foreign laws, governments, contracts, labor unions, as well as intercultural practices and communication styles (Box 5.2 and Figure 5.1).

Box 5.2

Walt Disney Company's Euro Disneyland*

After very successful ventures with Orlando's Disney World and the 1983 opening of Tokyo Disneyland, the Walt Disney Company was interested in the European market—a lucrative one due to a large population and previous high revenues from animated feature films.

Location, Contracts, and Master Plan
A small town 20 miles east of Paris, Marne-la-Vallée, was selected for Euro Disneyland (Euro Disney; current Disneyland Paris) for some of the following reasons: (1) close proximity to major highways, airports, and railways; (2) a lucrative market due to a large population: 50 million people within a two-hour drive and 310 million within a two-hour flight; (3) considerable farm acreage to develop park, and a planned development consisting of condominiums, office buildings, and retail stores; (4) a stable government that was interested in the project due to France's high unemployment and need to generate tax revenues; (5) available labor force; and (6) weather was comparable to conditions in successful Tokyo.

(Box 5.2 continued on page 134)

Box 5.2
Walt Disney Company's Euro Disneyland* *(continued)*

To "seal the deal" in 1987 required an agreement with the French Government: (1) property and revenue tax incentives; (2) enacted law of eminent domain to acquire farmland; and (3) direct access to the park by improving highways, railway lines, including a route from the Chunnel.

Euro Disney's master plan, including several hotels, was developed by Disney's "imagineers" (theme park designers) and architects who had won an international competition. Some of the original architects were Robert Stern, Michael Graves, Robert Venturi, Frank Gehry, Aldo Rossi, and Antoine Predock.

"Tragic Kingdom"
Euro Disney opened in 1992, but within six months had lost $36 million with projected annual losses of $150 million. The "Magic Kingdom" became known as the "Tragic Kingdom." Based on analyses conducted by many business experts, Euro Disney's troubles can be attributed to the following:

- Business decisions based on Disney's previous success in the United States and Japan rather than paying attention to France and Europe's customs and economy.

- Business decisions that lacked consideration of the seriousness of Europe's recession and inflation.

- Business decisions based on assumptions that the real estate market would continue to increase—hence enabling the corporation to sell properties for a considerable profit.

- Disney executives' assumptions that labor costs would be similar to previous contracts.

- Erroneous assumptions regarding insurance policies, negotiations, and employment policies.

- Disney executives' assumptions that French employees would adhere to Disney's policies and practices.

- Disney executives' assumptions that French farmers would not be upset that their farmland was taken for an amusement park.

- Disney executives' assumptions that French contractors would remain solvent.

- Disney executives' assumptions regarding negotiations that French subcontractors would use creative strategies to accommodate Disney's self-imposed deadlines.

- Disney executives' assumptions regarding culture and lifestyles that affected the amount of money spent on hotels, food, drinks, entertainment, and souvenirs.

- Assumptions that French families had the same travel lifestyle and built environment expectations as Americans.

Rescue Strategies
To avoid closing the park, the following actions occurred: (1) financial restructuring that reduced interest rates and payment deadlines, (2) financial investments from Saudi Arabia, (3) park and hotel operations were improved, (4) costs were reduced, including the elimination of administrative positions, and (5) a revamped marketing plan.

Adapted from: A. Lainsbury, *Once Upon an American Dream: The Story of Euro Disneyland* (Lawrence, KS: University Press of Kansas, 2000); A. Raz, *Riding the Black Ship: Japan and Tokyo Disneyland* (Cambridge: Harvard University Asia Center, 1999).

Figure 5.1 Aerial view of Euro Disney, located close to Paris. As discussed in Box 5.1, considerable farmland was consumed to develop the park and associated planned development, including condominiums, office buildings, and retail stores. (© *Lionel Cironneau/ ASSOCIATED PRESS*)

The Euro Disney case study illustrates the business-related issues, considerations, and problems that can be associated with international practice. This case study provides an example of some of the areas that are important to research when working on an international project, such as location, weather conditions, culture, economics, and government.

Euro Disney also illustrates business practices and requirements that are required for an international project. For example, Disney executives had to negotiate contracts with the prime minister as well as France's local governments. Legal transactions had to be based on France's civil law system. Loans were negotiated according to terms and conditions of local financial institutions. Disney's construction methods and insurance policies were revised to comply with French laws.

In response to protests, Disney's "cast member" dress and grooming standards were relaxed and employment policies were changed to reflect French labor laws. American pricing and operational policies had to be changed after low attendance figures, unoccupied hotel rooms, unsold merchandise, and complaints about long lines, food choices, and the lack of wine in restaurants. After considerable losses,

Disney executives also replaced Euro Disney's American management with French natives and revised marketing strategies to appeal to the French and European population.

International Practice: Regulations and Logistical Requirements

What if the Walt Disney Company had wanted to build a sustainable Euro Disney? How could this be done today? LEED is the best-known green certification system in the United States, but if you are working on an international project, you must be aware of other sustainable-related programs and organizations. For example, in the UK there is BREEAM (Building Research Establishment Environmental Assessment Method), in Australia Green Star, and in Japan CASBEE (Comprehensive Assessment System for Built Environment Efficiency).

In addition, other countries have adopted programs, such as LEED and BREEAM. For instance, Canada and India use LEED and the Netherlands uses BREEAM. France and Germany, among others, have developed their own green rating systems. Thus, when you are working on a sustainable international project, you must research the nation's rating system.

Other sources for international environmental programs are the UNEP, the World Green Building Council (WorldGBC), and the World Business Council on Sustainable Development (WBCSD). In addition, the International Initiative for a Sustainable Built Environment (iiSBE) is a nonprofit organization whose overall aim is to "actively facilitate and promote the adoption of policies, methods, and tools to accelerate the movement toward a global sustainable built environment" (iiSBE 2010).

From an energy perspective the International Energy Agency (IEA) is an excellent resource; this organization serves as an energy policy advisor for 28 countries, including Australia, Japan, the UK, and the United States. The European Union's (EU) active involvement with protecting the environment has resulted in some of the highest energy and sustainability standards in the world.

The world's largest developer of international standards is the International Organization for Standardization (ISO). The ISO standards are as follows (ISO 2010):

1. Make the development, manufacturing, and supply of products and services more efficient, safer, and cleaner.

2. Facilitate trade between countries and make it fairer.

3. Provide governments with a technical base for health, safety and environmental legislation, and conformity assessment.

4. Share technological advances, and good management practice.

5. Disseminate innovation.

6. Safeguard consumers, and users in general, of products and services.

7. Make life simpler by providing solutions to common problems.

Travel Logistics

Unless a project is conducted entirely via virtual space, international practice requires travel. How do you, in an era of travel alerts and warnings, prepare for business travel and perhaps living abroad as an **expatriate** at some point during the design process?

An excellent resource is the U.S. Department of State's Consular Information Program (Box 5.3). The State's Consular program provides the most updated, country-specific information regarding travel alerts, travel warnings, entry/exit requirements, currency regulations, health conditions, safety, security, crime, political disturbances, and addresses of the U.S. embassies and consulates abroad (U.S. Department of State 2010).

According to the State Department, "Travel Alerts are issued to disseminate information quickly about terrorist threats and other relatively short-term conditions overseas that pose significant risks to the security of American travelers. Travel Warnings are issued when the State Department recommends that Americans avoid travel to a certain country because the situation is dangerous or unstable" (U.S. Department of State 2010).

In addition to reading updated information on various websites, the State Department recommends that travelers or citizens living abroad register online or at a U.S. embassy (Box 5.3). When you register with the U.S. government, officials will know how to contact you in the event of a personal emergency or a security alert. For example, these procedures were enacted during the evacuation of U.S. nationals after the devastating earthquake in Japan in 2011.

International travel requires passports to any country outside the United States, including Canada and Mexico; a visa might also be needed. Passport and visa information is available at the National Passport Information Center (see http://travel.state.gov/).

Entry and exiting requirements can include immunization requirements or recommendations. The U.S. Centers for Disease Control and Prevention provides the most updated information, and the Center has health advisories as well as advice on food and drinking water safety for regions and countries.

The U.S. government also makes business-related information available on various websites (Box 5.3). For example, in addition to security information, the Overseas Security Advisory Council (OSAC) has regional news that can affect business operations for U.S. companies that are conducting business abroad. The export.gov website provides (1) export-related assistance, (2) market information, (3) trade leads, (4) free export counseling, and (5) help with the export process (OSAC 2010).

The U.S. Department of Commerce is another excellent resource for business and international trade information. The STAT-USA/Internet website was used to disseminate this information for free, but it was replaced in 2010 with a fee-based, USA Trade Online. This site (http://www.usatradeonline.gov/) has current and historical trade-related news releases,

Box 5.3

Sources for U.S. Travel Information

Organization	Website	Information
U.S. Department of State's Consular Information Program	http://travel.state.gov/	Country-specific information, travel alerts, and travel warnings. Country information includes information on entry and exit requirements, currency regulations, health conditions, safety/security, crime, and political disturbances, and the addresses of the U.S. embassies and consulates abroad.
U.S. Department of State	https://travelregistration.state.gov/ibrs/ui/	*Smart Traveler Enrollment Program* for emergency contacts; also enables people to receive up-to-date information on security conditions.
U.S. Department of State	http://www.travel.state.gov/	International local conditions and laws.
Centers for Disease Control and Prevention	http://wwwnc.cdc.gov/travel/	Most recent health advisories, immunization recommendations or requirements, and advice on food and drinking water safety for regions and countries.
U.S. Department of State	http://travel.state.gov/passport/passport_1738.html	Passports
U.S. Department of State	http://travel.state.gov/visa/visa_1750.html	Visas
U.S. Department of State—Bureau of Diplomatic Security	https://www.osac.gov/Pages/Home.aspx	Security information and regional news that impact U.S. companies working abroad.
Export.gov	http://www.export.gov/	Export-related assistance and market information offered by the federal government and provides trade leads, free export counseling, and help with the export process.
U.S. Department of Commerce	http://www.commerce.gov/	Authoritative economic, business, and international trade information from the federal government.

international market research, trade opportunities, country analyses, and provides access to the National Trade Data Bank.

Checking for Comprehension

* Identify three issues that are important to know when considering international ventures.

* Which two organizations would you contact to learn more about international sustainability standards?

International Business Cultural Dimensions: Attitudes, Values, and Beliefs

The general information in the above section is important for some of the logistics required for international practice; however, a solid understanding of foreign laws, governments, and environmental programs can be useless without an ability to successfully interact with people. For example, the Euro Disney theme park demonstrates how important it is to understand cultural attitudes, values, and beliefs.

To gain an understanding of cultural dimensions that affect business, this discussion is presented in three sections (Figure 5.2). This section reviews national cultures' perspectives regarding **individualism/collectivism, hierarchical/egalitarianism**, time orientation, and work/life balance.

The next section examines intercultural communication styles, and the last section in the chapter analyzes international business protocols, including arranging appointments, conducting meetings, making decisions, negotiating, and socializing.

Intercultural Relationships

Relationships are the essence of the design profession. The ability to build relationships is so important that many job requirements include items such as "Able to fully understand client needs and how this affects the development of design solutions" and "Able to build good professional relationships at all levels, internally and externally."

Building intercultural relationships requires an understanding of the characteristics of national cultures, including attitudes, values, beliefs, preferences, and behavior. First, and

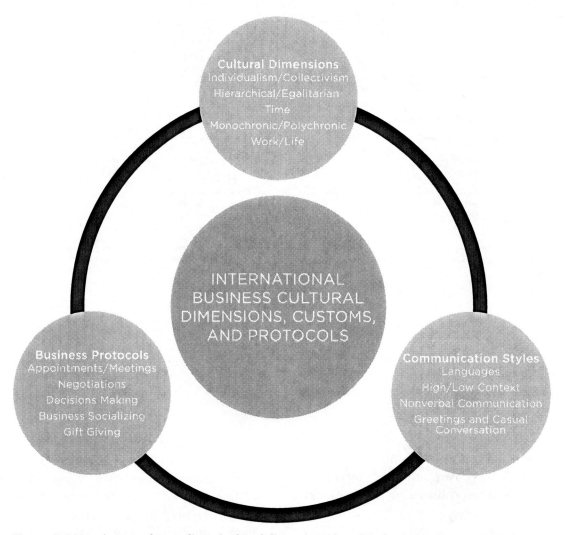

Figure 5.2 To gain an understanding of cultural dimensions that affect business, the content in this chapter is presented in three sections: (1) cultural dimensions, (2) communication styles, and (3) business protocols.

perhaps foremost, is to establish the mindset that *you should follow the business culture of the host country.*

What exactly is **culture**? Culture has many definitions, such as referring to someone as a cultured person when he or she has an appreciation for the visual and performing arts. Social scientists have a very broad view of culture by including all areas that affect the way people live, including housing, food, apparel, education, family, language, laws, ethics, and business practices. This chapter examines the beliefs, customs, language, values, and behavior that affect the business of interior design internationally.

Designers are accustomed to considering cultural context when designing facilities for people with diverse needs, backgrounds, and expectations—these same considerations must be applied to cross-cultural business interactions. Earlier in this book the statement was made that success as a designer required good business practices. Successful business practices require strong relationships. Relationships require trust, respect, honesty, reliability, and understanding (see Chapter 7). This, in turn, requires an understanding of business-related issues associated with culture, lifestyle, interests, customs, work habits, norms, communication protocols, and negotiation styles.

Individualism and Collectivism Orientations

Job descriptions often include the requirement that a candidate must be "able to fully understand client needs." In an era of globalization this is a significant request. Understanding the needs of clients born and raised in your own country can sometimes be a challenge itself. How can you understand the needs of clients in foreign countries?

Ironically, one of the best approaches to understanding other cultures is to first review your own attitudes, beliefs, and preferences. Understanding your values and behavior provides the context for understanding similarities and differences in other cultures. Thus, every topic

in this section and the next two sections will include characteristics of the United States as well as other nations.

As noted at the beginning of the chapter, cultural generalizations identified in these sections are intended to simply provide an overview of a society's culture with the understanding that there are *always* exceptions. Differences can be based on individual preferences as well as **subcultures**, or groups within a culture with their own patterns and expectations.

The important element is that you are aware that cultural differences exist, and that when you interact with people from countries throughout the world, either in person or through virtual means, you apply your knowledge of cultural differences to business practices as well.

Individualism Orientation

One area of cultural difference is how people view their role in an organization as well as society. This cultural dimension is categorized as individualism/collectivism and can affect teamwork (Table 5.1). For example, the United States generally has a culture that values individualism. In the workplace, people are rewarded for individual accomplishments by receiving promotions, raises, and awards.

Résumés and personal reviews tend to emphasize individual responsibilities and achievements. Meetings are viewed as a means to accomplish tasks rather than an opportunity to engage in collaboration. Decisions made by one person or by a majority are well accepted and are often the norm.

Individualism affects loyalties; people are inclined to change jobs when a new position can advance their career and salary. From an organizational perspective, individualism eases the difficulty of layoffs and downsizing.

Individualism results in people feeling comfortable working alone, but when working in a group, they must know their role and responsibilities. Recognition for successfully completing an assignment for a team is appreciated and at times expected.

Table 5.1 International Business Cultural Dimensions—Attitudes, Values, and Beliefs

	Individualism/ Collectivism	Hierarchical/ Egalitarian	Monochronic/ Polychronic	Work/life balance
U.S.	Individualism	Egalitarian	Monochronic	WORK/life
China	Collectivism	Hierarchical	Polychronic/mono	WORK/life
India	Collectivism	Hierarchical	Polychronic	WORK/life
Russia	Collectivism	Hierarchical	Polychronic/mono	WORK/LIFE
Japan	Collectivism	Hierarchical	Monochronic	WORK/life
UK	Individualism	Egalitarian	Monochronic	WORK/LIFE
Germany	Individualism/ Collectivism	Hierarchical	Monochronic	WORK/life
Brazil	Collectivism	Hierarchical	Polychronic	Work/LIFE
Arab World*	Collectivism	Hierarchical	Polychronic	WORK/LIFE

*Area from Morocco in North Africa to Oman along the Arabian Sea, including Algeria, Jordan, Egypt, Iraq, Kuwait, Saudi Arabia, and United Arab Emirates (UAE).

Sources: J. Al-Omari, *The Arab Way* (Oxford, UK: Howtobooks, 2005); M. K. Asante, E. Newmark, and C. A. Blake, *Handbook of Intercultural Communication* (London; Sage Publications, 1979); M. M. Bosrock, *Asian Business Customs & Manners* (New York: Meadowbrook Press, 2006); M. Bosrock, *European Business Customs and Manners* (New York: Meadowbrook Press, 2006); B. L. DeMente, *Etiquette Guide to China* (Rutland, VT: Tuttle Publishing, 2008); K. M. Diran, *Doing Business in Latin America* (New York: Prentice Hall Press, 2009); R. Gibson, *Intercultural Business Communication* (Oxford, UK; Oxford University Press, 2002).

Competitiveness is an element of individualism. Individual accomplishments requires that the person be competitive, which often surfaces during business negotiations. From an individualistic perspective, proposals or contracts are negotiated from the mindset that the terms favor the individual's position regardless of how the outcome affects a group or organization.

Collectivism Orientation

Collectivism focuses on doing what is best for a group (this, for example, is a feature of the Japanese culture). Groups are rewarded for achievements, and résumés highlight team accomplishments. Meetings are the most comfortable format to conduct work.

Decisions can take considerable time because everyone must participate in the decision-making process. Finalizing a decision could take even more time when people who are not involved with the meetings must participate in the process.

Collectivism fosters feelings of loyalty to units beyond the immediate family. Thus, people are loyal to extended family members, coworkers, employers, their community, as well as their country. Reciprocally, organizations and the state have a strong sense of commitment to their people and typically find eliminating positions much more problematic than in the United States.

Collectivism results in people feeling comfortable working in groups and using the group to make decisions. Roles and responsibilities are understood within the context of group tasks and accomplishments. Thus, relationships are highly valued and team membership is based on compatibility. Receiving individual recognition for an accomplishment is an embarrassment. Competitiveness is considered aggressive behavior; harmony is preferred. Thus, negotiations are approached from the perspective that the outcome should benefit a group, organization, nation, or the planet.

Hierarchical and Egalitarian Orientations

Decisions, negotiations, and communication styles are all affected by how people view power and authority. The two cultural dimensions are hierarchical and egalitarian, also known as vertical and horizontal/flat, respectively (Table 5.1).

Hierarchical Orientation

Many cultures, such as Japan, China, India, Germany, and the Arab world, have a hierarchical perspective. Cultures that have a hierarchical point of view associate position with power. Power can be derived from a variety of sources, such as owning the business, seniority, or social ranking. Thus, individuals at the top of the pyramid make decisions with or without input from others in the organization. Meetings are generally to announce decisions; people without authority often do not express their opinions.

Negotiations in organizations with hierarchical viewpoints can be lengthy when the people empowered to make the decisions do not participate in initial meetings—a situation that frequently occurs at the beginning stages of discussions. Thus, it is important to learn as quickly as possible who is responsible for final decisions. This is critical information for any business transaction, but in a hierarchical organization it is essential to learn the proper communication channels and use appropriate titles.

Hierarchical organizations have strict "chain of command" ethos that require employees to converse with the appropriate people at a particular time. Contacting someone near the top of an organization before meeting with those at lower levels can be viewed as rude and could prevent the development of business relations.

Egalitarian Orientation

Societies in the United States, Canada, and the UK tend to have an egalitarian perspective whereby people in a variety of positions can be empowered to succeed. Thus, power is associated with achievements, expertise, and often material wealth, such as expensive homes and cars.

In egalitarian organizations people can communicate with individuals regardless of their position or seniority; hence the reason for using the term "horizontal" or "flat." Meetings are often used for discussion purposes, and it is expected that anyone who wants to can voice an opinion. In these structures, people generally operate under the premise that their input is important. Therefore, bad feelings can result when someone's ideas are not used for a project. Inclusivity can be challenging when you must appease many people and are required to incorporate numerous design suggestions.

Negotiations in organizations with egalitarian perspectives can be lengthy when discussions must occur with various groups, but they could be very short when numerous people are empowered to make decisions. Once you have learned who is qualified to make decisions, determine what is important to that person and use the information as a basis for negotiations.

In addition, even though an organization might function from an egalitarian viewpoint, still try to learn the proper communication channels. There might be several people or even other organizations that need to be involved with a project. It is therefore imperative that you involve all relevant individuals and departments at every phase of the design process.

Time and Monochronic/Polychronic Orientations

Many cultural dimensions are associated with time; knowing the differences can mean success or failure. As always, the important element is that you are aware that cultures have several different ways of viewing time, and when you are establishing business relationships, you should respect dissimilarities and make appropriate adaptations.

Some of the time perspectives involve whether an organization views an opportunity within the context of the past or the future. For example, when people in China or Japan study a business proposition, they want to understand the project from a historical perspective. Often

Russians want to examine business proposals from a futuristic viewpoint.

Some cultures make decisions based on short- or long-term strategies. What do "short" and "long" mean? In the Netherlands engineers develop water management technology for the long term, which to them is 1,000 years.

Societies also have different ways of interpreting punctuality, which can affect project deadlines as well as business relationships. Some **monochronic** countries, such as Japan and Germany, are very strict about being punctual (Table 5.1). Being late is considered rude; it sends a message that the person does not have a sincere interest in building a relationship. In **polychronic** countries, for instance India and Brazil, people appreciate punctuality, but tardiness can be acceptable (Table 5.1).

To be on the safe side, the best policy is to arrive a few minutes early for appointments or meetings and avoid cancellations. Appointments should be scheduled at least two weeks in advance, and dates that might conflict with national holidays as well as undesirable travel times, such as the monsoon season, should be avoided.

Try to select a time of the day for the appointment that is conducive to a culture's work style. For example, preferred times in Latin America are late mornings, and businesspeople in Saudi Arabia might want an evening appointment to avoid the intense heat of the day.

Punctuality viewpoints are transferred to other business-related activities, such as projects, tasks, and relationships. For example, monochronic societies value the importance of completing a task within a prescribed timeline. Thus, meeting agendas have a list of activities along with a fixed amount of time for the specific action. Schedules have start and finish dates, and to be successful, a project must be "on time." In monochronic organizations, therefore, time is a primary driver of business operations, including projects—time is money.

In a polychronic culture, time is elusive; thus it becomes impossible to stipulate timelines. Building lifelong relationships is more important than meeting a deadline. How can one specify the amount of time needed to build and then sustain a relationship? Therefore, when working with a polychronic organization, you should allow time for business relationships and understand that deadlines are not incentives.

Monochronic and polychronic tendencies are also associated with the number of tasks that are completed during a particular period. Monochronic cultures tend to focus on the completion of one task at a time. An example of this is the time management suggestions in Chapter 4. In addition, monochronic perspectives contend that working long hours demonstrates hard work and is a prerequisite for promotions.

Polychronic societies believe that more than one task can be done at a particular time, as in multitasking. In this scenario, several people might talk at the same time in a meeting; interruptions are also common. A meeting time might interfere with another responsibility, and therefore it is understandable why someone might be late. Accepting multiplicity also translates into flexible schedules and revised plans. Moreover, a polychronic culture does not believe that working long hours equates to competency. In contrast, the inability to complete tasks within office hours conveys the impression that ineptness caused the need for more time.

Work/Life Orientations

How a society believes time should be used also transfers to balancing work and life responsibilities (Table 5.1). The general approach to examining this cultural dimension is to ask the following: Do you work to live or do you live for work?

The answer to these questions affects business practices. For example, for many cultures family vacation time is highly valued. Organizations in those cultures have generous paid vacation days, which can be four to six weeks in addition to holidays. Employees typically use their vacation benefits and avoid engaging in business, such as checking e-mail, while on vacation.

If you are working with people in countries such as France, Germany, and the Arab states, your work schedule might have to accommodate the vacation plans of members of your host culture. July and August are common vacation months in many countries, and some businesses completely shut down for vacations.

Preserving personal time also affects activities during evenings and weekends. Societies that believe you should "work to live" use non-business hours exclusively for family and friends. Thus, business-related activities, such as phone calls, e-mails, checking mail, or reading reports, are conducted during office hours. Moreover, discussing business during social events is not appropriate.

International perspectives regarding work/life balance practices also affect a company's policies regarding maternity and parental leave. A survey conducted by the World Economic Forum for the 2010 *Corporate Gender Gap Report* found that "the length of maternity leave and the percentage of salary paid during this period vary greatly from country to country as well as from company to company" (Schwab 2010).

Respondents from 20 countries reveal that the most generous maternity leave policies were the UK (42 weeks) and Norway (52 weeks). India, Mexico, and the United States had the least generous statutory leave provisions. In reviewing the countries that had the most generous maternity benefits, the report concluded that "in Norway 100% of the maternity benefit is covered by social insurance and in the United Kingdom it is compulsory for the employer to pay 90% (most of which is refunded by the state)" (Schwab 2010).

The importance of personal time is just one of the beliefs that underlie cultural behavior and affect business practices. Other topics include attitudes toward age, religion, status, education, and women in the workplace. For example, in Japan and China, seniors are revered and are the highest ranking executives. Seniors are the first to enter a room and to be greeted during introductions, and have the prominent seat at a conference table.

Subordinates always avoid a statement or action that could cause a senior, or other high ranking executives, to lose face. **Saving face**, or avoiding public humiliation, is a critically important Asian concept. Seniors are also highly regarded in several other cultures, such as in Latin America, South Korea, and Mediterranean countries.

Religious beliefs can affect attitudes and might determine when people work. The separation of religion and state, which exists in the United States, is not a universal principal. To uphold religious doctrines, some people will not work during specific observances or might pray five times a day (dawn, noon, afternoon, soon after sunset, nightfall), as is the case in the Islamic faith.

As discussed later in this chapter, religious teachings can also affect views on touching, food customs, and appropriate choice of business gifts. Moreover, religious conflicts have impacted international business (for example, the imposing of trade restrictions as well as other economic sanctions).

Religious beliefs can also influence a person's status—a cultural dimension that can impact business relationships. For example, Hinduism is associated with a five-tier caste system based on family ancestry and occupation. Priests, scholars, and philosophers are at the highest level, followed by warriors, merchants, laborers, and people assigned to cleaning duties or the "untouchables." In India, where Hinduism is the predominant religion, authorities have banned discriminatory practices associated with the caste system, but some people still continue to engage in the practice.

Status can also be determined by a person's ethnicity, gender, occupation, corporate position, family name, social class, wealth, or education. Hence, status might be earned or acquired at birth. People might expect to conduct business with individuals of the same their status.

Educational level as well as an institution's reputation can affect a person's status and subsequent business opportunities. In some cultures, such as in Germany and Mexico, educational level is so important that degrees as well as titles are printed on business cards. Some business cultures, as in South Korea, equate prestige with specific universities; hence, these graduates are afforded more respect.

Gender-based disparities still exist in educational attainment, as well as other issues that are being addressed by several global organizations, such as the World Economic Forum (WEF), the United Nations Development Programme (UNDP), United Nations Educational, Scientific and Cultural Organization (UNESCO), and the International Labour Organization. For example, the WEF globally monitors national gender-based disparities in education as well as economics, politics, and health.

In the WEF's annual report, *The Global Gender Gap Index*, the countries that have the least gender-based disparities are, in descending order, Iceland, Norway, Finland, Sweden, New Zealand, Ireland, Denmark, Lesotho, Philippines, and Switzerland (Hausmann, Tyson, and Zahidi 2010). Germany ranked 13th, the UK 15th, and the United States and Canada 19th and 20th, respectively. Russia was 45th, China 61st, Brazil 85th, Japan 94th, UAE 103rd, India 112th, and Saudi Arabia 129th; the last country on the list of 134 was Yemen.

Some of the same gender views that affect educational opportunities are transmitted to the business world. Thus, regardless of citizenship, women must be aware that gender inequalities exist in the business world, and they should be aware of discriminatory practices (see the next two sections). In an attempt to assess and improve this situation, the WEC has started to track gender inequalities in the corporate world. The organization published its results in *The Corporate Gender Gap Report 2010*.

In addition to examining work/life balance practices, the WEC surveyed topics that are listed in Figure 5.3. Based on these criteria, the results reveal that out of their sample of 20 countries that responded to the survey, India had the lowest percentage of female employees, followed by Japan, Turkey, and Austria.

The countries with the highest percentage of total female employees were the United States, Spain, and Canada. However, in nearly all countries female employees were concentrated in entry- or middle-level positions. The biggest barriers to leadership positions were attributed to "general norms and cultural practices in your country," "masculine/patriarchal corporate culture," and "lack of role models."

In the United States the first two barriers were "masculine/patriarchal corporate culture"

REPRESENTATION OF WOMEN IN BUSINESS.

MEASUREMENT AND TARGET SETTING FOR WOMEN IN BUSINESS.

MENTORSHIP AND TRAINING FOR WOMEN IN LEADERSHIP.

BARRIERS TO WOMEN IN LEADERSHIP.

EFFECTS OF ECONOMIC DOWNTURN ON WOMEN IN BUSINESS.

Figure 5.3 A list of gender inequality topics included in the WEC corporate survey. The results were published in *The Corporate Gender Gap Report 2010*.

and "general norms and cultural practices in your country," but in Canada the barriers were "lack of networks and mentoring" and "lack of role models." The report concluded that "Business leaders and policymakers must remove barriers to women's entry to the workforce and provide equal opportunities for rising to positions of leadership to ensure that all existing resources are used in the most efficient manner and to optimize the flow of future talent" (Schwab 2010).

Checking for Comprehension

* Describe the difference between individualism and collectivism.

* Identify your personal attitudes toward hierarchical/egalitarian orientations as well as monochronic/polychronic orientations.

Intercultural Business Communication Styles

Thus far in this chapter, we have reviewed international practice and logistics as well as several cultural dimensions that can affect business relationships. The focus on intercultural business continues in this section by analyzing communication styles, including languages, contextual factors, and nonverbal communication.

Greetings, introductions, and appropriate casual conversation topics are explored, as well as written business protocols and customs. As mentioned previously, for intercultural relationships to be successful, follow the business culture of the host country. To understand what is appropriate, research a nation's culture and then carefully observe and follow the behavior of people living in the host country.

Languages and Low/High Context

As evidenced by the 56 translations of the word "chapter" in this book, when engaging in international projects, you will be introduced to numerous languages as well as different ways to interpret English. Even if linguistics is not your

strength, you should attempt to at least know how to say a few words and phrases when working in a foreign country.

Trying to learn a host country's language demonstrates your interest in their customs—a gesture that can be viewed as a first step to building a long-term business relationship. At the very least, people will appreciate your effort and can help you to improve your pronunciation and word usage.

There are many programs and classes designed to teach you specifically what you should know to conduct international business. Materials are available online, via CDs and DVD, and in classes at local community colleges.

In addition to knowing some words and phrases in a foreign language, you should be aware of possible problems when communicating with someone whose first language is not English. Because English is becoming the international business language, this situation is common. However, problems and misunderstandings can occur when English is used for business communication between native and non-native English speakers.

For instance, non-native English speakers frequently feel they are at a disadvantage because they do not have the same level of language proficiency. Thus, they might be uncomfortable with discussion topics and contractual terms—a likely situation when forming new relationships. If you are in this position, what can you do to help alleviate these feelings of apprehension?

Helping someone feel comfortable transacting business in your native language requires a close analysis of how you use English, followed by identifying strategies for improving your language skills—important for accurate translations. Approaches to studying your use of English should include reviewing documents you have written, recording your speech, and observing how you use your hands, arms, eyes, and facial expressions when you are talking (see the next section). The last exercise could be done in front of a mirror or by using a video camera.

Your writing and speech should have the following characteristics: (1) accurate grammar; (2) short, concise sentences; (3) consistent usage of terms; (4) frequent summary statements; and (5) free of slang, idioms (i.e., "I could kick myself"), acronyms, industry jargon, and words that could have double meanings in a different language (see foreign language books for examples of double meanings). In addition, make a conscious effort to enunciate clearly, and speak using a moderate speed and volume. The volume of your voice should not decrease at the end of sentences (a common practice that can result in unheard words).

When people learn English as a second language, they are attuned to precise definitions and proper verb/noun usage. Deviating from proper grammar and word usage can confuse non-native English speakers. For example, in the United States a common question is, "What do you do?" A native would respond by talking about his or her job. The use of the two "do's" in the question is confusing to someone not familiar with the phrase. A better question would be: "What is your occupation?"

"How are you?" is another standard question that can be confusing. This question is frequently asked by store clerks or other service employees. Non-native English speakers are often perplexed by why a stranger would ask about their health.

Even when two cultures share English as their first language, there are different word usages. For example, in the UK the words for "elevator" and "apartment" are "lift" and "flat," respectively. Some foreign words, such as "la carpeta" in Spanish, appear to be similar to English words but have a completely different meaning. In this example, "la carpeta" translates to "folder" or "portfolio."

How can you prepare for accurate verbal and written communication? Obviously, you do not know every word and sentence in an upcoming conversation, but you can rely (at least to some extent) on patterns that have developed over the years. For example, what are some of the most common phrases you say when you meet someone?

When you are preparing to travel to a foreign country, write down what you hope to discuss at a meeting/presentation, and then analyze if there could be a problem with how someone translates your words, or if a word sounds like a word in the host country's language. Make the adjustments to your verbal comments as well as to any written documents, including presentation slides.

Frequently, when an organization is transacting business in a foreign country, it will hire **translators** and **interpreters** for written and verbal translations, respectively. Hiring people to translate documents is preferred to using automatic (or software-based) services available online; native speakers are able to translate within the context of the culture. In addition, hiring someone who is familiar with professional terms and practices can be very important for accurate translations.

Local people can help you to understand customs regarding nonverbal communication, taboo topics, social distances, and speaking styles. When using an interpreter, speak in short sentences and talk directly to your business associate—not the interpreter.

High/Low Context

Another consideration associated with intercultural communication is what Edward and Mildred Hall identified as **high and low context**. According to the Halls, "A high context (HC) communication or message is one in which *most* of the information is already in the person, while very little is in the coded, explicit, transmitted part of the message. A low context (LC) communication is just the opposite; i.e., the mass of the information is vested in the explicit code" (1987 p. 8).

Knowing the preferred context can be very useful for planning meetings, presentations, and proposals as well as for casual conversations. For example, a culture that lives with HC communication relies on receiving information from a variety of sources and then internalizes the material for future practice. Thus, if you were preparing a design proposal for an HC society, such as Japan, you would have to allow sufficient time for building relationships as well as preparing considerable background documents (Table 5.2).

These activities are ways that someone in an HC society can internalize information about you as well as your proposal. In an LC culture, such as Germany, facts and figures are important to the communication process. Avoid superfluous information. Thus, if you prepared a design proposal for a German organization, generally the document would focus on rational details and objective data.

High or low context preferences can also help you to understand the appropriate amount of information to give or to present to an organization. If you give too much information to someone who prefers LC communication, the person might think you are being condescending. In contrast, not giving enough information to someone who lives in an HC society could result in uncertainties because that person does not have enough details to make an appropriate judgment.

Nonverbal Communication

HC cultures rely especially on nonverbal communication. However, every culture uses various means to communicate that do not involve speaking or written words. Nonverbal communication is complicated by the ways cultures interpret gestures, facial expressions, eye contact, posture, touch, and use of space (Table 5.2).

As an intercultural businessperson, you must know how people react to nonverbal communication. Using the wrong gesture or facial expression can be very offensive and could cause an irretrievable breakdown in a business transaction. For example, the hand signal for "OK" (a thumb and index finger touch to create a circle) in the United States represents money in Japan, but is seen as vulgar in some countries, such as Brazil, Russia, and the Arab world.

Nodding the head for "yes" and shaking it for "no" is not a universally accepted practice. To communicate effectively, you must be aware of your own nonverbal communication practices as well as the customs of the host country.

In general, the most common uses for gesturing are to greet, beckon, congratulate, and insult. As illustrated in Table 5.2 and discussed in the next section, cultures have numerous forms of greeting that range from mild handshakes to a ritual involving bowing at an appropriate depth for the correct amount of time. Beckoning also involves different gestures; the form used in the United States is not frequently used in other countries. Moreover, using the index finger to motion someone to approach you is an offensive gesture in many countries, such as Japan, Australia, and Indonesia. A common gesture for beckoning in many countries is to have your palm facing down and flex your fingers.

To express appreciation or congratulations, members of most cultures applaud, but gestures that signal approval in the United States, such as the previously mentioned "OK," "thumbs up," or "V" for "victory" have dramatically different meanings. For example, in Australia and Nigeria using a thumb to signal "things are good" is interpreted as an obscene gesture. People in Australia and the UK can be offended when the victory signal is used with the palm facing the wrong direction. In general, avoid pointing or using signals and exaggerated gestures, including moving your hands and arms as you talk.

Depending on the situation, the people involved, and the culture, eye contact can be intimidating, rude, flirtatious, submissive, or respectful. As illustrated in Table 5.2, in Latin America, the United States, and Germany, people believe that direct eye contact demonstrates sincerity as well as interest in the conversation. The custom in the UK is to use direct eye contact with occasional breaks, but in Japan and China people are comfortable with occasional eye contact.

There are varying comfort levels with other movements, such as touching (Table 5.2). Some

Table 5.2 International Business Protocols—Intercultural Communication Styles

	U.S.	China	India	Russia	Japan	UK	Germany	Brazil	Arab World*
Nonverbal: Gestures/Facial Expressions	Moderate	Calm	Moderate	Active	Calm	Reserved	Reserved	Active	Active
Nonverbal: Eye Contact	Direct	Indirect	Broken direct	Direct	Indirect	Broken direct	Direct	Direct	Direct
Nonverbal: Personal Space	Arm length	Close but non-touch-oriented	3 feet space	Close	Distance	Arm length	Distant	Close	Very close
Nonverbal: Touch	Some touch	Close but non-touch-oriented	No touch opposite genders and never touch head	Touch	No touch	Semi no touch	Non-touch	Touch	Touch
Language	American English and Spanish	Mandarin Chinese	Hindi and 20 other languages	Russian	Japanese	British English	German	Portuguese	Arabic
High/Low Context	Low	High	High	High	High	High/low	Low	High/low	High
Greetings	Firm handshake	Slight bow or nod and Western handshake	Namaste and Western handshake	Handshakes; men may kiss women's hand friends kiss on cheeks	Formal bow and Western handshake	Moderate handshake	Handshake	Long handshakes; women kiss on cheeks	Handshake between men
Casual Conversations	Semi-important. No silence.	Important. Silence is normal.	Important. No silence.	Important. No silence.	Important. Silence is normal.	Important. No silence.	Very short talks. No silence partial.	Important. No silence.	Important. No silence.

*Area from Morocco in North Africa to Oman along the Arabian Sea, including Algeria, Jordan, Egypt, Iraq, Kuwait, Saudi Arabia, and United Arab Emirates (UAE).

Sources: J. Al-Omari, *The Arab Way* (Oxford, UK: Howtobooks, 2005); M. K. Asante, E. Newmark, and C. A. Blake, *Handbook of Intercultural Communication* (London; Sage Publications, 1979); M. M. Bosrock, *Asian Business Customs and Manners* (New York: Meadowbrook Press, 2006); M. M. Bosrock, *European Business Customs and Manners* (New York: Meadowbrook Press, 2006); B. L. DeMente, *Etiquette Guide to China* (Rutland, VT: Tuttle Publishing, 2008); K. M. Diran, *Doing Business in Latin America* (New York: Prentice Hall Press, 2009); R. Gibson, *Intercultural Business Communication*. (Oxford, UK: Oxford University Press, 2002).

cultures, such as Brazil's, are accustomed to touching, but the members of other cultures, for example, Germany, can be offended when touched by a business associate. In addition, some cultures differentiate touching according to gender. For example, in the Arab world, businessmen can touch each other, but men are generally not supposed to touch an Arab woman. In this situation, to avoid offense, the best policy is to refrain from shaking hands unless the Arab woman extends hers to you.

Views on touching often align with personal space requirements. Thus, people in the Arab world stand very close when having a business conversation. German businesspeople tend to value their personal space by maintaining long conversational distances (as well as using their office door for privacy).

In addition to respecting personal space in a business setting, it is also important to use proper posture. Generally, to present a professional appearance, you should stand or sit straight and avoid slouching (a sign of laziness in most every culture). Never put your feet on furniture unless the unit is an ottoman. Crossing your leg by putting the foot on the knee of the other leg is not an acceptable position in most countries and is very offensive in places such as India and the Arab world, where one should never show someone the bottom of the shoes—which is very unclean.

Dress

Another form of nonverbal communication is dress and appearance. Wearing inappropriate apparel, such as a short skirt or revealing blouse, to an international business meeting can be a disaster. Yet proper professional attire is fairly simple and generally universal.

Appropriate dress is affected by the person's profession; people in the design field tend to be more accepting of creative apparel. However, most of your clients will most likely be accustomed to professional business dress standards that are generally conservative. Thus, to err on the safe side, you should dress according to a host country's professional business dress code.

For the most part, business dress standards are similar to what was recommended for interviewing (see Chapter 3 and Figure 5.4). For business purposes most nations expect men to wear dark suits, with light-colored shirts and conservative ties. Some countries, such as Brazil and France, are more style conscious, but most people appreciate quality fabrics, a good fit, and a clean and neat appearance. Shoes should be clean and shined. Loafers, due to their casual look, are generally not a good choice.

Women should wear dark, skirted suits or business dresses. Pantsuits may be acceptable, but generally a dress or skirt is a more respected appearance. Blouses should have a high neckline, be in a neutral color, and never be

Figure 5.4 For business purposes most nations expect men and women to wear professional apparel. (© *Purestock/Getty*)

sleeveless. Jewelry should be conservative (avoid dangling earrings), and makeup and perfume should be limited.

Low heels are appropriate, especially in countries such as Japan and China, when high heels could cause you to be taller than your hosts. Shoe selection should also be determined by ease of removal when you are traveling to countries such as India and Japan, whose members remove their shoes when entering homes, temples, and mosques.

To respect Hindus, who believe that cows are sacred, avoid using leather belts, shoes, or handbags in those countries where that religion is prominent. In the Arab world women's bodies must be covered, including upper arms, necks, backs, and legs. To be prepared for an invitation to a religious institution, you should travel with a scarf, a required garment for many denominations.

Greetings and Casual Conversations

Proper professional dress will help to facilitate your greetings, especially the first introduction. Knowing that you are wearing appropriate business apparel can instill the confidence needed to build professional relationships. Equally important is how you greet someone.

As explained in Chapter 3, in the United States when you meet someone, you should stand, smile, make direct eye contact, and extend your hand for a firm handshake. Some of these protocols are used in other nations, but they are not appropriate for many cultures. However, standing to greet someone is an exception—people throughout the world follow this custom.

Smiling is generally a universal expression, but some people are not comfortable having a stranger smile at them. In addition, a smile does not necessarily mean happiness. Some people might smile because of anger, embarrassment, or disapproval, or because they simply like to smile.

Handshakes are another trait that varies across cultures. A firm handshake is generally expected in the United States, but in most other countries that use a handshake, a moderate grip is preferred. A firm handshake can be perceived as aggressive. Gender also plays a role in handshakes. For example, in Saudi Arabia and India men shake hands, but men do not shake hands with native women. Generally, to ease uncertainties regarding the appropriateness of men shaking hands with women, a woman should initiate a handshake by extending her hand first.

Other greeting styles include bowing, kissing, blowing kisses, hugging, and **namaste**. Traditionally nations that bow or nod include China and Japan. A bow is performed with lowered eyes, and the extent of the bow can be light, intermediate, or deep. In Japan the extent of the bow is associated with social status; deep bows are used in highly respectful situations.

Kissing might be on one or both checks and is generally reserved for friends in cultures such as Latin American, Mediterranean, and African. Men in some cultures, such as Latin American, may kiss a woman's hand, but when a man from the United States is a guest, he should not kiss the hands of women.

Hugging is also reserved for friends in several cultures, including Latin America, the Middle East, and Russia. However, as mentioned previously, some people are offended when touched by business associates.

A "namaste" is common in India and involves a slight bow as hands are placed in the praying position. Namaste is also a salutation.

Other considerations related to introductions include titles and business card etiquette. In general, err on the side of formality when meeting a business associate; this can prevent insulting the person. Thus, you should use titles such as Mr., Ms., Madame, Dr., or President followed by his or her last name.

Do not use the person's first name unless he or she has indicated this is what is desired. Be certain of the placement of surnames. For example, surnames are positioned first in China and Japan. In Latin American countries, two surnames are common: those of the person's father and mother.

A business card can have significant meanings to many cultures, so you should follow the host country's protocols regarding what is printed on a card, the colors used, and how a card is presented, read, and stored. In addition to basic contact information, some cultures expect titles, degrees, and details that demonstrate a company's success, such as a founding date and the number of employees.

As a courtesy to the recipient, one side of the card should have the information translated into the language of the host country. Generally, black ink on white card stock is the common color choice; however, the Chinese are impressed when their side is printed in gold ink.

The point at which you give your business card to someone can vary across cultures. Cards can be given immediately, after introductions, or at the end of a meeting. Follow the protocols of the hosts. When you give your card to a Japanese or Chinese person, you should present the card by holding it in both hands. The card should be faced so that the other person can read the card. Accept their card using both hands and pause to read the information and compliment some aspect written on the card, such as noting the person's impressive title.

How you handle the card is very important. Do not put the card in a wallet that is then placed in a back pocket, drop the card in a purse, or use it for an unintended purpose, such as a bookmark or toothpick. Carefully place the card in a business card case. During a meeting you might place the card on the table directly in front of you. When traveling internationally for business, bring several business cards because you will give them to many people.

Casual Conversations

At some point during a business meeting you will be engaged in casual conversation. Minimally, these conversations occur after introductions and prior to business discussions. However, you might be invited to a social event in the evening that will always involve casual conversation. How long should you talk? Can you interrupt someone? What should you talk about? What should you do when there is silence?

Engaging in successful intercultural communication requires an awareness of how answers to these questions vary across cultures. First, casual conversations should be viewed within the context of the meanings associated with nonverbal communication discussed in the previous section. Thus, perspectives regarding gestures, facial expressions, and use of exaggerated movements should also be applied to social conversations.

The amount of time for small talk is often based on a culture's views about the importance of building relationships (Table 5.2). Thus, conversations before a business meeting in Japan or in the Arab world could be very lengthy, but in Germany very little business time is dedicated to chitchat. Generally, in any culture the best strategy is to politely take turns talking, do not interrupt, and refrain from talking for a lengthy period. However, in some cultures, such as Brazil, people enjoy talking for extended periods and freely interrupt each other.

While in conversation, observe the behavior of the "locals" and follow the habits you note. This technique can be used for how long people talk, the use of interruptions, as well as voice volume, speed of conversation, and the use of silence. In the United States and the UK generally people are uncomfortable with silence and will often say something to break the awkwardness (Table 5.2). In Japan silence is important for the thought process and indicates that someone is seriously contemplating the information. Thus, the silence should not be interpreted as a problem or a "no."

Cultures have different attitudes toward the words "no" and "yes." Thus, you cannot assume that when someone says "yes," they are in agreement—or that the lack of a "no" means "perhaps" or even a "yes." A "yes" can be used to signal that someone has heard you or that he or she understands what you have said—a common practice when people are trying to communicate in dissimilar languages.

Some cultures, such as Japan and India, feel it is impolite to say "no" to someone. Thus, they say phrases that may substitute for "no," such as "This task would be difficult to accomplish," or "Thank you, we will take this under consideration."

In addition to knowing how a culture interprets "no" and "yes," it is very important that you know what topics are appropriate and inappropriate for conversations. Discussing a taboo topic will create an embarrassing situation and could completely alienate a business associate. Generally, acceptable subjects center on positive characteristics of a country, such as the beauty of the countryside, a city's architecture, economic progress, or successful sports teams.

Topics that should usually be avoided include religion, politics, personal information, incomes, ethnic conflicts, race, poverty issues, drug wars, stereotypes, social systems, regimes, wars, terrorism, catastrophes, and any criticism of the way the people in the host country live or work.

Demonstrating your humor when someone makes a joke is fine, but because of the various ways that jokes can be interpreted, avoid trying to be humorous. Conversations should be respectful, polite, and void of judgments.

Sensitivity to national heritage is also important. For example, many Brazilians consider themselves "Americans"; thus, people from the "U.S." should use this designation. The UK includes England *and* Scotland, Wales, and Northern Ireland. There are distinctions between the European continent and the UK—and some people in the UK do not consider themselves European.

In addition, be sure to be current on conditions associated with the EU and the euro (http://europa.eu/). These situations are in flux, and you will want to know EU members as well as which countries use the euro. As of 2012, there were 27 members as well as several countries that have applied for membership. The UK is a member of the EU but has retained its own currency, the British pound (GBD, £), rather than the euro.

Intercultural Business Communication Styles

An awareness of a culture's business customs also applies to communication styles. As discussed in Chapter 4, a professional image requires oral and written communication etiquette. Thus, when you are working internationally, your communication style should be adapted according to the customs of the host country. Why is this important?

Clients and businesses appreciate the respect that is demonstrated in using their native format, and a familiar style helps to facilitate the communication process—a critical element when transacting business in a foreign language or when English is a second language. The variances in business communication styles tend to focus on correspondence formats, and differences in words, punctuation, date, times, and numbers.

As previously discussed, business correspondence should be grammatically correct, with proper punctuation and flawless spelling. These rules become even more important when you are communicating internationally. To help ensure accurate translations, it is imperative that business communications have perfect grammar and spelling. How can someone translate a word that does not exist because of a spelling error? The situation could even be worse if the misspelled word can be translated into something offensive. A good solution to using words that can be accurately translated is to refer to basic language books written for a person studying English.

Intercultural communication often requires that business letters be written in a formal style. When writing an intercultural letter, use the appropriate format, address elements, titles, dates, salutations, content, complimentary close, and signature. Generally, use the format in correspondence sent to you or consult the *Merriam-Webster's Guide to International Business Communications*, which provides examples of communication standards for numerous countries.

An appropriate format includes the form of a letter as well as preferred reading direction, alphabet, or characters. Traditional business letters in the United States are **block form**, or all parts of the letter are flush left. In other countries, such as France, the **semi-block form** is used, which includes indenting the first line of paragraphs.

Numerous cultures read from left to right, but as illustrated at the beginning of Chapters 1 and 5, Arabic and Hebrew are read right to left. In addition to the 26-letter Roman alphabet used in the United States, other alphabets include Greek, Russian (Cyrillic), Hindi, and Arabic. Instead of an alphabet, the Chinese and Japanese use characters that represent words and syllables (Figure 5.5).

The way a culture writes elements in their address also varies, and the differences can include (1) how a title is written; (2) line location of a title, name, and position; and (3) line location of street number, city, state, and ZIP or postcode (Box 5.4). Placing a building number or postcode in the wrong format can result in lost mail. For example, in the United States ZIP codes are placed after the state, but in France the postcode precedes the name of the city (e.g., 75002 Paris).

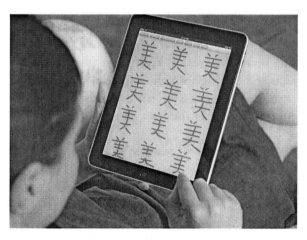

Figure 5.5 As shown on this tablet the Chinese use characters that represent words and syllables. (© *Iain Masterton/Alamy*)

Most often titles are very important for intercultural business correspondence and there are cultural preferences for titles, such as "Dr." for "doctor"; in China "Zhuxi" means "Chairman"; and "Mr." is "Herr," "Senhor," and "Monsieur" in German, Portuguese, and French, respectively. Titles and a person's surname should be used in salutations, but a colon or comma might be the preferred punctuation following the name. As illustrated in Box 5.4 notice that some nations, as in China, place a surname (family name) before the first name (given name).

Dates might appear above or below the inside address, and could be left- or right-justified, as in Germany. The date January 15, 2011 (1-15-2011) is often written 15-1-11 in Europe and 11/1/15 in China. To avoid confusion, the best approach is to use the word for the month.

As demonstrated by the following examples, there are various ways people can be confused with numbers. To prevent confusion about time, reference the time zone and use the 24-hour clock system. Thus, 8:00 p.m. in New York City should be written 20:00 ET.

Be aware that using commas or decimals with numbers can cause confusion. For example, some countries use a decimal point rather than a comma to separate numbers in the thousands, for example, 1.000. These distinctions can be very important when you are listing costs and quantities. Lastly, remember that most of the world uses the metric system of measurement (e.g., meters, centimeters, and square meters) rather than the United State's English system.

> **Checking for Comprehension**
> * What are the differences between high and low context?
>
> * What are some topics that would be appropriate for casual conversations in a foreign country?

Brazil
Ilmo. [honorific] Sr. [senhor or Mr.]
Gilberto [given name] Rabello Ribeiro [family names—Mr. Ribeiro]
Editores Internacionais S.A. [company name]
Rua [street] da Ajuda, [street name] 228 [building number] -6º-[6th] Andar [floor]
Caixa Postal [P.O. Box] 2574 [box number]
20040-000   [postcode followed by four blank spaces]RIO DE JANEIRO [city]—RJ [state abbreviation]

Note translations and explanations are in brackets.

China
Xia [family name] Zhiyi [given name]
International Publishing Ltd. [limited (Ltd.)—a corporation]
14 [building number] Jianguolu [street name—"lu" is "street"]
Chaoyangqu [district name—"qu" is "district"]
BEIJING [city name] 100025 [six-digit postcode]

Germany
Herr [to Mr.]
Gerhardt [given name] Schneider [family name]
International Verlag [company name] GmbH [Inc.]
Schillerstraße [street name—"straße" is "street"] 159 [building number]
44147 [postcode followed by one blank space]DORTMUND [city name]

India
Shyam [given name] Lal [second given name] Gupta [family name]
International Publishing (Pvt.) [private—privately owned] Ltd. [limited]
1820 [office 20 on 18th floor] Rehaja Centre [building name]
214, [building number] Darussalam [street name] Road [street]
Andheri East [suburb name]
BOMBAY   [city followed by a few blank spaces]- 400049 [postcode]

Japan
Mr. Taro [given name] Tanaka [family name]
Kokusai Shuppan [company name] K.K. [Kabushiki Kaisha – corporation]
10 [lot number 10] -23, [building number] 5-chome, [area 5] Minamiazabu [neighborhood name]
Minato-ku [district of the city]
TOKYO [city name] 106 [postcode]

Intercultural Business Protocols: Meetings, Negotiations, and Socializing

Knowing the correct date and time are obviously necessary when scheduling appointments and meetings. This section reviews additional important issues for successful intercultural business engagements, including negotiations and decision making.

Intercultural gatherings often involve socializing and gift giving. The chapter concludes by explaining cultural etiquette with regard to dining and protocols for selecting, presenting, and receiving business gifts. As has been emphasized throughout this chapter, intercultural business protocols require a mindset of following the culture of the host country.

Appointments and Meetings

When you are required to travel to a country to conduct business, you have to know the protocols for making appointments as well as meeting etiquette. As with any organization, some appointments must be made several weeks ahead or just a few days, but the logistics are far more complicated when long flights have to be scheduled or visas are required to enter the country.

Box 5.4

Examples of Addresses for Selected Countries* *(continued)*

Russia	
Natalya [female given name] Konstantinova [female family name]	
Mezhdunarodnoye Izdatel'stvo [company name] TOO [smaller corporation]	
Ulitsa [street] Plekhanova [street name] 6 [building number]	
MOSCOW [city name] 115201 [postcode]	
Saudi Arabia	
Ahmad [given name] Faraj [father's name] Al Ghamdi [family name]	
International Publishing Ltd. [corporation]	
P.O. Box 4732 [P.O. Box]	
RIYADH [city name] 11491 [postcode]	
United Kingdom	
Mr. G. R. [initials of two given names] Robinson [family name]	
International Publishing plc [public limited company—corporation publicly traded]	
Publishing House [building name]	
17 [building number] Swiss Cottage Road [street]	
LONDON [city name followed by six blank spaces]NW3 4TP [postcode]	
United States	
Dale [given name] C. [initial of second given name] Benedetto [family name]	
International Publishing, Inc. [incorporated]	
16850 [building number] S. [south] Union [street name] St., [street] Suite 2250 [suite probably on 22nd floor]	
LAKEWOOD, [city name] CO [state abbreviation followed by one or two blank spaces]80028 [ZIP code]–4892 [Zip code extension]	
Phone System	
IAC (International Access Code) + Country Code + City/Area Code + Local Number	

*Source: T. D. Atkinson, *Merriam-Webster's Guide to International Business Communications* (Springfield, MA: Merriam-Webster, Incorporated, 1998).

The best strategy, therefore, is to plan well in advance, but while you are visiting a country, you might or might not be able to schedule an impromptu meeting. However, some cultures, such as India, might request your attendance at an impromptu meeting, which of course is very important to attend.

As always, the most successful intercultural business relationships occur when you follow the norms of the host country, which includes the ability to contact an organization directly or through an intermediary. Connections through business associates might be needed to arrange a meeting with an organization, or in the case of China, you might need the assistance of the government.

Frequently, connections are essential in cultures that are relationship-focused, such as Brazil, India, Russia, and Japan. Make sure to consult a country's holiday schedule before contacting people to arrange appointments. Trying to schedule a meeting during a national or religious holiday could give the impression that you are unprepared or perhaps understand nothing about the country—not a good way to begin a long-term relationship.

These same understandings must be applied to the various ways that cultures conduct meetings (Table 5.3). In the United States, organizations schedule numerous meetings primarily for the purpose of sharing information and voting on issues. Agendas are sent before the meeting and include a list of tasks with suggested time frames. Meetings are supposed to start and finish on time, and often the chairperson leads the meeting by controlling the flow of information using **parliamentary procedures (Roberts Rules of Order)**.

Other cultures have very different structures for meetings. For example, in cultures that emphasize relationships, meetings are important conversations and discussions. Agendas might or might not be used, but in either case, they are do not drive discussions or timelines. Start times are flexible, although a non-native should always be on time. The end of a meeting is determined by the length of discussions, which could involve time needed to reach consensus on an issue.

The Chinese and Japanese also value time spent building relationships, and their meetings have elements of formality. For example, in China the top-ranking person in the organization enters the room first, followed by associates in descending order of rank. The top-ranking person sits at the head of the conference table, and each associate has a designated seat based on rank.

The Chinese leader makes the introductions and also demonstrates protocols associated with business cards. The presentation of business gifts (such high-quality pens) might be appropriate (Table 5.3). At the end of the meeting, guests leave first. Meetings in Japan also have a formal structure based on seniority and rank, but businesspeople also enjoy socializing in the evening as a means to building relationships.

Following the lead of your host is always the best strategy, which includes appropriate times to speak as well as what to say. Be prepared to avoid or resolve translation difficulties by hiring an interpreter and preparing materials in the host's language. Some cultures, such as Germany and Japan, want considerable information that might need to be sent before the meeting. And as mentioned previously, silence might be the preferred communication style, but try to gauge misunderstandings by asking if further explanations are necessary.

Negotiations and Decision Making

An effective approach to understanding intercultural negotiations and decision making is to examine how cultures view contracts (see Chapter 6). When a society, such as the United States, emphasizes contracts as the binding agreement between two parties, time and energy are dedicated to crafting the ideal contract. Thus, the negotiation process can proceed rather quickly and a signed contract is the final document. In addition, the organization's highest ranking executives are responsible for final decisions, but they might not participate in the negotiating sessions.

In contrast, when a contract is merely an outcome of an agreement created by two organizations seeking a long-term relationship, as in Japan, China, or Brazil, time and energy are devoted to understanding each other and how the partnership can ensure mutual prosperity (Table 5.3). Therefore, the negotiation process requires considerable time, and a signed contract is viewed as the start of the relationship and can be changed at any time. The organizations' highest ranking executives lead negotiating sessions and are responsible for final decisions.

These fundamental differences must be understood when you are entering into intercultural business transactions. Creating a business partnership with countries such as China and Brazil requires patience, and the highest ranking executives must be willing to travel to the host country and meet with authorities for as many times as needed to develop the relationship. Once established, the relationship is considered long-term with a sense of sincere loyalty.

Handshakes demonstrate the true commitment, and contracts are merely a formality that can be revised on the day they are signed as well as the following month or year. Operating under these conditions means that contracts do not require detailed descriptions and parameters. After all, how can one accurately predict what will be appropriate in one, two, or five years? Circumstances and conditions are in constant flux—in a relationship the parties work together to resolve any situations that affect the partnership.

Table 5.3 International Business Protocols—Customs, Etiquette, and Practices									
	U.S.	China	India	Russia	Japan	UK	Germany	Brazil	Arab World*
Meetings	Informal	Formal	Formal	Formal	Formal	Informal	Formal	Semi-formal	Semi-formal
Business Relationships	Semi-important	Important	Important	Important	Important	Semi-important	Semi-Important	Important	Important
Communication Approach	Direct	Indirect	Indirect	Direct	Indirect	Direct/indirect	Direct	Semi-direct	Indirect
Negotiation Process	Fast	Slow	Slow	Slow	Slow	Moderate	Moderate	Slow	Slow
Basis for Decisions	Objective data	Subjective data	Subjective data	Subjective and objective data	Subjective and objective data	Objective data	Objective data	Subjective data	Subjective data
Gift-giving	Not expected	Common	Common	Common	Common and formal	Not expected	Not expected	Common after relationship	Not expected

*Area from Morocco in North Africa to Oman along the Arabian Sea, including Algeria, Jordan, Egypt, Iraq, Kuwait, Saudi Arabia, and United Arab Emirates (UAE).

Sources: J. Al-Omari, *The Arab Way* (Oxford, UK: Howtobooks, 2005); M. K. Asante, E., Newmark, and C. A. Blake, *Handbook of Intercultural Communication* (London: Sage Publications, 1979); M. M. Bosrock, *Asian Business Customs and Manners* (New York: Meadowbrook Press, 2006); M. M. Bosrock, *European Business Customs & Manners* (New York: Meadowbrook Press, 2006); B. L. DeMente, *Etiquette Guide to China*. Rutland, VT: Tuttle Publishing, 2008.; K. M. Diran, *Doing Business in Latin America* (New York: Prentice Hall, 2009); R. Gibson, *Intercultural Business Communication* (Oxford, UK: Oxford University Press, 2002).

In addition to understanding how a culture views contracts, when you are negotiating an intercultural agreement, there are other important elements to consider (many of which were discussed previously in this chapter). For example, it is important to know the cultural dimensions associated with being hierarchical/egalitarian, individualistic/collectivistic, monochronic/polychronic, and low/high context (Tables 5.1 and 5.2).

As discussed previously, what is meant by "yes" and "no"? Should you refer to an organization or a person? For example, in collectivistic cultures it might be more appropriate to say, "We would like *your company* to consider this offer," rather than "We would like *you* to consider this offer." Furthermore, is the host country's communication style direct, indirect, fast, or slow (Table 5.3)? All of these variables affect decisions and negotiations.

Direct or indirect communication styles affect the way information is transmitted and the amount of time required for negotiations. A culture that uses a direct communication style transmits information by providing concise and complete details (German business practices are an example of this style). Generally, information is disseminated in a very linear or organized manner. Efficiency is achieved when people receive all the information needed for a business transaction. However, a direct style can offend people when they are confronted with issues, such as errors or missed deadlines.

Discussions in cultures that favor more indirect communication, such as China, use less detailed information and rely more on shared understandings. Rather than logical and sequential discussions, people might approach several different topics at one time as well as revisiting previous information. In addition, the indirect communication style tends to discourage negative comments and controversy. Consequently, the indirect style requires considerable time to uncover potential problems as well as conclude general discussions. In either communication style, during negotiations it is important to contain your emotions, avoid aggressive behavior, be patient and sincere, and never offer unrealistic promises.

In conducting intercultural negotiations, another issue that should be considered is the preference for attorneys. Some cultures (for example, Japan and Brazil) are comfortable conducting business only with local attorneys. Thus, it might be necessary to hire an attorney native to the host's country.

As mentioned previously in this chapter, gender inequalities exist in many countries. The negotiation process tends to bring gender perspectives to the forefront. In countries that are male-dominated and do not have many women in high-ranking positions, such as the Arab world, India, and Russia, people might feel uncomfortable negotiating with women. In these situations, it might be necessary for the woman to be in the background; if she is the negotiator, her behavior should be nonaggressive. It is also important to emphasize titles, advanced degrees, and credentials to help establish credibility. And as described previously, a businesswoman should wear conservative attire, colors, jewelry, makeup, and low-heeled shoes.

Business Socializing and Gift Giving

The members of many cultures might want to know you as a person before making a business commitment. Thus, international business often involves social events and gift giving, especially in cultures that use relationships as the basis for partnerships (Table 5.3).

Relationships require trust, compatibility, honesty, and sincerity—traits often difficult to uncover in the formality of an office setting. Social events provide the opportunity to learn if someone has the personal qualities necessary for lifelong relationships. Given the importance of business socialization, it is imperative that you are aware of cultural etiquette associated with dining and gift giving.

International business dining experiences occur mostly in restaurants rather than private homes. If you are invited to someone's home, consider that gesture a very high honor and never refuse the invitation. As discussed in the next section, determining what gift to bring the host depends on a culture. Also, you may ask the host or a hotel concierge about the appropriate dress for an event.

In Japan and the Arab world, people remove their shoes when entering someone's home. In Japan guests are given slippers, which they remove when entering the living room. Special slippers are placed in the bathroom for guests to use, and must remain in that room.

In most every situation the host expects to pay the bill (in male-dominated cultures a businesswoman hosting a meeting might have to arrange payment ahead of time with the restaurant staff). Whenever you are invited to a restaurant or someone's home, reciprocate by hosting another gathering at a restaurant. Select a quality restaurant with reasonable prices. Choosing a restaurant that is more expensive than your host's choice can be very embarrassing, especially in cultures that are sensitive to saving face. On the other hand, a cheaper restaurant could insult your guests. When reciprocating a dinner at someone's home, you can ask your guests to select the restaurant.

Lunch and dinner are the most frequent meals for business socialization, but breakfast meetings are popular in the United States and Germany. Keep in mind that cultures eat at a variety of times. Thus, lunch might be 14:00 and dinner could be at 22:00. Learn what the culture is accustomed to and adjust your eating schedule accordingly.

There are also different norms regarding when you should arrive and depart. The best approach is to ask your host what time you should arrive for a social event, but generally you should arrive close to the designated time—within 15 minutes. Departing at the appropriate time could be your preference, or you might have to take a cue from your host. In China, the host determines when an event is over; fruit is often served to signal the end of the evening.

People in most societies appreciate a verbal thank you as well as a handwritten note, but saying "thank you" is not appropriate in India. To show appreciation a guest should say to the host "namaste" (nuhm-uh-stey).

In many situations, business topics are taboo during dining and social events. The purpose of socializing is to get to know each other. Refer to the "Greetings and Casual Conversations" section earlier in this chapter for appropriate topics for casual conversations. When it is appropriate to discuss business, your host will initiate the conversation.

With regard to seating, some cultures, such as the Chinese, have very formal seating arrangements based on the proper seat for the guest of honor, host, and those with seniority. The safest practice is to ask your host to identify your seat.

Dining can be an extraordinary adventure by exposing you to new foods with interesting flavors, unusual textures, and visual delights. The Chinese can have very elaborate meals: 12- or even 20-course banquets. Do not show disgust for food choices or refuse an item. Politely take a very small portion and continue with the meal. Keep in mind that Hindus do not eat beef, and Muslims do not eat pork or generally drink alcohol.

Eating utensils—and their positions—can also vary according to cultural customs. People in the United States normally use a fork and knife in the right and left hands, respectively. Numerous countries use the continental style by reversing the hands used to hold the fork and knife.

Chopsticks are used in many Asian countries. When visiting these countries, such as China and Japan, you should attempt to use chopsticks and follow proper etiquette. For example, when you are not using your chopsticks, they should be placed on the chopstick holder in a parallel position. Chopsticks should never be pointed, crossed, stuck into rice, or used to tap on a surface.

In India and the Middle East you may use your hands as a utensil. In this situation, you will be presented with the amenities needed to wash your hands before and after the meal. Only the right hand should be used for eating, as the left hand is considered impure; it is supposed to be used only for personal hygiene.

Many societies consider toasting a very important custom and use toasts to express good wishes as well as friendship. Toasting protocols can be informal, as in the United States, or very formal, as in China. Protocols can prescribe body positions, expressions, frequency of the toasts, timing, drink quantities, the initiator of the toast, and the honoree's response. For example, in China the first of many toasts is for the honored guests and is done by the host. The first toast is done during or after the first course, and the guest is supposed to reciprocate by toasting the host during the next course.

In China a common expression used for toasts is "Gam bei" or "bottoms up." In Japan, another culture that values toasts, the word is "Kanpai." In Russia a common toasting phrase is "Na Zdorovie" or "Cheers."

Business Gifts

In addition to socializing, many cultures view gift giving as an important sign of friendship and use gifts as a symbol for the establishment of a business relationship (Figure 5.6). Thus, when forming intercultural business relationships, you must be prepared to present and accept gifts.

There are many gift-giving protocols to follow, and giving something that is inappropriate or presenting it to the wrong person or at the wrong time can sever a partnership. To follow gift-giving etiquette, some of the answers you should research are as follows: Is a gift expected? What type of gift is appropriate? What gifts, colors, numbers, and symbols are taboo? Should the gift be wrapped? What taboos are associated with gift wrappings? When should the gift be given? Who should give the gift and to whom? When should a gift be unwrapped?

As illustrated in Table 5.3 many cultures view gift giving as an important form of business

Figure 5.6 Many cultures view gift giving as an important sign of friendship and use gifts as a symbol for the establishment of a business relationship. This beautifully wrapped Japanese traditional money gift envelope illustrates the importance of gift giving and its presentation. ("© *Payless Images, Inc/Alamy*")

etiquette. Generally, gifts that tend to be universally appreciated are items that are representative of the guest's national heritage, local crafts, or chocolates. Other appropriate gifts are quality pens and items with a company's logo.

Gifts to avoid in many Asian and Latin American cultures include clocks, scissors, knives, and handkerchiefs. Clocks and handkerchiefs are associated with death, and cutting devices symbolize severing a relationship. Gifts should not be expensive, but should always be of fine quality. In countries that value saving face, the cost of your gift to the recipient should be considerably less than the value of the gift you were given.

There are intercultural taboo symbols, colors, and numbers to be aware of. Some of the items mentioned above are examples of things that symbolize death. Certain flowers, such as calla lilies, carnations, and chrysanthemums, symbolize death because they are used for funerals. In many Asian countries the colors white, black, and blue represent death, whereas in India green, red, and yellow are lucky colors.

The number of flowers or any other gift also has cultural significance. The Japanese and Germans prefer odd numbers, and the number 4 is unlucky to the Japanese. In addition, many cultures have superstitions about the number 13. Even numbers are auspicious to the Chinese. Taboo symbols and colors should be considered when selecting wrapping paper, and often ties around packages are associated with misfortune because they are usually broken when opening the package.

Generally, the highest ranking executive from each organization is the person to present and accept a gift. Gift giving and receiving should always be done using both hands. Most often gifts are not opened in the presence of the gift giver—another example of a courtesy that is associated with saving face. A gift giver would lose face by the embarrassment that would be caused if the person opened an undesirable gift in public. Generally, gifts are exchanged at the conclusion of a business meeting, but a gift may be presented during introductions. The best approach is to have a gift with you, and as with most intercultural business etiquette, follow the behavior used in the host country.

Checking for Comprehension
- How would you describe the basic differences between negotiations in the United States and in Brazil?

- Identify three issues that are important to business gift giving.

This chapter reviewed many aspects related to international practice, including logistical considerations and business cultural dimensions. Topics also included intercultural business communication styles as well as business protocols for meetings, negotiations, and socializing. As mentioned at the beginning of the chapter, knowledge of cultural attitudes, beliefs, and values are important for international projects as well as today's diverse workplace.

The importance of respectful attitudes becomes very apparent when considering long-term client relationships, as explored in Part III. Before discussing client relationships, we will complete Part II with Chapter 6, which addresses additional important elements associated with working in a design firm. The chapter begins by explaining professional compensation and fees, and continues with an overview of general accounting and administrative practices. The chapter ends with a summary of the U.S. laws that can be applicable to the work of an interior designer. Concluding Part II, *Working in a Design Firm* establishes the background for Part III, *Long-Term Client Relationships and Project Responsibilities*.

Knowledge and Skills Summary

Highlights
- Being successful in a global marketplace requires an understanding of international collaboration practices as well as logistical requirements critical to business operations.

- Global alliances are driven by market demands as well as accommodations provided by the host country.

- Contractual agreements with global alliances must concisely prescribe each party's responsibilities within the context of mutually understandable design and business practices.

- Cultural dimensions that affect business include individualism/collectivism, hierarchical/egalitarianism, time orientations, and work/life balance.

- Cultural dimensions affect attitudes, values, behavior, and beliefs.

- Intercultural business communication styles are affected by language and nonverbal communication.

- Intercultural business etiquette includes greetings, introductions, conversation topics, and written business protocols.

- Intercultural business protocols include arranging appointments and conducting meetings.

- Intercultural business transactions require appropriate strategies for negotiating and decision making as well as following socializing etiquette.

Key Terms

block form letter

collectivism

culture

egalitarian

ethnocentrism

expatriate

hierarchical

high context

individualism

interpreter

low context

monochronic

namaste

parliamentary procedures (Roberts Rules of Order)

polycentrism

polychronic

saving face

semi-block form letter

subculture

translator

Projects

Philosophy and Design Project

Refer to the tables in this chapter that summarize international business cultural dimensions and protocols. Select your native country and one other country listed in the tables. Research these two countries and conduct a comparative analysis of each country's profile. Identify key attributes that would be important for doing business in the foreign country.

Based on your cultural heritage, how would you have to adapt to the host country? Develop a presentation (approximately 10 minutes) of your analysis and include images that support your statements.

Research Project

There are many international programs and organizations, such as the World Bank, that are important to the work of an interior designer because they give us updates regarding economic issues, environmental concerns, and business opportunities. Use the Internet to identify international programs and organizations that could help you conduct business in foreign countries.

Create a summary table of the programs and include the following types of information: (1) purpose of the organization, (2) services, (3) news, (4) projects and operations, (5) events, (6) history, and (7) publications.

Human Factors Research Project

Imagine that your supervisor has asked you to collaborate on a project in Shanghai. In a team of three to five members, develop and implement a plan for preparing for your group's first visit.

Develop an oral presentation (approximately 15 minutes) that includes the following: (1) a detailed background on Shanghai, (2) attitudes, values, and beliefs of the people that could affect business, (3) business protocols related to communication styles, and (4) business protocols related to customs, etiquette, and other practices.

References

Association of Southeast Asian Nations (ASEAN). 2010. *Aims and Purposes*. http://www.aseansec.org/about_ASEAN.html. Accessed July 15, 2010.

Atkinson, T. D. 1998. *Merriam-Webster's Guide to International Business Communications*. Springfield, MA: Merriam-Webster, Inc.

Council for Interior Design Accreditation (CIDA). 2011. *Professional Standards*. http://www.accredit-id.org/. Accessed February 10, 2012.

European Union (EU). 2010. *Member Countries*. http://europa.eu/. Accessed November 22, 2010.

Fairtrade International (FLO). 2010. *What We Do*. http://www.fairtrade.net/what_we_do.html Accessed July 30, 2010.

Hall, E. T., and M. R. Hall. 1987. *Hidden Differences: Doing Business with the Japanese*. Garden City, NY: Anchor Press/Doubleday.

International Initiative for a Sustainable Built Environment (iiSBE). 2010. *About iiSBE*. http://www.iisbe.org/. Accessed November 22, 2010.

International Monetary Fund (IMF). 2010. *About the IMF*. http://www.imf.org/external/. Accessed July 14, 2010.

International Organization for Standardization (ISO). 2010. *Discover ISO*. http://www.iso.org/iso/about/discover-iso_what-standards-do.htm. Accessed November 17, 2010.

Lainsbury, A. 2000. *Once Upon an American Dream: The Story of Euro Disneyland*. Lawrence, KS: University Press of Kansas.

North American Fair Trade Organization (NAFTA). 2010. *North American Fair Trade Organization (NAFTA)*. http://www.ustr.gov/trade-agreements/free-trade-agreements/north-american-free-trade-agreement-nafta. Accessed July 29, 2010.

Overseas Security Advisory Council (OSAC). 2010. *Overseas Security Advisory Council (OSAC)*. https://www.osac.gov/Pages/Home.aspx. Accessed November 1, 2010.

Raz, A. 1999. *Riding the Black Ship: Japan and Tokyo Disneyland*. Cambridge: Harvard University Asia Center.

Schwab, K. 2010. *Corporate Gender Gap Report 2010*. http://www3.weforum.org/docs/WEF_GenderGap_CorporateReport_2010.pdf. Accessed November 22, 2010.

United Nations Environment Programme (UNEP 2010). *Environment for Development*. http://www.unep.org/. Accessed November 22, 2010.

United Nations Office on Drugs and Crime. 2010. *Data and Analysis*. http://www.unodc.org. Accessed November 22, 2010.

U.S. Department of State. 2010. *Travel.State.Gov*. http://travel.state.gov/. Accessed November 10, 2010.

USA Trade Online. 2010. *The Official Source for U.S. Merchandise Trade Data*. http://www.usatradeonline.gov/. Accessed November 22, 2010.

World Bank. 2010. *Economy Rankings*. http://www.doingbusiness.org/economyrankings/. Accessed September 6, 2011.

World Bank. 2011. *Environment*. http://data.worldbank.org/topic/environment. Accessed September 6, 2011.

World Bank. 2011. *Internet Users*. http://data.worldbank.org/indicator/IT.NET.USER.P2. Accessed September 6, 2011.

World Economic Forum. 2010. *The Global Gender Gap Index*. http://www.weforum.org/en/Communities/Women%20Leaders%20and%20Gender%20Parity/GenderGapNetwork/index.htm. Accessed November 22, 2010.

CHAPTER

6

6. Fejezet (Hungarian)
Kafli 6 (Icelandic)
Bab 6 (Indonesian)
Caibidil 6 (Irish)
Capitolo 6 (Italian)

After learning the content in Chapter 6, you will be able to answer the following questions:

* How do I charge for my design services?

* How do I estimate costs for a project?

* What are some of the forms I can use to manage projects?

* What are some of the basic business forms used by a design firm?

* How do U.S. laws affect my work as an interior designer?

Chapter 4 began Part II by examining personal management strategies, professional ethics, multidisciplinary collaboration, and Western business etiquette. Other important aspects of working as an interior designer were further explored in Chapter 5, which reviewed international practice ventures, cultural dimensions, and intercultural communication styles and business protocols. This chapter concludes Part II by examining other business aspects you should understand when beginning your career.

The first section of this chapter describes various methods used for compensation and fees, and includes an analysis of the variables that can affect fees, prices, and expenses. The chapter continues by providing an overview of some of the daily accounting and administrative forms and practices related to the work of an interior designer, such as purchase orders, invoices, employee expense reports, and **work orders**.

The last section in the chapter reviews how U.S. laws affect the design profession by specifically examining intellectual property law, tort law, contract law, and international law. After studying Chapter 6, you will be prepared to progress to Part III, "Long-Term Client Relationships and Project Responsibilities," and continue learning about many facets of the work of an interior designer.

Professional Compensation and Fees

Interior designers' salaries—an obviously critical element of your first job—have already been discussed in this book. The funds for your salary require compensations and fees that are paid to the firm by clients. How will you charge your clients? When should you charge nothing, as in **pro bono** work for community service?

When you begin your first job, you must understand the importance of fees as well as the various approaches to charging your clients. Charging too much can result in not being hired. Not charging enough can also affect business when low fees result in mediocre designs.

How? Inadequate compensation could reduce time needed to identify all the needs of the client, ideal products, or the most efficient space plan. To optimize profits, designers should estimate fees using at least two different methods, which are discussed in this section.

Over time, every firm establishes a formula that enables it to be profitable. Even though there could be many different ways to charge clients, fundamentally they are based on not supplying merchandise, supplying merchandise, or a combination of the two.

This section reviews the basic ways of charging clients, with the understanding that your company will have its own strategy that you will have to use. Your employer's strategy will include the consideration of many variables related to a project, such as the size of a project and past experiences with a client. Knowing the fundamentals of fee structures allows you to better understand your employer's procedures and how to implement those policies when you are working on projects.

Hourly Fees

As is the case with many other professions, **hourly fees** have become a very common way to charge clients for professional services. According to ASID approximately 60 percent of the interior design firms responding to its survey reported using hourly fees (ASID 2010). Basically, when using an hourly fee structure, a designer receives a **retainer** and is compensated by the hour for services provided to a client. Fees are deducted from the retainer.

The concept appears simple, but successfully implementing hourly fees to ensure profits requires several considerations that focus on determining (1) appropriate amounts, (2) **billable services**, (3) travel expenses, and (4) a system for logging time.

Often a firm's hourly rate is based on the local prevailing amount. Thus, in major cities, with greater overhead expenses, hourly rates tend to be higher than in rural areas. The local rate can be discovered by networking, discussing fees with clients, or reviewing national databases, such as those provided by *Interior Design* magazine in their annual "100 Giants" (Figure 6.1) international profile. For example, in 2011 *Interior Design* reported that the median hourly rates were the following: principal/partner $200; project manager $157; designer $115; and other design staff $93. The median annual salaries were principal/partner $140,000; project manager $97,000; designer $64,662; and other design staff $50,000.

To determine hourly rates, firms often use salaries as well as a **multiple** or **multiplier** to account for their other expenses, such as employee benefits, rent, utilities, supplies, equipment, and employee salaries that are typically not billable, such as accountants, attorneys, and cleaning staff (see Part IV).

Multipliers generally range from 2.5 to 3.5. For example, let's assume that a designer's

annual salary is $70,132 and that he or she works 40 hours per week for 50 weeks, which equals 2,000 hours per year. Using a multiplier of 3.5 times the designer's annual salary and dividing the amount by the number of hours worked per year results in charging a client $125 per hour for the designer's services:

$70,132 (annual salary) × 3.5 (multiplier)
= $245,462, or $250,000

$250,000 / 2,000 (hours per year)
= $125 hourly rate

For large projects a designer could be full-time for a year; using the example described above, the client would be charged $250,000 per year. In other situations the charge to the client is determined by multiplying the hourly rate by the number of billable hours. Thus, a client would be billed $7,500 for 60 hours of professional services for the designer in the above example. Or:

60 (hours of consultation) × $125 (hourly rate)
= $7,500 (total charges)

What are billable hours? Generally, clients are charged for any professional services that are associated with a project. An approach to conceptualizing "professional services" is to think about all the tasks that are completed at each phase of the design process. Thus, you would charge a client for programming, schematic drawings, design development, contract documents, and contract administration. Within these broad categories you would charge for tasks associated with the project, such as meetings with clients, other professionals, suppliers, and contractors as well as research that might be needed for products, codes, and green certifications.

Travel Expenses

Determining how to charge for time spent traveling to and from a site, or **portal-to-portal**, can be complicated. Some clients might object to being charged professional rates for time spent driving or flying. Yet the designer is traveling for the purpose of the project, and that time could have otherwise been spent providing a service that was billable at the professional rate. The solution that tends to appease both sides is to bill for travel at half the designer's hourly rate.

Fees might also be augmented with travel expenses, such as mileage for local destinations, airfare, taxis, hotels, and meals for distant locations. These items might be reimbursed according to the exact costs, or a firm might have a **per diem** (by the day) rate that is charged to the client.

Travel expenses as well as any billable services must be precisely outlined in an agreement (contract) with a client. Clients must know upfront what you will be charging them for, and at what rate. This is a significant part of conducting business in an ethical, fair, and professional manner.

Time/Activity/Travel Logs

Being able to bill a client for professional services requires keeping excellent records. Clients might receive a **billing statement** monthly, quarterly, or at the end of a project. At any time the client might ask you to explain an amount on his or her bill. Thus, from the very beginning you must learn to keep a log of project-related activities (Table 6.1). The information is essential for billing a client, and the data can be very helpful when estimating consultation fees (see

Table 6.1 Time/Activity/Travel Log

Client: Smith				**Week of:** May 3 – 8, 2012			
Project Number: 5656				**Project Phase:** Contract Administration			
	Monday May 3, 2012	**Tuesday May 4, 2012**	**Wednesday May 5, 2012**	**Thursday May 6, 2012**	**Friday May 7, 2012**	**Saturday May 8, 2012**	**Weekly Totals**
Individual(s)	Smith, Designer, Contractor	Designer & contractor	Designer	Designer	Smith, Designer, Contractor	Smith, Designer, Contractor	
Activity Code(s)	D, E	D	A, C	A, C	D	D, E	
Location(s)	New Orleans	New Orleans	New Orleans	New Orleans	New Orleans	New Orleans/ return	
Billable Time	5 hours	6 hours	7 hours	8 hours	6 hours	2 hours	34 hours
Airfare	$350						$350
Auto Mileage							
Parking/Tolls							
Hotel	$200	$200	$200	$200	$200		$1,000
Food	$75	$75	$75	$75	$75	$35	$410
Taxis	$50	$25	$25	$25	$25	$50	$200
Other							

Note project number and project phase.

Use these activities as a guide. Create a list that works for your tasks.

An Excel spreadsheet enables you to automatically total these rows.

Activity Codes
A—Drawing
B—Meeting
C—Shopping/Purchasing
D—Site Visit
E—Travel
F—Interviews/Observations/Charrettes
G—Writing Specifications
H—Presentation boards/models

the section "Determining Compensation and Fees" coming up in the chapter). To get into the practice of recording your time, complete the form as you work on class projects.

Using an Excel spreadsheet is an effective means of keeping records and executing the calculations. Basically, as illustrated in Table 6.1, your records should include a date, client, project number, project phase, amount of time, location, activities, and who was involved with the tasks.

Text messages are an excellent way to record data, especially when you are away from your computer. By texting at the start and finish time of an activity, you will automatically have the amount of time and the date. Your text message can be brief, just noting the client's name, location, and task. The text message can then be used as the basis for logging more detailed information into your client's records. There are also numerous apps for mobile devices that enable you to record data and images.

Flat or Fixed Fees

How can you quote an exact amount for professional design services? The **flat** or **fixed fee** method is used for this purpose, and according to ASID, is used by approximately 20 percent of the interior design firms that responded to the organization's survey (ASID 2010). As noted in the previous section, considerably fewer design firms use the flat fee than use the hourly fee. However, the effects of the recent recession, as well as other factors, are seemingly changing these percentages.

Flat fees are becoming more common because knowing a fixed amount makes it easier for an organization to develop and to adhere to a budget—a very important consideration when resources are limited. Some firms use a flat fee when it is unlikely that the firm will be supplying merchandise—a potential source of considerable income. In this situation receiving a flat fee helps to ensure that the design firm will be compensated for time expended on creating designs, as well as writing specifications for items purchased by the client or another firm—an escalating issue due to the ease of being able to acquire items online at discounted prices.

Estimating Flat or Fixed Fees

There are many ways that a design firm determines a flat fee, which might or might not include travel expenses. Some are determined by hunches, which have the potential of becoming financial disasters. Generally, profitable flat fees require considerable experience working with a specific client or type of project. Methods for determining flat fees include examining past records, using square footages/meters, and using a percentage of project costs.

To be able to use past records as a means to estimate flat fees requires excellent time/activity logs (Table 6.1). These records can serve as the basis for how long it takes a firm to execute its work, including the number of employees and the required expertise. For example, based on past experiences a firm can estimate that a project will minimally require the full-time expertise of a principal and a project director throughout the duration of the project (Table 6.2).

Another approach to estimating a flat fee is to base the compensation on the project's square footage/meters and include a factor that accounts for items that could increase costs, such as a client wanting expensive materials or custom furniture (Table 6.2).

Flat fees can also be determined by using a percentage of the project costs. In this method, a designer is compensated for his or her time and expertise based on the amount of the project's budget.

When a firm has considerable past experience and has attained a high level of stature, a supplemental amount or **value-oriented fee** might be applied to the fees for professional services.

No matter how the flat fee is determined, a very important clause that must accompany an estimate is a time limitation. The agreement must stipulate that design services are concluded by some condition, such as a specified date, phase of the design process, or number of hours.

Table 6.2 Estimating Fees Based on Time and Square Footage

Estimating Fees Based on Amount of Time Required for Past Projects					
Individuals Needed for New Project	Project Phase(s)	Salary/ Month	Total Months	Multiplier	Total Estimated Fee
Mary Designer	All phases	$6,200	12	3.5	$260,400
Tom Designer	All phases	$7,000	12	3.5	$294,000
Carl Designer	Contract administration	$5,000	6	3.5	$105,000
Total Estimated Fees for Project					$659,400
Estimating Fees Based on Square Footage					
Type of Project	Location	Square Footage/ Meter	Average Fees for Type of Project	Job Factor Multiplier*	Total Estimated Fee
Museum Renovation	Miami, Florida	25,000	$3.00	1.2*	$90,000

These figures are determined by multiplying the salary × the number of months × the multiplier.

This figure is the sum of the column.

This figure is determined by multiplying the square footage × the average fee × the multiplier.

*Job Factor Multiplier	
None	Do not expect additional costs
1.2	Expect some additional costs
1.4	Expect additional costs
1.6	Expect substantial additional costs

Cost Plus Percentage Fees

Interior designers can also be compensated by the **gross profits** that are realized through selling merchandise to a client. Gross profit is the difference between what a designer charges a client for an item and the designer's **cost** from a manufacturer or **wholesaler**. For projects that require considerable *new* merchandise the **net profit**, or money earned after expenses, can be considerable.

Compensation can be calculated by either adding on a percentage of the cost of an item (cost plus percentage) or deducting a percentage from the list price of an item (retail-based fees).

When supplying merchandise, a client provides a **deposit** of generally 50 percent with a signed contract. According to the ASID report, approximately 20 percent of the respondents used cost plus percentage or retail for their compensation method, with **markups** between 20 and 40 percent (ASID 2010). Often these methods are combined with hourly rates or flat fees.

Calculating the client's cost for an item requires knowing the designer's cost for the merchandise. For example, if the **net price** or the cost a manufacturer charges a designer for a chair is $800 and there is a 20 percent markup, the client would pay $960 for the chair:

$800 (net price) + $160 (20% markup of $800) = $960 (client cost)

Receiving $160 for one chair might not appear to be fair compensation, but if the order was for 1,000 new chairs, the gross profit is $160,000.

Note that $160,000 is the *gross* profit. If the designer is responsible for other expenses, such as delivery and repairs for any damaged goods, that amount is subtracted from the $160,000. When the percentage of the markup is low, as in this example, the client is normally responsible for any additional expenses. Again, percentages added to the cost of an item are between 20 to 40 percent.

Retail-Based Fees

From the other end of the spectrum, if a designer is using retail-based fees, then a percentage is subtracted from the manufacturer's **list price**. For example, a manufacturer's list price for the chair described above could be $1,600 ($800 × 2 = $1,600). A common percentage used in retail-based fees is 10 percent. Thus, the cost charged to the client is $1,440 and is determined using the following calculations:

$1,600 (manufacturer's list price)
− $160 (10% of $1,600)
= $1,440 (client cost)

Because the net cost of the chair was $800, the gross profit was $640 and was calculated in this manner:

$1,440 (client cost) − $800 (net cost to designer)
= $640 (gross profit)

Note that when using the retail-based fee structure, you must deduct any expenses from the gross profit. Thus, a designer would have to deduct from the $640 all expenses directly and indirectly associated with the purchase of the chair.

You might have noticed that there was a considerable difference in the amount of profit that was realized when using the cost plus percentage and retail-based methods: $160 and $640, respectively. Why would a designer use the cost plus percentage when the retail-based fee structure results in greater profit?

As discussed in the next section, there are many factors that must be considered when determining fees, but fundamentally a designer has to calculate a price that both provides a profit *and* is comparable to the competition. In the situation described above, a designer most likely would use the cost plus percentage fee for a project that required the purchase of a considerable amount of merchandise. The retail-based method could be used for a client who is purchasing only a few chairs.

Determining Compensation and Fees

Charging a client for professional services requires knowing more than how to calculate hourly rates, flat fees, cost plus percentages, and retail. When determining fees, a designer must consider numerous conditions that can affect the final compensation. In addition to the variable characteristics of each project and client, calculating fees requires an understanding of operational budgets, manufacturers' pricing policies, and general expenses.

Variables Affecting Compensation and Fees

As discussed previously, past experience can be an effective means for determining compensation and fees. But within these past records there are a multitude of variables that affected the fees and outcomes of that project. Knowing these variables is essential when a firm is developing an estimate, even if merely contemplating becoming involved in a project.

What factors affect compensation and fees? Generally, these factors can be categorized in the following manner: (1) a design firm's operating policies, (2) project-specific requirements, and (3) direct and indirect job costs (Figure 6.2).

Factors that are considered when establishing compensation methods include the firm's annual budgeted expenses such as rent, utilities, office equipment, supplies, insurance, and by far the biggest item—personnel salaries and benefits or the **direct personnel expense (DPE)**. (see Part IV.) Annual budgeted expenses and a profit dollar amount are used to determine the number of hours that must be billed to a client.

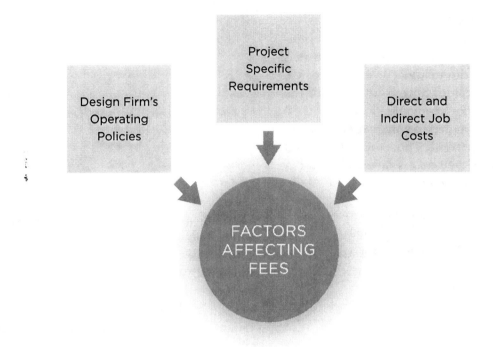

Figure 6.2 Factors that affect fees and compensation can be categorized into three areas.

Obviously, the larger the firm the greater the expenses, including the need for support staff, whose DPEs are not billable. In addition, larger firms are more likely to have a headquarters and other offices in major cities with high rents. As discussed in the previous chapter, more firms are opening offices in international locations. Thus, to cover all of these expenses and also earn a profit, larger firms generally charge higher rates and fees than design firms with low **overhead**.

In addition to a firm's annual expenses and selected profit, other considerations that affect fees are related to the organization's experience and areas of specializations. Both of these aspects can be used to justify higher or lower fees. For example, when a design firm has many years of experience, its fees might be high to reflect both the company's esteemed reputation as well as its high level of expertise.

On the other hand, a firm with considerable experience might elect to lower fees for certain projects because it has a personal interest in the design and realizes that its years of experience can reduce the amount of time normally

required to execute a project. There are many other reasons why a design firm would lower fees for a particular project. For example, the project might result in excellent referral business, or it might give the firm visibility in a high-profile city and perhaps throughout the world.

When a firm does not have considerable experience with a type of project or area of specialization, fees can be too high or too low. Additional amounts are intended to cover unexpected expenses that can occur when a firm is engaged in a new experience. For example, inexperience can increase the amount of time needed to research sources, interview clients, develop design concepts, and supervise installations. Fees that are too low are often due to a lack of awareness of real costs.

Project Variables

When determining fees, what should you know about a project? A primary consideration is a firm's experience or the lack of experience with a client. Direct experience with a client can inform you about characteristics that generally are unknown without personal contact, such as an individual's indecisiveness or perhaps the tendency to want to change decisions at the last moment. These actions require additional time and might result in increased expenses, such as extra shipping charges due to returns.

From the other perspective, when past experiences with the client were wonderful, there might be little concern that designers will be required to work extra hours or might have to pay for unexpected expenses. Thus, past experiences with clients could prompt designers to increase or lower compensation amounts.

When a client is new to the firm, the only option might be to charge according to the type of project, or you might be able to detect favorable or unfavorable characteristics during interviews (see Chapter 7).

Factors that affect the budget include the amount of square footage/meters, the number of people occupying the space, and the quantities of furniture, furnishings, and equipment. Generally, for large budgets, a designer can apply a small rate when using the cost plus percentage method. Hourly rates might also be lowered because of the high volume of work. The opposite generally occurs when projects have a small budget; percentage amounts increase when using the cost plus percentage method, and increases can be applied to hourly rates.

Any condition or factor that requires the designer's involvement beyond the expected responsibilities associated with the design process should be considered when determining fees. This could include LEED certification, custom designs, tight schedules, underdeveloped budgets, and collaboration with community representatives. The status of negotiating a lease can also affect fees. Without a signed lease a client might have to select another facility that might need substantial remodeling.

The decision-making process can also affect fees. Time is minimized when a designer can directly contact the decision maker for answers. When this is not possible, delays and misunderstandings can occur—two situations that can affect fees as well as the overall success of the project and the overall quality of the relationship.

The project's location is a significant consideration when setting fees. Designing locally is completely different than being responsible for a project in another state or on the other side of the world. In addition to travel expenses, which should be reimbursed by the client, out-of-town projects require a firm to research fees, billable services, codes, regulations, and tax laws. The firm must find and hire local warehouses, suppliers, contractors, delivery businesses, and installers.

Regardless of location, the designer must clarify charges, including the responsibilities of the designer and the client (see Chapter 7). If a designer has significant responsibilities, such as purchasing all merchandise and comprehensive supervision, the compensation schedule and contract must reflect these tasks. From the other perspective, fee structures should be altered and detailed in a contract when a client is responsible for aspects of the project such as purchasing products and working with contractors.

Remember, as you determine fees, be consistent across projects and clients. Clients can learn how much other people are paying for a designer's services. Different fees for equivalent services gives the impression that a designer is not being honest and cannot be trusted—two important attributes that a professional must have for successful client relationships (see Chapter 7).

Pricing Practices and Expenses

As you calculate fees for a project, two other important considerations are manufacturers' pricing policies and expenses. Numerous terms are used for prices; thus, it is very easy to be confused when trying to determine what price to charge a client. If you use the wrong price chart, you could charge a client too much or you could give them a product for an amount that is less than what the firm paid.

Generally, manufacturers, vendors, and suppliers use two separate price charts in order to prevent a client from discovering what a designer paid for a product or service. One price chart has the designer's cost, and the other chart has the list or **retail price** (Figure 6.3). Obviously, with the cost plus percentage method, a client will know the designer's cost—one of the reasons why clients prefer this compensation method. However, for most fee methods you must keep retail prices separate from designer's costs.

How can a designer know which price chart to use? When you need a price that is to be paid by the client, refer to a manufacturer's suggested retail price. When you need to know how much a designer will pay for an item, refer to the manufacturer's cost or net price.

When you are referring to a manufacturer's price list, be sure to note the effective dates. Manufacturers' prices are continually updated, and this possible change might not yet appear on the charts you are using for pricing. Check your manufacturers' website for current prices.

In addition, be aware that a considerable amount of time could transpire between when you quote a price and order an item. Thus, the price on the manufacturer's **invoice**, or bill, could be higher than what you had originally budgeted. In these situations you might have to increase the price to compensate for anticipated price changes.

Discounts

In addition to understanding pricing terms, be aware of potential discounts and how they can be applied to a price. For example, some manufacturers provide **quantity discounts** when you are purchasing a large number of items or significant yardages (as is the case with textiles).

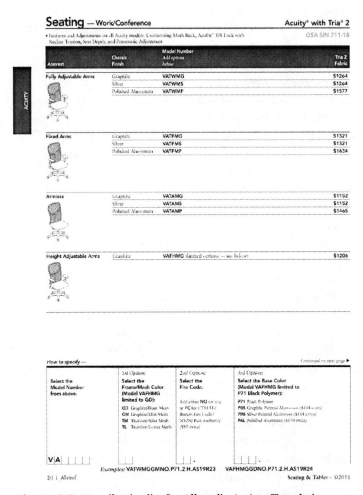

Figure 6.3 A retail price list for Allsteel's *Acuity* office chair. *Acuity* is Cradle to Cradle Certified ™ Silver by MBDC, a product certification firm. *(Allsteel)*

Multiple discounting can also be used for large quantity purchases, but the process involves applying a discount on top of other discounts. For instance, a manufacturer might give you a 50 percent discount on an item and then deduct another 20 percent:

$500 (list price) – $250 (50% discount) – $50 (20% discount) = $200 (designer's cost)

A **trade discount** is a reduction that can be provided to design professionals by a variety of businesses. Generally, a designer would request a trade discount when he or she is purchasing the items through a retail business. For example, designers frequently search for unique items at antique stores and art galleries. Many of these businesses as well as other retail establishments will give a trade discount to the designer; the percentage often ranges between 10 to 20 percent.

Pricing Codes

Codes can be used to price merchandise, especially at design centers because designers frequently bring their clients to see products at the centers and do not want the client to know the price charged to the designer. For example, a showroom might mark its fabrics with this number: 60/20. After confirming that the showroom applied a commonly used 10/20 code, you would determine the cost of the fabric per yard by subtracting 10 from 60 and 20 from 20. Thus, the designer's cost per yard is $50. Another frequently used code is 5/10 and is calculated in the same manner. A **keystone price** indicates that the designer receives a 50 percent discount off the retail price.

Some manufacturers use letters to represent numbers. For example, the word "Baltimore" can be used to code the numbers 1–9 (B-1, A-2, L-3, T-4, I-5, M-6, O-7, R-8, E-9), and the letter "X" is used for "0." Thus, the designer's cost for an item marked "TEI.XX" is $495.00. "Baltimore" is ideal because it has nine letters, none of which is repeated. When unique coding systems are used (as with the word "Baltimore"), you must ask the business owner to explain the system.

Project Expenses

In addition to salaries and the cost of merchandise, compensation must also include any expenses associated with the project. Examples of expenses are printing, renderings, models, copying, postage, and travel. When a designer is supplying merchandise, expenses can include charges for shipping, warehousing, servicing, delivery, and installation. Expenses are paid either by the designer, the client, or a combination of the two. Often designers do not mark up expenses; expenses are therefore charged to a client at invoice costs.

As with all business transactions, your agreement with the client should clearly specify all expenses, who is responsible for the amount, and who will pay the bill. When a delivery or installation is complicated, a **surcharge** should be applied to the final price. Examples of situations that could involve surcharges are deliveries to buildings that do not have elevators or installations in historic buildings.

Shipping costs should be closely monitored because the amount can be considerable, depending on the distances between the manufacturer and the final destination as well as other factors. Shipping charges can be determined by the size of the item, its weight, and special care that might be necessary, such as when delivering a crystal chandelier. Always ask the manufacturer to provide a quote for shipping.

It is very important to know terms used in the shipping industry because the descriptors indicate who is paying the freight charges as well as who is responsible for ensuring a safe delivery. **FOB (free/freight on board) destination** indicates that the manufacturer or seller pays the freight charges. A designer is responsible for the charges when the agreement is **FOB factory**.

 Pick This

---

Checking for Comprehension

• What is the direct personnel expense (DPE)?

• What is the difference between list and net prices?

Thus far in this chapter, we have examined professional compensation and fees as well as the variables that must be considered when determining costs. In addition to understanding how you will charge for your professional services, interior designers work with basic accounting policies and professional forms.

This section provides a general overview of accounting systems (the more comprehensive discussion is in Part IV). If you want to own your business, you will have to become very knowledgeable of business policies, operations, and requirements delineated in Part IV. But when you are working for an organization, you will be required to use employee expense reports, purchase orders, invoices, and work orders.

Accounting Systems: Employee Expenses and Purchase Orders

Determining fees and compensation does not translate into being paid. Once you have identified a fair and profitable compensation method, you must develop and implement a plan with the goal of being paid for your professional services and any merchandise you order for the client. As noted previously, there are ways to receive funds up front by using retainers and deposits, but these advance payments, and all subsequent funds, must be recorded and managed.

When you become involved with multiple concurrent projects, it is very easy to forget to record your time, order an item, and even bill a client for delivered merchandise. You must have an accounting system and forms for tracking your time, travel expenses, purchases, invoices, **transmittals**, **tradespeople work orders**, **work change orders**, and billings (Figure 6.4). Your project accounting system should be developed, in place, and functional before signing contracts with clients (reviewed in the next chapter).

Accounting systems are a means to record, maintain, and process all financial aspects related to a project. The time/activity log illustrated in Table 6.1 is an example of a timesheet

used for accounting purposes. The figures in the spreadsheet can be used to bill a client. Employee expense reports can be a separate form, or the information could be included with a time/activity log. In either situation, critical elements to record are the dates of travel, number of miles, mileage rate, parking, tolls, airfares, hotel charges, food, taxis, and any other travel-related expenses, such as professional conference fees.

Depending on your employer's policies or your agreement with your client, you might be given a per diem rate for meals or you could be reimbursed for each charge. Regardless, keep all food receipts as well as all other business-related receipts, including those for taxis.

Purchase Orders

Some of the most important documents you will handle are **purchase orders**. You might not have to complete and process the form that will be sent to a supplier or manufacturer, but you will be responsible for what is recorded on the form. It is therefore critical that you know every element of a purchase order as well as how many of the items on the form can affect your practice and the success of a project.

A purchase order is a legal contractual agreement between a buyer and a seller. In most

Figure 6.4 Having products made by tradespeople, such as carpenters, requires work orders that include detailed specifications. (© *Getty*)

situations your employer is the buyer, although as discussed previously, some clients prefer to be the buyer. In these situations you may or you may not be the person who drafts the purchase order. When the client is the buyer, he or she still might want you to write the purchase orders. A seller is any company that is supplying you with products.

Because it is a legal document, once the seller acknowledges receipt of the purchase order, the terms of the order cannot be changed without written approvals. Unless flawed, many items cannot be returned to a manufacturer, such as fabric cut from a bolt or custom cabinetry. Some products, such as unopened full bolts of wallcovering, might be returnable, but **restocking charges** will be applied and the return must be done within a prescribed period.

Fundamentally, all purchase orders should be written with the mindset that you are committed to the item. If a client changes his or her mind or does not like the item, a designer has three basic resolutions: (1) not allow the client to return the item, (2) accept the return and hopefully use the item for a future project, or (3) accept the return and use the item in the designer's facilities. Obviously, a client will not appreciate the first option, and this solution could have a negative impact on the relationship. The other two options are generally good for client relations, but the designer might have substantial losses as a result.

Given the legal commitment to purchasing items, it is very important that a purchase order is accurate and all the information is complete. As illustrated in Box 6.1 most purchase orders are preprinted with the design firm's name, address, telephone/FAX numbers, and purchase order number. Other information on a purchase order includes the vendor's name, address, telephone/FAX numbers, as well as an expected shipping date, shipping terms, preferred method of shipping, and delivery location.

Whenever possible, the expected shipping date should be coordinated within the context of the entire project. Ideally, items should be shipped when they can be installed in the building. Shipping merchandise too early can result in storage fees, and the items could be damaged due to extra handling or improper storage arrangements. In addition, because the merchandise has been shipped, the vendor will send an invoice to the designer, which could be thousands of dollars. The designer must pay the vendor, but generally the designer cannot collect money from the client because the merchandise has not been delivered to the site. Merchandise that arrives too late can delay a project, which becomes especially problematic when other work cannot be done until the item is installed.

Deliveries can be made to a storage facility, the design firm, the client's address, and/or to a manufacturer. As described above, problems can occur when products are shipped to storage facilities, but these arrangements might be inevitable when it is impossible to efficiently coordinate delivery and installation dates.

When deliveries are made to the design firm, there will be another delivery to schedule, but the designer has the opportunity to inspect the merchandise before showing the item to the client. If an item is wrong or is damaged, hopefully the designer can reorder the product without too much delay.

Deliveries to the client's address or **drop-shipped** are convenient, and storage fees are eliminated as well as additional transportation costs from either the designer's studio or storage facilities. However, the client should not be the person to receive the shipment. A representative from the design firm should be present to check the merchandise, verify any damage, and ensure that the installation is executed as planned. In addition, residential deliveries can be of special concern when a driver only does "tailgate deliveries." The client homeowner might have to lift the item off the truck and carry the piece into the house.

Items shipped to a manufacturer are generally materials needed for fabrication purposes. For example, **COM (customer's own material)** pieces require the shipment of fabric from one company to a furniture manufacturer. For COM orders you must make sure you are sending the correct amount of fabric. Manufacturers

Box 6.1

Purchase Order

PURCHASE ORDER			
XYZ Interiors 1122 West Avenue Miles, MA 11223-2323	**P.O. Number 12345** **Order Date** January 15, 2012 **Telephone** (112) 112-1122 **Fax** (112) 112-1123		*Preprinted numbers on forms.*
Vendor BBB Lighting Manufacturer 2323 Springfield Avenue Springfield, PA 34555-1234 **Telephone** (333) 333-3334 **Fax** (333) 333-3335	**Ship to** Ms. J. Smyth 123 East 3rd Street Miles, MA 11223-2323 **Telephone** (112) 112-4545 **Fax** (112)-112-4546	**Tag for** J. Smyth **Project** Reception Renovation **Floor** 2nd **Room** 2-234	*Name of client.* *Verify correct shipping address.*

Shipping Terms FOB	Estimate Date February 15, 2012	Acknowledge Order January 16, 2012	Rec'd February 10, 2012	*Requested date.*

Item Number	Quantity	Description	Unit Price	Total Cost	
4545-06	10	6" LED Recessed downlighting	$250.00	$2,500.00	
6544	10	Ceramic metal halide track system	$600.00	$6,000.00	*Verify numbers.*
			Subtotal	$8,500.00	
			Shipping/handling	$45.00	
			Tax	$400.00	
			Total	$8,945.00	

Ordered by

Signature _____   Date: _____

Print Name _____

See reverse side for terms and conditions of this purchase order.

will state the number of yards required for a piece, but additional yardage might be needed to match patterns. Remember: Once the fabric vendor cuts the yardage, you own the material.

Moreover, when reading a manufacturer's price sheet, be sure to locate the correct COM column. Some manufacturers list COM prices at the lowest end of the price range or far left column, and others charge the highest prices for a COM item, which is usually the far right column. In either case, the cost of the fabric is not included in the price and must be added to the furniture manufacturer's price.

COM orders provide an excellent example of the importance of completing the line: "**Tag for**" or "**sidemark**." Your client's name is written on this line, which becomes critical when you send materials to a manufacturer for fabrication. If an item, such as fabric, is sent to a manufacturer without a name, the fabricator might wait for that information or if there are other orders from the same design firm, the fabric could be used on a wrong piece. Always include the client's name as well as the project, floor, and room. Thus, if you are working on many projects with the same client, your records will have the complete information.

The purchase order also includes the quantity, manufacturer's product name/number, color, finish, measurements, unit cost, and total cost. This information should be checked, re-checked, and checked again. Some manufacturers use a name and a number for an item—use both. Be sure to verify the color and finish ordering details. Changing one digit when typing the color number could result in receiving black fabric rather than green.

Including the price can serve as a way to verify the accuracy of the item number and description. For example, if a manufacturer received your purchase order and the price and item do not match, there is an obvious problem (which should be corrected immediately).

Purchase orders can be e-mailed, faxed, or mailed to the vendor. The original purchase order is sent to the vendor; you will need several copies of the order. The number of copies depends on the design firm's policies, but minimally you need a copy for your client's file, the office manager, project manager, and perhaps a centralized filing system that tracks purchase orders.

Accounting Systems: Acknowledgments, Invoices, and Client Billings

After you have placed an order, the vendor will send you **confirmation** or an **acknowledgment** of the order via e-mail, a FAX, or through the mail. Unfortunately, you might receive notice that an item is **discontinued**. If an item is discontinued, the product is no longer being produced and you need to find an alternative.

The acknowledgment form includes an account number assigned by the vendor. This number must be used when corresponding with the vendor, such as checking on a delivery date. The form also includes payment terms that have been arranged with the design firm. For example, for firms with a solid credit rating a common payment term is **net 30**; a vendor does not require prepayments and the firm has 30 days

to pay a bill. Some vendors give a discount for payments that are made before the 30 days.

COD (cash on delivery) or **pro forma** payment plans are used for firms that have a weak credit rating or have never conducted business with that vendor. Under these arrangements the design firm must pay the entire bill before the vendor sends the merchandise.

A vendor's acknowledgment should have the *exact* product descriptions, quantities, and prices that were on the original purchase order. It is *very* important that the vendor's acknowledgment states what was listed on the purchase order. The two documents should be checked for accuracy right away. Any discrepancies should be reported to the vendor immediately. Waiting too long, even if the vendor was at fault for an error on the document, can result in the purchase of unwanted merchandise.

Another important item to check is the shipping information. In addition to noting the correct name and address, check the anticipated shipping date. Even though a designer requested a particular shipping date, a vendor might not be able to fulfill the request. You might receive notice that an item is **back-ordered**. Back orders will be shipped, but the date might be too late for your project and you might have to find an alternative.

If a delayed shipment is for a product that is subject to variances in dye lots, such as fabric or wallcoverings, you might have to wait to approve the item until you can receive a **cutting for approval (CFA)**. Dye lots can have slight color changes, which may or may not be an acceptable color (Figure 6.5). Thus, after the item has been produced again, the manufacturer can send you a current cut or swatch of the fabric and then you can determine the accuracy of its color. The CFA process can be used for back orders and whenever a design requires an exact color match.

Shipping dates can also be delayed, thus you should have a notification or "tickler" system that alerts you when orders are late and triggers a method for contacting the manufacturer in order to determine the cause for the delay and obtain the new shipping date (see Chapter 7).

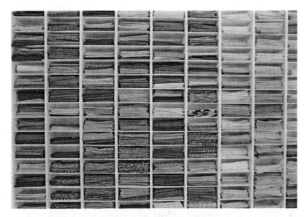

Figure 6.5 Each of these fabric samples were produced using a particular dye lot. Subsequent productions of a fabric may result in a color that is different than the samples. To verify a color, designers ask for a cutting for approval (CFA). (© *Radius Images/ Alamy*)

Invoices

When a product is shipped, the manufacturer sends an invoice to the buyer. The invoice lists all of the items that were shipped and includes the total amount due to the seller, including the payment terms. The invoice should be checked for accuracy by comparing the bill to the purchase order or acknowledgment. Again, if there are any discrepancies or disputes, contact the vendor.

Keep in mind that when purchasing items in quantities, such as chairs, all of the pieces might not be shipped at the same time, but the designer has to pay the bill according to the payment terms. The problem with this situation is that most often the merchandise is not delivered to the client until the ordered quantity arrives, thus, preventing the designer from sending a bill to the client. Some agreements with a client might allow a designer to bill as products are shipped, but for the most part it is essential to receive a deposit from the client that is large enough to cover payments to vendors.

Client Billings

Depending on the design firm's policies, clients can be billed at a variety of times, such as monthly, quarterly, after the completion of a construction phase, or at the end of the project. Designers are responsible for initiating the billing process by creating a statement of the goods and services that have been provided to the client. The design firm sends a billing statement to the client that includes fees, merchandise, and payments that were made by the client.

In accounting terms, charges are known as **debits (dr.)** and payments are **credits (cr.)**. A client should be billed at the agreed-upon time for a variety of reasons. Obviously, the sooner a client receives a bill, the sooner the design firm receives a payment—essential for maintaining an effective **cash flow**. Having access to funds enables a firm to pay its vendors as well as other operating expenses, including salaries.

Sending bills promptly is also good for client relations. A client can become concerned if he or she receives a bill several months after an installation. A very late bill might give the impression that the designer or the design firm does not have a well-managed business. In addition, the client might have forgotten some of the project's details, and thus possibly want to question specific charges.

The prolonged time period can affect a designer's memory as well. Therefore, if the client calls and asks for clarification, it could be difficult for the designer to provide adequate answers. When a designer cannot justify his or her fees, unnecessary adjustments might have to be made to the bill, which might appease the client at the time, but is likely to result in future lost business—including possible referrals.

Administrative Forms

To facilitate other business-related activities, design firms have forms that are used by all employees. Three major types are transmittal forms, tradespeople work orders, and work change orders. Templates of these forms are available online from a variety of sources, such as AIA and the construction industry.

Transmittal Forms

A transmittal letter or form is used to send an item to a business or tradesperson. For instance, a designer might want to send a catalogue to a colleague at another firm or paint chips to a painter. A transmittal form can be used to document these deliveries.

As illustrated in Box 6.2, the basic elements on the form include (1) names and addresses of the senders and recipients, (2) project number, (3) purpose of the transmittal, (4) items enclosed, (5) expected follow-up, and (6) means of sending the item.

Tradespeople Work Orders

Some administrative forms are used to communicate with tradespeople. For example, when specifying custom products, such as cabinetry, a designer must complete a work order. A work order form has the basic information needed to request the services of a tradesperson. Thus, the form includes product specifications, quantities,

approval stages, completion dates, quality assurances, delivery terms, price, and provisions related to ownership of designs, materials, and the final product. The form can be used to request estimates from a fabricator and can serve as a purchase order. When requesting a quote, the form should include a deadline date for receiving the information as well as a date that stipulates when the estimated price expires.

Work Change Orders

What if a contract has been signed with a tradesperson and your client changes his or her mind? First, contact the tradesperson and determine if it is feasible to change the order. This may or may not be possible, depending on the item's stage of development. If it is possible to

---

Box 6.2
Transmittal Letter Form

TRANSMITTAL FORM			
XYZ Interiors 1122 West Avenue Miles, MA 11223-2323	**Project** Forest Offices **Project Number** 5656 **Date** April 15, 2012 **Telephone** (112) 112-1122 **Fax** (112) 112-1123		Always reference project numbers on documents.
To BBB Energy Systems 23 Highway 4 Miles, MA 11223-2326 **Telephone** (112) 333-3334 **Fax** (112) 333-3335	**Sent via** Fax ☐ US Mail ☐ UPS ☐ Messenger ☐ **Other** FedEx	**For** Approval ☐ Revisions ☐ Estimate ☐ Review ☐ As requested ☐ **Other** Charrette April 20, 2012	How is the item sent? What do you want the person to do with the enclosures?
Enclosures			
Original drawings ☐ **Blueprints** ☐ **Specifications** ☐ **Photographs** ☐ **Catalogue** ☐ **Material swatch** ☐ **Paint/finish chip** ☐ **Documents** ☐ **Media** ☐ **Other** Draft of an agenda and presentation for the upcoming charrette. Please advise and return. **Notes**			What you are sending with this cover sheet.

---

change the order, ask the tradesperson to list the costs for the changes.

A description of the changes and costs can be recorded on a work change order form (Box 6.3). In addition, this form includes (1) the project number and client name, (2) names and contact information of fabricator and designer, (3) phase of the design process/contract date, (4) reason for the change, (5) who initiated the change, (6) how the change could affect the schedule, and (7) lines for signatures.

Each work change order form must be signed by the fabricator, designer, project manager, client, and any other people involved with the project or required by the design firm, such as the owner. Signatures are critical to ensuring that everyone is aware of the changes and the client is willing to pay the additional charges. In addition, because one change can delay or alter other aspects of a project, a signed work change order alerts people to the new arrangements and appropriate steps can be taken to revise the schedule as well as any activities impacted by the changes.

Checking for Comprehension
° What are purchase orders?
° What is a cutting for approval (CFA)?

Box 6.3
Work Change Order Form

WORK CHANGE ORDER FORM		
XYZ Interiors 1122 West Avenue Miles, MA 11223-2323	**Project** Forest Offices **Project Number** 5656 **Contract Date:** May 20, 2012 **Date** November 15, 2012 **Telephone** (112) 112-1122 **Fax** (112) 112-1123	Always reference project numbers on documents.
To CCC Cabinetry 2334 Fourth Street Miles, MA 11223-2326 **Telephone** (112) 333-4444 **Fax** (112) 333-5555	**Change Order Number** 34522 **Estimated Cost for Changes $350.00**	

The hiring parties and contractor agree to the following work order changes for the project listed above:

Original Description

The original dimensions for the oak conference table were 48" (depth) x 96" (width) x 28.5" (height)

Adjusted Description

The new dimensions for the oak conference table are 48" (depth) x 120" (width) x 28.5" (height)

Authorized signatures can include client, design firm, and contractors.

Authorized Signature _____ **Date:** _____

Authorized Signature _____ **Date:** _____

The discussion related to tradespeople work orders and ownership of designs is an excellent example of how laws affect the design profession. Ownership of creative expressions is one of numerous items under the category of **intellectual property law**.

This section reviews how you as an interior designer working for a firm can be affected by intellectual property law as well as **tort law**, federal laws, **contract law**, and **international law**. Areas of law that affect designers who own their business, such as tax and employment laws, are examined in Part IV of this book.

Working in a global marketplace necessitates an awareness of the differences in legal systems. U.S. laws are based on **common law**—a system with beginnings in the UK hundreds of years ago. Rulings in the common law system are reliant on case law or legal precedents.

Civil law is the other major type of system used throughout the world. Decisions in the civil law system are based on a nation's statutes rather than case law. In addition, as described in this section, some countries create their laws by combining elements from both the common and civic law systems.

U.S. Intellectual Property Law

When a client hires an interior designer, that person is seeking creative and technical skills.

Once a design concept or solution is presented to a client, how can a designer protect his or her work? After all, when someone sees a drawing, it can be easy to remember the design and hire someone else to execute the plan.

As long as the designer has a signed contract with the client, the designer is protected by the extent of its terms (see Chapter 7). But what if, regrettably, a contract does not exist or someone besides the client duplicates the design? Intellectual property law is intended to protect creative expressions and applies to a variety of professionals, such as writers, photographers, artists, musicians, and actors.

Intellectual property is a federal law based on the powers of Congress provided by the U.S. Constitution's Article 1, Section 8: "Congress shall have the power to promote the Progress of Science and useful Arts, by securing for limited Times to Authors and Inventors the exclusive Right to their respective Writings and Discoveries" (U.S. Government 2010). Thus, the designing of a built interior environment is considered "useful Arts," and the work of an interior designer is protected for a limited time.

Intellectual property law is divided into three categories: **copyright law**, **patent law**, and **trademark law** (Figure 6.6). Copyright applies to "works of authorship" and creative expression, and patent law regulates "new and useful" inventions. Thomas Edison had more than 1,000 U.S. patents for a variety of inventions, including the incandescent electric lamp.

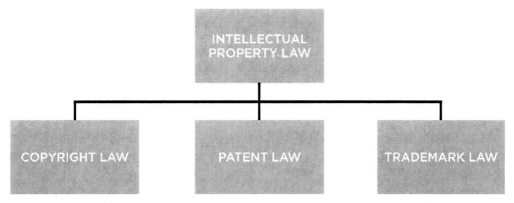

Figure 6.6 The three categories of intellectual property law. The overall purpose of the law is to protect the commercial value of the human mind.

Trademark laws protect words, symbols, or images that are distinctive to a company, product, or service. For example, the names "Google" and "Microsoft" are protected trademarks. Trademark laws can serve as a means to protect consumers, as might be the case when a company creates an inferior product, but packages the item to resemble an item that is well known for its quality.

For the most part, the work of an interior designer is protected under copyright law, but there could be situations where patent and trademark laws apply. For example, a designer could apply for a patent if he or she were involved with designing a new assistive device for operating a window treatment. A trademark might be registered for a distinctive design for an interior plan of a restaurant franchise.

Copyright provisions started in 1909 with the Copyright Act. The act delineated the exclusive rights of an author, including the ability to "print, reprint, publish, copy, and vend the copyrighted work" (U.S. Government 1909). The 1976 Copyright Act is the basis for current copyright laws.

As of October 2009, two copyright categories can be associated with the work of an interior designer: (1) pictorial, graphic, and sculptural works, and (2) architectural work. According to the U.S. copyright law, the pictorial category includes "two-dimensional and three-dimensional works of fine, graphic, and applied art, photographs, prints and art reproductions, maps, globes, charts, diagrams, models, and technical drawings, including architectural plans" (U.S. Government 2009).

The U.S. copyright law defines architectural work as "the design of a building as embodied in any tangible medium of expression, including a building, architectural plans, or drawings. The work includes the overall form as well as the arrangement and composition of spaces and element in the design, but does not include individual standard features" (U.S. Government 2009).

To be protected by the copyright law an item does not have to be registered; however, registration does create a public record. Refer to the U.S. Copyright Office for registration information (http://www.copyright.gov/eco/). As noted the U.S. Constitution's Article 1, Section 8, "Authors and Inventors" are protected for a limited time. In 1977, Congress defined the time limit as 70 years after the author's death for any work produced after 1978.

Ownership of copyrights can also apply under "work made for hire" whereby "the employer or other person for whom the work was prepared is considered the author for purposes of this title, and, unless the parties have expressly agreed otherwise in a written instrument signed by them, owns all of the rights comprised in the copyright" (U.S. Government 2009). Thus, unless otherwise stipulated in a contract, a client does not own work created by the hired interior designer. When copyright infringements occur, copyright owners can recover damages after proving "substantial similarity" between the two works.

U.S. Tort Law

Tort or "wrong" law is civil law based on a person or a property being injured or wronged. The injury could be caused by an act or an omission. Under tort law, a common remedy is monetary compensation for damages and could include remunerations for "pain and suffering."

Three types of torts are **intentional**, **negligence**, and **strict liability**. Intentional tort involves deliberate harm, such as battery, assault, false imprisonment, and trespass to land or personal property.

Negligent Tort

Negligent tort or what is referred to as "negligence" is "the failure to exercise the standard of care that a reasonably prudent person would have exercised in a similar situation; any conduct that falls below the legal standard established to protect others against unreasonable risk of harm, except for conduct that is intentionally, wantonly, or willfully disregardful of others' rights" (Garner 2009).

Negligent torts include personal injury cases, defamation, and professional malpractice. The key elements of negligence include: (1) an expected standard or duty of care, (2) a breach of the duty, (3) the breach causes an injury or wrong, and (4) there were damages.

Interior designers have an expected standard of duty to their clients. A standard of duty involves conducting business in a reasonable manner. For example, the courts expect interior designers to specify chairs that are safe to sit on. An interior designer can be found negligent when a breach of his or her duty—specifying a chair that collapses when occupied—results in injury as well as subsequent damages. What constitutes a breach of duty?

There are numerous items that could qualify as a breach of duty. The list can include all of the services that can legally be provided by an interior designer, such as those identified by the State of Illinois Interior Design Title Act (Box 6.4) and any activities executed by an interior designer that are not in their legal domain, such

as work that is legally to be performed by engineers and architects. Thus, it is imperative that an interior designer follows the licensing laws in *any* state where he or she is working on projects. In addition, the designer is required by law to comply with federal and state laws as well as local building codes and regulations (Box 6.4 and Beverly Hills Supper Club fire in Box 4.2).

As evidenced in Box 6.4, many laws are associated with the design profession, including building construction, fire safety, energy conservation, the Americans with Disabilities Act (ADA) of 1990, and several environmental regulations.

As an example, *U.S. v. Days Inns of America* is a case filed in 1996 because some newly constructed Days Inns hotels violated Title III of the ADA. The U.S. alleged that Days Inns violated Title III by designing and constructing the new Wall Days Inn in Wall, South Dakota, to be inaccessible to individuals with disabilities. In addition, the U.S. argument states that the corporation's actions or omissions were typical of its standard practices as evidenced by

Box 6.4

Licensing Act and International/Federal Laws and Standards

"The profession of "interior design", within the meaning and intent of this Act, refers to persons qualified by education, experience, and examination, who administer contracts for fabrication, procurement, or installation in the implementation of designs, drawings, and specifications for any interior design project and offer or furnish professional services, such as consultations, studies, drawings, and specification in connection with the location of lighting fixtures, lamps and specifications of ceiling finishes as shown in reflected ceiling plans, space planning, furnishings, or the fabrication of non-loadbearing structural elements within and surrounding interior spaces of buildings but specifically excluding mechanical and electrical systems except for specifications of fixtures and their location within interior spaces" (Illinois General Assembly, 2001, p. 1).

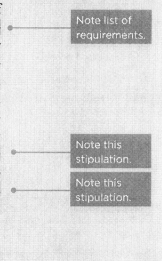
Note list of requirements.

Note this stipulation.

Note this stipulation.

Source: Illinois General Assembly 2001. *Illinois Interior Design Title Act.* http://ilga.gov/. Accessed March 22, 2012.

(Box 6.4 continued on page 186)

Box 6.4

Licensing Act and International/Federal Laws and Standards *(continued)*

International/Federal Laws and Standards*	Purpose
American with Disabilities Act (ADA) of 1990 *Title III Public Accommodations and Services* *Operated by Private Entities* http://www.ada.gov/statute.html	An act created to establish a clear and comprehensive prohibition of discrimination on the basis of disability.
American Society of Heating, Refrigeration and Air-Conditioning Engineers (ASHRAE) Standard 90.1, 2010 http://www.ashrae.org/	Standard 90.1 has been a benchmark for commercial building energy codes in the United States, and a key basis for codes and standards around the world for more than 35 years.
ASTM International (former American Society for Testing Materials—ASTM) http://www.astm.org/	A globally recognized leader in the development and delivery of international voluntary consensus standards. ASTM standards are used around the world to improve product quality, enhance safety, facilitate market access and trade, and build consumer confidence.
Architectural Barriers Act (ABT) http://www.access-board.gov/	Requires access to facilities designed, built, altered, or leased with federal funds.
Clean Air Act (CAA) http://www.epa.gov	The CAA is the law that defines EPA's responsibilities for protecting and improving the nation's air quality and the stratospheric ozone layer.
Clean Water Act (CWA) http://www.epa.gov	The statute employs a variety of regulatory and nonregulatory tools to sharply reduce direct pollutant discharges into waterways, finance municipal wastewater treatment facilities, and manage polluted runoff.
Comprehensive Environmental Response, Compensation and Liability Act (CERCLA) known as Superfund http://www.epa.gov	This law created a tax on the chemical and petroleum industries and provided broad federal authority to respond directly to releases or threatened releases of hazardous substances that may endanger public health or the environment.
Fair Housing Amendments Act (FHAA) of 1988 http://www.hud.gov/	Prohibits discrimination in the sale, rental, and financing of dwellings based on race, color, religion, gender, or national origin.
Federal Insecticide, Fungicide, and Rodenticide Act (FIFRA) http://www.epa.gov	The objective of FIFRA is to provide federal control of pesticide distribution, sale, and use.
International Building Codes (IBC) Former BOCA and ICC http://www.iccsafe.org/	Membership association dedicated to building safety and fire prevention. Develops the codes and standards used to construct residential and commercial buildings, including homes and schools.
International Energy Conservation Code (IECC) 2009 http://www.internationalcodes.net	Encourages energy conservation through efficiency in envelope design, mechanical systems, lighting systems, and the use of new materials and techniques.
International Fire Code (IFC) 2009 http://www.internationalcodes.net/	The comprehensive code includes regulations governing the safeguarding of life and property from all types of fire and explosions hazards.
National Environmental Policy Act (NEPA) http://www.epa.gov	Requires federal agencies to integrate environmental values into their decision-making processes by considering the environmental impacts of their proposed actions and reasonable alternatives to those actions. To meet NEPA requirements, federal agencies prepare a detailed statement known as an **Environmental Impact Statement (EIS)**.
National Fire Protection Association (NFPA) NFPA 101: Life Safety Code 2009 http://www.nfpa.org/	Incorporates the latest research, technological advances, and industry developments to provide the most advanced rules for sprinklers, alarms, egress, emergency lighting, smoke barriers, and special hazard protection.

Box 6.4

Licensing Act and International/Federal Laws and Standards *(continued)*

International/Federal Laws and Standards*	Purpose
Occupational Safety and Health Administration (OSHA) http://www.osha.gov/	Created by Congress to ensure safe and healthful working conditions for working men and women by setting and enforcing standards and by providing training, outreach, education, and assistance.
Resource Conservation and Recovery Act (RCRA) http://www.epa.gov	Gives EPA the authority to control hazardous waste from the "cradle-to-grave." This includes the generation, transportation, treatment, storage, and disposal of hazardous waste.
Section 504 of the Rehabilitation Act of 1973 http://www.hhs.gov/ocr/civilrights/	A national law that protects qualified individuals from discrimination based on their disability. The nondiscrimination requirements of the law apply to employers and organizations that receive financial assistance from any Federal department or agency.
Toxic Substances Control Act (TSCA) http://www.epa.gov	Provides EPA with authority to require reporting, record-keeping, and testing requirements, and restrictions relating to chemical substances and/or mixtures.

*Sources are the websites located in the first column.

many of its other hotels that were inaccessible to people with disabilities. Days Inns and its parent company had a "high degree of control or authority over the design and construction of the Wall Days Inn, and extensive involvement in the project itself" (*U.S. v. Days Inns of America* 1997).

Some of these violations of title III of the ADA included: (1) unequal treatment in features provided in guest rooms, (2) the lack of an elevator in buildings with two floors and a basement, (3) inaccessible height of registration desks for someone in a wheelchair, (4) controls for heating/air-conditioning units difficult to manipulate, (5) clothes rods and shelves too high for someone in a wheelchair, (6) narrow bathroom doors, and (7) the lack of insulation on hot water and drain pipes under the lavatories in public restrooms [insulation is intended to prevent burns on the legs of someone sitting in a wheelchair] (*U.S. v. Days Inns of America* 1997).

Days Inns did not dispute the facts; thus, the U.S. sought injunctive relief and the award of civil penalties against Days Inns and its parent company. Civil penalties were sought "to punish

wrongful conduct" and "to deter other potential violators." In 1997, a settlement was reached between the Justice Department and the owners, architect, and contractor of the Days Inn hotel in Wall, South Dakota. The agreement included civil penalties and the requirement that the hotel had to be more accessible to guests with disabilities.

Recently, **toxic tort** litigation has involved extremely hazardous substances, such as asbestos exposure in buildings and hazardous waste. A designer should be familiar with these litigations because the issues are associated with the built environment. For example, litigious items can include lead-based paints, radon, Environmental Tobacco Smoke (ETS), formaldehyde, Building-Related Injuries (BRI), and Sick Building Syndrome (SBS). (see Box 6.5.)

Other design areas prone to litigation involve: (1) ownership rights associated with electronic documents, such as CAD-prepared drawings, (2) liability issues when electronic documents are altered, (3) scheduling problems that can result in expensive construction delays, (4) inaccurate estimates that cause cost

Box 6.5

Mondelli v. Kendel Homes Corporation 1998–2001*

Nature of Case and Facts

Barbara and Vito Mondelli sought to recover damages for personal injuries allegedly sustained as a result of the defective construction of their home in Papillion, Nebraska, in 1998.

Mondellis signed a purchase agreement with Kendel to have a house built in Papillion.

The City inspected the building during construction according to the local municipal code and the Uniform Building Code (UBC). ●————— Note this reference.

Mondellis moved into the house in April 1992.

Mondellis noticed water in the basement beneath the dining room window and living room window. Kendel caulked between May 1992 and July 1993. Some brick work was done in May 1993.

During repair work after insulation was removed mud and tiny toadstools were discovered on the wall and stud plate.

In June 1993 Mondellis claimed that mold, fungi, and spores had circulated throughout the house and affected the air, carpeting, furniture, and clothing. Mondellis claimed that the mold caused health problems.

Mondellis alleged:

● City inadequately and negligently inspected the house. ● — Note the city's alleged negligence.

● City issued a building permit to Kendel when blueprints and construction design for the house were in violation of the Code, the UBC, and industry standards. — Note the city's violation.

● Kendel constructed a house with latent and dangerous defects.

● In connection with the construction and sale of the house, Kendel impliedly warranted that the house would be erected in a workmanlike manner and in accordance with the Code, the UBC, and industry standards. — Note the application of implied warranty.

● Strict liability and negligence for Mondellis' theory of relief. ● — Note the application of strict liability and negligence.

Court findings at the end of liability phase:

● Mondellis met their burden of proof that the house was defective. ● — Note the application of burden of proof in the liability phase.

● These actions were in violation of the Code, industry standards, and constituted a breach of implied warranty. ● — Note the breach of implied warranty.

● Mondellis failed to prove that the defects constituted a breach of warranty that the house would be fit for human habitation. ● — Note the failed proof for breach of warranty.

Box 6.5

Mondelli v. Kendel Homes Corporation 1998–2001* *(continued)*

Court findings of the theory of negligence:

- Kendel was negligent in constructing the house in violation of the Code, the UBC, and industry standards.

Note the finding of negligence.

- Judgment in favor of Mondelli against Kendel on liability under the theories of implied warranty and negligence and strict liability was an appropriate theory of recovery.

Note the finding of implied warranty, negligence, and strict liability.

- City was negligent in issuing a building permit when the house violated the Code, the UBC, and industry standards.

Supreme Court of Nebraska Court findings of the cross-appeals of the City and Kendel:

- City should have been granted immunity from suit under the act and that the City should be dismissed from the case.

Note City was granted immunity.

- The district court was correct in determining that Kendel was negligent in the construction of the house and that Kendel breached its implied warranty that the house would be erected in a workmanlike manner.

*Adapted from: Mondelli v. Kendel Homes Corporation. 2001. Case Nos. S-96-820 through S-96-823.

---

overruns, and (5) performing tasks that are outside the scope of a designer's responsibilities, such as altering construction methods.

To determine whether a person has breached his or her duty, the courts frequently rely on the profession's norms for the town or city of the offense. Thus, a comparison could be made between the defendant's actions and what another local interior designer would have done under the same circumstances.

To try to avoid litigation, an interior designer should always act in good faith by intending to be fair and honest, and make every attempt to follow the standards of the profession as well as local building codes and regulations. In addition, as described in the next section, contracts should not specify services and expectations

that are beyond the skills, expertise, and control of the designer.

Strict Liability

Strict liability, the third type of tort, does not rely on negligence or intentional actions. Strict liability is based on harm caused by a person's duty to ensure safe conditions. Working with very hazardous materials, such as those produced by building implosions, is an example. Thus, if someone located blocks away from the site was injured by the implosion's flying debris, the company working with the hazardous substances could be liable for injuries and damages.

Products liability can be based on strict liability theory. Products liability is "a manufacturer's or seller's tort liability for any damages or injuries suffered by a buyer, user, or bystander as a result of a defective product" (Garner 2009). The legal theory involves injury caused by a manufacturer's product due to design defects, manufacturing defects, or insufficient information regarding use and safety.

As illustrated in *Mondelli v. Kendel Homes Corporation* (see Box 6.5), the courts can determine that a building is a product. In this case Mondelli sued Kendel Homes for strict liability and negligence, as well as breach of **implied warranty** that the house would be built in a "workmanlike manner" (Figure 6.7). The courts found that Mondelli did not prove that the defective house "constituted a breach of **warranty**."

U.S. Contract Law and International Law

Tort law can apply when someone fails to fulfill the terms of a contract. A contract is a legal agreement when two or more individuals (parties) make voluntary promises to each other. Generally, the promises in a business contract are to provide goods, services, or labor in exchange for pay. For example, employers have employees sign contracts that stipulate conditions of employment, including salaries, benefits, start dates, and termination clauses.

A contract might be written, oral, or acknowledged by a handshake depending on the type of agreement. The terms of a contract generally include: (1) the names of the parties, (2) what will be supplied and/or performed, (3) start and end dates, (4) terms and conditions, and (5) signatures.

Digital or electronic signatures with a secure digital code attached to the electronic message might be used for Internet transactions. Electronic signature laws began with Utah's Act in 1995 followed by every state enacting some type of e-signature legislation. Subsequently, states passed the Uniform Electronic Transactions Act in 1999 and Congress enacted the Electronic Signatures in Global and National Commerce Act in 2000 (see http://www.fca.gov/).

You will be signing contracts with your clients that delineate what services you will provide, for what price, and for what period of time (see Chapter 7). As noted previously, the contracts you use for your clients as well as other parties should include **exculpatory** or exemption provisions that clear you of wrong. Some of these items reflect more recent practices, such as not being responsible for team members not completing their tasks, or not being liable for any hazardous substances that might exist on a site.

Other exculpatory provisions might include unforeseeable expenses due to natural disasters, unanticipated labor increases, or material increases. A good way to explain these provisions to a client is to provide them with a draft of a typical contract and discuss the details with them—another relationship building exercise.

Contracts must clarify the responsibilities of a designer as well as a client with special consideration to specifying the legal limits related to the interior design profession. For example, legally an interior designer cannot sign and seal

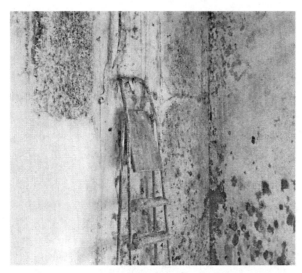

Figure 6.7 An example of the mold damage that can occur from defective construction practices. In *Mondelli v. Kendel Homes Corporation* (2001), the Mondellis claimed that mold, fungi, and spores had circulated throughout the house and affected the air, carpeting, furniture, and clothing. The Mondellis also claimed that the mold caused health problems. (© *Peter Geschwill/Alamy*)

technical submissions, such as the drawings and specifications for a building that will be constructed. Architects have this legal responsibility.

When there is a breach of contract, or disagreements with the terms of a contract, the best approach is to make every effort to resolve the issue without using the courts. The legal system is expensive, and the experience will result in the loss of a client no matter who wins the case. In addition, an angry former client can disparage your name and reputation to other people in the community.

Contracts become complicated when a design firm is located in one state and the project is in another state—or nation. Contracts must be written according to the laws that are applicable to the location of the project. Thus, given the growing number of international projects, it is important for an interior designer to at least be aware of international law and its relationship to U.S. law.

International Law

A definition of international law is "The legal system governing the relationships between nations; more modernly, the law of international relations, embracing not only nations but also such participants as international organizations and individuals (such as those who invoke their human rights or commit war crimes)" (Garner 2009).

Fundamentally, international law involves three major sources: (1) treaties, such as U.S. international agreements, (2) customary international laws that have been created by years of past practices, and (3) principles of law recognized by most nations. Principles of law are reflective of the laws used in nations with common law, such as the United States, Canada, and the UK. Decisions in the civil law system are based on a nation's statutes rather than case law, as in the common law system.

Typically, international law has been important for defining peace, war, and geographical boundaries. But international law has also been evolving to respond to the globalization of commerce, economics, and social issues. Thus, several international organizations and conferences have been developing agreements that are part of international law. For example, commercial interests have prompted the development of trade-related agreements, such as the North American Free Trade Agreement (NAFTA), the Association of Southeast Asian Nations (ASEAN), the World Trade Organization (WTO), and the Fairtrade Labelling Organizations International (FLO).

Other examples of international agreements involve intellectual property rights, including copyrights. The first agreement to protect copyrights internationally was in 1886 with the Berne Convention for the Protection of Literary and Artistic Works, referred to as the "Berne Convention." In 1952, to ensure that all countries had copyright protection of literary, scientific, and artistic works, agreements were formed at the Universal Copyright Convention (the 1952 convention). The convention was sponsored by United Nations Educational, Scientific and Cultural Organization (UNESCO).

At the 1952 convention, it was determined to use © as the international symbol for copyright. To further protect copyrights, in 1967, the United Nations created the World Intellectual Property Organization (WIPO). The purpose of WIPO is to develop a "balanced and accessible international intellectual property (IP) system, which rewards creativity, stimulates innovation and contributes to economic development while safeguarding the public interest" (WIPO 2010).

In 1988, to address copyright protection with respect to "new technologies," such as "television by cable, semiconductors, computer technologies, and new audio-visual recording techniques," a European Commission developed a plan to unify the copyright laws—including those related to information technology—of member nations. The plan was published in *Green Paper on Copyright and the Challenge of Technology*, or the *Green Paper*.

In 1994, the WTO created the Trade-Related Aspects of Intellectual Property Rights

(TRIPS) agreement. TRIPS was the first attempt to merge intellectual property rules with a multilateral trading system. Most recently, at the 2001 Convention of Cybercrime a treaty was signed to address crimes committed via the Internet and other computer networks, dealing particularly with infringements of copyright, computer-related fraud, child pornography, and violations of network security" (Council of Europe 2001).

Chapter 6 concluded Part II by examining several methods associated with professional compensation and fees as well as describing variables that can affect costs and fees. General accounting and administrative practices were then analyzed by explaining forms and procedures that designers must work with on a daily basis, such as purchase orders and invoices. The last subject explored in Chapter 6 was law and how laws impact the design profession.

Parts I and II serve as background for Part III, Long-Term Relationships and Project Responsibilities. Part III is dedicated to understanding how to establish and nurture client relationships as well as how to demonstrate value and implement best business practices throughout the design process.

Knowledge and Skills Summary

Highlights
* Methods to charge clients include hourly fees, flat/fixed fees, cost plus percentage fees, and retail-based fees.

* When determining fees, a designer must consider numerous conditions that can affect the final compensation, including the variable characteristics of each project and client.

* Factors that can affect fees include operational budgets, manufacturers' pricing policies, and general expenses.

* Interior designers should have an accounting system and forms that are used to track the designer's time and travel expenses.

* Forms used for projects include purchase orders, invoices, transmittals, tradespeople work orders, work change orders, and billing statements.

* U.S. laws that can impact the design profession include intellectual property law, tort law, federal laws, contract law, and international agreements

Key Terms
acknowledgment (confirmation)

back order

billable service

billing statement

CFA (cutting for approval)

COD (cash on delivery)

COM (customer's own material)

cash flow

civil law system

common law system

confirmation (acknowledgment)

contract law

copyright law

cost

credit (cr.)

debit (dr.)

deposit

direct personnel expense (DPE)

discontinued

drop-shipped

exculpatory

fixed fee (flat fee)

flat fee (fixed fee)

FOB (free/freight on board) destination

FOB factory

gross profits

hourly fee

implied warranty

intellectual property law

intentional tort

international law

invoice

keystone price

list price

markup

multiple (multiplier)

negligence

net 30

net price

net profit

overhead

patent law

per diem

portal-to-portal

pro bono

pro forma

product liability

purchase order

quantity discount

restocking charge

retail price

retainer

sidemark (tag for)

strict liability

surcharge

tag for (sidemark)

tort law

toxic tort

trade discount

trademark law

tradespeople work order

transmittal letter (form)

value-oriented fee

warranty

wholesaler

work change order

work order

Projects

Philosophy and Design Project

When you begin your first job, you must understand the importance of fees as well as the various approaches to charging your clients. To optimize profits, designers should estimate fees by using at least two different methods. Examine each of the methods discussed in this chapter, and develop advantages and disadvantages of each method based on your philosophical beliefs regarding how you want to work with your clients.

Your analysis can include considerations such as the size of a project and past experiences with a client. In addition, to gain insight from working professionals, you might want to initiate a productive IM exchange with interior designers and/or prepare an inquiry message to be posted on a professional blog. Write bulleted summary of your analysis and discuss your summary with your classmates.

Research Project

This chapter reviewed several different business forms that designers use with clients and suppliers. Many organizations and businesses have developed various versions of these forms. Research the forms discussed and develop recommendations for the key elements you think should be included in a purchase order, work order, contract, work change order, and invoice. Develop drafts of the forms that include your recommendations.

Human Factors Research Project

This chapter identified case laws associated with the design profession. In a team of three to five members, research another case. Prepare an oral presentation (approximately 15 minutes) that includes (1) introduction, (2) statement of the case, (3) summary of arguments, (4) conclusion, and (5) how the case could impact clients and the work of the design profession. You might want to consider using role play as the means to present the information.

References

American Society of Interior Designers (ASID). 2010. *The Interior Design Profession: Facts and Figures*. Washington, DC: American Society of Interior Designers.

Council of Europe. 2001. *Convention on Cybercrime*. http://conventions.coe.int. Accessed November 19, 2010.

Davidsen, J. 2010. "2010 Giants: A Spoonful of Sugar." *Interior Design Magazine*. http://www.interiordesign.net/article/483374-2010_Giants_A_Spoonful_of_Sugar.php. Accessed November 23, 2010.

Garner, B. A., ed. 2009. *Black's Law Dictionary*. St. Paul, MN: West.

Mondelli v. Kendel Homes Corporation. 2001. Case Nos. S-96-820 through S-96-823.

U.S. Government. 2010. *U.S. Constitution—Article 1 Section 8*. http://www.usconstitution.net/xconst_A1Sec8.html. Accessed October 30, 2010.

U.S. Government. 2009. *Copyright Law of the United States*. http://www.copyright.gov/title17/circ92.pdf. Accessed October 30, 2010.

U.S. Government. 1909. *Copyright Act of 1909*. http://www.copyright.gov/history/1909act.pdf. Accessed October 30, 2010.

U.S. v. Days Inns of America. 1997. Civil Action—96-5012.

World Intellectual Property Organization (WIPO). 2010. *What Is WIPO?* http://www.wipo.int. Accessed November 19, 2010.

PART

III

LONG-TERM CLIENT RELATIONSHIPS AND PROJECT RESPONSIBILITIES

Part I, *Launching a Career in the Interior Design Profession* began an exploration of professional practice by reviewing the fundamentals of the interior design profession, career opportunities, and strategies for attaining an entry-level position. This information served as the foundation for analyzing Part II, *Working in a Design Firm*. Part II examined professional business responsibilities and international business practices, and concluded with professional compensation, administrative practices, and legal obligations.

Part III, *Long-Term Client Relationships and Project Responsibilities* is dedicated to understanding how to establish and nurture client relationships as well as how to demonstrate your value by implementing best business practices throughout the design process. Part III begins with Chapter 7. This chapter analyzes strategies for establishing long-term client relationships. The next two chapters review working on projects from the perspective of best business practices as well as effective client relationships. Chapter 8 explores building long-term relationships with clients within the context of effective project management practices, and Chapter 9 covers the phases of the integrated design process (IDP).

Part III concludes the book's information related to working as an entry-level interior designer, and then Part IV, *Owning and Operating an Interior Design Business: An Overview* examines content that is relevant to designers who want to own their firm.

C H A P T E R

Enhancing Your Value: Client Relationship Skills

第7章 (Japanese)
7장 (Korean)
Nodaļa 7 (Latvian)
7 skyrius (Lithuanian)
Глава 7 (Macedonian)

After learning the content in Chapter 7, you will be able to answer the following questions:

* What do I need to know to develop and sustain long-term client relationships?

* How can I acquire clients?

* What should I do to get appointments with clients?

* How should I interact with clients?

* What contracts should I use with clients?

* How can I deliver successful presentations to clients?

It is well known that "interior design is a business" and that fabulous designs cannot succeed without sound business practices. This chapter expands on these points by exploring how the relationship between an interior designer and a client affects business. The interior design profession depends on relationships with clients. When none exists or they are very weak, interior design businesses have, do, and will fail.

How can an interior designer develop strong relationships with his or her clients? This chapter, as well as other content in the book, is dedicated to providing answers to this question. Your future success as an interior designer depends on knowing how to initiate, develop, and sustain client relationships or what can be termed the client relationship cycle (CRC). Figure 7.1 visually presents the CRC and includes critical elements that should be considered when working with a client.

The CRC serves as the organizational structure for the chapter. Thus, the first section examines how to initiate a relationship with a client. The next section analyzes the initial stages of developing a relationship with a client by reviewing effective dialogue, listening skills, and strategies for the first appointment. The last section in the chapter explores the next phase in the development of a relationship with a client—various types of contracts are explained in this section, as well as how to prepare and deliver excellent presentations to clients.

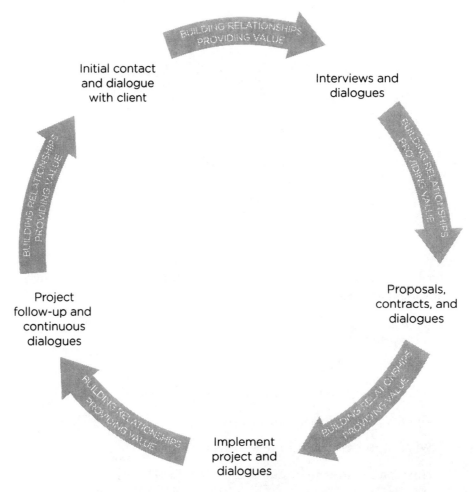

Figure 7.1 The client relationship cycle (CRC). Note that dialogue, providing value, and building relationships serve as continuous elements of the circle.

The process of understanding how to create long-term client relationships begins by explaining important stages in the relationship with a client, as well as the profiles of designers and clients. This section concludes by reviewing how to acquire your own clients by strategically analyzing a design firm's existing clients and identifying new clients.

To illustrate the importance of client relationships, let's examine a list of requirements included in job descriptions and note how often client/customer service skills are identified:

* "Strong skills in client relationship management and presentation."

* "The ability to build long-term relationships with clients, excellent communication, interpersonal and customer service skills and strong time management/project skills are critical."

* "Strong customer service orientation."

* "Strong customer service orientation with a sincere desire to satisfy client requirements."

* "Strong interpersonal and client relationship skills."

Client Relationships: The Client Relationship Cycle (CRC)

Developing "strong skills in client relationships" requires an examination of the word "client" as well as understanding a professional "relationship." Why does the profession use the term "client" with "relationship" rather than "customer"?

A client is someone "who engages the professional advice or services of another" (Merriam-Webster 2010). The definition appears straightforward, but when we compare the client's definition to that of a "customer," we begin to understand some of the responsibilities of an interior designer; hence helping to explain why the profession prefers the term "client." A definition of a customer is "one that purchases a service" (Merriam-Webster 2010).

Note the words "engages" and "purchases" in the two previous definitions. When someone hires an interior designer, that person "engages" rather than "purchases" the services. The word "engage" implies that there is an ongoing personal connection between the client and the interior designer, rather than a one-time impersonal "purchase" as with a customer. In addition, a client is not just seeking services or a product; that person wants professional services or advice.

Naturally, collaboration requires communication, a topic that has been emphasized many times in this book. But within the context of a client relationship, communication must be a **dialogue**. A "dialogue" is "conversations between two or more persons; an exchange of ideas and opinions; a discussion between representatives of parties to a conflict that is aimed at resolution" (Merriam-Webster 2010). Client relationships are based on dialogue, not talk. Thus, client relationships should have "conversations," "exchange ideas and opinions," and use "discussions" as the means to resolve conflicts.

The ultimate goal of a client relationship is loyalty. An interior designer needs loyal clients. Why? Loyal clients continuously return to the designer for professional services and are the most likely to recommend a designer to friends, family members, and colleagues. A loyal client knows you, likes you, and trusts your professional advice. The loyal client can also sense your loyalty to them.

To earn loyalty, an interior designer must be honest, dependable, and reliable while creating designs that add value by fulfilling the needs of the client. Once this relationship is formed, it is often a lifelong commitment; typically, the only time a client searches for an interior designer is when the relationship no longer exists.

One way to understand how to create loyal clients is to examine the development of the relationship within the context of the design process (see Chapters 8 and 9). For the purposes of explaining the CRC, "client" is a term that represents one or more individuals. Thus, "client" could be an individual homeowner, a couple, or a committee. As illustrated in Figure 7.1, the process can begin with (1) an interior designer contacting a client to offer professional services, or (2) a client contacting an interior designer because of a specific need or vision. The initial contact leads to interviews, a proposal, and agreements. Once a contract is signed, the project begins.

A signed contract signals the *formal* beginning of providing impeccable customer service. As noted in the list of sample job requirements, employers want designers who have strong customer service skills. Clients expect a designer's services to be reliable, responsive, and accommodating to their needs. Any problems or complaints must be promptly resolved to the satisfaction of the client. (Examples of how you can provide excellent customer service to your clients through the design process are described in Chapters 8 and 9.) Upon the completion of a project, the designer should conduct follow-up dialogues with the client to ensure that the final design addresses all of the client's needs.

As illustrated in Figure 7.1, creating a loyal client requires a continuous loop that involves additional customer service as well as future projects. Keep in mind that a client might not initially complete the entire project. Thus, future projects could include areas in the original plans that were not completed. For instance, designs for the original plans of a retail store might have included the entire facility, but perhaps only the first floor was initially renovated. Reconnecting with the client could result in renovations of additional floors. At any point in the cycle, a client might refer an interior designer to others, but this is most likely to occur when a solid relationship exists.

Client Relationships: Profiles of Interior Designers and Clients

To initiate a relationship with a client, you must first understand the strengths and weaknesses of your professional profile. Why would a client hire you? Why wouldn't he or she hire you? The professional profile you developed for interviewing purposes (see Chapter 3) could serve as a starting point, but you must update the profile to reflect your current situation, including integrating its content with the profile of your employer's firm. Thus, your new professional profile should highlight key features of your design firm, and how your skills and abilities reinforce these attributes. Your employer might have examples in brochures, publications, annual reports, **qualifications packages**, or videos, or on the company website. (Qualifications packages are discussed later in this chapter and are also reviewed in Part IV.)

A design firm highlights its strengths by listing its expertise and track record according to markets, services, and regions. Markets or types of facilities can include commercial office buildings, educational, entertainment, government, hospitality, residential, and retail facilities. Services could be just interior design or could also include architecture, brand design, global relationships, planning and urban development, and sustainability. As an example, Gensler has a brief statement that summarizes its expertise (2012):

> As architects, designers, planners, and consultants, we partner with our clients on some 3,000 projects every year. These projects can be as small as a wine label or as large as a new urban district. With more than 3,000 professionals networked across 41 locations, we serve our clients as trusted advisors, combining localized expertise with global perspective wherever new opportunities arise.

Regions or the company's geographical profile delineates the locations of its projects (Figure 7.2), and, as in the Gensler example, a firm might also include the number of offices. Projects featured on a firm's website illustrate the company's expertise in each market, service area, and region. Furthermore, the examples generally demonstrate a firm's range of experience, such as working on very small to large projects, as well as private, public, nonprofit, and for-profit enterprises.

A design firm might also identify other services or characteristics that distinguish it from the competition. For example, HOK's website includes this statement: "We Create. We Inspire. We Connect. We Care" (HOK 2010). Foster + Partners includes the following statements: "We believe the quality of our surroundings can lift the quality of our lives." "We are guided by a sensitivity to the culture and climate of place." "We design by challenging—by asking the right questions" (Foster + Partners 2010).

Figure 7.2 An example of an international project designed by American architect Marshall Strabala while Director of Design at Gensler.
The Shanghai Tower is a mixed-use building (offices, high-end hotel, retail space, restaurants, cafés, and a public observatory) that has several sustainable design elements and is scheduled to be completed in 2014. (© 2Define Architecture)

Unique strengths of a firm could also include (1) a reputation for quality designs as evidenced by awards and honors, (2) a commitment to sustainability, (3) adding value to the client's aspirations and profitability, (4) collaboration with clients and colleagues, (5) 24/7 services, (6) the number of languages spoken by members of the firm, (7) offices in construction locations, and (8) exceptional customer service.

Use your firm's profile as an umbrella for developing your professional profile. Your first profile should be viewed as the initiation of your **self-brand** or the image you want to portray to clients. Your profile should catch the attention of a prospective client as well as providing information. Your profile should give a client the reasons why he or she should arrange the first meeting with you. Focus on your strengths, your distinctiveness, and the type of work you enjoy the most.

As an entry-level designer, obviously you will not be able to feature your depth of experience. But you can emphasize the ability to take a fresh approach to a design and your enthusiasm for the profession and for launching your career. Someone recently graduating from college might also have unique skills or knowledge not covered in previous educational programs, such as sustainability, evidence-based design theories, or research methodologies. Moreover, as an associate in a design firm, you have access to people with experience and expertise who can help guide you and provide assistance. Concentrate on your collaboration skills, your willingness to learn, and your availability to provide excellent customer service.

Clients' Profiles

To "satisfy client requirements" is to understand who you are and who your clients are. Your professional profile helps you understand what you and your design firm can offer. Thus, the next step is to develop an overview of your design firm's current clients as well as **prospects** or potential clients. The more you know about your clients, the easier it is to build lifelong relationships.

To develop client relationships, you need to understand their general profile, including who they are, their values and their needs, how your services meet their needs, and the best approach to connecting with them. Your research should include examining cultural dimensions that were reviewed in Chapter 5 as well as generational attitudes, which are analyzed in this section.

An excellent approach to understanding your clients' profiles is to categorize them according to the variables you used in your professional profile. Thus, current and prospective clients could be grouped according to markets, services, and regions. Within each of these categories you could further define their characteristics according to demographics such as age, sex, gender, race, ethnicity, education, disabilities, income, life cycle, and location.

Existing clients, referring to past and current clients, could be further profiled according to their likes, dislikes, and preferences. Keep this simple fact in mind: Something attracted these clients to your design firm. These are the distinctive elements to discover or rediscover. Generally, these are the tangible and intangible features that attracted a client to your firm rather than to the competition. Was it the creativity? Ability to understand how to meet the person's needs? Impeccable service—such as responding to inquiries in a timely manner or immediately correcting a mistake? Personal relationships? Solutions that added value? Reasonable fees? International experience? Global reputation?

Within the demographic profile, age is an area that requires special consideration. How can someone's age affect your work as an interior designer? Increased longevity has created a unique situation for current designers. You might have clients from *four* generations—each with its own attitudes, expectations, and experiences. As described in Chapter 1, you might encounter clients from the Silent Generation, Baby Boomer Generation (Boomers), Generation X (Gen-Xers), and the Millennial Generation (Millennials), and in the future there will be what

has been tentatively termed either the Homeland, O, or Z Generation (born 2001–present).

In the past designers did not have to be concerned about working with clients and coworkers from so many generations. However, this has changed because of improvements in healthcare that enable people to live longer, and professionals are postponing retirement for a variety of reasons, such as financial security, rising mandatory retirement ages, and the desire to stay active. According to ASID (2010), 55 percent of the interior designers who completed their survey were between the ages 35 and 54, 20 percent were older than 55, and 25 percent were younger than 35. Thus, 75 percent of responding designers were older than age 35.

Therefore, not only is it critical for you to have a working knowledge of your client's generation, but this information is important when working with users of a client's building as well as your relationships with other professionals, supervisors, and fellow employees. Obviously, you will want to have good working relationships with all of these people. How can this be accomplished?

An essential step is to understand what events, conditions, and trends helped to shape the way they behave, what they value, their attitudes, and what motivates them. As discussed in Chapter 5, individual differences and preferences exist and must be considered when working with a client, but researchers have identified fundamental characteristics of each generation that can serve as a foundation for understanding generations (Pew Research Center 2010). Interestingly, some of these researchers have found that globalization has started to erode more recent generational differences across cultures. Thus, some of the same characteristics of the Gen-Xers and Millennials can be found in people throughout the world.

Characteristics of Generations

What is a generation? A **generation** is "a group of individuals born and living contemporaneously" (Merriam-Webster 2010). Thus, people in a generation grow up together during the same time period of approximately 20 years and are consequently shaped by the same events, situations, and conditions. The shared occurrences affect attitudes toward a variety of issues, such as gender roles, diversity, education, aspirations, motivators, finances, the environment, social responsibilities, life styles, and technology (Table 7.1).

Preconceived assumptions regarding someone's generation can affect the ability to both begin and develop a relationship with a client. For example, how do you think a potential client from the Silent Generation would perceive an interior designer with very visible tattoos and body piercing, and who uses an iPad? How do you think a potential client from the Millennial Generation would perceive an interior designer who is wearing a three-piece suit and gold cuff links, and uses the Rolodex on his desk?

As you review Table 7.1, closely examine the items listed with your generation. These can be the initial perceptions that people might have of you. For example, older generations have referred to Millennials as "me-oriented, distractible, fragile, pushy, needy, rude, impatient, thin-skinned, ruthless, irresponsible, reckless, overprogrammed, and timid" (Howe 2010). Thus, if your client is from this generation, he or she might have a preconceived idea that you have these characteristics.

Knowing how generations perceive each other is helpful when you must correct misperceptions. Study the events and conditions that shaped the attitudes of members of that generation to understand why someone views the world from a different lens. Consider these differences as you interact with clients, client users, and colleagues. Remember that currently, most of the clients who typically have the means or the authority to hire design professionals are members of the Silent and Boomer Generations, with Gen-Xers on the horizon.

Client Relationships: Existing and Prospects

How does an interior designer get clients? At the beginning of this chapter we reviewed the CRC and proceeded to explain the initial steps in starting a relationship with a client by developing profiles of an interior designer/firm and clients. This section continues the initial phase of the CRC and describes how to develop a clientele list by reexamining existing clients and creating strategies for acquiring new clients.

Obviously, finding new clients is important, but why would it be necessary to also focus on existing clients? After all, existing clients obviously already know the design firm exists and have conducted business with it. Let's take a look at the reasoning here.

Existing Clients

There are many reasons why existing clients are critically important to an interior designer and a design firm, among which is the emphasis on building loyal clients as well as lifelong relationships. Existing clients might be aware of a design firm and have done business with a designer, but that might or might not indicate that they *know*, like, or trust the designer or the firm. But the fact that a client has hired a designer clearly demonstrates an interest in those professional services, and as noted in the CLC, the relationship has progressed to an advanced stage.

The latter observation is significant from various perspectives. First, a great deal of time and energy can be expended in trying to attract clients. To target new clients, firms can spend considerable money on advertising, hiring marketing consultancy firms, and working with prospects who never become clients. In addition, even when marketing strategies are targeted to appeal to specific individuals, the approach is still from a broad perspective.

Obviously, marketing-related expenses are not necessary with existing clients; energies can therefore be devoted to addressing the specific needs of each client. Developing existing clients can also be an effective strategy during the downside of an economic cycle when a design firm is seeking business and its resources are scarce.

We do know that for a variety of reasons existing clients expressed interest in an interior

Table 7.1 Profile of Four Generations[+]

	Silent Generation (born 1925–1945)	Baby Boomer Generation (born 1946–1964)	Generation X (born 1965–1980)	Millennial Generation (born 1981–2000)
Demographics	White 80% Hispanic 7% Black 8% Asian 4% Other 1% **Male Education Level 18–28** Less than high school 32% High school 40% Some college 19% 4 years of college or > 9% **Female Education Level 18–28** Less than high school 31% High school 49% Some college 15% 4 years of college or > 6% **Marital Status when age 18–28** Married 54% Separated or divorced 3% Never married/single 43%	White 73% Hispanic 10% Black 11% Asian 4% Other 2% **Male Education Level 18–28** Less than high school 21% High school 41% Some college 25% 4 years of college or > 13% **Female Education Level 18–28** Less than high school 19% High school 47% Some college 23% 4 years of college or > 11% **Marital Status when age 18–28** Married 42% Separated or divorced 6% Never married/single 52%	White 62% Hispanic 18% Black 12% Asian 6% Other 2% **Male Education Level 18–28** Less than high school 18% High school 36% Some college 33% 4 years of college or > 13% **Female Education Level 18–28** Less than high school 16% High school 32% Some college 37% 4 years of college or > 15% **Marital Status when age 18–28** Married 29% Separated or divorced 5% Never married/single 67%	White 61% Hispanic 19% Black 13% Asian 4% Other 2% **Male Education Level 18–28** Less than high school 15% High school 35% Some college 34% 4 years of college or > 15% **Female Education Level 18–28** Less than high school 12% High school 28% Some college 40% 4 years of college or > 20% **Marital Status when age 18–28** Married 21% Separated or divorced 4% Never married/single 75%
Identity, Priorities, Outlook	**What makes your generation unique?** WWII, Depression (14%) Smarter (13%) Honest (12%) Work ethic (10%) Values/Morals (10%) **Respecting their elders:** A responsibility 38% Not a responsibility 52% **Views on state of the nation:** Satisfied 14% Dissatisfied 78%	**What makes your generation unique?** Work ethic (17%) Respectful (14%) Values/Morals (8%) "Baby Boomers" (6%) Smarter (5%) **Respecting their elders:** A responsibility 55% Not a responsibility 41% **Views on state of the nation:** Satisfied 23% Dissatisfied 71%	**What makes your generation unique?** Technology use (12%) Work ethic (11%) Conservative/Traditional (7%) Smarter (6%) Respectful (5%) **Respecting their elders:** A responsibility 67% Not a responsibility 30% **Views on state of the nation:** Satisfied 36% Dissatisfied 57%	**What makes your generation unique?** Technology use (24%) Music/Pop Culture (11%) Liberal/Tolerant (7%) Smarter (6%) Clothes (5%) **Respecting their elders:** A responsibility 63% Not a responsibility 33% **Views on state of the nation:** Satisfied 41% Dissatisfied 55%

	Silent Generation (born 1925–1945)	Baby Boomer Generation (born 1946–1964)	Generation X (born 1965–1980)	Millennial Generation (born 1981–2000)
Table 7.1 (continued)				
Technology & Social Media	**Internet behaviors/cell phones:** Social networking profile 6% Use Twitter 1% Use cell to text 9% Cell phone/no landline 5%	**Internet behaviors/cell phones:** Social networking profile 30% Use Twitter 6% Use cell to text 51% Cell phone/no landline 13%	**Internet behaviors/cell phones:** Social networking profile 50% Use Twitter 10% Use cell to text 77% Cell phone/no landline 24%	**Internet behaviors/cell phones:** Social networking profile 75% Use Twitter 14% Use cell to text 88% Cell phone/no landline 41%
	New technology makes life: More complicated 36% Easier 50%	**New technology makes life:** More complicated 30% Easier 60%	**New technology makes life:** More complicated 21% Easier 69%	**New technology makes life:** More complicated 18% Easier 74%
	Main news source: Television 82% Internet 13% Newspapers 50% Radio 15% Other 5%	**Main news source:** Television 76% Internet 30% Newspapers 34% Radio 20% Other 3%	**Main news source:** Television 61% Internet 53% Newspapers 24% Radio 22% Other 5%	**Main news source:** Television 65% Internet 59% Newspapers 24% Radio 18% Other 4%
Work	**% Who are employed:** Full-time: no data Part-time: no data Not employed: no data	**% Who are employed:** Full-time 54% Part-time 13% Not employed 32%	**% Who are employed:** Full-time 65% Part-time 10% Not employed 25%	**% Who are employed:** Full-time 41% Part-time 24% Not employed 35%
	% Who say likely to: Switch careers in work life: no data Stay at current job rest of work life: no data	**% Who say likely to:** Switch careers in work life: 31% Stay at current job rest of work life: 84%	**% Who say likely to:** Switch careers in work life: 55% Stay at current job rest of work life: 62%	**% Who say likely to:** Switch careers in work life: 66% Stay at current job rest of work life: 42%
Family Values	**Lived with growing up:** Both parents 80% Only 1 parent 14% Neither parent 6%	**Lived with growing up:** Both parents 80% Only 1 parent 16% Neither parent 4%	**Lived with growing up:** Both parents 68% Only 1 parent 25% Neither parent 7%	**Lived with growing up:** Both parents 61% Only 1 parent 31% Neither parent 7%
	Gay marriage Strongly favor/favor 24% Strongly oppose/oppose 66%	**Gay marriage** Strongly favor/favor 32% Strongly oppose/oppose 58%	**Gay marriage** Strongly favor/favor 43% Strongly oppose/oppose 46%	**Gay marriage** Strongly favor/favor 50% Strongly oppose/oppose 36%

(Table 7.1 continued on page 206)

	Silent Generation (born 1925–1945)	Baby Boomer Generation (born 1946–1964)	Generation X (born 1965–1980)	Millennial Generation (born 1981–2000)
Lifestyles	**% Who have a tattoo:** 6%	**% Who have a tattoo:** 15%	**% Who have a tattoo:** 32%	**% Who have a tattoo:** 38%
	Environment—% who: Recycle from home 77% Buy green products 51% Buy organic foods 27%	**Environment—% who:** Recycle from home 72% Buy green products 54% Buy organic foods 35%	**Environment—% who:** Recycle from home 77% Buy green products 55% Buy organic foods 38%	**Environment —% who:** Recycle from home 69% Buy green products 53% Buy organic foods 36%
	Vigorous exercise past 24 hours: 39%	**Vigorous exercise past 24 hours:** 42%	**Vigorous exercise past 24 hours:** 48%	**Vigorous exercise past 24 hours:** 56%
Government & Civic Engagement	**Most influence over how you live today:** Government 48% Business corporations 18% Both 12% Don't know 22%	**Most influence over how you live today:** Government 42% Business corporations 35% Both 10% Don't know 13%	**Most influence over how you live today:** Government 39% Business corporations 41% Both 7% Don't know 13%	**Most influence over how you live today:** Government 40% Business corporations 42% Both 10% Don't know 8%
	% Volunteered last year: 39%	**% Volunteered last year:** 52%	**% Volunteered last year:** 54%	**% Volunteered last year:** 57%
Influential Events, People, & Technologies	World War II, Great Depression, New Deal, GI Bill, Pearl Harbor, FDR, Hitler, Stock Market Crash, Radio	Vietnam War, Cold war, Civil Rights Movement, Women's Liberation, Kennedy and King Assassinations, Woodstock, Peace Sign, Landing on Moon, Television	Persian Gulf War, Challenger Explosion, AIDS, Computers, Microwaves, Computer Games, VCRs, MTV	Terrorism, 9-11, Iraq War, President Obama, Recession, Columbine, Cell Phones, Internet, Online Social Networks

Table 7.1 (*continued*)

*Adapted from Pew Research Center. 2010. *Millennials: A Portrait of Generation Next*. http://pewsocialtrends.org/files/2010/10/millennials-confident-connected-open-to-change.pdf. Retrieved November 20, 2010.

designer as well as the design firm. To strengthen these relationships, and potentially find new business, a design firm should undertake a review of its client files or **job books**. Regardless of the date of the last contact or who worked with the individual, each client should be reviewed within the context of the CRC. The goal is to identify the person's current stage in the CRC and develop a strategy to strengthen the relationship. The strategy should be customized to each client and focus on getting to know the person better while building a friendship, credibility, trust, and confidence.

This could be difficult for clients who have not been contacted for several years, who are disgruntled, or if the designer who worked with them is no longer with the firm. For clients in these types of situations an interior designer should attempt to contact the client and pursue reestablishing the relationship, which might involve resolving past problems and differences. The initiative might not be successful, but a client will note the consideration behind the effort and might contact you in the future. If the person had a bad experience, he or she might be talking negatively about that experience to others, and your efforts to resolve any issues might cause the person to stop making unkind remarks.

Hopefully, the majority of your firm's existing clients had good experiences that you can build on. The designer who worked with a client is the person who should contact previous clients. However, for various reasons an interior designer may be willing to allow another designer to make the contact. For example, the designer might contend that even though a project was successful, perhaps the two did not relate well to each other. Or the client might have wanted designs that were beyond that designer's area of expertise or interest. Or the designer might be very busy with current projects and does not currently have time to start new projects. Or perhaps a mentor wants to give a protégé a project. Thus, for these reasons or others it might be possible to assign a client to another interior designer, or perhaps it could be a collaborative arrangement involving two designers. In either situation the first designer should begin the transition by introducing the new designer to the client. The first designer should also be involved with selecting the new designer, because that person's experience with the client is invaluable to the matching process.

A designer should *never* assume that a client will contact him or her when services are needed. Moreover, lifelong relationships require that both parties connect with each other. Depending on the client's circumstances, there are several ways to rekindle a relationship. The first contact could be a phone call, an e-mail message, or a handwritten note. The goal is to make the contact and let the client know you are interested in him or her. Follow-ups could involve a lunch or coffee meeting, attending an event together, or perhaps sending update information about the firm or articles of special interest to the client.

When appropriate, the designer should try to learn more about the client's professional and personal life. This information could stimulate ideas for new projects that you could suggest, or the client might mention someone who needs professional design services. For example, a conversation with commercial clients could reveal restructuring or merger initiatives that could require new or renovated facilities. Residential clients might mention a family member looking for a new home or who is dissatisfied with an old kitchen.

With respect to current clients, again, a designer should *never* assume that a client will initiate contact when something is needed. Clients can have the impression that a designer's role in a project is to develop a design, order products, and send bills. Clients can develop these attitudes when the only time an interior designer connects with them is to present a design and send a bill for products and fees. A focus on the CRC can help to change these attitudes and practices.

Current clients should be contacted at every stage of the design process and at regular intervals after the completion of a project. Contacts should involve: (1) getting to know the client better, (2) mentioning aspects about the project that are exciting, (3) providing an update on the project's progress, (4) providing reassurance about any changes that had to be made to the original design, (5) explaining the next stages of the project, (6) thanking the client for working with you, and (7) asking if there are any problems or concerns (Figure 7.3). If there are problems, the client should be reassured that you will promptly resolve the issue and you will let him or her know when the problem will be resolved.

Prospects

By far the easiest way to find new work is to build existing client relationships. However, business expansions rely on new clients. Thus,

to build your clientele, you must nurture existing clients while pursuing prospects. There are many ways to identify prospects, but the most effective methods involve personal relationships. Your personal and professional networks are an excellent source, especially when someone provides you with a referral and is willing to serve as a reference.

Meeting people through blogs or at professional conferences, seminars, workshops, community events, and volunteer activities are all ways to learn who might need design services. Volunteering could expose you to potential clients, and the experience might help you to learn a new skill and acquire new knowledge.

From the other end of the personal spectrum, a design firm might attempt to attract clients by advertising in local publications, having articles published in mainstream magazines, joining

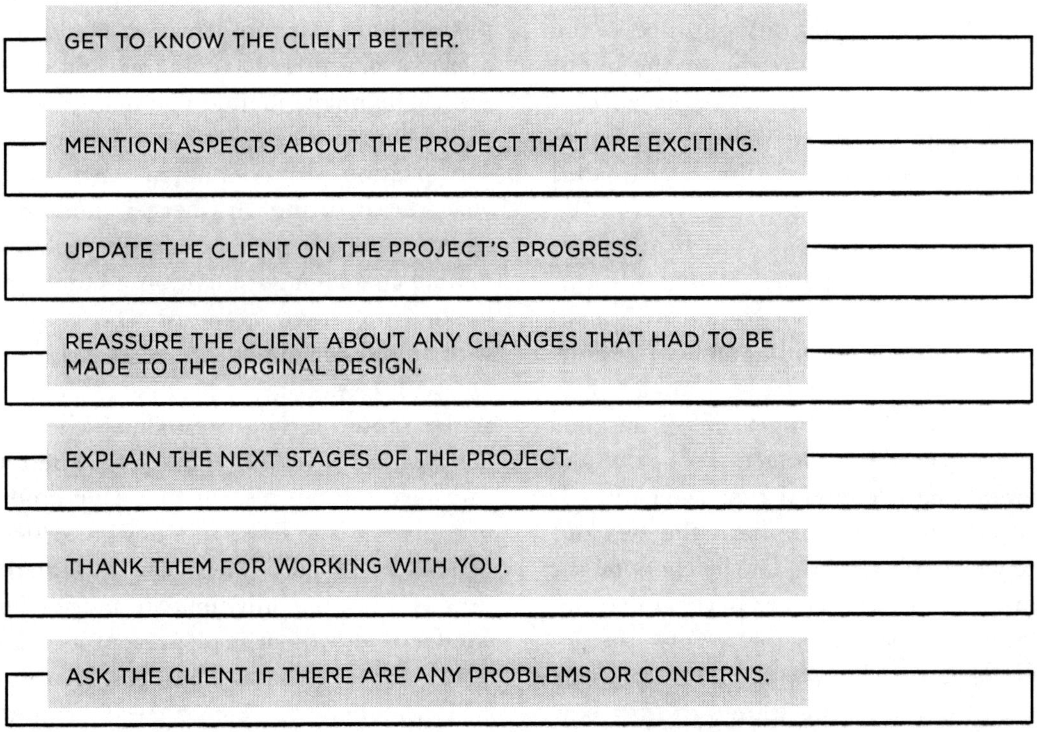

GET TO KNOW THE CLIENT BETTER.

MENTION ASPECTS ABOUT THE PROJECT THAT ARE EXCITING.

UPDATE THE CLIENT ON THE PROJECT'S PROGRESS.

REASSURE THE CLIENT ABOUT ANY CHANGES THAT HAD TO BE MADE TO THE ORGINAL DESIGN.

EXPLAIN THE NEXT STAGES OF THE PROJECT.

THANK THEM FOR WORKING WITH YOU.

ASK THE CLIENT IF THERE ARE ANY PROBLEMS OR CONCERNS.

Figure 7.3 Current clients should be contacted at every stage of the design process and at regular intervals after the completion of a project. Client contacts could be made for a variety of reasons, including the items listed in this illustration.

listings on websites of professional organizations, publishing newsletters, and distributing press releases of newsworthy accomplishments, such as the opening of a newly renovated local public building or the announcement of a new designer who has joined the staff.

A design firm might wait for prospects to contact the firm, or it might engage in cold calls. Waiting for prospects to contact a firm is a reactive approach to building clientele and generally is only effective when a firm has an esteemed reputation with an amazing track record.

Keep in mind that an excellent prospect might call any design firm; it is therefore imperative that the person answering the phone or e-mail message is prepared to provide accurate information and can ask appropriate qualifying questions. Without qualifying a prospect, a designer might have an appointment with someone who is not serious about hiring an interior designer. In some situations a designer might meet with a prospect, provide suggestions, and then discover that the prospect purchased the designer's ideas online.

As explained in the next section, strategies can be used to be ensure compensation when a designer first meets a prospect, but these methods should not preclude a qualification process. Generally, a prospect can be qualified by asking probing questions that include enquiring if design fees are in their budget. Clients who are not anticipating paying fees tend to hesitate and seem to lose enthusiasm for scheduling an appointment with a designer.

Other qualifying questions could focus on trying to obtain further details about a project. When a prospect is serious, he or she generally knows what problem is to be solved, how a designer can help solve the problem (at least in a general sense), a timeline, and an approximate budget.

Proactive Client Strategies

A very proactive strategy to acquiring clients is **cold calls**. If you are in a situation where you are supposed to make cold calls, instead of phoning people, you might have more success by taking the personal approach by visiting businesses. Whom do you contact? First you need to create a list of potential prospects. Your cold-call list could be generated by leads in newspapers, announcements of pending projects by local officials, or talking with your professional colleagues, such as landscape designers, graphic artists, contractors, realtors, and painters.

You could also develop a list of prospects by observing the interiors of commercial buildings that typically have not been designed by professionals. Sometimes the owners of these buildings have never considered having their facilities professionally designed by an interior designer. Examples tend to focus on service-oriented businesses, such as dry cleaners, dog kennels, or accountants. The list could also include doctor/dentist offices and any non-franchise restaurant or retail store.

Working with these businesses can help you to begin a client relationship with the owners, and you might attract other clients who visit these establishments. Future projects could be both residential and commercial interiors. For example, if the facilities are in dire need of a renovation, that business's customers will notice the upgrade and might want to contact you to redesign their facilities or residences. Furthermore, before-and-after photographs that illustrate these dramatic transformations of interiors can be excellent additions to your portfolio.

After you create your list of **suspects**, or potential prospects, the next step is to try to discover as much about the individual or business as feasibly possible. Information can be attained by speaking with local people as well as searching online and reading local publications.

If the only way to contact the person is by phone, then you should prepare a script that could be based on the following information: (1) your name and the name of the design firm, (2) one sentence that describes how your expertise can address the suspect's need, and (3) permission to continue or request a convenient time to return the call and/or schedule an appointment.

This script could be used for cold phone calls as well as cold walk-in visits.

Walk-ins can be done during regular business hours, but ideally you should visit during nonpeak periods. Visiting the business reveals a sincere interest in working with the potential client, and the face-to-face contact enables you to demonstrate your professionalism and confidence. Prior to the visit, make every attempt to discover the name of the person who is responsible for the facilities. Do not go to the business with the assumption that the person can talk with you immediately. When you enter the facility, you can basically follow the script outlined above.

Another way to acquire new clients is to enter competitions. Various organizations and corporations use competitions to determine who they will hire to design their facilities. Announcements can include a **request for proposal (RFP)**, **request for information (RFI)**, and **request for qualifications (RFQ)**.

Some competitions are by invitation only, and others are open to anyone. Competitions can be very time-consuming and expensive. Nonetheless, winning a competition is an excellent way to design a project and perhaps gain new clients as a result of publicity that might occur as a result of the selection process.

Depending on the competition, a design firm might have to go through the following steps: (1) comply with the qualifications of the project, (2) submit proposals to the organization, (3) upon request, present a proposal, and (4) if selected, negotiate a contract with the organization.

Generally, proposals for competitions include the firm's qualifications package, examples of completed projects that are similar to the proposed project, and how the design firm would approach the project, including a schedule, fees, and compensation.

Most firms will only become involved with a competition when it feels the firm is well qualified, has extensive experience with the client or the type of project, and is able to coordinate the project with its other commitments.

Checking for Comprehension
* Describe the CRC.

* Give examples of proactive strategies for building client relations.

Client Relations: Interpersonal Communication and Appointments

Once you have attracted the attention of a potential client, how should you proceed? This section continues an explanation of the CRC by reviewing the next steps in the process. The section begins by explaining best practices associated with interpersonal communication and specifically focuses on effective listening skills.

The section continues by reviewing how to arrange first appointments, including developing agendas and creating a dialogue with clients. The section concludes by explaining the importance of client job books and how to develop these files.

Client Relations: Dialogues, Observations, and Listening

Your first appointment with a client requires thinking about answers to questions, such as the following:

* What will you say at the first meeting?

* How will you react to what the prospect says to you?

* How will you react when the prospect says nothing?

* How will you react to the project?

* How will you respond to questions?

* How can you appear trustworthy?

* How can you show that you are interested in working with the client?

* How can you tell the person you are not interested in working with him or her?

In preparing for your first appointment with a prospect, you must think about these questions and develop a strategy for successful interpersonal communications. Your strategy should support the overarching goals of interactions with clients—to create loyal clients and long-term relationships.

In general, your communication strategy should follow many of the principles, including intercultural dimensions, that have already been discussed in this book. Your verbal and nonverbal communication should give the client the impression that you are a professional, very likable, honest, enthusiastic, ethical, trustworthy, and open-minded, and that you are interested in their needs, including helping them to be successful.

Remember, a prospect's first impression of an interior designer can significantly influence whether or not the person will work with (or continue working with) that designer. In fact, many times a prospect interviews several designers in order to find the perfect match because the prospect wants to make sure he or she is hiring a designer who understands his or her needs, is reliable, honest, and has the expertise and resources to create the best possible design.

Presenting the ultimate positive impression requires excellent interpersonal skills. You should be polite, pleasant, and considerate, and give the person your undivided attention. As is the case when you are interviewing for a job, your speech should be clear, concise, grammatically correct, and the appropriate volume and pitch. Do not use jargon, slang, derogatory statements, or industry terms that would typically be unfamiliar to a client. Avoid jokes and controversial topics, such as religion, politics, and social issues. Sentences should be short. Do not monopolize the conversation.

Engage the prospect in a dialogue, which involves each person contributing to the discussion. This conversation should be viewed as the beginning of a long-term relationship; therefore, take the time to get to know the person and the organization (when applicable). If you are talking with a quiet person, get him or her involved in the dialogue by asking questions in addition to inquiring about how he or she perceives the needs of the project.

Effective interpersonal skills also include the arts of observation and listening. Observe how the client says something, how he or she reacts to your comments, the body language, and periods of silence. Words and statements can mean many different things, depending on how they are said. For example, the word "really" can have multiple meanings: "Really!" "Really..." or "Really?" How a prospect states ideas or questions can reveal the person's enthusiasm, skepticism, or doubts.

Nonverbal cues can often indicate whether a person likes or dislikes ideas; they can also reveal confusion. To detect these nuances, pay attention to eye movement, posture, gestures, and if the person moves closer or farther away from you.

As mentioned in Chapter 5, silence can be a time to reflect on the dialogue, or it could be a sign that the person likes or dislikes your ideas, is confused, or has learned everything he or she wanted to know and is ready to conclude the meeting. When in doubt, clarify the reason for the silence by asking questions.

Listening Skills

Developing extraordinary listening skills is absolutely essential to developing lifelong relationships and being able to create designs that accommodate people's needs. Listening sounds simple. We hear people talk every day. However, as the definitions below illustrate, there is considerable difference between hearing and listening.

Hearing is "the process, function, or power of perceiving sound" (Merriam-Webster 2010). A definition of listening is "to hear something with thoughtful attention: give consideration" (Merriam-Webster 2010). Obviously, designers want to hear what clients say with "thoughtful attention" and "give consideration" rather than simply "perceive sound."

How can you learn to listen—not just hear?

Ralph Nichols and Thomas Lewis, academic experts in speech and rhetoric, researched listening and speaking. Based on their research results and their analysis of numerous other studies, they developed ten components of effective listening (Box 7.1).

Nichols and Lewis noted that most people lack essential listening skills, but these skills can be improved through exercises. Their work was done many years ago, but the principles have been supported by more recent research (Graham 2006, Macaro, 2006, Rost 2002, 1995, Vogely 1995) and remain applicable in the twenty-first century.

Box 7.1
Nichols and Lewis' Ten Components of Effective Listening*

Effective Learning Component	The Problem and Suggestions for Improvement
Previous experience with difficult materials	Poor listening can be caused by the lack of experience with difficult or technical language. Listening can be improved by acquiring more experience with challenging materials. Suggestions for improvement include acquiring assistance from speech experts, watching educational programs with technical content, and reading higher-level materials.
Interest in the topic at hand	Poor listening can be caused by not identifying interesting aspects of a topic. Suggestions for improvement include identifying an interesting aspect of a subject, and when a topic seems to be uninteresting, asking yourself, "Why am I here?" Use the reasons for being at the event as the motivating factor for becoming interested in the topic.
Adjustment to the speaker	Poor listening can be caused by being distracted by nuances of the speaker, such as a cough, poor eye contact, or monotone speech. Suggestions for improvement include not blaming the speaker and helping the speaker to improve by giving the speaker overt attention.
Energy expenditure of the listener	Poor listening can be caused by failing to expend the energy required for efficient listening. Suggestions for improvement include getting more sleep, avoiding thinking about personal problems, discussing the speaker's topic prior to listening, and behaving like a good listener.
Adjustment to the abnormal listening situation	Poor listening can be caused by reacting to poor physical conditions, such as noise, faulty heating/AC equipment, and idle chatter. Suggestions for improvement include sitting close to the speaker and, if necessary, asking people to be quiet.
Adjustment to emotion-laden words	Poor listening can be caused by reacting negatively to a word, phrase, or argument. Suggestions for improvement include identifying offensive words or phrases and then analyzing the causes of the offense. Understanding the cause of your reactions can help to reduce their impact.
Adjustment to emotion-rousing points	Poor listening can be caused by having a quick and violent disagreement with the main points or arguments of the speaker. Suggestions for improvement include withholding judgment until an argument is fully understood and avoiding looking for negative evidence.
Recognition of central ideas	Poor listening can be caused by not recognizing the main points. Suggestions for improvement include recognizing patterns of speech composition.
Utilization of notes	Poor listening can be caused by poor note-taking skills, including writing too much. The more notes that are recorded, the more people replace listening time with writing time. Suggestions for improvement include taking fewer notes and using reflection time after hearing a speaker. Reflection time could include reorganizing and transcribing notes.
Reconciliation of thought speed and speech speed.	Poor listening can be caused by the significant time difference between the rate of speech and the rate of thought. People talk between 100–125 words per minute. The average speed of thought is at least 400 words per minute. Suggestions for improvement include staying "on track" through intense concentration and eye contact.

*Adapted from: R. Nichols and T. Lewis, *Listening and Speaking* (Dubuque, IA: Wm. C. Brown Company, 1954).

Suggestions provided by Nichols and Lewis are invaluable when you are in a dialogue with prospects and clients. Understanding their likes, dislikes, preferences, and needs as well as what they value requires effective listening. Acquiring accurate information about a client helps you develop design solutions that accommodate the needs of that person, thereby increasing the likelihood that the client will engage your services. Moreover, when you demonstrate that you have been listening by developing a design that is customized to the client's needs, that person begins to form the impression that you care about him or her and that, in time, you are someone who can be trusted—critical elements to loyalty and lifelong relationships.

Effective listening skills are also relevant to nonverbal communication. When a client is talking and the designer is doing something besides listening—such as looking around the room, reading text messages, or tapping a pen, —the client will lack confidence that the designer is listening. Furthermore, the client might have the impression that the designer is distracted, bored, and disinterested.

Your nonverbal communication should be professional and reflect your interest in the prospect and the project. In addition to incorporating the suggestions provided by Nichols and Lewis, you should have excellent posture, yet not appear to be stiff. Norms concerning eye contact, touching, and spatial distances should be considered within the context of the cultural perspectives discussed in Chapter 5. Electronic devices should be on silent mode and out of sight.

Client Relations: First Appointments and Job Books

Planning the most effective communication strategy for the initial appointment is dependent on many variables, such as the location of the meeting, length of time, who will be involved with the meeting, and how much you know about the person or organization. In addition, you must plan what to bring to the meeting.

A meeting could be at the job site, the site of your previous projects, a client's office, your studio, or at a public place such as a restaurant or coffeehouse.

Each site requires a slightly different strategy. Generally, the best location is at the job site because it is easier for both the designer and the client to discuss the project by being able to see specific details as well as actually walk through the spaces. When the project is new construction, a designer might arrange to have the meeting at the site of a previous project that is similar to what the client wants to have built. Visiting a completed project can be an excellent way to showcase a designer's expertise as long as the design of the interior reflects the needs of the prospective client. If not, or if the client's preference is still unknown, then it is best to have the first meeting elsewhere.

Other locations might be at the client's office, a gesture that indicates consideration of that person's time. Or a designer could ask the client to come to their studio. Of course, the designer's studio is convenient for the designer, but this should not be the reason for selecting the site. The designer's studio can be an effective location for the first interview when you are trying to impress a client with perhaps a well-designed interior in a landmark building, touches of hospitality, an array of presentation boards from previous projects, or a large staff. A studio might also have other elements that can be useful when you are discussing a project with a client, such as displays, materials, product literature, sophisticated lighting systems, and a conference room with advanced technology for presentations.

From a marketing perspective, meeting someone at a restaurant or other public site is likely to be the least desirable of the choices because the conditions are unpredictable. On the day of the appointment the facility could be noisy and crowded, and you could be stuck sitting in an uncomfortable location, such as next to the kitchen doors, entrance, or restrooms. However, a public meeting spot might seem less intimidating to some prospective clients, thus these locations might be an appropriate site to begin a relationship with someone who is new to hiring a professional designer.

The location can affect the scheduled time as well as the real time of an appointment. For instance, a meeting at a crowded and noisy restaurant might result in a shortened meeting. This could be a problem when the discussion is productive. Generally, an hour is scheduled for first appointments, but if you are at the job site, the chances are very good that the meeting will be much longer.

A meeting at a client's office can often be shortened because of business commitments and interruptions. An appointment at the designer's studio can be scripted according to the scheduled time, but if the firm has extensive facilities with many professionals, the appointment time could be extended when the client wants to see spaces that were not on the schedule or meet people who were not included on the agenda.

There are various configurations possible in regard to the meeting participants: (1) designer and prospect; (2) designer, prospect, and other individuals; (3) design team and prospect; (4) design team, prospect, and other individuals; (5) designer and a committee; and (6) design team and a committee.

Prior to the appointment, ask the prospect who is expected to be at the meeting, and if possible, find out if the participants include the final decision maker. As the above scenarios suggest, each arrangement necessitates a unique communication strategy and can affect the number or type of materials that are brought to the meeting. A one-to-one conversation is considerably different than speaking with a committee. Moreover, conducting the entire meeting yourself is very unlike having one voice within a team of designers.

Agendas

After you know the meeting's location, amount of time, and its participants, you may plan the agenda and what you should bring to the meeting. Generally, items you would bring to a first appointment are a notebook, examples of your related work, brochures, business cards, camera, measuring tape, and perhaps a role of tracing paper for quick sketches. Other items, such as drawings, sample books, product **cutsheets**, or finishes, might be necessary depending on the project and the meeting location.

Whether or not the meeting requires a printed agenda, every appointment should have an outline of what will be discussed in a strategically arranged order. The agenda should be determined according to the overall goals of the meeting.

From a designer's perspective, the goals of a first appointment with a prospective client are to: (1) give the client the impression that the designer is professional, competent, knowledgeable, reliable, confident, trustworthy, and likeable, (2) learn as much about the client and the project as possible, and (3) be so successful that the meeting is the first step in a long-term relationship.

From the prospective client's perspective the goals of the appointment are to: (1) determine if the designer is someone he or she likes and feels he or she could work with on the project, (2) determine if the designer can understand the needs and aspirations for the design, and (3) comprehend the next steps in the process, including timelines and fees.

The designer should incorporate the goals of both parties in the agenda. Thus, prior to the appointment the designer should learn as much as possible about the person, the project, and when applicable, the organization. Obviously, when a designer already knows considerable information about a project, the agenda can focus on expanding this knowledge and probing for details.

When little is known about the project or people involved, the agenda must include very general discussions related to the basic parameters of the project. An example of an agenda for first appointments with provisions related to prior knowledge of the project is illustrated in Box 7.2. Items that would be listed on an agenda are in regular script; suggestions for what you might want to do at a particular point in a meeting are in italics. Think of the italics as ticklers that can prompt actions during an appointment.

Box 7.2

Agenda for First Appointment with Prospective Clients

(Note: Italics are suggestions for improving listening, showing collaboration efforts, etc. Think of the italics as ticklers in an appointment.)

AGENDA

First Appointment with Mr. Smyth
Date   June 12, 2012
Time   14:00 – 15:00
Place   Mr. Smyth's Office

- Introductions

- Background of XYZ Interiors and my design experience

- Explain my understanding of the project.

  Meets the goals of the designer and client by demonstrating professional competence, knowledge, and interest in the client.

- Ask Mr. Smyth to clarify and provide additional information about the project.

  (If he asks a question I don't have an answer for, I will get back to him.)

- Dialogue regarding the project

  (Connect my experiences with items Mr. Smyth has mentioned.)

  (Show how this will be a collaborative process between our design team and Mr. Smyth.)

  (Constantly qualify the project and Mr. Smyth.)

- Conclusion

  Meets the goals of the client by outlining timelines and fees.

  • Summarize the meeting.

  • Explain the next steps:

    · Letter of agreement
    · Fees
    · Contracts
    · Timeline
    · When I will contact Mr. Smyth

- Ask Mr. Smyth if he has any questions.

  (Make sure all information is gathered.)

  Meets the goals of the designer and client by initiating steps for a long-term relationship.

  (Record notes, send handwritten thank you note, update tickler file for promises, find follow-up answers, schedule a meeting with other people, order items, and arrange next meeting. If client seems hesitant and I like the project, identify ways to connect with him again.)

Qualifying Clients and Dialogues

There is a saying, "A designer is only as good as the client." In the long run, you do not want to work with clients who are unreasonable, unethical, irrationally demanding, inconsiderate, or unlikeable, and who do not understand how to work with a designer. Your first meeting with a prospective client gives you the opportunity to qualify the person.

Does the client seem interested in your skills and expertise? Does he or she value the work of an interior designer? Do you get the impression that the person thinks you are unqualified for the project? Is the prospect too busy to schedule the next appointment? Is he or she consumed with perceptions that designers charge too much for services? Is the person overly focused on the amount of your fees? Does he or she tell you the design solutions you are supposed to create for the project? Can you have a dialogue with the person?

During the course of a meeting with a potential client, be sensitive to your comfort level with that person. Initial instincts about people can give a heads-up regarding whether or not there is a good match—especially important when finances or your reputation could be on the line.

During your discussions with a client, be very careful how you respond to questions. Know exactly what you can and cannot deliver—and don't promise what you can't deliver. Making promises that cannot be fulfilled can happen when you are trying to impress a prospective client. Again: Don't promise what you can't deliver. False promises might enable you to get the business, but in the long term—always the driver in regard to client relationships—the results can be disastrous and can also end up in lawsuits.

Generally, issues to be watchful of are: (1) situations that are fundamentally out of your control, such as guaranteeing project completion dates, costs beyond a specific date, product availability, no changes to the design, performance of other professionals, and delivery dates; (2) requests to perform a service that is outside of your area of expertise; and (3) requests to do something unethical, such as providing free advice or free merchandise, revealing confidential information, or allowing the person to purchase items at unreasonably low prices.

If the client is asking for many things beyond your scope of services or control, this could be a hint the relationship will not work. It can be very difficult to turn down business when you are eager to design projects and acquire clientele. However, to have long-term relationships, you must ask yourself: Do I genuinely want to work with this person on this project? Note that there are two parts to this question.

The first issue addresses the likeability of the person, and the second concern is how you feel about the project. You might like a prospective client, but the project might not be appropriate for your area of expertise or experience. In this situation you might want to ask the client if it would be acceptable to invite other professionals to collaborate with you on the project. If you don't like the person but the project is exciting or interesting, you might want to again ask other professionals to become involved with the project, or it might be better to turn the entire project over to another associate in your firm.

Toward the end of an appointment, review what was covered and determine whether you have accomplished the goals of the meeting. Try to finish these tasks; then suggest to the client the next steps in the process and request permission to continue.

Generally, the next step is to enter into a contract with the client, but there might be some follow-up that needs to happen before developing an agreement. In this situation, the designer should list what needs to be done and suggest deadline dates. Sometimes the client has to provide more information, such as a budget, approvals from supervisors, or input from end users.

When the next step is a contract, the designer should review retainers, fees, payment schedules, and the date for sending the contract. The designer should also verify the client's preferred method of communication: mail, e-mail, texting, or phone calls. As always, within a day or two after the meeting, send the client a hand-written note thanking the person for his or her time and interest in your professional services.

Client Job Books

A successful appointment prompts the development of the client's job book—an invaluable file you will use throughout your involvement with the client, beginning with the first project and continuing with every project thereafter. Every contact, activity, transaction, schedule, and document associated with your client should be recorded in the client's job book.

Why? For a variety of reasons. First, every designer has to develop an effective method to organize the potentially thousands of items associated with a client's project. As the number of clients increases, well-organized files become even more important. For example, when a client contacts you about the delivery of a furniture piece, you will want to respond immediately.

Promptness not only demonstrates your efficiency, but it also sends a message to the client that you care about the person and his or her project. What if you received 20 or 40 calls in one day from a variety of clients and manufacturers who are requesting answers? Delaying your responses can appear rude and could seriously affect construction schedules to the extent that you might be held legally liable.

A client job book also becomes very important when you have not worked with a client for a period of time and that person contacts you because he or she wants to order an exact replacement of an item. You can't give the client the impression you don't recall him or her or the purchases the person made; doing so would damage the sense of connection between you and could harm the relationship.

Generally, it is very difficult to remember an exact item years later, and impossible to know the manufacturer's product number off the top of your head. However, this information can easily be retrieved when you maintain thorough and up-to-date job books. If the item has been discontinued, at least you will know what the item was so that you can look for an appropriate substitute and avoid disappointing a client.

Client job books are extraordinarily useful when an associate must work with a client during your absence or if you are no longer with the firm.

Job books can also be useful as a reference tool when you are preparing estimates for either a new project for the client or for other clients. These books can give you the number of hours required for specific services, fees recovered, cost breakdowns of items, expenses incurred, delivery times, installation fees, and any problems or complaints. In addition, documentation retained in job books might be very helpful for green certification programs and also in the unfortunate event of a lawsuit.

The client job book could be created using a paper file or a customer relationship management software program. Select the format you prefer; the goal is to use the file to store all of your client's records with ease and convenience.

What should be included in the job book? Everything related to contacts with the client and that person's projects. An organizational format helps you to understand what should be in the job book (Figure 7.4). The book could be organized in two major sections: one as a tickler system for active projects and the other for retaining records.

The tickler system is a means to track a project and to alert you when a deadline or task is approaching. Thus, as a project proceeds you could receive reminders for these examples: (1) when to order an item, (2) when to contact people providing service to a project, such as electricians, plumbers, painters, upholsterers, furniture deliverers, and flooring contractors, (3) expected installation and delivery dates, and (4) follow-ups to repairs.

In addition, the tickler file could be used to remind you when to contact clients, facility managers, or client representatives. Contacts could include: (1) routine project updates, (2) periodic post-occupancy inquiries that include asking if

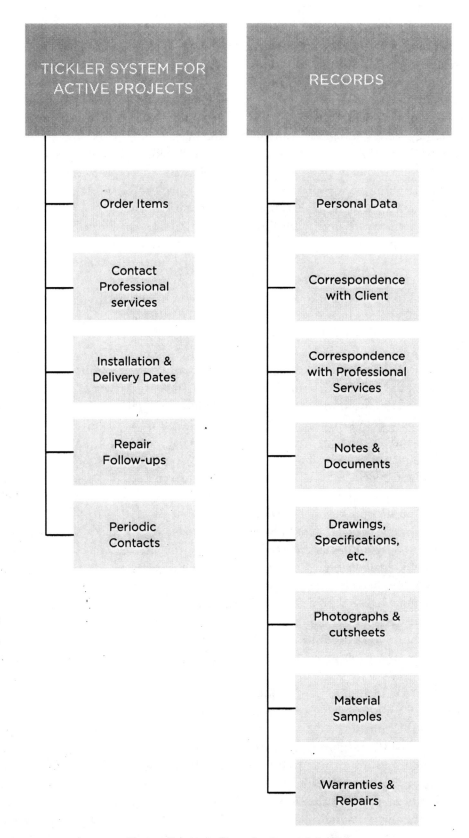

TICKLER SYSTEM FOR ACTIVE PROJECTS

- Order Items
- Contact Professional services
- Installation & Delivery Dates
- Repair Follow-ups
- Periodic Contacts

RECORDS

- Personal Data
- Correspondence with Client
- Correspondence with Professional Services
- Notes & Documents
- Drawings, Specifications, etc.
- Photographs & cutsheets
- Material Samples
- Warranties & Repairs

Figure 7.4 An outline of a client job book.

there are any problems to resolve, (3) personal notes to keep in touch, (4) thanking the client for working with you, (5) cards for birthdays and anniversaries, or (6) congratulations on the anniversary of an opening of a business or a building.

In addition to the tickler system, the client job book should have a method for retaining the following items:

- Personal data, such as the client's likes, dislikes, motivators, what is important to them, what they value, the best strategies for helping them to be successful, the best strategies for working with them, preferred means of communication, and articles about them or their business

- All correspondences between the designer and client, including copies of letters, e-mails, and notes

- All correspondences between the designer and other professionals, such as architects, contractors, developers, and electricians

- All contracts between the designer and client

- All contracts between the designer and other professionals associated with the client

- All notes from meetings, phone calls, text messages, discussions, and interviews that were associated with the client

- All documents associated with purchases, including purchase orders, invoices, and billing statements

- Drawings, sketches, contract documents, specifications, perspectives, photographs of models, and any other design-related documents, such as LEED reports, surveys, observation reports, and post-occupancy evaluations

- Before-and-after job site photographs

- Product cutsheets

- Small swatches of fabrics, carpet yarns, trimmings, finishes, wallcoverings, and paint samples

- Copies of product warranties

- Copies of documents relating to damages and repairs

Checking for Comprehension

- How can you improve your listening skills?

- What method would you use for a client job book? Why?

Client Relations: Contracts and Presentations

Thus far in this chapter we have discussed the CRC and profiles of interior designers as well as clients. This section analyzes some of the elements in the next phase of the CRC by reviewing contractual agreements, negotiation styles, and presentation techniques. Presentations are explained from the perspective that designers must present ideas and rationales on a daily basis.

Contracts and Negotiations

As defined in Chapter 6, a contract is a legal agreement when two or more individuals (parties) make voluntary promises to each other. Generally, the promises are to provide goods, services, or labor in exchange for pay. The laws that govern contracts as well as other commercial transactions between U.S. states and territories are the **Uniform Commercial Code (UCC)**. In addition, tort law might apply when someone fails to fulfill the terms of a contract.

This section reviews the most common contracts used by the design profession, but you should keep in mind that your firm might have its own forms, or **house forms**, that you will be required to use with your clients. In addition, some corporations might use their own contracts when engaging the services of professionals.

Any contracts used for business transactions should be reviewed with legal counsel. The attorney must be knowledgeable about the laws in force at the design firm's locale as well as laws that pertain to the location of a project. Furthermore, it is very helpful when the attorney has experience with the design profession.

You should *always* have a signed contract when you are working with a client. A signed contract creates the rights and obligations between you and the client. Furthermore, a contract might be needed to resolve mistakes, misinterpretations, and disputes involving the scope of services, fees, costs, schedules, and responsibilities.

When you are trying to begin what is hoped to become a lifelong relationship, it can be awkward to approach a client with the necessity of creating and signing a contract. You might fear that the client will have the impression that you are requiring a contract because you doubt the client's trustworthiness. Initially, a client could have this impression, but you can ease the person's anxieties by the way you approach the development of the contract as well as explaining how the contract protects the client's interests as well.

You will have clients with a wide range of experiences with contractual services. Clients who are accustomed to signing contracts for professional services understand and expect to sign the documents. Waiting to provide them with a contract presents an unprofessional image.

Clients who are not accustomed to working with a designer should be educated about the process, fees, and advantages of having a contract. This discussion should occur during the initial conversations with a prospective client. Explanations up front give the person the impression you are professional and you intend to be honest with him or her. In addition, if a client is not comfortable with fees or signing contracts, that person can decline services before you have provided any design advice.

Some designers will not schedule any appointment with a prospective client without a retainer and some type of a signed agreement, such as an **interim proposal**, formal contract, or **letter of agreement (LOA)**. In this situation,

a designer would send an agreement to the prospective client requesting that the person return the signed document and the retainer. Upon receipt of the agreement and retainer, the designer would proceed with arranging the appointment with the prospect.

Other designers are willing to meet with a prospective client for a limited amount of time without a signed agreement or a retainer. Thus, the designer might schedule the initial appointment and inform the prospect that the first half hour or full hour is free, but additional time is billable at a specific amount. Generally, in this situation, the fee quoted is by the hour and might require a minimum number of hours. When you are working with a client under these circumstances, the intent is to gather general *information* about the project without charging the client. This knowledge can help a designer to qualify the prospective client as well as the project.

When a designer does not want to work with the client, it becomes fairly easy to walk away from the project when fees or contracts have not been involved. But when you offer to waive initial fees, be careful of people who try to get free advice. The purpose of the free time is to gather information—not to provide design solutions. When asked for advice, explain to the prospective client that professional services require time, thought, collaboration, and the process of gathering relevant information.

Types of Contracts and Collaborative Negotiations

Signed contracts signal the beginning of the design process. What are the types of contracts? The residential and commercial contract documents produced by ASID illustrate the types of contracts available for the interior design profession (Boxes 7.3 and 7.4, and Appendix E).

As illustrated in Box 7.3, residential contract documents can be very open as in ID120-1996 or prescriptive as shown in the other contract documents. Thus, a designer could use ID120-1996 when he or she wants to delineate the

Box 7.3

ASID Residential and Commercial Contract Documents*

ASID Residential Interior Design Contract Documents

ID120-1996

Residential Interior Design Services Agreement (Short Form). This short-form document contains no printed description of design services or compensation arrangements. It is intended to be used by those wishing to set forth within the agreement their own description of design services to be rendered and method of compensation for such services. The short-form document does contain a section entitled "Miscellaneous" with printed terms and conditions.

ID121-1996

Residential Interior Design Services Agreement with compensation basis consisting of hourly fees with A Fixed Initial Design Fee and No Fee Charged on Purchases; or alternate language for a Fixed Initial Design Fee and Fees Charged on Purchases.

ID122-1996

Residential Interior Design Services Agreement with Fixed Fee Compensation Basis.

ID123-1996

Residential Interior Design Services Agreement with compensation basis consisting of cost plus on purchases, with A Fixed Initial Design Fee for Design Concept Services and Percentage of Contractor's Fees for Project Review; or alternate language for Hourly Fees for Design Concept Services with Initial Design Fee and Percentage of Contractor's Fees for Project Review.

ID124-1996

Residential Interior Design Services Agreement with compensation basis consisting of cost plus on purchases, with A Fixed Initial Design Fee for Design Concept Services and Hourly Fees for Project Review Services; or alternate language for Hourly Fees for Design Concept Services with Initial Design Fee and Hourly Fees for Project Review Services.

ID125-1996

Residential Interior Design Services Agreement with compensation basis consisting of presented price for purchases, with A Fixed Initial Design Fee for Design Concept Services and Percentage of Contractor's Fees for Project Review Services; or alternate language for Hourly Fees for Design Concept Services with Initial Design Fee and Percentage of Contractor's Fees for Project Review.

ID126-1996

Residential Interior Design Services Agreement with compensation basis consisting of presented price for purchases, with A Fixed Initial Design Fee for Design Concept Services and Hourly Fees for Project Review Services; or alternate language for Hourly Fees for Design Concept Services with Initial Design Fee and Hourly Fees for Project Review Services.

(Box 7.3 continued on page 222)

ASID Residential and Commercial Contract Documents* *(continued)*

ASID Commercial Interior Design Contract Documents

> Note contracts are for small/ medium sized commercial projects.

ID301-2008

Small/Medium sized Commercial Interior Design Service Agreement with compensation based on a Fixed Design Fee.

ID302-2008

Small/Medium Sized Commercial Interior Design Service Agreement with compensation based on an Hourly Design Fee.

ID303-2008

Small/Medium Sized Commercial Interior Design Service Agreement with compensation based on i) hourly charges for Project Program services; ii) a percentage of Interior Construction Costs, and; iii) a percentage of the vendor costs for Project Furniture, Furnishings and Equipment.

*Source: http://www.asid.org/NR/rdonlyres/EFE6458A-9C9F-4DF3-B136-42D6B8420305/0/ResandCommContractOrderFrom.pdf. Reprint from order form.

exact scope of services as well as the method of compensation. Some designers prefer to use this form because of the variability of each client and project. The form's lack of a description enables the designer to customize the contract for each client and for each project.

ASID's other residential contract documents are more specific. As illustrated in Box 7.3, most of the residential contract documents are based on a specific compensation basis, such as hourly fees, fixed fees, "cost plus on purchases," and "presented price for purchases." The compensation basis can be supplemented with various methods, including (1) fixed initial design fees, (2) no fee/fees charged on purchases, (3) fixed initial design fee for design concept services, (4) percentage of contractor's fees for project review, (5) hourly fees for design concept services with initial design fee, and (6) hourly fees for project review services.

ASID's contract documents for small/ medium commercial agreements include a compensation based on fixed design fees, hourly design fees, and a method to combine compensation by: (1) hourly charges for project program services and (2) a percentage of interior construction costs and vendor costs for project furniture, furnishings, and equipment.

Besides methods of compensation, what else should be included in a contract? As detailed in Box 7.4 and Appendix E, the basic elements of a contract should include the following: (1) names of the parties; (2) location and scope of the project; (3) scope of services provided by the designer; (4) scope of services provided by other parties; (5) contractual timeline; (6) compensation base and retainers; (7) means of payments and reimbursements; (8) extra services, taxes, shipping/delivery charges; (9) supplementary conditions; and (10) signature lines with dates.

Generally, retainers are applied toward payments for future services. Supplementary conditions could involve several items, such as ownership of merchandise, property of

ASID Document ID122

RESIDENTIAL INTERIOR DESIGN SERVICES AGREEMENT

This **AGREEMENT** is

made this _____ day of _____ . in the year of Two Thousand and _____

_____

BETWEEN the **CLIENT**:
(name and address)

and the **DESIGNER**:
(name and address)

The **CLIENT** and the **DESIGNER** agree as follows:

The Project pertains to the following areas within Client's residence located at

_____ :

(List areas below:)

ID122-1996   1

(Box 7.4 continued on page 224)

Box 7.4

ID122-1996 Residential Interior Design Services Agreement with Fixed Fee Compensation Basis *(continued)*

INTERIOR DESIGN SERVICES

1. **Design Concept Services**

1.1 In this phase of the Project, Designer shall, as and where appropriate, perform the following:

   A. Determine Client's design preferences and requirements.

   B. Conduct an initial design study.

   C. Prepare drawings and other materials to generally illustrate Designer's suggested interior design concepts, to include color schemes, interior finishes, wall coverings, floor coverings, ceiling treatments, lighting treatments and window treatments.

   D. Prepare layout showing location of movable furniture and furnishings.

   E. Prepare schematic plans for recommended cabinet work, interior built-ins and other interior decorative details ("Interior Installations").

1.2 Not more than _____ (_____) revisions to the Design Concept will be prepared by Designer without additional charges. Additional revisions will be billed to Client as Additional Services.

2. **Interior Specifications and Purchasing Services**

2.1 Upon Client's approval of the Design Concepts, Designer will, as and where appropriate:

   A. Select and/or specially design required Interior Installations and all required items of movable furniture, furnishings, light fixtures, hardware, fixtures, accessories and the like ("Merchandise").

   B. Prepare and submit for Client's approval Proposals for completion of Interior Installations and purchase of Merchandise.

2.2 Designer may, at times, request Client to engage others to provide Interior Installations, pursuant to the arrangements set forth in the Project Review services described in paragraph 3 of this Agreement.

2.3 Merchandise and Interior Installations to be purchased through Designer will be specified in a written "Proposal" prepared by Designer and submitted in each instance for Client's written approval. Each Proposal will describe the item and its price to Client (F.O.B. point of origin). The price of each item shall be the amount charged to Designer by the supplier of such item ("Client Price").

ID122-1996   2

Box 7.4

ID122-1996 Residential Interior Design Services Agreement with Fixed Fee Compensation Basis *(continued)*

2.4 No item can be ordered by Designer until the Proposal has been approved by Client, in writing, and returned to Designer with Designer's required initial payment equal to _____ percent (____%) of the Client Price. The balance of the Client Price, together with delivery, shipping, handling charges and applicable taxes, is payable when the item is ready for delivery to and/or installation at Client's residence, or to a subsequent supplier for further work upon rendition of Designer's invoice. Proposals for fabrics, wall coverings, accessories, antiques, and items purchased at auction or at retail stores require full payment at time of signed Proposal.

3. Project Review

3.1 If the nature of the Project requires engagement by Client of any contractors to perform work based upon Designer's concepts, drawings or interior design specifications not otherwise provided for in the Interior Specifications and Purchasing Services, Client will enter into contracts directly with the concerned contractor.

3.2 Designer will make periodic visits to the Project site as Designer may consider appropriate to observe the work of these contractors to determine whether the contractors' work is proceeding in general conformity with Designer's concepts. Constant observation of work at the Project site is not a part of Designer's duties. Designer is not responsible for the performance, quality, timely completion or delivery of any work, materials or equipment furnished by contractors pursuant to direct contracts with Client.

4. COMPENSATION

4.1 Designer's compensation for the Interior Design Services described above shall be a fixed fee of _____ dollars ($_____) payable as follows:

ID122-1996   3

(Box 7.4 continued on page 226)

4.2 Designer's compensation shall be subject to renegotiation if:

A. The scope of the Project changes materially; or

B. Through no fault of Designer, its Interior Design Services are not substantially completed within _____ (___) months of the date of signing this Agreement.

5. MISCELLANEOUS

5.1 Should Designer agree to perform any design service not described above, such "Additional Service" will be invoiced to Client at the following hourly rates:

Design Principal	$_____
Project Designer	$_____
Staff Designer	$_____
Draftsman	$_____
Other employees	$_____

Hourly charges will be invoiced to Client _____ and are payable upon receipt of invoice.

5.2 Disbursements incurred by Designer in the interest of the Project shall be reimbursed by Client to Designer upon receipt of Designer's invoices, which are rendered _____. Reimbursements shall include, among other things, costs of local and long distance travel, long distance telephone calls, duplication of plans, drawings and specifications, messenger services and the like.

5.3 Designer's drawings and specifications are conceptual in nature and intended to set forth design intent only. They are not to be used for architectural or engineering purposes. Designer does not provide architectural or engineering services.

5.4 Designer's services shall not include undertaking any responsibility for the design or modification of the design of any structural, heating, air-conditioning, plumbing, electrical, ventilation or other mechanical systems installed or to be installed at the Project.

5.5 Should the nature of Designer's design concepts require the services of any other design professional, such professional shall be engaged directly by Client pursuant to separate agreement as may be mutually acceptable to Client and such other design professional.

5.6 As Designer requires a record of Designer's design projects, Client will permit Designer or Designer's representatives to photograph the Project upon completion of the Project. Designer will be entitled to use photographs for Designer's business purposes but shall not disclose Project location or Client's name without Client's prior written consent.

Box 7.4

ID122-1996 Residential Interior Design Services Agreement
with Fixed Fee Compensation Basis *(continued)*

5.7 All concepts, drawings and specifications prepared by Designer's firm ("Project Documents") and all copyrights and other proprietary rights applicable thereto remain at all times Designer's property. Project Documents may not be used by Client for any purpose other than completion of Project by Designer.

5.8 Designer cannot guarantee that actual prices for Merchandise and/or Interior Installations or other costs or services as presented to Client will not vary either by item or in the aggregate from any Client proposed budget.

5.9 This Agreement may be terminated by either party upon the other party's default in performance, provided that termination may not be effected unless written notice specifying nature and extent of default is given to the concerned party and such party fails to cure such default in performance within _____ (____) days from date of receipt of such notice. Termination shall be without prejudice to any and all other rights and remedies of Designer, and Client shall remain liable for all outstanding obligations owed by Client to Designer and for all items of Merchandise, Interior Installations and other services on order as of the termination date.

5.10 In addition to all other legal rights, Designer shall be entitled to withhold delivery of any item of Merchandise or the further performance of Interior Installations or any other services, should Client fail to timely make any payments due Designer.

5.11 Any controversy or claim arising out of or relating to this Agreement, or the breach thereof, shall be decided by arbitration only in the _____ in accordance with the Commercial Arbitration Rules of the American Arbitration Association then in effect, and judgment upon the award rendered by the arbitrator(s) may be entered in any court having jurisdiction thereof.

5.12 Client will provide Designer with access to the Project and all information Designer may need to complete the Project. It is Client's responsibility to obtain all approvals required by any governmental agency or otherwise in connection with this Project.

5.13 Any sales tax applicable to Design Fees, and/or Merchandise purchased from Designer, and/or Interior Installations completed by Designer shall be the responsibility of Client.

5.14 Neither Client nor Designer may assign their respective interests in this Agreement without the written consent of the other.

5.15 The laws of the State of _____ shall govern this Agreement.

5.16 Any provision of this Agreement held to be void or unenforceable under any law shall be deemed stricken, and all remaining provisions shall continue to be valid and binding upon both Designer and Client.

5.17 This Agreement is a complete statement of Designer's and Client's understanding. No representations or agreements have been made other than those contained in this Agreement. This Agreement can be modified only by a writing signed by both Designer and Client.

ID122-1996   5

(Box 7.4 continued on page 228)

6. ADDITIONAL TERMS

CLIENT:

_____

_____

DESIGNER:

_____

_____

ID122-1996   6

Source: Reprinted from the American Society of Interior Designers, http://www.asid.org/.

drawings/designs, change order procedures, and provisions for additional expenses, delays, damages, injuries, and acts of nature.

Collaborative Contract Negotiations

At the beginning of this section, it was suggested that a designer can ease a client's apprehensions about contracts by how he or she approaches the development of the contract as well as by explaining how the contract protects the client's interests as well. Thus, when writing the contract, you should have the mindset that you are initiating a long-term collaborative relationship with your client. Consequently, you should develop drafts of the contract with your client. This collaborative approach helps you both to better define the parameters of the project, responsibilities, costs, schedules, and perhaps future alliances.

Reviewing drafts of a contract with a client can also help educate the client regarding the design process, how a designer is involved in each phase of the design process, and problems and setbacks that can occur during a project. Moreover, involving the client in drafts of the contract can help reduce or eliminate the need for negotiations. Thus, negotiations are integrated within the collaborative process of developing the contract.

A close examination of key elements in a contract can demonstrate how a contract can be collaboratively negotiated. One very important collaborative element is defining the scope of the project. Unless a client is very familiar with building, remodeling, or renovations, there tends to be little awareness of all the activities, expenses, and requirements necessary for a project. Clearly defining the scope of the project is the first step.

The client and the designer must clearly understand: (1) which rooms/spaces/buildings are involved with the project, (2) exactly what the client wants done to each room/space/building, and (3) which elements will remain and which elements are to be replaced or added. Identifying the exact scope of the project enables the designer and the client to learn if there are elements that were forgotten, as well as items that should be included in the project.

Within the context of the scope of the project, the designer and client can both gain an understanding of the designer's services. From this perspective every task and item within each area of the project should be reviewed to determine responsibility. For example, in an office, a designer might be responsible for ordering new desks, but the client might want to purchase the artwork. A thorough approach to this task is to follow the project through every stage of the design process (see Chapters 8 and 9).

Analyzing the project through the design process enables the designer and the client to think about tasks that should be prescribed in the contract, such as feasibility studies, programming procedures, design concepts, determining functional/aesthetic needs, contract documents/administration, and other services.

As you are discussing what items are included in your services, be sure to explain to the client exactly what is *not* provided in the contract. This gives the client the opportunity to decide if some services are not necessary, as well as adding other services. A clear understanding of responsibilities when the contract is signed helps to eliminate or at least reduce disappointments or frustrations that can occur during project implementation phases.

Reviewing the project via the design process can also help clarify and refine the schedule. Collaborating with the client on the project's schedule provides an excellent chance to explain unavoidable and unpredictable elements of a project, such as discontinued products, damaged goods, lost deliveries, installation problems, construction delays, fabricator delays, and holdups because of the late arrivals of materials, products, or equipment. When a client is aware that these problems can occur, then when or if they do occur, he or she is more likely to understand the normalcy of the events and less likely to become upset with the designer. Moreover, time and expenses associated with delays and setbacks can be factored into the terms of the contract—another attempt to prevent client anger during project implementation phases.

When a client has a thorough understanding of the scope of the project, the designer's services, and the amount of time required to complete a project, it is much easier to discuss fees, compensation, and reimbursements. Thus, this area of the contract should not be reviewed until the other elements are clarified and agreed upon.

A clear understanding of the project provides the basis for determining what fee structure would be best for the client as well as the designer. Thus, the entire project and services can be reviewed within the various options outlined in ASID's contract documents.

What is the best compensation strategy within the context of the project requirements, services provided, and time period? The compensation plan should be approached from the standpoint of initiating a long-term relationship. Thus, the arrangement should be cost-effective for the client while sustaining a reasonable profit for the designer and the design firm. In collaborating with the client, examine various options that could involve fixed fees, hourly rates, fees charged on purchases, percentage of contractor fees, hourly charges for project program services, or a combination of compensation methods.

While reviewing compensation strategies, the designer should work with the client to identify a payment plan that is convenient for the client and provides the funds the design firm needs to pay vendors, suppliers, and salaries in a timely manner. A review of costs should include determining who pays taxes, shipping/delivery charges, storage, installation expenses, registration fees, travel expenses, and any special services, such as renderings, models, and presentation boards. In addition, the client should fully understand that he or she is responsible for any expenses or delays that can occur as a result of requesting changes or revisions to the project.

Even after carefully collaborating with the client in the development of a contract, you still might have to engage in some form of negotiations—normally about price. The collaborative approach to contract development is intended to result in a win-win situation; this is the same mindset you should have when negotiating with a client. Remember: You are trying to establish a lifelong relationship with the client; thus, negotiations should not be adversarial but should be a means to reach an agreement with benefits to all parties.

When entering into negotiations with a client, you should be well prepared by understanding all parameters of a project, the needs of the client, your goals, and the limits of the negotiation process. It is very important to listen to your client closely during the dialogue and to present reasoned arguments for your perspective. Always be professional. In addition, you should look for signs that negotiations seem to be coming to a close and conclude the process before there can be an irretrievable breakdown.

Prolonged negotiations can result in disappointments, frustrations, and questions regarding a designer's trustworthiness and goodwill—all issues that are counterproductive to establishing a relationship. Thus, if reasonable, it might well be worth compromising to the appeasement of the client to sustain good relations. If the required compromise is unreasonable, the chances are very good that the project is not right for you or your design firm.

Informal and Formal Presentations

What do you think of when you are told you have to give a presentation? Chances are very good that you believe you will have to deliver a presentation by standing in front of a group of people. This is one presentation method used by designers, but just one of many approaches to providing information during the design process.

Nearly every day a designer has to present some idea, concept, or rationale to a variety of people, such as clients, end users, supervisors, coworkers, alliances, suppliers, installers, and fabricators (Figure 7.5). Thus, improving your

Figure 7.5 Nearly every day a designer has to present some idea, concept, or rationale to a variety of people. (© Somos Images/Alamy)

presentation skills can help you to effectively communicate with people on a daily basis.

There are *many* times when you will have to do some type of presentation to a client. Your first appointment with a client requires you to present your background, experience, and areas of expertise. Design proposals can be presented to clients, committees, end users, and competition judges. Project updates and post-occupancy evaluations can be presented to clients and their representatives. In other words, at every phase of the design process you might have to present information to a client as well as persuade that person to agree with and approve various elements associated with a project.

Throughout the design process you will have to inform and persuade a client about a wide range of conditions and expectations. Presentations can be very informal, as when presenting an idea to one person during lunch, and continue along the spectrum to a very formal presentation that involves presenting a design proposal for a complex of buildings to an audience of 100 people in a large auditorium.

Presentations might have to be delivered in a range of methods to a range of audiences: using no tech or high tech; cocktail napkins or presentation boards; sketches or models; spontaneous or planned; in person or online; seated or standing; alone or in teams; known or unknown audience; audience very familiar with design or audience that knows nothing about design; audience fluent in English or English as a second language; monoculture or multicultural; and single generation or multiple generations.

The wide range of potential scenarios illustrates situations you might encounter in your career and are included to demonstrate that designers must continually deliver some type of presentation to professionals as well as clients throughout the CRC. Informative presentations professionally delivered can contribute to long-term relationships with clients. Thus, it is very important that you overcome any anxieties about presentations. Becoming more comfortable giving presentations requires understanding how to prepare and deliver them effectively.

The preparation process should be used for every type of presentation. Obviously, some presentations will require more preparation than others, but each incorporates the same basic elements: introduction, body, and close. Once the presentation structure becomes routine, you can use the format to quickly organize your thoughts when asked to present your ideas at a moment's notice. For instance, during a casual conversation, if a client unexpectedly asks you to explain why you selected a particular furniture piece, you can provide a prompt and complete response by organizing your answer based on the critical elements of a presentation: introduction, body, and close.

Presentation Preparations

Within the context of the variety of presentations you will deliver as a designer, you might have no time to prepare, or several weeks, or perhaps even months. Regardless of the amount of preparation time, always consider: (1) the purpose of the presentation, (2) who is listening, (3) what you would like to accomplish with the presentation, and (4) how to appear credible and professional.

Most often the purpose of an interior designer's presentation is to inform or to persuade. For example, designers might deliver an

informative presentation to a committee when they are providing updates on the renovation of a library. In this situation the purpose of the presentation is to primarily disseminate facts and figures to the committee, such as what installations have been completed, which spaces are scheduled in the next phase, and when the entire project is expected to be completed.

An example of a **persuasive presentation** is when a designer presents a design proposal to a client for the purpose of convincing them that a design flawlessly accommodates their needs. Done well results in new business—done poorly results in no business. Thus, a well-prepared persuasive presentation can help to build a client base and acquire new projects.

Understanding the profile of your audience (who will be listening) is critical when preparing a presentation. As with preparing for an interview with a client, the more you know about the audience, the more you will be able to customize the presentation to their needs and background. The variability ranges described earlier provide examples of characteristics of your audience that you should try to identify, such as their knowledge of design, fluency with the language, and cultural norms. Might you need to hire an interpreter for your presentation?

You should also try to determine the audience's state of mind. Are they apprehensive because they are not familiar with your work? Are they complacent because they are too familiar with the work of your firm? Will they be excited about your presentation? Do they want to be there? Are they concerned about the cost of a designer? Are they thrilled that the project was completed on time? Are they angry with delays and cost overruns? Attempting to understand the audience's state of mind can help you to prepare a presentation that addresses the situation.

What you would like to accomplish with a presentation is tied to its purpose as well as the needs of the audience. Generally, when you are delivering an informative presentation, you want to ensure that the audience feels they have received and understand all of the necessary information. In addition, it is hoped that the presentation was able to inspire the audience and alleviate any ambivalence or negative feelings about the designer or the project.

Examples of successful persuasive presentations are winning the contract, convincing a client to purchase a specific furniture piece, or motivating him or her to pursue LEED building certification. Thus, as described in the next section, the content of your presentation should be targeted to these accomplishments. For example, if you were trying to motivate your client to pursue LEED certification and he or she was unfamiliar with the details of the process, the major points in your presentation should focus on the certification process as well as describing the benefits associated with green buildings. Another aspect that could be included in a persuasive LEED certification presentation is testimonies from prominent businesspeople who have certified buildings. Their credibility could be very persuasive to your client, but in addition to including testimonies from experts and renowned people, you must convince your audience that you and your design firm are credible and professional. How?

Generally, credibility can be demonstrated by experience, education, specializations, certifications, awards, and affiliations with prestigious organizations, businesses, and professionals. Thus, any attributes that reflect positively on your credibility should be stated at the beginning of the presentation and reflected in points addressed throughout the rest of the presentation. For example, in the previous LEED scenario, your credibility could be established at the start of the presentation by stating that you are a LEED-certified professional. Therefore, every time the points in your presentation addressed LEED certification, the information would appear to be credible.

Any credibility established at the beginning will be lost if the rest of the presentation is unprofessional, poorly prepared, or badly delivered. The importance of a professional image has been discussed many times in this book and is just as applicable to presentations. Your appearance and all of the items included in your presentation must be professional (see the next section). Pay particular attention to your audience profile, and their expectations and value systems. Refer to Chapter 5 for considerations when delivering presentations to various cultures and the issues related to generational differences discussed in this chapter. As always, building lifelong relationships requires empathy (understanding someone's perspective) and knowing how to meet the needs of a client.

Presentation Outlines

After you have created a profile of the audience and determined the purpose of the presentation, the desired accomplishments, and a means to establish credibility, the next step is to create an outline of the presentation. Like a letter, a presentation has an introduction, body, and closing, and should be developed by writing several drafts (Box 7.5).

As discussed in the next section, within each of the main areas you should consider visuals that support concepts or text. The introduction should be brief but should attract the attention of your audience, establish your credibility, and succinctly state how the presentation will proceed, including when you plan to respond to questions.

Generally, a good way to attract audience attention is to begin with a rhetorical question, interesting fact, or story that is germane to the presentation and the needs of the audience. Unless you know the audience very well, avoid starting out with jokes or humor.

Box 7.5

Outline of a Presentation to a Client

(Note: Italics are suggestions for visuals and other supporting materials. Think of the italics as ticklers during the presentation.)

Presentation to Smyth Corporation

Clear understanding of the purpose of the presentation.

Purpose To explain how XYZ Interiors can help the Smyth Corporation's headquarters building attain LEED Platinum status.

Introduction

Brief, but should attract the attention of your audience.

I. XYZ Interiors has worked on 25 LEED-certified buildings in the past 3 years; 5 of those buildings are LEED Platinum.

(Photographs of LEED Platinum buildings and positive testimonials from clients)

II. XYZ Interiors' strategy for achieving LEED Platinum certifications

    A. Staff qualifications

    B. Collaborative relationships with specialized professionals

    C. Comprehensive and integrative approach throughout the design process

(Box 7.5 continued on page 234)

Box 7.5
Outline of a Presentation to a Client *(continued)*

Body

III. Staff qualifications

(Photographs of design teams and award-winning projects)

    A. Design team qualifications that include LEED accreditations

    B. Design team qualifications that are reflected in being named the number one green design firm in the country and receiving the Green Award for LEED-certified buildings

IV. Collaborative relationships

(Photographs of charrettes in worldwide locations)

    A. Examples of collaborative networks in 18 offices on 3 continents

    B. Examples of successful LEED projects that involved collaborative relationships

V. Comprehensive and integrative approach

(Graphics depicting integrative processes and photographs of projects that illustrate our comprehensive approach throughout the design process)

    A. Explanations of how XYZ Interiors approaches projects from an integrative and comprehensive perspective

    B. Examples of successful LEED Platinum certified projects with an emphasis on client relationships, adding value, and flexibility

    C. Examples of successful LEED Platinum certified projects with an emphasis on energy conservation, sustainable performance, and 3D analysis tools

Three-to-five main points targeted to the purpose of the presentation.

Close

VI. XYZ Interiors' strategy for achieving LEED Platinum certifications includes:

    A. Design team qualifications

    B. Collaborative relationships with specialized professionals

    C. Comprehensive and integrative approach throughout the design process

VII. XYZ Interiors has experience with 25 LEED certified buildings; 5 of those buildings are LEED Platinum.

VIII. XYZ Interiors can help Smyth Corporation to be successful in attaining LEED Platinum status.

(Close with a video of our most impressive LEED Platinum building and include shots of people meaningfully engaged in the space.)

Reversal of the presentation.

The body of the presentation should have between three and five main points, with each point having between two and three subpoints. The points should be targeted to the purpose of the presentation and your intended accomplishments. Remember to consider the background of your audience. If they are unfamiliar with the design profession, avoid acronyms and be sure to define any terms, concepts, or technologies mentioned that are associated with the built environment. In addition, do not assume your audience understands how to read drawings. When drawings are elements in your presentation, consider including points that explain how to interpret the symbols, graphics, or abbreviations.

The presentation's closing should be a reversal of your introduction. Thus, the closing should summarize the main points of the presentation, reinforce your credibility, and conclude with remarks that leave the audience feeling positive and perhaps cause them to pause and reflect.

Once you have developed a draft of your presentation, then practice, practice, and practice at least one more time. The more you practice your presentation, the more comfortable you will become with its content, order, visuals, pauses, emphases, pronunciations, and length. And the better you will deliver it. As you practice your presentation, try to determine how you want to handle questions and answers (Q&A).

Some presenters invite the audience to ask questions or provide remarks at any time during what can then become a discussion. Other presenters prefer to stay focused on the content and request that the audience refrain from asking questions until the end of the presentation. Remember, because of potential technological problems, online presentations might require additional time for Q&A to ensure that participants are receiving information. In addition, you might want to send online participants handouts prior to the presentation.

You can determine which structure is most comfortable to you, but keep in mind that regardless of what you prefer, there can always be audience members who ask questions at any time during a presentation. Be prepared for the interruption and how you might handle the situation. Generally, a presenter will politely provide a brief response, but if the question is complicated, the presenter might suggest the two speak after the presentation. When you are asked a question, repeat the question to your audience before delivering a response. This helps to clarify the question and to ensure that all audience members have heard the question.

Presentation Visuals and Delivery

Practice your presentation with any visuals you plan to include with your presentation. For designers, visuals or props can be very extensive as well as costly. Thus, as you consider which, if any, visuals you will include in the presentation, you should be very selective so you don't overwhelm your audience.

A designer has many visuals that can be used in a presentation, including photographs, sketches, drawings, renderings, models, computer animation, material samples, product literature, presentation boards, hyperlinks, audios, and videos. Microsoft PowerPoint is an option, as well as electronic whiteboards, flipcharts, tracing paper, and blackboards. Thus, a designer can determine how passive or active (or a combination of both) to be during a presentation. Quite often an audience gets very excited to see designers actually sketching their ideas as they speak. However, whatever types of visuals you use must be professional and necessary, and must also be included in your rehearsals.

The size and type of visuals should be appropriate for the location of the presentation. Manipulating large presentation boards in a little, crowded office can be very awkward, and small models in a large auditorium become lost.

Location also plays an important role in the type of technology you use for a presentation. Thus, when planning a presentation, ask what type of technology and support staff is available at the site. And if you are delivering an online presentation, ask what type of system is being used, such as webcasts, screencasts, or virtual meeting systems.

When you are using PowerPoint slides, be sure to consider the number of slides, amount of content, fonts, multimedia elements, transitions, and colors. Strategize the number of PowerPoint slides used in your presentation. The most effective means of communication is face-to-face. When a PowerPoint slide is displayed on a screen, the audience is reading the information, not looking at you. Therefore, every sentence or phrase of your presentation outline does not have to be printed on a slide. Determine when you want your audience to read a point on the screen and when you want them to look at you. When you want them to pay attention to you, show a blank slide (these can also be useful for transitioning between topics).

Resist the urge to use slides as an "information dump." Each slide should have only one main idea supported with three to five lines. The size of the font will determine the number of lines and words on a slide. If you are presenting in a small room, you might want to use a font size between 32 and 44 points, but a very large room might require a font size between 130 and150 points. Thus, as illustrated in Figure 7.6, the smaller-size font allows for more words than the very large font. The most readable fonts for slides are **sans serif**, thus Arial and Helvetica are good choices.

Figure 7.6 A PowerPoint slide with different font sizes.

Color also affects the readability of slides. Dark backgrounds with light-colored text, such as cream, white, or light gray, work well when the lighting is dimmed. Remember: The goal is to have your audience focus on the purpose of your presentation and not distracted by the slides or other visuals. Backgrounds should always be subtle, as well as any other elements added to your slides, such as animation, graphics, and multimedia elements.

Consider cultural norms when you select colors for your slides; use colors that appeal to a culture, and avoid colors that might have an undesirable meaning. In addition, the number of colors used should be limited to three to present a unified appearance. More than three colors can be distracting and increases the probability of selecting a color that someone dislikes.

To demonstrate your creativity and skill, design your own slides instead of using the master slides supplied with PowerPoint. Every slide should have the same format. If you are using transition animations, be sure to select a subtle action and use the same animated feature throughout the presentation.

Keep in mind that most clients are not able to visualize a design. Thus, multimedia elements, such as drawings, photographs, and video clips, can enhance your presentation. But, again, these elements should not *be* the presentation.

Presentation Deliveries

Before your presentation, make sure the equipment, software, and so on is set up correctly, and if necessary, provide online participants with time to connect. Have your speaking notes and any visuals arranged for the greatest accessibility and convenience. Speaking notes should be used for reference purposes—*never* read your presentation to your audience. Practicing your presentation several times will help you to become so familiar with the material that you will be able to rely on cues, such as visuals, to guide you through each slide.

Practice will also help you to develop a calm and conversational style—two critically important elements to a successful presentation. Your dress should be professional, but select apparel and shoes that are comfortable (this helps you avoid distractions and look at ease). Your demeanor should be professional, confident, polite, energetic, and enthusiastic. If you are not excited about your presentation, how can the audience become interested?

An enthusiastic delivery must be accompanied with good eye contact, pauses at optimum times, and the avoidance of prejudices and biases, such as racist or gender remarks. In addition, avoid physical/visual/auditory distractions, such as touching your hair, shuffling your feet, chewing gum, looking at the ground, repeatedly waving your arms, and using words such as "um," "like," or "you know."

Observe your audience as you are delivering your presentation (Figure 7.7). Are they talking to each other? Are they texting? Are they tapping their feet? Are they gathering their materials to indicate they are ready to leave? Are there expressions of confusion? Are there frowns of disagreement? Are the audience members quiet because they are engrossed in what you are saying? Do they seem distracted by flickering

Figure 7.7 As you are delivering your presentation, observe your audience. Examine this photograph and respond to the following questions: Are there people who appear to be distracted? If yes, why do they seem to be distracted? Do people appear to be bored, confused, or interested? How can you tell? (© Paul Doyle/Alamy)

lights, noisy air conditioners, or telephones? Do they seem distracted by views of the outdoors, a cold room, or a hot room?

By observing your audience, you can determine if they are bored, confused, distracted, interested, or excited with your presentation. Use the information to adjust the elements under your control, such as explaining confusing material or maintaining eye contact. If you do not know the answer to a question, be honest and say you will research the information and follow up by an approximate time period. Elements that might be beyond your control, such as the room temperature or flickering lights, could be addressed by asking for assistance. At least the audience will know you empathize with them and that you too want to resolve the problem.

When presenting, face your audience. Do not turn your back to them. It is tempting to turn your back to the audience to look at slides on a screen, to see information written on a board, or to explain details of a floor plan. Always maintain face-to-face contact with your audience. Stand to the side of visuals and use a pointer to guide their focus to specific details.

In addition, when you are discussing details in a drawing, such as a floor plan, do not tell the audience what an object is without describing an important feature of the item. For example, a common approach to explaining a floor plan during a presentation is to say, "This is the desk, the guest chairs, and the fabrics for the guest chairs." This statement informs the audience that there is a desk, guest chairs, and suggested fabrics, but it does not give them a reason to buy the desk, guest chairs, and fabrics. Instead, be sure to always include the reason why an item is important to the overall design and the needs of the client. Thus, the previous quote could be "The desk, guest chairs, and fabrics were selected for their impeccable quality, stylistic features, sustainability characteristics, and reasonable costs."

Remember to *close* the presentation. Frequently, presenters will jump from the body of a presentation to the Q&A segment. The leap is awkward to listen to and the omission removes a critical element of a presentation: convincing the audience to take action. The closing should summarize the highlights of the presentation and could end with a statement, such as "I truly look forward to working with you on this project" or "I hope to have the opportunity to work with you on this project."

A solid close indicates that the presentation is over and also helps underscore your image as a professional—someone who takes care of the final details. The end of your closing is often a good time to distribute any handouts, such as brochures or executive summaries. When you give an audience these materials at the beginning of a presentation, they tend to read the documents rather than concentrate on what you are saying.

Follow up your closing and the Q&A session with a genuine "thank you" for both the opportunity and the audience's time and attention. Listen intently to remarks presented during the Q&A discussion. Soon after the presentation, jot down notes about audience members' questions, concerns, and what they seemed to like and dislike. Also record follow-up tasks, such as finding answers to questions, product substitutions, revised design concepts, phone calls, and writing thank you notes.

Checking for Comprehension

* Identify two important elements in a contract.

* Describe strategies for delivering an effective oral presentation.

This chapter reviewed absolutely essential information for becoming a successful interior designer: building long-term relationships with loyal clients. In doing so, the chapter reviewed the CRC and provided suggestions for working with existing clients as well as acquiring new clients.

Effective interpersonal communication skills were explored by examining the importance of having dialogues and being a good listener.

The last section in the chapter reviewed collaborative approaches to contract negotiations and provided recommendations for delivering informal and formal presentations.

These core elements of client relationships will be applied to the content in the next two chapters. Chapter 8 reviews project management strategies followed by an analysis in Chapter 9 of the phases of the integrated design process: programming, schematic design, design development, contract documents, and contract administration. Chapter 9 also discusses post-occupancy responsibilities and their role in the CRC.

Knowledge and Skills Summary

Highlights

* The CRC begins with acquiring a new client and proceeds by engaging in meetings, presenting proposals, signing contracts, and implementing design services. After completion of a project, a designer should maintain the relationship by keeping in contact with the client.

* To initiate a relationship with a client, you must first understand the strengths and weaknesses of your professional profile as well as the client's.

* Responsibilities of designers include reexamining existing clients and creating strategies for acquiring new clients.

* To prepare for appointments with prospects and clients, designers develop interpersonal communication strategies.

* Initial meetings with clients require a qualification process and discussions that focus on clarifying fees, contracts, and professional services.

* A client's job book is used throughout the CRC. Every contact, activity, transaction, schedule, and document associated with a client should be recorded here.

- Contracts with clients include interim proposals, formal contracts, and letters of agreement.

- Building long-term relationships with a client involves developing contracts through collaborative negotiations.

- Designers engage in informal or formal presentations on a daily basis. Presentations can be informative or persuasive.

- Presentations have an introduction, body, and a closing. Presentation deliveries should be practiced many times.

Key Terms

client job book

cold call

cutsheet

dialogue

generation

house form

informative presentation

interim proposal

letter of agreement (LOA)

persuasive presentation

prospect

qualifications package

RFI (request for information)

RFP (request for proposal)

RFQ (request for qualifications)

sans serif

self-brand

suspect

Uniform Commercial Code (UCC)

Projects

Philosophy and Design Project

The first step in being able to "satisfy client requirements" is to understand who you are and how you prefer to build relationships. For this project you should expand on the self-assessment exercise in Chapter 3 by including cultural dimensions reviewed in Chapter 5 as well as generational attitudes, which are analyzed in this chapter. Based on this information, develop an updated personal profile that includes your attitudes, beliefs, and values (if needed, refer to Tables 5.1, 5.2, and 5.3). Develop a table of your personal profile and include examples of how you would need to adapt to work in two other countries listed in the tables.

Research Project

A client's job book is an invaluable file that you will use throughout your involvement with the client, beginning with the first project and continuing with every project thereafter. Research items and various formats that could be used for a client's job book; the goal is to use the file to store client's records with ease and convenience.

Develop a plan for creating a client job book you would use when you begin working as an interior designer. The job book should have a way to record every contact, activity, transaction, schedule, and document associated with a client. The book could be organized in two major sections. One section could be a tickler system for active projects, and the second section could be used for keeping records. Submit an example of your client job book with an explanation of how the format will help to facilitate your work as an interior designer.

Human Factors Research Project

Examine the effective listening components listed in Box 7.1. Identify your listening challenges, and develop suggestions for improvement. To assess your listening skills, create a daily log of your reactions to listening situations in the classroom, at work, and during social events. You might also want to discuss listening skills with friends online and in person. Develop a written report (approximately three pages) of your analyses and include strategies for effective listening for your future work with clients.

References

American Society of Interior Designers (ASID). 2010. ASID Contract Documents. http://www.asid.org/NR/rdonlyres/EFE6458A-9C9F-4DF3-B136-42D6B8420305/0/ResandCommContractOrderFrom.pdf. Accessed November 17, 2010.

Foster + Partners. 2010. *Foster + Partners*. http://www.fosterandpartners.com/Practice/Default.aspx. Accessed November 23, 2010.

Gensler. 2012. *Gensler*. http://www.gensler.com/. Accessed March 27, 2012.

Graham, S. 2006. "Listening Comprehension: The Learner's Perspective." *System* 34, 165–182.

HOK. 2010. *HOK*. http://www.hok.com/. Accessed November 23, 2010.

Howe, N. 2010. *Millennials in the Workplace*. Great Falls, VA: LifeCourse Associates.

Macaro, E. 2006. "Strategies for Language Learning and for Language Use: Revising the Theoretical Framework." *Modern Language Journal 90*, 320–337.

Merriam-Webster's Dictionary. 2010. *Merriam-Webster's Dictionary*. http://www.merriam-webster.com/dictionary/ethic. Accessed November 1, 2010.

Pew Research Center. 2010. *Millennials: A Portrait of Generation Next*. http://pewsocialtrends.org/files/2010/10/millennials-confident-connected-open-to-change.pdf. Accessed November 20, 2010.

Rost, M. 2002. *Teaching and Researching Listening*. Harlow, UK: Longman.

Vogely, A. 1995. "Perceived Strategy Use During Performance on Three Authentic Listing Comprehension Tasks." *Modern Language Journal* 79, 41–56.

CHAPTER

8

Enhancing Your Value: Project Management Skills

Bab 8 (Malay)
Kapitolu 8 (Maltese)
Kapittel 8 (Norwegian)

After learning the content in Chapter 8, you will be able to answer the following questions:

* What do I need to know about project management strategies and project delivery methods?

* How can I define the scope of a project?

* How can I continuously improve the quality of my services?

* What should I do to create a schedule for a project?

* How should I help to facilitate a project's human resource management plan?

* How can I develop a project's budget and control costs?

* What should I do to facilitate communication processes during the life of a project?

* How can I create management plans for risks and procurement?

Design is a business that is dependent on client relationships. Chapter 7 began the exploration of understanding how to build long-term client relationships by explaining the client relationship cycle (CRC) and strategies for working with existing clients as well as prospects. The chapter reviewed the importance of interpersonal communication skills with an emphasis on dialogue and effective listening. Chapter 7 also described how to have productive appointments with clients and what should be included in client job books. The chapter concluded by examining various types of contracts, negotiation strategies, and dynamic presentations.

Chapter 8 continues to discuss business practices that are critical to providing value and building long-term relationships with clients by exploring the topic within the context of effective project management practices. The chapter begins by providing an overview of project management that includes examining project delivery methods, scope management, and strategies for managing quality.

The next section reviews approaches to managing key project resources: schedules, people, and budgets. The chapter's culminating section explores project communication channels as well as strategies for managing risks and procurement activities.

Project Management: Elements and Strategies

Descriptions of the design process generally begin with the programming phase; however, there are many predesign activities that precede this phase, including initial contacts with clients and signed contracts, as reviewed in Chapter 7. After the interior designer wins a contract the next predesign activity is planning the project by using **project management** strategies.

Project management requires comprehensive planning and effective strategies for organizing, monitoring, and controlling all elements of a project. Ineffective management can result in projects that are not completed on time, have

budget overruns, and do not fulfill the client's quality requirements—all potentially irretrievably damaging to client relations.

Excellent sources for project management are the Project Management Institute (PMI; http://www.pmi.org/), the Association for Project Management (APM; http://www.apm.org.uk/), and the IPMA International Project Management Association (IPMA; http://www.ipma.ch/Pages/default.aspx).

Project Management: Definition and Components

Regardless of the size or complexity of the built environment, every project should employ project management strategies. Large projects have **project managers**—the person responsible for planning and managing a project. To be successful, a project manager must have excellent leadership skills, interpersonal skills, organizational abilities, and a willingness to work with a variety of people in situations that have the potential to become stressful.

Generally, you will not be expected to manage a project until you have adequate experience, but you can become involved with project management strategies as a member of a design team. Therefore, before beginning your career, you should become very familiar with the most effective approaches to project management. Potential employers have this expectation, as illustrated in the following interior design job requirement: "Seeking applicants with knowledge of the total project process including fee and team management, schedules, and budgets."

What is project management? A credible source for this definition is the PMI, an organization associated with the project management profession and offering the project manager certification program. PMI created *A Guide to the Project Management Body of Knowledge (PMBOK Guide)*, a document that has become an internationally recognized standard (ANSI/PMI 99-001-2008; American National Standards Institute/Project Management Institute). The organization defines project management as "the application of knowledge, skills, tools, and techniques to project activities to meet the project requirements" (PMI 2008). The PMI suggests that managing a project includes the following (2008):

* Identifying requirements

* Addressing the various needs, concerns, and expectations of the stakeholders as the project is planned and carried out

* Balancing the competing project constraints including, but not limited to:

  * Scope

  * Quality

  * Schedule

  * Resources

  * Risk

Hopefully you or your design firm will be involved with several projects at the same time. In these situations the knowledge, skills, tools, and techniques required for all of the projects must be coordinated through **portfolio management**.

Project management software is available for portfolio management as well as a single project, but the software should be used to facilitate your policies and procedures, not as the means to create project management.

Some of the project management software programs available are Method 123 (see http://www.method123.com), Microsoft Project (see http://www.microsoft.com/project), and Primavera (see http://www.oracle.com).

Project Management Plan (PMP)

One of the first steps in project management is creating a **project management plan (PMP)**. The PMP serves as the guide for activities required to accomplish the goals of the project. Thus, if the project's goal is to design an efficient office space for 16 employees, the PMP outlines every step that must occur to complete the office on time, within budget, and according to the client's requirements.

To accomplish the goals of a project, the PMP includes a detailed description of the design requirements (**project scope**), quality assurances, schedules, team members, stakeholders, communication channels, budgets, procurement policies, and strategies to manage risks (see next sections).

The PMP is typically developed for the entire **project life cycle (PLC)**. For project management purposes, the PLC has four basic elements: (1) starting the project, (2) organizing and preparing, (3) carrying out the work, and (4) closing the project (PMI 2008). The activities and decisions that transpire during the PLC should be documented daily, and then used as the basis for continuously improve project management processes and policies.

The design team should focus on how to reduce costs, conserve time, exceed quality expectations, avoid conflicts, and control **scope creep**—additions to a project that are beyond the original requirements. Improving the management of a project can enhance the final results as well as long-term relationships with clients.

Some projects develop a PMP by specifying requirements for the initial phases of a project, and the remaining details are determined as the project proceeds. Referred to as **rolling wave planning**, this continuous planning approach can conserve time and resources because a project can begin before all of the details are prescribed, and later decisions can be based on updated information. By viewing planning as an ongoing process, the design team can identify solutions determined by the project's actual conditions. For example, a design team might want to use a rolling wave plan when remodeling a historic building because structural problems might not be discovered until after workers remove elements of the interior, such as plaster walls and flooring.

Project Delivery Methods

Elements associated with the PMP are affected by the **project delivery method** or the type of business approach used to design, construct, operate, and maintain a built environment. Project delivery methods include **Design-Bid-Build (DBB)**, **Design-Build (DB)**, **Construction Management at-Risk (CMaR)**, and Integrated Project Delivery (IPD). (see Figure 8.1.)

The DBB delivery method is the traditional process whereby a client hires a design firm to create a design and the construction documents. General contractors bid on the project,

Figure 8.1 Wight & Company in Darien, Illinois, is an example of a design firm that specializes in IPD—"Our integrated design/build approach provides numerous advantages to clients, including a single point of contact, reduced schedules, guaranteed costs and increased quality in design and value" (Wight 2011). Wight's Chicago office—The Powerhouse Building—is located in a designated landmark of the National Register of Historic Places and is LEED-CI certified. Wight's Interiors Group designed the space and the interior was recognized as one of "Chicago's Coolest Offices" by *Crain's Chicago Business* in December 2008. *(Wight & Company)*

and most often the contractor with the lowest bid is awarded the contract.

The DBB method involves two separate contracts: one with the designer and another with the general contractor. The client assumes the responsibility or risks associated with the project. DBB's segregate and potentially inefficient approach to the design process has prompted clients to pursue alternative project delivery methods, such as DB, CM, and IPD, which encourage collaboration and conserve resources. These alternatives to the traditional DBB also help reduce the client's responsibility for design and construction services.

The DB project delivery method uses a design team that is responsible for design and construction services. One contract is awarded to the design team, and they work together throughout the PLC. The DB method can conserve time and resources because activities conducted during the design phases of a project can overlap with construction. In addition, costly mistakes and problems can be avoided when designers and contractors identify optimum solutions during the initial phases of the design process.

The CM at-risk project delivery method involves hiring the most qualified construction manager in the earliest phases of the design process. As with the DB method, collaboration occurs between the designer and the contractor, but the construction manager is responsible for design and construction services.

Integrated Project Delivery (IPD)

IDP is a collaborative project delivery method that broadens who is involved in the PLC. Thus, the design team could include vendors, suppliers, fabricators, specialists, real estate agents, developers, IT, and a variety of project stakeholders.

According to the AIA (American Institute of Architects) California Council, "IDP is a project delivery approach that integrates people, systems, business structures, and practices into a process that collaboratively harnesses the talents and insights of all participants to reduce waste and optimize efficiency through all phases of design, fabrication and construction" (AIA California Council 2007).

Participants must support the following principles to be successful: (1) mutual respect, (2) mutual benefit, (3) early goal definition, (4) enhanced communication, (5) clearly defined standards, (6) appropriate technology, and (7) high performance (AIA California Council 2007).

Project Management: Scope

Regardless of the technology or the project delivery method, project management must begin with clear definitions of the project scope. The scope of the project is defined by what is and is *not* included in a project. From a project management perspective, project scope includes *all* of the products, processes, resources, and services needed to create the built environment.

To successfully complete a design project, a design team must manage the scope of the project. According to the PMI, **project scope management** has five basic components: (1) collect the requirements of the stakeholders, (2) define the scope, (3) create a **work breakdown schedule (WBS)**, (4) verify scope, and (5) control scope (PMI 2008).

Interior designers are very familiar with processes associated with gathering and analyzing the needs and wants of clients, users, and stakeholders of a project. As described in Chapter 7, some of the information is collected when an interior designer creates the contract with a client. However, facts gathered at the contractual phase are just the beginning of identifying the scope of the project.

Once a contract is awarded, a comprehensive programming process is initiated by the design team (see Chapter 9). Information can be gathered through interviews, focus groups, surveys, and observations. The design team develops the client program by identifying project requirements, conceptual statements, preliminary timelines, and budget estimates.

Information collected during the programming phase is used to define the scope or the detailed description of the project. A thorough and accurate description of the project is essential to the project's success. First and foremost, make sure you understand the requirements of your client, as well as have a clear understanding during the initial stages of the design process. Proceeding to the next stage without a clear definition can result in wasted resources and rework, and your client might have an unfavorable impression of your ability to handle the project.

Another reason to ensure you have a thorough understanding of a project's parameters is because the scope description is used as the basis for several elements of the project management plan, including quality assurances, schedules, budgets, risk analyses, and the WBS.

Work Breakdown Schedule (WBS)

The WBS is a systematic approach to identifying what activities must be performed for the scope of the project. People responsible for an activity should be consulted to determine the exact tasks and the appropriate sequence.

The WBS divides broad project activities into smaller and more manageable tasks. For example, the WBS for a bathroom remodeling project could begin with the following general tasks: (1) demolition, (2) walls, (3) flooring, (4) plumbing, and (5) finishing. These activities can be further divided into the following work breakdown:

- Demolition
  - Remove toilet, sinks, and tub.
  - Remove floor tile and interior walls.
  - Order fixtures.
  - Rough-in plumbing and electrical.
  - Conduct building inspection.

- Walls
  - Patch drywall.
  - Install drywall.
  - Paint walls and ceiling.

○ Flooring

  • Install subfloor.

  • Install floor tile.

  • Install and paint trim.

○ Plumbing

  • Install faucets and sinks.

  • Install toilet and shutoff valves.

  • Install tub.

  • Trim-out electrical, plumbing, and install light fixtures.

  • Conduct building inspection.

○ Finishing

  • Touch up paint.

  • Install towel bars and hooks.

  • Install window coverings and mirrors.

Each of those subtasks could be further divided to identify additional activities. The larger the project, the greater the number of subtask categories. The greater the complexity, the higher the number of subtask categories. The lowest level is referred to as a work package. Considerable time should be dedicated to creating a detailed WBS; the document is used to develop numerous other items in a project management plan, including the schedule, design team composition, budget, and risks.

Activities associated with managing project scope extend beyond determining the WBS. The scope of the client's program must be verified and controlled throughout the PLC. For example, the client's program can be verified by monitoring interior construction work, installations, and the delivery of furniture, furnishings, and equipment.

Controlling scope requires constantly tracking the progress of the project and ensuring that appropriate corrective as well as preventative actions are promptly taken when necessary. Deviations from the client's program can

affect many aspects of the project, including the schedule, budget, and quality assurances. Therefore, immediate corrections help to contain the extent of a divergence and reduce its impact on the overall goals of the project.

Project Management: Quality

In addition to scope management, the design team must employ strategies for managing quality. The design team is responsible for ensuring that the final design incorporates the client's quality expectations. Accomplishing this requires an understanding of the principles associated with **total quality management (TQM)**.

Originally formulated by an American statistician, W. Edwards Deming, TQM is a management philosophy that focuses on continuous improvement processes with an emphasis on the needs of the customer, leadership, collaborative relationships, education, and understanding processes from a systemic perspective. TQM was originally applied to manufacturers' processes, but currently the philosophy is used to manage people and organizations.

An overall tenant of TQM is Deming's **Shewhart cycle** or the **Plan-Do-Check-Act (PDCA) cycle**, which was developed for the Japanese in the 1950s (Box 8.1—Figure 8.2a). Theoretically, the PDCA cycle begins with a "Plan" that describes what needs to be accomplished, followed by the "Do" or executing the activity. The results of the activity are checked or evaluated by comparing the outcomes to the goals of the project.

Information retrieved during the "Check" process is then applied to the "Act" phase. During the "Act" phase, ineffective results are corrected and positive outcomes are retained. These initiatives are used to inform best practices for future plans and the cycle continues again by repeating the "Do," "Check," and "Act." These cycle iterations continuously improve the quality of products, policies, and processes.

Over the years Deming's PDCA cycle has expanded to include several business tools that are used to continuously improve the quality of

Box 8.1
Quality Management Business Tools

QUALITY MANAGEMENT BUSINESS TOOLS	FIGURES OF QUALITY MANAGEMENT BUSINESS TOOLS
PLAN-DO-CHECK-ACT (PDCA) CYCLE (Figure 8.2a) **Description:** A business tool used to continuously improve a process, product, or entity. A plan is created to accomplish goals. The plan is implemented and then checked or evaluated. Actions are taken to improve the outcomes and this information is then used to improve the next plan. **Application Example:** Assessments of existing buildings can be used to improve new designs of interiors.	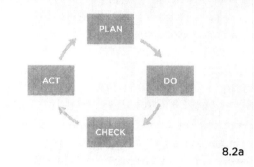 8.2a
AFFINITY DIAGRAM (KJ – KAWAKITA JIRO METHOD) (Figure 8.2b) **Description:** A business tool that can be used to organize large amounts of data acquired from stakeholders. **Application Example:** Excellent for the programming phase of the integrated design process. Affinity diagrams can organize information gathered using surveys, charrettes, focus groups, and interviews.	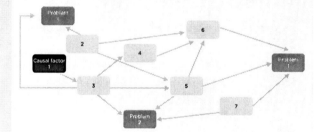 8.2b
RELATIONS DIAGRAM (INTERRELATIONSHIP DIGRAPH) (Figure 8.2c) **Description:** A business tool that can be used to analyze the causes and effects of complex problems. Affinity themes can be used to generate the diagram. The diagram reveals the causes that have the greatest effect on the problem. Solutions focus on addressing high impact causes. **Application Example:** Excellent for any phase in the design process when the design team must solve a problem with multiple causes. Can be used to improve the schedule, costs, quality, communication, and onsite construction processes.	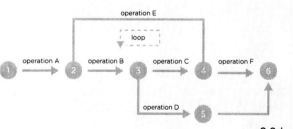 8.2c
ARROW DIAGRAM (Figure 8.2d) **Description:** A business tool that a design team can use to plan daily schedules and visualize the interrelationships between phases, activities, schedules, and people. **Application Example:** Excellent for any phase in the design process when the design team must schedule people and activities	8.2d

processes and products. Some of these include the **affinity diagram**, **relations diagram**, **systematic diagram**, **process decision program chart (PDPC)**, **matrix diagram**, and **arrow diagram**. As illustrated in Figures 8.2a–d (Box 8.1), these business tools have a specific purpose and can be used at various stages of the design process.

The tools are especially useful for large projects that have substantial amounts of information and numerous stakeholders. For example, affinity diagrams can be used to organize large amounts of information gathered during a brainstorming session. After all ideas have been recorded on Post-its, participants silently organize the data by grouping similar concepts together. Themes are identified for each group of ideas. Themes can be used to analyze relationships as well as prioritizations.

Design Quality Indicator (DQI)

Another approach to quality improvements is the **Design Quality Indicator (DQI)**, a tool initiated and managed by the United Kingdom's Construction Industry Council (CIC). The CIC is a nonprofit organization that serves as a forum for design professionals, research organizations, and businesses in the construction industry. According to the CIC (2011), DQI is

> A method of evaluating the design and construction of new buildings and the refurbishment of existing buildings. DQI is a process that actively involves a wide group of people in the design of buildings. Those involved are people responsible for the design and construction and those who will use the building or be affected by it. DQI can be used at all stages of a building's development and plays a fundamental role in contributing to the improved quality of building projects.

The DQI process uses structured workshops and online tools to involve designers, architects, engineers, contractors, and stakeholders, such as the client, users of the space, facility managers, and representatives from the local community. Stakeholders use the forums to communicate their needs, wants, and priorities to the design team. The design team then applies the information provided by the stakeholders to the designs of the building project. The collaborative dialogues help to create quality designs by addressing the functional requirements of the stakeholders.

Ideally, DQI begins at the earliest stages of the design process and continues through post-occupancy evaluations. However, as illustrated in the case study described in Box 8.2, DQI can be used to evaluate the success of an existing building and the results can inform design solutions for new buildings. This strategy is an excellent example of implementing Deming's PDCA cycle—the positive and negative characteristics of the International Manufacturing Centre were used to improve the quality of the design for the Warwick International Digital Laboratory (Box 8.2 and Figure 8.3).

From an international perspective you should be aware of quality management processes prescribed in ISO 9000 Family of Standards by the International Organization for Standardization (ISO). The voluntary management and leadership standards delineated in ISO 9000 are used by over a million organizations in 176 countries (ISO, 2011). Architects, engineers, and designers use ISO 9000 principles to improve design practice, provide excellent service, enhance profitability, and reduce risks.

ISO 9000's international consensus standards are based on the following eight principles (ISO 2011): (1) customer focus, (2) leadership, (3) involvement of people, (4) process approach, (5) system approach to management, (6) continual improvement, (7) factual approach to decision making, and (8) mutually beneficial supplier relationship.

Checking for Comprehension
- Describe five important elements in a project management plan.
- Identify two quality management business tools and how you would use the tools in a project.

Using the Design Quality Indicator (DQI) Method*:
Warwick International Digital Laboratory

Client and Background

Warwick Manufacturing Group (WMG), Coventry, UK (http://www2.warwick.ac.uk/). WMG is a research center located at the University of Warwick with private and public funding. WMG hired Edward Cullinan Architects to design new facilities for the Warwick International Digital Laboratory. WMG's goal was to achieve the BREEAM (Building Research Establishment Environmental Assessment Method) green building excellent rating (Figure 8.3).

DQI Process

- To assist in the development of the design for the Warwick International Digital Laboratory, Edward Cullinan Architects utilized DQI. The building used for the DQI process was the International Manufacturing Centre, a WMG facility, located at the University of Warwick. A facilitator processed the DQI using the following procedures:

  - WMG identified stakeholders for the sessions.

- Introduced the principles associated with DQI to the participants as well as the importance of quality designs and fulfilling functional requirements.

- Developed questions based on the design of the International Manufacturing Centre. The items were used to create dialogue between participants.

- Regardless of a person's hierarchical status all positive and negative responses were respected, and then posted online for immediate access. Priorities were identified and participants determined that the design of the new laboratory should be a marketing tool for WMG's research activities.

- Based on the most optimum design features of the International Manufacturing Center, a consensus process was used to identify the vision for the new building, the Warwick International Digital Laboratory.

*Adapted from: http://www.cabe.org.uk/case-studies/international-digital-laboratory/process.

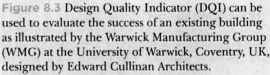
Figure 8.3 Design Quality Indicator (DQI) can be used to evaluate the success of an existing building as illustrated by the Warwick Manufacturing Group (WMG) at the University of Warwick, Coventry, UK, designed by Edward Cullinan Architects.

The DQI process determined that to facilitate cross-disciplinary work and cooperation, the interior should be informal and have open plan spaces.
(© Simon Feneley)

To accomplish the goals of a project, the PMP must have a strategy to manage resources. This section reviews three areas that must be managed well for a successful project: schedule, people, and budget. Regardless of the size or complexity of a project, there must be a plan for organizing activities, projecting timelines, managing personnel, and controlling costs.

Project management software programs can help you document and update information, but the programs are useless without a solid understanding of project management, including resource management policies and procedures.

Project Management Resources: Schedules

The project's scope and quality assurances are intrinsically connected to the schedule. Adequate time must be planned to fulfill the requirements of the project. Delays or incomplete scheduling might require the client to eliminate important elements of a project, lower quality expectations, or pay more. Therefore, it is essential that you understand the critical elements of a schedule, effective coordination methods, and the principals associated with project time management.

Fundamentally, creating a schedule for a project requires the following steps: (1) develop a list of the activities that must be done to finish the project, (2) determine the sequence of the activities, (3) estimate the resources required for each activity, (4) estimate the amount of time required for each activity, and (5) incorporate the preceding items into a chart.

Identifying and Sequencing Project Activities

Creating a list of project activities should begin with the WBS. As described previously in this chapter, the WBS is important for determining the scope of the project as well as other items required in the PMP. The WBS should be very detailed, and the design team should be able to identify a **deliverable** for each activity. For example, in the bathroom remodeling example described earlier, freshly painted surfaces and the new tub are deliverables in the later phases of the project.

The design team must determine how to accomplish each deliverable. The WBS should be reviewed by people involved with the tasks to ensure the list of activities is complete. Any task missing from the WBS can result in delays and cost overruns, and could possibly affect the quality of the end results.

The list of activities must be reviewed within the context of sequence. Several questions can be asked to determine the order of activities. For example, which activities must be done **sequentially**? Which activities can be done in **parallel** or concurrently? Which activities can be done at the beginning of the project? Which activities cannot be done until the end of the project? Which activities can be done at any time during the project? From a management perspective, your responsibility is to create a sequence of activities that conserves time and resources.

Activity Resources and Timelines

The design team must identify every resource required for each activity. Resources can include people, equipment, materials, supplies, and facilities. The list of people for each task should be accompanied by information about who is responsible for ensuring the activity is completed accurately, by its deadline, and within budget. In collaboration with the person(s) responsible for an activity, the design team must estimate task durations for every deliverable.

Time estimates and resources required for each deliverable must be analyzed within the context of the entire project. For example, if a carpenter is assigned a specialized task that will take three consecutive months to complete, the carpenter cannot be assigned to another assignment during that period. Therefore, to complete both tasks at the same time, a project manager might have to hire another carpenter. Another important consideration related to resources and estimated timelines is the number of people assigned to a task. A task completed by one person might take six days, but if two people are hired, the task should take only three days to complete.

Estimating timelines for deliverables can be complicated. Design firms that have considerable experience with a specific service or building type can refer to past projects as a reference point. However, because every project is unique, past timelines should only be used as a basis for estimating new schedules. Estimated timelines for a project must be developed within its prescribed parameters and conditions. Slight alterations between projects, such as the number of people installing drywall or the availability of a floor tile, can affect the timeline.

One approach to creating time approximations is to use **three-point estimates** via the **Program Evaluation Review Technique (PERT)** formula. The PERT formula requires three different estimates: an *optimistic* estimate that represents the most hopeful time required for a task, the *most likely* amount of time needed for the assignment, and a *pessimistic* or the worse estimated time period (6 in the denominator of the formula is the total standard deviation—optimistic estimate [3 standard deviations] and pessimistic estimate [3 standard deviations]). The PERT formula is as follows:

$$\frac{\text{Optimistic estimate} + \left(4 \times \text{Most likely estimate}\right) + \text{Pessimistic estimate}}{6} = \text{Estimate}$$

Therefore, with the PERT formula, if the optimistic estimate for completing a tile installation was 20 days, the most likely time estimate was 35 days, and the pessimistic estimate was 60 days, the approximate time estimate for the tile installation is 37 days, as shown:

$$\frac{\text{20 Optimistic} + \left(4 \times \text{35 Most likely}\right) + \text{60 Pessimistic}}{6} = \frac{37}{\text{estimated days}}$$

After a preliminary outline of the duration of the activities, reanalyze the information to identify ways to fulfill the project's scope while conserving time. One approach to **schedule compression** is to reduce sequential activities and identify tasks that can occur in parallel. The goal of this activity, known as **fast tracking**, is to reduce the overall time required for a project by overlapping stages and tasks.

Schedule compression can also occur by consolidating tasks that will be performed in repeated processes. For example, a large building could require the installation of hundreds of window treatments. Rather than scheduling the installations on a room-by-room basis, time and resources can be conserved by scheduling several installations simultaneously.

Another method for schedule compression is **crashing**. Projects that use the crashing technique supplement various resources to shorten the amount of time. For example, additional carpenters could be hired to rapidly complete a construction stage, or additional money could be spent to purchase a more expensive light fixture because of its immediate availability.

Crashing can obviously have a negative impact on the project's budget. Therefore, when crashing is being considered, the client must be involved with the decisions and a comprehensive analysis must be performed to determine its overall affect on the project's scope.

Developing a Gantt Chart

The next step in developing a project's schedule is to incorporate the data gathered into a **Gantt** or **time chart**. A time chart is an excellent way to visually review a project's activities, sequence of events, resources-per-task, as well as the amount of time scheduled for each activity. Industrial engineer Henry Gantt developed the chart in 1915 to organize military operations during World War I, and it is still used today with various modifications. Gantt charts can be created with computer spreadsheets as well as project management software programs.

The basic elements of a Gantt chart include the tasks and resources listed in the left columns; the timeline appears in the remaining columns

(Figure 8.4). The timeline indicates the planned (**baseline**) and actual start/finish dates for every task. The timeline should also include project **milestones** or major events that reflect significant progress as well as the project's **critical path**.

The critical path is the series of activities that take the longest to complete. The critical path represents the absolute minimum amount of time needed to finish the project. Therefore, any event that affects activities along the critical path will affect the project's duration.

To help ensure all activities are included in the schedule, as well as appropriate durations and start/finish dates, the design team and other relevant persons should review a draft of the Gantt chart. After the development of the baseline schedule, designated individuals must monitor and track the daily progress of the project—especially tasks associated with the project's critical path and change requests.

Deviations from the baseline must be analyzed as soon as they are detected and must be communicated to those affected by the changes. The tracking system should also monitor overruns and have predetermined, acceptable costs. Schedule updates are included in project progress reports that are distributed to internal as well as external audiences.

Project Management Resources: People

A project's schedule can include who is responsible for completing a task by a designated date. Coordinating people, activities, costs, and timelines requires effective human resource management techniques. For the purposes of facilitating a project, the basic human resource management

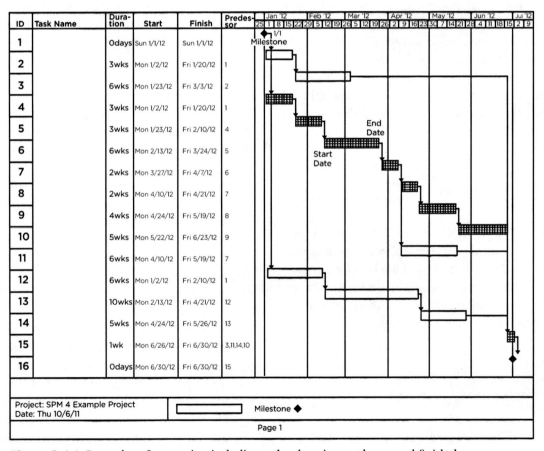

Figure 8.4 A Gantt chart for a project including tasks, duration, and start and finish dates.

procedures include: (1) identifying the team members, (2) establishing the team, (3) managing the team, and (4) disbanding the team.

Identifying Team Members

The first step in identifying team members is to determine an organizational structure for the project. Small projects usually have just one team consisting of key personnel, such as the architect, designer, engineer(s), and perhaps stakeholders. Large and complex built environments generally require a central team and what is referred to as "support teams."

A central team consists of people representing major disciplines as well as functional requirements for a project. For example, the central team for a school project might include an architect, a designer, a structural engineer, a civil engineer, a mechanical engineer, an electrical engineer, a landscape architect, a commissioning agent, a school superintendent, a contractor, and the project manager.

The central team is involved with the project from the planning phase through post-occupancy evaluations. Generally, the best scenario is when the same people serve on the central team throughout the project because they can use their tacit knowledge to help solve problems and make critical decisions.

The composition of support teams can vary depending on what is required for a project. For example, when the task is designing classrooms, the support team for the school project could include the architect, designer, project manager, principal, teachers, students, parents, technology specialists, and furniture manufacturer representatives.

Regardless of the number of teams, their membership is based on the project deliverables outlined in the WBS. Tasks delineated in the WBS should be used to identify who and how many people are needed for each activity. The human resource plan includes the list of people, roles, responsibilities, and their qualifications, such as years of experience, skills, expertise, and certifications.

Depending on the requirements of the project and the design firm's area of expertise, the human resource manager might have to hire new personnel, consultants, or subcontract work to other organizations. Training of personnel might have to be planned in addition to obtaining professional certifications.

Personnel hiring should be conducted as early in the planning process as possible because the individuals who will perform the tasks should be the ones who plan the activities, such as determining optimum start times, duration estimates, costs, equipment needs, and any other resources. When an individual is able to plan the activity, there is a greater probability that the tasks will be completed accurately, on time, and within budget. Moreover, allowing the person to be involved with the process from the very beginning promotes a sense of ownership for the endeavor, which generally translates into outstanding results. However, a caveat to this supposition is that the task providers are empowered by giving them the authority to make decisions and acquire the necessary resources.

After the identification of team members, there are tools that can be used to visually organize departments, people, reporting responsibilities, and activities (Figure 8.5 and Table 8.1). Developing a clear understanding of responsibilities as well as the reporting lines helps to reduce potential conflicts that can occur in teams.

A hierarchical organizational chart can be used to visually depict reporting lines and responsibilities (Figure 8.5). A project might have several hierarchical organizational charts that illustrate a variety of conditions. For example, a chart could provide a general overview of the project by including the primary functions and reporting lines. Other charts could specifically illustrate one department or a phase of the project.

A matrix responsibility chart using the RACI (responsible, accountable, consult, inform) format (PMI 2008) is another tool that can be used to visually organize team members (Table 8.1). The matrix provides a quick reference to who

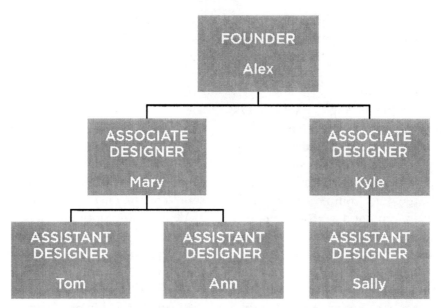

FOUNDER

Alex

ASSOCIATE DESIGNER

Mary

ASSOCIATE DESIGNER

Kyle

ASSISTANT DESIGNER

Tom

ASSISTANT DESIGNER

Ann

ASSISTANT DESIGNER

Sally

Figure 8.5 A hierarchical organizational chart can be used to visually depict reporting lines and responsibilities. A matrix responsibility chart using the RACI (responsible, accountable, consult, inform) format (PMI 2008) is another tool that can be used to visually organize team members (see Table 8.1).

Table 8.1 Matrix Responsibility Chart						
RACI Chart	**Team Members**					
Activity	**Alex**	**Mary**	**Kyle**	**Tom**	**Ann**	**Sally**
Develop design concept	C	A	I	R	R	I
Schematic designs	C	I	A	I	I	R
Presentations to client	R	A	A	C	C	C
Preliminary drawings	C	I	A	I	I	R
Preliminary specifications	C	A	I	R	R	I
Preliminary budget	C	A	I	R	R	I

Key: R=Responsible A=Accountable C=Consult I=Inform.

is working on which activities, and the format makes it easy to identify people who are responsible for multiple tasks. As shown in Table 8.1, Tom and Ann are responsible for developing the design concept, and Mary is accountable for the task. When decisions regarding the design concept are made, Alex must be consulted, and Sally and Kyle are informed of the results.

Team members should be consulted when determining the RACI designations as well as other human resource management policies, such as assessment standards, recognition guidelines, and conflict resolution procedures.

Soliciting input from team members is especially critical for successful intercultural business practices. As discussed in Chapter 5, national cultures have varying perspectives regarding individualism/collectivism, hierarchical/egalitarianism, and time orientations. Thus, human resource management policies must incorporate the views of the team members to help ensure the most effective approaches to facilitate processes, motivate people, and establish schedules.

Establishing a Team

Understanding cultural differences is just one of the considerations when formulating teams. An assortment of people from different disciplines, experiences, skills, cultures, and locations—many of whom might not know each other—are suddenly expected to work together as a team. How can this be accomplished in a timely manner?

Fundamentally, the project manager is responsible for creating an environment that fosters effective teamwork. But team members also bear responsibility for interactions. Therefore, as a future member of a team, you should have an understanding of the best methods to transform a group into a team.

From a project management perspective, the stages of a team are: (1) forming, (2) storming, (3) norming, (4) performing, and (5) adjourning (PMI 2008).

Team members are introduced to each other during the forming phase. Team members who already know each other should make a special effort to include "outsiders" in their conversations. The first meeting should be in-person and whenever possible include virtual team members. Face-to-face interactions are important for establishing a connection with fellow team members. During the forming stage, team members should learn each person's professional background and role in the project. As the source of commonality among the team members, discussions that focus on the requirements of a project help to initiate collaborative attitudes.

A collaborative mindset is essential to the team development's storming phase. At this stage team members are expected to brainstorm ways to approach the project. The development of a collective understanding about the project requirements might elicit a reexamination of the initial WBS, reporting responsibilities, and human resource management policies. Any necessary refinements of responsibilities and procedures will set the required foundation for the team's norming stage.

As the name of the stage implies, during norming, team members employ established behavioral expectations based on shared values, attitudes, and understandings. Norming is essential to develop trust—an absolute necessity for effective teamwork.

Without successful norming, it is difficult for a team to execute the performing phase. Successful performance requires a work environment that supports collaboration, respects diverging opinions, encourages open communication, and promptly resolves conflicts. The final product is a built environment that meets the needs of the client. When a team performs successfully, advancing to the next phase—adjourning—is difficult because team members miss the excitement, connectivity, and pride they experienced during the performance. However, the adjourning phase can be productive by conducting an assessment of the team process and applying the results to continuously improve future practice.

Team Management and Disbandment

Through every stage of a team, the project manager is responsible for managing people, activities, and processes (Figure 8.6). To manage the team, the project manager schedules meetings, tracks performances, provides feedback, facilitates communication channels, and implements program changes.

Depending on the project and the needs of its participants, the project manager might have to implement training workshops, team-building programs, and conflict resolution sessions. The quality management business tools described in Box 8.1 can be very helpful for team management, and they are often enlarged and displayed in rooms where team members engage in collaborative activities.

Team management can be especially challenging for project managers because they often do not have direct authority over all members

Figure 8.6 Through every stage of a project the project manager is responsible for managing people, activities, and processes. The Vancouver Convention Centre West in Vancouver, British Columbia, Canada, designed by LMN Architects is an excellent example of a project that required comprehensive management of people, activities, and processes. The design team included architects, an interior designer, engineers, and 40 sub-consultants.

Over a three-year period the team was involved with presentations to urban design guideline authorities, design review boards, citizens, and stakeholders. The building is Canada Green Building Council (CaGBC) LEED-NC Platinum certified and was also recognized as an *AIA/COTE* [Committee on the Environment] *Top Ten Green Projects* in 2011. *(© Nic Lehoux)*

of the team. For example, a manufacturer's representative might be a member of the team, but formally that person reports to his or her boss at the manufacturing company, not to the project manager. Therefore, for a variety of reasons, including commitments to other projects, the manufacturer's representative might not promptly respond to requests from the project manager. Written agreements can be helpful, but it still can be difficult to acquire the information in a timely manner. Often success depends on the project manager's persuasive skills, patience, and his or her willingness to provide assistance. However, the project manager should avoid **micromanagement** because frequently people do not respond well to someone telling them how to do their job.

In lieu of micromanaging individuals, the project manager should dedicate considerable time to assessing the performance of the team

and identifying strategies for improvement. To continuously improve teamwork, assessments should be conducted on a regular basis. Informal assessments can be performed routinely, such as weekly, or on an as-needed basis (for example, when a new person joins the team or a new technology is introduced).

Informal assessments performed on a regular basis are an excellent way to identify conflicts before an issue escalates into a systemic problem. Some of the primary causes of team conflicts are scarce resources, communication barriers, and personal factors (see Chapter 4). Early identification enables early resolutions.

Formal assessments can be aligned with project milestones. Generally, the goal of informal or formal assessments is to evaluate the team's progress. Are deliverables as prescribed by the project's scope? Are deliverables in compliance with quality expectations? Are deliverables on time? Are deliverables within budget? What works? What does not work and why?

The project manager should promptly share the results of the team assessment process with its members and solicit suggestions for improvement. The team's feedback should be incorporated into an action plan that could include reorganizing reporting lines, hiring more people, revising communication channels, requesting more resources, improving decision-making processes, and resolving conflicts via mediation sessions.

Generally, team assessment results are included in **project performance reports**. A primary reason for these reports is to compare the project's progress with baseline projections and then determine corrective and preventative actions for any variances. Project performance reports can help to verify and control the scope, schedule, costs, and quality expectations. In addition, a formalized documentation process provides an excellent record that can be used as a guide to estimate time and expenses for future projects.

The last phase in the human resource management plan is disbanding the team. At this stage the project has been completed and in-house personnel as well as external team members have been assigned to other work. Immediately before the disbandment it is very useful to ask the team members to evaluate policies and procedures related to project management. Information could be gathered via focus groups, online surveys, interviews, or a combination of methodologies. The goal is to learn from the team members what was successful and what could be done to improve project management in the future.

Project Management Resources: Budgets and Cost Management

How much will a project cost? This is one of the most pressing questions you will be asked—and one of the most difficult answers to determine. A project might have a professional cost estimator, but there are still design items in the budget that you or your colleagues will have to provide, and as a member of the design team, you will participate in budget discussions. Therefore, the more you understand budgets, the greater your contributions to the team.

Budget knowledge becomes absolutely essential in situations where you have sole responsibility for the entire project. Project management software programs are available that can help to facilitate budget processes; however, as is the case with all computer programs, their usefulness depends on the user entering complete and accurate information.

Estimate Costs

An excellent way to understand how to develop budgets is to review the process via the three major areas identified by PMI: (1) estimate cost, (2) determine budget, and (3) control costs (PMI 2008). As a word of caution, some projects skip the estimate cost phase and begin with a budget—an unadvisable approach because of the significant possibility of missing expenses and inaccurate figures.

Cost estimation involves determining approximate expenses for a project, which is critical

for developing the budget. Cost estimates are determined by analyzing items in the project scope, WBS, schedule, and human resource plan.

There are expenses specifically associated with the project, such as labor hours/rates, billing rates, building materials, plumbing, mechanical systems, furniture, furnishings, equipment, lighting systems, equipment leases, supplies, subcontractor quotes, and travel. Expenses can also include an inflation allowance, profits, administrative services, and a geographical allowance for projects in expensive urban areas. Some projects include **contingency funds**—money that is reserved for unanticipated expenses.

The estimated costs for the project become the budget's **cost baseline**, a figure used to determine if a project is under or over budget.

When estimating project costs, use realistic figures. Avoid overestimating or underestimating costs. Either situation can give the client the impression that you are unqualified to manage the project. Overestimating costs or **padding** could eliminate your proposal from a bidding process. Underestimating costs could result in project cutbacks or degradation of quality standards—unfortunate situations that dissatisfy clients and could result in legal action.

A critical step in developing authentic cost estimates is to gather as much information and as many details about the project as possible. One effective approach is referred to as **bottom-up estimates**. With this method, cost analysis begins by examining tasks at the most simplistic level and proceeding to the most complex activities. The bottom-up approach helps ensure the inclusion of all tasks required for the project and their associated costs.

Other methods that can be used to estimate costs include **analogous estimating**, **parametric estimating**, and three-point estimates using the PERT formula. Analogous estimates are based on actual costs expended for a similar project that ideally was recently built in the same geographic area.

Parametric estimates use statistical calculations to approximate costs. For example, estimates could be determined by using the project's square footage/meters. Additional considerations could be factored into the calculations, such as inflation or allowances for locations with expensive labor and materials.

As with estimating time, the PERT formula can be used to approximate costs by determining an optimistic cost, most likely cost, and a pessimistic cost. For example:

$$\frac{\underset{\text{Optimistic}}{\$300,000} + \left(4 \times \underset{\substack{\text{Most} \\ \text{likely}}}{\$350,000} \right) + \underset{\text{Pessimistic}}{\$450,000}}{6} \quad \begin{array}{l} \$358,000 \\ = \text{estimated} \\ \text{cost} \end{array}$$

A very important aspect of any cost estimating technique is to describe the assumptions used to approximate costs. For example, the estimated costs for labor could be based on the assumption that a pay raise will not occur throughout the PLC. It could be assumed that the cost for materials will not increase more than 5 percent or that the existing plumbing will not have to be replaced in a remodeling project.

As we will learn in the "Control Costs" section, identifying assumptions for cost estimates become very important when a project is behind schedule or there are overruns—assumptions can provide insight to cost variances. Thus, in the plumbing assumption, if there were cost overruns during the remodeling project, the reason could be attributed to the need to replace old plumbing—a problem that could not be discovered until the walls were removed.

Knowing that the cost estimates were based on not having to replace existing plumbing does not eliminate the expense, but the designer now has a very reasonable explanation for the overrun to present to the client—important for building strong client relationships (see "Project Management Communication" section later). In addition, if the cost overruns were due to the plumbing assumption, then the other estimated costs should still be realistic and would not require corrective actions. However, because of the additional plumbing expense, the client

might want to revise the original design to stay within budget. Whenever these situations occur, demonstrate to the client your problem-solving skills, maintain a positive attitude, and make sure your client is satisfied with the solutions.

Determine Budget

Cost estimates are used to create the project's budget (Table 8.2). As with personal budgets, a project budget is merely a projection for anticipated costs and expenses. It is impossible to know the exact cost of every task or to predict events, such as flooding or discontinued products, that can affect a budget. However, the greater the detail, the more likely the result will be an accurate budget. Moreover, the greater the detail, the easier it is to identify the causes of overruns or delays. It is critically important to find the causes of problems as quickly as possible because immediate corrective and preventative action can help avoid additional overruns, setbacks, and delays.

Detailed budgets include all projected costs and expenses during every phase of a project. Identifying costs at each phase of the design process is very useful for cost management and can help reduce additional expenses. Knowing how much money is required and when provides the client with the ability to plan cash flow and request loans at the appropriate time. Depending on the loan specifications, waiting to withdraw funds could reduce interest charges or increase funds in interest-bearing accounts. The amounts can be substantial for large projects requiring years to complete.

To help ensure you have included all required items and the costs are reasonable, a proposed budget should be reviewed by several people, such as the client, team members, contractor, and specialists. The review process could include comparing the proposed budget to recent completed projects as well as identifying ways to reduce costs, such as substituting materials, eliminating wasted steps, or finding a supplier with better prices.

Table 8.2 Project Budget

Happy Valley Community Center

Funding Sources:

A.	State Funds from 2002	$	27,750
B.	State Funds from 2003	$	45,000
C.	State Funds from 2004	$	100,000
D.	City G.O. Bonds 2001	$	250,000
E.	City G.O. Bonds 2002	$	1,500,000
F.	City G.O. Bonds 2003	$	4,000,000
	Total Project Funds	**$**	**5,922,750**

Project Costs

	Item	Notes	Area	Cost	
A	Demolition of Existing Building		13,872 sf x	5 $/sf = $	69,360
B	New Construction				
B.1	Regular Ceiling		20,774 sf x	140 $/sf = $	2,576,000
B.2	High Ceiling		6,400 sf x	160 $/sf = $	1,024,000
C.	Site Development (@ 20% of B1+B2)			$	720,000
D.	Special Equipment (@ 5% of B+C)			$	87,200
E.	**Construction Cost**			**$**	**4,476,560**
F.	Site Acquisition (not applicable)			$	-
G.	Furniture and Equipment (@8% of B)			$	288,000
H.	Computer Equipment	1		$	20,000
I.	Telephone Equipment	2		$	8,000
J.	Architects/Engineer Fees	3		$	326,789
K.	Asbestos Abatement	4		$	33,000
L.	Site Survey			$	2,800
M.	Soils Tests			$	2,400
N.	Acoustical Consultant			$	2,000
O.	Taxes on J, K, L, M, and N (@.058125)			$	21,331
P.	Contingency (@ 10% of E)			$	447,656
Q.	City Overhead (@2% of Funds)			$	30,000
R.	Site Observation (@ 5% of E)			$	223,828
S.	Misc. Administrative Expenses	5		$	22,000
T.	**Total Project Cost**			**$**	**5,904,364**
U.	**Total Gross Square Footage**				**27,174**
V.	**Building Cost/sf**			**$**	**135.69**
W.	**Construction Cost/sf**			**$**	**164.74**
X.	**Total Project Cost/sf**			**$**	**217.28**

Notes

1 City Vendor provides equipment, wiring (Cat 6), and terminate divices. Contractor provides conduit and cable trays.
2 Leased.
3 City Fee Schedule calls for 7.3% of E for a project of this cost.
4 Prior to demolition of existing building. Use City On-Call Abatement Company.
5 Printing Bid Sets, Plan Check, Bid Ad, Demo Storage Shed.

Source: Reprinted from *Whole Building Design Guide* (WBDG), 2008, Architectural Programming Exhibit B: Example of a Total Project Budget, http://www.wbdg.org/pdfs/archprogramming_exhibit_b.pdf. Retrieved May 24, 2011.

A **cost-benefit analysis (CBA)** might be conducted to analyze the cost of items within the context of their advantages and disadvantages. Reviewers should identify the optimum time to order and purchase items. The goal is to have materials available when they are needed, and to avoid early shipments that require payments and storage fees. The evaluation of the budget should also include determining the need for a contingency fund. When it is necessary to access the fund, the team should determine the appropriate amount.

After reviewing the proposed budget, the design team should revise the budget as appropriate and initiate steps for approval. The approved budget becomes the project's cost baseline: the source for monitoring and controlling costs.

As described in the next section, variances from the cost baseline can help reveal problems in the project that are not directly related to expenditures, such as an unrealistic schedule or insufficient personnel. Therefore, as a measure of the financial as well as the functional performance of a project, the budget should be monitored on a daily or at least weekly basis.

Control Costs

The control costs phase involves monitoring project activities and comparing accomplishments with the budget. Depending on the scope of the project and its location, monitoring project activities can be very complex, challenging, and time-consuming.

To thoroughly monitor a project, the design team must determine: (1) what information is needed, (2) who is responsible for reporting progress, (3) when updates should be submitted, (4) who is responsible for gathering and analyzing the reports, and (5) processes for corrective and preventative actions.

Establishing these protocols for monitoring a project helps ensure that all relevant items are studied in a timely manner. The earlier that variances are identified, the sooner they can be corrected in a manner that minimizes negative impacts on the project.

A useful tool to facilitate cost controls by measuring the project's progress is **earned value management system (EVMS)** or simply **earned value (EV)**. The PMI defines EV as "The value of work performed expressed in terms of the approved budget assigned to that work for a schedule activity or work breakdown structure compound" (PMI 2008).

EV is a tool for tracking the progress of a project by examining time and costs. EV can provide a quick summary of which activities are on schedule and within budget based on how much has been accomplished.

Major elements of EV are **planned value (PV)**, earned value (EV), and **actual cost (AC)**. The PV represents the project's budget. The EV reflects the work accomplished based on the budget, and the AC is how much money was spent.

As illustrated in Table 8.3, the PV, EV, and AC are used to calculate schedule and cost variances. The equation used to determine the schedule variance is:

$$EV - PV = \text{Schedule variance}$$

The cost variance is:

$$EV - AC = \text{Cost variance}$$

As examples, the figures in Table 8.3 reveal that the installation of the floorcovering and window treatments is behind schedule and over budget (negative figures are in parentheses). Deliveries of desks are behind schedule and under budget.

When a task is finished, the schedule variance is 0 (EV – PV = 0). When a task is finished, the cost variance (EV – AC) can be 0, over budget, or under budget.

When variations from the cost baseline occur, assigned individuals should examine how much money, time, and resources were actually expended to accomplish the activities. These

Table 8.3 Project Progress Analysis Using the Earned Value (EV) Tool					
Activity	Planned Value (PV)	Earned Value (EV)	Actual Cost (AC)	Schedule Variance EV – PV	Cost Variance EV – AC
Floorcovering installation	$50,000	$45,000	$48,000	($5,000)	($3,000)
Desk deliveries	$55,000	$35,000	$33,000	($20,000)	$2,000
Window treatments installation	$25,000	$22,000	$30,000	($3,000)	($8,000)
Totals	$130,000	$102,000	$111,000	($28,000)	($9,000)

figures are then compared to the original project scope, schedule, cost estimates, assumptions, and human resource plan. A comparison of the two documents should reveal the causes of the cost variances, which could be from:

* Price increases, unanticipated expenses, or timing overruns

* Incorrect assumptions, project scope misinterpretations, miscalculations, or quality misunderstandings

* Inaccurate vendor invoices, rework, or wrong purchases with expensive replacement costs

* Unapproved purchases, padding, unrealistic costs, or authorized changes

An important consideration is how cost variances might affect the success of future activities. Thus, variance reports should be monthly and include a summary of how the assumptions that formed the basis for the budget affected the actual schedule and costs. When corrective actions are necessary, appropriate people must be informed and solutions developed in collaboration with people who are directly involved.

Checking for Comprehension
* Describe the PERT formula and how you can use the formula to create time estimates.

* What are key considerations for determining a budget?

Project Management: Processes

To accomplish the goals of a project, the PMP also includes a communications plan, strategies to manage risks, and procurement policies and procedures. This section explores communication through the lens of project management and specifically addresses how to communicate with team members, and provides guidelines for communication channels.

Risk management is discussed by reviewing how to identify, analyze, evaluate, treat, and monitor risks—activities that are critical to the success of a project. This section and the chapter conclude by examining effective strategies for managing procurement processes. Given the enormous number of items and services that could be purchased during the life of a project, solid procurement procedures are crucial to effective project management.

Project Management: Communication
Written and verbal communication skills are so vitally important to the interior designer's professional practice that the topic has already appeared in Chapters 4, 5, and 7. The communication information presented in previous chapters should be integrated with project management communication strategies—absolutely essential to the success of a project.

Think about all the information and details that must be communicated during a PLC: design concepts, site measurements, programming results, agendas, meeting minutes, schematics, drawings, specifications, construction schedules, permits, certification documents, purchase orders, invoices, billing statements, maintenance recommendations, and post-occupancy evaluations.

Then consider all the people who must be informed, the numerous communication methods, and the ways to distribute information. The lists become even more complicated for large, collaborative, multinational projects—especially when change orders are necessary and numerous people must be informed of project modifications.

Communications Plan: People
Coordinating project communication requires a plan that should be included in the PMP. The project communications plan should include: (1) who needs to be informed, when, by whom, and for what reason; (2) communication methods; and (3) communication guidelines. The communications plan should be developed

as early in the project as possible and should delineate strategies for every stage of the PLC.

The communications plan is an iterative document—its contents are modified on an as-needed basis. The plan is also an excellent way to document a project, which can be used as an historical database for future projects.

The first step in the communications plan is to identify all the people involved with the project, including stakeholders. The list should include internal and external individuals, such as architects, designers, MEP/FP (mechanical, electrical, plumbing/fire protection) engineers, contractors, builders, real estate agents, developers, IT (information technology) professionals, code consultants, legal counsel, board members, end users, suppliers, and community members. The project scope, WBS, and human resource management plan are excellent sources for this information. The design team should develop a draft of the names of those people and distribute the list to relevant persons and organizations for corrections, additions, and deletions.

For each person on the list, the design team should identify his or her role and responsibilities associated with the project (Box 8.3). This information is useful for determining when someone should be informed, by whom, and for what reason.

For example, to install a new tile floor in a lobby, the tradesperson must know when to schedule the installation. The person who receives the tile delivery might be responsible for contacting the tradesperson. The tradesperson should definitely be notified when there is a delay with the preparation of the lobby or a problem with the tile. Who contacts the tradesperson under these situations should also be included in the communications plan. If the tradesperson is not contacted when there is a delay or a problem, there is a good chance that when the floor is ready for the tile installation the tradesperson might be committed to another project. Consequently, the installation might have to be scheduled for a later·date, which could contribute to other delays and additional expenses. This scenario is even more likely when working with quality tradespersons because their services are in high demand.

Other important considerations that should be included in the communications plan focus on personal attributes related to the project. For example, a team member who is highly respected in a community might be helpful in persuading people to approve the installation of unconventional green technologies, such as wind turbines. A team member who has excellent experience working with a subcontractor might be of assistance when requesting a change order.

Another characteristic to examine is a team member's level of interest in the project. People with a strong interest should be continuously updated and might have to be consulted when there are problems with the project. Generally, people with low levels of interest do not have to receive regular contacts; the information they receive consists of merely project highlights.

Communication strategies should also be based on the recipients' knowledge of design. People without design knowledge should receive design-related materials that include explanations, definitions, and clarifying illustrations. Technical terms should be avoided as well as any drawings or specifications that would be difficult for a layperson to understand. Enabling someone to understand technical information is especially important when the individual is involved with making decisions—another key element of the communications plan.

It is critical to identify who must be consulted when making decisions, in addition to who ultimately is responsible for determining a decision. These details should be supplemented with identifying the type of decision. For example, a plumber might be involved with decisions related to plumbing requirements but not with furniture specifications. Decision-making profiles are used to determine communication strategies, such as who needs what materials and when.

Accommodations that fulfill an individual's personal and professional needs help to build

Box 8.3

Example of a Personnel Profile Register for a Communications Plan for XYZ Industries

Profile Items	Mr. Smith	Ms. Jones
Organization and contact information	XYZ Industries 2233 Trade Avenue Cleveland, OH Cell phone: 112.334.3334 E-mail: rjsmith@xyz.com	MJJ Lighting Consultants 1122 Parkway Drive Cleveland, OH Cell phone: 112.122.1222 E-mail: mjjones@mjj.com
Role/Responsibilities	Director of Marketing/responsible for providing input to the project and serving as the lead communications person for XYZ's directors.	Lighting Designer/responsible for the lighting plans and coordinating lighting with other sustainable designs.
Team membership	Member of the director's support team.	Member of the central team.
Project duration	All phases of the PLC.	All phases of the PLC.
Reasons to contact the person	Solicit information pertaining to the XYZ directors; notify change orders related to directors and project updates.	Any issues involving the central team and specific items related to lighting and sustainability.
Person responsible for initiating contacts	Project Manager	Project Manager
Contact frequencies	As-needed basis and important milestones.	Weekly as a minimum.
Level of influence*	5—Senior director of XYZ Industries, highly respected and very influential in the company and community.	4—Has an excellent reputation in the nation for outstanding lighting designs and is LEED AP.
Level of involvement*	3—Very busy professional, but must be contacted to report project progress and accomplishments.	5—Very important for the lighting design and acquiring LEED certification.
Level of design knowledge*	1—Requires explanations, definitions, and illustrations.	5—Design professional.
Decision-making responsibilities	Consulted for decisions involving the overall project. Responsible for decisions related to XYZ directors.	Consulted for decisions involving details of the project. Responsible for decisions related to the lighting design.
Preferred communication method(s) (e.g., telephone, e-mail, texts, FAX, audio/video conferencing, U.S. post office, FedEx)	E-mail and interoffice mail system.	Telephone/texts for immediate responses and e-mail for other reasons. FedEx for deliveries.
Attendance requirements (e.g., staff meetings, charrettes, design team meetings, presentations, workshops)	Charrettes, interviews, directors support team meetings, and formal presentations of project updates.	All central team meetings and lighting support team meetings.
Access to technology and software	Access to project management software.	Access to project management software and BIM.
Documents/materials recipient (e.g., agendas, minutes of meetings, progress reports, invoices, change orders)	Agendas and minutes of directors support team meetings and project progress reports.	Agendas and minutes of central team meetings. Agendas and minutes of lighting support team meetings. All documents related to the lighting design. Project progress reports.
Other (e.g., work environment conditions, public events, community initiatives)	Prefers morning meetings in a casual setting— preferably outdoors when possible. Actively involved with local charitable organizations.	Prefers to work at her studio. Actively involved with local USGBC chapter.

*Very Low (1); Low (2); Moderate (3); High (4); Very High (5) relationships and enhance the success of the project. Therefore, the communications plan should include items that are specific to the needs of team members and stakeholders. For example, to enhance task performance, the design team can ask individuals to indicate their preferred work environment. Someone might be most productive working in a home office, or members of a sub-team might want their offices close together.

To meet the needs of stakeholders, the design team might want to invite local government officials to milestone events, such as ground-breaking ceremonies. Or the design team might want to send progress reports and press releases to a local businessperson who is contemplating a similar project.

Communication Plan: Communication Methods

Fulfilling the needs of project participants includes identifying each person's preferred communications method (Box 8.3):

* Does the person prefer to be contacted by telephone, text messages, e-mail, or fax?

* Does the person prefer to communicate in-person, or via telephone, e-mail, audio/video conferencing, web conferencing, or computer chats?

* Will the person only engage in virtual interactions?

* Should the person receive hard copies or electronic documents?

* Should the format be formal or informal?

* Should hard copies be sent via interoffice mail system, U.S. post office, FedEx/UPS, or common carrier?

Addressing communication needs also involves determining which activities and events require the person's attendance. Should the person attend meetings with the client, design team, staff, suppliers, manufacturers, contractors, subcontractors, or community representatives?

Should the person attend presentations, charrettes, focus groups, interviews, conferences, workshops, or manufacturers' demonstrations?

Communicating with team participants also requires a coordinated technology plan. Does every person have access to the same technology? Do they have the same software and the same version of that software? Do they have access to electronic databases? Can they use the scheduling and project management software? Do they have access to technical support staff?

The design team must decide what type of information each person should receive and when. Does the person prefer oral or written communication, and in what language? Should someone receive confidential documents, committee reports, meeting minutes, progress reports, revised PMPs, memorandums, press releases, change order requests, or change order authorizations? Should someone receive drawings, illustrations, specifications, commissioning reports, LEED certification documents, or product literature?

Key to the usefulness of this information, as well as the other items discussed in this section, is acquiring the details as early as possible. Early adoption helps to ensure that people receive the information they need for successful performance and to avoid uncompleted tasks because someone was unaware of an assignment.

Communication Plan: Guidelines

Preferred communication methods should be used to develop project communications guidelines. Fundamentally, the guidelines outline policies and procedures related to project communications, and could include a breakdown of costs associated with communications management.

The design team should determine an appropriate format and its content. Large and complex projects require guidelines with the most details. Some of the topics in a communications guideline include format suggestions for project materials as well as operational policies and procedures.

Providing consistency in content, presentation, and delivery requires the development of guidelines. The design team can determine format suggestions for oral presentations in addition to written documents, such as agendas, e-mails, letters, and memorandums. Materials for external parties might require a very polished appearance.

Along with format recommendations, the design team could specify the required content for important documents that help keep the project on track, such as project performance or **progress reports**. For example, project performance reports should include accomplishments, current activities, schedule/cost variances, and forthcoming tasks as well as future events.

The communications guideline document might also include project operational policies and procedures. For example, the design team might want to formalize procedures for analyzing risks, distributing information, or conducting PMP revisions and updates. The team might want to create a glossary of terms associated with the project to help ensure consistent usage throughout the PLC.

A very important item to specify is project record-keeping policies. Project records are very important for green certification programs, estimating resources for future projects, and for developing recommendations for continuous improvement. The design team should determine what type of information should be included in the project records, who is responsible for maintaining the records, how the records be retained (hard copies/electronic/both), and document accessibility.

Project Management: Risks

Designers must deal with the inevitable risks that impact projects. Completing a project on time, within budget, and according to the needs of the client requires a comprehensive process to manage risks. There are two excellent sources for risk management processes. From an international perspective, *ISO 31000:2009—Risk Management—Principles and Guidelines* was developed to assist organizations in a variety of types and sizes to effectively manage risk (see http://www.iso.org/). The PMI also has recommendations for project risk management (PMI 2008).

Both organizations view risk assessment as a means to identify threats as well as opportunities within the context of the project's objectives. This philosophy is reflected in PMI's definition of risk: "An uncertain event or condition that, if it occurs, has a positive or negative effect on a project's objectives" (PMI 2008).

The risk management guidelines developed by ISO and PMI have similar recommendations for the risk assessment process: (1) planning and establishing the context, (2) risk identification, (3) risk analysis and evaluation, (4) risk responses and treatments, and (5) monitoring and review (Figure 8.7). The processes require cross-functional collaboration and a comprehensive communications plan.

An extremely important aspect of risk assessment is to begin the process as early in the project as possible. The earlier the identification, the easier it is to avoid a problem or take advantage of an opportunity. Therefore, a plan for risk management should be developed in the predesign phases of a project and ideally, the steps prior to the last process—*monitor and review*—should be completed by the end of the project's schematic phase.

Risk Management Plan

The risk management plan includes policies and procedures for risk management, such as roles, responsibilities, assessment methodologies (e.g., brainstorming, focus groups, and interviews), communication/reporting mechanisms, costs, and timelines.

Project objectives provide the context for the risk management plan as well as **risk categories** and **risk criteria**. Risk categories are areas of possible causes of risk, such as organizational, financial, programmatic, economic, natural environment, and technical.

Risk criteria are used to determine the importance of a risk. A risk management team

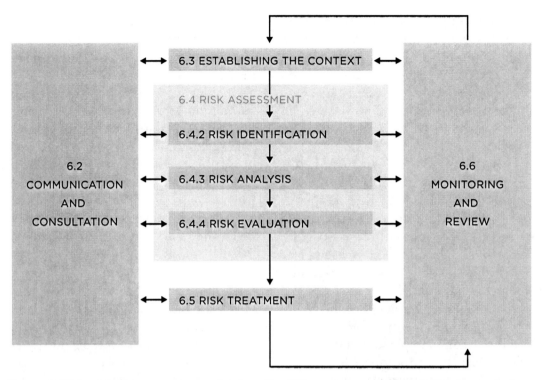

Figure 8.7 The risk assessment process developed by ISO requires communication and consultation with internal and external stakeholders as well as a plan for monitoring and reviews.

might identify hundreds of potential risks for a project—impossible numbers to resolve and monitor. Risk criteria tend to focus on the likelihood of an event occurring and its importance to the project. Risks that have the most significant impact on the outcome of the project have the highest priority.

Risks that are most likely to occur are also prioritized. A risk that has a *very high* probability of happening and has a *very high* impact on a project becomes a top priority. Risks that have a *very low* probability of occurring and have a *very low* impact on the project generally are eliminated from the risk management process.

Risk Identification

Risk management cannot occur without a **risk register**—a comprehensive list of potential risks and their characteristics. Past experiences and surveys can be used to help inform risk management. However, to create an all-encompassing list of risks that are relevant to

the current project requires collaborative sessions with representatives from each area in a firm.

Collaborative sessions should be done for every project, regardless of the team's experience with a building type or market. Every project has unique nuances that are accompanied by unique risks.

The most effective approach to identifying risks is to use brainstorming sessions, as with the affinity diagram tool (see Figure 8.2b). Brainstorming is very effective for risk identification because it encourages participants to suggest as many ideas as possible in a very receptive environment. Participants are told that every idea will be considered and suggestions are not evaluated or discussed. This open and nonthreatening format encourages a proliferation of ideas, which increase as ideas serve as a stimulus to even more ideas. Generally, listening in person is the most effective setting to inspire thoughts.

Another important element for idea generation is involving the right people. There should be a representative from every major area in the project, such as the project manager, architects, interior designers, engineers, end users, and community stakeholders. Cross-functional collaboration is needed to ensure a comprehensive list of risks and their characteristics and possible mitigation.

To help ensure a comprehensive risk register, some groups will brainstorm by using the **SWOT (strengths, weaknesses, opportunities, threats) analysis**. SWOT is often used for strategic planning purposes (see Chapter 12) but can be useful for risk identification because participants examine positive and negative factors. The initial risk register is considered an evolving document that is revised as the project progresses.

Risk Analysis and Evaluation

After the development of the risk register, a designated team must prioritize the list by conducting a thorough risk analysis and evaluation. The intent is for the team to understand each risk and how it might have a positive or negative effect on the project. Risks that have the greatest impact on a project have the highest priority.

Risks are also prioritized according to the likelihood that they will occur. Events with a low probability of occurring might be eliminated from the register, or if they are important to the project, the team could decide to monitor the risk. For example, a furniture delivery for an office might have a low probability of not arriving on time, but if the furniture isn't delivered on time people can't move into the space—a high impact on the project.

Risk analysis also involves examining the causes of a risk and their overall effect on the entire project. A cause might affect several risks; thus, the design team might elect to prioritize the cause, which ultimately impacts several risks. For example, a rise or fall in interest rates could have a negative or positive effect on the cost of materials, supplies, and equipment.

Closely monitoring interest rates might allow a firm to purchase items at the optimum time.

The risk analysis and evaluation process should conclude with priority rankings of risks from very high to very low. The rankings could be grouped according to function. For example, the team might rank the risks associated with the budget and create a separate ranking for technical issues. The team might want to create a separate ranking for risks requiring immediate attention, those that will need attention at midterm, and toward the end of the project. The overall goal is to identify the risks that require some type of response and treatment.

Risk Treatments (Responses)

The next step in the risk management process is to determine appropriate treatments or responses for the prioritized risks. To identify risk treatments, the team must understand the client's **risk tolerance**. How much is the person willing to lose or gain given a condition or event?

Clients with low risk tolerance are very interested in treatments that will moderate or eliminate a risk. Clients with high risk tolerance are more willing to take their chances that a risk will not affect the project. Thus, they are less interested in **risk treatments**. Costs, time, and effort all become factors when deciding the most appropriate risk treatment. The basic options from a negative and positive approach include avoidance/exploitation, mitigate/enhance, transfer/share, and accept/accept.

Risk Treatments: Avoidance/Exploitation

The avoidance treatment is selected when it is likely that a risk could have a negative impact on a project. For example, to avoid the risk of not completing a project on time, the team might recommend that more people are hired or suggest a revised schedule. From the positive perspective, the exploitation treatment involves taking advantage of a risk for the benefit of the project, such as purchasing items when interest rates are low.

Risk Treatments: Mitigate/Enhance

Risk mitigation involves identifying ways to lessen the negative impact of a risk. For example, the risk of using inaccurate measurements of a room could be mitigated by having several people measure and record the figures. Risk enhancement can be used to improve a positive outcome of a project, such as hiring a professional photographer to enhance the probability that an interior will appear in a popular magazine.

Risk Treatments: Transfer/Share and Accept/Accept

The transfer treatment shifts the risk to a third party, such as an insurance company or a subcontractor. In contrast, a share treatment splits the responsibilities associated with a risk.

Lastly, the accept treatment is used when the team recognizes that the risk is inevitable and the other options are not plausible for a variety of reasons, such as high costs, lack of expertise, or significant consumption of time. Therefore, the project proceeds without treatment interventions. The acceptance treatment is used for positive and negative situations. Accept treatments and all other proposed risk treatment strategies are recorded in the risk register.

Risk Monitor and Review

The risk register becomes very important for the monitor and review phase in the risk management process. The primary tasks in the risk monitor and review stage include: (1) tracking the decisions formulated in the previous phases of risk management—risk identification, risk analysis, and risk treatments; and (2) scanning the environment to discover new potential risks.

Generally, the risk monitor and review process entails responding to a series of reoccurring questions, such as:

- What is the status of risks that had a high probability of occurring and a significant impact on the project?

- What is the status of risks that had a moderate or low probability of occurring?

- Should changes be made to the list of possible causes of risks?

- Should the team revise the prioritized list of risks?

- Are there risks that can be eliminated from the register?

- How have the risks and risk treatments affected the project's scope, quality standards, schedule, human resource plan, communications plan, budget, and contingency fund?

Periodic reviews of conditions and events must be performed to determine the probability of new risks and their potential impact on the project. Any new risks would be added to the project's risk register for continuous monitoring and review.

Project Management: Procurement

Project procurements can be simplistic when a client is purchasing only a few items, or it can be very complex as in the case of designing and building a multipurpose high-rise. However, in either situation, it is still very important to have procurement management policies and procedures. Obviously, procurements are associated with finances and the budget—critical elements of a project. But, purchases are also closely tied to the project's scope, quality assurances, and the schedule—equally as important to the project's success. Therefore, a well-managed procurement program is vital to the budget and indirectly impacts other essential components of a project. The ideal arrangement is to develop efficient procurement management practices as you work on small projects and then transfer those skills to larger projects in the future.

Procurement management begins in the contract document phase of the design process and continues through contract administration (see Chapter 9). Project FF&E (furniture, furnishings and equipment) manuals might be developed that list furniture, furnishings, and equipment and manufacturers' specifications.

Some design firms have formal procurement management guidelines; other firms use a less-structured approach. In either situation procurement management basically involves: (1) developing criteria for products, materials, services, and equipment required for the project; (2) determining qualifications of suppliers, vendors, and service providers; (3) processing bids, proposals, and contractual arrangements; and (4) monitoring work performance, change orders, and contracts.

Criteria for Products, Equipment, and Services

The first step in the procurement management process is to develop the specifications for all products, materials, equipment, and services needed for the project (see Chapter 9). The information is derived from the construction drawings and schedules (doors, windows, finishes, and lighting). For large projects, items such as furniture are coded to ensure accuracy (see Chapter 9).

Specifications must be thorough and accurate. Various requirements can be included in specifications, such as manufacturers, quantities, quality expectations, delivery timelines, performance standards, warranties, and certifications.

Closed specifications are used when an exact item must be purchased and substitutes are not acceptable. In this situation, the specifications include the manufacturer, item number/name, dimensions, and any other descriptors, such as color, finish, hardware, and fabric.

Open specifications are used when it is unnecessary to purchase a specific product. Open specifications provide more flexibility; however, it is imperative that descriptions are very thorough and do not allow a supplier to interpret what is needed for a project. In addition, missing details can delay the entire procurement process because of the time required for clarification.

Supplier Qualifications

Specifications might also indicate that a supplier, vendor, specialists, contractor, or subcontractor has specific qualifications. For example, they could require a minimum number of years of experience with a particular product, activity, or service. Requirements might include specific technical skills, expertise, certifications, and licenses. Past performance records might be required as well as financial standing and references.

Specifications might also request company policies related to legal issues, such as risk responsibilities, warranties, intellectual property rights, safety performance, security measures, and quality assurances. The company might have to document any existing **proprietary rights**, such as patents or copyrights.

Similarly, a company might be required to demonstrate a particular business practice, such as a commitment to the environment, the community, diversity, innovation, or the health and well-being of its employees. Statements alone are not acceptable; the company must verify its business practices with authentic documentation and references. For example, if a company claims to have a commitment to the environment, then this philosophy should be evident in every aspect of its operations, such as using sustainable materials and manufacturing processes. The company should be able to provide examples of recycling, working with a sustainable supply chain, and green certifications.

All of these requirements, which might be included in specifications, are reflective of a business philosophy that is fundamentally derived from total quality management. Price is just one of the items to consider in acquiring products and services. Other factors, such as establishing long-term relationships and continuous improvement policies, are critical to the overall success of the project and should be delineated in specifications. Eventually, successful experiences result in a company being included on a design firm's list of qualified sellers.

Bids and Proposals

Specifications are used to create purchase orders or solicitation documents, such as **bids** and **proposals** (see Chapters 6 and 9). Solicitation processes should be well organized and thorough, and all bidders should be given the same information at the same time.

Bids or **tenders** typically are used to solicit price requests for stock items, such as standard office chairs and desks. Proposals are used when costs and other requirements, such as expertise or technical background, are requested.

Prior to accepting bids the design team might schedule a bidder session or conference—common with large and complex projects. Ideally, the session should be held at the project location. The purpose of a bidder session is to clarify project specifications by responding to questions posed by potential bidders. When the bidders have a clear understanding of the project, they are able to address the requirements with their most cost-effective price in a very timely manner.

The submitted bids and proposals are evaluated from a variety of perspectives. A designated multidisciplinary team must review the documents for timeliness, accuracy, omissions, deletions, and substitutions. The bidder's qualifications must be verified; references are contacted for this purpose. At times the team might create a ranked short list and request the top-ranked bidders to submit additional information. In coordination with the client, the team selects a seller and then awards the contract.

Procurement Contractual Arrangements

The three major types of procurement contracts are the **fixed-price**, **cost-reimbursable**, and **time and materials (T&M)**. Fixed-price contracts can have various provisions. Some fixed-price contracts have a firm price for products and services throughout the life of the contract. Any changes to the scope of the project are paid by the client.

A fixed-price contract can also have an incentive clause or an economic price adjustment. Incentives are used to motivate the seller to accomplish some activity, such as completing a task early or under budget. Economic price adjustments can be necessary for long-term projects.

The fixed price might be adjusted for inflation or some other designated monetary index.

Cost-reimbursable contracts are similar to some of the designer-client contracts discussed in Chapter 7. The cost-plus-fixed-fee contract specifies that the client pays a fixed fee to the seller and any other costs associated with the project. In addition to fixed fees, cost-plus contracts can link the amount of a fee to specific incentives, as previously discussed, or to awards. A cost-plus-award fee contract has prescribed accomplishments that must be achieved to receive full fees.

Time and material contracts have the flexibility to adjust costs within specified limits. Thus, clauses in T&M contracts can specify maximum fees, number of hours, or cost of materials.

Monitoring Work and Product Performance

Contracts can include several provisions, including statement of work/deliverables, deadline dates, roles/responsibilities, costs, payment terms, inspection criteria, warranties, liability limitations, penalties, incentives, insurance/performance bonds, work approvals, change request policies, and termination/alternative dispute resolution mechanisms (PMI 2008). These items must be monitored and coordinated with other project management areas, such as the schedule, budget, and human resource plan.

Work and product performance must be in compliance with the terms of the legal contract. Deviations or omissions must be reported in writing and accompanied with the desired remedy. To help build solid relationships with suppliers and vendors, complaints should be handled carefully, and legal action should be avoided whenever possible.

Change orders should be processed according to the terms of the contract and should include signatures of authorized personnel (see Box 6.3 in Chapter 6). Payments based on the work performed or products delivered should be distributed as prescribed in the contract.

Monitoring procurement activities also includes maintaining excellent records. Documentation should include all contracts, correspondences, oral/written agreements, invoices, payments, penalties, incentives, awards, claims, disputes, resolutions, early terminations, and inspection reports.

An assessment of the work performance should also be included in the records. Procurement records become invaluable for assessing the qualifications of sellers in the future as well as providing input about the continuous improvement of business policies and procedures.

Checking for Comprehension

- Which components of a project management communication plan do you think are most important?

- Identify positive and negative risks that might affect a project.

This chapter reviewed effective strategies for project management. Regardless of the type or size of a built environment, you will be involved with project management. To accomplish the goals of a project, you will be involved with creating the PMP, which includes the project scope, quality assurances, schedules, personnel, communication channels, budgets, strategies to manage risks, and procurement policies.

A thorough understanding of the elements of a PMP will enable you to participate in team initiatives as well as oversee project management plans for your clients. The project management information discussed in this chapter is integrated with the content presented in the next chapter. The primary purpose of Chapter 9 is to review the phases of the integrated design process from the perspective of client relationships and best business practices—areas that require knowledge of project management.

Knowledge and Skills Summary

Highlights

- The PMI defines project management as "the application of knowledge, skills, tools, and techniques to project activities to meet the project requirements" (PMI 2008).

- Project delivery methods include Design-Bid-Build (DBB), Design-Build (DB), Construction Management at-Risk (CMaR), and Integrated Project Delivery (IPD).

- Project scope management has five basic components: (1) collect the requirements of the stakeholders, (2) define the scope, (3) create a work breakdown schedule (WBS), (4) verify scope, and (5) control scope.

- The design team is responsible for ensuring that the final design incorporates the client's quality expectations.

- To create a schedule for a project requires the following steps: (1) develop a list of the activities, (2) determine the sequence of the activities, (3) estimate the resources required for each activity, (4) estimate the amount of time, and (5) incorporate the preceding items into a chart.

- For the purposes of facilitating a project, the basic human resource management procedures include (1) identifying the team members, (2) establishing the team, (3) managing the team, and (4) disbanding the team.

- Developing a budget involves estimating costs, determining the budget, and controlling costs.

- The project communications plan should include (1) who needs to be informed, when, by whom, and for what reason; (2) communication methods; and (3) communication guidelines.

- The risk assessment process involves (1) planning and establishing the context, (2) risk identification, (3) risk analysis and evaluation, (4) risk responses and treatments, and (5) monitoring and review.

- Procurement management consists of the following activities: (1) developing criteria for products, materials, services, and equipment required for the project; (2) determining qualifications of suppliers, vendors, and service providers; (3) processing bids, proposals, and contractual arrangements; and (4) monitoring work performance, change orders, and contracts.

Key Terms

actual cost (AC)

affinity diagram

analogous estimating

arrow diagram

baseline

bid (tender)

bottom-up estimate

closed specification

Construction Management at-Risk (CMaR)

contingency fund

cost baseline

cost-benefit analysis (CBA)

cost-reimbursable contract

crashing

critical path

deliverable

Design-Bid-Build (DBB)

Design-Build (DB)

Design Quality Indicator (DQI)

earned value (EV)

earned value management system (EVMS)

fast tracking

fixed-price contract

Gantt chart

matrix diagram

micromanagement

milestone

open specification

padding

parallel activities

parametric estimating

Plan-Do-Check-Act (PDCA) cycle

planned value (PV)

portfolio management

process decision program chart (PDPC)

Program Evaluation Review Technique (PERT)

progress report (project performance report)

project delivery method

project life cycle (PLC)

project management

project management plan (PMP)

project manager

project performance report (progress report)

project scope

project scope management

proposal

proprietary right

relations diagram

risk category

risk criteria

risk register

risk tolerance

risk treatment

rolling wave plan

schedule compression

scope creep

sequential activities

Shewhart cycle

strengths, weaknesses, opportunities, threats (SWOT)

systematic diagram

tender (bid)

three-point estimate

time and materials (T&M) contract

time chart

total quality management (TQM)

work breakdown schedule (WBS)

Projects

Philosophy and Design Project

TQM (total quality management) is a management philosophy focusing on continuous improvement processes with an emphasis on the needs of the customer, leadership, collaborative relationships, education, and understanding processes from a systemic perspective. Based on the principles of TQM, develop strategies you could use when working with clients, coworkers, colleagues, and stakeholders. For example, you should identify strategies for continuous improvement and collaborative relationships.

Discuss (online or face-to-face) your ideas with other designers and develop a bulleted list of your TQM strategies that includes examples of how you would implement the strategies while working with clients, coworkers, colleagues, and stakeholders.

Research Project

Search the Internet to find a design-related RFP (request for proposal) sponsored by a state agency or the U.S. government. Note the agency/office/location and posting/due dates. Record the contact names/phone numbers, type of project, estimated price range, and details regarding the building (e.g., drawings, site visits, and restrictions).

Research the agency and view demonstration videos of the submission and review processes. In a group of two to three classmates, develop an outline of what should be included in a document package that would be submitted in response to the RFP. Submit a copy of the RFP with your outline.

Human Factors Research Project

A critical element of project management is knowing how to establish teams. From a project management perspective the stages of a team are: (1) forming, (2) storming, (3) norming, (4) performing, and (5) adjourning (PMI 2008).

Identify an occasion when you were a member of a team that was required to design an interior environment. Relate this experience to the five stages of a team, and analyze similarities and differences. Based on this analysis develop teaming policies for best practices.

Present your ideas to the class and solicit feedback for changes, additions, and deletions. Revise your teaming policies for best practices, and submit a summary of the recommendations (approximately three pages).

References

AIA California Council. 2007. *Integrated Project Delivery: A Working Definition*. http://www. aia.org/contractdocs/AIAS077630. Accessed January 4, 2011.

Construction Industry Council (CIC). 2011. *What Is DQI?* http://www.dqi.org.uk/. Accessed January 12, 2011.

International Organization for Standardization (ISO). 2011. *ISO 9000 Family*. http://www .iso.org/. Accessed January 13, 2011.

International Organization for Standardization (ISO). 2011. *Quality Management Principles*. http://www.iso.org/. Accessed January 13, 2011.

International Organization for Standardization (ISO). 2009. *ISO 31000:2009—Risk Management—Principles and Guidelines*. http:// www.iso.org/. Accessed January 28, 2011.

Project Management Institute (PMI). 2008. *A Guide to the Project Management Body of Knowledge* (*PMBOK Guide*)—ANSI/PMI 99-001-2008. Newtown Square, PA: Project Management Institute.

U.S. Green Building Council (USGBC). 2010. *Intro—What LEED Is*. http://www.usgbc.org. Accessed December 8, 2010.

Whole Building Design Guide (WBDG). 2011. *About the WBDG*. http://www.wbdg.org/ about.php. Accessed January 3, 2011.

Wight, M. 2011. *About Us*. http://www.wightco .com/. Accessed May 26, 2011.

CHAPTER 9

Enhancing Your Value:
Knowledge of the Total Design Process

لصف 9 (Persian)
Rozdział 9 (Polish)
Capítulo 9 (Portuguese)

After learning the content in Chapter 9, you will be able to answer the following questions:

- What is the integrated design process (IDP) within the context of project management strategies and cultivating client relationships?

- How can I integrate evidence-based design (EBD) with my project management strategies?

- How can I use project management strategies and cultivate client relationships in the predesign and programming phases of the IDP?

- How can I use project management strategies and cultivate client relationships in the schematic and design development phases of the IDP?

- How can I use project management strategies and cultivate client relationships in the contract documents, contract administration, and post-occupancy phases of the IDP?

Chapter 9 continues the discussion of business practices valuable to building long-term relationships with clients by exploring the topic within the context of the total integrated design process (IDP). (see Figure 9.1.) Chapter 7 defined the client relationship cycle (CRC) and reviewed many of the important strategies for establishing and building long-term client relationships, including interpersonal communication, developing collaborative contracts for design services, and presentations. Chapter 8 solidified this information by reviewing ways to nurture client relationships within the context of project management.

This chapter continues to review how to build long-term client relationships by providing suggestions for each phase of the IDP. These recommendations are particularly important during the initial stages of the CRC—a designer is focused on the client and eager to win the contract. As the CRC progresses designers have to shift their attention to the work necessary for the project. Consequently, designers might be less concerned about client relations—potentially disastrous for the development of loyal clients and referrals. Therefore, suggestions

The firm's design for the LEED Platinum certified Center for Neighborhood Technology (CNT) is an excellent example of their collaborative philosophy. (© Mark Ballogg)

for cultivating client relationships are reviewed throughout the chapter and a summary of these activities at each phase of the IDP is provided in Tables 9.1–9.3.

As a way to synthesize key practices and topics reviewed in the book with each phase of the IDP, Tables 9.1–9.3 include: (1) examples of deliverables, (2) each area of the project management plan (PMP; e.g., project scope, quality, and schedule), (3) contract/communications, (4) client relationship strategies, (5) **Leadership in Energy and Environmental Design (LEED)** certification activities, (6) examples of how interior designers add value, and (7) personal management strategies. This list illustrates the totality of the design process.

Don't be discouraged by the length of the chapter. In contrast, you should be impressed! The chapter's extensive coverage illustrates the many ways our profession provides value to clients and society.

Integrated Design Process (IDP)

You might be wondering why the IDP is used in this chapter, and what is the integrated design process (IDP)? The content in this chapter is based on the IDP because the approach is essential to the development of high-performance, sustainable built environments. Interior designers must be prepared to respond to the continuously growing demand for efficient and cost-effective buildings as well as green building certifications, such as LEED or Canada LEED. Thus, reviewing a project life cycle (PLC) within the context of the IDP will provide you with an understanding of IDP's operational procedures, resource requirements, and the role and responsibilities of interior designers. In addition, you will be able to analyze how the IDP differs from typical approaches even though the phases of the design process are essentially the same: **programming, schematic design, design development, contract documents**, and **contract administration**.

Fundamentally, the IDP evolved in the twenty-first century because of global interest in creating high-performance sustainable designs for the built environment. The Whole Building Design Guide (WBDG) is an organization that promotes high-performance buildings and the IDP (see http://www.wbdg.org/).

Sponsored by the National Institute of Building Sciences (NIBS), the WBDG has a web-based portal that provides current information on "building-related guidance, criteria and technology from a 'whole buildings' perspective" (WBDG 2011). Information is created through a collaborative effort involving numerous federal agencies, private companies, nonprofit organizations, and educational institutions (WBDG 2011).

Explanation of the IDP
The WBDG provides an explanation of the IDP and how it differs from a traditional design process: "The 'integrated' design approach asks all the members of the building stakeholder community, and the technical planning, design, and construction team to look at the project objectives, and building materials, systems, and assemblies from many different perspectives. This approach is a deviation from the typical planning and design process of relying on the expertise of specialists who work in their respective specialties somewhat isolated from each other" (Prowler 2008).

The WBDG further explains that the IDP involves "the knowledge pool of all the stakeholders across the life cycle of the project, from defining the need for a building, through planning, design, construction, building occupancy, and operations" (Prowler 2008).

The business-related responsibilities associated with each phase of the integrated design process are reviewed through the lens of achieving LEED certification as well as developing relationships with clients (Tables 9.1–9.3). Thus, this chapter "walks through" the integrated design process and describes the designer's business-related responsibilities at each phase of the process, including what must be done for LEED certification requirements.

To provide a background of LEED and its certification process, a summary is provided in Box 9.1. As we discuss these topics, you will learn that to achieve LEED certification there are *many* requirements that must be addressed at every phase of the integrated design process, especially at the beginning of a project. Waiting to address LEED requirements can result in compromised high-performance goals, increased costs, missed credits, and redesigns that require additional time and resources.

Client and Project Management Strategies: Predesign and Programming

Building long-term relationships requires a successful implementation of project management strategies beginning with predesign and programming. This section reviews important tasks associated with these two phases of the IDP by examining predesign initiatives, such as conducting feasibility studies and identifying relevant research studies as well as professional resources. This section also explains building permit procedures and how to cultivate client relationships during the predesign phase.

A review of project management strategies in the programming phase begins by examining various categories of design objectives and methodologies that can be used to gather design-related information from end users of a building. Strategies for collecting information about the built environment are also included in this section. As with the predesign phase, approaches to cultivating clients are provided for the programming phase.

Predesign Initiatives
Predesign activities fundamentally begin when a client contacts you for professional design services. The project might be redesigning an existing space, new construction, pre-lease building evaluations, feasibility studies, or the development of a master plan. Redesigning an existing space could involve a relatively simple task, such as rearranging furniture in a space, or providing space planning suggestions for thousands of square feet in an office building. Design services for new construction

Box 9.1

LEED for Commercial Interiors Rating System Profile*

Definition of LEED*

"LEED is an internationally recognized green building certification system, providing third-party verification that a building or community was designed and built using strategies aimed at improving performance across all the metrics that matter most: energy savings, water efficiency, CO_2 emissions reduction, improved indoor environmental quality, and stewardship of resources and sensitivity to their impacts. Developed by the U.S. Green Building Council (USGBC), LEED provides building owners and operators a concise framework for identifying and implementing practical and measurable green building design, construction, operations and maintenance solutions."

USGBC Rating Systems	Description
New Construction	LEED for New Construction and Major Renovations is designed to guide and distinguish high-performance commercial and institutional projects.
Existing Buildings: Operations & Maintenance	Provides a benchmark for building owners and operators to measure operations, improvements, and maintenance.
Commercial Interiors	A benchmark for the tenant improvement market that gives the power to make sustainable choices to tenants and designers.
Core & Shell	Aids designers, builders, developers, and new building owners in implementing sustainable design for new core and shell construction.
Schools	Recognizes the unique nature of the design and construction of K–12 schools and addresses the specific needs of school spaces.
Retail	Recognizes the unique nature of retail design and construction projects and addresses the specific needs of retail spaces.
Healthcare	Promotes sustainable planning, design, and construction for high-performance healthcare facilities.
Homes	Promotes the design and construction of high-performance green homes.
Neighborhood Development	Integrates the principles of smart growth, urbanism, and green building into the first national program for neighborhood design.

*Source: U.S. Green Building Council (USGBC). 2010. *Intro—What LEED Is*. http://www.usgbc.org. Retrieved December 8, 2010.

Key Areas of Performance*

Areas of Performance	Descriptions
Sustainable Sites (SS)	Choosing a building's site and managing that site during construction are important considerations for a project's sustainability. The Sustainable Sites category discourages development on previously undeveloped land; minimizes a building's impact on ecosystems and waterways; encourages regionally appropriate landscaping; rewards smart transportation choices; controls stormwater runoff; and reduces erosion, light pollution, heat island effect, and construction-related pollution.
Water Efficiency (WE)	Buildings are major users of our potable water supply. The goal of the Water Efficiency credit category is to encourage smarter use of water, inside and out. Water reduction is typically achieved through more efficient appliances, fixtures, and fittings inside and water-wise landscaping outside.
Energy & Atmosphere (EA)	According to the U.S. Department of Energy, buildings use 39% of the energy and 74% of the electricity produced each year in the United States. The Energy & Atmosphere category encourages a wide variety of energy strategies: commissioning; energy use monitoring; efficient design and construction; efficient appliances, systems and lighting; the use of renewable and clean sources of energy, generated on-site or off-site; and other innovative strategies.

Box 9.1

LEED for Commercial Interiors Rating System Profile* (continued)

Areas of Performance	Descriptions
Materials & Resources (MR)	During both the construction and operations phases, buildings generate a lot of waste and use a lot of materials and resources. This credit category encourages the selection of sustainably grown, harvested, produced, and transported products and materials. It promotes the reduction of waste as well as reuse and recycling, and takes into account the reduction of waste at a product's source.
Indoor Environmental Quality (IEQ)	The U.S. Environmental Protection Agency estimates that Americans spend about 90% of their day indoors, where the air quality can be significantly worse than outside. The Indoor Environmental Quality credit category promotes strategies that can improve indoor air as well as providing access to natural daylight and views and improving acoustics.
Locations & Linkages (LL)**	The LEED for Homes rating system recognizes that much of a home's impact on the environment comes from where it is located and how it fits into its community. The Locations & Linkages credits encourage homes being built away from environmentally sensitive places and instead being built in infill, previously developed, and other preferable sites. It rewards homes that are built near already-existing infrastructure, community resources and transit, and it encourages access to open space for walking, physical activity, and time spent outdoors.
Awareness & Education (AE)**	The LEED for Homes rating system acknowledges that a green home is only truly green if the people who live in it use the green features to maximum effect. The Awareness & Education credits encourage home builders and real estate professionals to provide homeowners, tenants, and building managers with the education and tools they need to understand what makes their home green and how to make the most of those features.
Innovation in Design (ID)	The Innovation in Design credit category provides bonus points for projects that use new and innovative technologies and strategies to improve a building's performance well beyond what is required by other LEED credits or in green building considerations that are not specifically addressed elsewhere in LEED. This credit category also rewards projects for including a LEED-Accredited Professional on the team to ensure a holistic, integrated approach to the design and construction phase.
Regional Priority (RP)	USGBC's regional councils, chapters, and affiliates have identified the environmental concerns that are locally most important for every region of the country, and six LEED credits that address those local priorities were selected for each region. A project that earns a regional priority credit will earn one bonus point in addition to any points awarded for that credit. Up to four extra points can be earned in this way.

**Note that Locations & Linkages (LL) and Awareness & Education (AE) are applicable for the Homes rating system.

LEED Point System*

LEED points are awarded on a 100-point scale with an additional 10 bonus credits. A project must satisfy all prerequisites and earn a minimum number of points to be certified.

- Certified 40–49 points
- Silver 50–59 points
- Gold 60–79 points
- Platinum 80 points and above

LEED Certification Process*

- Project Registration
- Prepare Application
- Submit Application
- Application Review
- Certification

*Source: U.S. Green Building Council (USGBC). 2010. *Intro—What LEED Is.* http://www.usgbc.org. Retrieved December 8, 2010.

might involve a purchased site, or the client might want you to help select the ideal location.

Pre-lease building evaluations can be requested when a client wants to relocate his or her firm to a different facility for a variety of reasons, such as lower rent, reduced space utilization, better building services, or a more convenient location.

Feasibility studies could include pre-lease evaluations, but they can also involve determining the success of several features associated with the built environment, such as the energy efficiency of a mechanical system or the durability of a fabric or floorcovering.

A master plan is requested for long-term projects that could encompass multiple buildings constructed over a period of many years. The master plan provides the client with a guideline for a comprehensive scheme that has a unified conceptual design and strategy.

Box 9.2

Evidence-Based Design (EBD) used in a Design Firm—Ellerbe Becket*

Design Firm Profile

*   Founder—Franklin Ellerbe in 1909. (Currently practicing as AECOM)

*   450 professionals in seven international locations.

*   Ranked one of the top architectural/engineering/interior design firms in the country by several trade magazines, including *Interior Design* and *World Architecture*.

Selected "Practice-based Research Efforts" at Ellerbe Becket

*   **In-House Healthcare Research Database**—Database of over 200 peer-reviewed research articles and healthcare-related websites.

*   **Funds Practice-based Research—Goals are to:**

    *   Promote the role of practice-based research

    *   Explore the role of research in understanding the world of healthcare design

    *   Experiment with research methods that focus on identifying the connections between social sciences and healthcare

*   **Healthcare Connection**—Monthly firm-wide meetings to share healthcare project information, current research, and updates on healthcare conferences.

*   **Speaker Series and Industry Participation**

    *   Employees present their integration of research at conferences throughout the world.

    *   Firm co-sponsors (with the University of Minnesota Center for Spirituality and Healing) a speaker series on Optimal Healing Environments.

    *   *Creating Optimal Healing Environments in a Health Care Setting*. (Publication that discusses research findings related to healing design.)

    *   *Step Inside the Patient Room of the Future: Flexibility is Essential to Accommodating Multiple Needs*. (Publication that explores an adaptable patient room of the future.)

*   **Research Used in Projects**—Client-driven requests to integrate research into the design decision-making process.

* Adapted from: http://www.ellerbebecket.com/success/efforts/index.html

Predesign Initiatives: Preliminary Studies

Regardless of the services required, or the project type, you must conduct preliminary studies of the project. Chapter 7 reviewed many activities that occur in the predesign stage of the design phase, such as interviewing the client, visiting the site, defining the scope of the project, developing preliminary schedules, estimating budgets, determining the designer's services, and signing a contract for interior design services. Information gleaned from these activities should be used as a basis for additional predesign initiatives.

From an integrated design perspective, the predesign phase should focus on acquiring as much information as possible from a variety of sources, including professionals representing various disciplines, local building inspectors, research articles, professional publications, professional networks, and green building certification programs. The sooner the design team has information, the easier it is to resolve conflicting solutions and create designs that incorporate features required for high-performance built environments.

To ensure comprehensive information is obtained, each problem should be analyzed by personnel from a variety of disciplines. One approach to acquiring this information is to send RFIs (requests for information) to the relevant personnel. An RFI might be used to ask respondents to provide solutions to a problem. To help control expenses, the instructions might stipulate that at least one of the suggested solutions must be achievable without additional costs.

Other information that should be obtained during the predesign phase is local city, state, and federal codes and regulations—laws that help to protect the health, safety, and welfare of the public. Legal requirements can include deed restrictions, covenants, standards, and zoning regulations.

Some projects, such as government institutions, schools, and hospitals, have specific standards and guidelines required for various reasons, such as licensures and accreditations. All projects must be in compliance with local ordinances, standards, and regulations.

Therefore, the sooner the facts are understood, the easier it is to incorporate the requirements into the project's design.

Evidence-Based Design (EBD)

Two other important sources for information that should be obtained in the predesign phase are the results of research studies and professional publications (Box 9.2 and Figure 9.2). There are few topics related to the design profession that have not been analyzed via **informal** or **formal research** methodologies.

Informal research methods lack a systematic approach to solving a problem or pursuing facts. Thus, someone making casual observations of

Figure 9.2 An excellent example of integrating "practice-based research efforts" into a project is the Southcentral Health Center in Anchorage, Alaska designed by NBBJ. Based upon best practices the Southcentral Foundation facilities were designed to have positive effects on patients and staff. *(Southcentral Foundation)*

consumers' behavior in a retail store is an example of informal research.

InformeDesign, a web-based entity sponsored by the University of Minnesota, has thousands of formal research summaries related to design and the built environment posted on its website (http://www.informedesign.org). InformeDesign categorizes the research summaries according to *Space*, *Issues*, and *Occupants*.

As an example of InformeDesign's extraordinarily large number of research summaries, one can examine the *Issues* category. Within this category there are seven major topics encompassing approximately 14,000 research summaries (numbers in parenthesis): *Building Materials, Finishes, and Systems* (1,587); *Codes and Safety* (1,200); *Design and Aesthetics* (2,084); *Design Business and Process* (1,833); *Furnishings, Fixtures, & Equipment (FF&E)* (827); *Personal/Individual Needs and Factors* (5,165); and *Social Needs and Factors* (1,287) (InformeDesign 2011).

To provide a succinct and useful format, InformeDesign's research summaries are divided into eight sections: *Introduction*, *Design Issue*, *Design Criteria*, *Key Concepts*, *Research Method*, *Limitations*, *Commentary*, and *Adapted From* (Box 9.3). The one- to two-page summaries are an excellent source for obtaining an overview of the research conducted on a topic and how the results can be applied to practice. When more detailed information is needed, the article's full citation is located in the *Adapted From* section.

The summaries provided by InformeDesign are derived from research articles published in **refereed journals**. Authors of these academic articles have used formal research methodologies and their work is scrutinized through a peer-review process. Formal research studies include: (1) a review of previous research (literature review), (2) a statement of the problem and objectives, (3) research procedures, (4) research findings, and (5) a summary and discussion.

A researcher determines the research procedures or methodologies. Basically, the choices are **quantitative research**, **qualitative research**, or a combination of both methods. Quantitative research methods involve numbers and statistical analyses of data. Qualitative research methods use non-numerical data to identify meanings and interpretations (Box 9.3). Research techniques can include surveys, interviews, observations, charrettes, and focus groups (see the "Programming" section).

Using the results of research studies to inform practice, or evidence-based design (EBD), is an excellent way to optimize design solutions and demonstrate added value to your clients. For example, InformeDesign states: "There is a broad range of benefits to be gained by the design community, clients, occupants, participants, and other users through the interior designer's use of research. The public at large will be the ultimate beneficiary of the designers' increased knowledge, which will enable them to design environments that protect and enhance the public's health, safety, and welfare, and respect the limitations of the earth" (InformeDesign 2011).

Applying EBD to Practice

Applying EBD to practice can be done by directly integrating research results with design solutions. For example, if you were involved with designing a healthcare project, the research findings in Box 9.3 could be used to improve the design of the psychiatric inpatient facility. Thus, based on the research findings in this study your design team would consider designing new inpatient facilities that: (1) encourage interaction with the local community (first bullet in *Design Criteria*), (2) provide public space (second bullet), and (3) have a homelike environment and an efficient patient discharge area (third bullet) (InformeDesign 2011). In addition, based on the last bullet in the *Design Criteria* list, your design team would be aware of some of the limitations and risks associated with community-based psychiatric inpatient facilities.

You also can use EBD as the basis for informal research activities. For example, for the healthcare project mentioned in the previous paragraph, your design team could decide to conduct your own research study by following the research method used by Sarah Curtis and the other authors. Doing your own research is especially important because of the limitations of the study that are listed in Box 9.3—small sample size and only English-speaking subjects.

When using a research summary for your research, obtain a copy of the original article (see *Adapted From* section). The full article will provide you with specific research details, including a review of the literature—an excellent source for results of other research studies. The *Commentary* section in Box 9.3 noted that the review of the literature included information

---

InformeDesign Newsletter

5/24/2011   © InformeDesign: Print View

InformeDesign®
Where Research Informs Design

CREATING AN OPTIMAL ENVIRONMENT FOR MENTALLY ILL PATIENTS

Author's Title: New Spaces of Inpatient Care for People with Mental Illness: A Complex 'Rebirth' of the Clinic?
Author(s) Name: Sarah Curtis, W. Gesler, Stefan Priebe, and Susan Francis
Year of Publication: 2009
Search Related Keywords: Environmental Control Mental/Cognitive/Learning Neighborhood Patient Personalization of Space Preference/Attitude Quality of Life and Well Being Resident/Occupant Residential Treatment Facility Social Needs and Factors Stress

Design Issue

This case study investigated the effect of a community-based model of inpatient care for mental illness on patients and staff in a psychiatric inpatient unit in East London, England.

- A new model for psychiatric care has recently emerged that offers patients contact with the surrounding community. Although deinstitutionalization has been considered a beneficial development, it has also possibly resulted in more patients being relocated to prisons or ending up in poor living conditions after they are discharged (Dear & Wolch, 1987).

Design Criteria

Author Identified:

- Design community-based models of psychiatric inpatient units that foster interaction within the community the unit is located.
- Include public spaces in psychiatric inpatient units for visitors, staff, and patients to use.
- Create psychiatric inpatient units that offer a familiar, homelike environment to the patients (e.g., allowing them to personalize their space) but also support efficient patient discharge.
- Recognize that the community-based psychiatric inpatient care model discussed in this study creates ambiguous boundaries, having the opportunity for independent living experiences (e.g., allowed to leave at-will) but also presenting risks (e.g., difficulty checking-in emergency patients).

Key Concepts

- Characteristics of the emerging community-based psychiatric inpatient care model include: new geographical locations within community settings (as opposed to isolated settings); open wards that allow patients to leave the hospital at-will (instead of locked down); and an overall culture that encourages interaction with the outside world (Quirk et al., 2006).
- The transitional nature of the unit made it difficult for staff to determine the right time to release a patient and to create a home-like environment where patients could practice autonomy (e.g., decorating their rooms).
- Access to the local community (e.g., local neighborhood activities) created a sense of

www.informedesign.org/PrintView.aspx   1/

(Box 9.3 continued on page 284)

Box 9.3

InformeDesign Newsletter *(continued)*

5/24/2011 © InformeDesign: Print View

connectedness to the outside world. However, informal activities made it more difficult to get patients to engage in structured activities they perceived as regimented.

- Doors that were unlocked from the inside allowed patients to easily leave the ward, creating a relaxed attitude among patients and staff and a more permeable boundary between the community and hospital.
- Increasing incoming security made it more difficult for both wanted (e.g., family, friends) and unwanted (e.g., drug dealers, prostitutes) visitors to enter the facility and made emergency check-ins more difficult.
- Community spaces were created within the facility to bring the outside world in, creating a connectedness to the community.
- The new inpatient hospital was perceived as a place of refuge breaking from the past negative associations of the old "asylum" model (located in isolated areas, lock-down wards, separation from communities). The new, more therapeutic environment offered better quality of care, improved self-esteem among patients, and encouraged them to keep their environment looking nice as compared to the previous, unattractive institutional-looking facility.
- Patients formed attachments to the building as a place of refuge, sometimes becoming anxious when it was time to be discharged. However, the new facility did not have walking grounds or gardening spaces that traditionally create places of refuge in asylum settings.

Research Method

- Subjects (20; 7 formerly mentally ill patients; 10 nursing staff/managerial staff; 3 psychiatrists) who had experience in a new psychiatric inpatient facility located in East London (run through a private-public relationship under the Private Finance Initiative) took part in group (separated into patient, staff, or psychiatrist groups) or individual interviews. Former patients were recruited with the help of a local psychiatric volunteer organization. Staff and psychiatrists volunteered to participate by responding to an invitation.
- Specific interview questions (2) were asked to determine 1) features of the hospital (physical layout) that interviewees felt were good for patient and staff well-being; and 2) features they felt were not good for patient and staff well-being. After questions were posed, informal discussions were encouraged. Interviews were tape recorded and transcribed. Major themes were identified to determine the features of the hospital subjects thought were important in response to the two questions; and to understand how and why they deemed the features important.
- Attributional coding (Sylvester, 1998) was used to analyze the data.

Limitations

- The small sample size from one hospital setting may limit the generalizability of the findings.
- Non-English speakers were not included in the sample, potentially excluding an important population, considering the ethnically diverse location of the study.
- Staff and psychiatrists volunteered leading to potential self-selection bias among subjects.

Commentary

A review of literature on the traditional asylum and the new inpatient model of care for the mentally ill was included. A discussion of how findings might relate to theories of therapeutic landscapes can be found elsewhere (Curtis et al., 2007).

Adapted from
Author(s): Sarah Curtis, Durham University, UK; W. Gesler, Department of Geography, University of North Carolina, Chapel Hill; Stefan Priebe, University of London, Unit for Social & Community Psychiatry, Newham Centre for Mental Health, London, UK; and Susan Francis, Commission for Architecture and the Built Environment, London
Article Title: New SPaces of Inpatient Care for People with Mental Illness: A Complex 'Rebirth' of the Clinic?
Publisher: Interior Design Educators Council
Publication: Health and Place;
Publication Type: Refereed Journal;
Date of Publication: 20089
ISSN: 1353-8292
Volume: 15
Issue: 1
Pages: 340-348

2/3

Source: Reprinted from http://www.informedesign.org/Rs_detail.aspx?rsId=3476.

related to the traditional asylum and new inpatient model of care for the mentally ill.

To re-create the research study, your design team would have to find at least 20 subjects, including formerly mentally ill patients, nursing/managerial staff, and psychiatrists with experience in inpatient facilities. The subjects would be involved with group or individual interviews. Questions would focus on identifying the features of a hospital that are good and not good for the well-being of patients and staff.

The sessions should be tape recorded and transcribed for analysis and evaluation. Your results could be compared and contrasted to the findings in the Sarah Curtis et al. study. Your design team would then determine which design criteria should be incorporated into the design of the new facilities.

Professional Resources and Project Management Planning

The predesign phase is also an excellent time to conduct a review of current information related to the design profession and other industries. Basically, you are trying to identify the latest developments in design and current issues that are affecting the project type as well as your client's business.

In researching the project type, you can examine typical spaces, square footages (square meters), average costs, regional differences, and special requirements. There are numerous sources for this information, including print/online publications, social networks, online communities, blogs, bulletin boards, webinars, newsletters, books, **white papers**, case studies, events, and conferences.

Many professional resources can be accessed via international trade publications (Figure 9.3), such as *Interior Design* (http://www.interiordesign.net/), *Azure* (http://www.azuremagazine.com/), *Blueprint* (http://www.blueprintmagazine.co.uk/), *Architectural Record* (http://archrecord.construction.com/), *Contract Magazine* (http://www.contractdesign.com/), *DesignBuild-Network* (http://www.

Figure 9.3 DesignIntelligence's website is an example of an online source for professional design information, including news, conferences, blogs, videos, books, and articles. *(DesignIntelligence)*

designbuild-network.com/), *DesignIntelligence* (http://www.di.net/), *Environmental Design + Construction* (http://www.edcmag.com/), *Interiors & Sources* (http://www.interiorsandsources.com/), and *Metropolis Magazine* (http://www.metropolismag.com/cda/).

White papers are professional reports that focus on one specific issue. For example, in 2011 some of the white papers posted on the *Environmental Design + Construction* magazine's website were "The Green Building Boom Continues," "Water/Energy Correlation," and "Glass for the Masses."

As discussed in Chapter 1, professional organizations are excellent sources for current design information, such as the American Society for Interior Designers (ASID), International Interior Design Association (IIDA), Interior

Designers of Canada (IDC), The American Institute of Architects (AIA), United States Green Building Council (USGBC), Canada Green Building Council (CaGBC), Environmental Design Research Association (EDRA), and the International Furnishings and Design Association (IFDA).

You also should explore the international websites of professional design firms as well as manufacturers. Websites of professional design firms provide an overview of current projects and their solutions to design problems. Some design firms post white papers, videos, and publications on timely topics. For example, Gensler's website has free access to videos and PDF files that review a variety of topics, such as "Design for Learning," daylighting, conservation, and "Workplace Survey" research results (see http://www.gensler.com/#viewpoint/research). Commercial furniture manufacturer Herman Miller posts on its website research summaries, solution white papers, and case studies (see http://www.hermanmiller.com/Research).

During the predesign phase you should locate non-design information that is important to your client. For example, for commercial projects you should have the most recent version of documents produced by your client's business, such as annual reports, company timelines/history, awards/recognition, newsletters, profiles of board of directors, community service programs, marketing brochures/pamphlets, strategic plans, and operational policies. Generally, you can access these documents online. When they are not online, contact your client or the client's representative for the most current documents. You should become familiar with the company's profile on websites, such as Facebook, Twitter, and YouTube. To have the most current news and announcements, you should provide your e-mail address when a website has this feature.

You also should research current information related to your client's business. Thus, if the project is a hospital, you should locate current information that is affecting local hospitals as well as the healthcare industry. Your client

can provide you with the names of relevant professional organizations, publications, regulatory agencies, and other resources that are important to their industry. Current information regarding your client's business is extremely important for developing design solutions that address their needs and is very helpful for identifying stakeholders that should participate in the programming phase of the design process.

Building Permit Procedures

Early in the design process your design team should research the proper local authorities for approvals and permits. Learning the permit process as early as possible provides you with the information that must be incorporated into design solutions. By knowing these details early, you can avoid a lot of problems that can occur when construction is expected to begin and authorities deny issuing a permit because they have not approved the design.

Every jurisdiction has a set of procedures that must be followed to obtain permits—absolutely essential for construction. Generally, the sources for requirements are available from building departments and fire marshals. Municipalities post information on their website, but it is also important to visit with the authorities because it is important to begin a collaborative approach with them. These individuals can help you to understand the permit and inspection process, identify critical resources, and provide you with answers related to approvals and your design intent.

There are several questions you should ask the authorities, but keep in mind that the answers vary depending on the jurisdiction and the specifics of a particular project. One of the first questions should be, What activities require a permit? For example, is a permit needed to remodel a bedroom? Is a permit needed to paint an office?

Other questions can focus on identifying the codes, standards, and ordinances used by the municipality. Does it use the International Building Code and the National Fire Protection

Association's Life Safety Code? What are the accessibility codes? Are there energy-conservation codes? What are the zoning ordinances? What are the land use ordinances? What are the use groups and categories? What are the building height and area limits? Are there special interior environment codes? What are the fire resistance codes? What are the fire detection systems codes? What are the exiting codes? If codes have conflicting requirements, what is the resolution?

You must also understand the local building permit procedures. What applications must be completed and by whom? Who must submit the application—a licensed contractor, architect, or an engineer? Who is responsible for the approval and inspection processes? How long does it take to obtain the suggested revisions on the **redline plans** and a permit? What has to be inspected and when? What are the procedures for obtaining an occupancy permit? Is it possible to use a permit processor? How much are the fees? What is the process when changes are made to approved work?

These sample questions should make it apparent that there are many issues that should be resolved early in the design process, and the importance of understanding the permit process. In addition to ensuring code compliance, having full details of the permit and inspection processes will allow you to allocate sufficient time and resources for the events in the PMP.

Predesign: Cultivating Client Relationships and the Project Management Plan (PMP)

In addition to reviewing and understanding relevant building codes and acquiring documents associated with your client's company and industry, many other considerations are associated with cultivating client relationships during the predesign phase (Table 9.1). What

Table 9.1 Integrated Design Process Matrix: Predesign and Programming

	Predesign (Document all Activities)	Programming (Document all Activities)
Deliverables	Preliminary project scope, schedule, and budget. Contract for design services. Results of any design charrettes. Client job book. Determine construction delivery method. Beginning of CRC Process credit applications with potential new companies and vendors. Identify local building ordinances, including the processes and departments required for permits. Design proposal presentation. Project documentation.	Draft of the client's program, including initial design concept. Signed client written approval of client program. Project goals and objectives. Results of design charrettes, surveys, observations, focus groups, and observations. Results of site surveys, including delivery options. PMP with preliminary budget and schedule Documents filed with local statutory authorities. Updated client job book. Building client and professional relationships. Initiate relationship with sales reps of potential new companies and vendors. Initiate discussions with local authorities designated to approve permits. Project documentation.
PMP: Project Scope/(WBS)	Review project scope. Initiate use of BIM software.	Develop project scope: (1) identify requirements of stakeholders, and (2) define the scope and WBS. Monitor and control scope creep.
PMP: Quality	Implement PDCA cycle. Identify quality assurances. Utilize quality management business tools. Implement DQI and ISO 9000.	Implement PDCA cycle. Verify quality assurances. Utilize quality management business tools. Implement DQI and ISO 9000.
PMP: Schedule	Identify preliminary timeline.	Develop initial schedule with a list of activities using the WBS, sequence of tasks, resources, and time duration. Time estimates with PERT formula. Consider schedule compression and fast tracking. Create Gantt chart(s). Identify baseline, milestones, and critical path.

(Table 9.1 continued on page 288)

Table 9.1 *(continued)*

	Predesign (Document all Activities)	Programming (Document all Activities)
PMP: Human Resource Management	Identify design team members and their roles, responsibilities, and qualifications. Identify training and certification programs. Consider cultural and generational dimensions.	Identify design team members and their roles, responsibilities, and qualifications. Identify and facilitate training and certification programs. Establish and manage the team—forming and storming stage Develop reporting line charts and RACI matrix. Ask individuals for input on implementing tasks. Monitor conflict resolution sessions and decision-making. Informal assessment of performance. Consider cultural and generational dimensions.
PMP: Budget/ Cost Management	Identify preliminary budget.	Develop estimate costs, and determine initial budget and cost baseline. Estimate costs using bottom-up estimates, analogous estimating, parametric estimating, and the PERT formula. Initial client approval. Develop descriptions of the assumptions used for cost estimates. Estimate contingency fund.
PMP: Communication	Initial development of communications plan, including guidelines. Structure virtual team, and confirm communication channels, and virtual technologies/tools. Consider cultural and generational dimensions.	Determine who needs to be informed, when, by whom, for what reason, technology access, and use of communication methods. Determine decision-making policies and levels of influence, involvement, and design knowledge. Finalize communications plan. Structure virtual team, and confirm communication channels, and virtual technologies/tools. Consider cultural and generational dimensions.
PMP: Risk Management	Preliminary list of risks—threats and opportunities. Preliminary planning and establishing the context. Preliminary risk identification, analysis, and evaluation. Preliminary responses and treatments. Determine client risk tolerance level.	Developing list of risks—threats and opportunities. Developing risk planning and establishing the context—risk categories, risk criteria, and prioritization. Developing risk identification, analysis, and evaluation. Developing responses and treatments. Monitor and review risk register.
PMP: Procurement Management	Preliminary list of suppliers, vendors, consultants, and tradespersons.	Preliminary list of suppliers, vendors, consultants, and tradespersons.
Contracts/ Correspondence/ Documents	Contract or Letter of Agreement/RFI Stakeholders	RFI and transmittals. Project performance reports.
Client Relationships	Beginning of CRC. Cultivate relationship by providing excellent customer service, and being reliable and responsive to the needs of the client and team members. Initiate client job book. Present professional and design firm's profiles. Consider cultural and generational dimensions. Initial interviews, presentations, dialogues, listening sessions, and observations. Develop a collaborative working arrangement. Identify best interpersonal communication strategy. Identify client risk tolerance level. Design proposal presentation. Collaboratively develop the contract for design services. Signed contract or LOA for design services.	Cultivate relationship by providing excellent customer service, and being reliable and responsive to the needs of the client and team members. Consider cultural and generational dimensions. Promptly resolve problems and complaints. Client input needed for programming activities and risk management plan. Client updates: Progress with programming and final results. Develop fair estimates of costs and sound assumptions for the estimates—no padding and not too low. Create a budget that works with client's cash flow. Client signs document approving programming results. Focus on developing loyalty.

Table 9.1 (continued)

	Predesign (Document all Activities)	**Programming (Document all Activities)**
LEED Certification*	Hire LEED AP. Determine LEED level, register, and pay fees. Designate LEED team leader. Search for LEED certified buildings or buildings with best practices, such as brownfield redevelopment, stormwater management plan, reduces heat island effect, developed density, connectivity to community, and public transportation. Review energy efficiency of potential tenant space—energy and water utility bills. Evaluate natural ventilation and daylighting. Review waste management services. Research regional recycling options. Research local climate, energy efficiency, and occupant comfort ranges. Discuss long-term lease. Set water-use goals and strategies. Research and set targets for regional materials, rapidly renewable materials, and FSC-certified wood. Research low-emitting materials—adhesives, sealants, paints, coatings, flooring systems, composite wood, agrifiber products, systems furniture, and seating. Begin energy commissioning activities. Purchase green power. Complete LEED calculations and documentation.	Continue energy and other commissioning activities. Develop a purchasing policy for ENERGY STAR-qualified equipment and appliances. Determine best spaces for daylighting and views. Develop building reuse strategies. Develop construction waste management plan. Identify materials reuse strategies. Inventory FF&E and determine reuse. Identify materials with recycled content. Identify regional materials, rapidly renewable materials, and FSC-certified wood. Identify low-emitting materials. Establish air quality standards. Identify users' lighting needs and document tasks. Identify HVAC system for thermal comfort needs. Determine client's equipment requirements and usage patterns. Develop smoking policies. Engineers develop ventilation mechanical system. Determine using measurement and verification (M&V) credit. Purchase green power. Complete LEED calculations and documentation.
Value-Added Examples	Knowledge of CRC, global context, organizations, design process, and regulations. Skills in collaboration, communication, listening, project management, consensus building, leadership, and customer service. Ability to envision what could be done to improve spaces or design a built environment.	Knowledge of trade sources, human behavior theories, socioeconomic factors, research methodologies, Skills in defining design problems, gathering and analyzing data, collaboration, communication, listening, and customer service. Ability to conserve costs and resources due to collaborative and experienced decision-making.
Personal Management Strategies	Complete time/activity log and expense reports. Develop and review prioritized goals that address daily, weekly, monthly, quarterly, and annual responsibilities. Identify a time management organizational format to schedule appointments, tasks, and reminders. Develop information management strategy for project, products, and services. Practice knowledge management techniques to build tacit knowledge and maximize explicit knowledge.	Complete time/activity log and expense reports. Review and revise prioritized goals of responsibilities. Assess time management skills, including repetitive tasks and procrastination. Check reminders. Update information management files for project, products, and services. Practice knowledge management techniques to build tacit knowledge and maximize explicit knowledge.

*LEED Certification section adapted from U.S. Green Building Council. (2009). *Green Interior Design and Construction*. Washington, DC: U.S. Green Building Council.

else can you do to build long-term client relationships and demonstrate your value?

The predesign phase is the opportune time to establish a collaborative working arrangement with your client. For example, ask your client or that person's representative to participate in the preliminary development of the PMP. The client might be interested in only answering your questions, or the person might want to partake in the discussions. Either way, demonstrate your sincerity in wanting to work with the person to create the best possible design.

During the predesign phase your client should assist you with the initial development of the project scope, timeline, budget, quality assurances, risks, and risk tolerance levels. Your client can be very helpful in developing the human resource plan by identifying potential team members, such as employees, end users, and stakeholders.

To assist with the development of a multidisciplinary team—critical to the integrated design process—your client might be able to identify specialists he or she has worked with, such as real estate agents, developers, and legal counsel. Other professionals to consider for the team are code consultants, MEP (mechanical, electrical, and plumbing) engineers, and FP (fire protection) engineers.

As you create the potential list of team members, your client might be able to help with determining roles, responsibilities, and qualifications. Cultural dimensions and generational differences should be identified for further exploration and considerations.

The IDP requires a great deal of work early in the PLC. Therefore, people who are not familiar with the IDP should participate in workshops preferably during the predesign phase and definitely by the end of the programming phase.

Your client might be interested in attending IDP workshops. If not, ask if the person wants a synopsis of the process, including an explanation of its importance to the final outcome of the project.

The predesign phase also is an excellent time to ask about your client's communication preferences and any recommendations for the preliminary communications plan. To communicate effectively during a project, you must know an organization's culture. Your client might have suggestions for how to contact team members and preferred communication channels—a potentially critical issue for some business operations because in strict hierarchical organizations, there are protocols for communicating with those at the highest level in the corporation.

Very important to remember during the predesign phase and onward is providing excellent customer service. Be reliable, honest, ethical, and responsive to the needs of your client as well as team members. How you interact with your team members affects your relationship with your client. Somehow the client will learn if team members are disgruntled with your work, but he or she will also learn when people are enthusiastic about working with you.

The most challenging times are when there are problems: address these issues immediately for mutually beneficial resolutions. The ability to resolve conflicts is one of the added values you can contribute to the project. Beginning with the predesign phase, document how you are adding value to your client's project and, if appropriate, that person's business. Record the services in your client's job book. When you are communicating with your client, you might have the opportunity to mention these in your *Value-Added* document (another way to cultivate your long-term relationship).

Programming Phase: Activities and Deliverables

Programming should be considered the most important phase of the entire project, especially when using an IDP. Most often you will be actively involved with programming activities, but you could also work with a facility programmer. Through programming, the design team develops the client program by identifying project requirements, conceptual statements, preliminary timelines, and budget estimates.

The importance of programming is evident in several student learning expectations prescribed in the 2011 Council for Interior Design Accreditation's (CIDA) *Standard 4. Design Process*: "Students are able to: a) identify and define relevant aspects of a design problem (goals, objectives, performance criteria); b) gather, evaluate, and apply appropriate and necessary information and research findings to solve the problem (predesign investigation); c) synthesize information and generate multiple concepts and/or multiple design responses to programmatic requirements; and d)demonstrate creative thinking and originality through presentation of a variety of ideas, approaches, and concepts" (CIDA 2011).

To begin the programming phase, the design team must identify goals and objectives for the project from psychological and physiological perspectives. Fundamentally, the goals and objectives should focus on the project's site, design, construction, users' satisfaction, building performance, maintenance, and its impact on finances, the natural environment, and the community. The WBDG suggests the following alphabetized categories for design objectives (2010):

- Accessible: Pertains to building elements, heights and clearances implemented to address the specific needs of disabled people.

- Aesthetics: Pertains to the physical appearance and image of building elements and spaces as well as the integrated design process.

- Cost-effective: Pertains to selecting build elements on the basis of the life cycle costs (weighing options during concepts, design development, and value engineering) as well as basic cost estimating and budget control.

- Functional/Operational: Pertains to functional programming—spatial needs and requirements, system performance as well as durability and efficient maintenance of building elements.

- Historic Preservation: Pertains to specific actions within a historic district or affecting a historic building whereby building elements and strategies are classified into one of the four approaches—preservation, rehabilitation, restoration, or reconstruction.

- Productive: Pertains to occupants' well-being—physical and psychological comfort—including building elements such as air distribution, lighting, workspaces, systems, and technology.

- Secure/Safe: Pertains to the physical protection of occupants and assets from man-made and natural hazards.

- Sustainable: Pertains to environmental performance of building elements and strategies.

Gathering Information from People

Based on the goals and objectives of the project, the design team must develop a strategy to collect the appropriate information relevant to each topic (Figure 9.4). Data needs to be collected regarding the needs and priorities of the client, end users, and the stakeholders—activities that must be planned in the PMP. Many techniques can be used to gather information from people, including design charrettes, **focus groups**, **in-depth interviews**, **surveys**, **observation studies**, and **triangulation** (multiple mixes of methodologies).

All techniques begin with defining a problem or an issue, and require appropriate research procedures, such as posing clear and unbiased questions. Active listening is required for interaction techniques. Technical terms should be avoided as well as lengthy questions, especially those with two or more questions embedded in one sentence.

Given the assortment of research techniques, how do you decide which one to use? How do they affect the PMP? Answering these questions

Figure 9.4 As evidenced by the collaborative processes used for the project— Greensburg Schools/Kiowa County Schools in Greensburg, Kansas—design teams must collect information that is relevant to the needs and priorities of the client, end users, and stakeholders. For example, to accommodate the needs of the school and the Greensburg community, the school's library was prominently located on the site.
Designed by BNIM the targeted LEED Platinum certified building was also recognized as an *AIA/COTE* [Committee on the Environment] *Top Ten Green Project* in 2011. (© *Farshid Assassi*)

requires an overview of the research techniques and the elements that affect the PMP, such as the required personnel and time allotments.

As described in Chapter 4, charrettes are used to generate initial ideas for design solutions. The process involves the collaborative efforts of designers and the project's stakeholders. Charrettes have been used for the IDP because they are an effective way to efficiently involve stakeholders, encourage full participation, and examine problems from a holistic perspective.

Gathering Information from People: Group Interactions

Focus groups also engage people in group interactions, but they are different than charrettes. For example, in contrast to charrettes' intensive multi-day workshops, focus group sessions generally last only two hours. In addition, the continuous feedback loops between designers and stakeholders, which are so important in developing design solutions in charrettes, do not typically occur during focus group sessions.

The basic format of focus groups is to: (1) define the problem or issue; (2) identify the participants or **subjects** (6–10), taking into consideration balances in relevant diversity issues, such as wanting representation from multiple disciplines; (3) develop the questions or topics that will be discussed during the session; (4) conduct an open discussion using a professional moderator and a recording device; and (5) evaluate the results.

The differences between the two group interaction methods can be useful to a design team. The design team can select the format that best accommodates the information they need to obtain, from who, and when. An example of a question for group interactions is, "How can the design of the new library best serve the needs of the community?"

Gathering Information from People: Interviews and Surveys

In-depth interviews and surveys are also information-gathering options that can be used during the programming phase. Interviews are one-to-one or one-to-many question and answer sessions. Interviews can be **structured**, **semi-structured**, and **unstructured**. Structured interviews use the same items for each participant, such as "Using a scale from 1 to 5 (with 5 best), rate the aesthetics of the XXX conference facilities."

Semi-structured interviews use a combination of specific items (as in the previous example) and questions that might be tailored to a specific person: "Why did you rate the aesthetics of the XXX conference facilities so low?" Unstructured formats have the flexibility to change questions as an interview progresses.

Some important considerations while interviewing include maintaining eye contact, engaging in active listening, avoiding interruptions, and not visibly reacting to responses.

Surveys are a data-collection technique that uses a standardized list of items. The basic forms of surveys are **closed-ended** and **open-ended**. As the names imply, a closed-ended survey provides a list of responses, as in a multiple-choice exam. The open-ended form has a blank space for subjects to write a response—similar to a short-answer essay.

To make sure people will understand how to respond to the items, pretest the instrument by asking a small sample of representative subjects to complete the form. This is especially important when the survey will be distributed to large numbers of people. People tend to not complete poorly written surveys, and the embarrassment could compromise perceptions of your professionalism—which could be a significant issue during the earliest stages of the design process when you are trying to establish credibility with your client and stakeholders. To encourage people to complete a survey, you might want to mount an iPad tablet in a convenient location and encourage people to complete the survey using this electronic device.

Gathering Information from People: Observation Studies

One approach to develop your credibility and demonstrate your value is to master the art of observation studies. Members of the design profession have the unique ability to improve their work by purporsefully watching people in public spaces. By observing how people interact with a space, with each other, and with objects, a designer can learn the successes and failures of the built environment. These findings can then be applied to improve practice.

To make observing easier, develop a form with a list of items that are specific to the building type and end users. Be sure to watch at different times of the day, week, or perhaps month to get a clear understanding of peoples' behavior in a variety of circumstances (think about the differences in a shopping mall during the Christmas season and a snowstorm in January).

Observation studies can be combined with other research techniques to gain a comprehensive perspective of the data. Using multiple methods lets you compare and contrast information and issues, thereby attaining the most accurate results.

As you are deciding which research technique to use, remember that generally, the most meaningful information is obtained via face-to-face interactions (hence, charrettes and focus groups are usually quite successful). Therefore, whenever possible interviews should be used to gather information, but when there are large numbers of people who must participate—especially when they are located at different sites—surveys can be the most practical instrument.

Gathering Built Environment Information

In addition to gathering information from people, the programming phase requires a thorough survey of the built environment when working with an existing structure. The amount of time and personnel to allocate for this task depends on the size of the building and the existence of drawings.

Unfortunately, some clients will not have the original construction drawings. Or clients might not have the **as-built drawings**—excellent resource for accurate measurements, configurations, and details. When as-built drawings must

be drawn for large and complicated buildings, the task can consume considerable time—a situation that must be accounted for in the project's schedule, budget, and human resource plan.

From an integrated design perspective you must allocate time to review the building's surrounding context, such as neighboring buildings and topography, as well as characteristics of the building's façades and interior. As noted in the discussion on LEED certification, a building's surrounding context impacts the success of sustainable designs, such as providing access to nearby amenities or determining optimum daylighting by analyzing the path of the sun.

Generally, most of your time will be allocated to collecting information about the interior spaces, such as square footages (square meters), location of openings, structural elements, finishes, furniture, equipment, built-ins, and technical requirements (lighting, electrical, telecommunications, plumbing, HVAC, and acoustical).

Create an inventory of existing items and record what activities are performed in each space. Required adjacencies—people and spaces that should be in close proximity—should also be noted during a site visit. Photographs and sketches of the spaces are very helpful for recording purposes.

Set aside time for analyzing the condition of FF&E, such as worn areas, broken elements, fingerprints, scratch marks, and dusty spots. From a sustainability perspective, attempts should be made to repair, refurbish, and retain as many items as possible.

Sketch or photograph the spaces as well as the future FF&E delivery routes. This is the ideal time to note potential delivery problems, such as small elevators, no elevators, narrow staircases, or restricted openings—constraints that often exist in older buildings. There have been occasions when a large furniture piece had to be delivered through a window using a crane mounted on the roof of the apartment building.

A very serious situation can occur when you have sold an item to your client and it is impossible to deliver the piece to the appropriate space. Or perhaps the item can be delivered to the room but at considerable cost because of the building's physical constraints. In either situation you want to take these factors into consideration during the earliest phases of the design process.

Built Environment Information: Data Analysis

The PMP schedule also requires time and resources for analyzing the data collected from people and the built environment. Quantitative methods require statistical calculations that can be done with computer software programs, such as SPSS (Statistical Package for Social Sciences). There are qualitative research software programs for analysis purposes, such as CAQDAS (Computer Assisted Qualitative Data Analysis Software). These programs are useful for coding, organizing, storing, and retrieving research data.

You might discover you can gain significant insight regarding participants' comments and suggestions by typing in the responses yourself. This activity itself prompts you to think about each response at least twice. As you continue to type responses, you begin to remember previous comments and discover both commonalities and differences in the responses. Consequently, by simultaneously typing and thinking, you begin identifying the themes or patterns in the research.

With or without a software program, such as CAQDAS, a key element to analyzing qualitative data is reading the responses several times. This repetition helps you identify themes or categories as well as patterns, such as a group of people wanting control of their lighting system. When the results show inconsistencies, your design team might want to follow up with additional interviews to clarify the responses. For further analysis your informal findings can be compared and contrasted to the results of formal research studies.

The results of the programming processes are used to develop the client's program. The program should be given to the client for his or her review and feedback. Upon agreement the client should sign a written statement acknowledging approval of the program.

Programming: Cultivating Client Relationships and the Project Management Plan (PMP)

Collaborating with a client to develop the program is just one of the important activities in cultivating client relationships. A client or that person's representative should be actively involved with charrettes, interviews, surveys, and/or focus groups to help make sure their ideas and preferences are included in the program. A designer also needs assistance with surveying the facilities, such as acquiring access to private spaces.

The programming phase can provide you with extensive knowledge of the project and its requirements. Therefore, verifying the results and collaborating with your client to create the program is one of the most important elements for building long-term relationships. The more you understand what is important to your client, the more you will be able to anticipate that person's decisions and preferences as the project evolves.

Intuitive knowledge of your client's interests can help to save time and costs because you will be able to present ideal solutions—and not waste time by showing designs the client would never approve. Furthermore, when a client is aware that you understand his or her needs, that person gains confidence in your ability to accomplish the project's goals and objectives.

In addition to demonstrating to the client your knowledge of the needs and requirements of the project, excellent client relations include focusing on the PMP. A comprehensive PMP is absolutely critical to the success of a project, yet clients might not expect a designer to show much interest in creating the document. Thus, by involving your client with the development of the PMP, you can demonstrate your desire to address the design solutions as well as other elements equally important to a client: completing the project on time and within budget.

As discussed in Chapter 8 and summarized in Table 9.1, the IDP requires collaborative up-front management plans, involving the client, design team, and stakeholders. Therefore, the information gathered during programming can be used to develop the project scope, including the WBS, and to establish quality management processes.

The programming phase is also an excellent time to reevaluate the project's schedule, including the sequencing of activities, required resources, durations, baselines, milestones, and the critical path (see Chapter 8). The client can help you to develop the human resource management plan, such as verifying team members, their responsibilities, and reporting lines. Your client might also be interested in attending workshops pertaining to specialized training or certifications.

Client input is essential for developing cost estimates, the initial budget, and the cost baseline. Ensure that your client is comfortable with cost estimates and that he or she feels the amounts are fair, honest, and have been based on sound assumptions. The client should also review the preliminary budget from the perspective of anticipated cash flow.

The budget and cost control policies can be tied to procurement management. To control costs and for other reasons, such as following accreditation standards, the client might suggest or require specific suppliers, vendors, and consultants. The client's recommendations should be incorporated into a preliminary list of businesses and tradespersons to be involved in the project.

Client collaboration with the PMP at the programming phase also involves asking that person's advice regarding the communications plan. The client might be able to help you to accurately complete the personnel matrix as well as offer ideas to address cultural and generational aspects.

The client should also help identify items for the risk management plan, such as SWOTs, prioritizing risk categories, and developing responses and treatments. The design team should routinely request the client to provide an assessment of the risks associated with his or her business.

Checking for Comprehension
- Provide at least two advantages to using EBD to solve design problems.
- Describe information that should be gathered during the programming phase.

Client and Project Management Strategies: Schematic Design and Design Development

Building long-term relationships requires a successful implementation of project management strategies, continuing with schematic designs and design development. The schematic design section reviews trade sources and how to develop an FF&E manual. Suggestions are also provided for cultivating client relationships and demonstrating your value during the schematic design phase of the project.

A review of project management strategies in the design development phase begins by providing an overview of the required drawings, specifications, and schedules. Strategies for performing a **life-cycle cost analysis (LCCA)** are also included in this section.

Schematic Design

The results of the programming phase—the client program—are used to begin the project's design concept, followed by sketches and schematic models. The design concept is the basis for designs. Therefore, the design team should review a draft of the design concept with the client and stakeholders before beginning any sketches, drawings, or specifications. After the client concurs with the design concept, the design team can proceed by creating schematic designs.

As "schematic design phase" implies, the design team creates concept sketches of design solutions, such as space allocations, furniture layouts, lighting plans, elevations, sections, perspectives, colors, finishes, and decorative details.

While exploring various options, create your ideas within the context of your client's budget, project scope, schedule, and the data collected during the programming phase; developing unrealistic designs more often than not is a waste of your time and resources, and can irritate a client. However, this doesn't preclude you from generating new ideas—many clients are impressed and excited when a designer suggests something that was never considered in previous discussions. Unexpected solutions that meet the needs of the client is another example of how designers add value to a project.

The goal is always to meet the needs of your client from every aspect of the project, including the critical elements detailed in the PMP. Therefore, sufficient time and resources should be allocated for numerous exploratory sketches as well as bubble diagrams, adjacency matrices, stacking diagrams, and the preliminary FF&E manual.

From an integrated design perspective it is critical to coordinate preliminary designs with other professionals involved with the project, such as architects, engineers, commissioning agents, and consultants. Full participation is needed to holistically examine the design and to help prevent omissions.

Trade Sources: Preliminary FF&E Manual

How does a designer assemble an FF&E manual? Creating the preliminary FF&E requires you to first know where to look for products and services. Visiting design centers, marts, and international trade fairs (see Appendix D) is an excellent way to: (1) see a wide range of products for the built environment, (2) scrutinize the characteristics and quality of products and materials, (3) acquire Continuing Education Units (CEUs) by participating in seminars, (4) attend educational sessions, (5) develop networks, and (6) build relationships with people employed by manufacturers and vendors:

showroom managers, **manufacturers' representatives (sales reps)**, and **territory sales representatives** (outside sales reps) (see Figure 9.5).

Trade Sources: Design Centers and Marts

In the past, design centers and marts, such as the Merchandise Mart in Chicago, were open *To-the-Trade-Only*, whereby only design professionals were allowed to visit showrooms. Clients had to accompany designers to walk into the spaces. Many showrooms still operate this way, but there has been an increase in the number of spaces that are open to the public. For example, the Merchandise Mart has nearly an entire floor dedicated to kitchen and bath showrooms that are always open for public viewing, but not purchases. The goal is to expose people to the high-end products available through the design profession.

As a design professional you will have access to wholesale showrooms. Visiting showrooms is the best way to see colors, textures, and to experience sitting on chairs and sofas. Other advantages to going to design centers and marts are to see products that are not available from other sources as well as being reassured by showroom personnel that an item is current and in-stock.

Figure 9.5 Visiting international trade fairs, such as the 100% Norway Exhibition during the London Design Festival, is an excellent way to network and see new products. The LK Hjelle's Duo sofa was designed by Norway Says and Hallgeir Homstvedt. (© *MarianneWie.net*)

Ordering items that are discontinued or are currently not available can have severe consequences to a project's schedule. With or without a showroom visit, before showing an item to a client, *always* contact the manufacturer to check on its availability.

To give you time to show your client a product or samples, you might want to request that the company hold the item or perhaps a specific number of yards of fabric or rolls of wallcoverings. Generally, the hold period is relatively short—perhaps two weeks. Thus, to use this service, you must coordinate your consultation with the client with the dates of the hold. Because some companies do not notify you when the hold expires, put the date in your tickler file. It can be very frustrating and embarrassing to learn that an item that was enthusiastically approved by a client is no longer on reserve and has been discontinued.

To maximize the usefulness of showrooms, you must know how they operate, including layouts, pricing policies, sample procedures, and account restrictions. The first time you visit a mart or design center, you will most likely feel overwhelmed by the vast amount of merchandise. In addition, you might find it difficult to keep track of the showrooms and what merchandise they handled. Take the time to understand how a space is organized by asking the showroom personnel to explain their layout and policies.

Record information in your cell phone/tablet to reference and organize later. When conducting a tour of the facilities, showroom personnel will review their pricing and coding policies. As reviewed in Chapter 6, pricing practices include differences between the designer's cost and retail. Generally, when a showroom is *To-the-Trade-Only*, pricing information on the tags is coded and the amount is the designer's cost—not retail.

When a design firm has an account with a company that sells fabric and wallcovering, the designer can obtain a **memo sample**—a piece of a fabric or wallcovering used for client presentations. A memo sample is a fairly large (approximately 25″ × 25″, or 63.5 cm × 63.5 cm) piece of fabric or wallcovering, large enough to see an entire pattern. Memos are stocked in the showroom. Therefore, by completing the company's form (available in the space), you can request the memo and have the sample immediately.

When the stock is depleted, showroom personnel will have the memo sent to your design studio. Most companies allow you to borrow the memo for 30 days and perhaps longer by request. If the memo is not returned, the design firm can be charged for the sample.

Showrooms also have very small fabric (approximately 2″ × 3″, or 5 cm × 7.6 cm) and wallcovering samples that are available without charge. These **cuttings** do not have to be returned to the showroom. For the most part, because of their small size, cuttings tend to be useful only for solid and small patterns.

Be sure to always use the correct term when ordering a fabric sample: "memo" or "cutting." The differences as described above are used consistently throughout the industry.

An important project management consideration related to fabric, wallcovering, carpets, rugs, furniture, lighting fixtures, and other items is the amount of time that must be scheduled for custom orders. Manufacturers have in-stock items in specific finishes, sizes, colorways, and patterns. When these are not acceptable you might want a custom order.

A custom order can be a totally new design or an adaptation of an existing item, such as changing all of the green objects in a fabric to red. Either situation can take several months, but by far a new design consumes the most time. In addition, custom orders require minimum orders that—depending on the manufacturer and the product—could be very high. For example, a manufacturer might require a minimum of 200 yards (183 meters) for custom fabric orders.

Another factor that affects the PMP is whether or not your design firm has an established account with a showroom, manufacturer, or a **jobber**. A jobber is an entity that purchases large quantities of merchandise from the manufacturer and then sells the product in smaller quantities to designers. Because account processing and credit reference checks takes time, it is very helpful to identify potential suppliers as early in the design process as possible and when necessary begin the process of applying for credit.

Establishing accounts is reviewed in Part IV of this book because the procedures are associated with owning a business. But to place orders for your client, you must be aware of the need for accounts as well as the basic arrangements.

Established accounts are required for all orders other than CODs or pro forma. An **open account** is the preferred way of working with a company. With this arrangement you can immediately order items, shipments are delivered before payments, and the design firm generally has 30 days to pay the vendor.

Some showrooms are open only during trade shows, such as NeoCon in Chicago. Therefore, you should keep an eye on exhibition schedules in order to see products in these showrooms. International trade show information (Appendix D), such as dates, locations, and special events, is available from convention centers, design centers, and marts in major cities.

Trade show news is also provided in professional magazines, including *Metropolis* and *Azure* (see http://www.metropolismag.com/cda/live.php and http://www.azuremagazine.com/IDS/ids.php) and organizations such as Biz Trade Shows (see http://www.biztradeshows.com/architecture/).

Manufacturers' representatives are very important for learning about new products, placing orders, helping to facilitate shipments, and resolving problems. Typically, sales reps are available in showrooms; territory sales reps visit design studios.

As the name implies, territory sales reps are responsible for a specific geographical area. That person will generally call to make an appointment with the design staff. During the visit the sales rep will show samples of new products and explain their features. He or she will also update the firm's library by adding new product information and samples as well as removing any discontinued materials, brochures, price charts, or **tearsheets**.

Trade Sources: Online Resources

In the age of easy online access it might appear that the best approach to finding products and information is to use the Internet. Searching for products and information online has advantages, such as the ability to discover several manufacturers of a product with a range of features and prices. However, online resources might not be able to provide some customer services, such as flexible pricing, quantity discounting, customization, rush deliveries, or merchandise returns. Moreover, from an integrated design perspective, collaborative activities require the involvement of suppliers, vendors, and consultants—especially important for design charrettes. Therefore, focus on building long-term relationships with your suppliers as well as your service providers.

In addition to building long-term relationships with vendors, you must be knowledgeable about online resources, such as manufacturers' websites and buyer's guides. For example, the website for Steelcase (see http://www.steelcase.com/en/)—an office furniture manufacturer—organizes the company's products according to category (e.g., education, healthcare, seating, storage, and tables), brand (e.g., Coalesse, PolyVision, and Designtex), and surface materials (e.g., fabrics and finishes).

If you are interested in a Steelcase conference table employing interactive technology, you could click on "media:scape" and review all the features for HD videoconferencing (Figure 9.6). You could also download an assortment of materials developed for media:scape, such as a spec guide, electronically updated price list, software updates/downloads, planning ideas, furniture symbols, an environmental profile, indoor air certification, and videos.

Steelcase also includes online information related to purchasing its merchandise via dealers, online, and retail. As with many office

Figure 9.6 Interior designers must be knowledgeable about online resources, such as manufacturers' websites and buyer's guides. For example, the website for Steelcase featured *media:scape*—the integration of furniture and technology enables people to collaborate globally via HD videoconferencing. *(© Steelcase)*

furniture manufacturers, most Steelcase products and services are available through the company's authorized dealers. Steelcase's independent and company-owned dealers are located in more than 200 and 400 cities in the United States and worldwide, respectively.

Dealers are responsible for placing orders, monitoring shipments, installing products, and responding to service requests. Dealers can also be involved with design and selling their product line. Thus, from an integrated design perspective, when appropriate, a dealer should be involved with design charrettes and other relevant collaborative activities.

Steelcase purchasing policies allow you to buy some products online by going directly to Steelcase or one of their authorized online retailers, such as Crate & Barrel or CSN Chairs. Shopping retail for some products can also be done by visiting authorized stores, such as Crate & Barrel or Healthy Back.

Interior Design magazine's buyer's guide has a digital library that enables you to search for products and create your own "binder" of favorite items (see http://goto.interiordesign.net/). The buyer's guide organizes information by: (1) product/company (e.g., accessories, art/antiques, building products, flooring, furniture, kitchen/bath, lighting, textiles, wallcoverings/

finishes, window treatments, craftsmen, and services/consultants); (2) location (the United States, Canada, and outside those two countries); (3) market segment (e.g., education, government/institution, healthcare, hospitality, kitchen/bath, office, residential, and retail); (4) style (contemporary, modern, and traditional); (5) U.S. General Services Administration (GSA) products; and (6) green and eco interior design products.

The buyer's guide has features that enable you to read the product description, save the item to your online binder, e-mail the information, view different images, print tearsheets, and request additional product information.

Whether you are using online or brick-and-mortar establishments, you must always check available stock, current prices, and shipping details, preferably during the schematic design phase. As mentioned previously, products can be discontinued, stocks can be depleted, and manufacturers routinely increase prices. In addition, more time might have to be planned for products that are manufactured throughout the world.

All this information is needed in the earliest stages of the design process so you have adequate time to find items that are current, are in the project's price range, and can be delivered at the appropriate time.

Schematic Design: Cultivating Client Relationships and the Project Management Plan (PMP)

As a means to cultivate client relationships and demonstrate your value, you should have the most current product information when you meet with your client to discuss the schematic designs. Once you have shown a client a sample, such as fabric, and the client is enthusiastic for the selection, it can be very difficult to recapture that excitement with alternatives. Moreover, searching for substitutes takes time, and it could be difficult to find an appropriate substitution with the same price and the required delivery date. Your client also has to find the time to view and consider the substitutes—a potential annoyance that could affect that person's confidence in your design abilities.

Speed bumps, such as discontinued items, will occur in the life of a project. To build long-term client relationships, your goal should always focus on avoiding and preventing the bumps whenever possible.

As mentioned previously, another way to avoid speed bumps during the schematic phase is to not create unrealistic designs. Be sure to design within the context of the programming results, codes, standards, and the project's budget and time restrictions. Furthermore, from collaborative and integrative perspectives be very careful how you present your designs as well as the type of information shared.

The schematic design phase should be seen as a way to brainstorm preliminary design solutions with your client and other stakeholders. Your client and others should have the opportunity to provide their input by making suggestions, deleting unfavorable items, and adding important elements. These interactions can be hindered when a client has the impression that the designer is essentially presenting the final design solution—thoughts that can be fueled by computer-generated drawings with a polished appearance.

Hand-drawn sketches typically have the opposite effect. Sketches can present the impression that your design ideas are conceptual, are fluid, and need further contributions. In addition, presenting sketches provides an opening for you if the client does not like the design. Sensing the person's lack of enthusiasm for designs in the schematic phase allows you the opportunity to reconsider the design and perhaps suggest alternatives as you are presenting a sketch.

Hand-drawn sketches allow you the flexibility to redraw plans and details as you are conversing with your client—another example of how your skills add value to your client's project. However, you must carefully select the sketches you present and not overwhelm the client with too many images.

Ideally, the sketches should have an artistic appearance, but with enough detail so that someone without design experience can understand the drawings. Be selective—consider quality over quantity. The chosen sketches should reinforce the design concept, themes, and information gathered during the programming phase, most notably during discussions with your client.

Clients also can have a sense of design finality when a designer shows just a few samples during the schematic design discussions. There is a very fine line between showing a client too many samples and showing too few. Presenting too many choices of an item, such as eight different upholstery fabrics for a chair, can be confusing and overwhelming, and the client might begin to question your ability to suggest something appropriate. Moreover, some clients contend that they hire a designer to make these decisions, and asking them to weed through numerous choices can indicate that the designer is not doing his or her job.

Conversely, showing a client just one or two options can become a problem when the client is seeking a collaborative partnership and when the client dislikes the choices. Ideally, the insights you gained during the programming phase should activate your intuition about collaborative activities as well as likes and dislikes. Therefore, depending on these insights, you should select samples that first address the client's criteria and within that category, whenever possible, choose approximately three items.

For reasons described above—as a guideline—fewer or more than three samples can be problematic. When it is not possible to offer alternatives, you should feel confident that the client will enthusiastically agree with the choice.

Following these recommendations will help you to cultivate client relationships and support the requirements outlined in the PMP as well as the integrated design approach (see Chapter 8 and Table 9.2). Discussing schematic designs with your client and stakeholders allows you

Table 9.2 Integrated Design Process Matrix: Schematic Design and Design Development

	Schematic Design (Document all Activities)	Design Development (Document All Activities)
Deliverables	Conceptual design and refine estimate of costs, budget, and timeline. Concept sketches, schematic models, bubble diagrams, adjacency matrices, and stacking diagrams. Preliminary floor/furniture plans, lighting, colors, and FF&E. Material boards. Risk management plan. Signed client written approval of estimate of costs, budget, and preliminary design. Proposals for consultants. Updated PMP and client job book. Building client and professional relationships. Project documentation.	Detailed drawings, schedules, and specifications. Adjustments to preliminary cost estimates, etc./ design development documents. LCCA calculations. Updated PMP. Presentation to client. Signed client written approval of the design development documents. Updated client job book. Building client and professional relationships. Continue discussions with local authorities designated to approve permits. Identify local storage and delivery businesses that focus on quality service. For existing buildings, review construction conditions with clients. As necessary, discuss move management during construction with the client. Project documentation.
PMP: Project Scope/(WBS)	Verify project scope. Monitor and control scope creep. Track project progress and deviations. Take corrective and preventative actions promptly.	Monitor and control scope creep. Track project progress and deviations. Take corrective and preventative actions promptly.
PMP: Quality	Implement PDCA cycle. Monitor and control quality assurances. Utilize quality management business tools. Implement DQI and ISO 9000.	Implement PDCA cycle. Monitor and control quality assurances. Utilize quality management business tools. Implement DQI and ISO 9000.
PMP: Schedule	Review and update initial schedule with a list of activities using the WBS, sequence of tasks, resources, and time duration. Monitor and track baseline schedule, critical path, change requests, and deviations. Distribute deviation notices.	Review and update schedule with a list of activities using the WBS, sequence of tasks, resources, and time duration. Monitor and track baseline schedule, critical path, change requests, and deviations. Distribute deviation and adjustment notices.
PMP: Human Resource Management	Verify design team members and their roles, responsibilities, and qualifications. Identify training and certification programs. Manage the team—storming, norming, and performing stage. Informal assessment of performance. Verify reporting line charts and RACI matrix. Ask individuals for input on implementing tasks. Monitor conflict resolution sessions and decision-making. Formal assessment of performance. Consider cultural and generational dimensions.	Verify design team members. Manage the team—norming and performing stage. Monitor conflict resolution sessions and decision making. Informal assessment of performance. Consider cultural and generational dimensions.
PMP: Budget/Cost Management	Several people should review estimate costs, initial budget and cost baseline. Add more details to the budget for every phase of the design process. Conduct a CBA. Initial client approval. Develop descriptions of the assumptions used for cost estimates. Estimate contingency fund.	Several people should review estimate costs, initial budget, and cost baseline. Client approval becomes project's cost baseline. Determine what information needed for cost control, who is responsible, when updates submitted, and processes for corrective and preventative actions. Institute EVMS procedures.
PMP: Communication	Reexamine and update communications plan. Implement communications plan and involve people in appropriate events and activities. Consider cultural and generational dimensions.	Develop design presentation and coordinate the event. Reexamine and update communications plan. Implement communications plan and involve people in appropriate events and activities. Consider cultural and generational dimensions.

(Table 9.2 continued on page 302)

Table 9.2 (continued)

	Schematic Design (Document all Activities)	Design Development (Document All Activities)
PMP: Risk Management	List of risks—threats and opportunities. Risk plan and the context—risk categories, risk criteria, and prioritization. Risk identification, analysis, and evaluation. Responses and treatments. Monitor and review risk register.	Monitor and review risk register. When necessary, implement risk identification, analysis, evaluation, responses, and treatments.
PMP: Procurement Management	Preliminary list of suppliers, vendors, consultants, and tradespersons.	All project specifications (e.g., FF&E, finishes, materials, and colors). Preliminary list of suppliers, vendors, consultants, and tradespersons.
Contracts/ Correspondence/ Documents	RFI and transmittals. Project performance reports	RFI and transmittals. Project performance reports
Client Relationships	Request client to review estimate costs, initial budget, and cost baseline. Request client to approve risk management plan. Cultivate relationship by providing excellent customer service, and being reliable and responsive to the needs of the client and team members. Consider cultural and generational dimensions. Promptly resolve problems and complaints. Client input needed for schematic approvals. Client updates: Progress with schematic designs. Client signs document approving schematic designs. Focus on developing loyalty.	Request client to approve budget, quality, schedule, and project scope. Cultivate relationship by providing excellent customer service, and being reliable and responsive to the needs of the client and team members. Consider cultural and generational dimensions. Promptly resolve problems and complaints. Client input needed for design development. Client updates: Progress with design development and final results. Client signs document approving design development results. Focus on developing loyalty.
LEED Certification*	Continue energy and other commissioning activities. Energy simulation modeling. Develop plan for tracking energy usage. Determine best spaces for daylighting and views. Develop comprehensive lighting design intent, including daylight, fixtures, and occupancy responsiveness. Identify footcandle target levels for each space. Inventory FF&E and determine reuse. Identify materials with recycled content. Identify regional materials. Research low-emitting materials. Run preliminary calculations of rapidly renewable materials. Develop building reuse strategies. Identify materials reuse strategies. Identify entryway locations and ensure compliance. Examine areas with chemicals and isolate the rooms. Purchase green power. Complete LEED calculations and documentation.	Two-phase LEED reviews submit documents after end of design phase. Continue energy and other commissioning activities. Develop a photometric floor plan to determine areas over- or under-lit and refine lighting design. Mark collection and storage areas for recyclable materials. Locate central collection and storage recycling area in convenient areas. Incorporate M&V equipment into design and develop M&V plan. Determine FF&E reuse, and repair and refurbish as needed. Identify materials with recycled content. Identify regional materials. Research low-emitting materials. Require contractor to develop and implement a construction IAQ plan. Design strategies for high level of thermal comfort. Run preliminary calculations of recycled content and set targets. Incorporate building reuse strategies into design. Incorporate materials reuse strategies into design. Determine placement of outdoor air sensors and intakes. Purchase green power. Complete LEED calculations and documentation.

Table 9.2 *(continued)*

	Schematic Design (Document all Activities)	**Design Development (Document All Activities)**
Value-Added Examples	Knowledge of sustainability, human behavior, anthropometric data, universal design, history of design, space, form, and color. Skills in synthesizing data, solving design problems, creativity, drawing, collaboration, communication, listening, project management, and customer service.	Knowledge of building methods, materials, sustainability, human behavior, anthropometric data, universal design, history of design, space, form, color, FF&E, environmental systems and controls, and regulations. Skills in solving design problems, creativity, drawing, specifications, schedules, collaboration, communication, listening, project management, and customer service. Ability to design safe and healthy interior environments because of knowledge of codes, regulations, IAQ, and EIQ.
Personal Management Strategies	Complete time/activity log and expense reports. Review and revise prioritized goals of responsibilities. Assess time management skills, including repetitious tasks and procrastination. Check reminders. Update information management files for project, products, and services. Practice knowledge management techniques to build tacit knowledge and maximize explicit knowledge.	Complete time/activity log and expense reports. Review and revise prioritized goals of responsibilities. Assess time management skills, including repetitious tasks and procrastination. Check reminders. Update information management files for project, products, and services. Practice knowledge management techniques to build tacit knowledge and maximize explicit knowledge.

*LEED Certification section adapted from: U.S. Green Building Council. (2009). *Green Interior Design and Construction*. Washington, DC: U.S. Green Building Council.

to verify the project scope, help control scope creep, and avoid deviations that can delay the project and cause overruns. Moreover, at this early stage of the design process, you will be able to promptly correct or prevent any activities that could impact the scope of the project and quality assurances.

From an integrated design perspective, the schematic design phase is an ideal time for the design team, client, and stakeholders to review and update the initial schedule, human resource plan, cost estimates, and preliminary budget. With the WBS as a guide, the review process should concentrate on the baseline schedule, the critical path, team compositions, and the stage of team development.

Are teams in the storming, norming, or performing stage? Ideally, teams that have been working together for an extended period should be in the performing stage. If this is not the situation, the project manager might have to consider resolution sessions. Your client should

receive updates of informal performance assessments of the team. Depending on the interests of your client or his or her representative, you might also want to develop an outline of task assignments and reporting lines.

The schematic design phase is a critical stage for controlling scope creep and associated costs and expenses. Therefore, at the conclusion of the phase, numerous people, including the client, design team, contractor, and consultants, should review cost estimates, the initial budget, and the cost baseline. To help assess options, your client should be involved with any cost benefit analyses (CBA). In addition, your client should have a clear understanding of the assumptions formulated for cost estimates as well as the rationale for the contingency fund.

Review and update the project's communications plan with your client, including attaining verification of the team members listed in the plan and requests to attend specific meetings, events, and educational sessions. Your client should be involved with the final approval of the risk register as well as other fundamentals in the risk management plan, the elements of which should be implemented as early in the design process as possible. Your client should also receive updates regarding procurement processes, such as distributing RFIs and transmittals, and developing the preliminary list of suppliers, vendors, and tradespersons.

At the conclusion of the schematic design phase, your client should receive an updated project performance report and a request to sign off on the preliminary design of interior construction work. After receiving a written approval from the client, the design team can proceed to the design development phase.

Design Development

Design development begins with the client's signed approval of the preliminary designs developed in the schematic design phase. The sketches created in the schematic design phase are translated into *detailed* schedules (e.g., lighting, hardware, door, and windows) and technical drawings, including floor plans, elevations, sections, reflected ceiling plans, and three-dimensional views.

Schedules and drawings are used to illustrate space planning, lighting, furniture, millwork, art, architectural woodwork, wayfinding, graphics/signage, accessories, details, and the electrical/power/data/communications plan. Specifications are written for the FF&E, finishes, colors, and materials. The design team might create models to study volumetric space and to work out dimensioning details, such as projections of built-in cabinets.

All of the tasks that must be performed during design development must be accounted for in the PMP. Obviously, given the amount of work that potentially has to be done at this phase of the design process, the design team will want to collaborate with other professionals involved with the project to ensure there is agreement about what drawings, schedules, and specifications must be developed, who is responsible for

the work, and what policies regarding file sharing should be instilled. The larger the number of drawings, the more time that must be allocated to the design development phase.

Rendered perspectives, sample boards, and finished models can be very time-consuming and require considerable resources. Does the client want to pay for these services? Should professionals be hired to draw the perspectives, create the sample boards, or build the model? The design team has to be particularly mindful of time-consuming tasks, such as designing custom furniture, built-ins, and millwork, such as mantels, baseboards, and crown molding.

As the design team is determining the time and resources needed for design development, the planning should be done within the context of developing accurate and complete drawings and specifications. This statement might appear to be obvious; however, it is very easy for mistakes and omissions to occur when adequate time is not allocated to developing the essential *details* of a design.

Drawings are necessary for documentation purposes *and* for developing the precise details of the design. Develop every type of drawing possible to ensure complete and accurate designs. For example, elevations and sections can verify details of a floor plan. The floor plan can verify details in elevations and sections. How do the interior elevations coordinate with the exterior elevations? How do the light fixtures in the reflected ceiling plan coordinate with other elements, such as mechanical systems, occupancy sensors, and egress signage? How are all of these elements affected by volumetric space? How do all of the elements affect functionality and aesthetics?

These examples are important for the overall success of a design, but they also have an enormous impact on the PMP as well as your relationship with your client. How? When details are wrong or are missing in drawings, schedules, and specifications, the problem will surface at some point in the PLC—and the later the discovery of this, the worse it is.

Wrong or missing details can prevent the successful installation of many items, such as cabinets, light fixtures, flooring, windows, doors, and window treatments. These problems might be resolved only by retrofits, replacements, or exclusions—solutions that are expensive and time-consuming, and can seriously affect your reputation, quality assurances, and the project's schedule.

Wrong or missing details can result in designs that are not compliant with codes and standards—leading to the denial of building permits. Moreover, mistakes, omissions, unnecessary expenses, and wasted time can cause undue stress to client relations and affect your reputation with team members, suppliers, vendors, and contractors. The problem can become even worse if a design flaw is not noticed until it is discovered by end users and the community. The public exposure to poor designs can have a long-term impact on your relationships with your client and referrals, as well as your career.

Paying attention to details includes making every attempt to finalize specific design solutions. Knowing exactly what is included in a design is necessary to develop all of the required details described above. In addition, specificity is essential for cost estimates, the budget, and the schedule. For example, obtaining approval for a specific office chair without selecting the fabric can be a very costly mistake because there can be a significant difference in the cost of fabrics. In addition, a manufacturer might have a substantial **upcharge** for a specific finish or for using a particular type of fabric or pattern.

Before developing the specifications, cost estimates, and the budget, know what you are using, where the item is located in the space, and all of the variables associated with installations, operation, and maintenance. This might appear to be a challenge for an entry-level designer, but remember to talk with your teammates to benefit from their experience and expertise.

Acquiring details also involves identifying any tradespeople who might be needed for the project. Quality tradespeople require long lead times for projects and command higher fees. Contracts for these services might be between the tradesperson and the client or the designer. Only recommend or hire people you know who do quality work. The design development phase is the ideal time to determine who you want to hire, obtain estimates, and if possible, schedule tentative delivery dates.

Life Cycle Cost Analysis

Issues related to costs, operations, and maintenance can be addressed by performing a life cycle cost analysis (LCCA). (see Figure 9.7.) The WBDG defines this as "a method for assessing the total cost of facility ownership. It takes into account all costs of acquiring, owning, and disposing of a building or building system. LCCA is especially useful when project alternatives that fulfill the same performance requirements, but differ with respect to initial costs and operating costs" (WBDG 2010). Other terms used for LCCA are cost estimating, value engineering, and economic analysis (WBDG 2010).

As described in WBDG's definition, LCCA can be very complex (as in the case of examining facility ownership), but LCCA can also be performed for individual components, such as light fixtures or appliances.

To facilitate the calculations, LCCA-related software programs are available (see Building Life-Cycle Cost: http://www1.eere.energy.gov; ECONPACK: http://www.hnd.usace.army.mil; or Energy-10: http://sbicouncil.org/store). However, to use these programs, you should have a basic awareness of the LCCA method and the importance of performing the calculations early in the design process.

Fundamentally, the LCCA method involves identifying costs and the cost period for a particular design and its alternatives. Costs identified by WBDG include purchase, acquisition, construction, energy, water, operations, maintenance, repairs, replacements, resale, salvage values, disposals, loan interest payments, and nonmonetary benefits. In other words *all* of the costs associated with the life cycle of a facility or

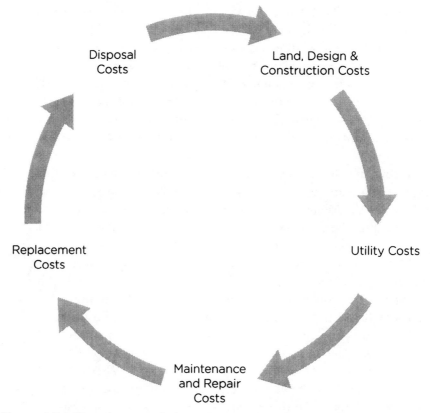

Disposal
Costs

Land, Design &
Construction Costs

Utility Costs

Maintenance
and Repair
Costs

Replacement
Costs

Figure 9.7 A life cycle cost analysis (LCCA) examines the long-term cost of a building, including design/construction, maintenance, and disposing of a building or building system.

specific item, such as an appliance, floorcovering, or piece of furniture.

To calculate the LCCA using software programs, you must identify all the relevant costs for several alternatives. The program provides the total life cycle costs for each alternative. The design team should discuss the results of the LCCA with the client and appropriate stakeholders to determine which alternative best fits the scope of the project, quality assurances, the budget, and the schedule. Performing an LCCA is another excellent example of how you can add value to your client's project.

Design Development: Cultivating Client Relationships and the Project Management Plan (PMP)

You can cultivate client relationships various ways during the design development phase. Many of these strategies are associated with the PMP and the integrated design process (Table 9.2). Discussions about the development of the *detailed* drawings and specifications with your client, contractor, vendors, tradespeople, and stakeholders provides an ideal time to ensure the maximum level of coordination between the interior construction and other aspects of the project, such as codes, standards, mechanical systems, daylighting, acoustics, and security provisions.

The parameters of the project scope can be verified, including a close examination of scope creep, quality assurances, and the risk register. The design development phase is an opportune time to avoid mistakes that could eventually increase costs, compromise quality standards, or delay the project.

The development of project details provides the design team with the information needed to verify and refine the schedule, personnel requirements, and the budget. After reviewing each of these areas, the designer should immediately communicate any adjustments to the client and other pertinent individuals, businesses, and stakeholders. As is the case in the schematic design phase, to verify the project's cost estimates, the client as well as other professionals, such as architects and engineers, should review the initial budget.

In coordination with the client, the interdisciplinary team might determine which items will or will not undergo a bidding process. The design team reviews and refines the preliminary list of vendors, tradespersons, and consultants listed in the procurement management plan. A client-approved budget becomes the project's cost baseline. To monitor the budget, schedule, and work performance, the design team can develop the earned value management system (EVMS)—an excellent tool for succinctly communicating project progress to clients and stakeholders (see Chapter 8).

Monitoring the schedule and work performance might also require a **move management plan** (see the next section under "Contract Administration"), which includes helping the client find reliable storage and delivery companies. For new construction the move management plan has procedures for moving into the new facilities. For remodeling or new additions the move management plan could involve moving to other facilities or identifying the best ways to accommodate people who want to remain at the site during construction. Under these circumstances businesses sometimes close or people take vacations.

If a client intends to live or work at the site during construction, you should inform them that conditions can be horrific: noisy saws; hammering; boards falling; dust from sanding drywall joints; power shutoffs; and water shutoffs, which means no toilets, sinks, or showers. To better explain the turmoil, you could show them a photograph of a space during renovation. The design development phase is an ideal time to discuss these situations with your client and work with him or her to find solutions

that fit the person's schedule and budget. The goal is to demonstrate to the client that you are concerned for their well-being and you want to make certain they are completely satisfied.

Communications come to the forefront when the design team must present its design to the client and stakeholders. As reviewed in Chapter 7, presentations have a variety of formats, including one-to-one, many-to-many, informal discussions, and formal addresses.

The cost of the presentation might be limited by the terms of the contract for design services. Some materials used for presentations can be very costly and time-consuming to create, such as detailed models, mockups, and elaborate sample boards, or they can be very inexpensive with little preparation, as when arranging fabric swatches and images from manufacturers' catalogue on a conference table.

Costs and time influence the type of presentation, as well as your perceptions of what is important to your client and stakeholders. The goal is to develop a presentation that will totally impress the client while providing that person with the information needed to approve the final design. Some clients appreciate short, flashy presentations. Others prefer thought-provoking, discussion-rich presentations.

When building a relationship with a client, you might have to ask the person's preference. Once you have established the relationship, the type of presentation will become intuitive. Moreover, after a series of successful projects you might discover that a client no longer requests detailed information.

Regardless of the stage of the CLC, you might invite appropriate people to the presentation, including local community representatives and the press, depending on the interests of the client. Some clients will not approve the design development package without input from various constituents.

Verify the guest list with your client as well as the best location, date, and time. Invitations or notes should be distributed as early as possible, preferably four to six weeks in advance. After the presentation, solicit feedback from your client and other relevant people. In consultation with the client the design team will then revise the design. Before proceeding to contract documents, the design team must obtain the client's written approval of the design development package.

Client and Project Management Strategies: Contract Documents, Bidding Procedures, Contract Administration, and Post-Occupancy

Building long-term relationships and demonstrating your value requires a successful implementation of project management strategies, beginning with predesign and continuing through post-occupancy. This section opens by examining project management strategies for contract documents, including bidding procedures. It also explains how to cultivate relationships with clients during the contract document phase and the bidding process.

The section concludes by reviewing project management strategies that are important during contract administration and post-occupancy. Topics include move management, deliveries, and site supervision. As with the other phases of the IDP, the chapter concludes by examining approaches to cultivating clients during contract administration and post-occupancy.

Contract Documents

The client's signed approval of the design development package triggers the drafting of the project's contract documents. These documents include technical construction or working drawings, schedules, and specifications. A set of drawing sheets for interior construction can include: (1) a cover sheet (e.g., project, location, design firm, seals, and index); (2) legend/general notes (e.g., symbols, abbreviations, and notes to the contractor); (3) plans (e.g., floor, reflected ceiling, interior demolition, partition, FF&E, and power/communication); (4) plans from engineers and licensed consultants (e.g., mechanical, electrical, fire protection, and lighting designer); (5) elevations; (6) cross-referenced detail drawings; and (7) schedules (e.g., doors, windows, light fixtures, and hardware).

To protect the health, safety, and welfare of the public, contract documents executed by an interior designer are limited to applicable laws, and may *not* include services of other professionals, such as architects, engineers, or contractors. As legally binding agreements, contract documents must be accurate, comprehensive, and in compliance with local building codes and federal regulations. Contract documents serve as the legal contract between the client and the contractor. Thus, contract documents are used for bidding, obtaining building permits, and construction.

The contract document phase also involves the development of the project's *comprehensive* FF&E manual, including all product specifications. Your client should have the opportunity to review the FF&E manual and to provide suggestions for suppliers, vendors, and tradespeople. After the client's written approval, the FF&E manual serves as the guide for writing purchase orders.

As discussed in Chapter 6, purchase orders are legal contracts between a designer and a supplier, vendor, fabrication workroom, or tradesperson. A client might also be the purchasing agent. In this situation the client might ask you to prepare the purchase order and monitor progress during the contract administration phase.

Very critical to remember: Problems with the contract documents can affect the project scope, quality assurances, schedule, budget, legal proceedings, and your reputation with your client, stakeholders, and other professionals involved with the project.

Given the importance of contract documents, it is essential that adequate time and resources are allocated in the PMP to allow for the coordinated efforts between various professionals as well as ensuring that the documents are accurate, understandable, complete, consistent, and compliant with all relevant codes and standards. To help make sure that details and instructions are clear, you might need to include additional notes to drawings.

The design team should review the documents to eliminate any details or instructions that are needlessly redundant. Wading through useless information is time-consuming and can be perceived as an annoyance by contractors, subcontractors, and others hired to execute the contract documents. In addition, working drawings must clearly indicate existing conditions and new construction, when appropriate.

When using the IDP, many of the important components that must be included in the contract document package will have already appeared in the earliest phases of the design process. Thus, at this stage of the project's life cycle, the process should be very smooth and can quickly move to the construction phase.

Construction drawings, schedules, and specifications must be submitted to the authorities legally responsible for reviewing the documents and issuing permits for a specific jurisdiction. As discussed previously, when the design team researches local permit requirements early in the design process and reviews the design intent with the proper authorities, the approval process should be very smooth at the end of the contract document stage. A rapid and efficient permitting process is critical to keeping on schedule, and can help to avoid the embarrassment as well as additional costs that could be incurred if some aspect of the project must be modified or eliminated to be code compliant.

Bidding Procedures

Depending on the project, you might be involved with bidding or tendering procedures. Bidding is used in Design-Bid-Build (DBD) project delivery methods, commercial projects, and when required by law, projects involving public institutions and government agencies.

Bids are used to ascertain competitive costs for products and services. Generally, the lowest bidder is awarded the contract. The design team must allocate adequate time and resources in the PMP for the various steps in the bidding process, including creating the bid package, prequalifying bidders, conducting bidder sessions, and evaluating bids (see Chapter 8).

The bidding process begins with you discussing requirements with your client, including legal conditions, performance criteria, advertisements for bids, and the bid package. Legal conditions encompass the responsibilities of the client, contractor, subcontractors, and vendors, including payment schedules, guarantees, termination clauses, and arbitration rules.

Performance criteria for bidders must be established, such as areas of expertise, years of experience with the project's building type, comments from references, and the bidder's track record for being on time, within budget, and fulfilling the requirements of the project. Your client might also be interested in the bidder's experience with LEED certifications.

Bidding Documents

According to the AIA, the bidding documents include bidding requirements as well as the contract documents. Components in the bidding requirements include: (1) Advertisement or Invitation to Bid, (2) General Conditions, (3) Instructions to Bidders, and (4) the bid form.

The Invitation to Bid serves as the means to announce that the client is soliciting bids for their project. An Invitation to Bid must be publicly announced when you are working with governmental agencies because of laws requiring an open and competitive procurement process.

General Conditions in the bidding documents includes items such as definitions, contract administration, changes in the work, insurance, bonds, payments, termination of contracts, dispute resolutions, ownership of documents, and protection of persons and property (see AIA Document A201-1997 at http://www.aia.org/).

The Instructions to Bidders document provides an overview of the bidding process (see AIA Document A701-1997—Instructions to Bidders). Article 3 in the document delineates how to obtain the sets of bidding documents and explains procedures for submitting requests for interpretations, corrections, and changes to the documents.

The Instructions to Bidders document also describes substitution policies and addenda protocols. In consultation with the client, the design team should carefully determine whether or not substitutes will be allowed, and if acceptable, under what conditions. Inappropriate substitutes can seriously affect quality assurances and the design intent. Addenda protocols basically delineate procedures for transmitting copies of materials that have been modified after the initial distribution of the bidding documents.

Instructions to Bidders documents also include details regarding bidding procedures, such as the preparation of bids, **bid security**, and submission of bids. An essential element of preparing a bid is completing the project's bid form. The bid form might have to be accompanied with a bid security, such as providing a **bid bond** that is guaranteed by a financial institution to cover all payments associated with the work. Bid preparation might also involve an approved **alternate bid**, including the amount added or deducted from the base bid.

The next step in the bid process is termed Consideration of Bids. At this stage the bids are opened and the client has the option of accepting or rejecting the bids. The accepted bidder receives a written acknowledgement and is awarded a contract with the owner.

Post-bid information could require the verification of a contractor's qualification statement and the owner's statement of financial capability to the contractor.

Contract Documents and Bidding Processes: Cultivating Client Relationships and the Project Management Plan (PMP)

Cultivating client relationships and demonstrating your value during the contract document phase involves keeping your client and stakeholders apprised of the design team's progress with developing the drawings, schedules, and specifications. Your client should also be informed when you have been issued approvals and permits from the local building department—an accomplishment that can trigger excitement because legally, construction can then begin.

Depending on the project, completing contract documents can also initiate a bidding process. An interior designer can demonstrate considerable added value to a project by being actively involved with coordinating the bidding process and helping review and evaluate the bids. Clients appreciate when you find problems with a bid, such as omissions, improper substitutions, unwanted additions, and unreasonable costs.

In addition to continuously updating your client and stakeholders through the development of contract documents phase, you should inform them about the status of the PMP, including the project scope, quality assurances, schedule, WBS, budget, and risk register (Table 9.3). Critical items to report to your client include the degree to which you are controlling scope creep, the baseline schedule, the cost baseline, and risks that could significantly affect the project.

Politely share information about any corrective or preventative actions you initiated (another example of how your work adds value to the project). Your updates should also include the most current EVMS and an executive summary of the teamwork assessment report.

The development of contract documents activates a very important phase of procurement management. In collaboration with the

	Contract Documents (Document All Activities)	Contract Administration (Document All Activities)	Post-Occupancy (Document All Activities)
Deliverables	Final working drawings, schedules, and specifications for interior construction. Verification of compliance with local building codes and federal regulations. Signed client written approval of construction documents. Contract documents submitted to local building departments for permits. Bid package. Bids and proposals distributed—contracts awarded. Issue addendums. Affirm schedule. Approved project FF&E manual. Confirm local storage and delivery businesses. As necessary, finalize move management strategies with the client. Updated client job book. Building client and professional relationships. Project documentation.	Completion of interior construction according to design intent. Contracts implemented. Approve workrooms and mechanics. As necessary implement move management. Process purchase orders, work orders, and freight claims. Track orders, deliveries, and installations. Approve shop drawings, materials, and finishes. Evaluation of site visits. Building inspections. Performance of interior construction design related services, including responding to RFI, processing change orders, finding alternates, and monitoring the PMP. Begin project closeout. Develop punch list and complete repairs, omissions, etc. Signed client written approval of change orders and final inspection. Certificates of payment. Certificate of occupancy. As-built drawings. Updated client job book. Building client and professional relationships. Project documentation, including approving certificates of payments.	Assessment and TQM Reports. Postoccupancy evaluation (POE). Post-project assessment. Thank you notes to client and stakeholders. Operational/maintenance policies and costs. Warranties to client. Signed client written approvals. Updated client job book. Project documentation. Assess project documentation policies and procedures. Complete project closeout. Building client and professional relationships. Suggestions for continuous improvement of design services and client relationships.
PMP: Project Scope/(WBS)	Monitor and control scope creep. Track project progress and deviations. Take corrective and preventative actions promptly.	Monitor interior construction work and installations. Supervise delivery of FF&E. Monitor and control scope creep. Track project progress and deviations. Take corrective and preventative actions promptly.	Assess extent of scope creep. Assess project progress and deviations. Assess corrective and preventative actions. Develop suggestions for continuous improvement.
PMP: Quality	Implement PDCA cycle. Monitor and control quality assurances. Utilize quality management business tools. Implement DQI and ISO 9000.	Implement PDCA cycle. Monitor and control quality assurances. Utilize quality management business tools. Implement DQI and ISO 9000.	Implement PDCA cycle. Assess quality assurances. Assess the use of quality management business tools. Assess DQI and ISO 9000. Develop suggestions for continuous improvement.
PMP: Schedule	Review and update schedule with a list of activities using the WBS, sequence of tasks, resources, and time duration. Monitor and track baseline schedule, critical path, change requests, and deviations. Distribute deviation notices.	Review and update schedule with a list of activities using the WBS, sequence of tasks, resources, and time duration. Monitor and track baseline schedule, critical path, change requests, and deviations. Distribute deviation notices.	Assess schedule with a list of activities using the WBS, sequence of tasks, resources, and time duration. Assess baseline schedule, critical path, change requests, and deviations. Assess process for distributing deviation notices. Develop suggestions for continuous improvement.

(Table 9.3 continued on page 312)

Table 9.3 *(continued)*

	Contract Documents (Document All Activities)	Contract Administration (Document All Activities)	Post-Occupancy (Document All Activities)
PMP: Human Resource Management	Verify design team members. Manage the team—performing stage. Monitor conflict resolution sessions and decision making. Formal assessment of performance. Consider cultural and generational dimensions.	Verify design team members. Manage the team—performing stage. Monitor conflict resolution sessions and decision making. Informal assessment of performance. Consider cultural and generational dimensions.	Assess team management and disband the team. Assess training and certification programs. Assess reporting line charts, WBS, and RACI matrix. Assess conflict resolution sessions and decision making. Formal assessment of performance. Consider cultural and generational dimensions. Develop suggestions for continuous improvement.
PMP: Budget/Cost Management	Monitor and control cost baseline on regular basis. Implement cost control processes, including corrective and preventative actions. Implement EVMS procedures.	Monitor and control cost baseline on regular basis. Control costs by monitoring activities, and compare accomplishments with budget. Implement cost control processes, including corrective and preventative actions. Implement EVMS procedures.	Assess accuracy of cost baseline. Assess cost control processes, including corrective and preventative actions. Assess EVMS procedures. Develop suggestions for continuous improvement.
PMP: Communication	Reexamine and update communications plan. Implement communications plan and involve people in appropriate events and activities. Consider cultural and generational dimensions.	Reexamine and update communications plan. Implement communications plan and involve people in appropriate events and activities. Consider cultural and generational dimensions.	Assess communications plan, including events and activities. Consider cultural and generational dimensions. Develop suggestions for continuous improvement.
PMP: Risk Management	Monitor and review risk register. When necessary implement risk identification, analysis, evaluation, responses, and treatments.	Monitor and review risk register. When necessary implement risk identification, analysis, evaluation, responses, and treatments.	Assess risk management policies and procedures. Assess accuracy of risk register. Develop suggestions for continuous improvement.
PMP: Procurement Management	Develop criteria and specifications (closed and open) for products, materials, services, etc. based upon drawings and schedules. Develop Project FF&E manual. Determine qualifications of sellers, including proprietary rights. Process bids, proposals, and contracts.	Determine qualifications of sellers. Process bids, proposals, and contracts. Monitor work performance, change orders, and contracts (fixed price, cost reimbursable, T&M). Monitor work performance with other PMP components. Monitor payment distributions.	Assess procurement management procedures and policies. Update firm's qualified seller's list. Update firm's list of green sellers. Develop suggestions for continuous improvement.
Contracts/ Correspondence/ Documents	Process purchase orders— check for accuracy and correct shipping dates and locations. Process COM orders, CFAs, transmittals, work orders, and work change orders. Develop ticker system for shipping dates. Process client billings. Project performance reports.	Process purchase orders—check for accuracy and correct shipping dates and locations. Process COM orders, CFAs, transmittals, work orders, and work change orders. Verify acknowledgements and pay attention to discontinued notices and backorders. Monitor ticker system for shipping dates. Verify accuracy of invoices. Process client billings. Project performance reports.	Finalize any remaining purchase orders—check for accuracy and correct shipping dates and locations. Verify accuracy of invoices. Process client billings. Project performance reports. Develop suggestions for continuous improvement.

Table 9.3 (continued)

	Contract Documents (Document All Activities)	Contract Administration (Document All Activities)	Post-Occupancy (Document All Activities)
Client Relationships	Cultivate relationship by providing excellent customer service, and being reliable and responsive to the needs of the client and team members. Consider cultural and generational dimensions. Promptly resolve problems and complaints. Client input needed to respond to questions related to drawings and specifications. Client updates: Progress with development of drawings, specifications, bids, and proposals. Client signs document approving contract documents. Focus on developing loyalty.	Cultivate relationship by providing excellent customer service, and being reliable and responsive to the needs of the client and team members. Consider cultural and generational dimensions. Promptly resolve problems and complaints. Client input needed for change orders and billings. Client updates: Schedule, budget, quality assurances, project scope, risks, completion date, and progress with construction. Client signs document approving changes. Focus on developing loyalty.	Cultivate relationship by providing excellent customer service, and being reliable and responsive to the needs of the client and team members. Consider cultural and generational dimensions. Promptly resolve problems and complaints. Client input needed for assessment inputs. Client updates: Results of assessment process. Client signs any documents needed to close project. Develop plans to conduct postoccupancy evaluations at later dates. Identify any potential future projects with the client and/or referrals. Focus on developing loyalty. Develop suggestions for continuous improvement of client relationships.
LEED Certification*	Specify water efficient fixtures and appliances. Continue energy and other commissioning activities. Perform daylighting calculations. Purchase green power. Complete and record building reuse strategies. Complete and record materials reuse strategies. Specify products with recycled content. Specify regional materials, rapidly renewable materials, and FSC-certified wood. Specify air quality standards. Specify low-emitting materials. Complete LEED calculations and documentation.	One- and two-phase LEED reviews submit documents after end of construction. Confirm proper selection of fixtures, installation, and operation of fixtures, fittings, and systems. Continue energy and other commissioning activities. Ensure placement of recycling bins. Implement building reuse strategies. Confirm installation of materials with recycled content. Confirm installation of regional materials, rapidly renewable materials, and FSC-certified wood. Confirm installation of low-emitting materials. Confirm calibration of lighting controls with installer and commissioning agent. Post IAQ policies on-site. Install absorbent materials after any products with VOCs. Purchase green power. Complete LEED calculations and documentation.	Complete energy and other commissioning activities. Educate end users about recycling practices, lighting systems, and thermal comfort controls. Survey end users to determine satisfaction with lighting systems, daylighting, views, and thermal comfort controls. Conduct IAQ testing. Enforce smoking policies. Complete LEED calculations and final documentation. Develop suggestions for continuous improvement.
Value-Added Examples	Knowledge of regulations, business practices, bidding, ethics, sustainability, project delivery methods, business contracts, and organizations. Skills in drawing, specifications, schedules, collaboration, communication, listening, project management, and customer service.	Knowledge of regulations, sustainability, building inspections, contracts, and project delivery methods. Skills in site supervision, tracking orders, financial management, project communication, problem solving, collaboration, communication, listening, project management, and customer service.	Knowledge of human behavior theories, socioeconomic factors, research methodologies, and continuous improvement strategies. Skills in gathering and analyzing data, problem solving, and collaboration, communication, listening, and customer service.

(Table 9.3 continued on page 314)

Table 9.3 (continued)

	Contract Documents (Document All Activities)	Contract Administration (Document All Activities)	Post-Occupancy (Document All Activities)
Personal Management Strategies	Complete time/activity log and expense reports. Review and revise prioritized goals of responsibilities. Assess time management skills, including repetitive tasks and procrastination. Check reminders. Update information management files for project, products, and services. Practice knowledge management techniques to build tacit knowledge and maximize explicit knowledge.	Complete time/activity log and expense reports. Review and revise prioritized goals of responsibilities. Assess time management skills, including repetitive tasks and procrastination. Check reminders. Update information management files for project, products, and services. Practice knowledge management techniques to build tacit knowledge and maximize explicit knowledge.	Complete final time/activity log and expense reports. Review and revise prioritized goals of responsibilities. Assess time management skills, including repetitive tasks and procrastination. Check reminders. Update information management files for project, products, and services. Assess project to capture tacit knowledge. Develop suggestions for continuous improvement.

*LEED Certification section adapted from: U.S. Green Building Council. (2009). *Green Interior Design and Construction*. Washington, DC: U.S. Green Building Council.

client, the design team must verify criteria and the FF&E manual. Open or closed specifications must be determined, as well as seller qualifications and proprietary rights. Your client must approve the final FF&E manual.

Contract Administration

The contract administration phase is the most exciting time in the IDP—and the most stressful. At this stage of the project all of the time, energy, and resources expended in the previous phases of the design process are transformed into an actual built environment—conceptual designs become reality.

Concurrently, there are many aspects of a construction project that can create anxiety, such as staying within budget, adhering to quality standards, finishing the project on time, and hoping that the client and end users will like the results. Stress levels can increase dramatically if the client has to leave his or her facilities during construction—or must live and/or work in the midst of construction workers, materials, equipment, dust, and debris.

For the transformation to be a success, the design team must closely monitor interior construction and pay special attention to the needs of the client and stakeholders. Deviations from either primary task can cause havoc and ruin

the relationship with your client. Therefore, it is very important that the PMP provides sufficient time and resources for contract administration responsibilities—especially activities that affect client relationships (Table 9.3).

What are the design team's responsibilities during contract administration? Depending on the agreement between the designer and client for design services, the design team's tasks can include move management, purchasing FF&E, observing field conditions, and supervising interior construction. The design team's involvement with the project might increase when an IDP is used because of requests to collaborate with various professionals, such as the contractor, subcontractors, consultants, and specialists.

All of the activities must adhere to the extent permitted by applicable laws. To successfully execute contract administration activities, you must have a comprehensive PMP, effective project management, and a continuous focus on providing excellent service to your client, stakeholders, and other parties involved with construction.

Move Management

Projects, such as renovation and remodeling, that require the client to contend with construction or evacuate the space, require very special considerations. Move management is generally not considered a task for an interior designer, but helping your client through the tribulations of a construction project can be excellent for client relations, and a positive experience makes it more likely that a client will be willing to do another project in the future. Moreover, unexpected assistance demonstrates another way that you are adding value to the project. A bad experience with construction activities can affect how a client reacts to any change orders as well as how much a client likes or dislikes the final product.

Move management assistance is project-specific, but there are key considerations affecting most situations. For example, generally people remain in their residence during remodeling, but they might want to stay at a hotel for a few days to avoid trying to live with truly inconvenient arrangements, such as no sink in a kitchen or the removal of the toilet when the residence only has one bathroom.

Inconveniences with commercial projects depend on the extent of the renovation and the building type. For the most part, businesses that rely on customers for income such as restaurants, hotels, and retail stores must stay open during renovations. Thus, for small facilities most construction work must be planned to take place during off-hours. For larger facilities renovation work can be planned in stages.

When the client remains in the space, you should make every effort to minimize disruptions and accelerate the construction time. Safety is a primary concern; unsafe situations should be reported immediately to the contractor, followed by a written statement describing the violation. Make sure workers use drop cloths over furniture and floors and contain dust and dirt by using plastic sheeting, and so on.

Whenever possible, schedule utility shutoffs and the noisiest and messiest activities when occupants are gone from the space. When they return, make sure the space is clean and that dangerous tools and equipments are stored in a remote location.

For very extensive renovation—as was the case with the La Samaritaine department store in Paris—an entire building could be closed for an extended period. La Samaritaine completely closed in 2005 to be compliant with safety codes, including replacing antiquated electrical circuits, and was scheduled to be reopened in 2012 (Figure 9.8).

Offices and schools have different concerns. For a comprehensive renovation of an office building, the occupants can lease space in a different building. A great amount of the construction at schools can be done during the summer months, and if necessary, during the school year classrooms can be transferred to temporary trailers situated on school grounds.

As mentioned earlier in this chapter, when it is necessary for the client to move to another building during construction, you should discuss the move early in the design process and offer planning assistance. You can help by suggesting reliable moving and storage companies.

You can also help to coordinate the move by monitoring real-time construction activities. The goal is to plan **just-in-time** moves. In other words, develop a plan that enables the moving company to pack and remove items just prior to the start of construction. This strategy can

Figure 9.8 Some move management strategies during construction involve closing a facility, as was the case with the La Samaritaine department store in Paris. La Samaritaine completely closed in 2005 to be compliant with safety codes and was scheduled to reopen in 2012. (© Karl Johaentges/ageFotostock)

allow the client to remain in the space as long as possible, thus reducing the amount of rent and utilities at the temporary location.

Purchasing FF&E

As discussed in Chapter 6, acquiring merchandise for the project involves writing purchase orders and work orders, reviewing acknowledgements, and checking invoices. From a PMP perspective the designer will want to carefully coordinate purchases and the timing and sequencing of the project activities as described in the WBS. The goal is to have the item delivered at the exact time of the installation. Items arriving too early can incur storage fees. Items arriving too late can trigger a cascade of project delays.

To coordinate delivery dates with interior construction, you must know the sequence of events. When will the walls be painted? When will the cabinets be installed? Will the carpet be installed—before or after the walls are painted? How long will it take to install the window treatments? When can the furniture and artwork be delivered to avoid dust, dirt, and damage?

Coordinating delivery dates also requires knowing how long it takes to obtain an item. Factors affecting the amount of time include shipping destinations, means of transportation, availability of an item, and the extent of customization. As noted earlier, custom designs, especially items that involve multiple tradespeople, require considerable time for production—plan accordingly. Contact manufacturers and tradespeople to obtain delivery estimates.

Procurement tasks continue after orders are submitted to manufacturers, vendors, subcontractors, and tradespeople. Acknowledgments and invoices must be checked for accuracy as well as delivery dates. Unacceptable delivery dates or discontinued items force the design team to find alternates and present the new item to the client. After the client approves the alternate, the design team must complete the change order form and disseminate the information to all relevant parties.

Quality Expectations—Tradespeople and Deliveries

The amount of time required for custom designs is just one of the considerations when working with tradespeople. Having the knowledge and skills to partner with quality tradespeople is another example of how you add value to the project.

As a professional interior designer, you must know who to hire to execute work in a professional manner. Are they honest? Do they complete work on time? Are their cost estimates accurate? Do they adhere to the design intent? What is the quality of their workmanship? How much experience do they have? How do they handle change requests from a client? What do their references say about them and can you see past work in person? Do they have the current license required by state or local authorities? Do they have insurance and a contractor's license bond?

To provide excellent service to clients, interior designers must know who has the license, talent, and professionalism to construct buildings and produce interior items, such as cabinetry, window treatments, reupholstering of furniture, and specialized painting techniques. Interior designers must also know who can professionally as well as legally install window treatments, wallcoverings, and flooring.

A **general contractor (GC)** can be hired to coordinate and oversee a construction project, which includes hiring **subcontractors** (subs) to perform specialized services, such as installing flooring, electrical systems, and plumbing.

General contractors as well as most subcontractors must be licensed. For example, California requires floorcovering and painting contractors to have a license. To supervise work or provide instructions, some states require an interior designer to have a contractor's license. You can verify contractors' license numbers by contacting the Contractors State License Board.

In addition to having a current license for the location of a project, make sure the contractor has workers' compensation insurance for employees, and request a copy of the certificate of insurance. States also require licensed contractors to have a contractor's license bond—a promise to pay the costs of projects the contractor agrees to perform. Hiring *or* recommending unlicensed contractors can result in lawsuits and significant financial harm.

Depending on the item, you might have to meet with the tradesperson at the construction site to verify measurements and field conditions. For example, you might want to review a complicated window treatment with the person who will fabricate the unit. Or discuss with a woodworker how custom cabinets can be installed within the space.

As with FF&E purchases, there is considerable paperwork that must be processed when you are working with tradespeople as well as contractors and subcontractors. To verify accuracy, you must respond to **contractor's submittals**, such as shop drawings and materials. You might be be required to distribute and respond to RFIs and **RFCs (requests for comments)**. Transmittal letters are used as well as change order forms. Copies of the documents must be filed in the client's job book.

Storage and Deliveries

Storage and deliveries also require paperwork, such as the **bill of lading, packing lists, freight bills**, and **freight claims**. The bill of lading is a document from the carrier to a shipper that lists the products shipped to the site. Prior to signing the bill of lading, the containers must be inspected for damage, and the actual contents must match the list of goods. A packing list is a document that itemizes what is in the container. Manufacturers usually place the packing list inside the container.

A freight bill is the document that lists shipping charges. Damaged or lost merchandise must be noted on the freight bill or bill of lading. To file a claim for lost or damaged merchandise, you must complete the carrier's freight claim form. Depending on the extent of damage, the designer might have to send a letter to the manufacturer requesting permission to return the item.

Often a designer or the delivery/storage company has people who can make minor repairs. When a repair can be done well, this is generally the preferred solution because of the considerable time required to send the item back to the manufacturer, followed by the wait for its replacement to arrive.

As reviewed in Chapter 6, deliveries can be made to a storage facility, the design firm, the client's address, and a manufacturer. When items must be shipped to a storage facility, make sure you are working with a reputable company known for excellent service.

The storage and delivery company should understand the importance of handling fine objects with care, storing materials in climate-controlled conditions, and delivering merchandise to the space without damaging the item or any other elements in a room.

A reputable company also uses responsible movers who are honest, wear uniforms, use "white glove" service (an expression meaning helping set up and cleaning up afterwards), and are properly groomed. After the delivery the handler should make sure the item and space are clean and then remove all cartons and packing materials. The mover must also receive a signed acceptance of the delivery from the client.

Problems with deliveries can reflect negatively on your level of professionalism. Quality delivery and storage companies are expensive, and these fees should be included in the preliminary budgets.

Monitor Field Conditions

Fees for monitoring field conditions during construction should be included in contracts for design services. The amount of time required to supervise work can be considerable for large projects involving several years of construction. Therefore, it is very important that your client has a clear understanding of, and written documentation detailing, how much time you will dedicate to site supervision—to the extent permitted by licensing laws. Unless your client has hired you to monitor all construction activities during the early stages of work, most of your responsibilities involve attending meetings with the contractor, responding to RFIs, processing change orders, and monitoring progress.

As the project advances to interior construction, there can be numerous times when you must visit the site. For projects using the IDP, site supervision can be simplified because the people performing the work were involved with decisions at the earliest phases of the design process. To make sure the design intent is followed, you should observe tasks such as painting and the installation of wallcoverings, flooring, window treatments, light fixtures, and cabinetry.

When the tradespeople are ready to execute these tasks, make sure that items are not damaged and that these team members understand the specifications. For example, make sure that painters have the correct colors for the right rooms and surfaces. Clarify the placement of seams with the carpet installers. Clarify the layout of tile or wood flooring.

Make sure window treatments are mounted correctly and operate as intended. Fabric window treatments should be neatly pressed, and folds should fall as designed. Light fixtures must be mounted in the correct location with the proper lamps. During the very last stages of construction, you will be involved with fine-tuning the directional qualities of lighting and positioning furniture and accessories.

As you are observing work related to interior construction, you must note any errors, omissions, and safety concerns. In addition, with or without the intention of acquiring LEED certification, construction waste management, including a recycling center, should be a consideration. The contractor should have a plan for reducing and recycling the solid waste from demolition and construction. Any problems with the contractor's work or third-party professionals must be documented in writing. Notifications should be submitted to the client, contractor, and any other appropriate entities.

The last major task in the contract administration phase is the **walk-through** with the contractor. During the walk-through you must create a **punch list** of problems that must be corrected by the contractor or others. Once the problems have been rectified, on behalf of your client you might be required to review that work has been completed and approve a **certificate of payment**.

A final walk-through by the local building department inspector is required to receive a **certificate of occupancy**—a document indicating the building is in compliance with building codes, and people can move in to the facilities.

Post-Occupancy Activities

At this stage of the project, to continue to cultivate your relationship with your client, you should monitor move-in activities and immediately resolve any problems that might occur with the initial operation of the facilities, such as defective lamps or misplaced occupancy sensors.

Be aware that some problems could be the result of a person being displeased with an item—even though the piece is exactly what the client approved and wanted the designer to purchase. Resolving this problem is complicated and might depend on the design firm's policies. Legally, you might not be obligated to accept returns, but when you are very interested in developing a long-term relationship with the client, the best decision might be to replace the item at no or minimal cost to the client.

To **close out** the project, you should assemble materials your client needs for operation and maintenance, including warranties, cleaning recommendations, and as-built drawings. Closeout procedures can also involve educational sessions with users of the space and facility staff. Session topics might include how to adjust furniture, lighting systems, indoor air quality (IAQ) devices, and window treatments.

Training might also be required for operation of mechanical systems, recycling initiatives, and commissioning requirements. Finally, consider providing your client with "before" and "after" photographs (another excellent way to illustrate your added value to the project).

At different intervals the design team should conduct a post-occupancy evaluation (POE). The purpose of the POE is to assess the degree of satisfaction with the project. The assessment process could be done via interviews, focus groups, or online surveys. As is the case with gathering information during the programming phase, for large facilities you might want to mount an iPad tablet in a convenient place to let people complete the survey that way.

Items on a POE survey typically focus on satisfaction with work performance, FF&E, communication strategies, and overall customer service. The respondents should be asked to assess the strengths and weaknesses of the project, and whether they are willing to refer the design firm to others. A POE is generally distributed to the client, end users, and stakeholders approximately 6 months after occupancy and perhaps again 1 to 2 years later.

The design team should make every effort to immediately resolve any problems identified in the POE. This is an excellent way to continue to build the relationship with your client and stakeholders. Another way is stay in regular contact with your client using his or her preferred mode of communication. Consider also inviting your client to special events sponsored by your design firm, and make sure he or she receives newsletters and press announcements.

In addition to focusing on enhancing client relationships, post-occupancy activities should include an assessment of the project by the design team. In following the tenets of quality management practices, the purpose of the assessment is to identify ways to continuously improve designs, project management, and customer service.

Ideally, the review should be done when details can be easily recalled, such as immediately after occupancy. To conduct a comprehensive assessment of their work and to solidify collaborative relationships, the design team might also want to solicit feedback from others involved in the project, such as the contractor, subcontractors, vendors, and tradespeople.

The conclusions from all these assessments should be used to improve future practice and relationships.

Contract Administration and Post-Occupancy: Cultivating Client Relationships and the Project Management Plan (PMP)

As described above numerous opportunities exist to cultivate client relationships and demonstrate your value during contract administration and post-occupancy. In many ways this could be the stage of the project that is most important for client relationships because it is the last experience remembered by the client. Therefore, every effort should be made to create a positive and professional impression. To demonstrate a high level of professionalism, the design team must be in regular communication with the client as well as others involved with the project, including the contractor, subcontractors, tradespeople, and vendors.

The topics of communication focus on the elements in the PMP (Table 9.3). Activities in the contract administration phase are directly correlated with the PMP. Success or failure depends on the parameters in the PMP. Thus, the design team must constantly monitor the project scope, quality assurances, the baseline schedule, team performance, the cost baseline, and the risk register.

Deviations must be identified immediately and responded to by appropriate corrective actions. This level of vigilance can increase the chances that problems are discovered well before the client notices errors or omissions.

Any problems associated with FF&E and interior construction come front and center during contract administration. Therefore, make sure procurement management is successful. As mentioned previously in this book, be sure to check, recheck, and recheck again the information on purchase orders, work orders, or any other agreements with suppliers, vendors, and tradespeople. These are legally binding documents, and the buyer is committed to their terms.

As items are shipped from manufacturers, you are held responsible for inspections, needed repair work, and transport to the proper location in a space. Any problems can have serious consequences to the project's scope, schedule, quality assurances, and budget, as well as your relationship with the client, your employer, stakeholders, the design team, and manufacturers.

Chapter 9 continued to build your knowledge of how to work in a design firm by reviewing strategies for enhancing client relationships, adding value, and managing projects for each phase of the integrated design process (IDP): predesign, programming, schematic design, design development, contract documents, contract administration, and post-occupancy.

This chapter concludes Part III *Long-Term Client Relationships and Project Responsibilities* and serves as the transition to Part IV *Owning and Operating an Interior Design Business: An Overview.* Business ownership is the basis for the chapters in Part IV, but the topics are also approached from the perspective of building long-term client relationships.

Knowledge and Skills Summary

Highlights

* According to the WBDG, the "integrated" design approach asks all members of the building stakeholder community, and the technical planning, design, and construction team to review all aspects of the project.

* Predesign activities fundamentally begin when a client contacts you for professional design services and continues with conducting preliminary studies and identifying research studies (evidence-based designs), professional resources, and building permit procedures.

* Project management strategies must include planning for all phases of the integrated design process: predesign, programming, schematic design, design development, contract documents, contract administration, and post-occupancy.

* Bidding is used in design-bid-build (DBD) project delivery methods and commercial projects, and when required by law, such as in projects involving public institutions and government agencies.

* Throughout the integrated design process—predesign, programming, schematic design, design development, contract documents, contract administration, and post-occupancy—you should collaborate with your client to develop the project management plan (PMP), as well as focusing on cultivating client relationships and demonstrating your value.

Key Terms

alternate bid

as-built drawing

bid bond

bid security

bill of lading

certificate of occupancy

certificate of payment

closed-ended survey

closeout

contract administration phase

contract document phase

contractor's submittal

cutting

design development phase

focus group

formal research

freight bill

freight claim

general contractor (GC)

in-depth interview

informal research

jobber

just-in-time

Leadership in Energy and Environmental Design (LEED)

life cycle cost analysis (LCCA)

manufacturers' representative (sales rep)

memo sample

move management

observation study

open account

open-ended survey

packing list

programming phase

punch list

qualitative research

quantitative research

redline plan

refereed journal

requests for comments (RFCs)

schematic design phase

semi-structured interview

showroom manager

structured interview

subcontractor

subject

survey

tearsheet

territory sales representative

triangulation

unstructured interview

upcharge

walk-through

white paper

Projects

Philosophy and Design Project

This chapter examined ways to cultivate relationships with clients and demonstrate your value during each phase of the integrated design process (IDP): predesign, programming, schematic design, design development, contract documents, contract administration, and post-occupancy. These practices should become elements of your professional philosophy.

Identify a team of three to five members. Your team has the following assignment: (1) develop a professional philosophy based on cultivating relationships with clients—the philosophy should reflect each phase of the IDP, and (2) provide suggestions for implementing the philosophy. Post these results on a blog and prepare an oral presentation (approximately 15 minutes) to a team of professional designers.

Research Project

Applying evidence-based designs (EBD) to practice is an excellent way to demonstrate to your client that you are adding value to his or her project. Locate a recent research article that focuses on some topic or issue related to the work of interior designers.

Develop a one-page summary of the article that includes (1) a review of the literature, (2) research methodologies, (3) findings, (4) author's discussion, and (5) your suggestions for how you could use the results of the research to improve practice. Submit your summary with a copy of the article.

Human Factors Research Project

The programming phase involves identifying goals and objectives for the project from psychological and physiological perspectives.

The WBDG developed categories for design objectives: accessible, aesthetics, cost-effective, functional/operational, historic preservation, productive, secure/safe, and sustainable.

Identify a team of three to five members. Your team has the following assignment: (1) based on WBDG's categories for design objectives, develop a survey that would be given to users of a space; (2) distribute the survey to 10 to 15 people; (3) evaluate the results and determine if revisions, additions, or deletions are needed; and (4) develop a written report (approximately five pages) of your results. Include a copy of the survey with your written report.

References

Council for Interior Design Accreditation (CIDA). 2011. *Professional Standards 2011*. http://www.accredit-id.org/professional-standards. Accessed February 16, 2011.

Farr Associates. 2011. *About Us*. http://www.farrside.com/. Accessed May 26, 2011.

InformeDesign. 2011. *Benefits of Applying Research to Practice*. http://www.informedesign.org/Page.aspx?cId=203. Accessed February 12, 2011.

InformeDesign. 2011. *Creating an Optimal Environment for Mentally Ill Patients*. http://www.informedesign.org/Rs_detail.aspx?rsId=3476. Accessed February 14, 2011.

Prowler, D. 2008. *Whole Building Design*. http://www.wbdg.org/. Accessed January 3, 2011.

U.S. Green Building Council. 2009. *Green Interior Design and Construction*. Washington, DC: U.S. Green Building Council.

Whole Building Design Guide (WBDG). 2010. *Design Objectives*. http://www.wbdg.org/design/designobjectives.php. Accessed February 16, 2011.

OWNING AND OPERATING
AN INTERIOR DESIGN BUSINESS:
AN OVERVIEW

Parts I, II, and III reviewed strategies for launching a career and information that an interior designer should know to work in a design firm, such as establishing long-term client relationships, providing value, and project management.

Do you think you want to own an interior design business? The first step to owning your own business is to acquire considerable years of experience. Professional experience will help you to avoid costly mistakes and will enable you to build a roster of clients who can provide you with the operating dollars that are required for a business.

Part IV *Owning and Operating an Interior Design Business: An Overview* is dedicated to content that is relevant to designers who want to own their firm by reviewing how to develop a business plan, operate a green business, create a marketing program, and manage human resources.

CHAPTER 10

Business Requirements

Capitolul 10 (Romanian)
Глава 10 (Russian)
Поглавље 10 (Serbian)

After learning the content in Chapter 10, you will be able to answer the following questions:

* Am I ready to be an entrepreneur?

* Where can I get advice about starting a new business?

* What is a business plan?

* For the purposes of a business plan, what should be included in a description of a business?

* What should be included in the market analyses section of a business plan?

* What should be included in the management and operations section of a business plan?

* What should be included in the financial data section of a business plan?

The purpose of Chapter 10 is to begin the process of providing an overview of the fundamentals related to owning and operating an interior design business. The first section of the chapter reviews the qualities and characteristics required to be an entrepreneur, including the ability to take financial risks, manage a business, and possess a willingness to commit substantial amounts of time, energy, and resources. The section features an analysis of the advantages and disadvantages of various types of business, and there is a discussion of organizations that help people start a new business.

The next section of the chapter focuses on how to develop a business plan—critical for determining your business readiness. Each area of a business plan is discussed, including business descriptions, marketing analyses, management, operations, and finances.

Topics include business structures (sole proprietorship, partnerships, and corporations), professional liability insurance, insurance policies, business permits, licenses, resale taxes, and financial data.

The content in this chapter is focused on what should be included in a business plan. Supplemental information needed to manage and operate a business is reviewed in Chapters 11, 12, 13, and 14, including green businesses, financial management, marketing plans, and employment taxes.

Entrepreneurship

Considering owning your own business should begin by understanding what it means to be an entrepreneur. This section explores characteristics of an entrepreneur and topics essential to starting a new business, such as purchasing an existing interior design firm. The section concludes by outlining various organizations that can provide assistance, counseling, and training to small businesses, such as the U.S. Small Business Administration (SBA).

Are You an Entrepreneur?

Do you think you want to be an **entrepreneur**? What is an entrepreneur? According to the dictionary, an entrepreneur is "one who organizes, manages, and assumes the risks of a business enterprise" and business is defined as a "commercial or mercantile activity engaged in as a means of livelihood" (Merriam-Webster 2011). Is this what you think you want to do?

Given the substantial number of interior design firms in the United States and Canada, it is apparent that many interior designers elect to own their own business. However, is entrepreneurship the best choice for you and your career aspirations? You really can't answer this question until you have had several years of experience working as an interior designer. But at this stage of your career, it is important to be aware of what is required to own a small business in the event you eventually establish your own design firm. The knowledge can also help you understand what the owner of your design firm has to contend with on a daily basis—empathy can be very important in collaborative relationships.

Entrepreneurship should be considered *only* after several years of professional experience. In Chapter 3, it was suggested you might be interested in owning a business after 15 years of experience. Why is experience necessary? Experience is essential to owning a business. Advisors and organizations associated with small businesses urge potential entrepreneurs to have a solid understanding of their industry.

Acquiring this solid understanding requires several years of work experience. You will make mistakes early in your career. Hopefully your boss will be able to correct your mistakes before they're installed. But as a new business owner, you can't afford to make expensive mistakes. Moreover, as a business owner you must have numerous clients—which happens only after years of experience.

Exploring the world of business ownership requires a reexamination of your career plan, including engaging in another self-assessment process and identifying items that are important to you professionally as well as personally (see Chapter 3). The self-assessment process can be done by creating another bulleted summary of successful activities (see Box 3.1). However, now your list can be derived from experiences involving numerous projects. The self-assessment process also should involve reprioritizing the self-assessment items according to your perceived level of ability and interest (see Table 3.1).

To help determine your level of ability and interest in owning a business, you should also prioritize the items listed in Table 10.1. Remember: To own your business, you must continue to work with your clients *while* you are assuming the responsibilities of running a small business.

As you are reviewing the items in Table 10.1, think about why you want to own a business. A rating of 3 or lower on any item might be cause to reconsider business ownership. A low rating on an item, such as managing finances, could suggest that you should consider partnering with someone who has finance skills or outsource the task to an accredited accounting

Table 10.1 Self-Assessment of Entrepreneur Skills, Knowledge, and Abilities		
Self-Assessment of Specific Business Skills/Knowledge/Abilities	My Level of Interest*	My Level of Ability*
Understanding of and ability to demonstrate leadership.		
Understanding of and ability to be a self-starter.		
Understanding of and ability to perform every task required to own a business.		
Understanding of and ability to manage people.		
Understanding of and ability to manage resources.		
Understanding of and ability to manage budgets.		
Understanding of and ability to plan and manage financials.		
Understanding of and ability to manage accounting procedures.		
Understanding of and ability to manage administrative duties.		
Understanding of and ability to manage marketing strategies.		
Understanding of and ability to manage legal requirements.		
Understanding of and ability to identify opportunities.		
Understanding of and ability to manage projects.		
Understanding of and ability to make business decisions.		
Understanding of and ability to sell products, services, and concepts.		
Understanding of and ability to organize documents.		
Understanding of and ability to manage suppliers and vendors.		
Understanding of and ability to resolve conflicts.		
Understanding of and ability manage time.		
Understanding of and ability to collect overdue bills.		
Understanding of and ability to collaborate with the local community.		
Understanding of and ability to collaborate with local professionals.		
Understanding of and ability to collaborate with professional interior designers.		
Understanding of and ability to keep abreast of the interior design profession.		
Understanding of and ability to keep abreast of global events.		
Understanding of and ability to manage risks.		
Dedicate numerous hours (70–80) each week to the business.		
Dedicate substantial funds to the business.		
Dedicate substantial resources to the business.		

Scale: 1–5 (5—Very high; 4—High; 3—Neutral; 2—Low; 1—Very low or not applicable).

professional, such as a **certified public accountant (CPA)**.

Again, why do you want to own a business? Are you bored with the work you are doing and believe that if you had your own business you would no longer be bored? Are you unhappy working with your boss or coworkers? Are you uncomfortable with your boss's operating policies and procedures? Starting a business might not be the solution for being discontent with current work arrangements. The best solution might be to resolve differences by discussing the problems with your boss or perhaps searching for new opportunities (see Chapter 2). Therefore, you must seriously contemplate why you want to start a business. For this career option to make sense, your answer should focus on a desire to be an entrepreneur and the willingness to perform all the tasks and handle all the responsibilities associated with business ownership.

Identifying Your Type of Business

Why you want to start a business is naturally tied to your interest in wanting to own a specific type of business. What type of business do you want to own and why? What services do you want to provide and why? Do the services you want to provide align with the needs of your current clients? Is there a future market for the services you want to provide? Who or what is your competition? These questions are very important to address while you are contemplating starting a business—your answers help to determine the feasibility of the business proposition. If opportunities do not exist for the type of business you are interested in operating, then you should pursue other career options.

The answers to these questions should revolve around your work experience. To start a business, you *must* understand the industry and have professional experience performing the work. You need experience to have an immediate clientele base that can provide you with **revenues** (income). You also need the experience in order to obtain **loans**. You need experience to understand how to operate and manage the business. Therefore, within the context of your professional experiences, identify the type of design firm you would like to own and what services you want to perform for your clients. This information serves as the basis for discussing your business proposal with small business advisors and developing your business plan.

A useful approach to identifying the type of business you want to own is to research design firms using the Internet and to network with designers at national interior design conferences sponsored by ASID, IIDA, and IDC. As previously mentioned, the number of design firms in the United Sates is impressive: According to ASID 2010, in 2009 there were 13,388 interior design firms in the United States, and approximately 80 percent of these firms had fewer than five employees (ASID 2010).

The number of small businesses in the United States becomes even more impressive when we examine its entire profile: The U.S. Small Business Administration reported that in 2008 there were 5,911,663 small business employers, defined as fewer than 500 employees (SBA 2011). Obviously, most of these businesses are not interior design firms. However, the significant number of small businesses demonstrates the feasibility of owning your business, and regardless of the industry, small business owners are excellent resources for learning how to start, operate, and expand a business.

Buying an Existing Business?

One of the owners of the 13,388 interior design firms might be interested in selling his or her business. Your boss might be interested in selling his or her business. An owner can have a variety of reasons for selling a business, such as wanting to retire, change careers, or move to a distant location. The owner might have personal problems, poor health, or financial issues. Knowing the reason can be very useful in determining whether or not you want to buy a particular business. Buying a business that has substantial debt could be a disaster.

Understanding the firm's business operations and knowing its reputation are absolute prerequisites to ownership. The best way for you to completely understand a business is to actually work for the firm. When this is not possible, you must do extensive research and rely on information from the owner's clients and employees, in addition to other design-related professionals and those connected to relevant businesses.

Advantages and Disadvantages of Purchasing an Existing Business

Buying an existing business has both advantages and disadvantages—all of which must be considered in the context of your situation and the circumstances surrounding the business. Some of the advantages focus on established relationships with clients, employees, suppliers, vendors, contractors, tradespeople, the landlord, and others.

An excellent location that is well-known and accessible to clients is an asset when purchasing an existing building. Existing facilities can also help to reduce start-up costs, such as those for equipment, furniture, inventories, manufacturers' catalogues, and a sample library.

However, these advantages can also be disadvantages when purchasing an existing business. For example, existing relationships with clients, employees, or businesses might be problematic when there have been unresolved conflicts or unpaid debts. The building that accompanies the purchase might be located in a remote area or lack adequate parking.

Undesirable elements included with the purchase price can increase costs and might have to be eliminated or replaced. For example, the sales price might include outdated or unattractive merchandise. Furniture and equipment might be in disrepair, or the sample library might be loaded with discontinued items.

Is buying an existing business a good option for you? Answering this question requires a thorough analysis of the proposition in the context of your professional experience and other issues. For example:

* Do you have professional experience with the firm's areas of specialization?

* What services and merchandise has the firm been providing, and to whom?

* What is the reputation in the community?

* What is its **brand** identity (see Chapter 13)?

* Does it have a national or international reputation?

* How would a change in ownership affect the business?

* Do you think the owner's clients would remain with the firm?

* Do you think the owner's departure could encourage the arrival of new clients?

* Are you comfortable with the working conditions?

* Do you like the current employees? Would they stay with a new owner? Would you want them to stay?

* Who are their suppliers, vendors, and tradespeople? Is the firm in good standing with these entities and other professionals and businesses?

In addition to addressing these questions, you should investigate business operations with an experienced accountant, attorney, and perhaps a local banker. What is the value of the business? This includes intangibles, such as an esteemed reputation, and tangibles, including the income, property, building, equipment, furniture, and the inventory. Documents that can reveal the value of a business include recent audited financial statements and tax returns, balance sheets, and income statements.

The value of the business must be analyzed within the context of what is included with the purchase price. Does the purchase price include the client list, current projects, furniture, equipment, inventory, vehicles, trademarks, copyrights, or contracts with suppliers and tradespeople? What is the status of receivables? Will you be able to collect?

The purchase price of the business must be evaluated with respect to the terms of the contract. For example:

* How much is required for a down payment—20 percent, 30 percent, 50 percent?

* Does the seller sign a **non-compete clause**, agreeing not to establish a business that would be in competition with the existing business?

* Is the seller willing to assist with the transition process?

* If a building lease is involved, what are the terms? Is the lease transferable to a different party?

* How will utility bills be proportioned?

* Are there equipment leases? How will these be handled?

* What are the financial commitments to employees, such as salaries and benefits?

* How will any unpaid taxes be resolved?

Small Business Organizations, Programs, and Mentors

Fortunately, there are many resources available that can help you find answers to small business operations and management questions. Professional organizations such as ASID, IIDA, IDC, and AIA are excellent sources, as well as trade magazines (e.g., *Interior Design*, *Contract Design*, *Perspective*, and *Architectural Record*). Professional organizations post business articles on their websites, sponsor web events, post blogs, send Twitter updates, and host conference sessions dedicated to business operations.

Trade magazines have features and editorials that focus on emerging issues related to business. In addition, research studies pertaining to business are published in academic journals such as the *Journal of Small Business Management*, *International Small Business Journal*, *Entrepreneurship Theory and Practice*, and *Journal of Small Business and Entrepreneur Development*. As an example, in 2010 the *Journal of Small Business Management* included an article titled "Social Networks: Effects of Social Capital on Firm Innovation." Topics in *Entrepreneurship Theory and Practice* include venture financing, family-owned businesses, and minority issues in small businesses.

From a small business organizational perspective, the government sponsored U.S. SBA and Canada Business have extensive information on a broad range of small business topics, such as advocacy, permits, licenses, financial assistance, counseling, training, and disaster assistance (see http://www.sba.gov/ and http://www. canadabusiness.ca/eng/). These organizations also sponsor blogs, small business organizations and gatherings, and provide access to laws, regulations, and public notices related to the operations of small businesses.

There are also nonprofit small business professional organizations with membership fees, including the Small Business and Entrepreneurship Council (SBE Council; see http://sbecouncil.org/home/index.cfm), the National Small Business Association (NSBA, http://nsba.biz/), and the United States Association for Small Business and Entrepreneurship (USASBE, http://usasbe.org/). Membership in USASBE includes membership in the International Council for Small Business (ICSB, http://icsb.org/).

Generally, the purposes of small business professional organizations are to promote the growth and development of small business through advocacy, research, education, and global networks.

SBA Assistance, Counseling, and Training Programs

In addition to small business professional organizations, there are several programs that can provide assistance, counseling, and training to small businesses. Most of the counseling and training is free, but there are also some low-cost options. The SBA has district offices for this purpose, and its website offers several free online courses and podcasts featuring interviews with experts in the field. Topics include how to start a business, creating a business plan, financing a business, hiring employees, and strategies for working with the government.

In collaboration with colleges and universities, the SBA sponsors Small Business Development Centers (SBDCs; see http://www.sba.gov/content/small-business-development-centers-sbdcs). Located throughout the United States, SBDCs provide assistance and training to owners of small businesses.

The SBA sponsors many programs directed toward a specific population or activity (http://www.sba.gov/). (see Figure 10.1.) For example, the organization supports Women's Business Centers, Veterans Business Outreach Centers, People with Disabilities, and Minority-Owned Businesses.

SBA programs that address a specific activity include Starting a Green Business, Home-Based Business, International Business Planning, and U.S. Export Assistance Centers. Procurement

Technical Centers (PTACs) help businesses wanting to sell products or services to federal, state, and local governments.

When the word "Center" is in the name of a program, as is the case in the name "Women's Business Centers," it usually offers local in-person training, counseling, and mentoring (http://www.sba.gov/content/womens-business-centers). The other programs provide information online and are especially useful for their links to important resources. For example, the online information related to Starting a Green Business includes important tips, articles, certification programs, ecolabel resources, industry partnerships, and case studies (http://www.sba.gov/content/starting-green-business).

One of the free programs sponsored by the SBA is SCORE (Service Corps of Retired Executives, http://www.score.org/index.html). SCORE is a volunteer-based organization that has provided assistance to more than 9 million entrepreneurs since it began in 1964. SCORE is "dedicated to entrepreneur education and the formation, growth and success of small business nationwide" (2010). More than 13,000 volunteers mentor entrepreneurs and small business owners.

One-to-one counseling is available at SCORE's 350 chapters or online by selecting a mentor from a list and asking a business question. SCORE also sponsors free workshops at the local chapters and online. Topics range from what to consider when thinking about becoming an entrepreneur to strategies for growing an established business. Some of SCORE's success stories include Vera Bradley Designs, Jelly Belly Candy Company, and Vermont Teddy Bear.

Figure 10.1 The SBA sponsors many programs that are directed to a specific population, such as women. Arcturis, a multi-disciplined design firm in St. Louis, is a registered Woman-Owned Business.
Arcturis designed the BJC HealthCare New Primary Data Center & Medical Office Building in O'Fallon, Missouri. The Medical Office Building is LEED Gold, Core & Shell certified. (© Sam Fentress)

Checking for Comprehension
*   How would you prioritize your successful professional activities for a self-assessment process?

*   Describe two of the advantages to purchasing an existing interior design business.

Business Plans

SCORE is a superb resource when you are ready to write your **business plan**. Writing a business plan might appear to be a daunting task, but considerable assistance is available from a host of organizations.

This section outlines the basic elements of a *typical* business plan, including how to write the business description, the market analysis, management and operations, and the financial data section. Writing a business plan helps you to understand what is required to own a business, and the exercise might cause you to reconsider the endeavor—or reinforce your enthusiasm for owning an interior design firm.

What Is a Business Plan?

An excellent way to further explore the feasibility of owning your business is to write a business plan. A business plan is a professional document that describes the major considerations associated with starting or expanding a business, such as defining the business, determining the market, managing the business, and understanding the financials.

Developing the business plan provides a profile of what you would have to do to establish, operate, and expand your business. Business plan templates are available from a variety of sources, including the SBA and Canada Business. In addition, professional design organizations might have sample interior design business plans.

After you have written the business plan and decide to continue with your entrepreneurial endeavor, this document continues to be very useful for several purposes. For example, when applying for loans, entrepreneurs must provide a business plan to bankers and investors. In addition, some suppliers and vendors might want to examine a business plan to establish accounts.

The business plan is very helpful as a management tool, especially during the first year of operation. Subsequently, the business plan can be viewed as a document that is revised and updated on a regular basis—important when you must provide an overall assessment of your business to existing or potential investors.

When considering what to include in your business plan, keep in mind you will be giving it to professionals (e.g., bankers, accountants, and attorneys) accustomed to reading these documents. Therefore, your business plan must have all the essential elements and a professional appearance.

As illustrated in Box 10.1, a business plan should begin with a cover sheet and continue with an **executive summary**, a table of contents, and the body of the document (A., B., C., and D.). It should conclude with supporting materials in the appendix of your business plan.

Standard business writing practices must be followed and the document should have a professional presentation. For example, hard-copy forms should be printed on high-quality paper with no marks or smudges.

Executive Summary

The executive summary is a synopsis of the business plan and provides a succinct description of the business, the market, its competitive advantage, your management skills, and the financial request (if applicable). The executive summary is extremely important because this one- to two-page document is usually read first, and some people might read only the executive summary. Therefore, the content should evoke excitement by highlighting your strengths and how your unique business can be a success. You might find it is easier and more effective to write the executive summary last because this is the stage in the writing process when your ideas have been fully developed and it is easy to identify highlights in the document.

Body of the Document

The body of the document is essentially divided into four major categories: (1) Description of the Business, (2) Market Analysis and Competition, (3) Management and Operations, and (4) Financial Data. Generally, a business plan begins with the description of the business

Outline of Key Elements in a Business Plan

Cover Sheet (name of the business, contact information)

Executive Summary

Table of Contents

    A. Description

        1. Professional Background
        2. Type of Business
        3. Services and Products
        4. Business Profile
        5. Location

    B. Market Analysis and Competition

        1. Interior Design Industry
        2. Target Market
        3. Competition
        4. Marketing Strategy

    C. Management and Operations

        1. Business Structure
        2. Registrations, Taxes, Licenses, and Permits

        3. Personnel
        4. Business Insurance

    D. Financial Data

        1. Start-Up Cost Estimate
        2. Breakeven Analysis
        3. Forecasted Income Statement
        4. Cash Flow Forecast
        5. Balance Sheet

    Appendix (Examples)

        Résumés
        Portfolios
        Personal Financial Statements
        Job Descriptions
        Proposed Lease
        Copies of Licenses
        Market Studies
        References

and ends with the financial data. Other content, such as marketing, operating procedures, and personnel management, can be organized so that your strongest points are described early in the document. For example, if you have considerable management and administrative experience, you might want to place this section after the description of the business. Information that should be included in the major categories of a business plan are reviewed in the remaining sections of this chapter.

Writing the Business Plan: Description of the Business

The Description of the Business section should include the following areas: (1) Professional Background, (2) Type of Business, (3) Services and Products, (4) Business Profile, (5) Location, and (6) Location Contractual Arrangements.

Professional Background

As you are writing your business plan, remember that the reader might not be familiar with or understand the design profession—and people do not invest in entities they do not understand. Keep in mind an old saying: "The confused mind says 'No.'" Therefore, it is imperative that you include information that helps to explain the profession as well as the type of business you would like to establish. But how do you do this?

The answer is fairly easy when you have substantial design experience. Thus, it is assumed that your new business is related to your previous experiences and many of your current clients will follow you to your new business. Some clients might have allegiances to your previous employer, but chances are excellent that, after years of positive experiences with you, your long-term clients are committed to continuing the relationship. Therefore, an excellent way to educate the reader of your business plan is to describe previous projects and how you were involved with making them successful.

One approach to writing a synopsis (or short summary) is to identify one project that exemplifies your expertise and helps explain the type of business you want to own. For example, if you were interested in starting a design business that specialized in healthcare facilities, you could describe a recent healthcare project and include how your responsibilities contributed to the project's success. The project profile could include testimonials from clients, end users, stakeholders, and other professionals.

In addition to explanations related to your design skills and abilities, your narrative should emphasize other activities that are critical to owning and operating a business, such as your experience with leadership, interpersonal communications, management, accounting, financial data, marketing, and operations.

Another way to inform your reader is to highlight your professional accomplishments in an updated résumé and design portfolio. Résumés and examples of projects should be included in the appendix of your business plan, along with other materials that support your achievements, such as exemplary employer evaluations, reference letters, articles in journals (either by you or about you or one of your projects), photographs, and testimonials from clients and colleagues.

Type of Business

An explanation of your professional background, skills, abilities, and knowledge serve as the foundation for the description of the type of business you would like to operate. Writing this section requires a very thoughtful analysis of your business *type*.

Your first response to this task might be a statement such as "XYZ Interiors specializes in designing healthcare facilities." This is a true statement, but to adequately explain your new venture, you should describe the *type of business* rather than focusing on the type of building. For example, let's reexamine XYZ Interiors' statement within the context of the healthcare industry.

Healthcare professionals and their customers want facilities that help to improve healing and reduce anxieties while presenting a professional image. Therefore, XYZ Interiors' *type* of business could be enhancing the healing process, reducing anxieties associated with healthcare procedures, or promoting the highest level of professional healthcare. In other words, your business is *how* your design services are fulfilling the needs and wants of your clients, end users, and stakeholders.

The essence of your type of business is summarized in your firm's **mission statement**. A mission statement is a succinct statement that reflects the essence of a business. Generally, businesses prefer very brief mission statements: one to two short sentences that can be remembered easily by employees as well as clients and the public.

For example, the mission statement for M-Architects, a firm in Houston offering interior architecture services, is "We believe in making dependable services and design excellence our highest concern. We provide thoughtful design solutions and create a better built environment resulting in a higher value" (M-Architects 2011). Fowler Design Associates, Inc., located in Atlanta, has this mission: "Fowler Design Associates, Inc., is a collaborative, multidisciplined professional services firm, effecting value in the design of communities and work places, and in personalized service for our clients" (Fowler Design Associates, Inc. 2011).

As illustrated by the examples above, the mission statement should indicate how your business is making a difference in the lives of your clients and end users. Both firms emphasize the importance of providing value. What is special about your business, and how does your uniqueness separate your firm from the competition? Is it "dependable services," "design excellence," "thoughtful design solutions," or "personalized service"? Or perhaps it is "Improving the quality of life," "A commitment to the client," "Respect for environmental resources," or "Being socially responsible."

The mission statement is important for your business plan and subsequently should be used to guide the direction of your firm. As a reflection of the essence of a firm, a mission statement becomes a declaration of the purpose of your business. Although a mission statement is infrequently revised, it is used as the foundation for developing items that do change, such as goals and objectives (see Chapter 12).

Services and Products

After you have explained your business, the next step is to identify the services and products you will provide to clients. Questions to consider are:

* Will you be a full-service design firm by working with your client from the first appointment until the project is built?

* In addition to interior design, do your services include sustainability advice, product design, communications, preservation, reuse, research, graphics, model making, or project management?

* Which type of buildings do you provide services for—commercial, corporate, residential, multi-family residential, mixed-use developments, healthcare, retail, hospitality, libraries, museums, higher education, K–12 education, or government?

* Do you sell products: furniture, lighting, textiles, flooring, window treatments, wallcoverings, accessories, kitchen, or bath?

Services and Products: Virtual Business

Your design services could be a **virtual business**. Generally, online interior design services involve a two-step process: (1) the customer

sends to the service their room measurements, furniture measurements, photographs, and often a completed survey of their design preferences, and (2) based on this information the design service develops solutions and sends the customer a variety of items, such as floor plans with furniture arrangements, specifications, and color boards.

Design fees are often on a per-room basis, and products might be available for purchase. Services are provided using Skype, instant messaging, phone calls, e-mail, and mail. Google Engage, a program for web professionals, includes training and tools for getting online and growing a virtual business.

Virtual businesses must register a **domain name** (web address), select a **web host**, and register with **search engines** and directories. Registering a domain name can be done by contacting the Internet Corporation for Assigned Names and Numbers (ICANN). To ensure that a computer can find each address, ICANN "coordinates unique identifiers across the world" (see http://www.icann.org/). To combat people who register Internet domain names for the purpose of profiting by selling the name, the Anticybersquatting Consumer Protection Act (ACPA) was signed into law in 1999.

Several companies offer a service to register a website URL with search engines and directories (see Google Search Engine Registration at www.google.com). In addition, for monthly fees a web host service can provide disk space, technical support, e-mail accounts, and the means to set up and promote a website.

The website also must be in compliance with online advertising, marketing, and business laws, as well as U.S. trademark and intellectual property laws (see http://www.sba.gov/content/patents-trademarks-copyright).

Fundamentally, the same consumer laws used for other commercial activities apply to Internet advertising, marketing, and sales. However, to help explain how the laws apply to the Internet, the Federal Trade Commission (FTC) describes several examples (see www.ftc.gov and the FTC's Bureau of Consumer Protection Business Center:

http://business.ftc.gov/). For instance, to ensure that information about a product or service are clear and conspicuous, the FTC explains that ideally disclosures should be on the same screen as a claim, or a consumer should be enticed to scroll down a web page to read disclosures.

The FTC has recommendations for making sure that hyperlinks are concisely written when they are linked to a disclosure. In addition, the FTC recently noted that Commission rules associated with terms such as "written," "writing," "printed," or "direct mail" are applicable to text displayed on the Internet and that "direct mail" includes e-mail (FTC 2011). Information regarding online advertising and marketing laws can also be found at the SBA website (http://www.sba.gov/).

Services and Products: Identifying Your Niche and Future Plans

Within the context of identifying your services and products, you must determine what is unique about your business. For example, design firms are distinguishing themselves from the competition by publicizing the number of LEED-certified buildings they've contributed to (Figure 10.2). What services and products will you provide that distinctively address the needs of the market and are far superior to the competition? For example:

* Do you design energy-efficient buildings that are socially responsible by conserving and protecting the natural environment?

* Do you specialize in creativity?

* Do you have relationships with specialized disciplines, suppliers, tradespeople, or craftspeople?

* Are your business operations green?

* Are you known for being an innovator?

* Do you want to emphasize your business's philanthropic activities?

* Do you view diversity as strength?

Figure 10.2 A business plan includes a description of the design firm's niche. For example, Perkins + Will promote their sustainable design services as evidenced by the announcement of its 100th LEED certified building, *Dockside Green*, a mixed-use residential and commercial real estate development in Victoria, British Columbia, Canada.

Dockside Green was awarded LEED Platinum certification by the Canada Green Building Council (CaGBC). (© *John Scratchley*)

To reiterate: Demonstrate how your products and services are needed for your market, and surpass those of the competition.

Another consideration related to services and products that should be included in a business plan is how you intend to adjust to changes in the future. What type of services and products will you provide if there is a global economic boom or if the needs of your market change? What are your expansion plans? Do you foresee expanding your services to another type of building or opening international offices? What is required to enable you to expand? Would you require a certain dollar amount in design fees or a particular number of design staff?

Identifying approaches to future situations demonstrates you are knowledgeable about the inevitable ups and downs of business ownership and are prepared to ensure the success of your business by minimizing any threats while maximizing opportunities.

Business Profiles

An excellent way to summarize your business, including its services and products, is to compose a **business profile**, or what has been referred to as the "elevator pitch" (so named because you should be able to state your profile during a one-to-two minute elevator ride). Your business profile should be included in the business plan and can also be used for marketing materials.

Similar to the professional profile described in Chapter 3, a business profile should provide a summary of your business (Box 10.2). In approximately 250 words a business profile should identify: (1) historical details—years of experience, number of clients, client profile, amount of revenues, and type of buildings; (2) design philosophy, beliefs, and values related to client relationships, design process, built environment, and solving problems; and (3) business philosophy, beliefs and values related to the community, environment, global affairs, and social responsibility.

Location

The type of business, services, and products you intend to provide are important factors when you identify a location. Options include having a professional studio in your home, commercial office space, or a space in an executive office complex. A business could also be located in a retail space or exist solely online as previously discussed. A key consideration in determining

---

Box 10.2
Summary of a Design Firm's Business

LOCUS Architecture is committed to providing clients with innovative design solutions for particular projects that result from a highly investigative design process, a studied analysis of traditional and unconventional construction methods, and an ongoing commitment to researching sustainable technologies and resource-efficient construction methods.

Each of our projects strives to enrich one's experience of space, light, context, materials, and craftsmanship through the experience of architecture. It is our belief that exemplary architecture not only provides functional space, but acts as a lens through which we view, understand, and appreciate the natural and man-made world. In this way, architecture can offer order, beauty, and inspiration. Architecture, as we view it, is art.

It is our belief that architecture should be harmoniously linked to microclimate, context, and both local and global sites. As a result, we promote the sale and use of local building materials, employ energy- and resource-efficient design strategies, and actively practice "green" architecture. In conjunction with these aims, we produce designs which are bold and unique to each client and site.

Collectively, we have over 50 years of on-site construction experience and over 20 years of construction observation experience to back our design efforts. Our methods and practices are tested and reviewed on site where their performance can be evaluated. In this way, we can provide inventive and creative designs for environmentally and socially responsible residential, commercial and public projects.

At LOCUS we deliver a unique and personal product. Although projects range from new construction at the civic scale to the smallest residential remodels, each design opportunity brings creative potential. LOCUS Architecture's strength is transforming this potential into reality.

Source: Reprinted from http://www.locusarchitecture.com/about_us/mission.html. Accessed 2011.

the location is how you plan to work with your clients. For example:

* Are you planning to nearly always go to the client's home or place of business?

* Are there times when you want the client to come to your studio?

* Are you hoping to get new clients from walk-ins?

* Do you only want to have a virtual business?

As discussed in the next sections of this chapter, other considerations related to determining a location include **zoning ordinances**, taxes, insurance, rent, property lease terms, and real estate prices.

Location: Home-Based Business

A home-based business is a *possibility* when you anticipate that nearly all of your contacts with clients will be scheduled at their home or their place of business. Many designers start a business in their home because activities are initially part-time, and they can begin without the expense or commitment of leasing or buying commercial office space. However, it is important to separate professional and personal responsibilities—a task that can be challenging in the home setting.

Note the word "possibility" in the first sentence of the previous paragraph. Depending on your local zoning ordinances, you might not be able to have a home-based business. You must engage in **due diligence** by researching local zoning ordinances as well as any restrictions or **covenants** prescribed by homeowners' associations.

City and county zoning ordinances stipulate land use practices, and you must comply with current **municipal codes**. The codes may or may not allow nonresidential uses; this depends on the activities required for the business. Counties and cities are generally concerned about home-based businesses that involve considerable parking, customer traffic, large deliveries, noise, bright lights, and exterior signs.

Code information is posted on city websites under titles such as "zoning ordinances,"
"municipal code," or "inspections and planning department." Typically, codes classify uses according to "permitted by-right," "special use approval required," "planned development approval required," and "not allowed."

"R" is usually the designated code for residential districts, including single-unit detached houses on individual lots, and multi-unit buildings with designated densities and the scale (size and mass) of buildings.

What if the local municipal code does not allow a home-based business? You may be able to apply for a **special use permit** or **zoning variance**. Special use permits are allowed on a case-by-case basis. Procedures include submitting an application and having the request reviewed by the local zoning board of appeals. If the permit is denied, you can submit an appeal.

Location: Commercial and Retail Businesses

Usually designers move their business from their home to a commercial building when more space is needed, they want to attract new business, or they want to present a more professional image. Moving to a commercial site is also an excellent way to separate professional and personal responsibilities when this has become an issue. From a different perspective, some designers start their business in a commercial building and never have a home-based business.

As with residential codes, city and county zoning ordinances also apply to commercial office space and retail businesses. "B" and "C" are the designated codes for business and commercial districts, respectively. Complying with municipal codes is the first consideration when you are searching for a location, followed by many other factors, such as:

* Is it important that your clients can get to the business easily? If yes, is the area safe and will it continue to be in the near future?

* To encourage sustainable practices, can you, your clients, and employees use public transportation? If not, can people drive to the location with ease and is there adequate and convenient parking?

- Do you need excellent visibility to encourage walk-ins? If yes, is the location in an area where your potential clients visit?

- Do you want to find a location close to trade showrooms so it is easier to search for samples?

- Do you want to find a location that is close to trade showrooms to make it convenient to bring a client to a showroom while he or she is visiting your business?

- For visibility or collaborative purposes do you want to be in an area with other design firms?

After determining an area for your business, other factors to consider are the type of building, square footage requirements, and whether you plan to rent or buy the property. The type of building and the interior architecture should reflect your brand. For example, a business specializing in historic preservation should be located in a building that has historical relevance.

Design studios need space for basic business operations as well as design-related activities (Figure 10.3). For example, items and spaces can include computers, printers, office furniture, file cabinets, supplies, equipment, **inventory**, area for meetings/presentations, space for an office manager/receptionist, and a sample library.

The size of the sample library depends on your firm's range of products and the business's proximity to trade showrooms. Design firms with comprehensive product lines and long distances from showrooms require ample space for the sample library (e.g., material samples/books and manufacturers' brochures/catalogues/binders/tearsheets).

A new business might not be able to afford a full-time office manager or receptionist. In these situations a designer might look for an executive office complex that includes a full-time receptionist and other amenities associated with an office, such as a lobby, conference space, public restrooms, storage facilities, and break rooms.

A retail-based business needs considerable space for displays, and ideally a storage area for inventory and client purchases. Space is required to facilitate sales transactions and retail operations also need staff and adequate security. Conveniently located loading docks are necessary for businesses that display large quantities of furniture or allow customers to pick-up their merchandise.

Location Contractual Arrangements: Buy or Rent?

Often the answer to this question is easy when starting a new business. Due to finances, many new businesses rent rather than buy the property. Not only is it expensive to buy a building, the monthly payments, taxes, and insurance reduce your cash flow. Regardless of whether you are buying or renting, many factors must be considered when you are searching for the ideal location. For example:

- What is the condition of the building?

- How much are the utilities?

- How much is insurance?

- How much are the property taxes?

- How is the building maintained and at what cost?

Figure 10.3 Regardless of whether you are buying or renting, many factors must be considered when searching for the ideal location for a design firm, including adequate space for a library, equipment, work areas, and storage. (© Beau Lark/Corbis)

- How much is the deposit?

- How much are the parking fees?

When renting a building or space some of the charges mentioned above are included with the monthly rent. But, you must understand what you are financially responsible for as well as other terms in the property lease, such as:

- How much is the rent and predetermined **escalations** or increases?

- How long is the lease and what are the conditions for renewals?

- Is it possible to buy the property at a later date?

- What are the sublease provisions?

- Will the landlord pay for renovations?

- Can there be a reduction in the rent if you pay for renovations?

- What are the conditions for termination by you or the landlord?

Writing the Business Plan: Market Analysis and Competition

Whether you're starting a virtual or **brick-and-mortar business**, your business plan must include an analysis of the market and the competition. This section reviews the elements related to **marketing** that are important to include in a business plan. (Chapter 13 provides the details for developing a comprehensive plan for marketing, branding, **advertising**, and **public relations** with an emphasis on expanding your business.)

What is marketing? Marketing is a common term that is often misunderstood and frequently confused with advertising. According to the American Marketing Association (AMA), marketing is "... an organizational function and a set of processes for creating, communicating, and delivering value to customers and for managing customer relationships in ways that benefit the organization and its stakeholders" (AMA 2011).

The AMA defines advertising as "The placement of announcements and persuasive messages in time or space purchased in any of the mass media by business firms, nonprofit organizations, government agencies, and individuals who seek to inform and/or persuade members of a particular target market or audience about their products, services, organizations, or ideas" (2011).

As the definitions indicate, there is quite a distinction between marketing and advertising. These distinctions are applied to the discussions in this chapter as well as marketing-related information presented in the next chapters. For example, in analyzing the two definitions, you might notice that marketing is important for establishing a new business, but advertising could be viewed as a strategy explored and executed when a firm has the resources to purchase time or space. Thus, first versions of a business plan tend to focus on marketing and deemphasize advertising.

The overall goal for the marketing section of the business plan is to demonstrate your knowledge of (1) the interior design industry, (2) the target market, (3) the competition, and (4) marketing strategies.

Marketing: Interior Design Industry Knowledge

To demonstrate your knowledge of the interior design industry, you should describe the current state of the profession, and how global events and conditions are affecting business. Because the reader might not be knowledgeable about the interior design profession, provide an overview of the profession by describing interior design firms, services, types of products specified, salary ranges, professional organizations, social media applications, and legislation (see Chapters 1 and 2).

The "purchasing power" of interior designers should be emphasized, because "designers specify about 80 percent of all products purchased in the A&D [Art and Design] industry" (ASID 2010). Use the client relationship cycle (CRC) to explain how interior designers obtain and retain clients, focusing on the importance of loyal clients, networking, reputation, referrals, and securing relationships with existing clients while pursuing prospects (see Chapter 7).

Data related to the interior design industry can be obtained by contacting professional design organizations and reading trade journals.

For example, *Interior Design* magazine annually profiles the "Top 100 Interior Design Giants," "Jolly Green Giants," "Healthcare Giants," and "Hospitality Giants." An article in *Interior Design* magazine, "Universe Study of the Interior Design Profession," provides a summary of the global interior design profession (Box 10.3).

Box 10.3
Summary of the 2009 Survey, "Universe Study of the Interior Design Profession"*

Profile of Interior Designers in the Universe

- Number of Interior Designers—87,502
- Number of Design Firms—25,248
  - Interiors Firms—84%
  - Architecture Firms—15%
  - Office Furniture Dealers—1%
- Design firms specify products worth $46.25 billion per year
- On average, designers have 15 years of experience—41% have 20 or more years of experience
- Fee-per-hour the most popular method to bill clients—66%
- Approximately 65% of a designer's time is billable

Time Spent on Weekly Activities

- Working on drawings and designing—22%
- Meeting with clients and end users—16%
- Specifying products—14%
- Researching products on the Internet—11%
- Preparing presentations—9%
- Meeting with project team—9%

- Meeting with vendors—7%
- Researching products in the library—5%
- Meeting with consultants—5%
- Other—2%

Top Three Favorite Work Activities

- Meeting with clients and end users—34%
- Working on drawings and designing—19%
- Specifying products—15%

Perceived Strengths of a Successful Firm

- Acquiring clients—73%
- Fostering innovation –53%
- Diversifying/Creating business—44%
- Marketing—42%
- Charging appropriate fees—38%
- Recruiting/retaining staff—34%
- Other—3%

*Adapted from Interior Design. 2010. *Universe Study of the Interior Design Profession*. http://www.interiordesign.net/slideshow/1422-The_Universe_Study_Profile.php?photoId=319742&photoUrl=/photo/319/319742-35746.gif. Retrieved March 26, 2011.

Figure 10.4 Industry awards provide information about the profession, such as *Architectural Record*'s "Good Design is Good Business Awards." In 2011, one of the winners was the Trumpf Campus project in Stuttgart, Germany, designed by Barkow Leibinger in Berlin.

To help Trumpf GmbH & Company achieve its goals, the buildings were designed with energy-saving technologies, and workplaces were created to instill pride in employees, improve performance, and attract as well as retain the best talent (Lentz 2011). (© *Christian Richters/VIEW*)

The online survey involved 40,000 design industry professionals, resulting in "3,527 qualified respondents who work on interiors projects and specify design products" (Interior Design 2010).

Industry awards can also provide details about the profession, such as *Architectural Record*'s "Good Design is Good Business Awards," which acknowledges designs that help businesses reach their goals (Figure 10.4).

Other sources of information include the U.S. Census Bureau (http://www.census.gov/), the U.S. Bureau of Labor Statistics (BLS; http://www.bls.gov/), the U.S. Equal Employment Opportunity Commission (EEOC; http://www.eeoc.gov/), the Pew Research Center (http://pewresearch.org/), Service Canada (http://www.servicecanada.gc.ca), and *Statistics on Canadian Industries and Products* (http://www.canadabusiness.mb.ca/).

Comprehensive salary data can be found at Salary.com (http://www.salary.com/) and an excellent source for commercial information and business records is Dun & Bradstreet (D&B; http://www.dnb.com/).

Many of these sources also provide excellent information about how events and conditions affect the interior design profession. For example, the results in "Universe Study of the Interior Design Profession" also included the top issues facing designers at the end of 2009: (1) how the economic downturn was the primary cause for shifting business practices, (2) acquiring new business, (3) challenges associated with acquiring new clients, and (4) getting clients to understand design value and to pay what it is worth.

From a different perspective, after Japan's devastating earthquake and tsunami in 2011, D&B posted a free search tool that let users connect with businesses that were potentially impacted by the natural disasters.

These examples demonstrate that the profession can be affected by a variety of situations, including economic circumstances, social attitudes, the environment, and natural disasters. Other issues and concerns that can impact the field include sustainability, technology, terrorism, fires, energy crises, homeland security, generational trends, digital communities, and new regulations. The goal is to outline the critical global events and conditions that affect the interior design profession as well as your business.

An event can also be the stimulus for your business to provide a unique service. For instance, during the initial years of implementing the ADA (Americans with Disabilities Act) regulations, a design firm with expertise in this area could offer a specialized service. Of course, today ADA requirements are integrated into the design process. Thus, a niche can become mainstream, and your business plan must reflect your awareness of the situation and how you plan to adjust to future changes.

Marketing: Target Market Knowledge

A profile of the interior design industry provides the background for a description of your **target market**. The explanation often includes a general profile of the market and a specific targeted market. A profile of the general market can also help to reveal prospective clients. For example, your **general market** could be potential clients who own residences worth over $500,000 and your targeted market could be people who want their kitchen remodeled.

Thus, to demonstrate knowledge of your market you should describe characteristics of your prospective as well as existing clients. Descriptions should include **demographics**, such as age, gender, employment, income, education, family life cycle, and location (this information can be gleaned from government sources listed above).

Local Chamber of Commerce and SBA offices can often help with data gathering. Other resources for statistics include MarketResearch. com (http://www.marketresearch.com/), the Economics and Statistics Administration (ESA; http://www.esa.doc.gov/), and the BLS for information on employment, income, and earnings.

A profile of clients should also include **psychographics**, such as their lifestyle, behavioral patterns, and **AIO (attitudes, interests, and opinions)**. What type of services do they need? The description should outline their design-related needs and how your business can fulfill those needs. For example:

- Do they need planning, sustainability, product design, architecture, lighting design, engineering, or consulting? Which services will you provide?

- Do you have a niche, such as expertise in international design services or sustainable design?

Design-related problems also should be identified and how your services and products can solve these problems. For example, is the problem renovating a historical building, conserving energy, or acquiring LEED certification? How can your business solve these problems?

Focus on *why* clients want to hire you to fulfill their needs and solve their problems. Is the demand for your unique services increasing or decreasing? For a business to succeed there must be an increase in demand. As you are developing your business plan, if you discover that statistical data indicate a decrease in demand, you should reconsider how you want to approach your new business.

In your explanation of why clients would want to hire your design firm, include a description of how you became involved with your existing clients and if that approach could be successful with prospective clients. For example, if you acquired clients because they were attracted to the reputation of your employer's firm, it could be difficult to attract new clients. If, however, the majority of your existing clients were from referrals, then it can be assumed that your client base will continue to grow after you start your own business.

Marketing: Competition Knowledge

Depending on the circumstances, your previous employer could be your biggest competitor. If this is the situation, how can you differentiate your design services from this firm as well as other design firms in the area? Moreover, in the future you might be competing regionally, nationally, and globally.

To demonstrate that your business's services surpass those of other design firms, you must provide a comparative analysis of your competition. Identify design firms in your area offering similar services and products. To ensure a complete list you can search the online local Yellow Pages, contact the Chamber of Commerce, and ask the people in your networks.

Research each firm to determine: (1) philosophy, values, and leadership; (2) services, products, and types of buildings; (3) areas of expertise, work style, and years in business; (4) fee rates and billing methods; (5) clients and location of their projects; (6) publications, press releases, and awards; (7) size of the firm and number/location of offices; and (8) if possible, comments from clients, end users, and professionals who have worked with the firm.

Fortunately, a great deal of this type of information is usually available on a design firm's website, but keep in mind that facts might be outdated and negative situations will be absent. This is when your networks as well as any published articles can be very helpful.

How do your competitions' characteristics impact your business? If there are numerous design firms specializing in your area of expertise, how can you carve a niche in that specialty that is either unique or surpasses their operations? Based on the needs and problems of your targeted market, how can you provide better services and products than the competition? This is known as **market positioning**. Your business plan should have answers to all the questions posed here.

Marketing: Marketing Strategy Knowledge

Creating a business that will be prosperous requires a marketing strategy that gives you credibility, visibility, and networking opportunities. You must have a plan for how you will retain existing clients and acquire new clients. Central to the business plan is strategizing ways to establish long-term relationships with loyal clients.

Chapter 7 outlined several ways to nurture existing clients and to reach prospective clients when you are a design firm employee. These approaches are important for client relations; however, there are additional considerations when you are establishing your own business, such as finding the money and the time to implement a marketing plan—a challenging task when new owners typically have limited funds and could be the only employee. This section introduces market strategies for the purpose of

developing the first business plan—specifics regarding creating strategic marketing programs are reviewed in Chapter 13.

The results of your market research described in the previous sections are used to create marketing strategies. Thus, information pertaining to the interior design industry, global conditions, economic conditions, target market profiles, and your competition is the basis for your marketing strategies.

Fundamentally, marketing strategies are developed according to your target market and the basic **Four P's** of marketing: product, price, promotion, and place (distribution). Another term for the Four P's is **marketing mix**.

The marketing strategy in your business plan should: (1) identify clients needing your products/services rather than your competitors', (2) develop products/services addressing the needs of your targeted clients as well as exceeding competitors' products/services (Product), (3) create a design services fee and compensation schedule that your targeted clients perceive as both fair and a better value than your competitors (Price), (4) promote your products/services directly to your targeted clients and demonstrate how your firm can address their needs better than your competitors (Promotion), and (5) determine ways of distributing your products/services that are convenient for your targeted clients (Place).

As you are developing your marketing strategies, note the importance of differentiating your products/services, fees (price), and promotions from those of your competitors. You must demonstrate why your targeted clients will hire your firm rather than your competitors. In addition, your marketing strategies must be unified. For example, your design fees should be appropriate for the products and services you are providing, and your promotions must accurately portray your products/services.

In addition to identifying your marketing strategies, your business plan should address issues that are critical to successful implementation, such as ambitious timelines, marketing budgets, and long-term strategic marketing considerations. Timelines that outline how you plan to immediately initiate your marketing strategies demonstrate that you understand the importance of acquiring new clients. Your intent to actually implement marketing strategies can be demonstrated by specifying a marketing budget—often a percentage of your gross income.

Outlining an ambitious plan for time and resources must be accompanied with long-term planning. How do you plan to sustain marketing strategies that will continue to differentiate your firm from your competitors in the minds of your targeted clients? The proposed long-term initiatives might never come to fruition, but the reader of your business plan will take note that you consider your new business an ongoing endeavor.

Checking for Comprehension

* What would you include in a description of an interior design business?

* Identify three important things to know about a competing interior design business.

Writing the Business Plan: Management and Operations

In addition to outlining your marketing strategies in your business plan, you must provide an overview of how you intend to manage and operate your business as well as who else will be involved in managing the firm, employees, and perhaps an advisory board.

Other requirements associated with starting a new business—discussed in this section—can include registrations, filing fees, licenses, permits, tax identification number, and insurance. Your business plan should specify the requirements based on city, county, state, and federal regulations. If you work on projects in other jurisdictions, you must make sure you are also in compliance with those regulations, such as earthquake codes in California.

As a caveat to the following "Business Structures" sections (as well as the legal sections below), the information here is presented to provide an overview of legal requirements. Because of the differences in the requirements, you must contact your local jurisdictions to obtain specific information. Moreover, when you are deciding on a business structure, you should review your options with an attorney and an accountant.

Business Structures

One of the first decisions you will have to make is the business structure and the name of your business. There are advantages and disadvantages to each type of business structure, and many of the differences center on legal issues, finances, and taxes. For example, limited partnerships, corporations, and LLCs must file organizational documents with the appropriate government agency, usually the office of the Secretary of State. The type of business structure can also affect your time, **expenses**, management abilities, and the permanence of the business.

The major types of business structures include sole proprietorship, **partnership (general** and **limited)**, corporation, **limited liability company (LLC)**, and **S corporation**. Interior designers often create the business as a sole proprietorship or partnership when starting out, but as a business grows, owners might elect to establish a corporation. Regardless of the business structure, separate personal and business records, accounts, and transactions.

Business Structures: Sole Proprietorship

A sole proprietorship or an unincorporated business is very easy to form because it does not require legal paperwork or filing fees. Thus, a sole proprietorship requires very little time and expense. Another advantage of a sole proprietorship is the ability to make all decisions related to the business because you are the only owner.

Sole proprietorship might be easy to establish, but this type of business structure does have disadvantages that can affect your business as well as your personal life (Figure 10.5). One of

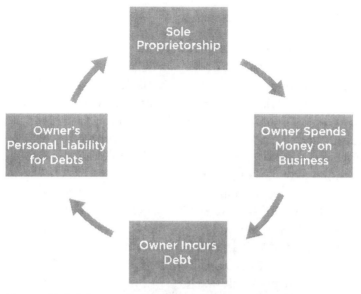

Figure 10.5 Sole proprietorships might be easy to establish, but this type of business structure does have disadvantages that can affect your business as well as your personal life. As a sole proprietor you are legally liable for any debts, actions, and decisions associated with the business.

the most important issues is liability. As the sole proprietor, you are legally liable for any debts, actions, and decisions associated with the business. Thus, your personal assets can be used to satisfy creditors. The liability issue can also affect your ability to establish credit and obtain loans. Some owners purchase insurance to help protect their assets (see the "Management and Operations" section).

Sole proprietorship also affects your state and federal income tax returns. The Internal Revenue Service (IRS) uses **pass-through taxation** for this type of business structure (for details, see http://www.irs.gov/). Under this arrangement any profits or losses associated with the business are reported on your personal income tax returns. In addition, when operating a sole proprietorship, the business ceases to exist when the owner is no longer involved with the business.

Business Structures: Partnership (General and Limited)

When there is more than one owner, a sole proprietorship can become a partnership. Partners contribute to the business by providing something of value, such as money, labor, skills, or a clientele base. As is the case with a sole proprietorship, a partnership is fairly easy to form. However, it is important to develop a written agreement with all partners.

The agreement should delineate how the partnership will operate, including decision-making policies, capital requirements, work responsibilities, profits/losses distributions, and terms of dissolution. For example:

- Do all partners have to agree when deciding to spend money, or is one person responsible for expenses?

- Do all partners make equal financial contributions to the business, or are the amounts prorated based on alternative contributions, such as a partner's specialized skill or another's considerable clientele?

- How will the work be distributed?

- Who will manage finances, records, or employees?

- How will profits and losses be distributed among the partners?

- If a partner wants to leave the partnership, what happens to the business—will the business continue or be dissolved, and if so, under what terms?

These questions are just a few examples of issues that you must thoroughly address before committing to a partnership.

A partnership can be advantageous when two or more people combine their skills and experiences for the benefit of one firm. But the arrangement can fall apart when the partners are not able to work together on a daily basis and can't agree on how money should be spent or invested. Thus, developing a partnership agreement could take considerable time, and if the document is not agreeable to the parties, that could be a red flag about the partnership.

Decision-making responsibilities could be determined by creating a general or limited partnership. A general partnership is as described previously—management decisions are determined by the details in the agreement.

A limited partnership involves at least one general partner; the limited partner often becomes involved as an investor of the business but is not involved with decisions or the management of the business. Limited partnerships file organizational documents with the appropriate authorities, usually the office of the Secretary of State.

A partnership might be convenient, but as with a sole proprietorship, there are disadvantages, such as personal liability and pass-through taxation. In a general partnership, you are legally liable for all debts, actions, and decisions made by you as well as your partner. Again, your personal *assets* can be used to satisfy creditors. But the personal liability of a limited partner is restricted to the amount of his or her investment.

As with a sole proprietorship, the IRS requires pass-through taxation for partnerships. The partnership agreement can stipulate how new partners can be added to the business as well as the terms of the partnership's dissolution, including buy-out conditions.

Business Structures: Corporations

To avoid personal liability, owners often elect to form a corporation—a separate legal entity owned by **shareholders**. Unlike the sole proprietorship and partnership, a corporation is complicated and expensive to both form and maintain. This business structure requires considerable administrative work that includes legal counsel, special registrations, **articles of incorporation**, stockholders, **stock offerings**, **stock options**, a board of directors, annual shareholder meetings, and corporate taxation. As with all business structures, legal requirements are defined by government agencies at the local, state, and federal levels.

Items that a government agency could require in the articles of incorporation include the purpose of the corporation, authorized shares, estimated gross amount of business income for a given year, and the names of its directors. Generally, a board of directors establishes a corporation's policies and strategic direction.

As a separate entity, a corporation conducts business, realizes losses, and is taxed on its profits rather than the owners. What is known as a **double tax** occurs when the corporation pays an additional tax on the dividends it pays to its shareholders.

Regular or **C corporations** pay double taxes, but an S corporation has pass-through taxation, whereby the profits are paid by the owners. According to the IRS, S corporations are entities "that elect to pass corporate income, losses, deductions and credit through to their shareholders for federal tax purposes" (IRS 2011).

In addition to limited personal liability, this type of business structure does feature some other advantages. For example, the ability to sell stock is an excellent way to acquire capital for business operations, and the availability of stock options can attract talented employees to your business. Furthermore, it is easier for a corporation to establish credit and acquire loans. One more advantage: The business continues to exist even after the death of its founder.

Business Structures: Limited Liability Company (LLC)

A limited liability company (LLC) is a business structure that combines elements of a corporation with a partnership. Thus, an LLC has limited personal liability as with a corporation, but pass-through taxation as with a partnership. The owners of an LLC are referred to as "members," and depending on state legislation, members can include individuals, corporations, and foreign entities.

As is the case with a partnership, members rather than shareholders are responsible for the management of the LLC. This translates to fewer administrative expenses, such as record keeping, stockholders, stocks, and annual shareholders' meetings. In addition, the members are able to determine the distribution of profits and losses.

An LLC must file **articles of organization** with its Secretary of State's office. Generally, information that must be provided for the articles of organization includes the location of the business, the purpose for organizing the LLC, and names and addresses of managers and members.

The form used to file the articles of organization might request a date of dissolution when appropriate. This illustrates one of the potential disadvantages of an LLC—again depending on the state. Some states have declared that an LLC must be dissolved when a member is no longer involved with the business.

Legal Requirements: Business Name and Registrations

Obviously, you must also decide on a name for your business. This is often the name of the founder(s)/owner(s), such as Gensler or Perkins + Will. Frequently the first initial of the last name of each partner becomes the name of the design firm as in RTKL (Archibald Rogers, Francis Taliaferro, George Kostritsky, and Charles Lamb).

Using initials for the name of the firm makes it easy to add another initial when a partner joins, for example, Rogers and Taliaferro were the first two partners in 1946 (Figure 10.6). In addition, a short name can be simple to remember and stylized to reflect the firm's brand.

Using your name or initials can make it easier to create a business name that does not already exist. However, to ensure that the proposed name of your business is not being used by others in the vicinity of your business and is not a trademark, you must research your proposed name to avoid potential litigations involving false claims. Generally, you can find this information by Googling the name and examining resources, such as business directories, phone books, registered trademarks (U.S. Patent and Trademark Office (USPTO; see http://www.uspto.gov/), and unregistered trademarks (see The Thomas Register; http://www. thomasnet.com/). Other sources are the local County Clerk's office and the Business Services

Figure 10.6 Along with the business structure, you must decide on a name for your business. Often the first initial of the last name of each partner becomes the name of the design firm, as in RTKL (Archibald Rogers, Francis Taliaferro, George Kostritsky, and Charles Lamb). The firm started with Rogers and Taliaferro in 1946.

Currently, RTKL is a global architecture, design, and planning firm. An example of its work is the Shanghai Science and Technology Museum in Shanghai, China. (© Tim Griffith)

Department of a Secretary of State's office. Generally, these two offices can also help you register your business name. You might want to trademark your name by completing the registration (®) process with the Trademark Office of the USPTO (http://www.uspto.gov/).

If you are not using your personal name, then you must register the assumed name—also referred to as the **Doing Business As (DBA)** name. Registration is legally required to conduct business with a different name. Each state has different protocols for handling DBAs; therefore, you need to contact your state office for proper filing procedures. Often the requirements are determined by the business structure.

Once you are confident your proposed name can be used for your business, you must contact agencies, such as the County Clerk and Secretary of State, to register both the business name and the business. Registration generally involves completing a form and paying filing fees.

Legal Requirements: Taxes

Another important registration is required by the IRS. To identify a business entity, the IRS uses an **Employer Identification Number (EIN)**—also known as the Federal Tax Identification Number. To determine whether or not your business must have an EIN, refer to the IRS Business Department on its website (http://www.irs.gov/). To apply for the EIN, you can go to the IRS website and complete the online form or the process can be done by phone, fax, or mail.

You also must register the business with your state and local revenue agencies. Generally, information required for a state's department of revenue's registration form includes an EIN, type of business structure, name(s) of owners/officers, and a description of the business activity (employees, sales, services, rent, and utilities).

Once approved, the state issues a **tax registration certificate** and taxpayer ID (your tax number). Your business is assigned a category and its respective tax rate. There also could be departments in a city or county that require

businesses to pay additional taxes, such as mass transit district taxes or a water commission tax.

In addition to a tax registration certificate, most states require a **seller's permit**, which requires a business to collect state *and* local taxes for merchandise sold to consumers. State and local tax agencies are generally housed in a Department of Revenue or Department of Taxation/Finance.

According to the IRS, taxes associated with businesses are classified into four areas: (1) income tax, (2) self-employment tax, (3) employment taxes, and (4) excise tax. The IRS requires that "all businesses except partnerships must file an annual income tax return. Partnerships file an information return" (IRS 2011). However, there are specific forms for each business structure. Federal taxes are a "pay-as-you-go" tax: Taxes must be paid as you earn the income.

The IRS describes the self-employment (SE) tax as "a social security and Medicare tax primarily for people who work for themselves" (IRS 2011).

Employment taxes are required when you have employees and include: (1) federal income tax, (2) Social Security and Medicare taxes, and (3) federal unemployment (FUTA) tax (IRS, 2011) (see Chapter 14). Employers must file appropriate forms and pay according to IRS requirements.

Payments and forms also are required for the excise tax depending on certain activities, such as the manufacture or sale of certain products, such as alcohol, cigarettes, and gasoline.

Legal Requirements: Licenses and Permits

All states and most local government agencies require businesses to have a license. Depending on the jurisdiction, you might also need permits. There are different license and permit requirements at the federal, state, county, and local levels.

This section therefore provides an overview of business licenses and permits, but you must contact state agencies for specific information. If you intend to work on a project in a different state, you must comply with that state's regulations as well.

As reviewed in Chapter 1, depending on the location of your business and where you practice, some states have professional regulations for interior designers, which include licensure and registration. For information as well as the rules and license application form, contact the state office responsible for professional regulations. And when you are working with other professionals who must be licensed, such as electricians and architects, you must be certain they have the license required for the jurisdiction.

In addition to professional regulations, some municipalities require zoning and local permits for certain businesses. In addition to meeting zoning requirements, local laws might require permits issued by governmental agencies, such as building inspectors and fire departments. Information on these issues can generally be obtained from the county clerk or a department of finance/taxation.

Management and Operations

A *Management and Operations* section in an initial business plan for an interior design firm is usually straightforward because most often the business is started with very few employees. Thus, the owner can easily identify who is involved with the firm and their roles and responsibilities. A typical organizational chart delineating reporting lines and divisions is unnecessary. However, personal profiles as well as how business transactions and records will be managed should be included in every business plan.

The Management and Operations section for starting a business should have a profile of the owner that focuses on items included in a résumé and design portfolio, such as professional experience, skills, expertise, responsibilities, education, and projects.

When more than one owner is involved with the business, there should be a description of how the background and skills of the individuals bring synergy to the firm and how the work,

hours, finances, salaries, benefits, profits, and losses will be handled on a weekly or monthly basis. When relevant, indicate the percentages of ownership.

A business plan also should include the personal profiles of your advisory board members. An advisory board includes professionals who have provided and will continue to provide you with legal and financial advice, such as attorneys, accountants, bankers, real estate agents, and insurance brokers. Their profiles should include the name of their business, position, years of experience, professional highlights, educational background, and role in the success of your business.

A very important consideration is who will handle the day-to-day operations, such as answering phone calls, e-mails, processing payroll, signing contracts, writing purchase orders, sending invoices, paying bills, hiring installers, responding to vendor inquiries, and arranging deliveries. Do you plan to hire a bookkeeper, office manager, designers, or assistants?

Your business plan should include a job description for new hires and include their roles, responsibilities, and salary information. The plan also could include employee screening protocols, benefits, and an employee handbook (see Chapter 14). This information, as well as job descriptions, résumés, and portfolios, should be included in the appendix of the business plan.

Management and Operations: Business Insurance

There are several different types of insurance for interior designers, including **professional liability (errors and omissions) insurance, commercial general liability (CGL) insurance, product liability insurance, business interruption/continuation insurance, key person insurance, commercial property insurance**, and **home-based business insurance**.

Generally, states do not require liability or property insurance for your business, but having business insurance is highly recommended. Moreover, states mandate liability insurance for vehicles, and lenders and investors might require business insurance.

In differing from liability and property insurance requirements, according to state and federal laws, businesses with employees must have **workers' compensation insurance, unemployment insurance**, and possibly **disability insurance**, depending on state regulations (see Chapter 14). In addition, insurance usually is required when you work on a project for a government agency.

As illustrated with the long list described above, determining your insurance coverage can be daunting—as well as potentially expensive. A good way to start is to locate an **insurance broker** who has experience working with interior design businesses. An insurance broker represents you when searching for insurance policies. An **insurance agent** is a representative from an insurance company or companies and should be licensed by the state.

Discussions with an insurance broker should focus on a description of your business, including the type of products and services. In addition, review your inventory of business **assets**, such as furniture, equipment, computers, merchandise, material samples, and items owned by clients that are stored in your facilities. For example, a client's sofa could be in your building for reupholstery work.

The inventory should also include items owned by the business but are not at the premises of the business. Examples could include material samples at a client's office, an oriental rug that is in client's home on a trial basis, or materials at a craftsperson's studio.

The goal of the discussion is to provide the information so that the insurance broker can recommend the insurance and the coverage that will protect you and your business for a reasonable price. Insurance **premiums** are correlated with the amount of **deductibles**. Thus, premiums tend to be the high when the deductibles are low and vice versa—premiums tend to be low when the deductibles are high. Low premiums can help your monthly cash flow, but keep

in mind that a lawsuit could require the business to pay an expensive deductible.

Even with the advice of an insurance broker, it is imperative that you thoroughly review every insurance policy and pay particular attention to: (1) what is covered, (2) what is excluded, (3) how the insurer defines business property, and (4) the amount of premiums, payouts, deductibles, and co-payments.

A thorough review should be done before you first purchase insurance and at various intervals after the policy is active. Periodic reviews help to ensure that your coverage is appropriate as your business changes and grows.

Note the amount the insurance company will pay to replace business property because of loss or damage. Will the insurer pay the current replacement cost or the amount you paid for the item? Are you paying several times for a specific coverage because it is included in different policies?

Keep in mind that insurance policies do not cover criminal actions or intentional acts of harm—legally, harm can include physical *and* mental injury.

Types of Business Insurance

Professional liability insurance protects you from litigious situations arising from your acts, mistakes, errors, or omissions. Examples can include errors in cost estimates, material overruns, construction delays, specifying materials that pollute indoor air quality, failing to comply with ADA regulations, or providing services beyond the state licensing requirements for interior designers.

CGL insurance protects an owner if someone is injured at his or her place of business, such as falling down the stairs. The CGL policy should also cover acts of negligence.

Injuries due to merchandise sold or specified to a client can be covered by product liability insurance.

There are also specialized types of insurance, such as business interruption/continuation insurance, which covers expenses when a business must stop operations due to some condition specified in the policy, such as an earthquake or flooding.

Another approach to continuing a business is coverage provided in a key person insurance policy. This insurance covers the death of a firm founder when that person had been essential to the success of the business. The policy provides money to conduct business operations while the remaining owners attempt to hire a replacement and/or determine the fate of the business.

States mandate vehicle liability insurance, and when the vehicle is used for business, the state might also require commercial auto insurance (see your state's Department of Motor Vehicles). When your employees use their own cars for business, such as traveling to meet with a client or visit a construction site, consider liability coverage offered by a **non-owned vehicle liability insurance**.

Commercial property insurance protects the assets of your business in the event of loss and damages due to a situation prescribed in your policy. Common events in a policy are vandalism, fires, high winds, and smoke. Not all policies include flooding, or theft, or cover damages to accounting records. Therefore, you must know what is covered in the policy and when necessary, you might want to purchase additional coverage through a **rider**.

Be aware that home-based businesses might not be covered by homeowner's insurance. Thus, to protect your business property, you might have to purchase a rider that is appended to your homeowner's insurance.

If renting a space for your business, you should have commercial property insurance for your business assets (this might be a requirement in your lease).

Writing the Business Plan: Financial Data

Insurance costs must be included with your financial information. This section reviews how to develop financial projections for your business plan and serves as a foundation for understanding accounting practices and financial management (see Chapter 12).

The financial section of your business plan should demonstrate that you have an understanding of what is required to manage the finances of your business and of basic accounting practices. This section of the plan shows that you understand your expenses and will be able to pay your bills. Considerations include **start-up costs**, the amount of money you have when you start the business, and expected income from clients.

Frequently, financial information is located toward the end of a business plan because you must first explain what you want to do before outlining expenses and income. But people most interested in the monetary aspects of the business, such as lenders and investors, will often go directly to the financial section. Thus, as the first topic that might be read, this section should be very professional in appearance, concisely written, and thorough, and it should use graphics to illustrate data. Keep in mind, financial calculations can be performed using a spreadsheet program, such as Microsoft Excel.

To understand how to conduct financial analyses, you must become familiar with basic accounting terms and their calculations. The main goal here is to determine your profit after paying all your costs. Costs are separated into variable and fixed.

Variable costs are associated with the cost of a sale, such as fees you might pay for a consultant on a project. These will vary according to the client and the project.

Fixed costs (expenses) or **overhead** do not vary month-by-month and generally include expenses such as rent and insurance.

To determine your **gross profit (gross income),** you must subtract the variable costs from the sales revenue:

Sales – Variable costs = Gross profit

The **net profit (net income)** is then calculated by subtracting the gross profit from your fixed costs:

Gross profit – Fixed costs = Net profit

Taxes are subtracted from the net profit. The finance section should begin with a written synopsis of your financial situation and projections. The description should provide an overview that includes:

1. Financial goals, such as annual growth rates and average sales-per-month in the first three years

2. Assumptions that were used to create the financial goals, such as expecting a continuous demand for your services, low operating costs, and a healthy economy

3. Business risk analysis, such as unexpected new competitors, problems collecting payments from clients, and severe spikes in the cost of materials, transportation, or equipment

4. Plan for contending with problems identified in the risk analysis

5. An analysis of your financial data and industry **benchmarks** to demonstrate that your projections are aligned with comparable design firms

Start-Up Cost Estimates and Loans

Your financial projections include your estimate of start-up costs, such as:

* Rent, security deposits, utilities, insurance, and business registration fees

* Furniture, sample books/binders, material samples, equipment, and merchandise

* Office supplies, stationery, brochures, and consultant fees (e.g., attorney, accountant, webmaster)

Try to minimize these costs because any initial expenses, such as sample books and security deposits, require cash up front. On the other hand, monthly expenses, such as rent, affect your monthly cash flow.

The start-up cost estimate should be accompanied by your start-up funding sources—potentially problematic due to banks' reluctance to loan money to new businesses.

Start-ups might qualify for a loan guaranteed by the SBA (http://www.sba.gov/content/sba-loans) and/or a Community Development Financial Institution (CDFI; http://www.cdfi-fund.gov/). However, typical sources for new businesses are personal savings and loans from family and friends (see Chapter 12 for business's loans).

Some of the start-up costs could be paid over several months, such as those for furniture or equipment. But these expenses will have to be offset with sufficient income.

To help reduce the initial costs of starting a business, some owners rent rather than buy equipment. In addition, designers can rely on memo samples rather than purchasing material books/binders. They can also minimize their inventory by taking clients to trade showrooms instead of buying furniture or accessories for their own offices.

Finances: Break-even Analysis

A **break-even analysis** illustrates at what point your expenses and income are equal—no profits or losses. To calculate this analysis, first estimate your annual sales based on your design fee schedule (see Chapter 6). Fortunately, when you have years of experience and an established clientele base, you can use these historical records as a basis for your estimate, or you can refer to industry standards.

To account for seasonal differences as well as various phases of a design process, your annual sales revenue could be estimated by calculating earnings on a month-to-month basis.

Break-even Analysis Step 1

Break-even analysis can be examined as a three-step process. As an example, the owners of XYZ Interiors are anticipating $120,000 in annual sales based on the number of clients and the average hourly billings and merchandise. XYZ Interiors expects to have 10 clients per month with average hourly billings and merchandise at $1,000 per client. Their variable costs per client are $250. The gross profit per client is $750:

$1,000   – $250   = $750
(average client   (variable   (gross profit
billing)   costs)   per client)

Break-even Analysis Step 2

A break-even analysis requires you to calculate the gross profit percentage. For XYZ Interiors this is determined by dividing the gross profit per client by the average hourly billings and merchandise:

$$\frac{\$750 \text{ (gross profit per client from step one)}}{\$1,000 \text{ (average client billing)}} = 75\% \text{ (gross profit \%)}$$

Break-even Analysis Step 3

The next step is to examine how fixed costs affect profits. Thus, you must estimate your annual fixed costs. XYZ Interiors anticipate that its fixed costs will be approximately $50,000 per year. The break-even amount is then determined by dividing the annual fixed costs by the gross profit percentage:

$$\frac{\$50,000 \text{ (estimated fixed costs)}}{.75 \text{ (gross profit \%) from step two}} = \$66,666 \text{ (break-even amount)}$$

Thus, XYZ Interiors can anticipate breaking even when sales reach $66,666 or in approximately six months with estimated annual sales of $120,000.

Finances: Forecasted Income Statements (Profit and Loss Statements)

Figures used in the break-even analysis are also used to create forecasted **income statements**, also known as **profit and loss (P&L) statements** (Table 10.2). For a new business the figures used in the income statement are projections. Existing businesses use historical financial data generally from the most recent three to five years.

Fundamentally, income statements are a summary of monthly sales, cost of sales, gross profits, fixed expenses, and net profit. A business plan could include monthly projections for the first year and then quarterly forecasts for the second and third years. For accounting purposes, negative numbers are in parentheses.

Finances: Cash Flow Forecast

A forecasted P&L statement is an excellent overview of the potential success of a business based on monthly sales revenues and fixed expenses. A **cash flow forecast** is used to project how other income sources as well as irregular expenses can affect a business on a monthly basis. Thus, financial data for a cash flow statement include monthly cash transactions: cash sales, loans, cash expended, and the amount of cash at the beginning and end of each month (Table 10.3).

Why is a cash flow forecast necessary when a net profit is projected in the P&L statement? A cash flow forecast demonstrates *when* you might need additional funds to meet your expenses in a given month. For example, even though XYZ Interiors projected a net profit at the end of the year, its cash flow forecast projects having several months without enough cash to pay expenses (Table 10.3).

Cash flow can be a significant problem when manufacturers must be paid and clients are delinquent in their payments, or designers are unable to bill clients as the result of project delays. Your cash flow forecast helps you to plan how you will have the cash to cover monthly business expenses during the first year of operation.

What are some ways to ensure enough cash to cover monthly business expenses? When you are working with projected expenses and income—as in the above XYZ Interior example—an excellent way to reduce the negative cash flow in the early months is to spend less. For a new business, areas to consider include reducing start-up costs, avoiding start-up

Table 10.2 One-Year Forecasted Income Statement (Profit and Loss Statement) for XYZ Interiors

	JAN	FEB	MAR	APRIL	MAY	JUNE	JULY	AUG	SEPT	OCT	NOV	DEC	YEAR TOTAL
SALES	$10,000	$10,000	$10,000	$10,000	$10,000	$10,000	$10,000	$10,000	$10,000	$10,000	$10,000	$10,000	$120,000
Cost of Sales	$ 2,500	$ 2,500	$ 2,500	$ 2,500	$ 2,500	$ 2,500	$ 2,500	$ 2,500	$ 2,500	$ 2,500	$ 2,500	$ 2,500	$ 30,000
Gross Profit	$ 7,500	$ 7,500	$ 7,500	$ 7,500	$ 7,500	$ 7,500	$ 7,500	$ 7,500	$ 7,500	$ 7,500	$ 7,500	$ 7,500	$ 90,000
Gross Profit %	75%	75%	75%	75%	75%	75%	75%	75%	75%	75%	75%	75%	75%
FIXED EXPENSES													
Payroll	$ 1,500	$ 1,500	$ 1,500	$ 1,500	$ 1,500	$ 1,500	$ 1,500	$ 1,500	$ 1,500	$ 1,500	$ 1,500	$ 1,500	$ 18,000
Rent	$ 1,500	$ 1,500	$ 1,500	$ 1,500	$ 1,500	$ 1,500	$ 1,500	$ 1,500	$ 1,500	$ 1,500	$ 1,500	$ 1,500	$ 18,000
Utilities	$ 500	$ 500	$ 500	$ 500	$ 500	$ 500	$ 500	$ 500	$ 500	$ 500	$ 500	$ 500	$ 6,000
Insurance	$ 500	$ 500	$ 500	$ 500	$ 500	$ 500	$ 500	$ 500	$ 500	$ 500	$ 500	$ 500	$ 6,000
Misc.	$ 200	$ 200	$ 200	$ 200	$ 200	$ 200	$ 200	$ 200	$ 200	$ 200	$ 200	$ 200	$ 2,400
Total Fixed Expenses	$ 4,200	$ 4,200	$ 4,200	$ 4,200	$ 4,200	$ 4,200	$ 4,200	$ 4,200	$ 4,200	$ 4,200	$ 4,200	$ 4,200	$ 50,400
Net Profit	$ 3,300	$ 3,300	$ 3,300	$ 3,300	$ 3,300	$ 3,300	$ 3,300	$ 3,300	$ 3,300	$ 3,300	$ 3,300	$ 3,300	$ 39,600

Table 10.3 One-Year Cash Flow Forecast for XYZ Interiors*(Note: Arrows illustrate the transfer of funds from one month to the next month.)

	JAN	FEB	MAR	APRIL	MAY	JUNE	JULY	AUG	SEPT	OCT	NOV	DEC
Beginning Cash Balance	$ 1,000	$(18,200)	$(16,400)	$(14,600)	$(11,300)	$(8,000)	$(4,700)	$(1,400)	$ 1,900	$5,200	$ 8,500	$11,800
CASH RECEIVED												
Sales/Billable Fees	$10,000	$10,000	$10,000	$10,000	$10,000	$10,000	$10,000	$10,000	$10,000	$10,000	$10,000	$10,000
Loans	$15,000	0	0	0	0	0	0	0	0	0	0	0
Receivables	0	0	$ 1,500	$ 1,500	$ 1,500	$ 1,500	$ 1,500	$ 1,500	$ 1,500	$ 1,500	$ 1,500	$ 1,500
Total Cash Inflows	$26,000	$(8,200)	$(6,400)	$ (3,100)	$ 200	$ 3,500	$ 6,800	$ 10,100	$13,400	$16,700	$20,000	$23,300
EXPENDITURES												
Start-Up Costs	$25,000	0	0	0	0	0	0	0	0	0	0	0
Product/Operation Expenses	$12,000	$ 1,000	$ 1,000	$ 1,000	$ 1,000	$ 1,000	$ 1,000	$ 1,000	$ 1,000	$ 1,000	$ 1,000	$ 1,000
Payroll	$ 1,500	$ 1,500	$ 1,500	$ 1,500	$ 1,500	$ 1,500	$ 1,500	$ 1,500	$ 1,500	$ 1,500	$ 1,500	$ 1,500
Rent	$ 1,500	$ 1,500	$ 1,500	$ 1,500	$ 1,500	$ 1,500	$ 1,500	$ 1,500	$ 1,500	$ 1,500	$ 1,500	$ 1,500
Utilities	$ 500	$ 500	$ 500	$ 500	$ 500	$ 500	$ 500	$ 500	$ 500	$ 500	$ 500	$ 500
Insurance	$ 500	$ 500	$ 500	$ 500	$ 500	$ 500	$ 500	$ 500	$ 500	$ 500	$ 500	$ 500
Misc.	$ 200	$ 200	$ 200	$ 200	$ 200	$ 200	$ 200	$ 200	$ 200	$ 200	$ 200	$ 200
Loan Payments	$ 3,000	$ 3,000	$ 3,000	$ 3,000	$ 3,000	$ 3,000	$ 3,000	$ 3,000	$ 3,000	$ 3,000	$ 3,000	$ 3,000
Total Cash Spent	$44,200	$ 8,200	$ 8,200	$ 8,200	$ 8,200	$ 8,200	$ 8,200	$ 8,200	$ 8,200	$ 8,200	$ 8,200	$ 8,200
Ending Cash Balance	$(18,200)	$(16,400)	$(14,600)	$(11,300)	$(8,000)	$(4,700)	$ (1,400)	$ 1,900	$ 5,200	$ 8,500	$11,800	$15,100

*Note: For accounting purposes, negative numbers are in parentheses.

loans, and waiting to hire employees. Note that XYZ Interiors was planning to spend $25,000 for start-up costs, an amount that significantly affected the ending cash balance for several months.

To improve the cash flow, some owners readjust the figures by increasing the projected sales for each month; this is not a sound business solution. The best solution for projecting cash flow is to forecast reasonable sales *and* to reduce your expenses.

Finances: Balance Sheet

A **balance sheet** illustrates the assets, **liabilities**, and **owner's equity (net worth)** of a business for a given period (Table 10.4). As reflected in its name, assets must be balanced with liabilities and the owner's equity. A business has current (liquid) and fixed (long-term) assets.

Current or liquid assets include cash, money in savings accounts, checking accounts, stocks, **accounts receivable**, inventory, and other items that can easily be converted into cash.

Table 10.4 One-Year Balance Sheet	
	Year 1
Current Assets	
Cash	$20,000
Accounts Receivable	$15,000
Inventory	$40,000
Total Current Assets	**$75,000**
Long-Term Assets	
Furniture and Light Fixtures	$10,000
Computers and Equipment	$ 5,000
Accumulated Depreciation	$ (500)
Total Long-Term Assets	$14,500
TOTAL ASSETS	**$89,500** **(Total Current Assets + Total Long-Term Assets)** **($75,000 + 14,500 = $89,500)**
Current Liabilities	
Accounts Payable	$20,000
Taxes	$10,000
Total Current Liabilities	**$30,000**
Long-Term Liabilities	
Bank Loans	$35,000
Total Long-Term Liabilities	$35,000
Total Liabilities	**$65,000** **(Total Current Liabilities + Total Long-Term Liabilities)** **($30,000 + $35,000 = $65,000)**
Owner's Equity (Net Worth)	
Paid-In Capital	$10,000
Retained Earnings	$14,500
Total Owner's Equity	**$24,500**
TOTAL LIABILITIES and EQUITY (NET WORTH)	**$89,500** **(Total Liabilities + Total Owner's Equity)** **($65,000 + 24,500 = $89,500)**

Note cash is a current asset.

Note furniture is a long-term asset.

Note the total asset amount is the same amount shown in the last row—total liabilities & equity.

Note taxes are a current liability.

Note loans are a long-term liability.

Accounts receivable are basically IOUs, or money that is due from clients. Inventory is considered to be items owned by the business that are for sale.

Fixed or long-term assets include items of value but typically are associated with business operations, such as a building, office furniture, and equipment. Assets that decrease in value over time, such as computers and equipment, are **depreciable assets**.

Liabilities also are categorized by whether they are current or long-term. **Current liabilities** include **accounts payable**, payroll, taxes, and short-term loans. Accounts payable is the amount owed to a creditor. **Long-term liabilities** are debts not due for an extended period, such as a mortgage.

The owner's equity includes items such as invested capital and retained earnings (money kept within a company). Note in the balance sheet example in Table 10.4 that total assets ($89,500) equal total liabilities and owner's equity ($89,500). Chapter 12 discusses financial management and accounting procedures in greater detail.

> ### Checking for Comprehension
> * What are the differences between a sole proprietorship and a corporation?
>
> * How would the owner of an interior design business use a cash flow forecast statement?

Chapter 10 begins to examine some of the requirements associated with owning and operating an interior design business. Having an overview of the requirements can help a designer decide if ownership is the most appropriate career path. Key to this understanding is developing a business plan.

Chapter 10 provided a background for exploring business policies and operations outlined in Chapters 11 and 12. Specifically, Chapter 11 examines how to operate and manage a green

business and Chapter 12 explains accounting practices, financial management, and strategic management planning.

Knowledge and Skills Summary

Highlights

* An entrepreneur is "one who organizes, manages, and assumes the risks of a business enterprise;" business is defined as a "commercial or mercantile activity engaged in as a means of livelihood" (Merriam-Webster 2011).

* There are both advantages and disadvantages to purchasing an existing interior design business.

* Many resources, including professional organizations and government agencies, are available for those wanting help to start a business.

* A business plan is a professional document describing the major considerations associated with starting or expanding a business.

* The essential elements of a business plan are (1) Description of the Business, (2) Market Analysis and Competition, (3) Management and Operations, and (4) Financial Data.

* Both virtual and brick-and-mortar businesses must include in the business plan an analysis of the market *and* the competition.

* Major types of business structures include sole proprietorship, partnership (general and limited), corporation, limited liability company (LLC), and S corporation.

* Legal requirements for a business include deciding on a name for the business, paying (and, in some cases, collecting) taxes, and obtaining the appropriate licenses and permits.

* There are several different types of insurance for an interior design business.

- Financial projections in your business plan serve as a foundation for understanding accounting practices and financial management.

- Financial data includes start-up cost estimates, break-even analysis, forecasted income statements, cash flow forecasts, and balance sheets.

Key Terms

accounts payable

accounts receivable

advertising

AIO (attitudes, interests, and opinions)

articles of incorporation

articles of organization

asset

balance sheet

benchmark

brand

break-even analysis

brick-and-mortar business

business interruption/continuation insurance

business plan

business profile

C corporation

cash flow forecast

certified public accountant (CPA)

commercial general liability (CGL) insurance

commercial property insurance

covenant

current asset (liquid asset)

current liability

deductible

demographics

depreciable asset

disability insurance

Doing Business As (DBA)

domain name

double tax

due diligence

Employer Identification Number (EIN)

entrepreneur

escalation

executive summary

expenses

fixed asset (long-term asset)

fixed cost (overhead)

Four P's (marketing mix)

general market

general partnership

gross income (gross profit)

gross profit (gross income)

home-based business insurance

income statement (profit and loss or [P&L] statement)

insurance agent

insurance broker

inventory

key person insurance

liability

limited liability company (LLC)

limited partnership

liquid asset (current asset)

loan

long-term asset (fixed asset)

long-term liability

market positioning

marketing

marketing mix (Four P's)

mission statement

municipal code

net income (net profit)

net profit (net income)

net worth (owner's equity)

non-compete clause

non-owned vehicle liability insurance

overhead (fixed cost)

owner's equity (net worth)

pass-through taxation

premium

product liability insurance

professional liability (errors and omissions) insurance

profit and loss (P&L) statement (income statement)

public relations

psychographics

revenues

rider

S corporation

search engine

seller's permit

shareholder

special use permit

start-up cost

stock offering

stock option

target market

tax registration certificate

unemployment insurance

variable cost

virtual business

web host

workers' compensation insurance

zoning ordinance

zoning variance (special use permit)

Projects

Philosophy and Design Project

Several agencies provide assistance to individuals wanting to start a new business. Some of the advice is translated into business philosophies. Research national and international business philosophies, and identify key elements that appear to be consistently included in the philosophies.

Develop two business philosophies—one for a new interior design business and another for an established interior design business. Create a collage of images that reflect your two business philosophies.

Research Project

A business plan is a professional document describing the major considerations associated with starting or expanding a business. In a team of three to five members, develop a draft of a business plan for a starting interior design business based on these four areas: (1) Description of the Business, (2) Market Analysis and Competition, (3) Management and Operations, and (4) Financial Data.

Present your team's business plan to an owner of a local business, and ask the person to evaluate the plan. Revise the business plan based on the evaluation.

Human Factors Research Project

Identify a team of five members. Your team should develop a plan to interview designers who are business owners. Your team should identify the questions, the interview format, and three to five owners of design firms. The questions should focus on the pros and cons of owning a business.

Your team should interview the owners, and compare and contrast the responses. Develop a bulleted list of your results, and include your interview questions and how this exercise influenced your thinking about owning a business.

References

American Marketing Association (AMA). 2011. *Dictionary*. http://www.marketingpower.com. Accessed March 25, 2011.

American Society of Interior Designers (ASID). 2010. *The Interior Design Profession: Facts and Figures*. Washington, DC: American Society of Interior Designers.

Federal Trade Commission (FTC). 2011. *Dot Com Disclosures: Information About Online Advertising*. Washington DC: Federal Trade Commission.

Fowler Design Associates, Inc. 2011. *Mission*. http://www.fowlerdesignassociates.com/ fowler-design/fowler-design-mission-statement.php. Accessed March 21, 2011.

Interior Design. 2010. *Universe Study of the Interior Design Profession*. http://www. interiordesign.net/slideshow/1422-The_Universe_Study_Profile. php?photoId=319742&photoUrl=/ photo/319/319742-35746.gif. Accessed March 26, 2011.

Internal Revenue Service (IRS). 2011. *Business Taxes*. http://www.irs.gov/. Accessed March 29, 2011.

Internal Revenue Service (IRS). 2011. *Selecting a Business Structure*. http://www.irs.gov/. Accessed March 31, 2011.

Lentz, L. (May 2011). "Good Design is Good Business." *Architectural Record* 199 (5): 83–106.

M-Architects. 2011. *Mission Statement*. http:// www.m-architects.com/. Accessed March 21, 2011.

Merriam-Webster's Dictionary. 2011. *Merriam-Webster's Dictionary*. http://www.merriam-webster.com/dictionary/business. Accessed March 7, 2011.

Service Corps of Retired Executives (SCORE). 2010. *About Score*. http://www.score.org/ index.html. Accessed May 30, 2010.

United States Small Business Administration (SBA). 2011. *Creating a Marketing Strategy*. http://www.sba.gov/. Accessed March 7, 2011.

United States Small Business Administration (SBA). 2011. *Small Business Profile*. http://www.sba.gov/sites/default/files/files/ AllProfiles10.pdf. Accessed March 7, 2011.

11
C H A P T E R

Operating and Managing a Green Interior Design Business

Kapitola 11 (Slovak)
Poglavje 11 (Slovenian)
Capítulo 11 (Spanish)

After learning the content in Chapter 11, you will be able to answer the following questions:

- How can I manage and operate a sustainable building for a green interior design business?

- What should be included in a *Green Business Handbook* for a green interior design business?

- What should I know to purchase sustainable products for a green interior design business?

- How can I conserve resources and minimize waste for a green interior design business?

- What should be included in a marketing and communications plan for a green interior design business?

Many design firms provide sustainable design services and demonstrate a commitment to the principles of sustainability by operating a green business. This chapter examines what is required to operate and manage a green interior design business. The information is intended to be useful to an owner of an interior design firm, but the material can also be helpful to designers' clients who are business owners and want to also operate a green business.

Some of the green business requirements are related to topics addressed in green building certification programs, such as LEED. But there are many other considerations associated with operating an environmentally friendly business, such as working with green suppliers, having a green marketing and communications plan as well as developing a comprehensive *Green Business Handbook*.

A green business begins by developing a green business management plan. Each section of this chapter describes one of the areas that should be included in the green business management plan as well as the *Handbook*. The chapter's first section reviews the essential elements of a sustainable building, including green certification programs, sustainable sites/buildings, and conservation strategies.

The chapter continues by examining approaches to green office policies, sustainable purchases, and conserving resources via recycling policies. The concluding section of the chapter completes the green business management plan by identifying sustainable resources and explaining how to create a green marketing and communications plan.

Green Business Management Plan: A Sustainable Building

You might decide that your new business will specialize in designing sustainable built environments. How will you respond if your potential client—who wants a sustainable building—asks you to discuss your business's green operational policies and procedures? Do you think you will work with this client if you say your business does not incorporate the principles of sustainability into practice?

Implementing green business practices is an excellent way to demonstrate your knowledge of (and commitment to) sustainability. From a public relations perspective, green business practices reveal to clients, potential employees, stakeholders, investors, and the community that you are serious about social and environmental responsibilities. Moreover, savings attributed to green business practices, such as reduced energy costs, can illustrate your ability to make sound financial decisions. Your green business initiatives can also become associated with your brand. Thus, a green business can be an important component of your marketing strategy.

Green Certification Programs for Businesses
One of the best ways to demonstrate your commitment to sustainability is to have your business certified by ISO 14001 Environmental Management Systems (http://www.iso.org). To make it easier for small- and medium-sized business to implement the standards, the ISO (International Organization for Standardization) created a workbook, *ISO 14001 Environmental Management Systems—An Easy-to-Use Checklist for Small Business—Are You Ready?*

The ISO recently identified the following benefits to implementing ISO 14001: (1) preservation of the environment, (2) business performance and profitability, (3) improved corporate image, (4) enhanced access to export markets, and (5) a common reference for communicating environmental issues with customers, regulators, the public, and other stakeholders (ISO 2011).

There are many design firms that specialize in designing sustainable built environments *and* "walk the talk" by managing and operating a green business (Box 11.1 and Figure 11.1). What does owning a green business require? Fundamentally, many of the practices are associated with LEED (see Chapter 9). This knowledge can

Box 11.1
A Green Design Business—Perkins + Will

Design Firm Profile

- Founders—Lawrence B. Perkins and Philip Will Jr. in Chicago (1935).

- 1,500 professionals in 24 international locations.

- One of three recipients of the 2010 National Building Museum Honor Award in recognition of the firm's commitment to civic innovation in design, construction, and education.

- Have designed more than 100 LEED-certified buildings (Figure 11.1).

Moving Toward a Sustainable Future: Our Vision

Sustainable design is a result of a creative and collaborative process that realizes synergies between all design disciplines and produces thoughtful, intelligently integrated work. Dedication to design excellence, research, education, and operational excellence will allow us to apply the latest knowledge of the science and art of sustainable design, enabling us to learn from our designs and continuously inform our future projects. Our work will conserve water and energy, work to restore and regenerate the natural environment, enhance the ecological systems, and offer healthier and more vibrant buildings and communities. We are committed to creating work which will sustain healthy lives and ecosystems, benefit our clients, our company, our community, and our world. By honoring these broader goals, we will set the course for global sustainable design leadership. (Perkins + Will 2011)

Selected Green Workplace Practices at Perkins + Will

- Sustainable Design Initiative (SDI) strategic plans (2004, 2007, and 2011).

- Green Operations Plan in 2005—Tracked and benchmarked operational performance:
  - Energy and water use
  - Greenhouse gas emissions associated with travel and office operations

- Every office renovated or constructed is designed to LEED Platinum standards and metered to monitor performance.

- Carbon-neutral organization—Offsetting carbon emissions.

- Investing in renewable energy technologies.

- Supports a diverse culture of sustainable design:
  - Applied research
  - Internal education
  - Public advocacy
  - Outreach

- Develops sustainable tools, publications, and research reports that are publicly available:

  - *Precautionary List* (Document that lists substances that should be eliminated from buildings.)

  - *2030 Estimating + Evaluation Tool* (Tool that enables teams to set energy mix goals by 2030.)

  - *Sustainable Advisory Services Digital Booklet* (Publication to help clients attain their sustainability goals.)

  - *Energy Modeling Guidance* (Research article on designing energy efficient buildings.)

(Box 11.1 continued on page 366)

Box 11.1

A Green Design Business—Perkins + Will *(continued)*

- *Stormwater Reuse and Whole System Design: Insights from a 'Living Lab'* (Publication that describes a whole system approach to water management and sustainable design.)

- *Sanford-Burnham Medical Research Institute—A Model of Sustainability and Collaboration* (Publication in *R&D*

Magazine's Laboratory Design newsletter that describes how Perkins + Will created a sustainable, state-of-the-art research facility.)

*Adapted from: Perkins + Will. 2011. *Broader Goals: The Sustainable Leadership Plan 2011–2015*. http://www.perkinswill.com/. Retrieved May 25, 2011.

Figure 11.1 One Haworth Center in Holland, Michigan, designed by Perkins + Will is LEED-NC Gold certified. *(Steve Hall © Hedrich Blessing)*

therefore serve as a foundation for establishing a green business.

An excellent way to learn LEED certification requirements is to work on LEED projects and to acquire LEED's professional credential, LEED AP (see http://www.usgbc.org/). LEED's professional credential for commercial interiors is LEED AP ID+C (Interior Design + Construction). The credential for designing high-performance homes is LEED AP Homes.

In addition to being knowledgeable about green certification programs, the owner of a green business should have an operations and management plan that outlines green policies and procedures. The principles of the plan should be based on the tripartite of sustainable development: society, the environment, and economics. Thus, the policies and procedures should benefit (1) current and future generations, (2) the natural environment, and (3) the finances of the firm, its clients, professional partners, and the community.

The plan should include policies associated with the firm's building, FF&E, purchases, suppliers, vendors, recycling, maintenance, and marketing. Policies and procedures should be incorporated into a *Green Business Handbook* to be shared with employees, collaborative partners, suppliers, bankers, investors, and community representatives.

Sustainable Sites and Buildings

If sustainable design is one of the services provided by your firm, then your business should be housed in a sustainable building. Thus, an essential element in the *Green Business Handbook* is sustainable requirements for the firm's building.

To demonstrate the firm's commitment to conserving resources, the business should be located in an existing building rather than new construction. Ideally, the building is LEED certified, but when this is not the situation the firm should work toward achieving LEED certification at the highest possible level, preferably platinum.

LEED certification covers many of the characteristics that are important for a green business's building, such as a sustainable site, water efficiency, energy/atmosphere strategies, conservation of materials/resources, and a healthy indoor environmental quality (IEQ). (see Chapter 9, Box 9.1.)

Based on LEED's performance criteria, the building for your green business should have a minimal impact on ecosystems and feature regionally appropriate landscaping (USGBC 2011). The building's site should have a means, such as a green roof, to control stormwater runoff while reducing erosion and heat island effect. The building's exterior lighting must be energy efficient and should not contribute to light pollution. In addition, fixtures must be directed to avoid light trespass.

The building site should have convenient access to public transportation networks, community amenities, and trade showrooms (if possible). Your business should have energy-efficient vehicles and policies that encourage employees to use public transit and ride bicycles to work. The building should have cycle storage facilities as well as showers and lockers.

A building with close proximity to public transportation also can be helpful to clients, professional partners, and employees when they must travel to a client's business or residence. Thus, green business operations also should include green business travel policies, such as restricting air travel, minimizing site visits, and encouraging remote meetings via free services, such as Skype (http://www.skype.com) or TokBox (http://www.tokbox.com).

Policies also could include encouraging designers to consolidate trips by scheduling several appointments when traveling to a specific area rather than scheduling appointments in various locations in a city on a given day. Consider creating incentives for ride-sharing as another way to show your commitment to environmental issues. These sustainable practices can conserve time, minimize travel costs, and help reduce the negative effects of transportation on the natural environment.

Conservation of Natural Resources and Energy

A green business must conserve natural resources and energy and document these policies in the *Green Business Handbook*. Land can be conserved by selecting an existing building and economizing on space utilization. Conduct a thorough analysis of your studio/office space needs and identify strategies, such as multifunctional areas, that can result in a very efficient space. Small spaces help to both conserve resources and reduce many business expenses, such as rent, utilities, insurance, furniture, lighting, and flooring.

A small business can conserve water in many ways. First, have a water audit performed for your building and repair any leaking pipes, seals, faucets, showerheads, or fixtures. Ideally, your building should have efficient fixtures and fittings, such as low-flow fixtures (faucets and showerheads), high-efficiency/waterless urinals, and ENERGY STAR–qualified dishwashers and water heaters.

Small businesses can help to conserve energy and reduce **greenhouse gas (GHG)** emissions. ENERGY STAR recently reported that 30 percent of energy used in buildings was inefficient or unnecessary. In addition, commercial buildings were responsible for 17 percent of the U.S. GHG emissions; if the energy efficiency of commercial buildings was improved by 10 percent, the reduction in GHG emissions would be equivalent to approximately 30 million vehicles (ENERGY STAR 2011). ENERGY STAR has a free energy consulting service for small business owners (see http://www.energystar.gov).

Reducing energy consumption helps to decrease GHG emissions, which contribute to global climate change. To analyze energy consumption patterns and usage, have an energy audit conducted for your building, including an analysis of daylighting. Energy use should be monitored, and whenever possible, consider using renewable energy sources, such as wind, solar, and geothermal. Conserving energy also involves the commissioning of building systems, such as HVAC, lighting/daylighting controls, and hot-water systems.

In addition, green business policies and procedures should include energy conservation strategies for lighting systems, equipment, and computers. Electronic equipment, including computer monitors and water coolers, should be ENERGY STAR qualified to conserve energy, save money, and help protect the environment. For existing lighting systems, consider switch plate occupancy sensors and lighting retrofits.

Some of the ways to retrofit lighting systems involve adding reflectors to the existing fixtures to maximize light output and replacing lamps with energy-efficient CFLs, T-8's, or T-5's. Employees should be encouraged to turn off lights, equipment, and machines after use and activate power management features. Keep in mind that multifunction devices that combine printing, copying, and scanning, use less energy than separate units.

An office's indoor environmental quality (IEQ) affects energy consumption and the health, safety, satisfaction, and productivity levels of employees. Your employees must have healthy and adequate ventilation and should be able to control their lighting and thermostats.

Employees should have natural daylight with effective control of direct sunlight. Ideally, employees should have views of the outdoors from seated areas, such as an office desk or a conference room. Additional policies related to indoor air quality (IAQ) are addressed in the next section.

Green Business Management Plan: Purchases and Supply Chain

Typically, a new business needs to purchase furniture, office equipment, computers, lighting, and perhaps appliances, flooring, window treatments, and new wall finishes. For a green business the first priority is to try to retain existing items by refurbishment and repairs. If you must purchase an item, explore the used market to conserve both natural resources and costs.

The *Green Business Handbook* should establish criteria for business purchases focusing on conserving energy, minimizing waste, and creating a healthy indoor environment. In addition, products and materials should be manufactured in a location close to the business to reduce transportation costs.

Items such as furniture, window treatments, flooring systems, and paints should be made from environmentally friendly materials. Examples include rapidly renewable materials, bio-based products, postconsumer recycled content, certified woods, and low-emitting materials. For example, your green policies should specify that the firm's wooden furniture should be certified by the Forest Stewardship Council (FSC; http://www.fscus.org/) and have the GREENGUARD Indoor Air Quality certificate (http://www.greenguard.org) because their guidelines focus on conserving and protecting the natural environment.

Carpet should have at least 25 percent recycled content, and textiles must be made from recycled materials or bio-based products (see The Carpet and Rug Institute [CRI]; http://www.carpet-rug.org). To improve the IAQ, paint should comply with the volatile organic compound (VOC) content limits created by Green Seal Standard GS-11 (http://www.greenseal.org). Policies also should include a plan to monitor the IAQ by determining emission levels of VOCs, formaldehyde, and 4-phenylcyclohexene (4-PCH).

Green Office Policies and Procedures

These same sustainable principles should be applied to policies regarding office paper, presentation materials, office supplies, and cleaning supplies documented in the *Green Business Handbook*. Green Seal has several standards for these types of products as well as other items for the built environment (Box 11.2).

A green business also has policies about the type of paper and ink used in the office. For example, paper should be chlorine-free (**Processed Chlorine Free**, or **PCF**) and 100 percent

---

postconsumer recycled. However, some products are only available with lower percentages of postconsumer materials. Postconsumer fibers and materials are obtained from consumer waste. Other examples of green paper products are art paper, sketching pads, drawing paper, flipcharts, printer paper, stationery, and self-stick notepads.

Sustainable ink and toners are also available for most printer models. Soy and vegetable ink (with zero VOCs) should be used. Professional printing should use chemical-free plate processing.

Most types of office supplies are now available as green products. For example, green office supplies include binders, desk accessories, dry erase boards, shipping supplies, hanging folders, markers, highlighters, pencils, and pens. The percentage of postconsumer content is relevant to some of these items, such as binders and hanging files, but depending on a product's material composition, there are additional green considerations. For example, green binders should have postconsumer content *and* be biodegradable and have low VOCs. Highlighters should be biodegradable and nontoxic.

Shipping cartons should be shipped flat and have postconsumer content. Packing materials, such as peanuts, should be made from approximately 100 percent renewable resources, biodegradable, and dissolvable in water.

In addition to specifying green products, sustainable office procedures should focus on reducing, reusing, and recycling. Thus, employees should be encouraged to reduce the amount of paper, presentation materials, and office supplies used on a daily basis.

Paper use can be reduced by enacting green policies, such as using both sides of a sheet, reserving printing for final versions, and using reusable envelopes for office correspondence. Another option is to implement a "paperless office" policy. Finally, recycling materials can include using shredded paper as a packing material, and reusing presentation boards.

Green office policies and procedures must also include cleaning supplies and maintenance procedures. Toxic substances in some cleaning supplies can affect the IAQ and, hence, the health of people. Cleaning and custodial products that should be green include glass/surface cleaners, insecticides, restroom hand towels/tissues, sponges, vacuums, and floor cleaning machines and chemicals.

Glass/surface cleaners should be Green Seal certified, non-caustic, nontoxic, biodegradable, and free of harsh fumes. Sponges should be biodegradable, and paper products should have postconsumer content and be PCF. To protect the IAQ and ensure high cleaning standards, vacuums should be certified by The Carpet and Rug Institute.

Green Business: Supply Chain

A green business works with other green businesses. Thus, you should establish policies that stipulate green criteria for your manufacturers, vendors, and suppliers, and document these policies in the *Green Business Handbook*.

An excellent way to know that you are working with a sustainable company is by asking if the business is certified by *ISO 14001 Environmental Management Systems* (see http://www.iso.org). In addition, consider working with companies that manufacture GREENGUARD Indoor Air Quality-certified products. Certified products include adhesives/sealants, cabinetry, ceiling systems, flooring, and furniture (see http://www.greenguard.org).

To determine which companies support and practice the principles of sustainability, ask their representatives questions that reflect operations and management policies. For example:

* Does the company have a *Sustainability Report* that explains its environmental and socially responsible activities?

* Are issues related to sustainability included in the company's code of conduct and ethics document?

* Is it using sustainable practices to acquire raw materials?

* Does it have policies that conserve energy and water during production?

- Is it working toward being carbon neutral?

- Is it reducing GHG emissions and managing soil, water, and air contamination?

- Is it managing chemical substances?

- Does the company produce quality, environmentally conscious products?

- Does it reuse and recycle products and materials?

- Does it reduce waste and the use of chemicals?

- Does the company's packing and shipping practices reflect the principles of sustainability?

- Is it involved with continuously improving practices by engaging in the PDCA cycle?

Answers to these questions, and others related to green production and business activities, can provide the information needed to establish relationships with green business partners.

Checking for Comprehension

- What do you think should be included in a *Green Business Handbook*?

- Explain the importance of green office policies and procedures when operating a green interior design business.

Green Business Management Plan: Conserving Resources and Minimizing Waste

The questions above related to minimizing waste are issues your green business should delineate in its *Green Business Handbook*. Your firm needs to develop policies and procedures regarding waste, collection methods, processing requirements, and strategies for the storage, management, and disposal of hazardous materials.

The overall goal is for the business to generate zero waste. The policies and procedures must be developed within the context of your business's type of waste, the quantity of items, and where/how the waste is generated. Waste from most offices includes paper products, office supplies, cardboard, aluminum, glass, plastic, and packing materials. Offices with kitchens and/or employee break rooms also have food waste.

In addition, design offices have waste from sample books/binders, materials, presentation boards, model building, and any other items used in the design and selling processes. Firms that sell furniture have considerable waste from large boxes and packing materials. In addition, a design firm might have to comply with environmental laws and regulations that are applicable to certain products, such as paint, carpet, and light sources.

An inventory of the type of waste must be coordinated with appropriate strategies for reducing, reusing, and recycling products and materials. Examples of reduction and reuse strategies were previously described in this chapter. Waste can be eliminated when fewer items are used and reuse strategies are employed, such as donating discontinued sample books or used furniture to a local community center.

Waste Quantities and Recycling Policies

The quantity of waste can affect recycling policies. For example, special containers and storage facilities might be needed for large quantities of office paper or cardboard. The quantity as well as the type of waste affects which waste hauler will pick up and transport the waste to a processing site. These operations might already be prescribed by your building's property manager.

The quantity and category of waste also affects the type of container used to collect recyclables as well as the placement of the units. For example, in an office, paper waste is often generated at a workstation. Thus, small blue plastic containers (marked with the recycling symbol) are located next to desks.

Large blue plastic containers are located in a remote location to collect all paper generated in an office. Each category of recyclables should have a unique container, unless the facility has single-stream recycling. Recycling policies should specify how the materials will be collected, stored, and transported to the dock for pickup by the waste hauler.

Management of Hazardous Materials

The management of recyclable materials, such as paper and aluminum, is fairly straightforward. Managing materials that are hazardous to people, ecosystems, and the natural environment is complicated and requires compliance with laws and regulations. The best source of information is the Environmental Protection Agency (EPA; http://www.epa.gov/). The EPA is responsible for ensuring that "federal laws protecting human health and the environment are enforced fairly and effectively" (EPA 2011).

According to the EPA, hazardous waste is "waste that is dangerous or potentially harmful to our health or the environment. Hazardous wastes can be liquids, solids, gases, or sludges. They can be discarded commercial products, like cleaning fluids or pesticides, or the by-products of manufacturing processes" (EPA 2011).

The EPA's hazardous waste regulations are related to business operations as well as the design profession and include batteries, pesticides, mercury-containing thermostats and mercury-containing lamps (such as fluorescent lamps).

Regulations associated with the management and disposal of mercury-containing lamps by a business are presented in the Resource Conservation and Recovery Act (RCRA) Universal Waste Rule (UWR) and Subtitle C hazardous waste regulations (EPA 2011). The EPA also has information for recycling mercury-containing lamps (see http://www.epa.gov/).

Another hazardous waste related to lighting is PCBs (polychlorinated biphenyls), found in fluorescent ballasts prior to being banned in 1979. Thus, old fluorescent fixtures might have ballasts with PCBs. If your office or any of your clients have these fixtures, you must comply with the laws and regulations that prescribe the management, cleanup, and disposal of PCB wastes.

Laws and regulations also exist for lead-based paints. Exposure to lead can occur when lead-based paints deteriorate or when children eat fragments of lead-based paints. Municipalities might regulate the proper disposal of leftover products that potentially have hazardous ingredients, such as paint, cleaners, pesticides, and electronic equipment.

In addition, communities and the EPA are trying to encourage people to **e-cycle** by recycling electronic equipment, such as computers, cell phones, monitors, and printers. Your *Green Business Handbook* should include these recommendations as well as the proper reuse, recycling, and disposal of construction and demolition materials.

These recommendations are critically important because of the large quantity of debris that might be landfilled, and the likelihood that waste contains hazardous substances. In addition, the cost of recycling can be less than disposal. Reuse should be the first option, followed by recycling and environmentally friendly disposal (when necessary).

Green Business Management Plan: Marketing and Communications

Successful examples of your business's recycling program can be integrated with your marketing plan for a green business. Your *Green Business Handbook* should include a green marketing and communications plan. Fundamentally, the plan incorporates sustainability into the basic marketing strategies described in Chapters 10 and 13. Thus, a green/sustainable marketing plan includes: (1) your knowledge of the green/sustainable design industry, (2) target green/sustainable market, (3) green/sustainable competition, and (4) marketing strategies emphasizing green/sustainable design.

Green/Sustainable Resources

In addition to professional design organizations and trade journals, excellent sources for green/sustainable industry information include the USGBC, EPA, World Green Building Council (http://www.worldgbc.org/), Build It Green (http://www.builditgreen.org/), Building Green (http://www.buildinggreen.com/), and the World Council for Sustainable Development (http://www.wbcsd.org/).

A resource for learning about new environmental research is the *Environmental e-Market Express*, sponsored by the U.S. Department of Commerce—U.S. Commercial Service (see http://www.buyusa.gov).

The *Environmental e-Market Express* allows U.S. firms to electronically submit requests for environmental market research developed by overseas staff. The reports are free, but the product or service associated with the firm must have at least 51 percent U.S. content. Examples of the reports include *The European Eco-Label; China, Environmental Technologies Market in Shanghai's 3-Year Environmental Action Plan*; and *Japan, The Solar Panel Industry in the Kansai Region* (Figure 11.2).

Figure 11.2 The *Environmental e-Market Express* allows U.S. firms to electronically submit requests for environmental market research developed by overseas staff. One of its reports, *China, Environmental Technologies Market in Shanghai's 3-Year Environmental Action Plan*, features the city of Shanghai. (© *Tom Bonaventure/Getty*)

In addition, the U.S. Department of Commerce sponsored *Global Enviro Team* can be followed on Twitter (http://www.twitter.com/enviroteam).

At the request of U.S. companies involved with architecture, construction, and engineering services, the U.S. Commercial Service also created the *Design Build Product & Services e-Market Express*. Examples of market research reports in this category include *Germany, Green Building; Italy, Green Building Market*; and *Saudi Arabia, Green Building Market*.

The *Design Build Product & Services e-Market Express* also includes reports that describe a variety of business opportunities for the design profession, including future projects. Documents include *United Kingdom: Sustainable Construction*, and *Bangladesh: Clean Air and Sustainable Environment Project*.

The organizations described above as well as local offices, such as Green Building Councils, can provide information for determining your target green/sustainable market and identifying your competition. Depending on the size of your firm, your green competition might include global businesses. Analyze the extent of your competitors' commitment to green design. For example:

* Do their philosophical beliefs include sustainability?

* How many LEED-certified projects have they designed?

* How many designers are LEED AP's?

* Have they received awards for sustainable designs?

* Are their service activities focused on sustainability?

Your knowledge of the green/sustainable industry, target market, and competition should be used to create green/sustainable marketing strategies. Your strategies should focus on creating a green/sustainable brand (see Chapter 13).

Information and materials distributed to internal and external audiences should highlight your firm's involvement with green/sustainable projects, products, and activities.

An excellent approach is to develop a *Sustainability Report* that includes your management philosophy, code of conduct and ethics, green/sustainable projects, socially responsible initiatives, and environmental activities. All marketing strategies must demonstrate your firm's commitment to practicing the principles of sustainability as well as designing sustainable interiors.

Marketing and Communications: Greenwashing

A very important area for demonstrating your firm's commitment to sustainability is to ensure the accuracy of any green marketing claims. Are the "green" products you are specifying credible? Unfortunately, the popularity of the green movement has prompted manufacturers to engage in **greenwashing** or deceptively claiming that their products are green.

To have a green brand, you must ensure that the products you specify are truly green, and that your suppliers and vendors have environmentally friendly policies regarding management and operations.

Products and organizations should have the proper third-party certifications as described previously in this chapter. Green credibility can also be determined when an environmental claim conforms to the standards delineated in the ISO 14020 Series—Environmental Labels and Declarations.

In addition, the Ecolabel Index—the world's largest directory of ecolabels—can provide reliable information for hundreds of ecolabels throughout the world (see http://www.ecolabelindex.com). For example, the Australian Forest Certification Scheme ecolabel states that the certification "Enables users and consumers of timber and wood-based products to be assured that the origin of timber wood or wood-based products are derived from sources that have been independently, third-party certified from sustainable managed forests. The Australian Forest Certification Scheme covers both forest management (FM) and chain of custody (CC) certification" (Ecolabel Index 2011).

The Federal Trade Commission (FTC) has developed *Guides for the Use of Environmental Marketing Claims* (*Green Guides*), based on Section 5 of the FTC Act. The *Guides* applies to environmental advertising and marketing practices, including labeling, promotional materials, digital/electronic means, and other forms of marketing.

Environmental claims can be associated with a product, package, or service. Principles that can be applied to environmental marketing claims are: (1) qualifications and disclosures; (2) distinction between benefits of product, package, and service; (3) overstatement of environmental attribute; and (4) comparative claims (FTC 1998).

Furthermore, the FTC identified several topics whereby it is deceptive to misrepresent—directly or by implication—that a product, package, or service has specific environmental attributes unless the claim is substantiated with reliable scientific evidence. This guideline applies to products or packages that claim the following properties: (1) degradable, biodegradable, or photodegradable; (2) compostable; (3) recyclable; (4) recycled content; (5) source reduction; and (6) ozone safe or ozone friendly.

The *Green Guides* also states that it is deceptive to misrepresent that a product, package, or service offers general environmental benefits. The FTC is currently revising the *Green Guides*, and it appears the document will include guidelines for environmental claims related to "certifications and seals of approvals," "free-of and non-toxic," and "refillable."

Checking for Comprehension

* Why do you think a design firm specializing in sustainable services should also be a green business?

* Describe how a design firm could institute a green marketing and communications program.

Chapter 11 provided an overview of areas that are important for operating and managing a green interior design business. As more clients seek sustainable built environments, it becomes increasingly important for interior designers to "walk the talk" by owning a green business.

As described in the chapter, an important step is to have a certified sustainable building and to create a *Green Business Handbook*. The *Handbook* should outline policies and procedures related to business operations, including purchasing strategies, conserving resources, and a green marketing and communications plan.

The content in Chapter 11 serves as background for topics covered in *Chapter 12 Business Policies and Operations*. Chapter 12 reviews topics that are critical to owning a business, such as accounting procedures, financial management, and strategic management planning.

Knowledge and Skills Summary

Highlights

- Implementing green business practices is an excellent way to demonstrate your knowledge of sustainability.

- One of the best ways to demonstrate your commitment to sustainability is to have your business certified by ISO 14001 Environmental Management Systems.

- Policies and procedures should be incorporated into a *Green Business Handbook* to be shared with employees, collaborative partners, suppliers, bankers, investors, and community representatives.

- A green business must conserve natural resources and energy.

- The *Green Business Handbook* should establish criteria for business purchases that focus on conserving energy, minimizing waste, and creating a healthy indoor environment.

- A green business must have policies and procedures regarding waste, collection methods,

and processing requirements, and strategies for the storage, management, and disposal of hazardous materials.

- A *Green Business Handbook* should include a green marketing and communications plan.

Key Terms
e-cycle

greenhouse gas (GHG)

greenwashing

postconsumer

Processed Chlorine Free (PCF)

Projects

Philosophy and Design Project
In an era focused on sustainable designs, a design firm should have the expertise to design sustainable built environments and demonstrate its commitment to the principles of sustainability by being green.

Create a green business philosophy and outline strategies for operating and managing a green interior design business. Develop a written report (approximately five pages), and prepare an informal presentation to the class that includes questions for a class discussion.

Research Project
A green interior design business should have criteria for business purchases that focus on conserving energy, minimizing waste, and creating a healthy indoor environment.

In a group of three to five students, research products and materials that an owner of a green interior design business could purchase that would conserve energy, minimize waste, and create a healthy indoor environment. Create a virtual notebook of your products.

Human Factors Research Project
A problem with instituting green policies and procedures is identifying strategies that will encourage people to willingly engage in sustainable practices. Identify human factors research

studies that have examined this situation. Based on the results of these studies, develop a short survey that asks people to describe their willingness to engage in sustainable practices.

Prepare a written summary of the human factors research studies and the results of your survey. The summary (approximately three pages) should include recommendations for future practice.

References

Ecolabel Index. 2011. *All Ecolabels*. http://www.ecolabelindex.com. Accessed April 12, 2011.

ENERGY STAR. 2010. *Fast Facts*. http://www.energystar.gov/index.cfm?c=home.index. Accessed June 2, 2010.

Environmental Protection Agency (EPA). 2011. *Our Mission*. http://www.epa.gov. Accessed April 7, 2011.

Environmental Protection Agency (EPA). 2011. *Wastes—Hazardous Waste*. http://www.epa.gov. Accessed April 7, 2011.

Federal Trade Commission (FTC) 1998. *Guides for the Use of Environmental Marketing Claims (Green Guides)*. Washington, DC: Federal Trade Commission (FTC).

ISO (International Organization for Standardization). 2011. *ISO 14001*. http://www.iso.org. Accessed April 7, 2011.

U.S. Department of Commerce. 2011. *The Environmental e-Market Express*. http://www.buyusa.gov. Accessed April 3, 2011.

U.S. Green Building Council (USGBC). 2011. *Intro—What LEED Is*. http://www.usgbc.org. Accessed April 5, 2011.

12

Business Policies and Operations

Sura ya 12 (Swahili)
Kapitel 12 (Swedish)
บทที่ **12** (Thai)

After learning the content in Chapter 12, you will be able to answer the following questions:

* What are the basic accounting terms and practices?

* How can I interpret my business's financial reports?

* How can I use accounting software programs to help me to record and manage financial data?

* Why is it important for an interior design firm to have a strategic plan?

* What should be included in a strategic plan?

* How should I develop, implement, and assess a strategic plan for my interior design firm?

Owning an interior design firm requires an understanding of business policies and operations. This chapter reviews what is required for the management of finances and strategic plans. The chapter's first section explains basic accounting terms and practices, the role of business credit agencies, and approaches to financing a business.

The second section of the chapter explores how to develop a direction for the design firm's future by creating a strategic management plan. The section begins by describing the components and processes involved with strategic planning, including developing mission statements, goals, objectives, strategies, and tactics.

The strategic planning discussion also examines how to perform a SWOT (strengths, weaknesses, opportunities, and threats) analysis, which involves researching the design industry and the design firm's operating environment. The last unit in the chapter completes the strategic management plan by explaining procedures for implementation and continuous improvement.

Accounting Procedures and Financial Management

A business must have a way to record and manage its revenues and expenses. How do you get started? Many small businesses, including interior design firms, use an accounting software program, such as *QuickBooks Pro* or *Peachtree*. A small business might hire a **bookkeeper** and/or an **accountant** to handle the firm's financial data. In either arrangement you must have a basic understanding of accounting procedures and financial management. Without this awareness it is more difficult to understand what information you must provide to run the software or give to the bookkeeper (as the old saying goes, "Garbage in, garbage out"). Accounting fundamentals are also needed to interpret the financial reports generated by the software.

This section reviews basic accounting procedures and financial management so that you can properly organize and manage your revenues and expenses. The content builds on information presented in Chapter 10 *Writing the Business Plan: Financial Data* by relying on an understanding of accounting terminology and financial reports.

This section begins by reviewing basic accounting terms and practices, followed by an overview of the proper setup of the data files in an accounting software program. Interpreting financial reports using actual rather than projected costs (see Chapter 10) is examined, as well as how to establish business credit. The last topic in this section covers opportunities for business loans.

Understanding Basic Accounting Terms and Practices

Your first step in creating accounting policies and procedures is to discuss your business with an accountant specializing in small businesses and tax preparation—preferably someone who has experience working with design firms. Usually, a start-up business is not able to afford an accountant on a regular basis, but a professional is essential for two important tasks: (1) creating the proper setup and accounts for the business's accounting software program and (2) preparing financial statements and documents required for filing tax returns. An excellent resource for IRS regulations for small businesses is *IRS Publication 334— Tax Guide for Small Businesses* (see http://www.irs.gov/pub/irs-pdf/p334.pdf).

It is very easy to understand the need to hire a professional for tax preparation purposes, but why is it necessary to employ someone to set up a user-friendly software program?

Accounting software programs have become very easy to input data and generate reports. But a proper setup is crucial for accuracy, creating the accounts that are relevant to your business, and generating the most relevant financial reports that can help you understand how to reduce expenses and increase profits. As reported by an accounting software consultant who has helped hundreds of businesses with program problems,

"I have found that improper set up of the data file was most often the primary cause, second only to judgment errors in posting transactions to the incorrect account" (Madeira 2009).

You might not be able to afford an accountant for day-to-day operations, but you might want to hire a part-time bookkeeper or outsource the work. A bookkeeper's job can involve numerous tasks, such as entering data into the accounting software program, monitoring work/purchase orders, and preparing the payroll, purchase orders, invoices, and billing statements (see Chapter 6).

Hiring a part-time or full-time bookkeeper is generally dependent on the type of services provided by the design firm as well as the size of the business. For example, large businesses and firms that sell substantial quantities of merchandise require full-time bookkeepers.

To work with bookkeepers and accountants, as well as accounting software programs, you must be familiar with basic accounting terminology and practices. For example, you must know the difference between **cash** and **accrual accounting methods**. Should you use a **double-entry** or **single-entry accounting system**? How does a **journal** differ from a **ledger**?

Fundamentally, accounting focuses on five areas: revenues, expenses, assets, liabilities, and owner's equity. Most calculations involve addition, subtraction, multiplication, and division. Keep these basics in mind as you read the following sections.

Cash and Accrual Accounting Methods

Understanding the differences between cash and accrual accounting methods provides a good start to seeing the "big picture" of accounting practices. This is important because your accountant must know which method you will be using to set up your accounting software program. To comply with IRS regulations, you might not have an option (see *IRS Publication 334—Tax Guide for Small Businesses*). For example, large businesses with inventory are required to use the accrual accounting method.

Software programs allow you to switch between the two methods, but it is much easier to create the proper program from the very beginning (see the next section). In addition, IRS regulations might not allow you to change to a different accounting method.

The fundamental difference between the cash and accrual methods is when revenues and expenses become effective. When using the cash method, revenues are recorded when you actually receive the cash, and expenses are recorded when you pay the bill. For example, a sofa sold on June 1 will not be recorded until your client pays the bill, which could be in October. From the expense perspective an office desk purchased on June 1 will not be recorded until your business has paid off the entire amount, usually within 30 days.

With the accrual method, revenues and expenses are immediately recorded. Thus, using the examples described above, the income from the sofa sold on June 1 is recorded on June 1 and the expense of office desk purchased on June 1 is also recorded on June 1.

Cash and accrual accounting methods can affect the revenues and expenses reported on your tax return. For example, with the cash method, a sofa sold on December 15, 2013, will not be recorded until the client pays the bill, which could be January 15, 2014. In this situation the income from the sale of the sofa *is not* reported on the 2013 tax return.

With the accrual method, a sofa sold on December 15, 2013, will be recorded on December 15, 2013. In this situation the income from the sale of the sofa *will* be reported on the 2013 tax return. The same scenarios apply to when expenses are reported on a tax return.

Given the various ramifications associated with cash and accrual accounting methods, you must discuss the topic with your accountant to determine the best option for your particular business.

Another issue to initially discuss with your accountant is whether your business will use the **calendar** or **fiscal year** accounting period. The calendar accounting period ends on December 31.

The fiscal calendar has 12 months, but the ending date is not December 31. A common beginning date is July 1 and the ending date is June 30. The period selected can affect how the business taxes are reported to the IRS (see *IRS Publication 334— Tax Guide for Small Businesses*). Most small businesses use the calendar accounting period.

Single-Entry and Double-Entry Accounting Systems

Generally, whenever possible, accountants recommend that small businesses use the cash method because it is easier to use a single-entry accounting system. A single-entry system is easy to process because **transactions** are entered in only one record. Transactions are any occurrences—such as paying rent or selling a sofa— that affect the business's financial situation.

The accrual method requires the double-entry accounting system, which is more complicated due to having to enter transactions in separate records—balanced debits and credits.

Do not confuse conventional definitions of these terms (debits and credits) with the accounting rules used for double-entry accounting systems. According to the accounting rules used in double-entry systems, debits (dr.) (1) *increase* assets and expenses and (2) *decrease* liabilities, owner's equity, and revenues. For example, a rent expense of $2,500 is recorded in the debit column, an increase in expenses (Figure 12.1). Because of the balancing requirement of a double-entry system, the $2,500 rent expense must also be recorded as a credit.

According to the accounting rules used in double-entry systems, credits (cr.) (1) *increase* liabilities, owner's equity, and revenues and (2) *decrease* assets and expenses. For example, the $2,500 rent expense is recorded in the loan account's credit column—a decrease in assets (cash). (see Figure 12.1.) Credits are always listed on the right-side column of an account. Debits are always listed on the left-side column of an account.

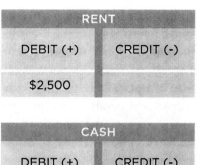
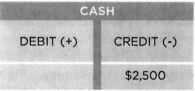

Figure 12.1 In double-entry accounting systems a rent expense of $2,500 is recorded in the debit column and the $2,500 rent expense is also recorded as a credit. Notice the large "T" used to separate debits and credits—hence the term "T-account."

Notice how the *increases* and *decreases* are balanced with the two entries. Debits *increase* assets and expenses, while credits *decrease* assets and expenses. Debits *decrease* liabilities, owner's equity, and revenues, while credits *increase* liabilities, owner's equity, and revenues. Remembering that these two entries must be made and must balance will help you avoid many mistakes when using a double-entry accounting system.

As illustrated in Figure 12.1, accountants use the term **T-account** to illustrate debit and credit entries. Accountants draw a large T with the name of the account. The words "debit" and "credit" are written under the line on the left and right sides, respectively. T-accounts are useful for visualizing where debits and credits are recorded for various accounts.

Source Documents and Journals

Accounting transactions begin with **source documents**, such as purchase orders, sales receipts, check stubs, or invoices. These documents must be accurate and have all information needed for accounting purposes. Critical information includes the date, description, amount, form of payment, and the name/address of a client or vendor.

When required, the amount must be categorized according to the pre-tax amount of the merchandise and the exact amount of state and local sales taxes. Consult with your accountant to establish policies and procedures for (1) using the correct forms, (2) completing essential information, (3) entering the data into an accounting software system, and (4) retaining all records.

Either you or your bookkeeper is responsible for entering all transactions into what accountants refer to as a "journal." Transactions entered in a journal are recorded in chronological order. Thus, a journal provides a detailed record of transactions that occur every day within a month.

Ledger Accounts

Transactions in a journal are then transferred, or **posted**, into ledger accounts. Postings might be done daily, weekly, monthly, or quarterly depending on the number of transactions. Businesses with a high number of daily transactions process postings every day. The important element is to keep up with postings so you have an accurate understanding of your financial situation.

Separate accounts are used for each asset, liability, owner's equity, revenue (income), and expenses. Accounts receivable is an example of an asset account; accounts payable is a liability account. Accountants use a numbering system to organize the accounts. For example, asset accounts often begin with the number 1.

To allow for several accounts, the numbers for your business's asset accounts could be 10–19 or 100–199. Liability accounts usually begin with the number 2 (20–29 or 200–299); owner's equity is 3 (30–39 or 300–399); revenue is 4 (40–49 or 400–499); and expenses is 5 (50–59 or 500–599). A list of ledger account names and numbers is provided in the **chart of accounts**.

Your accountant can provide the best advice regarding the type of accounts you will use in your software program. It is important that you understand the need to familiarize yourself with the fact that the number used to start an account number is related to the categorization scheme.

Your accountant also can help you to create accounts for your business checking account, business savings account, business credit cards, and a petty cash account. These business accounts are critical for establishing your business credit profile and for separating your personal and business revenues and expenses.

To track transactions and comply with IRS regulations, create customized categories for accounts (see *IRS Publication 334—Tax Guide for Small Businesses*). For example, to organize your business assets, you might have a category for cash, petty cash, inventory, and fixed assets. Liability categories could include accounts payable and **notes payable** (loans). Categories for owner's equity could be XYZ's capital and XYZ's **drawings**—owner's cash withdrawals for personal use.

Your business revenues could include a category for design fees, interest income, and sales tax. Examples of categories for business expenses are rent, utilities, telephone, postage, automobile, delivery/shipping, and travel. As discussed in the next section, accounting software programs have excellent formats for customizing categories.

For double-entry systems you or your bookkeeper must verify the accuracy of your ledger accounts once a month. Known as the **trial balance**, the task involves listing the balances in the general ledger and determining if the debits and credits are equal. If the total debits do not equal the total credits, the error must be found and corrected. Accuracy is critical because data in the trial balance are used for financial reports such as income statements.

Interpreting Financial Reports

Chapter 10 explained financial reports that are important to include in a business plan, including income profit and loss (P&L) statements, cash flow statements, and balance sheets. As illustrated in Chapter 10, the figures used in these reports were projected or forecasted numbers because the business plan was written for a starting business. An established business uses the same statements but with actual figures. Thus, data posted in the general ledger are used to create P&L statements, cash flow statements, and balance sheets.

The P&L statement is a summary of monthly sales, cost of sales, gross profits, fixed expenses, and net profit over a year (see Chapter 10, Table 10.2). This report therefore allows you to track your monthly revenues and expenses, and determine if you have a net profit or a **net loss**. A net loss occurs when your expenses exceed your revenues.

The P&L statement allows you to easily track one particular expense or source of revenue throughout the entire year. For example, you might want to track your travel expenses for the year and compare this figure to billable fees charged to clients. To identify trends in the business, you could compare revenues and expenses for a particular month for several years.

As described in Chapter 10, a cash flow statement is used to project how other income sources as well as irregular expenses can affect a business on a monthly basis. Financial data for a cash flow statement includes monthly cash sales, loans, cash expended, and the amount of cash at the beginning and end of each month (Table 10.3).

Established businesses can use a cash flow statement for the same reasons described for a starting business (see Chapter 10). An established business uses actual numbers for the first month. These numbers serve as the basis for making the projections for the remaining months in a year.

An established business uses actual numbers from the ledger accounts to generate the balance sheet. A balance sheet illustrates the business's assets and liabilities as well as the owner's equity for a given period (see Chapter 10, Table 10.4).

Assets must be balanced with liabilities and the owner's equity. For an established business the balance sheet is important for revealing the overall financial health of the business. The statement succinctly indicates what a business owns as well as what it owes. An accounting software program can easily generate a balance sheet as well as P&L statements.

Accounting Software Programs: An Overview

As previously mentioned, many interior design firms use accounting software programs such as *QuickBooks Pro* or *Peachtree*. This section provides an overview of *QuickBooks Pro* so you are aware of software features and the information needed to create various business files. An excellent way to learn how to use the software and become more familiar with accounting practices is to take a course at a community college. Many of these schools offer introductory and advanced courses in accounting software programs.

Accounting software programs let you easily and efficiently organize, manage, and store financial records required for your business. Accounting software also has banking business features that allow you to transfer funds, manage credit card transactions, and reconcile accounts.

Additionally, you can use the software to view bank reports and to bank online. As described below, the software can also help you to manage your client's records/transactions, estimate projects, track time, organize vendor records/transactions, manage inventory, facilitate payroll, and generate financial reports.

Client Records and Transactions

Accounting software programs allow you to organize and process many of the tasks required for client (customer) transactions and records. For example, programs enable you to create files for each client that include the name, contact information, shipping/billing addresses, project (job) information, payment details, and a section for additional information that is important for a client, such as project descriptions.

Any design services provided to the client and the fees can be recorded in an "Item List." The Item List is used to automatically create invoices. Creating invoices prompts a program that allows you to receive payments (accounts receivable) from your client and deposit the funds into the appropriate account. The software also has a sales receipt function for cash sales.

All of the data entered for a client can be used to generate client-related reports, such as a summary of how much a client owes, payments received, unpaid invoices, and project-related expenses that must be charged to the client.

In addition, *QuickBooks Pro* allows you to create and manage "classes" or special categories. These classes can be very useful to interior designers because the program allows you to track the revenues and expenses of a specific activity or team. For example, if you were working on a project with several teams, you could designate a class for each team. Class tracking would allow you to compare and contrast how each team was generating revenues and managing its expenses.

Classes could be created for specific types of buildings or locations of projects. Again, class tracking enables you to compare and contrast revenues and expenses for different types of buildings or project locations. To avoid duplicating processes, *QuickBooks Pro* notes that classes should not be used to track types of clients or vendors because the program already creates profiles of these entities.

There are many other useful features for interior designers in *QuickBooks Pro*, including the format for creating estimates for a project and converting the estimate to an invoice. You can also track your time according to the client, project, design service, location, date, duration, fees, and billable time. These timesheets can be used to invoice a client and to create paychecks for the designer. In addition, you can access business data using your mobile device—iPhone, BlackBerry, and Android (Figure 12.2).

Vendor Transactions and Inventory

Many of the same software features used to organize and manage clients also apply to vendor records. Thus, you can create files for each vendor that include the name, contact

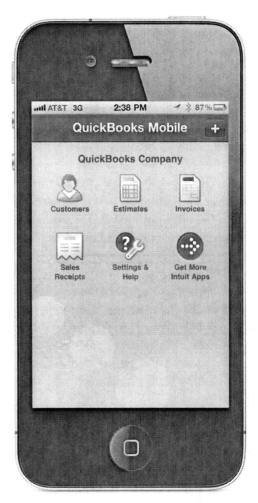

Figure 12.2 Business data stored in QuickBooks accounting software program can be accessed using a mobile device—iPhone, BlackBerry, and Android. (*Intuit*)

information, addresses, account number, and payment terms. Items purchased from the vendor are recorded in that company's file as well as accounts payable.

When the item was purchased for a specific client, *QuickBooks Pro* can automatically generate an invoice for the client. The program has a feature to write and print checks as well as generate vendor reports detailing all transactions with that vendor.

For design firms that have inventory, *QuickBooks Pro* enables you to create a file for each item that includes the item name/number, manufacturer, description, cost, sale price, and vendor. The program can also notify you when inventory is low on a particular item as well as charge and collect sales tax.

Purchase orders can be created with the program. When the item is received with additional charges, such as postage or freight, these amounts are stored in an expense file.

The program can generate inventory reports that include a summary of existing items, the number on hand, and when an item should be reordered. After an item is sold, the program allows you to create invoices, apply any applicable discounts, indicate payment terms, and ship items when necessary.

QuickBooks Pro has a feature to accept electronic payments from clients and assess finance charges for late payments. When sales tax has been collected, the manage sales tax program helps you to both determine the amount you owe and complete the local and state sales tax forms.

Payroll and Financial Reports

Managing payroll is complicated because of local, state, and federal legal requirements (see Chapter 14). In addition, to maintain good relationships with your employees, always make sure paychecks are accurate. Therefore, many small businesses outsource their payroll activities. For business owners wanting to manage their payroll, *QuickBooks Pro* has a program that enables you to process the payroll, manage your employee list, and create paychecks.

The program can also allow you to track and pay payroll liabilities, such as taxes collected for the federal government and other deductions. You can also generate basic payroll forms, such as W-2, W-3, 940, 941, 1099 MISC, and 1096 (see *IRS Publication 334—Tax Guide for Small Businesses*).

In addition to generating payroll forms, accounting software programs can produce P&L statements and balance sheets. P&L reports can be created after all revenue and expense transactions have been entered. As illustrated in

Table 10.4, the balance sheet report displays all the business's asset, liability, and owner's equity accounts. Software programs can "memorize" the report, enabling you to use the same format for future balance sheets.

Business Credit Agencies

To facilitate financial transactions, businesses should be creditworthy and registered with credit agencies. Registration with a credit agency serves multiple purposes, such as verifying the business, establishing a business credit/profile, and accessing other companies' business reports.

A strong business credit rating is needed to acquire loans and create accounts with vendors and suppliers. A solid credit rating might improve the terms of a loan, interest rates, insurance premiums, and lease terms for office space.

How does a business acquire a solid credit rating? Generally, financial institutions and businesses focus on the 4 C's of credit: Character, Capacity, Capital, and Conditions. Dun & Bradstreet (D&B), one of the most reliable credit agencies, provides the following definitions of the 4 C's of credit (2001):

> *Character* includes factors such as size, location, number of years in business, business structure, number of employees, history of principals, appetite for sharing information about itself, media coverage, liens, judgments or pending law suits, stock performance, and comments from references.
>
> *Capacity* assesses the ability of the business to pay its bills, i.e., its cash flow. It also includes the structure of the company's debt—whether secured or unsecured—and the existence of an unused lines of credit. Any defaults must also be identified.
>
> *Capital* assesses whether a company has the financial resources (obtained from financial records) to repay their creditors. **In general, this portion of the credit report is the one most closely reviewed by the credit analyst.** Heavy weighting is given to such

balance sheet items as working capital, net worth, and cash flow.

Conditions consider the external factors surrounding the business under consideration—influences such as market fluctuations, industry growth rate, political/legislative factors, and currency rates.

Many companies establish their business credit with D&B and apply for a **D-U-N-S number**. A D-U-N-S number is a business classification system and is required in order to work for some governmental agencies. To determine a credit profile, D&B examines various financial transactions, such as payment and banking data from suppliers, lien holders, financial reports, and loans.

Based on their investigation, a "complete D&B business credit report includes the following proprietary scores and ratings: (1) D&B Rating: an overall assessment of your business's creditworthiness and visibility, (2) PAYDEX Score: a predictive indicator that measures the likelihood of your business paying within an agreed upon timeframe, (3) Credit Limit Recommendation: D&B's guideline as to how much credit should be extended to your business, and (4) Financial Stress Score: a measurement of the likelihood that your business will experience financial stress in the next 12 months (D&B 2011).

Two credit agencies are associated with the design profession. For annual dues you can become a member of the Allied Board of Trade (ABT) credit agency (see http://www.allbusiness.com/). Members of the ABT include interior designers, interior decorators, and design firms. ABT provides business services such as arbitration, collection assistance, source information, and credit reports. It also provides trade information about manufacturers and jobbers in the United States. ABT publishes *Interior Designer Classification Directory* and the *National Directory of Professional Interior Decorators and Designers*.

The Lyon Mercantile Group, Ltd (Lyon Furniture Mercantile Agency) began in 1876 by providing credit information and collection services to the furniture trade (see http://www.lyoncredit.com/). By 1909, credit ratings posted in the *Lyon Red Book* became the definitive resource for the furniture industry. Over the years the organization expanded its services to include the textile, bedding, lighting, and gift industries. Members have access to the organization's database of thousands of businesses related to interior design, including retail and manufacturing. Currently, the Lyon Mercantile Group publishes Lyon Credit reports and hosts industry credit groups for the purpose of primarily managing risk.

Financing a Business

Excellent business credit reports and scores are very important when you need financing. Methods for acquiring funds include **equity financing**, loans, and establishing a **line of credit** with a financial institution.

Equity financing is a method of acquiring funds by selling a percentage of ownership to investors. Equity financing does not involve repayments, but the transaction can result in relinquishing some control of the business.

Loans from financial institutions are considered **debt financing** because of the repayments. A business loan involves receiving cash and paying back the amount with interest for a designated period. The document for loans is called a **promissory note**.

Generally, short-term loans are less than a year, intermediate loans are one to five years, and long-term loans are greater than five years. Typically, short-term loans require a lump-sum payment; long-term loans are repaid with monthly payments. Interest rates for short-term loans are usually higher than long-term loans.

Short-term loans usually cover immediate expenses, such as purchasing inventory or making vendors' payments while waiting for clients to pay your firm. Intermediate and long-term loans are often used for fixed assets, such as equipment or land for a building.

A business can establish a line of credit with a bank whereby a specified amount of cash is available in an account for withdrawals on an as-needed basis. Interest is charged only for the amount borrowed.

As noted in Chapter 10, it can be difficult for new businesses to acquire loans, but successful, established businesses can obtain loans with low interest rates and favorable terms. To evaluate your loan application, banks (as well as suppliers and vendors) will examine the items discussed in the previous section, such as the 4 C's of credit and your credit score and report. Lenders also want to see balance sheets and P&L statements for at least the two most recent years.

In reviewing financial statements, lenders will examine your business's **debt-equity ratio** or the total amount you owe (liabilities) compared to what you totally own (owner's equity).

To calculate the ratio, you divide total debt by your total equity (debt/equity = debt-equity ratio). A high number indicates a high risk due to a large amount of debt. Thus, lenders prefer the lowest number possible, generally between 50 and 150.

As noted under "Capacity," a financial risk consideration is whether a loan is **secured** or **unsecured**. A secured loan requires the borrower to provide **collateral**, such as a building or equipment, and is often required for long-term loans. The asset serves to protect the lender in case of a default.

An unsecured loan does not involve collateral and is basically granted due to creditworthiness. Unsecured loans are frequently used for short-term borrowing.

Checking for Comprehension

* Explain cash and accrual accounting methods.

* Identify two ways an interior designer could use an accounting software program.

Strategic Management Planning

Chapter 10 explained the major elements that should be included in a business plan. **Strategic**

plans and business plans share some of the same categories, such as management, marketing, and finance. Thus, a business plan can serve as a foundation for developing a strategic plan, but as reviewed in this section, a strategic plan is focused on identifying strategies that will improve your business within the context of its capabilities and external conditions. What are some of the differences between the two plans?

A business plan is focused on the feasibility of starting or expanding a business and is typically shared with external financial audiences, as in the case of preparing documents for potential investors. Generally, a strategic plan is an internal management document and is used to (1) assess the business's current situation, (2) determine the vision and direction of the business, and (3) identify the best approaches for the business to successfully reach its goals.

Strategic Management Plan: Components and Processes

Once a business is started, the owner must use management tools that can help to continuously improve every aspect of the business, including operations, management, marketing, finances, and public relations. Thus, a good time to begin identifying improvement strategies is approximately one year after the opening of the business. At this time you will be able to gather enough information to determine your business's strengths and weaknesses within the context of the design industry, your competition, and global events. You can then use this data to create strategies that will improve your business. All of these items as well as other considerations become elements of a strategic plan—often a five-year vision for the business.

The basic elements of a strategic plan include the (1) mission statement, vision, and values; (2) SWOT analysis; (3) goals, objectives, **strategies**, and **tactics**; and (4) communication, implementation, assessment, and continuous improvement.

This list provides an overview of the strategic plan's content as well as the order of the process (see Figure 12.3 for a graphic version of the list). Thus, to create a strategic plan, begin with the first items in the list (e.g., mission statement, vision). Then do the **SWOT analysis**. The items in the first two steps are used to create the goals, objectives, strategies, and tactics for the business. All the information gathered in the initial steps are communicated to employees so the plan can be implemented and then continuously improved.

Strategic Plan: Processes

Creating an effective strategic planning document requires considerable time and resources. For very small businesses the owner is responsible for creating the document. For intermediate and large businesses the process should be collaborative and can involve using the business tools described in Chapter 8, such as affinity diagrams, relations diagrams, and matrix diagrams.

Creating a sense of ownership related to the strategic plan requires that people take part in this; successful implementation depends on participation. Therefore, the firm's owner and a team of employees should develop the document.

Ideally, to help ensure that all topics are considered, team members should include an individual from every area/division in the business.

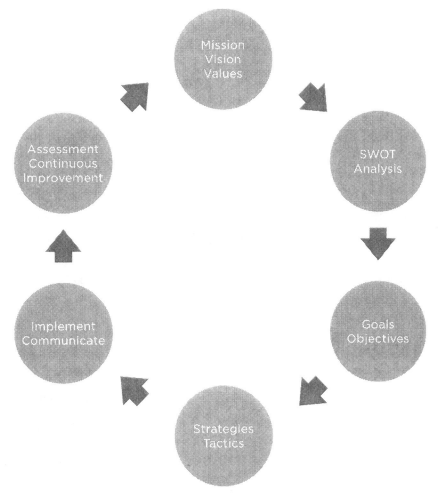

Figure 12.3 The basic elements of a strategic plan are (1) mission statement, philosophy, values, and vision; (2) SWOT (strengths, weaknesses, opportunities, and threats) analysis; (3) goals, objectives, strategies, and tactics; (4) communication, implementation, assessment, and continuous improvement.

All employees should also have the opportunity to provide input by commenting on drafts of the document. Every year the document development process should be repeated and the analyses results used to create a new five-year strategic plan.

Integrating Knowledge of Strategic Planning with Design Services

Learning the processes used to create a strategic plan as well as its critical components are very useful for your business. How? This knowledge can be used to provide additional services to clients. For example, in addition to interior design and architecture, HOK's services include strategic planning. HOK, an international firm, is consistently one of the top five firms in industry rankings, including *Interior Design*'s *Giants* and AIA's "Top 10 Green Projects List."

According to the firm, *HOK Advance Strategies* aligns "an organization's business strategies with their people, real estate, facilities, workplaces and information systems to achieve business objectives and gain competitive advantage. Our innovative strategies help clients make value-based decisions, make effective changes and achieve quantifiable results" (HOK 2011) (Box 12.1 and Figure 12.4).

Therefore, as illustrated in Box 12.1, HOK integrates its knowledge of strategic planning with its design expertise. Consequently, design-related considerations, such as workspace, technology, human factors, and sustainable design, are elements of the firm's clients' strategic plan. An example of incorporating the principles of sustainability is HOK's loop for continuous improvement in the *GSA Workplace 20/20 Process* (Figure 12.4).

Strategic Management Plan: Current Assessment

The development of a strategic plan begins by gathering data and performing an assessment of your firm's current situation. Gathering information helps you create a snapshot of your current business, such as your mission statement,

---

Box 12.1
A Design Firm Offering Strategic Planning Services*

Client Profile: GSA (Government Services Administration) Headquarters, Washington, DC

Project: GSA Workplace 20-20 Research Program

Locations: 22 Pilot Projects in 11 GSA regions

HOK Advance Strategies Responsibilities:

* Primary partner in developing a workplace strategy and processes for GSA's Workplace 20/20. The program helps GSA offices to develop effective workplaces that:

  * Support work processes

  * Enhance performance and satisfaction

  * Contribute to the bottom line

* Developed a toolkit for pilot project teams.

* Created a communication and training strategy for projects throughout the United States.

*Adapted from: HOK. 2011. *Advance Strategies*. http://www.hok.com/. Retrieved April 6, 2011.

GSA WORKPLACE 20•20 PROCESS

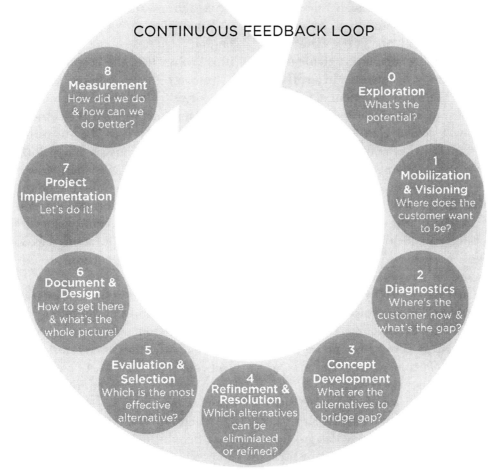

CONTINUOUS FEEDBACK LOOP

8 **Measurement** How did we do & how can we do better?

0 **Exploration** What's the potential?

1 **Mobilization & Visioning** Where does the customer want to be?

7 **Project Implementation** Let's do it!

6 **Document & Design** How to get there & what's the whole picture!

2 **Diagnostics** Where's the customer now & what's the gap?

5 **Evaluation & Selection** Which is the most effective alternative?

4 **Refinement & Resolution** Which alternatives can be eliminated or refined?

3 **Concept Development** What are the alternatives to bridge gap?

Figure 12.4 The GSA Workplace 20/20 Process with a continuous feedback loop (HOK 2011).

vision, values, revenues, clients, projects, expenses, suppliers, and vendors. When available, also have data for at least the previous year.

The business records provide the basis for examining your firm's strengths and weaknesses. In addition, you might want to gather perceptions of your business by asking employees, clients, and stakeholders to complete an online survey and/or to participate in interviews or focus groups.

Identifying your firm's strengths and weaknesses is only half of the information needed for a SWOT analysis. A current assessment of your firm's position also requires an examination of external conditions and events that can affect your success—opportunities and threats. An excellent method to identify business opportunities as well as real or potential threats is to have brainstorming sessions with people who are knowledgeable about your firm and the design profession, such as employees, contractors, suppliers, and vendors.

Current Analysis: Mission Statement, Vision, and Values

An analysis of a firm's current condition should begin by reexamining the mission statement (see Chapter 10). The mission statement is the basis for making many of the decisions required for a strategic plan. Is the statement still accurate? Are there significant changes to your business that must be included in a revised version? Because a mission statement is a declaration of the purpose of your business, chances are good you will not have to make changes, but it is important to either reaffirm or revise its contents for the development of a strategic plan.

While reviewing your mission statement, make sure that it succinctly states: (1) the purpose of the business, (2) the clients you are serving, (3) the value your firm is adding, (4) how your business is unique, and (5) your social responsibilities and business ethics.

As noted in Chapter 10, a business might want a two- or three-sentence mission statement (this will make it easy to remember). However, longer statements, as illustrated in Herman Miller's corporate mission statement, are an effective way to ensure the essentials are addressed as well as other items of importance, as with a **vision statement** (Box 12.2). Herman Miller, Inc. is a global company that designs furnishings and provides related services. In fiscal year 2010 the company's net sales were approximately $1.3 billion.

A vision statement is a declaration that describes your highest expectations for your business in the future. Use your imagination and dare to think big—the intent of the vision is your source of inspiration for long-term planning. For example, a visionary statement in Herman Miller's mission statement is "Ultimately, our aspiration is to design and build a better world around you" (Herman Miller 2010). A vision statement often includes references to being the world leader in a particular service or product—the best of the best.

To become the best of the best requires the *implementation* of corporate values that are universally respected. Values or beliefs serve as the

principles for behavior and business decisions. The business's values indicate its modes of operation as well as how it intends to interact with customers, stakeholders, the community, and perhaps the world.

For example, at Herman Miller one of the company's values is "curiosity and exploration" (Box 12.2). Thus, the corporation is interested in "research-driven designs" and wants to sustain curiosity "by respecting and encouraging risk" (Herman Miller 2011). Another value is "transparency," which "begins with letting people see how decisions are made and owning the decisions we make" (Herman Miller 2011).

Note in the previous paragraph that "implementation" is italicized to emphasize the importance of assimilating values into business practices. Some corporations develop a list of core values, but their actions do not reflect the stated ethos.

In order to be respected by clients, the design industry, and the community, the behavior of every person connected with the business must embody the values proclaimed by the business. For example, a customer of Herman Miller expects "transparency" regarding decision making.

When values are not upheld, the disappointment people feel can lead to cynicism, which can result in a search for a different design firm. Simply stated, walk your talk.

Current Analysis: Business Statistics

In addition to reexamining values as well as the mission statement and vision, an assessment of your firm's current situation requires an analysis of the basic components of an interior design business: clients, finances, human resources, management, and marketing. When available you should have data for at least the previous year and preferably for the past three years.

An analysis of your clients requires gathering all data associated with them and their projects. One way of doing this is by creating a list of your existing clients, locations, type of buildings (market), services provided, products purchased, and interior design fees. Project details

Box 12.2

Herman Miller, Inc.: Corporate Mission Statement*
and Corporate Values—*What We Believe***

We will be the leading provider of thoughtfully designed interior products for places where people work, heal, learn, and live. Our products will solve real problems, delight the eye, complement the ways our customers choose to express their environments, and they will be affordable. We will be an inspiration to our customers in the ways we create a great place to work for our employees, achieve operational excellence, provide a solid investment for our shareholders, advocate for the environment, unite a diverse and talented group of people, and exemplify a force for positive change in the communities in which we live and serve.

*Ultimately, our aspiration is to design and build a better world around you. Whether you are an employee, a customer, a shareholder, or a neighbor, we will use our energy, our creativity, and our resources to improve the places where you work, heal, learn, and live.**

Corporate Values**

Things That Matter—These beliefs unite all Herman Miller employees. They are the basis on which we build relationships and contribute to the community.

Curiosity & Exploration—These are two of our greatest strengths. They lie behind our heritage of research-driven design.

Engagement—For us it is about being owners—actively committed to the life of this community called Herman Miller, sharing in its success and risk.

Performance—Performance is required for leadership. We want to be leaders, so we are committed to performing at the highest level possible.

Relationships—We work hard to create and keep relationships. With customers, designers, dealers, suppliers, contractors, and among ourselves.

Inclusiveness—To succeed as a company we must include all the expressions of human talent and potential that society offers.

Design—Design for us is a way of looking at the world and how it works – or doesn't. It is a method for getting something done, for solving a problem.

Foundations—The past can be a tricky thing—an anchor or a sail—a tether or a launching pad. We value and respect our past without being ruled by it.

A Better World—This is at the heart of Herman Miller and the real reason why many of us come to work every day.

Transparency—Transparency begins with letting people see how decisions are made and owning the decisions we make.

*Source: Herman Miller. 2010. *A Better World Report*. http://www.hermanmiller.com/. Retrieved April 19, 2011.

**Source: Herman Miller. 2011. What We Believe. http://www.hermanmiller.com/About-Us/What-We-Believe. Retrieved April 19, 2011.

should include the phase of the design process, square footages (meters), and the dollar value of the installations. Client data also should include how you acquired your current clients and your list of prospective clients.

Financial data needed for planning purposes include previous and updated P&L statements, balance sheets, and cash flow statements. Specifically, identify total fees earned, billing rates, cost of sales, fixed expenses, accounts receivable, inventory, and accounts payable. As illustrated in the next section, these statistics are useful for many reasons, including analyzing the relationship between revenues and employee expenses. Therefore, create a list of all your employees and their respective areas of expertise and fees earned. This list should also include employees who are not responsible for earning fees, such as bookkeepers or administrative assistants.

Other information related to human resources you should gather includes any documents related to employee policies and procedures, such as job applications, benefits brochures, and employee handbooks.

Management data can include a summary of your firm's leaders, the board of directors, and publications created by the firm, such as annual reports, sustainability reports, case studies, research summaries, and design essays. These publications are also important for analyzing your marketing initiatives.

Other items related to marketing can include industry rankings, awards, competition submissions, exhibitions, community service, innovations, environmental initiatives, articles, press releases, blogs, social networks, and videos.

SWOT Internal Analysis: Strengths and Weaknesses

After all the data related to your firm's clients, human resources, management, finances, and marketing activities have been collected, your strategic planning team can begin analyzing the firm's current situation. The most common way of doing this is determining the firm's strengths and weaknesses (Figure 12.5).

In addition, the analysis must be performed within the context of the firm's mission statement, vision, and values. Thus, for example, when strengths have been identified, such as high revenues, ask if the revenue-producing projects were aligned with the purpose of the firm as described in the mission statement.

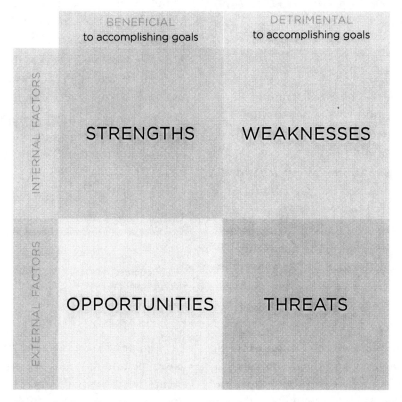

Figure 12.5 A SWOT (strengths, weaknesses, opportunities, and threats) grid.

Were the projects reflective of where the firm wants to be in the future? Were the corporate values evident in the actions required to generate the revenues?

When disconnects occur between a business's philosophical beliefs and its outcomes, corrective actions are needed. The strategic planning process is an ideal format to identify and resolve these differences.

Strengths and Weaknesses: Clients

What are the strengths and weaknesses of your current client portfolio? An immediate response could be "We don't have enough." This might be viewed as a weakness of your firm. However, depending on the capacity of your firm, the number of clients could actually be considered one of its strengths.

There must be a balance between the number of designers and the number of clients and projects. Too many designers for the number of clients can affect profits when the payroll exceeds revenues. Too many clients and projects for the number of designers can affect client relationships when there isn't adequate time to address the clients' needs. This scenario illustrates an important consideration as you are determining your strengths and weaknesses. As your team identifies strengths and weaknesses, be sure to determine the classification within the context of various issues, including your firm's capacity to appropriately accommodate the needs of all your clients.

Again, what are the strengths and weaknesses of your current clientele? Are your actions creating loyal clients? As your team members analyze client data, they must answer several questions. These should focus on client relationships, design knowledge, project management skills, and continuing education. For example, your team should answer client-relationship questions such as:

* How well do we understand the needs of our clients and their business?

* Do we know exactly what our clients are trying to achieve with their projects?

* Do we understand our clients' competitive advantages?

* What is their level of satisfaction with our designs and customer services?

* Are we building long-term relationships with our clients?

* How would our clients evaluate our communication skills?

* How would they evaluate our listening skills and presentations?

* Do our clients feel we are adding value to their projects?

* Do our clients believe our fees are properly aligned with the services we provide?

* Are clients happy with the products we specify?

* Are we happy with how we are working on building long-term relationships and pursuing prospective clients?

Strengths and Weaknesses: Design Knowledge

Questions related to the firm's current design knowledge could focus on types of buildings, technologies, and services. Questions related to buildings could be categorized according to the type as well as the greatest and least number of projects. For example, your team might want to analyze the strengths and weaknesses of all projects completed for educational facilities, retail stores, or residences. If most of the projects involved one type of market (such as commercial office buildings), questions could focus on determining whether the firm's design solutions were specific to the needs of the client, or if the solutions were primarily determined by the type of building (for example, a commercial office building). If appropriate, how well did your firm handle large and complex projects?

Analysis of the firm's design knowledge could also focus on its ability to solve interior problems:

* How well did you solve your clients' space problems?

- How well did you understand new products, materials, and technologies?

- How well did you understand the elements of a building that affect the design of an interior, such as mechanical systems, structural systems, building codes, building methods, ceiling systems, electrical, security systems, and fire safety?

- How well did you design for human behavior and universal needs?

- Did you use the results of research to solve problems?

Questions related to design services should be framed within the context of services provided, client/end user satisfaction, and services not provided:

- Given the services performed, how would your clients and end users evaluate the outcomes?

- Which services would your clients and end users evaluate as exceptional, average, or weak?

- Why weren't specific services performed? Does your firm lack personnel or expertise? Were your clients unaware of design services?

- If your firm did not win a particular contract, what was the reason?

- How would international clients evaluate your firm's business protocols and your understanding of cultural dimensions and diverse communication styles?

An evaluation of services also includes your firm's project management skills:

- Were your projects completed on time and within budget?

- Were there problems with your drawings or specifications?

- How well did the firm execute the phases of the design process—predesign, program-

ming, schematic design, design development, contract documents, and contract administration?

- Were postoccupancy evaluations performed appropriately and in a timely manner?

Strengths and Weaknesses:
Education and Human Resources

Answers to the questions posed during the strengths and weaknesses assessment should be reviewed within the context of educational needs. Do you or your employees need to take courses, attend seminars, network with professionals, or study research articles to develop a better understanding of areas where your firm is either strong or weak?

Accommodating the educational needs of employees is the responsibility of management. Thus, employees' educational opportunities should be evaluated as well as other issues connected to a firm's human resource policies and procedures:

- What are the strengths and weaknesses of your firm's human resources and management?

- Are employees satisfied with the firm's benefits package?

- Do employees believe their salaries and wages are in line with comparable firms?

- Do employees feel they are rewarded for activities associated with the firm's corporate values, such as community service?

- How would employees rate team cohesiveness and the effectiveness of collaboration?

- How would employees rate their own time management skills?

- How would employees rate the firm's ability to manage information and knowledge?

- What are the strengths and weaknesses of the design firm's location, facilities, equipment, computers, supplies, inventory, and sample library?

Human resources and management effectiveness also involves office procedures and relationships with stakeholders:

* How would employees and recipients evaluate the efficiency of processing paperwork, such as purchase orders, contracts, and invoices?

* How effective are your methods for tracking orders and deliveries?

* Are your suppliers paid promptly?

* How would suppliers, vendors, and tradespeople rate your communication skills?

* How would employees rate your firm's relationship with suppliers, vendors, and tradespeople?

* How would suppliers, vendors, and tradespeople rate their relationship with your firm?

Strengths and Weaknesses: Finances and Marketing

The SWOT analysis also involves finance questions:

* What are the strengths and weaknesses of your firm's finances compared to industry standards?

* Do your financial policies, such as fees and service charges, help to create loyal clients?

* Are your compensation and fees appropriate?

* Was your billable time equivalent to the actual hours spent on a particular project?

* Are you considering all the variables that can affect fees?

* Are you accurately reporting billable hours?

* What is your ratio of billable hours and square footages (meters)? Is the ratio reasonable and aligned with industry standards?

* What is your ratio of installed square footage (meters) and number of designers as

well as number of employees? Are the ratios aligned with industry standards?

The marketing program also has to be addressed:

* What are the strengths and weaknesses of your firm's marketing program and branding?

* Is your marketing program focused on creating loyal clients (e.g., targeting prospects who need your services or including current clients in mailings and/or social events)?

* Why would clients want to hire your firm?

* Is your firm able to fulfill their needs and solve their problems? In what ways?

* How did you acquire your current clients?

* What are you doing to maintain contact with your current clients?

* How are you trying to earn new clients?

* Do employees feel knowledgeable about your target market?

* Does your firm have updated and comprehensive target market data, such as demographics and psychographics?

An evaluation of your marketing program also involves examining your competitors and your marketing position:

* Do employees feel knowledgeable about your competition and how competitors impact your business?

* Do your marketing strategies promote your firm's branding, credibility, visibility, and networking opportunities?

* Are all elements of your business, including customer service and relationships with suppliers, directed toward developing your brand?

* How would employees, clients, stakeholders, and the community rate the quality of

your presentations, website, social media strategies, drawings, material boards, specifications, proposals, correspondence, brochures, and reports?

Your firm's list of strengths and weaknesses must then be prioritized. To develop priorities, the strategic planning team can use the business tools described in Chapter 8. Fundamentally, criteria used for prioritization should be based on the firm's mission statement, vision, values as well as its current capacity to serve clients. The prioritized list of your business's strengths and weaknesses are just two of the components in the SWOT analysis. The next section explains the other two elements—opportunities and threats.

SWOT External Environmental Analysis: Opportunities and Threats

Identifying strengths and weaknesses is basically an internal analysis of your business (Figure 12.5). Exploring opportunities and threats is approached using an external perspective. Thus, to identify opportunities and threats, the strategic planning team engages in brainstorming that includes gathering data related to the external environment, the design industry, and your operating environment.

Chapter 10 introduced the concept of assessing the environment within the context of writing the business plan's marketing section. Some of the sources of information identified in Chapter 10 can also be applied to the SWOT analysis. However, creating marketing strategies is different than developing a strategic plan. Marketing strategies are focused on promoting your credibility, visibility, and networking opportunities.

Marketing is an element of a strategic plan, but to reach its goals, a business must consider all areas that affect revenues and expenses— hence, the importance of strategic planning. Your strategic planning team must understand the distinctions between marketing and strategic planning when analyzing the external environment. Events and conditions that can present opportunities as well as threats must be examined from a holistic, big-picture perspective.

What are opportunities and threats? For strategic planning purposes, opportunities are viewed as any factor or situation that could promote the success and profitability of your business. A threat is a factor or situation that has the potential to be unfavorable to your business. A design firm could have both immediate and long-term opportunities and threats.

As your team examines the external environment, keep in mind that some threats can present opportunities with the development of an appropriate strategic plan. For example, the team might identify a global shortage of cotton fiber as a threat to your design firm. This situation should prompt the team to brainstorm ways to convert the shortage of cotton into an opportunity for the firm. Thus, the strategic plan could indicate that designers should try to avoid specifying materials produced with cotton and demonstrate their innovativeness by selling textiles made from recently developed fibers.

Opportunities and Threats: Extended Environment

What opportunities and threats in the extended environment could affect your design business? Extended environmental factors are situations out of your control, such as a hurricane or a war in a foreign country. Even though remote situations are uncontrollable, a business must constantly keep abreast of global conditions and develop strategies for either taking advantage of opportunities or addressing threats.

Generally, areas to monitor include economics, politics, social factors, demographics, cultural issues, legal systems, technology, ecology, and globalization. Sources for general public information can include credible websites, TV and radio news programs, newspapers, and weekly newsmagazines. Information can also be derived from publications targeted to non-design professionals, such as economists, sociologists, psychologists, and environmental scientists.

Opportunities and Threats: Design Industry

What opportunities and threats in the design industry could affect your design business?

Extended environmental factors can obviously impact the design industry, but there are also specific factors and situations that can affect a particular industry. For example, the ability for consumers to purchase discounted furnishings online affects the entire design industry.

When your team is identifying opportunities and threats in the design industry, areas to consider include suppliers, technology, government regulations, and consumer behavior. For example,

* What is the current status of suppliers?

* Are they creating new products?

* Are items discontinued?

* Are there new projects that could transform practices?

* Are there technological innovations or new government regulations that can affect business?

* How have consumer behavior and preferences changed?

Information related to these issues can be discovered via networking, attending professional conferences, reading trade journals/newsletters/blogs, and interacting with sales representatives.

Opportunities and Threats: Operating Environment

What opportunities and threats in your firm's operating environment could affect your design business? Opportunities could come from new construction activities, renovation projects, or increases in the local population. Examples of other potential opportunities could include the closure of a competitor's design firm or new professionals to partner with, such as tradespeople, architects, engineers, or contractors.

Threats to your design business could include the opening of a potential competitor's business or an established firm's expansion of services. Changes in your competitor's compensation and fees schedule could be a threat, as could be the closing of a supplier or service provider, such as an upholsterer or painter. Your business could be threatened when a major employer in your community decides to close its offices or when officials no longer support a proposed major highway through your city.

Reexamine the preceding suggested opportunities and threats, and notice that learning this important information requires your involvement with other local professionals, in addition to participation in community activities. Thus, excellent data sources about potential opportunities and threats in your operating environment are local professional organizations and community organizations, such as the chamber of commerce, city councils, historical societies, and museums. Other sources of information are local newspapers and regional publications.

As with the process used to assess strengths and weaknesses, your list of opportunities and threats must be prioritized according to your firm's mission, vision, and values. At this stage of the strategic planning process, the team can identify your firm's competitive advantages by combining its strengths with external opportunities. Your firm's competitive challenges are its weaknesses and external threats.

Strategic Management Plan: Determining a Direction and Reaching Goals

Your firm's competitive advantages and challenges are used to develop goals as well as the mission, vision, and values. Goals are then used to develop objectives, which serve as the basis for creating strategies. Tactics are then used to implement the strategies.

This developmental chronology is crucial for the success of a strategic plan. As illustrated in Figure 12.3, your firm's direction begins with the mission/vision/values → SWOT analysis → goals → objectives → strategies → tactics. Following this path helps ensure that all actions (tactics) support the firm's mission, realize the firm's vision, and adhere to the firm's values. The path therefore begins with a very broad perspective and ends with very detailed plans for action.

Strategic Management Plan: Goals and Objectives

Note in the path described above that goals are developed *before* objectives. This chronology helps to explain some of the differences between goals and objectives. Knowing the difference between these two terms is imperative when you are developing a strategic plan because each term represents a unique concept. In addition, goals are the basis for developing objectives.

Goals should be tackled after you develop your mission/vision/values. Goals are broad statements about what your business wants to accomplish in the long term. As broad statements, goals must be applicable to every employee and operational area within your firm. A broad perspective translates to having very few strategic planning goals—perhaps just three. Goals must be feasible and practical. In other words, the business must have the ability to accomplish the goals at a reasonable cost.

An excellent way to develop your strategic planning goals is to answer the following question: What are we trying to accomplish? For most businesses, one answer to this question is to be "profitable." Thus, a goal could be to *improve the net worth of our design firm*. Another goal could be to *increase our international operations* or *improve relationships with clients*. Note that these goals are broad statements requiring the involvement of the entire organization. Accomplishing these broad goals requires many initiatives over several years. In addition, achieving these goals benefits the business and promotes the purpose of the organization.

Every goal in a strategic plan is accompanied by objectives. In contrast to the broad and long-term perspectives associated with goals, **objectives** are very specific and are used for short-term accomplishments. Goals are applicable to the entire organization; objectives are directed to a specific area or function. Goals are general intents, whereas objectives are measurable outcomes.

Thus, objectives can be viewed as specific directives for accomplishing a task that includes how achievement is quantitatively measured. For example, an objective for the goal to *improve relationships with clients* could be as follows: *Improve client satisfaction by 20 percent in 12 months*. In addition, for this objective the team must identify how client satisfaction would be evaluated, such as using an online customer survey or focus groups.

Measurability is essential for objectives because quantitative figures are the means to determine if you are accomplishing your objectives. For example, if the objective is *Improve client satisfaction by 20 percent in 12 months*—client satisfaction levels could be periodically analyzed to determine progress or setbacks. If an objective does not include a means for measurement, such as *Improve client satisfaction*, there is no way of knowing if any improvements actually occurred, and the open-endedness of the statement could imply that designers had years and years to improve client satisfaction.

Strategic Management Plan: Strategies, Tactics, and Performance Indicators

Strategies are identified for every objective in a strategic plan. Strategies focus on *how* you will accomplish each objective, with an emphasis on maximizing your competitive advantages and overcoming challenges. Thus, developing strategies requires a thorough reexamination of your SWOT analysis while keeping in mind your mission, vision, and values. These elements are the basis for strategies and are very useful for prioritizing (including prioritizing the list of potential strategies).

Generally, each objective has several strategies, and a strategy might be directed to one particular area of a business, such as management or marketing. For example, for the objective *Improve client satisfaction by 20 percent in 12 months*, the team might have four strategies: (1) *track projects to ensure completions on time and on budget*, (2) *plan social event for clients*, (3) *schedule regular personal contacts with previous and current clients*, and (4) *conduct an assessment of unrealized projects and one-time clients*.

One approach to integrating the results of your SWOT analysis with the strategies is to use a 4-x-4 matrix; one axis represents strengths/weaknesses, and the other is for opportunities/threats (Table 12.1). A strategy can be developed for each quadrant in the matrix. For the example in Table 12.1, a design firm's competitive advantages are its ability to attract new clients (strength) and the closure of a local competitive design firm (opportunity). The firm's competitive challenges are its project management skills (weakness) and the economic downturn (threat).

As illustrated in Table 12.1, the design firm has identified a strategy in each quadrant that maximizes its competitive advantages and minimizes its disadvantages.

Every strategy requires tactics. Basically, tactics are the actions that must be done to accomplish a strategy. For example, for the strategy *Track projects to ensure completions on time and within budget*, the team might have four tactics: (1) *utilize a project management software program*, (2) *monitor estimated and actual costs*, (3) *track project deliveries and installations*, and (4) *increase site supervisions*.

These examples illustrate several important considerations related to developing and implementing tactics. Note that the tactics are for a particular task, but they lack the details required to actually execute the task. Ideally, the person responsible for implementing the task should be the one who provides the details, such as the activities, costs, timelines, and personnel requirements. These details are developed in **action plans**.

To avoid creating tactics that are not reasonable or cost-effective, some businesses ask people who are not on the strategic planning team to help draft tactics for each strategy. Involving the person who will actually be accountable helps to ensure appropriate tactics; that participation gives the person a sense of ownership to the activity, which is important for successful implementation.

Strategic Management Plan: Implementation and Communications

A strategic plan is useless without successful implementation. Therefore, the owner of the design firm in coordination with the strategic planning team must develop a thorough and comprehensive implementation plan. The first step is to create the document. At this stage of the strategic planning process, the team has collected and analyzed all data required for the plan and has developed goals, objectives,

Table 12.1 SWOT Matrix

	Strengths		
Opportunities	Closing businesses enables us to acquire new clients. We must develop strategies to use our strength in attracting clients.	The economic downturn could be the cause of businesses closing. We must develop strategies to work through the economic situation by using our strength in being able to attract new clients.	**Threats**
	Closing businesses enables us to acquire new clients. To retain new clients, we must improve our project management skills.	The economic downturn could be the cause of businesses closing. To avoid the closure of our firm, we must develop strategies to improve our project management skills	
	Weaknesses		

Strength: Attracting new clients

Weakness: Project management skills

Opportunities: Closure of a local competitive design firm

Threats: Economic downturn

strategies, and tactics. These materials must be assembled to create the strategic planning document.

The contents of a strategic plan generally includes: (1) an executive summary; (2) a brief business profile; (3) the firm's mission statement, vision statement, and values; (4) SWOT analysis; (5) goals and objectives; (6) strategies and tactics; and (7) an appendix with supporting documents and information, such as client survey results, demographic statistics, and new government regulations.

Several elements are important for successful implementation of the plan. First, determine the audience of the document. Is the plan for internal use only, or will you also share it with external constituents, such as stakeholders? Internally, should only the owner and team members receive the document, or should it be distributed to some or all of the employees?

Basically, as the number of people who will receive the document increases, the size of the document itself should decrease. Therefore, you might want to share the entire document with very few people and prepare an abbreviated version for other individuals and groups.

In general, the document should be very succinct and accessible online. The easier it is for people to understand as well as access it, the more likely it is that the plan will be implemented.

Successful implementation also requires a comprehensive communications plan. People involved with implementing the plan should be able to provide suggestions for their assigned tasks. The communications plan should include when and how the strategic plan is discussed with the entire design firm and any other relevant entities.

Various communication channels should be considered, such as newsletters, internal blogs, e-mail, and intranet. Integrating the strategic plan with topics covered during weekly or monthly staff meetings can be a very effective approach for demonstrating the importance of the plan, and how successfully implementing the strategies and tactics can improve the profitability of the design firm.

The communications plan should also identify who is responsible for tracking the implementation process, and procedures for any conflicts and corrective actions.

Strategic Management Plan: Assessment and Continuous Improvement

In addition to a communications plan, there should be a plan to routinely assess the strategic plan's activities. Implementation processes must be assessed for several important reasons. First, you will want to make sure that people are actually trying to implement strategies and tactics.

A somewhat frequent source of frustration associated with strategic plans is that considerable time and resources are expended to create the plan, but nothing is ever done with the plan—documents are tucked away on a shelf until it is time to revise the plan again. Thus, you will want to assure people that the time they spent on creating a strategic plan was not wasted and that the owner expects the improvement strategies to be implemented. Assessment is excellent for this purpose, and routinely performed assessments can help identify and correct problems with the recommendations of the strategic plan.

The basic purposes of an assessment are to obtain an overview of how well the strategic plan is being implemented and to indicate when (and if) revisions to the plan are needed. To conduct the assessment, the strategic planning team should examine each objective in the plan and determine what has been accomplished and what areas are problematic. In addition, the team should: (1) reexamine the original SWOT analysis, (2) decide the current relevancy of each SWOT item and make revisions as needed, and (3) add any new SWOT items to the strategic plan.

An assessment plan is aligned with the Plan-Do-Check-Act (PDCA) cycle described in Chapter 8; an assessment (check) must be conducted to improve future practice. Thus, assessments could be done monthly, quarterly, or at expected milestones. The frequency of the assessments can depend on the complexity of the activities and/or their importance to the design firm.

Thus, highly complex tasks that are very important to the firm's profitability require a series of assessments.

Minimally, an assessment of the strategic plan should be done after 12 months of implementation. At this stage of the process, the goals, objectives, strategies, tactics, and action plans of the SWOT analysis should be thoroughly reviewed.

Information gathered during the assessment should be used to improve current activities—this data serves as the foundation for the next version of the plan. In addition, to create the new plan, the strategic planning team should reexamine every element in the original document and make the appropriate additions, deletions, and revisions.

The anniversary of a strategic plan should be marked with a special event, correspondence, or perhaps awards. Some employees will be motivated by receiving accolades for accomplishments—this can help create positive attitudes about the strategic management planning process at your firm.

Checking for Comprehension
* What is the difference between a mission statement and a vision statement?

* Describe the SWOT analysis process.

Chapter 12 continued the overview of owning and operating an interior design business by first examining basic accounting terms and practices with an emphasis on accounting software programs. The second section of the chapter explained key components of strategic management planning, including analyses of current business values and statistics. The SWOT analysis process was reviewed by examining a design firm's clients, the design industry, and the firm's operating environment.

The chapter concluded by explaining the elements of a strategic management plan related to identifying a direction for a design firm and accomplishing goals. Understanding strategic management planning serves as a foundation for the next chapter, *Promoting an Interior Design Business*. Chapter 13 reviews topics relevant to an established business, including strategic marketing and brand development.

Knowledge and Skills Summary

Highlights

* Owners must have a basic knowledge of accounting procedures and be astute at financial management.

* Basic accounting practices involve cash/accrual accounting methods, double-entry and single-entry accounting systems, journals, and ledger accounts.

* Accounting software programs enable an owner to easily and efficiently organize, manage, and store financial records required for a business.

* To facilitate financial transactions, businesses should be creditworthy and registered with credit agencies.

* Methods for acquiring funds for a business include equity financing, loans, and establishing a line of credit with a financial institution.

* A strategic plan is an internal management document and is used to (1) assess the business's current situation, (2) determine the vision and direction of the business, and (3) identify the best approaches for the business to successfully reach its goals.

* A SWOT analysis includes identifying a design firm's strengths and weaknesses, and a current assessment of external conditions and events—opportunities and threats.

* A strategic plan is developed by addressing areas in this sequence: mission/vision/values → SWOT analysis → goals → objectives → strategies → tactics → implementation/communications → assessment → continuous improvement.

Key Terms

accountant

accrual accounting method

action plan

bookkeeper

calendar accounting period

cash accounting method

chart of accounts

collateral

debt-equity ratio

debt financing

double-entry accounting system

drawings

D-U-N-S number

equity financing

fiscal year accounting period

journal

ledger

line of credit

net loss

notes payable

objective

posted

promissory note

single-entry accounting system

secured loan

source document

strategic plan

strategy

SWOT analysis

T-account

tactic

transaction

trial balance

unsecured loan

vision statement

Philosophy and Design Project

A SWOT analysis is influenced by participants' philosophy toward what is perceived to be strengths, weaknesses, opportunities, and threats (see Figure 12.5).

Identify an international design firm. Based on the philosophical beliefs and information presented on the firm's website, develop a list of potential strengths, weaknesses, opportunities, and threats that could affect that firm. Create a graphic design reflecting the firm's philosophy as well as the results of your SWOT analysis.

Research Project

Research accounting software programs and develop a summary of their features, including how the programs can help manage client records/transactions, estimate projects, track time, organize vendor records/transactions, manage inventory, facilitate payroll, and generate financial reports.

Submit your summary in a written report (approximately three pages) that includes an assessment of how software programs can help a business owner to efficiently organize, manage, and store financial records.

Human Factors Research Project

A strategic plan is an internal management document used to (1) assess the business's current situation, (2) determine the vision and direction of the business, and (3) identify the best approaches for the business to successfully reach its goals.

In a team of three to five members, develop a draft (approximately five pages) of a strategic plan with an emphasis on addressing the needs of clients.

References

Dun & Bradstreet (D&B). 2011. *Understanding the Basics of Business Credit*. https://eupdate.dnb.com/. Accessed April 15, 2011.

Hakola, T. 2008. *QuickBooks Pro 2008: Level 1 of 2*. El Sobrante, CA: Labyrinth Learning.

———. 2008. *QuickBooks Pro 2008: Level 2 of 2*. El Sobrante, CA: Labyrinth Learning.

Herman Miller. 2011. What We Believe. http://www.hermanmiller.com/About-Us/What-We-Believe. Accessed April 19, 2011.

———. 2010. *A Better World Report*. http://www.hermanmiller.com/. Accessed April 19, 2011.

HOK. 2011. *Advance Strategies*. http://www.hok.com/. Accessed April 6, 2011.

Internal Revenue Service (IRS). 2011. *IRS Publication 334— Tax Guide for Small Businesses*. http://www.irs.gov/pub/irs-pdf/p334.pdf. Accessed April 14, 2011.

Madeira, L. 2009. *QuickBooks 2009: Solutions Guide*. Indianapolis: Que.

Merriam-Webster. 2011. s.v. "strategic." http://www.merriam-webster.com. Accessed April 18, 2011.

———. 2011. s.v. "tactics." http://www.merriam-webster.com. Accessed April 18, 2011.

CHAPTER 13

Promoting an Interior Design Business

Bölüm 13 (Turkish)
Глава 13 (Ukrainian)
باب 13 (Urdu)

After learning the content in Chapter 13, you will be able to answer the following questions:

* How do I create a strategic marketing and communications program?

* How should I develop the brand of my design firm?

* What are the best strategies for digital and web-based communications?

* How can I market my design firm via social media, public relations, and events?

* How should I manage my marketing program?

To improve the success of an interior design business, many firms develop a strategic marketing and communications program. This chapter explains the components of this program and provides recommendations for best practices. The chapter's first section examines how to create a business profile and research targeted markets as well as those of a competitor.

The second section of the chapter explores the different types of brand communications, including print, digital, and web-based forms. Strategies for creating effective brand communications are highlighted. At the conclusion of the chapter the discussion focuses on brand activities and marketing program management. Areas explored include how to enhance the reputation of a design firm as well as how to establish working relationships with the media.

Figure 13.1 Gensler has a "Brand Design" service that includes "Brand Strategy," "Environmental Graphic Design," "Graphic Design," and "User Research."

An example of its brand design services is the CityCenter Sales Pavilion and Marketing Material in Las Vegas. A team of brand specialists created the space, concepting videos, and printed sales collateral. (© *Michael Weber*)

Strategic Marketing and Communications Programs

Various aspects related to marketing have already been discussed in this book. For example, in Chapter 5, marketing was examined from the perspective of the global marketplace. Chapter 7 examined the importance of marketing for building long-term client relationships. Chapter 10 introduced marketing strategies for the purpose of developing the first business plan, and Chapter 12 explained marketing activities from the perspective of strategic management planning.

This book's various discussions of marketing demonstrate several significant facets of the topic. First, understanding marketing strategies is important when you are an employee in a design firm, as illustrated in material covered in Chapters 5 and 7, as well as when you own a business (Chapters 10–14).

We will now explore another, broader idea: that marketing very often is integrated with various activities required for professional practice. In fact, in addition to implementing marketing strategies, some design firms have added design services associated with marketing, such

as branding or visual communications (Figure 13.1). The breadth of the marketing coverage in this book also illustrates the importance of marketing strategies to interior design firms in the twenty-first century, for both large and small businesses.

Why large *and* small? It might appear that marketing is important for large firms because they have intense competitors and often global markets. Large firms also have the resources to develop a comprehensive marketing program, hire in-house marketing professionals, and fund an expensive marketing budget.

Marketing *is* important to large firms, but it is equally critical to small businesses. Unfortunately, owners of small businesses frequently do not have effective strategic marketing programs, and researchers have reported that this omission is a major reason behind many failures.

For example, Stanley Stasch, a professor at Loyola University Chicago, researches successful and unsuccessful small new businesses and found that "small new business failures can often be linked to marketing causes, such as questionable marketing analysis, weak or nonexistent marketing strategies, poor selection of marketing strategies, and poor marketing planning and implementation" (Stasch 2010). In general, approximately 80 to 90 percent of small businesses fail within the first two or three years (Stasch 2010).

To be competitive in the global marketplace, interior designers must have an understanding of marketing, and large *and* small design firms need marketing strategies. Developing and sustaining a profitable interior design business requires a comprehensive marketing program based on developing long-term relationships with clients.

Remember, loyal clients are the lifeblood of an interior designer's business. Thus, your marketing program must focus on the strategies that will attract and retain members of your targeted market.

The basic components of a marketing program should include your (1) business profile; (2) profiles of targeted and competitors' markets; (3) objectives and tactics for branding, positioning materials, web marketing, public relations, and positioning activities; (4) action plans; (5) marketing budget; and (6) assessment and continuous improvement strategies.

Business Profile and Markets

You might recall from Chapter 12's section on strategic management planning that marketing, along with clients, finances, human resources, and management, were identified as basic components of an interior design business. Therefore, as a key element of an interior design business, marketing was addressed in business-related areas of the strategic management plan, including current business statistics, SWOT (strengths, weaknesses, opportunities, and threats) analysis, strategies, and tactics.

The results of the SWOT analysis are essential to the development of the marketing program. Therefore, to extract essential information for your marketing program, refer to your business plan and strategic planning document (see Chapters 10 and 12).

These documents are also excellent sources for developing your business profile. For example, your strategic planning document provides an analysis of your firm's current situation, including your mission statement, vision, values, business statistics, SWOT analysis, and goals. These items should be included in your business profile. You can also refer to the business profile you developed in your business plan (see Chapter 10) for additional details.

The business profile for your marketing program should include historical details and your design philosophy related to client relationships. The profile might also include your business philosophy related to the community, environment, global affairs, and social responsibility.

Marketing Research: Targeted Market

Fortunately, your business plan as well as your strategic planning document (SWOT analysis) should already have market research data related to your targeted and competitors' markets (see Chapters 10 and 12). Refer to these documents as you create a profile of your targeted and competitors' markets.

For the summary of your targeted market you will need the marketing research on the characteristics of your prospective as well as existing clients: demographics, psychographics, and their AIO (attitudes, interests, and opinions).

An analysis of your existing clients requires data associated with their projects, such as locations, type of buildings (market), LEED certifications, square footages (meters), services provided, products purchased, dollar value of the installations, and interior design fees and compensations.

Your targeted market profile also needs marketing-related information identified in your SWOT analysis, including the strengths and weaknesses of your current clientele. Develop a summary of the strengths and weaknesses of your current clients from the perspectives of client relationships, design knowledge, project management skills, and continuing education (see Chapter 12).

Your marketing program should explore and articulate the reasons why clients want to hire your design firm to fulfill their needs and solve their problems. The marketing program must include the details associated with your marketing strategies, including the targeted market and the basic Four P's: product, price, promotion, and place (distribution). In addition, include a brief summary of how you became involved with your existing clients and whether those methods could be successful with prospective clients.

Marketing Research: Competitors' Market

Your SWOT analysis as well as your business plan should also have marketing research data related to your competition. For your marketing program you will need your competitors' profiles, including their mission statements, clients, services, products, types of buildings, areas of expertise, fee rates, publications, firm size, and comments from clients and stakeholders (see Chapter 10).

If you are anticipating the opening of a new design firm, try to acquire as much information about the business as possible. Most important, determine if the new firm will compete with your firm's specialization. How will the new firm as well as current businesses affect your market position?

Your marketing program needs to take into account the strengths and weaknesses of your competition as well as how competitors are impacting your business. For example:

- Based on the needs and problems of your targeted market, are you providing better services and products than your competitors?

- What are the opportunities and threats in your firm's operating environment that could affect your design business?

- Is a competitor closing or expanding his or her business?

- Is your competitor changing design fees and compensation schedule?

- How would you compare your firm's credibility and visibility to that of your competition?

Your marketing strategies should differentiate your design firm from your competition by:

- Identifying clients needing your products/services rather than those of your competitors.

- Developing products/services addressing the needs of your targeted clients as well as exceeding the products/services offered by your competitors.

- Creating a design services fee and compensation schedule your targeted clients perceive as fair and a better value than your competitors.

- Promoting your products/services directly to your targeted clients and demonstrating how your firm can address their needs better than your competitors.

- Determining ways of distributing your products/services that are convenient for your targeted clients.

Brand Development

An excellent way to differentiate your design firm from the competition is to create, build, and sustain your brand. Thus, your marketing program must have objectives and tactics enabling your firm to have a strong brand.

According to the American Marketing Association (AMA), a brand is "A name, term, design, symbol, or any other feature that identifies one seller's good or service as distinct from those of other sellers" (AMA 2011). A brand is the ideal image for your business and should encompass your values and beliefs. A highly valued brand attracts new business and creates loyal customers—exactly what an interior design business needs.

Your brand must be created within the context of the interior design industry, your target market, and your competition. Moreover, a brand differentiates your firm and reflects your type of *business*, rather than the *type* of building, product, or service (see Chapter 10).

For example, think about the brand Ritz-Carlton Hotels and Resorts. Of course, Ritz-Carlton Hotels provide the basics (beds and food), but their *business* as well as their brand are reflected in this statement posted on Ritz London's website: "Immerse yourself in a world of style, sophistication and grace the likes of which can only be found in this hotel, in this city." Given Ritz-Carlton Hotels' *business*, how would you design a guest room at the Ritz that reflected its brand? How would your design differentiate the Ritz from other elite hotels, such as the Four Seasons or Peninsula?

Having a strong brand requires an understanding of consumer behavior and how people ultimately become brand loyal. An excellent way to conceptualize clients' relationship with a brand is through the BrandDynamics Pyramid, developed by several marketing researchers (Hollis and Brown 2008; Dyson, Farr, and Hollis 1996). The BrandDynamics Pyramid has five levels of increasing attitudinal loyalty that drives consumer purchases: presence → relevance → performance → advantage → bonding (Hollis and Brown 2008).

The BrandDynamics Pyramid can be applied to a design firm's marketing program. For example, to create brand loyalty, your marketing program must first focus on *presence*—attracting prospective clients. After clients are aware of your firm, your marketing program must have strategies that demonstrate *relevance*—your firm can meet the needs of prospective clients better than your competitors.

After clients hire your firm because they believe you can meet their needs, your marketing program must focus on *performance*—providing exceptional service and products.

To ensure repeat business, your marketing program must demonstrate to current clients your firm's *advantages* over your competitors—value derived from services and products that exceed your competition. After a client believes your firm is advantageous, then your marketing program must have strategies that reinforce the *bond*—continuing to provide exceptional service and products.

The steps to developing a strong brand described here illustrate important considerations for your marketing program. First, having a strong attitudinal connection with a brand is essential for creating long-term relationships with loyal clients; this process begins by focusing on *presence* and continues through the entire client life cycle (CLC).

Second, your marketing program must have strategies that continuously reinforce your brand in the minds of your clients, prospects, end users, colleagues, suppliers, vendors, the community, and the profession (Figure 13.2).

Third, your brand must be infused in your marketing materials as well as everyday tasks and activities. For example, your design firm routinely creates drawings. From a marketing perspective your drawings should reinforce your brand in the following ways: (1) the quality of your drawings should reflect your brand, (2) what you draw should reflect your brand, (3) the price for your drawings should reflect your brand, (4) how you present your drawings

Figure 13.2 As illustrated in this Google office designed by Scott Brownrigg, the facilities of a business should be elements of its brand. (© *Philip Durrant*)

to a client and other professionals should reflect your brand, and (5) and how you resolve any problems with your drawings should reflect your brand.

You marketing program should identify activities associated with your work as an interior designer as well as a business owner; it should also develop ways to infuse your brand into everyday policies and practices. Thus, your brand should be evident in your website, text messages, online social networks, blogs, e-mails, correspondence, brochures, business cards, proposals, newsletters, press releases, competitions, presentation boards, drawings, specifications, employee relations, team meetings, discussions with vendors, conflict resolution policies, conference presentations, exhibitions, volunteering, teaching lectures, and community speeches.

Brand development includes consistency in the type of built environment you design (e.g., contemporary or traditional), the type of client you work with (e.g., conservative or avant-garde), and the amount of fees you charge for what services.

Note in the long list cited previously that there are many activities, such as delivering community speeches and writing and sending press releases, that do not require a significant amount of time or resources but can create visibility and networking opportunities.

Most important, to move your clients from *presence* → *bond*, you must have quality standards that are consistently evident in every aspect of your work, including your design services, products, and customer service. It might be necessary to turn down projects that do not reinforce your brand. The goal is for your clients to associate your brand with positive attributes, such as honesty, truthfulness, and reliability. These positive perceptions result in loyal clients, referrals, and excellent testimonials—essential to the interior design profession.

Loyal clients continue to provide you with work, and when their excitement for your design services is communicated to their family, friends, colleagues, and associates—the ripple effect can be tremendous for your business. Referrals are extremely important, but remember that it is also very important to provide exceptional service to these new clients. Why? The client who made the recommendation might be embarrassed or disappointed if you do not fulfill the new client's expectations. Thus, you might lose both clients as a result of unfilled promises.

Branding: Identity Packages

A critical element of creating and reinforcing your brand is a professionally developed **identity package**. Generally, an identity package begins with the firm's name and a logo, which is then used on a variety of materials, such as stationery, business cards, mailing labels, and business documents (e.g., purchase orders, specifications, and transmittals).

As mentioned earlier in this book, the name of a design firm is frequently either the name of the founder (e.g., Gensler) or a combination of the first letter of the last names of the founders and/or principals (e.g., HOK).

To achieve distinctiveness (from the simplicity of having just a name or three letters), graphic designers creatively explore possibilities with typography, color, spatial arrangements, and perhaps an abstract form or pattern. The firm's name is combined with an image to create its logo.

Carefully consider the appearance of your logo; its design communicates your brand and is used for a variety of materials and purposes, such as stationery, business cards, brochures, websites, contracts, and business forms (Figures 13.3a–b). Your logo must reflect your brand. For example, do you want to present a conservative or innovative image?

Generally, to create the ideal image, think about how you apply the elements and principles of design to the built environment. For example, as with interior spatial arrangements, symmetrical and asymmetrical logos tend to be more formal and informal, respectively. Bright and intense colors can symbolize boldness; soft colors suggest a subdued approach. Abstract forms imply innovativeness, and realistic images hint at rationality.

(a)

(b)

Figure 13.3a–b The design of a logo communicates a design firm's brand and is used for a variety of materials and purposes, such as stationery and business cards (Figure 13.3a) as well as websites (Figure 13.3b). *(Specto Design)*

As you are considering the basic elements of a logo, think about what the image will look like in a variety of sizes and presentations. Will your logo read well when printed on envelopes, large presentation boards, business cards, and your website? Does the logo appear to be timeless or trendy?

Obviously, there are many important issues to be considered when developing your identity package. Fortunately your design background can help you to make good decisions with the assistance of a graphic design firm or an in-house visual communications professional.

Brand Communications

Your identity package and the steps outlined in the BrandDynamics Pyramid are critical considerations when you are developing marketing materials. Thus, your communications, such as brochures, news releases, and newsletters, must also reinforce your brand. Categories of brand communications include print, digital, and web-based. Brand communications also can include materials used for special purposes, such as office portfolios, presentation boards, proposals (e.g., RFP, RFI, and RFQ), exhibition displays, calendars, and posters.

Materials should be developed according to your clients' level in the pyramid: presence, relevance, performance, advantage, or bonding (Hollis and Brown 2008). Thus, as you develop the various elements of brand communications, think about the purpose and the audience. Are you creating a piece to: (1) attract clients (presence), (2) cultivate clients (relevance), (3) demonstrate exceptional products and service (performance), (4) reinforce your exceptional products and services (advantage), or (5) sustain long-term client relationships (bonding)?

Consider these stages of the CLC as you develop your brand communications. How do you think a *long-term* client would feel if you sent that person a brochure describing your *basic* design services? Customizing interactions with clients based on the stage or your relationship, as well as other strategies discussed in the book, is another means of demonstrating how your firm provides value by fulfilling their needs.

Print Communications

There are many forms of print communication or **collateral materials** that can serve a purpose at every stage of the CLC. Pieces commonly used by design professionals include **brochures**, tearsheets, postcards, **newsletters**, and **press releases**. These pieces become **direct mail** when the item is sent through the mail. Some design firms have books that feature their projects and accomplishments.

Collateral materials are used to attract new clients as well as updating current clients. Every piece should reflect your firm's brand, including a consistent use of your logo, typography, color, ink, imagery, spatial arrangements, paper quality, and contact information. The text should be simple, concise, and free of grammar or spelling errors. The text should be composed for the intended audience, so avoid using technical terms and design jargon.

Photographs should be taken by professionals, and the images selected for the pieces should communicate a story that addresses the needs of its reader. For example, photographs used for a sustainability brochure should illustrate an array of sustainable features of the building. The text would support the images by highlighting how your firm solved the client's needs in a manner that exceeds services provided by competitors. To reinforce an environmentally friendly brand, brochures should be printed on recycled paper with nontoxic inks.

Brochures, Tearsheets, and Postcards

As illustrated above, brochures can be used for a variety of audiences and purposes. For example, your design firm might want to have a brochure that introduces potential clients to your business by providing an overview of the firm, your expertise, projects, and staff. You might want a brochure that is useful for current clients by featuring specialized services, such as project management or visual communications.

A brochure that outlines the highlights of a speech you deliver can be helpful as a handout after a presentation to an organization. Often these are **two- or three-fold brochures**, that fit into a standard business envelope and are ideal for mailings.

Design firms use tearsheets to provide a one-page summary of a project. Generally, this includes a description of the problem and how the design firm's expertise solved the problem. Photographs of the project illustrate solutions and can be supplemented with bulleted highlights and the names of the design team members. Tearsheets can easily be mailed to prospective and current clients to announce the grand opening of the facilities, and can also be distributed to a client or committee during a proposal presentation.

Postcards can also be sent to prospective and current clients. However, their small size can present challenges. How can you entice people to read the card? A bigger challenge is persuading people to keep the card for future reference. To address both of these issues, designers have become very creative with the images used for postcards—in addition to the factual information conveyed.

For example, images might include a collage of beautifully photographed local projects. Information on the postcard could be the dates of upcoming design-related events and tours in the local area. Dates and events could be categorized by the seasons, thus providing you with the opportunity to send four postcards every year.

Newsletters and News Releases

Newsletters are an excellent way for your firm to provide value to your clients. Generally, newsletters are one to two pages in length and are published quarterly. They are an important tool for sharing updates such as announcing awards, featuring completed projects, and describing innovative design solutions.

Newsletters should be a resource for clients for improving their facilities and solving their problems. Thus, in addition to promoting the work of a firm, newsletters should have information that provides value to the client, such as an article about a new lighting system that will reduce energy costs or an easily maintained, durable textile.

Design firms use **news** or press **release**s to communicate accomplishments to a wide audience. News releases are therefore used to announce the opening of a building; awards; LEED certifications; presentations to local, regional, or national organizations; publications in trade magazines; new offices; and new hires.

News releases are written by a member of the design firm and can be distributed to a variety of outlets, such as local newspapers and trade magazines. News releases can also be posted on a firm's website.

News releases should have descriptive headlines and include just the basic facts. For example, a news release to announce the grand opening of a project could be divided into three areas of content: (1) key summary information, (2) supplemental details of the design, and (3) a brief profile of the design firm (Box 13.1).

It is very important to include essential information on the first page of a news release because this might be the only page read by journalists searching for interesting news for their magazines or newspapers. Thus, to announce the opening of a new building, the first page should have contact information, the name of the design firm, names of the design team members, the structure, its location, and the date of the opening.

Project details should include square footage (meters), cost, date of the start of construction, LEED certification rating (if applicable), and whether the structure is new, renovated, or an addition. The first page should also reinforce a design firm's expertise by including similar projects completed by the firm, how unique challenges were solved, and/or the firm's approach to the design concept.

A news release should conclude with a profile of the design firm that includes areas of specialization, services (e.g., interiors, architecture, and lighting), markets (e.g., corporate, commercial, and institutional), and a statement about the firm's social responsibilities if appropriate. When the facts are impressive, the profile should also include the founding date and number of offices.

Digital and Web-Based Communications

Design students are already familiar with various drawing and modeling software, such as AutoCAD, SketchUp, Revit, BIM (Building Information Modeling), and Photoshop, as well as

Box 13.1

First Page of a News Release by HOK

NEWS RELEASE

January 10, 2011

Contact: Tara Michelle Hustedde
tarahustedde@pureprinc.com
813.785.5320

Corinne Drobot
corinne.drobot@hok.com
416.342.7026

HOK Designs New Dalí Museum in St. Petersburg, Fla.

*New Building Houses More of Salvador Dali's
Masterworks than any Other World Collection*

ST. PETERSBURG, Florida — The grand opening for the new Dalí Museum is on January 11, 2011, at 11:11 a.m. Located on a scenic waterfront site in downtown St. Petersburg, Fla., the 68,000-square-foot structure doubles the size of the original 1982 Dalí Museum, a one-story warehouse. Exhibits include oils, watercolors, sketches, sculptures and other works from a 2,140-piece permanent collection.

Despite the complex processes required to construct the building, which stands more than 75 feet tall and is adorned by 1,062 unique, triangular glass panels, the $29.8 million building project was completed on time and $700,000 under budget. Construction began in December 2008.

Internationally recognized architect **Yann Weymouth, AIA, LEED AP,** director of design for HOK's Florida practice, and led the design team. The Dali is HOK's fourth museum project completed in the state in the past 6 years, including: John and Mable Ringling Museum and Cultural Complex in Sarasota, the Hazel Hough Wing of the Museum of Fine Arts in St. Petersburg, and the Patricia and Phillip Frost Art Museum at Florida International University in Miami. Weymouth also served as chief of design for I.M. Pei for both the East Wing of the National Gallery of Art in Washington, D.C., and for the Grand Louvre in Paris.

HOK's **design concept** is drawn directly from the building's purpose. It is inspired both by Dalí's surrealist art and by the practical need to shelter the collection from the hurricanes that threaten Florida's west coast.

knowing how to create electronic portfolios and animations. These skills and others should be used for developing marketing communications.

Consider using digital communications to both attract prospective clients and update current clients. For example, to provide a prospective client an overview of your firm, give that person a CD or DVD featuring areas of specialization, projects, and profiles of the design team. The CD could be the standard size, a minidisk (approximately the size of a credit card), or a minidisk printed as a business card.

For current clients your firm might want to create a CD or DVD featuring projects relevant to their interests. For example, a client who owns retail stores might be interested in a DVD of recently completed LEED-certified retail projects with state-of-the-art lighting systems and sustainable design strategies. This DVD might prompt the client to renovate his or her retail stores and seek LEED certification.

As with other forms of marketing communications, **digital media** must be developed for your targeted market and demonstrate how your products/services provide benefits and solutions that exceed those of your competitors. Ideally, to enable people to feel like they are moving physically through spaces, these marketing communications should include video clips

Figure 13.4 An example of an architectural and digital media company that produces visual communication for designers is Archimation.
One of the company's projects was a conceptual design of the Victoria & Albert (V&A) Museum's Boilerhouse Yard (2010) in London, UK, by Heneghan Peng Architects. (*Archimation*)

and animations (Figure 13.4). These and other content forms, such as photographs, graphics, and audio, are used to create **multimedia presentations**. Some design firms use multimedia presentations as a substitute for the traditional office video.

Web-Based Communications

Multimedia presentations can be viewed on your design firm's website—another marketing communications tool. As with other communications, your website must be a reflection of your brand and should be developed by a professional. Websites can be created that enable you to manage the site, including adding or deleting sections, photographs, pages, and menus.

Generally, design professionals use the name of their firm followed by ".com" for their domain name. Domain names are not owned; registering your domain name gives you exclusive rights to use that name for a specific period, such as 10 years. For information contact the Internet Corporation for Assigned Names and Numbers (ICANN; http://www.icann.org/).

Design firm websites are globally viewed by many audiences, including clients, prospective clients, employees, potential employees, allied professionals, competitors, investors, vendors, manufacturers, suppliers, and members of the general public. Your content must therefore provide information for people who know nothing about your firm as well as loyal clients who might want to see their building featured on your site.

Your website might also provide information for job seekers and financial data for potential investors. To avoid confusing clients and revealing too much information to competitors, your website should not disclose specific details, such as fees and compensation schedules.

Generally, to serve the various audiences listed above, design firm websites tend to be organized by the following topics: firm profile (often called "About us"), philosophy/mission statement, leadership, locations, services (e.g., interior design, architecture, and sustainability), markets (e.g., commercial, hospitality, and healthcare), projects, careers, news, and contact information. Additional topic headings can include videos, publications, research studies, white papers, annual reports, blogs, and social networks.

The overall goal is to organize your website based on the needs and problems of your current and potential clients. To appeal to individual interests, examples of projects can be viewed according to the service provided, the type of building (markets), and locations. For example, if a client was searching for a design firm specializing in sustainability, that person could click "Projects—Service" and view your sustainable projects. Or all of your healthcare buildings can be viewed by clicking the heading "Projects—Market." Project information should include a brief description, photographs, location, and date of completion.

In addition, some websites have features that enable viewers to easily print images, download brochures, share projects, or create a "book" of favorite projects. The description should include the name of the client, square footage (meters), problem statements, and services provided by the firm that solved the problems.

Solutions should be evident in the accompanying photographs of the project. Typically five to eight images provide a good overview of the solutions; these should be presented one image at a time.

Another consideration associated with viewing photographs of projects is ease of navigation. Generally, when people want to see a new image, they want to be able to click themselves rather than watching images in a timed sequence. Time is also a factor with studying photographs and linking to other sections of the website: people want quick transitions between images and pages.

Large images, multimedia, and **flash animations** can unfortunately result in slow loading times. However, many design firms use flash animations because of the sophisticated effects that can be created with the multimedia format—an

expectation of many clients. To ease the frustration of waiting for a page, many websites have a "skip intro" link or miniature clock and/or a countdown image showing when the new page will appear.

Other user-friendly considerations include making sure information is current and that links are connected to the appropriate internal as well as external sites. Generally, links to external sites connect to an article about the firm or one of its projects that is featured in a magazine or newspaper.

An effective marketing strategy is to implement reciprocal links. For example, a design firm listed in *Interior Design* magazine's "Top 100 Giants" could have an **outbound link** to *Interior Design* magazine's article on its website—and the article in *Interior Design* would have an **inbound link** to the design firm's website.

Social Media

Websites of some design firms have a link to their blog, Twitter, YouTube, and to social networking sites such as Facebook and LinkedIn. Social media are quickly becoming essential elements of marketing programs because of their ability to build relationships through digital interactions.

The term **Web 2.0** is used to demarcate today's current online interactivity from the static nature of first-generation websites **Web 1.0** (prior to 2003). During the Internet's early years, people used Web 1.0 to locate specific facts and information.

Web 2.0 builds on being a repository for information by enabling people to participate, reciprocate, and interact with others. Thus, where Web 1.0 provided an encyclopedia—Web 2.0 has Wikipedia, where users can contribute information to the site. The major difference between Web 1.0 and Web 2.0—static versus interactive—is critical to your marketing program, especially since most of your clients will be accustomed to Web 2.0.

The question is, how can the interactivity of social media promote a design business? A critical element to this answer is the word "social" and its definition: "to form cooperative and interdependent relationships with others" (Merriam-Webster 2011). Thus, social media should be used to enhance relationships with your clients as well as other professionals and your employees. You can use social media to interact with clients, discuss new products, provide a profile of your design firm, reinforce your brand, and generate leads.

As discussed in Chapter 3, to be effective on the Web, a design firm must follow online protocols, such as responding to inquiries professionally and politely, sharing expertise, participating in discussions, being respectful, and demonstrating that the design firm is more interested in giving than taking.

In addition, viewers are turned off when a social media site is used to advertise products and services because the sites are intended for networking—not advertising. Therefore, business-related social media sites should not be used as a vehicle for self-promotion, but as a tool for enhancing *social* relationships.

Given the enormous number of social media tools available, your firm will have to determine the best ones for your business. It is fairly easy and inexpensive to start a blog or social networking site, but the time required to maintain the sites can become a critical element.

Effective social media requires dynamics and interactions. Therefore, consider appointing a "social media manager" who is responsible for maintaining your social media on a daily basis. The primary task here is to oversee the firm's website content, such as deleting spam, monitoring blog content, and forwarding messages to the appropriate people. Large firms might need a full-time social media manager, but smaller businesses might be able to assign the task to a current employee.

Blogs are an example of a very time-consuming tool. As an online journal, blogs are an excellent way to converse with clients and employees, but the content must be fresh to be effective. In addition, blogs must have links to other blogs as well as additional resources, such as magazine articles, newsletters, or brochures.

Microblogging devices, such as Twitter, are another means to converse with people and are important because this device allows you to send blogs to mobile phones—a quick and convenient way for people to access information. The challenge is to craft your message (a "tweet") in fewer than 140 characters.

From a business owner's view there are additional important considerations. For example:

- Social networking sites are excellent for interactions. Therefore, who is responsible for developing and maintaining interactions?

- Do you want your social network sites to have a theme, such as sustainability?

- How much personal information should be disclosed?

- How will the topics be determined?

- Will you write articles? Will those articles be open for comments?

- How will you manage new as well as dedicated readers?

- How can you keep track of visitors?

- Do you want to offer e-newsletters or white papers in exchange for visitors' e-mail addresses?

Remember, what you offer must be valuable to the user. Sending a brochure of your design firm tends to be more valuable to you, and therefore this type of marketing communication should *not* be offered as a means of establishing a relationship.

Checking for Comprehension

- Which print communications do you think are the most effective? Why?

- How do you think an interior design firm should use social media for promotional purposes?

Digital and web-based communications have a role in your marketing program, but by far the most effective way to build long-term relationships with clients is face-to-face because human interaction enhances and enriches communication. Thus, your marketing program must feature events and activities that promote your brand, enhance your visibility, establish or emphasize your credibility, and create networking opportunities. Some of these initiatives are categorized as public relations.

Ideally, you want control of your design firm's image, but events can occur that make it difficult to sustain your brand. For example, a recent public relations disaster was the 2010 BP oil spill crisis in the Gulf of Mexico that endangered wildlife and water quality. BP CEO Tony Hayward appeared to aggravate this situation by saying, "We're sorry for the massive disruption it's caused in their lives. There's no one who wants this over more than I do. I'd like my life back" (Durando 2010). This comment elicited an immediate storm of outrage and protest, and Hayward resigned from his position a few weeks later.

Design professionals also can have challenging public relations circumstances, especially when they are involved with public projects. For example, when the State of Illinois Center (currently the James R. Thompson Center) in Chicago was completed in 1985, there was public criticism for cost overruns and problems caused by excessive heat in the building (indoor temperatures exceeding 90 degrees Fahrenheit, 32 degrees Celsius). Subsequently, insulated glass was replaced with single-pane windows in the 17-story atrium (Figure 13.5).

Problems with the State of Illinois Center were featured in various media outlets, such as local newspapers and television/radio newscasts. The original public opinion crisis became worse when the state initiated litigation against 13 firms involved in the design, engineering, and construction of the building (Devall 1987).

Figure 13.5 As evidenced by problems associated with the design of the State of Illinois Center (currently the James R. Thompson Center) in Chicago, design professionals can face challenging public relations circumstances when involved with public projects. *(© Sandy Felsenthal/CORBIS)*

Public Relations: Reputation Enhancement

A focus on reputation recently has been added to the beginning of the traditional definition of public relations: "Public relations is about reputation—the result of what you do, what you say and what others say about you. Public relations is the discipline which looks after reputation, with the aim of earning understanding and support and influencing opinion and behaviour. It is the planned and sustained effort to establish and maintain goodwill and mutual understanding between an organisation and its publics" (Chartered Institute of Public Relations [CIPR] 2011).

Large and small design firms must have public relations strategies that can effectively respond to any problems associated with their projects as well as outlining proactive initiatives. Generally, when there is a crisis the most effective strategy is to acknowledge the wrong, apologize, and fix the problems as quickly as possible. This problem-solving approach illustrates to the **media**, the public, and stakeholders that your firm is willing to take responsibility for errors and is committed to excellence.

Proactive public relations strategies involve many different areas, including sales/marketing, publicity/promotion, **media relations**, and

event management. Several chapters in this book have already reviewed many of the issues associated with sales/marketing, such as client relationships, customer service, and product/service branding. This chapter has focused on the publicity/promotion aspect by discussing identity packages, brochures, and publications.

Public Relations: Media Relations

Media relations encompass online strategies as well as *the* media: television news programs, radio, newspapers, and magazines. **Online public relations** involve identifying the most effective ways to influence the media as well as other people by using communication channels such as blogs, forums, and social networks. Thus, depending on the purpose of your online presence, your firm must identify the best web-based communications.

To attract your targeted audience to your website, search engine optimization (SEO) must be used when you are composing blogs and documents, such as online news releases and e-newsletters. In addition, a "news" or "press" section on your website makes it easy for media members to find information, such as news about awards and grand openings of buildings. But remember: Your firm must have considerable news to have a "news" section on your website. Outdated or very few news releases can reflect poorly on your firm.

To maximize your potential with *the* media, identify stories that will appeal to their audiences for a particular geographical area: National media are interested in national news and local media search for local connections and angles.

"Breaking news" and "features" are two categories of stories most applicable to design firms. For example, a design firm's breaking news could be the opening of a public exhibition featuring projects designed by the firm or announcing that the firm has won a competition. Feature stories could focus on a trendy area of specialization or new products just introduced at an international furniture market.

Which story is selected is often determined by an editor or reporter, or is **pitched** by someone from the community, such as an interior designer. You should therefore develop relationships with editors and reporters in the same way you would build relationships with your clients: by engaging in face-to-face interactions.

You could invite a journalist to coffee, lunch, or special events sponsored by your firm. You could also ask the reporter what items he or she likes to receive in a **public relations kit**, and the ideal format. Generally, a design firm's public relations kit features numerous colorful images and includes a brochure, firm profile, tearsheets, reprints, articles, newsletters, and business cards.

To enhance a firm's reputation, many designers focus on writing articles for publication in major trade magazines, such as *Interior Design* or *Contract* (Figure 13.6). Trade magazines are an excellent way to attain high visibility throughout

Figure 13.6 To enhance the reputation of a firm, many designers focus on writing articles for publication in major trade magazines, such as *Interior Design* or *Contract*. Reprints of articles are excellent marketing tools and can be included in public relations kits. *(Contract Magazine)*

the world. Having an article published in the top tier of magazines is very difficult to accomplish because of extreme competitiveness, but if you are able to achieve this, you can purchase **reprints** of the article. They make excellent marketing tools and can be included in your public relations kit as well as your **office portfolio**.

Articles should include a brief description of the project, the client's program, your design solutions, high-resolution photographs, floor plans, size of the space in square footages (meters), a list of manufacturers' sources, and the project cost. In addition, writers should submit brief professional biographies with portraits of the designer(s). Editors require exclusive rights to an article; therefore, articles already printed in other publications are not acceptable.

Feature articles in trade magazines can be impressive in your office portfolio, but remember that the magazines are primarily read by other designers. Thus, to attract prospective clients, you should write articles for magazines targeted to these readers too.

For example, if your firm specializes in designing healthcare facilities, write articles for magazines published for health facility administrators or managers. To appeal to these audiences, you must write about a topic that is relevant to their professional interests. Illustrate your expertise by connecting the topic to one of your projects. For example, most health facility administrators are interested in indoor air quality (IAQ). Thus, you could write an article about current research associated with IAQ from a built environment perspective and include your recently completed project that was designed to enhance IAQ.

Public Relations: Event Management

Feature articles on a current topic could be the basis for presentations or vice versa. Presentations and published articles could be announced in news releases. These suggestions are provided to both stimulate your thinking about how you can maximize your opportunities and save time by exploring ways to work with various communication channels (also known as "repurposing"). Thus, the IAQ article could be revised into a presentation to local healthcare administrators or a hospital's charitable organization.

Presentations to a variety of local organizations, such as civic groups, clubs, and historical societies, should be one of the activities in your event management plan. These opportunities are an excellent way to educate people about your firm's services and perhaps interest someone to hire you or make a referral.

Event management also can include presenting at local, national, and international seminars, conferences, workshops, and trade shows. The goal is to enhance your reputation by demonstrating your expertise to other professionals as well as prospective clients.

Public presentations should be approached from a professional responsibility perspective rather than self-promotion. Therefore, the content should focus on educating the audience; references to your design firm should be limited to providing business cards at the end of the presentation and perhaps a tearsheet or small brochure. Any materials used to enhance the presentation, such as PowerPoint slides, presentation booklets, and presentation boards, must have a professional appearance and reflect your brand (see Chapter 7).

In addition to presentations, there are other ways to improve your credibility, enhance your visibility, and create networking opportunities. For example, you might be able to teach interior design courses at a local college or university, enter competitions, or do volunteer work. Volunteering (see Chapter 1) could include serving on a board, sponsoring a community event, or designing the facilities of a charitable organization. The amount of volunteer time should be coordinated with the responsibilities of owning a business and working with clients.

Event management also can include sponsoring holiday parties, open houses, cultural events, and tours. The type of event should be based on the interests of prospective and current clients. Thus, clients who enjoy the visual arts could receive invitations to the opening of a new art gallery. Clients interested in Frank Lloyd Wright could be invited to a private tour of residences designed by Wright. You could also give clients tickets to a cultural event, such as a theater or symphony performance. Again, make sure the event is appropriate for the recipient; this shows an added level of thoughtfulness.

Marketing Program Management

Note that CIPR's definition of public relations included "It is the planned and sustained effort to establish and maintain goodwill and mutual understanding between an organisation and its publics" (CIPR 2011).

For your marketing program to be successful you must have a "planned and sustained effort" that includes action plans, a marketing budget, and management strategies. As discussed in Chapter 12, action plans outline the steps required to accomplish a strategy. Your marketing action plans should include the tasks, who is responsible for each activity, timelines, materials/equipment/facilities, and costs.

Develop a calendar of marketing events/ activities every year with action plans outlining the steps to execute each item. For example, you might want to have two social events for prospective clients each year, in June and December. Identify someone to be responsible for reserving the facilities, ordering the food, beverages and invitations, mailing the invitations, and providing anything else needed for the occasion. In addition, after the event there should be follow-up strategies that could involve calling clients to provide them with answers to their questions, arranging appointments with clients, or **lead-tracking**: contacting people who indicated an interest in your design services.

Action plans should include several marketing strategies, such as a combination of print communications, direct mail, social media, news releases, presentations, and events. Strategies should be determined by your goals for prospective clients and how your firm cultivates relationships with clients.

For example, a firm needing to increase its client base might focus its marketing strategies on activities that attract prospective clients, such as cold calls, direct mail, and news releases. However, this firm must still schedule activities that strengthen its relationship with current clients, such as inviting them to events, seminars, or the grand opening of a new building. A firm with a well-established client base would tend to focus on marketing strategies that fulfill the needs of its existing clients, but it should still have some activities directed toward acquiring prospective clients.

The costs identified in your action plans are used to create a marketing budget. If the costs exceed the funds available, then prioritize your marketing communications according to the goals in your strategic plan. In addition, concentrate on strategies that do not cost additional funds, such as providing excellent customer service, networking, referrals, and sharing testimonials from current clients. A testimonial from a client might describe your creativity, level of professionalism, and how well your design addressed that person's needs.

While executing your action plans, record every expense as well as the results of each activity, such as the number of prospective clients who wanted a designer to contact them or the number of phone calls generated by a news release. The goal is to collect the data needed to assess your marketing costs, marketing strategies, and new business from prospective as well as current clients. This data is important for managing your marketing strategies and budget, and for identifying ways to continuously improve your marketing program.

Evaluations should be done at least once a year and perhaps mid-year when strategies have not been successful. Keep in mind that some marketing strategies take considerable time before they work, and certain marketing expenses, such as those for professional print communications, are indispensible because of their importance in promoting and operating a design business.

Chapter 13 provided additional information that is important for operating and managing an interior design business by examining initiatives that can improve the profitability and success of a firm via strategic marketing and communications programs.

In addition to identifying strategies for promoting an interior design business, ownership responsibilities include knowing U.S. tax and employment laws as well as developing effective human resource management policies and procedures. These topics are reviewed in Chapter 14—the concluding chapter of *Professional Practice for Interior Designers in a Global Marketplace*.

Knowledge and Skills Summary

Highlights
* To be competitive in the global marketplace, interior designers must have an understanding of marketing; both large and small design firms need marketing strategies.

* The basic components of a marketing program include (1) a business profile; (2) profiles of targeted and competitors' markets; (3) objectives and tactics for branding, collateral materials, web marketing, public relations, and marketing activities; (4) action plans; (5) marketing budget; and (6) assessment and continuous improvement strategies.

* An excellent way to differentiate a design firm from the competition is to create, build, and sustain a brand.

* Business owners can use both print and digital/web-based communications to attract prospective clients and update current clients.

* Social media are quickly becoming essential elements of marketing programs because of their ability to build relationships through interactions.

* A marketing program should have events and activities that promote a design firm's brand, enhance its visibility and credibility, and create networking opportunities. Some of these initiatives are categorized as public relations.

* A successful marketing program requires a planned and sustained effort that includes action plans, a marketing budget, and management strategies.

Key Terms
brochure
collateral materials
digital media
direct mail
event management
flash animation
identity package
inbound link
lead-tracking
media
media relations
microblogging
multimedia presentation
newsletter
news release (press release)
office portfolio
online public relations
outbound link
pitch

press release (news release)

public relations kit

reprints

two- or three-fold brochure

Web 1.0

Web 2.0

Projects

Philosophy and Design Project

A brand is the ideal image for a business and should encompass values and beliefs. A highly valued brand attracts new business and creates loyal customers—exactly what an interior design business needs.

Develop a written report (approximately three pages) with visual images that responds to the following items: (1) If you owned an interior design business what would you want as the ideal image for your business? (2) Based on your image create a brand philosophy and identify the values and beliefs that serve as the foundation for your philosophy. (3) Identify ways you would implement your brand philosophy in practice.

Research Project

Establishing a brand is a very important activity for a business. Research the topic of branding by carefully reviewing the websites of three major design firms. Use your branding research to analyze the firms' sites. Do the design firms appear to have a brand? If yes, how is each brand reinforced? If no, how could a brand be developed? Develop an oral presentation (approximately 10 minutes) of your analyses, and include images that summarize your branding research.

Human Factors Research Project

Digital and web-based communications have a role in a marketing program, but by far the most effective way to build long-term relationships with clients is still face-to-face. Research effective approaches for face-to-face interactions, and develop an outline for a marketing program that emphasizes face-to-face communication.

Develop a written summary (approximately three pages) of your research findings and the outline of your marketing program. Prepare an informal presentation to the class that includes questions about the topic for group discussions.

References

American Marketing Association (AMA). 2011. *Dictionary*. http://www.marketingpower.com. Accessed April 30, 2011.

Chartered Institute of Public Relations (CIPR). 2011. "What Is PR?" http://www.cipr.co.uk/. Accessed May 6, 2011.

Devall, C. 1987. "Architect to Countersue on State Center." *Chicago Tribune*, April 6, 1987.

Durando, J. June 1, 2010. "BP's Tony Hayward: 'I'd Like My Life Back.'" http://content. usatoday.com. Accessed May 5, 2011.

Dyson, P., A. Farr, and N. Hollis.1996. "Measuring and Using Brand Equity." *Journal of Advertising Research* 36 (6): 9–21.

Hollis, N., and M. Brown. 2008. *The Global Brand: How to Create and Develop Lasting Brand Value in the World Market*. New York: Palgrave Macmillan.

Merriam-Webster. 2011. s.v. "social." *Merriam-Webster Dictionary*. http://www.merriam-webster.com/dictionary/social. Accessed May 5, 2011.

Stasch, S. 2010. *Creating a Successful Marketing Strategy for Your Small New Business*. Santa Barbara, CA: Praeger.

CHAPTER

14

Managing, Growing, and Leading
a Profitable Interior Design Business

Chương 14 (Vietnamese)
Pennod 14 (Welsh)
לטיפֿאַק 14 (Yiddish)

After learning the content in Chapter 14, you will be able to answer the following questions:

* Which employment laws apply to a design firm?

* Which tax and business laws apply to a design firm?

* What do I need to know to hire and retain employees?

* What should be included in an employee handbook?

* As an owner of a design firm, how can I demonstrate leadership?

A prosperous, growing interior design business will need more employees to help serve its clients. This chapter therefore reviews what an owner must do when hiring employees. The first section examines employment laws and regulations—with the caveat that the information is only an overview of complicated and detailed requirements. Understanding how to implement employment laws requires the assistance of an attorney and an accountant.

The last section of Chapter 14 reexamines the book's main theme: the importance of relationships. However, this discussion focuses on the relationships between employers and employees. Solid employer-employee relationships are critical to the success of a business and are essential to an interior design firm.

Why? Because clients can sense when a problems exist between a firm owner and his or her designers, and these problems can affect long-term relationships among all three parties. Thus, the chapter's discussion on human resource management is presented from the perspective of humanism in business—an approach centered on human interests or values.

Human Resources Management

An effective marketing program (discussed in the previous chapter) might contribute to your firm's need for more employees. You must know numerous federal and state labor laws when hiring **employees** or **independent contractors**. This section provides a basic overview of employment and labor laws relevant to design firms. Comprehensive information is available from the U.S. Department of Labor (DOL; http://www.dol.gov/) and in the *Employer's Tax Guide* published by the Internal Revenue Service (IRS; http://www.irs.gov/).

The DOL site can direct you to specific statues and regulations, and the Department's *e-laws* (Employment Laws Assistance for Workers and Small Businesses), an interactive program that provides online assistance to business owners (see http://www.dol.gov/elaws/). For information regarding Canadian employment and labor laws, see the Canada Revenue Agency (http://www.cra-arc.gc.ca/menu-eng.html). Keep in mind you must understand and abide by the employment laws of a specific nation when working internationally.

Laws of the U.S. Department of Labor (DOL)

Businesses must be in compliance with federal labor laws as well as state and local employment laws. Compliance includes mandatory filings, recordkeeping, reporting, and posting of notices. Many of the laws and regulations associated with small businesses are part of the U.S. Department of Labor's Wage and Hour Division, which is responsible for labor laws associated with federally financed and assisted construction projects—Davis-Bacon and Related Acts (DBRA). The Division also enforces the laws associated with employees of contractors and subcontractors who provide services to agencies of the U.S. government—the McNamara-O'Hara Service Contract Act (SCA).

Additional labor laws administered by the Wage and Hour Division that can be applicable to design firms include the Fair Labor Standards Act (FLSA), Family and Medical Leave Act (FMLA), Consumer Credit Protection Act (CCPA), and the Immigration and Nationality Act (INA).

The DOL requires employers to maintain records and post information explaining federal and state laws and regulations; these notices and posters must be displayed in a location accessible to employees, such as break rooms.

Fair Labor Standards Act and Family and Medical Leave Act

The FLSA was created in 1938 to establish minimum wages, overtime pay, recordkeeping mandates, and child labor terms and provisions (DOL 2011). These laws apply to full-time and part-time employees working for public and private businesses.

Since July 2009, the federal minimum wage has been $7.25 per hour, but states might have a minimum wage that exceeds federal mandates. In addition, businesses are required to "pay at least one and one-half times the employees' regular rates of pay for all hours worked over 40 in the workweek" (DOL 2011).

Recordkeeping requirements prescribed in the FLSA involve maintaining current employee data including name, Social Security number, address, birth date, occupation, gender, day/time of start of workweek, hours worked each day/week, basis of pay (e.g., per hour or per week), and overtime pay.

The FMLA was created in 1993 to allow employees to "balance their work and family responsibilities by allowing them to take reasonable unpaid leave [up to 12 weeks] for certain family and medical reasons [e.g., birth of a child or serious illness of an employee's child, spouse, or parent]" (DOL 2012). The law applies to "employers with 50 or more employees each working day during at least 20 calendar weeks in the current or preceding year" (DOL 2011). The law also applies to state and federal agencies as well as local private and public education institutions.

Consumer Credit Protection Act and Immigration and Nationality Act

The Consumer Credit Protection Act (CCPA) of 1968 was created to look after and serve the interest of consumers. The wage garnishment provisions in the CCPA limit the amount of an employee's income that can be legally garnished for a debt (e.g., IRS or state collection agency) (DOL 2011). In addition, an employer cannot fire an employee whose wages are garnished for payment of a debt.

The INA of 1952 requires employers to hire only U.S. citizens, U.S. nationals, and aliens authorized to work in the United States. Employers must verify the identity of employees and their employment eligibility. This information is recorded by having an employee complete *Form, I-9, Employment Eligibility Verification Form (I-9)*. Employers are responsible for making sure employees complete the form and must retain the

I-9 on file for at least three years or one year after employment, whichever date is longer.

Employee Retirement Income Security Act and Occupational Safety and Health Act

In addition to laws administered by the Wage and Hour Division, the DOL oversees other laws that can pertain to an interior design business, such as the Employee Retirement Income Security Act (ERISA) and the Occupational Safety and Health Act (OSHAct).

The ERISA delineates requirements for employee benefit plans, such as retirement income, healthcare, vacation, and so on. Labor laws do not require an employer to have employee benefit plans, but when plans exist the ERISA has provisions for how an employer must manage and control the funds.

The OSHAct was created in 1970 to help protect the health and safety of employees at the workplace. The Act states that the Occupational Safety and Health Administration (OSHA) is responsible for setting standards and conducting inspections. Employers are required to follow OSHA's standards, which are designed to protect employees and eliminate all hazardous conditions. In addition, employers must maintain records of work-related injuries and illnesses that caused "death, days away from work, restricted work activity or job transfer, medical treatment beyond first aid, and loss of consciousness" (DOL 2011).

Workers' Compensation

States have workers' compensation laws that are required for *most* businesses with employees. The purpose of the laws is to provide benefits (medical care and wages) to employees who sustain injuries caused by the employment. Businesses must have workers' compensation insurance, unemployment insurance, and possibly disability insurance, depending on state regulations.

A business must comply with its state's requirements for compensation and reporting injuries. Businesses can buy insurance through a commercial insurance carrier, self-insurance, or state insurance programs.

Other U.S. Business Laws and Regulations

Federal and state governments have also created numerous laws prohibiting discrimination and harassment. Federal laws are administered by the Equal Employment Opportunity Commission (EEOC; http://www.eeoc.gov/).

Some of the laws enforced by the EEOC include Title VII of the Civil Rights Act of 1964, the Equal Pay Act of 1963 (EPA), the Age Discrimination in Employment Act of 1967 (ADEA), the Pregnancy Discrimination Act of 1978 (amended to Title VII), Title I of the Americans with Disabilities Act of 1990 (ADA), and the Genetic Information Nondiscrimination Act of 2008 (GINA).

Title VII prohibits employment discrimination based on an individual's race, color, religion, gender, or national origin. As an amendment to Title VII in 1978, the Pregnancy Discrimination Act prohibits employment discrimination based on pregnancy, childbirth, or medical condition related to pregnancy or childbirth (EEOC 2011). Title VII stipulates that employers cannot retaliate against a person who complained about discrimination, filed a discrimination complaint, or participated in a discrimination investigation or lawsuit.

In the 1986 case *Meritor Savings Bank v. Vinson*, the Supreme Court affirmed that sexual harassment violates Title VII. In 1990 EEOC published *Policy Guidance on Current Issues of Sexual Harassment*—a document that provides guidance for issues related to sexual harassment laws, including hostile work environments and preventive actions.

Equal Pay Act and Age Discrimination in Employment Act

The EPA and ADEA were created to prohibit employment discrimination based on gender and age, respectively. The EPA law makes it illegal to "pay different wages to men and women if they perform equal work in the same workplace" (EEOC 2011).

The ADEA "protects people who are 40 or older from discrimination because of age" (EEOC 2011). As with Title VII, both the EPA and the ADEA state it is illegal to retaliate against a person who complained about discrimination, filed a discrimination complaint, or participated in a discrimination investigation or lawsuit.

Title I of the Americans with Disabilities Act and Genetic Information Nondiscrimination Act

The EEOC also is responsible for administering Title I of the ADA of 1990 and the GINA of 2008. Title I of the ADA applies to employers with 15 or more employees. The general rule for Title I of the ADA of 1991 is "No covered entity shall discriminate against a qualified individual on the basis of disability in regard to job application procedures, the hiring, advancement, or discharge of employees, employee compensation, job training, and other terms, conditions, and privileges of employment" (EEOC 2011).

Title I of the ADA has a requirement that is particularly important for interior designers because of facility implications: "the law also requires that employers reasonably accommodate the known physical or mental limitations of an otherwise qualified individual with a disability who is an applicant or employee, unless doing so would impose an undue hardship on the operation of the employer's business" (EEOC 2011).

The GINA affects issues related to employment and health insurance (Figure 14.1). As of November 2009 the GINA prohibits discrimination "against employees or applicants because of genetic information. Genetic information includes information about an individual's genetic tests and the genetic tests of an individual's family members, as well as information about any disease, disorder, or condition of an individual's family members (i.e., an individual's family medical history)" (EEOC 2011).

As with other discrimination laws, GINA as well as Title I of the ADA prohibits retaliation against a person who complained about discrimination, filed a discrimination complaint,

Figure 14.1 DNA molecules are key to the Genetic Information and Nondiscrimination Act (GINA) legislation, which prohibits discrimination against employees or applicants because of genetic information. *(© Science Photo Library/Alamy)*

or participated in a discrimination investigation or lawsuit.

Privacy Act and the Personal Responsibility and Work Opportunity Reconciliation Act

A different government agency—the U.S. Department of Health and Human Services (HHS)—is responsible for administering other important laws associated with employment: the Privacy Act of 1974 and the Personal Responsibility and Work Opportunity Reconciliation Act (PRWORA) of 1996.

The Privacy Act law basically delineates procedures for maintaining the records of individuals. The law defines a record as "any item, collection, or grouping of information about an individual that is maintained by an agency, including, but not limited to, his education, financial transactions, medical history, and criminal or employment history that contains his name, or the identifying number, symbol, or other identifying particular assigned to the individual, such as a finger or voice print or a photograph" (HHS 2011).

These records, which include a person's Social Security number, are protected by the Privacy Act. The law stipulates that individuals are entitled to access their records and to request corrections when applicable. In addition, records cannot be disclosed without the written consent of the person unless there is a disclosure exception prescribed in the Act, such as employees of the business who need the records to fulfill their responsibilities or U.S. Census Bureau activities associated with surveys or the census.

The PRWORA of 1996 was enacted to improve the nation's welfare program. One of the comprehensive child support enforcement requirements was to establish a Federal Case Registry and National Directory of New Hires. The purpose of this national new hire reporting system is to track delinquent parents across state lines. Consequently, the law "requires that employers report all new hires to state agencies for transmittal of new hire information to the National Directory of New Hires" (HHS 1996).

Compliance with the law requires employers to report new employees or rehires to their state's New Hire Reporting System within 20 days after hiring the person. For information and New Hire forms, contact your state's New Hire Reporting System.

Uniform Commercial Code (UCC)

Another legal requirement for business owners is compliance with their state's Uniform Commercial Code (UCC) laws. The UCC is not a federal law but was created by a nonprofit organization—the Uniform Law Commission (ULC; also known as the National Conference of Commissioners on Uniform State Laws, or NCCUSL) and the American Law Institute (ALI) (see http://www.nccusl.org/ and http://www.ali.org/).

Every state has some adaptation of the UCC laws. Thus, for complete information you must contact your office of the Secretary of State.

The UCC is a "comprehensive modernization of various statutes relating to commercial transactions including sales, leases, negotiable instruments, bank deposits and collections, funds transfers, letters of credit, bulk sales, documents of title, investment securities, and secured transactions" (ALI 2011). The UCC has several articles addressing commercial transactions, including sales, leases, letters of credit, and bulk sales.

UCC Article 2—Sales is important for transactions that involve the sale of goods. In general, the purpose of Article 2 is to ensure sellers and buyers are acting in good faith, and to promote commerce. For example, when an interior designer is a merchant in a sale, UCC prescribes the designer has an obligation of "good faith" by being honest and complying with reasonable commercial standards.

There are many parts in *UCC Article 2—Sales* that can pertain to the work of an interior designer. For example, *Part 2 Form, Formation and Readjustments of Contract* stipulates formal requirements for a contract for the sale of goods, including records, signatures, and timelines.

Part 2 also prescribes guidelines for firm offers (§ 2-205), contract confirmation conditions (§ 2-207), buyer's right to inspect goods (§ 2-513), and buyer's rights regarding improper deliveries (§ 2-601). For current and complete UCC information refer to the Legal Information Institute (http://www.law.cornell.edu/ucc/ucc.table.html).

U.S. Tax Laws and Employer Requirements

To hire employees, you must comply with several U.S. tax laws administered by the Internal Revenue Service (IRS). Again, when you are ready to hire employees, seek the advice of lawyers and accountants with small business expertise.

One of the first considerations is to determine if the person you want to hire is an employee or an independent contractor based on the IRS criteria. The distinctions are important; an employer "generally must withhold income taxes, withhold and pay Social Security and Medicare taxes, and pay unemployment tax on wages paid to an employee. You do not generally have to withhold or pay any taxes on payments to independent contractors" (IRS 2011).

According to the IRS, "employees are defined either under common law or under statues for certain situations." The employee status under common law states, "Generally, a worker who performs services for you is your employee if you have the right to control what will be done and how it will be done. This is so even when you give the employee freedom of action. What matters is that you have the right to control the details of how the services are performed" (IRS 2011). For more information about this topic, the IRS advises that employers read *Publication 15-A* (see http://www.irs.gov/pub/irs-pdf/p15a.pdf).

An interior design firm can hire employees as well as independent contractors. For example, an interior designer who works on staff for just one firm typically would be an employee. But a person who is hired by the design firm to paint a client's residence is generally an independent contractor.

A business owner must know who is considered an employee or an independent contractor. For clarification, complete and file IRS *Form SS-8, Determination of Worker Status for Purpose of Federal Employment Taxes and Income Tax Withholding*. The IRS can provide the determination, but the process can take at least six months (IRS 2011).

When hiring employees, you must have an Employer Identification Number (EIN) from the IRS. As explained in Chapter 10, the nine-digit number (XX-XXXXXXX) is used by the IRS to identify tax accounts of employers. Your EIN is used for all forms and items sent to the IRS and the Social Security Administration (SSA).

As a business owner with employees, your tax responsibilities include withholding, depositing, reporting, and paying employment taxes. Employers are also responsible for providing employees with certain IRS forms and sending the forms to the IRS and to the SSA.

Patient Protection and Affordable Care Act (PPACA) of 2010

The PPACA of 2010 (also known as the Affordable Care Act) includes provisions that have implications for small and large businesses. The information presented in this section is intended to provide an overview of the new law; revisions might occur in the near future. For specific information, refer to websites related to this law (http://www.healthcare.gov/) or the IRS (http://www.irs.gov/).

According to the law, a new tax credit is allowable to certain small employers that provide healthcare coverage to their employees. The credit is targeted to those with low- and moderate-income workers.

The PPACA also "requires employers to report the cost of coverage under an employer-sponsored group health plan" (IRS 2011). Information is reported on IRS *Form W-2* (see the next section). The reason for the reporting is for "informational purposes only, to show employees the value of their health care benefits so they can be more informed consumers" (IRS 2011).

Figure 14.2 According to the IRS, employers are required by law to withhold federal income tax from their employees' wages (IRS 2011). In addition to an employee's gross income, fringe benefits—such as a free vacation to London—are also subject to income tax withholding and employment taxes. (© *Tony Watson/Alamy*)

Employment Taxes

As mentioned in Chapter 10, employment taxes are required when you have employees and include: (1) **federal income tax**, (2) **Social Security and Medicare taxes**, and (3) **Federal Unemployment Tax Act (FUTA)** (IRS 2011). In addition, most states require employers to withhold **state income taxes** (see state requirements for information). Employers who outsource their payroll duties should refer to the IRS website "Outsourcing Payroll and Third Party Payers" (http://www.irs.gov/bus).

According to the IRS, employers are required by law to withhold federal income tax from their employees' wages. In addition to an employee's gross income, **fringe benefits** (e.g., free commercial flights, vacations, discounts on services) are subject to income tax withholding and employment taxes (IRS 2011). (see Figure 14.2.) For complete information refer to *IRS Publication 15-B, Employers' Tax Guide to Fringe Benefits* (http://www.irs.gov/bus).

In differentiating health plans from fringe benefits, the IRS has other rules for the former: "if an employer pays the cost of an accident or health insurance plan for his/her employees,

including an employee's spouse and dependents, the employer's payments are not wages and are not subject to Social Security, Medicare, and FUTA taxes, or federal income tax withholding" (IRS 2011). Therefore, employment taxes do not apply to the cost of health plans when paid by an employer.

To begin the withholding process, the employee must compete and sign IRS *Form W-4, Employee's Withholding Allowance Certificate* at or before the start of employment. The employer must send the employee's form to the IRS and keep a copy for employment records.

In addition to federal income tax, employers must withhold part of Social Security and Medicare taxes from their employees' wages, and must pay an amount that matches the employees' taxes. The self-employed must withhold their own Social Security and Medicare taxes (**self-employment tax**); the amount is similar to the taxes withheld from the pay of most wage earners (IRS 2011).

The amount of taxes to withhold is described in *IRS Publication 15, Employer's Tax Guide* and *Publication 15-A, Employer's Supplemental Tax*

Guide (http://www.irs.gov/bus). Employers must report federal income taxes, and Social Security and Medicare taxes by using IRS *Form 941, Employer's Quarterly Federal Tax Return* (http://www.irs.gov/bus).

Note that the explanation provided above does not discuss the FUTA (unemployment) tax. This tax is paid and reported separately from federal income tax, and Social Security and Medicare taxes. Based on IRS regulations, employers pay these taxes; employees do not pay the FUTA tax, and the FUTA tax is not withheld from their pay (IRS 2011).

FUTA taxes also are delineated in *IRS Publication 15, Employer's Tax Guide*, and *Publication 15-A, Employer's Supplemental Tax Guide* (http://www.irs.gov/bus). When employees are hired employers must report FUTA taxes on IRS *Form 940, Employer's Annual Federal Unemployment (FUTA) Tax Return* (http://www.irs.gov/bus).

In addition to the requirements associated with federal income tax and Social Security and Medicare taxes, the law requires that at the end of the year employers must prepare and file IRS *Form W-2, Wage and Tax Statement*. All wages, fringe benefits, tips, and other compensation paid to an employee must be reported on IRS *Form W-2*.

The employer must give a copy of IRS *Form W-2* to the employee by January 31 of the following year. A copy of IRS *Form W-2* must also be submitted to the SSA.

Recordkeeping Requirements

The IRS recommends that employers use good recordkeeping practices that document income and expenses, including gross income receipts, purchases (items bought and resold to customers), expenses (costs other than purchases), travel, transportation, entertainment, gifts, assets, and employment taxes.

You can select the type of system used for recordkeeping, such as accounting journals and ledgers. The business checkbook is the main source for entries in business books (IRS 2011). Supporting documents can include sales slips, paid bills, invoices, receipts, deposit slips, and canceled checks.

Records must be retained that "support an item of income or deductions on a tax return until the period of limitations for that return runs out" (IRS 2011). The IRS stipulates that records of employment taxes must be retained for at least four years after filing the fourth quarter for the year.

Employment tax records must include names, addresses, Social Security numbers, dates of employment, and income tax withholding allowance certificates (IRS *Form W-4*). For complete information, refer to the IRS website and *IRS Publication 583, Starting a Business and Keeping Records* (http://www.irs.gov/bus).

Checking for Comprehension

* Describe how a law of the U.S. Department of Labor (DOL) might apply to a design firm.

* Which employment taxes are employers required by law to pay?

Humanism in Human Resource Management

Naturally, an owner of an interior design firm has to comply with federal, state, and local employment laws and regulations to *stay* in business. But compliance does not translate into a successful community of employees—people who can help you to not just *stay* in business; they can make significant contributions that result in enhanced profits and longevity for the business. Therefore, in addition to developing operating policies and procedures that meet legal obligations, you must formulate strategies for attracting, hiring, and retaining the best employees.

How?

Dating back to Frederick W. Taylor's 1911 views on scientific management in factories, there have been many approaches to managing people. Many business experts, such as Taylor (an American industrial engineer), focused on management strategies from an economistic perspective—policies and procedures centered on making profits for the organization regardless of the employees' work environment.

Actually the mindset of placing the organization first and thereby enacting unfair and discriminatory employment practices contributed to the need for government agencies to create many of the laws previously discussed. For example, the FLSA was created to ensure that employees had fair wages and worked reasonable hours, and that children were not exploited for economic gain.

OSHAct had to be enacted to force employers to create and maintain safe and healthy working conditions. To prevent employers from discriminating against qualified individuals based on a disability, the U.S. government created Title I of the ADA of 1990.

Rather than focusing on human resource management from an economistic approach, this discussion examines the topic from a **humanistic** perspective—ideal for a profession reliant on interpersonal relationships.

One way to understand humanism in business is to review a basic definition of the word: "a doctrine, attitude, or way of life centered on human interests or values; *especially* a philosophy that usually rejects supernaturalism and stresses an individual's dignity and worth and capacity for self-realization through reason" (Merriam-Webster 2011).

This definition of humanism identifies many key elements of the philosophy that are relevant to business practices, such as focusing on "human interests and values" as well as an "individual's dignity and worth and capacity for self-realization." Therefore, these are the elements that form the basis for the topics discussed next. The first step is to apply the philosophy to hiring policies and practices.

Hiring Employees

How do you use a humanistic perspective to develop hiring policies and procedures? One approach to thinking about hiring practices from a

humanism viewpoint is to remember when you were seeking your entry-level interior design position (see Chapter 3). For example:

- Where did you look for a position?

- How did you search for jobs?

- Who did you talk with?

- After you found a design firm you wanted to work for, how did you perceive the application process? Did the employer's representatives give prompt and courteous responses?

- How did you feel when they contacted you for an interview? Were you confused about the interview process? Did they make you feel important?

- How did you feel during the interview? Did people make you feel welcome? Did they seem to be interested in speaking with you, or did they appear to be preoccupied?

- Did people seem interested in your résumé or portfolio?

- How did you feel after the interview? Did you know the next steps? Did the employer or employer's representative contact you in a timely manner?

- How did you feel during negotiations? Again, did you feel like you were important to the organization?

Lastly, recall how you felt when you started your first professional job;

- Did people make you feel welcome?

- Were you introduced to other employees?

- Did you have orientation sessions and perhaps an "office buddy" to help you get settled in your job during the first week?

- Did people ignore you because they were busy or thought you were someone else's responsibility?

- Did people expect you to immediately know how to do your job?

Some of the best ways to develop humanistic policies and procedures in your business is to incorporate the practices you valued as an employee—and avoid any behavior or attitudes that made you feel you were not worthwhile to the organization. The process can begin by incorporating humanistic principles in the following personnel areas: (1) **job analyses**, (2) compensation and benefits, (3) hiring procedures, and (4) an **employee handbook**.

Job Analyses

The owner of an interior design firm might need to hire a variety of people depending on the needs of the business. For example, the owner might need an administrative assistant to help answer phone calls, track orders, arrange appointments, and schedule installations. Or the person might need an assistant designer who can help by searching for samples, writing specifications, or preparing drawings and presentation boards. Perhaps the owner wants to expand the business by developing a marketing department or hiring designers with considerable experience in large design firms. In addition, there are part-time and full-time positions.

Therefore, one of the first steps in hiring employees is to do a job analysis by determining what tasks need to be completed and what attributes an employee should have to successfully perform those tasks.

On the surface the job analysis process—writing a list of activities—might appear simplistic or unnecessary. But you should take considerable time and thought in performing job analyses. First make sure to identify all the tasks, and then determine the appropriate profession for the tasks. For example, given your list of tasks and responsibilities, you might need to hire another interior designer as well as an administrative assistant.

These distinctions are important for various reasons. From a humanistic perspective you want to make sure that someone applying for a position is fully aware of all the tasks required for a job; someone applying for an interior design position expects to work as a designer, not

to maintain the accounting software. Similarly, someone applying for an administrative assistant job expects to handle business operations and not work as an interior designer.

Unclear distinctions between positions can also have economic ramifications. For example, hiring overqualified people for positions might force you to pay higher salaries than what is normally expected for those jobs. Or you might pay full-time salaries for part-time work.

As discussed later in this chapter, incomplete and ambiguous job descriptions could result in legal problems during the search process, performance reviews, and terminations. Hence, every employer should do a thorough job analysis and use the results to develop employment policies and procedures.

Compensation and Benefits

After identifying who you need to hire for full- or part-time work, determine appropriate ranges of compensation as well as employee benefits. Networking with others in professional organizations and researching industry practices can provide an overview of typical salaries, wages, and bonuses.

Make sure you are financially able to offer a salary that is commensurate with the person's skills, knowledge, abilities, and experience. Offering less than industry expectations can offend candidates, resulting in the loss of a potentially valuable employee or the hiring of someone under awkward conditions. Depending on the circumstances, a poor beginning with a new employee could be difficult or perhaps impossible to overcome.

People expect to have fair and equitable compensation packages. However, when business is approached from a humanistic perspective, many other issues besides salary are considered important. Non-salary issues take center stage every year when *Fortune* magazine announces the "100 Best Companies to Work For," a list determined by feedback from employees. The article includes the highest-paying companies, but that list is supplemented with the companies that have the best perks. Moreover, most of the companies with the highest pay did not rank high as the best ones to work for.

For example, software company SAS was ranked as the top company to work for in 2010 and 2011, but was not listed as a high-paying company (Figure 14.3). As of 2011, SAS had been on the list for 14 years, and its employees raved about company perks: on-site healthcare, high-quality childcare at $410 per month, summer camp for kids, car cleaning, and beauty salon (Moore and Vandermey 2011). In addition, a manager noted that "people stay at SAS in large part because they are happy, but to dig a little deeper, I would argue that people don't leave SAS because they feel regarded—seen, attended to, and cared for. I have stayed for that reason, and love what I do for that reason" (Moore and Vandermey 2011).

The annual *Fortune* magazine article also identifies companies with the best benefits: healthcare, childcare, work-life balance, telecommuting, sabbaticals, and "unusual perks." Items included as "unusual perks"? Access to wine bars, auto tune-ups, shopping malls, on-site gym/gym discounts, a compressed workweek, gay-friendly benefits/policies, a life coach, and job sharing.

These "unusual perks" as well as the positive testimonials from SAS employees illustrate

Figure 14.3 As of 2011 SAS had been on *Fortune* magazine's list of *100 Best Companies to Work For*, for more than a dozen years. Employees rave about company perks and feel they are "cared for." *(SAS)*

the importance of humanism in business and also provide examples of benefits to consider when developing your design firm's policies. Obviously the perks identified in *Fortune* magazine are not required by law but are provided because employers have learned that incentives focused on the needs of people help to attract and retain outstanding employees.

Your benefit package must, however, include the legally required benefits discussed earlier in this chapter—Social Security and Medicare taxes that match employees' payments, workers' compensation, and unemployment insurance (FUTA). Also, some states require that employers offer disability insurance (as of 2012: California, Hawaii, New Jersey, New York, and Rhode Island).

Other possible elements of the employment picture to consider include personal leave policies, such as **paid time off (PTO)** for vacation, holidays, illness, and bereavement as well as personal leave guidelines that comply with the FMLA. Employers are not required by law to offer paid health plans, but most employers have some type of health plan for full-time employees and their dependents. Health plans might include dental, vision care, and short-term and/or long-term disability.

As discussed in Chapter 2, most employers offer some type of retirement or future planning benefit, such as company-sponsored pension plans, 401(k) retirement plans, and profit sharing. Most retirement plans require shared contributions from the employer and employee.

The IRS and the DOL developed a publication, *Choosing a Retirement Solution for Your Small Business*, outlining retirement savings plans for business owners (http://www.dol.gov/). The three retirement vehicles are the Individual Retirement Arrangements (IRAs), **defined contribution (DC) plans**, and **defined benefit (DB) plans**.

All of the plans have tax advantages for the employee as well as the employer (see http://www.irs.gov/retirement/index.html). In addition, the plans have specific requirements, such as employer responsibilities, maximum annual contribution per participant, and vesting provisions.

Employees and employers are both able to set up and contribute to IRAs, a tax-deferred retirement fund. IRA-based plans include a payroll deduction IRA, SEPs (Simplified Employee Pensions) plan, SIMPLE (Savings Incentive Match Plan for Employees of Small Employers) IRA plan, and Safe Harbor 401(k).

The SEPs plan allows employers to set up IRA retirement accounts for themselves as well as their employees. Under the SIMPLE IRA plan, employers with 100 or fewer employees can create a retirement account that "allows employees to contribute a percentage of their salary each paycheck and requires employer contributions" (DOL 2010). The Safe Harbor 401(k) plan is used by "businesses with highly compensated employees whose contributions would be limited in a traditional 401(k) plan" (DOL 2010).

DC plans include an automatic enrollment 401(k), a traditional 401(k), and profit sharing. A major difference between an automatic enrollment and a traditional 401(k) is the contributor's options. Under the automatic enrollment 401(k), "employees, unless they opt otherwise, must make salary contributions specified by the employer" (DOL 2010).

Using the traditional 401(k) plan an "employee can decide how much to contribute pursuant to a salary reduction agreement" (DOL 2010). Profit sharing allows an employer to make large contributions to employees.

DB plans provides a fixed amount at retirement that is determined by the employee's number of years of service and a percentage of that person's salary.

Hiring Policies and Procedures

A legal perspective that is important to understand when hiring is known as the **employment-at-will doctrine**. Fundamentally, this states that unless there is a written contract employees can leave a place of employment for any or no reason and employers can terminate an employee for any or no reason. Therefore, the employment-at-will doctrine should be considered as you develop your hiring policies, employee contracts, and termination procedures.

You do not want to hire people who leave for any or no reason—you *do* want to hire people who will not have to be terminated. Therefore, you should acquire as much information about a job applicant as is legally possible before making a job offer. This process begins with creating an employment application form. (Many job application form templates are available online.)

The form must comply with antidiscrimination laws by avoiding biased questions, such as those referencing birthplace, gender, age, religion/creed, race/color, height/weight, or marital status. Photographs must not be requested, and questions regarding disabilities may be mentioned only within the context of asking how an applicant would perform the essential functions of the job.

Generally, an employment application form is divided into five areas: (1) personal data—name, address, phone, and e-mail address; (2) education (most recent first)—school, major, start date, and completion date; (3) work experience (most recent first)—company name, address, phone, job title, job description, immediate supervisor's name, start date, end date, and reason for leaving; (4) additional information and corresponding dates—licenses, certificates, and professional courses; and (5) references (preferably persons familiar with work experience)—name, address, and phone number.

Job Descriptions

In addition to an employment application form, you must develop job descriptions for every position. A well-written, thorough, and concise job description is important for attracting and retaining ideal employees.

From a humanistic perspective, people want to have a clear understanding of what they are applying for and don't usually welcome surprises after accepting a position. The job description should give an accurate portrait of the type of position as well as the responsibilities, tasks, qualifications, and working relationships accompanying that job.

After an employee has been hired the requirements in a job description should be used for performance reviews and might initiate the need for professional development when an employer determines that an employee should have skills that were not included in the job description.

Generally, a job description can be divided into five areas (Box 14.1): (1) fundamentals—job title, location, starting date, career level (e.g., director/senior/junior/intermediate/intern or associate/assistant or 1/2/3/4), and employment status (full-time or part-time); (2) brief description of the job and employer; (3) list of job requirements (responsibilities and tasks); (3) qualifications (e.g., education, work experience,

---

Example of a Job Description for a Design Position at SOM*

This details all the information about the job posting. To submit your resume, click on the "Submit Your Resume to This Job" button.

Job Title
SF–Architectural Assistant

Location
San Francisco, CA

Open Date
04/29/2011

Career Level
Entry Level

Job Type
Full-time

Category
Architectural Services

Division
Architecture Design

Education
College—University

Job Description
The San Francisco office of Skidmore, Owings & Merrill LLP is looking for exceptionally talented designers with strong conceptual skills, capable of fulfilling supporting design roles on projects.

Summary:
* Performs work on basic segments of a project.

* Contributes to general preparation of master planning and site planning documents and models.

* Exhibits understanding of basic programming, massing, building, open space and urban planning typologies.

* Exhibits understanding of general design philosophy relating to assigned work.

* Performs basic documentation and presentation work, including diagrams, scale comparisons and visualizations.

* Organizes own work efforts.

(Box 14.1 continued on page 438)

Box 14.1

Example of a Job Description for a Design Position at SOM* *(continued)*

Job Requirements

Qualifications:

* Completion of a five-year or six-year architectural degree program (including minimum one year professional experience) and graduate of 1- to 2-year urban design/planning program.

* Limited experience in the architectural and/or urban design and planning profession.

* Demonstrated general knowledge and abilities in documentation, urban history and theory, urban design and planning.

* Demonstrated general knowledge of building materials, detailing, construction techniques related engineering principles and building codes.

* Excellent communication, problem-solving, and organizational skills.

* Ability to work in a team environment.

* Excellent MS Office skills.

* Proficiency in 3D modeling such as Revit, Rhino, and 3D Studio Max. Rendering using mental ray or V-Ray, AutoCAD Architecture 2008, Photoshop, Illustrator, PowerPoint.

All applicants must send a resume, cover letter and work samples/portfolio for consideration.

SOM is an Equal Employment Opportunity employer. We conduct all employment-related activities without regard to sex, race, color, religion, national origin, ancestry, age, medical condition, disability, sexual orientation, or marital status (except where certain characteristics are essential bona fide occupational requirements or where a disability is a bona fide occupational disqualification), as required by applicable law. SOM welcomes diversity in the workplace. SOM will make reasonable accommodation in the application process for applicants with disabilities, as required by applicable law. Please contact the Human Resources department at the location of interest to request accommodation.

Questions

If you have questions about the SOM Career Center, please e-mail **career.assistance@ som.com**. Please note that resume/portfolio submissions will not be accepted via e-mail. You should submit your resume and portfolio through the SOM Career Center. If you are unable to submit through the Career Center, please send your resume, cover letter, and work samples via regular mail, to the appropriate office mailing address

We realize that all candidates may not wish to complete an online application. If you would prefer to apply for a position via regular mail , please submit your resume, cover letter and 3 to 4 work samples to the appropriate office (C/O Human Resources). Clearly indicate in the cover letter the position and location of the position you are applying for. For a complete listing of SOM locations and addresses, please visit the "Contact" section of our website.

*Source: http://www.som.com/content.cfm/careers.

licenses, certificates, knowledge, skills, and proficiencies); (4) requests for supplemental materials (e.g., résumé, cover letter, work samples/portfolio); and (5) policy statements related to equal opportunities.

As illustrated in Box 14.1, the language in a job description is very succinct and is written in the present tense. For example, in the list of job responsibilities rather than writing, "An interior designer is responsible for preparing and developing drawings, models, images and other documents associated with a project." A job description should read, "Prepares and develops drawings, models, images and other documents associated with a project."

As is the case with an employment application form, a job description must not have biased terminology that discriminates against people because of a person's race, color, religion, gender, pregnancy, national origin, age (older than 40), disability, or genetic information (EEOC 2011).

Recruitment and Interview Practices

Avoiding discriminatory practices is also applicable to recruitment strategies, interpreting job referrals, and interviews. Thus, to develop hiring policies and procedures, refer to federal, state, and local employment laws, most notably those administered by the EEOC, such as Title VII of the Civil Rights Act of 1964, EPA of 1963, ADEA of 1967, and Title I of the ADA of 1990 (see http://www.eeoc.gov/).

In addition, you must comply with the Fair Credit Reporting Act (FCRA) of 1997 when seeking consumer reporting information. The FCRA was enacted in 1997 "to protect the privacy of consumer report information and to guarantee that the information supplied by consumer reporting agencies is as accurate as possible" (Federal Trade Commission [FTC] 1999).

From a legal as well as a humanistic perspective, your firm's recruitment and interviewing policies and procedures should be fair by treating every applicant in a consistent manner.

Therefore, job advertisements should be available to all potential candidates. This can be accomplished by using your website, Internet job boards, design newsletters, and the websites of professional organizations and trade magazines.

Newspaper advertisements are an option, but generally are not used by design firms because of the expense and low response rates of qualified applicants. Word-of-mouth recommendations from employees, clients, and allied professionals are also an effective way to recruit designers. In addition, you might be able to obtain leads through networking sites, such as LinkedIn and Facebook.

To conduct interviews in a fair and lawful manner, prepare an interview schedule and list of questions that are used for every applicant. Every candidate's schedule is therefore identical; they all interview with the same people, in the same facilities, for the same amount of time. Every candidate is also asked the same questions; the items should focus on the responsibilities of the job and the applicant's qualifications.

Laws prohibit discriminatory questions related to a person's race, color, religion, gender, pregnancy, national origin, age (older than 40), disability or genetic information (EEOC 2011). Within a seemingly structured format you can ask open-ended questions that provide candidates with the chance to reveal their strengths and communication skills. For example, an open-ended interview question could be "Explain how you worked with clients to determine functional and spatial requirements." Interviewers also can ask follow-up questions based on candidates' responses.

The hiring process can involve background checks. Generally, background searches are conducted for people you intend to hire. Searches can include contacting former employers, obtaining college/university transcripts, and perhaps reviewing the person's credit history, criminal history, and driving record. Some employers also conduct online searches for information about a potential employee, most notably by checking social networking sites.

As is the case with all employment practices, you must comply with laws pertaining to accessing and using personal information, including the Privacy Act of 1974 and the FCRA. In addition, questions you ask people such as former employers and references, and information you receive from these individuals must not discriminate against a candidate based on race, color, religion, gender, pregnancy, national origin, age (older than 40), disability, or genetic information (EEOC 2011).

Employee Policies and Practices

After you have found the ideal employees, continue to focus on the needs of each new hire. This statement might seem obvious, but the reminder is needed; some employers become so busy with their own work that new employees can feel somewhat forgotten during their first few weeks on the job. This can be a costly mistake when employees are not able to perform to their potential. In addition, discontented employees are not motivated to perform and often search for new job opportunities. Therefore, make sure your policies and procedures focus on the needs of new employees as well as other employees, regardless of years of service.

Policies and practices for newly hired designers should include orientation strategies and a mentorship program. Orientation should begin on the first day of employment. So that the new designer feels welcome, he or she should meet everyone working in the firm or that division; the person should also be given a tour of the facilities.

To provide an overview of co-workers' responsibilities, meetings should be scheduled with people who will be working with the new designer. The new designer should also be given assignments during the first week of employment to help that person feel he or she is making a contribution to the firm.

Often the best way to facilitate new assignments is to assign a mentor to the new designer for a reasonable period. The mentor can talk about and show how the design firm operates, including strategies for building long-term relationships with clients. For example, in Box 14.2 two new designers at Perkins + Will: Eva Maddox Branded Environments reveal in an interview how mentors helped to make their efforts successful and "they are learning how to work effectively with management, clients, and each other" (Olivieri 2011).

In addition to mentorships, there should be a plan for how the new designer will acquire his or her own clients. The process is simplified if the designer already has an established clientele from previous employment, but even when this is the situation, there still needs to be a plan for assigning clients to a new designer. The first priority is to address the needs of the client followed by being fair to designers who have years of service to the firm.

Employee Handbook

Employment policies and practices should be delineated in an employee handbook. An employee handbook is very useful to new employees, but it also serves a legal purpose. Detailing a design firm's policies and procedures can help to avoid complaints associated with discriminatory practices and can serve as the basis for termination procedures.

Creating an employee handbook can be made easier by customizing the template provided by the Small Business Administration (SBA) (http://www.sba.gov/content/employee-handbooks). Based on the SBA template, an employee handbook could include employment policies, standards of conduct, compensation, benefits, and employee communications (Box 14.3).

Note in Box 14.3 that "Internet Use" is included in "Standards of Conduct." For this topic the SBA template has a policy for using the Internet and e-mail. Fundamentally, employees are supposed to use the Internet and e-mail for company business and activities, and not disturb the organization's computer network nor interfere with the employee's productivity. Employees using the Internet must do so in an ethical

Box 14.2

Selected Interview Excerpts from *Q&A: Emerging Talent* by Gregory Olivieri* (January 6, 2011)

Gregory Olivieri interviewed Lynette Klein and Liz Potokar of Perkins + Will: Eva Maddox Branded Environments on January 6, 2011.

Gregory Olivieri: What are your current titles and responsibilities?

Liz Potokar: I was hired as a Designer 1 after graduating from the University of Cincinnati in 2008, with my Bachelor of Science in Interior Design. In this position, I assist in the preparation of presentation materials and digital models for clients, help with the preparation of plans, sections, and elevations, as well as furniture, color, finish, and material research, specifications, and selection.

Lynette Klein: I also started as a Designer 1, when I was hired after graduating from the University of Nebraska in 2006 with a Bachelor of Science in Interior Design. Two years ago, I was promoted to a Designer 2, which includes similar responsibilities to a Designer 1, but now I actively participate in the preparation of client presentations, documentation, details, and schedules.

GO: What prepared you to assume the responsibility that comes along with being a professional designer?

LK: On the job, we have great role models in Eva Maddox and Eileen Jones. They've taught us to take a strategic approach to our projects, and now this is second nature to us.

GO: How did senior leadership empower your work?

LK: Most important was the sense of trust to get the job done right and on time. That made for a less authoritative environment, in which we didn't fear being wrong.

LP: Because of our strategic approach, we agreed on a set direction. We knew we would have a limited amount of time with senior leadership, so we did our homework and researched answers to potential questions before our meetings. That made our review sessions more efficient. They were comfortable handing out the work, letting us learn on our own, and supervising the process in an unassuming manner.

GO: What makes your efforts successful?

LP: We trust each other. We also challenge each other, which increases our confidence.

LK: Eva's and Eileen's good intuition, knowledge base, and mentorship have also made a big difference.

*Source: http://www.metropolismag.com/pov/author/georgy-olivieri.

and lawful manner. For clarity, remind employees that messages sent from the firm's computers are considered public, and not private; the firm has the right to access and monitor files and messages.

Employee Handbook: Information Technology Policies
Information technology presents contemporary issues that should be addressed in an employee handbook. The author of the template

Box 14.3

Table of Contents for an Employee Handbook*

CONTENTS

SECTION 1—INTRODUCTION
1.1 Employment Applications

SECTION 2—DEFINITIONS OF EMPLOYEE STATUS
2.1 "Employees" Defined

SECTION 3—EMPLOYMENT POLICIES
3.1 Non-Discrimination
3.2 Non-Disclosure/Confidentiality
3.3 New Employee Orientation
3.4 Office Hours
3.5 Personnel Files
3.6 Performance Review and Planning Sessions
3.7 Outside Employment
3.8 Corrective Action
3.9 Employment Termination
3.10 Safety
3.11 Health-Related Issues
3.12 Employee Requiring Medical Attention
3.13 Building Security
3.14 Insurance on Personal Effects
3.15 Supplies; Expenditures; Obligating the Company
3.16 Expense Reimbursement
3.17 Parking
3.18 Visitors in the Workplace
3.19 Immigration Law Compliance

SECTION 4—STANDARDS OF CONDUCT
4.1 Attendance/Punctuality
4.2 Absence without Notice
4.3 Harassment, including Sexual Harassment
4.4 Telephone Use
4.5 Public Image
4.6 Substance Abuse
4.7 Tobacco Products
4.8 Internet Use
4.9 Mobile Devices, Social Media, and Blogs

SECTION 5—WAGE AND SALARY POLICIES
5.1 Wage or Salary Increases
5.2 Timekeeping
5.3 Overtime
5.4 Paydays

SECTION 6—BENEFITS AND SERVICES
6.1 Insurance
6.2 COBRA Benefits
6.3 Social Security/Medicare
6.4 Simple IRA
6.5 Vacation
6.6 Recordkeeping
6.7 Holidays
6.8 Jury Duty/Military Leave
6.9 Educational Assistance
6.10 Training and Professional Development

SECTION 7—EMPLOYEE COMMUNICATIONS
7.1 Staff Meetings
7.2 Bulletin Boards
7.3 Suggestion Box
7.4 Procedure for Handling Complaints

*Adapted from http://www.sba.gov/content/employee-handbooks.

in Box 14.3 has added other items below the "Internet Use" section that are relevant to the digital age, including mobile devices (personal smartphones, tablets), social media (Facebook, Twitter, and LinkedIn), and blogs. These items were added to the SBA employee handbook's Table of Contents because business in the twenty-first century is centered on information technology. Thus, business owners must create employee policies and procedures for using the range of technologies that exist beyond the Internet and e-mail.

The policies developed for the Internet and e-mail described above are also applicable to mobile devices, social media, and blogs. Policies regarding social media and blogs should focus on issues concerning confidentiality and inappropriate postings.

From a different perspective businesses are encouraging employees to use social media and blogs to improve information management and collaboration. The purpose is to encourage employees to participate on a daily basis and to collaboratively develop new ideas and solutions.

To ensure a firm has policies and procedures that reflect current business practices as well as new laws and regulations, the employee handbook should be updated annually.

Humanism in Human Resources: Leadership
Policies and procedures are useful for providing structure, but authentic performance of employees requires leadership. The owner of a business must be a **leader**—someone who can influence people to accomplish goals. Scores of articles and books have been written on the topic of leadership (see Bibliography); to have a better understanding of leadership, you can study any of the abundant examples.

This section of the chapter provides an overview of leadership theories by examining the philosophy developed by W. Edwards Deming and illustrates how Deming's tenets can be applied to an interior design firm.

Deming was a statistician hired by the Japanese government to help transform Japanese businesses after the devastation caused by the atomic bombings in World War II. On the surface it might not appear that a statistician would advocate a humanistic perspective; however, as described in this section, Deming's philosophy centered on the importance of employees and leadership. Moreover, it might seem that a leadership philosophy developed in the 1940s would not be relevant today. Again, as illustrated by the following examples, Deming's philosophy is applicable in the twenty-first century for the same reason previously mentioned—its focus on the needs of people.

Dr. Deming summarized his leadership philosophy into 14 interdependent points and translated those points into practice by identifying the role of someone who manages people (Box 14.4). Some of Deming's terminology was written for managers of production facilities, but the essence of his philosophy is applicable to any organization, including interior design firms.

Key elements of Deming's philosophy that can be applied to design firms include the importance of (1) a clearly defined mission statement (Point 1); (2) understanding systems and the Plan-Do-Check-Act (PDCA) cycle (Points 4, 5, and 11); (3) teamwork (Points 9 and 14); (4) instituting leadership (Points 2 and 7); (5) appropriate performance reviews and motivation strategies (Points 3, 8, 10, 11, and 12); and (6) training and education (Points 6 and 13).

Leadership in the Twenty-first Century
Many of the elements outlined above have already been discussed in this book, such as mission statements, systems, the PDCA cycle, and teamwork. As illustrated by Deming's philosophy, organizations must have leaders who understand their responsibilities, including helping people to perform at their optimum level.

Today's leaders are challenged to understand how to manage a workforce that includes several generations as well as diversity in gender, cultures, languages, races, ethnicities, lifestyles, values, and abilities. Within this pluralism

Box 14.4

W. Edwards Deming's Leadership Philosophy*

14 Interdependent Points

1. **Constancy of Purpose**—Create constancy of purpose toward improvement of product and service, with the aim to become competitive and to stay in business, and to provide jobs.

2. **Adopt the New Philosophy**—We are in a new economic age. Western management must awaken to the challenge, must learn their responsibilities, and must take on leadership for change.

3. **Cease Dependence on Mass Inspection**—Cease dependence on mass inspection to achieve quality. Eliminate the need for inspection to achieve quality. Eliminate the need for inspection on a mass basis by building quality into the product in the first place.

4. **Cease Doing Business on Price Tag Alone**—End the practice of awarding business on price tag. Instead, minimize total cost. Move toward a single supplier for any one item, on a long-term relationship of loyalty and trust.

5. **Continual Improvement of Process**—Improve constantly and forever the system of production and service, to improve quality and productivity, and thus constantly decrease cost.

6. **Institute Training on the Job.**

7. **Adopt and Institute Leadership** (see Point 12)—The aim of leadership should be to help people and machines and gadgets to do a better job. Leadership of management is in need of overhaul, as well as leadership of production workers.

8. **Drive Out Fear**—Drive out fear, so that everyone may work effectively for the company.

9. **Break Down Barriers between Departments**—People in research, design, sales, and production must work as a team, to foresee problems of production and in use that may be encountered with the product or service.

10. **Eliminate Slogans, Exhortations, and Targets**—Eliminate slogans, exhortations, and targets for the work force asking for zero defects and new levels of productivity. Such exhortations only create adversarial relationships, as the bulk of the causes of low quality and low productivity belong to the system and thus lie beyond the power of the work force.

11(a). **Eliminate Numerical Quotas**—Eliminate work standards (quotas) on the factory floor. Substitute leadership. 11(b). Eliminate management by objective. Eliminate management by numbers, numerical goals. Substitute leadership.

12(a). **Allow Pride in Workmanship**—Remove barriers that rob the hourly worker of his right to pride of workmanship. The responsibility of supervisors must be changed from sheer numbers to quality. 12(b). Remove barriers that rob people in management and in engineering of their right to pride of workmanship. This means, inter alia, abolishment of the annual or merit rating and of management by objective, management by numbers.

13. **Institute a Program of Self-Improvement**—Institute a vigorous program of education and self-improvement.

14. **Do It**—Put everybody in the company to work to accomplish the transformation. The transformation is everybody's job.

*Source: Deming, W. E. 1992. *Quality, Productivity, and Competitive Position*. (seminar presentation). Seattle: Quality Enhancement Seminars, Inc.

W. Edwards Deming's Leadership Philosophy* (continued)

Selected Examples of W. Edwards Deming's Roles of a Manager of People**

Someone who manages people should

- Understand and convey to people the meaning of a system.

- Understand that people are different from each other.

- Optimize an individual's family background, education, skills, hopes, and abilities.

- Be an unceasing learner.

- Be a coach and counsel, not a judge.

- Create trust.

- Not expect perfection.

- Listen and learn without passing judgment.

- Develop an understanding of each individual's aims, hopes, and fears.

- Understand the benefits of cooperation and the losses from competition between people and between groups.

**Adapted from W. E. Deming, *The New Economics: For Industry, Government, Education* (Cambridge: Massachusetts Institute of Technology, Center for Advanced Engineering Study, 1993).

---

a leader must effectively communicate with individuals, project teams, transnational teams, virtual teams, stakeholders, and the public.

Effective communication is dependent on trust. To earn trust requires a leader to care about people and to be honest, reliable, and competent. To trust a leader's actions and decisions, people have to believe the person is acting on behalf of their best interests.

Being benevolent is tied to honesty. A leader demonstrates honesty by being truthful, accepting responsibility, and doing what he or she promised. Honesty also involves being open with people—asking for advice and sharing information in a collaborative manner.

To earn trust also involves being reliable and competent. People must know a leader will consistently follow through and is dependable.

Reliability can be demonstrated by competence. Competent leaders are knowledgeable, effective communicators, and can perform

expected tasks. Leadership competency also involves being able to make sound decisions, and resolving problems and conflicts in a fair and equitable way.

Leadership in the Twenty-First Century: Social Responsibilities

Leaders today are often expected to fulfill their organization's social responsibilities. Depending on the interests of the business, there are various ways that this can be done, such as designing green buildings, enacting green business policies and practices, engaging in charitable initiatives, or volunteering in the community. For example, an international design firm, NBBJ, has three socially responsible programs: "sustainable design," "partnership," and "building community."

A description of the firm's "sustainable design" program states, "NBBJ is dedicated to actively pursuing sustainable solutions that contribute to a more livable world" (NBBJ 2011). NBBJ's "dedication to sustainable solutions" is illustrated by the LEED-certified buildings the firm has designed as well as its innovations for indoor air quality (Figure 14.4).

NBBJ's explanation for its "partnership" program is "We have a unique opportunity and responsibility to accelerate the shift to more sustainable design practices in all market sectors we serve and cities we live and work in. Such a shift requires collaboration" (NBBJ 2011). An example of NBBJ's "partnership" program is its service on a task force formed by the USGBC (U.S. Green Building Council). The purpose of this team is to develop LEED benchmarks for high-performance green healthcare buildings.

The firm's third socially responsible program is "building community": "NBBJ seeks opportunities to contribute positively wherever we have a presence. Our activities focus on building healthy, sustainable communities and strengthening the design profession" (NBBJ 2011). An example of its "building community" initiative is the "San Francisco Sandcastle Building Classic." NBBJ employees collaborated with local school children to compete in

Figure 14.4 An international design firm, NBBJ, has three socially responsible programs: "sustainable design," "partnership," and "building community." One of its LEED certified projects—the Bill & Melinda Gates Foundation Headquarters in Seattle— illustrates the importance of social responsibilities, partnerships, and building community. (© *Benjamin Benschneider*)

building sandcastles. The event is organized by a local group that encourages children to engage in the arts.

Leadership in the Twenty-First Century: Inspiration, Motivation, and Innovation

Refer to the items listed in Box 14.4 and notice the most dominant responsibility of a leader: understanding how to create a work environment that inspires and motivates people to care about an organization's mission, values, vision, goals, and social responsibilities (as evidenced by NBBJ). When people are inspired and motivated, they achieve their goals and do so in an enthusiastic manner.

How can a leader inspire and motivate people, or, for the purposes of this book, how can an owner of a design firm inspire and motivate designers and other employees?

As evidenced by the people working for SAS, one of the companies described earlier in this chapter, first and foremost, an owner must understand each designer's needs, aspirations, skills, abilities, knowledge, and fears as well as the person's role within the entire operations (system) of the design firm.

The entire system includes internal as well as external elements. Understanding these elements enables the owner to assign appropriate tasks and provide training, education, or assistance when an assignment exceeds the person's abilities. Understanding each person also helps the owner create customized motivational strategies, such as allowing someone with children to have days off for family events.

One critical element in this context is having a comprehensive awareness of the entire system. A person cannot perform to his or her potential if adequate information or resources are not available. Employees' potential cannot be realized when co-workers are not willing to collaborate or resources are not available.

Some employees cannot perform to potential if they are afraid of losing their job or are worried about not meeting design fee quotas. As explained by Deming, management by numbers, such as requiring a specific number of new clients in a month, can instill fear and "robs" people of their "right to pride of workmanship."

Leaders are responsible for creating a work environment that is positive and free from fear and mistrust. The leader's role is to "not expect perfection" and to "listen and learn without passing judgment" (Deming 1993).

Leaders and organizations are successful when employees are **intrinsically motivated**—the work itself brings fulfillment. Intrinsically motivated people seek employment that allows them to design their own work environment and empowers them to make decisions and innovations. They also value a sense of community as well as opportunities that enable them to grow professionally and personally.

Employers can help to inspire intrinsic motivation by assigning employees appropriate tasks and then giving them the resources to do the job. When there are problems, the employer should listen to the concerns and address the issues in a timely manner.

When someone is **extrinsically motivated**, fulfillment is derived from awards, usually monetary. A leader can be successful with employees who are extrinsically motivated; however, when this is the primary motivator, it can become difficult to constantly provide financial incentives. In addition, when money is the issue, there is a chance the person will quit to pursue a more lucrative job offer.

Inspired and motivated designers innovate—a critical element in an era of global competitiveness. Leaders must create an environment that encourages designers to use their creativity and reach beyond the expectations of the firm—or even the entire industry. Perhaps every designer should be given one or more hours every week for creative brainstorming that is *not* associated with a current project. These ideas might or might not be shared with others—the intent is to just let the mind explore. The results could be inspirational for everyone involved with the firm.

Checking for Comprehension

- When you interviewed for your first job as an interior designer, what actions and/or comments made you feel good about the design firm? What actions and/or actions made you feel uncomfortable?

- What do you want in a leader of an organization? Do you want that person to tell you how to do your job? Or to leave you alone? Do you want him or her to evaluate your performance every year or month?

This chapter concluded the book by examining programs that are essential for growing, managing, and leading an interior design business—critical areas for the owner of a design firm.

The chapter content contributed to the material discussed previously in the book with an emphasis on legal issues related to hiring employees as well as human resource management. The focus of the chapter's final discussion was the importance of demonstrating leadership by inspiring and motivating the people they work with on a continuous basis.

Knowledge and Skills Summary

Highlights

- There are numerous federal and state labor laws employers must know when hiring employees or independent contractors.

- Federal and state governments have created numerous laws prohibiting work-related discrimination and harassment.

- Hiring employees requires compliance with several U.S. tax laws administered by the Internal Revenue Service (IRS).

- Employers must pay employment taxes, which consists of (1) federal income tax, (2) Social Security and Medicare taxes, and (3) Federal Unemployment Tax Act (FUTA). In addition, most states require employers to withhold state income taxes.

- This book examines human resource management from a humanistic perspective—ideal for a profession that relies on interpersonal relationships.

- Employers usually offer some type of retirement or future planning benefit, such as company-sponsored pension plans, 401(k) retirement plans, and profit sharing.

- A legal perspective that is important for hiring and retaining employees is the employment-at-will doctrine.

- A well-written, thorough, and concise job description is important for attracting and retaining ideal employees.

- Discriminatory practices should be avoided in recruitment strategies, interpreting job descriptions, and employment interviews.

- Employment policies and practices should be delineated in an employee handbook.

- An owner of a business must be a leader—someone who can influence people to accomplish goals.

Key Terms
defined benefit (DB) plan

defined contribution (DC) plan

employee

employee handbook

employment-at-will doctrine

extrinsic motivation

federal income tax

Federal Unemployment Tax Act (FUTA)

fringe benefit

humanistic

independent contractor

intrinsic motivation

job analysis

leader

Medicare tax

paid time off (PTO)

self-employment tax

Social Security tax

state income tax

Projects

Philosophy and Design Project
Dr. Deming summarized his leadership philosophy into 14 interdependent points and translated the points into practice by identifying the role of someone who manages people.

Locate leadership books and articles written by Deming. Based on these readings, how can Deming's leadership philosophy be adapted by an owner of an interior design firm? Develop a written summary (approximately three pages) of your analyses and post some of your suggestions online.

Research Project
Research the employment policies and practices for five international interior design firms. In a table compile the following information: (1) develop a summary of the employment policies and practices, (2) conduct an analysis that compares and contrasts the design firms' employment policies and practices, and (3) identify strategies for improving the design firms' employment policies and practices.

Human Factors Research Project
Federal and state governments have created numerous laws addressing work-related discrimination and harassment. Reexamine the employment laws discussed in this chapter by locating the laws online and reading them carefully.

Based on your analysis of the laws, which ones do you think would not have to exist if all business owners operated from a humanistic perspective? Why? Are there new laws that should be enacted to protect people? Develop a summary of your analyses, and prepare an informal presentation (approximately 10 minutes) to the class that includes questions for group discussions.

References

American Law Institute (ALI). 2011. *Codifications and Studies – Commercial Law – Uniform Commercial Code*. http://www.ali.org/. Accessed May 11, 2011.

Equal Employment Opportunity Commission (EEOC). 2011. *Title VII of the Civil Rights Act of 1964*. http://www.eeoc.gov/. Accessed May 10, 2011.

———. 1990. *Policy Guidance on Current Issues of Sexual Harassment*. http://www.eeoc.gov/. Accessed May 11, 2011.

Federal Trade Commission (FTC). 1999. *FTC Facts for Business: Using Consumer Reports*. Washington, DC: Federal Trade Commission (FTC).

Internal Revenue Service (IRS). 2011. *Affordable Care Act Provisions*. http://www.irs.gov/. Accessed May 12, 2011.

———. 2011. *Employee Benefits*. http://www.irs.gov/. Accessed May 13, 2011.

———. 2011. *Independent Contractor (Self-Employed) or Employee?* http://www.irs.gov/businesses/small/article/0,,id=99921,00.html. Accessed May 11, 2011.

———. 2011. *Publication 15 (2011), (Circular E), Employer's Tax Guide*. http://www.irs.gov/publications/p15/ar02.html#en_US_2011_publink1000202292. Accessed May 11, 2011.

———. 2011. *Recordkeeping*. http://www.irs.gov/. Accessed May 12, 2011.

Merriam-Webster. 2011. s.v. "humanism." *Merriam-Webster Dictionary*. http://www.merriam-webster.com/dictionary/humanism. Accessed May 5, 2011.

Moore, T., and A. Vandermey. February 7, 2011. "100 Best Companies to Work For." *Fortune* at http://money.cnn.com/magazines. Accessed May 16, 2011.

National Conference of Commissioners on Uniform State Laws (NCCUSL). 1998. UCC Article 9, Secured Transactions (1998) Summary. http://www.nccusl.org/. Accessed April 30, 2011.

NBBJ. 2011. *Approach: Future Friendly*. http://www.nbbj.com. Accessed May 19, 2011.

Olivieri, G. 2011. *Q&A: Emerging Talent*. http://www.metropolismag.com/pov/author/georgy-olivieri. Accessed March 1, 2011.

U.S. Department of Health and Human Services (HHS). 1996. *The Personal Responsibility and Work Opportunity Reconciliation Act (PRWORA) of 1996*. http://aspe.hhs.gov/HSP/abbrev/prwora96.htm#TOC. Accessed May 11, 2011.

———. 2011. *The Privacy Act of 1974—5 U.S.C. § 552A—As Amended*. http://www.hhs.gov. Accessed May 11, 2011.

U.S. Department of Labor (DOL). 2010. *Choosing a Retirement Solution for Your Small Business*. http://www.dol.gov/. Accessed May 17, 2011.

———. 2011. *Employment Law Guide*. http://www.dol.gov/. Accessed May 10, 2011.

———. 2012. *Employment Law Guide*. http://www.dol.gov/. Accessed February 15, 2012.

———. 2005. *Employer's Guide to Group Health Continuation Coverage Under COBRA: The Consolidated Omnibus Budget Reconciliation Act of 1986*. http://www.dol.gov/ebsa/pdf/cobraemployer.pdf. Accessed May 16, 2011.

Resources: Organizations, Research, Design Blogs, and Government

Professional Organizations

(Note: All URLs were accurate as of press time.)

American Academy of Healthcare Interior Designers (AAHID)
http://www.aahid.org/

American Society of Interior Designers (ASID)
http://www.asid.org/

Associação Brasileira de Designers de Interiores
http://www.abd.org.br/

Association of Interior Designers of Nova Scotia (IDNS)
http://www.idns.ca/

Association of Registered Interior Designers of New Brunswick (ARIDNB)
http://www.aridnb.ca/

Association of Registered Interior Designers of Ontario (ARIDO)
http://www.arido.ca/

British Institute of Interior Design
http://www.biid.org.uk/

China National Interior Decoration Association (CIDA)
http://218.247.4.32/english/Associations/38.htm

Colegio de Decoradores y Diseñadores de Interiores de Puerto Rico
http://www.coddi.org/

Design Institute of Australia (DIA)
http://www.dia.org.au/

Himpunan Desainer Interior Indonesia (HDII)
http://www.hdii.or.id/

Institute of Indian Interior Designers (IIID)
http://www.iifaindia.com/IIFA-PROFESSIONAL/iiid.html

Interior Design Association Hong Kong (IDAHK)
http://www.hkida.org/

Interior Design Society
http://www.interiordesignsociety.org/

Interior Designers Association of Saskatchewan (IDAS)
http://www.idas.ca/

Interior Designers Institute of British Columbia (IDIBC)
http://www.idibc.org/

Interior Designers of Alberta
http://www.idalberta.ca/home.html

Interior Designers of Canada (IDC)
http://www.idcanada.org/

International Federation of Interior Architects/Designers (IFI)
http://www.ifiworld.org/#Homepage

International Furnishings and Design Association (IFDA)
http://www.ifda.com/

International Interior Design Association (IIDA)
http://www.iida.org/

Japan Interior Designers' Association (JID)
http://www.jid.or.jp/index_en.shtml

Korean Society of Interior Designers
http://kosid.or.kr/

Professional Interior Designers Institute of Manitoba (PIDIM)
http://www.pidim.ca/

South African Institute of the Interior Design Professions (IID)
http://www.iidprofessions.com/

Thailand Interior Designers Association
http://www.tida.or.th/

Affiliated Professional Organizations

Acoustical Society of America (ASA)
http://acousticalsociety.org/

American Design/Digital Drafting Association (ADDA)
http://www.adda.org/

American Institute of Architects (AIA)
http://www.aia.org/

American Institute of Graphic Arts (AIGA)
http://www.aiga.org/

American Society of Furniture Designers (ASFD)
http://www.asfd.com/

American Society of Landscape Architects (ASLA)
http://www.asla.org/

Energy Design Resources
http://www.energydesignresources.com/

GreenerBuildings
http://www.greenbiz.com/buildings

Illuminating Engineering Society of North America
http://www.iesna.org/

Industrial Designers Society of America (IDSA)
http://www.idsa.org/

Institute of Store Planners (ISP)
http://www.ispo.org/

International Association of Home Staging Professionals (IAHSP)
http://www.iahsp.com/

International Association of Lighting Designers (IALD)
http://www.iald.org/

International Council of Societies of Industrial Design (ICISD)
http://www.icsid.org/

International Facilities Management Association (IFMA)
http://www.ifma.org/

National Association of the Remodeling Industry (NARI)
http://www.nari.org/

National Kitchen & Bath Association (NKBA)
http://www.nkba.org/

New Buildings Institute
http://www.newbuildings.org/

Organization for Black Designers (OBD)
http://www.core77.com/OBD/welcome.html

Retail Design Institute
http://www.retaildesigninstitute.org/about

Society for Environmental Graphic Design (SEGD)
http://www.segd.org/

Affiliated Academic Professional Organizations and Research Resources

Allsteel Knowledge Center
http://www.allsteeloffice.com/AllsteelOffice/Knowledge+Center/

Association of University Interior Designers (AUID)
http://www.auid.org/

Carnegie Mellon Green Design Institute
http://www.ce.cmu.edu/GreenDesign/

Carpet and Rug Institute Publications
http://www.carpet-rug.org/index.cfm

Center for Inclusive Design and Environmental Access
http://www.ap.buffalo.edu/idea/Home/index.asp

Center for the Built Environment
http://www.cbe.berkeley.edu/

Center for Universal Design
http://www.ncsu.edu/project/design-projects/udi/

Council for Interior Design Accreditation (CIDA) (Formerly FIDER)
http://www.accredit-id.org/

Design Exchange
http://www.dx.org/

Environmental Design Research Association
http://www.edra.org/

GREENGUARD Environmental Institute
http://www.greenguard.org/en/index.aspx

Haworth Knowledge
http://www.haworth.com/en-us/Pages/Home.aspx

Herman Miller Research
http://www.hermanmiller.com/

IIDA's Knowledge Center
http://knowledgecenter.iida.org/Index.aspx

InformeDesign
http://www.informedesign.org/

Interior Design Educators Council (IDEC)
http://www.idec.org/

Intypes (Interior Archetypes)
http://intypes.cornell.edu/

Knoll Research
http://www.knoll.com/research/index.jsp

National Association of Schools of Art and Design (NASAD)
http://nasad.arts-accredit.org/index.jsp

National Council for Interior Design Qualifications (NCIDQ)
http://www.ncidq.org/

Research Design Connections
http://www.researchdesignconnections.com/

Steelcase 360 Research
http://www.steelcase.com/en/Pages/Homepage.aspx

The Center for Health Design
http://www.healthdesign.org/

The Center for Real Life Kitchen Design
http://www.ahrm.vt.edu/center_for_real_life_kitchen_design/index.html

The Centre for Sustainable Design
http://www.cfsd.org.uk/

Universal Design Learning Lab
http://www.hdfs.hs.iastate.edu/centers/udll/

Interior Design Blogs

Art That Fits
http://blog.artthatfits.com/

Benjamin Moore—Living in Color
http://www.livingincolorwithsonu.typepad.com/

CATALYST—Strategic Design Review
http://catalystsdr.wordpress.com/

COLOURlovers
http://www.colourlovers.com/

Contract Magazine—Talk Contract
http://www.talkcontract.com/

CoolBoom
http://coolboom.net/

Design Spotter
http://www.designspotter.com/

Design Thinking
http://designthinking.ideo.com/

Designing Better Libraries
http://dbl.lishost.org/blog/

Dialog
http://dialog.paulettepascarella.com/

Dwell Studio
http://www.dwellstudio.com/blog

Health Care Design Magazine—Blogs
http://www.healthcaredesignmagazine.com/blogs

IDesign Arch
http://www.idesignarch.com/

Interior Design Magazine—Design Green
http://www.interiordesign.net/blog/Design_Green/index.php

Kravet—Inspired Talk
http://kravet.typepad.com/inspiredtalk/

Make Studio
http://makestudio.blogspot.com/

Restaurants by Design
http://www.restaurantsxdesign.blogspot.com/

The Design Hub
http://thedesignhub.wordpress.com/

The Design Observer Group—Design Observer
http://designobserver.com/

The Design Traveller
http://designtraveller.blogspot.com/

American Society for Testing and Materials (ASTM)
http://www.astm.org/ABOUT/overview.html

Americans with Disabilities Act (ADA)
http://www.ada.gov/

Federal Trade Commission (FTC)
http://www.ftc.gov/

Internal Revenue Service (IRS)
http://www.irs.gov/

International Code Council
http://www.iccsafe.org/Pages/default.aspx

International Organization for Standardization (ISO)
http://www.iso.org/iso/home.html

Leadership in Energy and Environmental Design
http://www.usgbc.org/DisplayPage.aspx?CategoryID=19

National Fire Protection Association
http://www.nfpa.org/index.asp?cookie_test=1

U.S. Bureau of Census
http://www.census.gov/

U.S. Copyright Office
http://www.copyright.gov/

U.S. Department of Commerce
http://www.commerce.gov/

U.S. Department of Health and Human Services
http://www.hhs.gov/ocr/privacy/

U.S. Department of Housing and Urban Development
http://portal.hud.gov/hudportal/HUD

U.S. Department of Labor
http://www.dol.gov/

U.S. Department of State
http://www.state.gov/

U.S. Environmental Protection Agency (EPA)
http://www.epa.gov/

U.S. General Services Administration
http://www.gsa.gov/portal/category/100000

U.S. Green Building Council (USGBC)
http://www.usgbc.org/

U.S. Small Business Administration (SBA)
http://www.sba.gov/

APPENDIX

B

CIDA Professional Standards

Council for Interior Design Accreditation's (CIDA) *Professional Standards 2011*	
Standards	**Descriptions**
I. Mission, Goals, and Curriculum	
Standard 1. Mission, Goals, and Curriculum	The interior design program has a mission statement that describes the scope and purpose of the program. Program goals are derived from the mission statement and the curriculum is structured to achieve these goals.
II. Interior Design: Critical Thinking, Professional Values, and Processes	
Standard 2. Global Perspective for Design	Entry-level interior designers have a global view and weigh design decisions within the parameters of ecological, socioeconomic, and cultural contexts.
Standard 3. Human Behavior	The work of interior designers is informed by knowledge of behavioral science and human factors.
Standard 4. Design Process	Entry-level interior designers need to apply all aspects of the design process to creative problem solving. Design process enables designers to identify and explore complex problems and generate creative solutions that support human behavior within the interior environment.
Standard 5. Collaboration	Entry-level interior designers engage in multi-disciplinary collaborations and consensus building.
Standard 6. Communication	Entry-level interior designers are effective communicators.
Standard 7. Professionalism and Business Practice	Entry-level interior designers use ethical and accepted standards of practice, are committed to professional development and the industry, and understand the value of their contribution to the built environment.

Standards	Descriptions
III. Interior Design: Core Design and Technical Knowledge	
Standard 8. History	Entry-level interior designers apply knowledge of interiors, architecture, art, and the decorative arts within a historical and cultural context.
Standard 9. Space and Form	Entry-level interior designers apply elements and principles of two- and three-dimensional design.
Standard 10. Color	Entry-level interior designers apply color principles and theories.
Standard 11. Furniture, Fixtures, Equipment, and Finish Materials	Entry-level interior designers select and specify furniture, fixtures, equipment, and finish materials in interior spaces.
Standard 12. Environmental Systems and Controls	Entry-level interior designers use the principles of lighting, acoustics, thermal comfort, and indoor air quality to enhance the health, safety, welfare, and performance of building occupants.
Standard 13. Interior Construction and Building Systems	Entry-level interior designers have knowledge of interior construction and building systems.
Standard 14. Regulations	Entry-level interior designers use laws, codes, standards, and guidelines that impact the design of interior spaces.
IV. Program Administration	
Standard 15. Assessment and Accountability	The interior design program engages in systematic program assessment contributing to ongoing program improvement. Additionally, the program must provide clear, consistent, and reliable information about its mission and requirements to the public.
Standard 16. Support and Resources	The interior design program must have a sufficient number of qualified faculty members, as well as adequate administrative support and resources, to achieve program goals.

Source: Adapted from Council for Interior Design Accreditation (CIDA). 2011. *Professional Standards 2011*. http://accredit-id.org/wp-content/uploads/Policy/Professional%20Standards%202011.pdf. Accessed February 17, 2012.

APPENDIX C

State/Province Boards and Agencies

Alabama—Board for Registered Interior Designers
http://www.idboard.alabama.gov/

Alberta—Interior Designers of Alberta
http://www.idalberta.ca/intro_ida.html

Arkansas—Board of Registered Interior Designers
http://www.arkansas.gov/directory/detail2.cgi?ID=1148

British Columbia—Interior Designers Institute of British Columbia
http://www.idibc.org/

California—Council for Interior Design Certification
http://www.ccidc.org/

Colorado—Interior Design Coalition
http://cidc-colorado.org/new/

Connecticut—Department of Consumer Protection
http://www.ct.gov/dcp/cwp/view.asp?a=1622&q=446464

Florida—Board of Architecture and Interior Design
http://www.myfloridalicense.com/dbpr/pro/arch/index.html

Georgia—State Board of Architects and Interior Designers
http://sos.georgia.gov/plb/architects/default.htm

Illinois—Board of Interior Design Professionals
http://www.idfpr.com/dpr/WHO/intd.asp

Indiana—Professional Licensing Agency
http://www.in.gov/pla/interior.htm

Iowa—Interior Design Examining Board
http://www.state.ia.us/government/com/prof/interior_design/home.html

Kentucky—Board of Architects and Certified Interior Designers
http://boa.ky.gov/

Louisiana—State Board of Examiners of Interior Design
http://www.lsbid.org/

Maine—Board for Licensure of Architects, Landscape Architects and Interior Designers
http://www.state.me.us/pfr/professionallicensing/professions/architects/index.htm

Manitoba—Professional Interior Designers Institute of Manitoba
http://www.pidim.ca/public/organizations.php

Maryland—Board of Certified Interior Designers
http://www.dllr.state.md.us/license/cid/

Michigan—Interior Designers Regulation
http://www.michigan.gov/lara/0,1607,7-154-35299_35414_40920—-,00.html

Minnesota—Board of Architecture, Engineering, Land Surveying, Landscape Architecture, Geoscience and Interior Design
http://www.aelslagid.state.mn.us/

Missouri—Interior Design Council
http://pr.mo.gov/interior.asp

Nevada—State Board of Architecture, Interior Design and Residential Design
http://nsbaidrd.state.nv.us/?page=1

New Brunswick—Association of Registered Interior Designers of New Brunswick
http://www.aridnb.ca/

New Jersey—State Board of Architects
http://www.njconsumeraffairs.gov/arch/

New Mexico—Board of Interior Design
http://www.rld.state.nm.us/Interior/index.html

New York—Office of the Professions
http://www.op.nysed.gov/prof/id/

Nova Scotia—Association of Interior Designers of Nova Scotia
http://www.idns.ca/

Oklahoma—Board of Architects, Landscape Architects and Interior Designers
http://www.ok.gov/Architects/

Ontario—Association of Registered Interior Designers of Ontario
http://www.arido.ca/

Puerto Rico—Departamento de Estado, Junta Examinadora de Diseñadores de Interiores
http://www.pr.gov/Estado/inicio/decoradores.htm

Saskatchewan—Interior Designers Association of Saskatchewan
http://www.idas.ca/

Tennessee—Board of Architectural and Engineering Examiners
http://www.state.tn.us/commerce/boards/ae/interior.shtml

Texas—Board of Architectural Examiners
http://www.tbae.state.tx.us/

Virginia—Board for Architects, Professional Engineers, Land Surveyors, Certified Interior Designers, and Landscape Architects
http://www.dpor.virginia.gov/dporweb/ape_main.cfm

Washington, DC—Board of Architecture and Interior Design
http://obc.dc.gov/obc/cwp/view,a,3,q,521181.asp#architects

Wisconsin—Department of Regulation and Licensing
http://drl.wi.gov/profession.asp?profid=101&locid=0

APPENDIX **D**

Design Centers and International Exhibitions

Design Centers

AmericasMart Atlanta
http://www.americasmart.com/markets/
market-dates

Architects and Designers Building—New York City
http://www.adbuilding.com/

Arizona Design Center
http://www.arizonadesigncenter.com/

Atlanta Decorative Arts Center (ADAC)
http://www.adacatlanta.com/

Berkeley Design Center—Berkeley, California
http://www.berkeleydesigncenter.com/

Boston Design Center (BDC)
http://www.bostondesign.com/

Contract Furnishings Mart—Portland, Oregon
http://www.cfmfloors.com/

Decoration & Design Building—New York City
http://www.ddbuilding.com/

Decorative Center—Dallas
http://www.decorativecenterdallas.com/

Decorative Center—Houston
http://www.decorativecenter.com/

Denver Design District
http://www.denverdesign.com/

Denver Merchandise Mart
http://www.denvermart.com/

Design Center of the Americas (DCOTA)
http://www.dcota.com/

Designers Walk—Toronto Canada
http://www.designerswalk.com/

Domus Design Center (DDC)—New York City
http://www.ddcnyc.com/

Forty-One Madison—New York City
http://www.41madison.com/

Gentry Pacific Design Center—Honolulu
http://www.gentrycenter.com/

Hickory Furniture Mart—High Point, North
Carolina
http://www.hickoryfurniture.com/

International Design Center—Estero, Florida
http://esterofl.org/Issues/international_design_
center.htm

International Home Furnishings Center—
High Point, North Carolina
http://www.ihfc.com/

International Market Square—Minneapolis
http://www.imsdesigncenter.com/

L.A. Mart Design Center—Los Angeles
http://www.lamart.com/

Laguna Design Center—Laguna, California
http://lagunadesigncenter.com/

Las Vegas Market
http://www.lasvegasmarket.com/

Longworth Hall Design Center—Cincinnati
http://www.longworthhall.com/

Marketplace Design Center—Philadelphia
http://www.marketplacedc.com/

Michigan Design Center—Troy, Michigan
http://www.michigandesign.com/

Miromar Design Center—Southwest Florida
http://miromardesigncenter.com/

New York Design Center (NYDC)—
New York City
http://www.nydc.com/www/index.php

Ohio Design Centre—Beachwood, Ohio
http://www.ohiodesigncentre.com/

Pacific Design Center (PDC)—
West Hollywood, California
http://www.pacificdesigncenter.com/

San Francisco Design Center (SFDC)
http://www.sfdesigncenter.com/

Seattle Design Center (SDC)
http://www.seattledesigncenter.com/

The Manhattan Art & Antiques Center
http://www.the-maac.com/

The Merchandise Mart—Chicago
http://www.merchandisemart.com/

The Washington Design Center—
Washington, DC
http://www.dcdesigncenter.com/

International Exhibitions and Fairs

Adana Furniture—Decoration Fair—Turkey
http://www.tuyap.com.tr/en/

Ambienta—Croatia
http://www.zv.hr/default.aspx?id=1353

Australian International Furniture Fair
http://www.aiff.net.au/

Bashran Expo—Iraq
http://www.basrahexpo.com/

Best5 Algeria
http://www.best5algeria.com/

BIEL Light and Building Buenos Aires
http://www.biel.com.ar/ingles/index.htm

Cairo International Wood Show
http://www.cairowoodshow.com/

Central Asia Trade Exhibitions
http://www.catexpo.kz/en/default.asp?itemID
=10&itemTitle=Central%20Asia%20Home+

Copenhagen Design Fair
http://copenhagendesignfair.dk/

Decorex International—London
http://www.decorex.com/page.cfm/Link=4/
t=m/goSection=1

Ela—Mexico
http://www.e-la.mx/

Expo Casa Romania
http://expo-transilvania.ro/eveniment/2011/
Expo%20Casa%2012-16.10.2011/0/despre-targ

Furnitech Woodtech—Thailand
http://www.furnitechwoodtech.com/

Furniture Salon—Russian Federation
http://eng.uv2000.ru/vys/text/furn_2010/

Home Fair—Slovenia
http://www.ljubljanafair.com/fairs/
calendar-of-fairs/home-fair/

Hotex—Israel
http://www.stier.co.il/english/fair_hotex.htm

IFFINA—Indonesia
http://www.iffina-indonesia.com/

Index Fairs
http://www.indexfairs.com/aboutus.asp

Innbau—Germany
http://www.innbau-leipzig.de/

Interior World—Philippines
http://www.tradechakra.com/events/
manila-philippines/interior-world-2010-5420
.php

International Construction Technology and Building Materials Exhibition Saudi Arabia
http://www.recexpo.com/exhibition_overview
.php?id=166

International Furniture Fair—Bulgaria
http://www.bcci.bg/fairs/furniture_au/index.htm

International Furniture Mart—Malaysia
http://www.ifm.net.my/

Le Salon Habitat Design—France
http://www.tradeshowz.net/trade-event-detail/
le-salon-de-le-habitat.html

LED Lightfair—Japan
http://www.ledlightfair.com/ft/en/

LED Japan Strategies in Light
http://www.sil-ledjapan.com/index.html

Moacasa—Italy
http://www.cooperativamoa.com/

Moda Textile—Morocco
http://www.biztradeshows.com/trade-events/
moda-textile.html

Modern Home Exhibition—Greece
http://www.domusdeco.gr/

Ofitec—Spain
http://www.ifema.es/web/ferias/ofitec/default
.html

Prago Interier Czech Republic
http://www.pragointerier.cz/

Qatar Expo
http://www.qatar-expo.com/index.php

Salon Résidence et Bois—France
http://www.salon-residence-bois.com/

SibFurniture. Interior Design. SibFurnitech—Russian Federation
http://sibfurniture.sibfair.ru/eng/

SIDIM—Canada
http://www.sidim.com/

Techtextil India
http://www.techtextil-india.co.in/

Union Pan Exhibitions—Bulgaria
http://www.unionpan.com/event-calendar/
show-event.php?gallery_id=179&ha=99

Vietnam Furniture and Home Décor
http://www.biztradeshows.com/trade-events/
vifa.html

World Furniture Online
http://www.worldfurnitureonline.com/
Exhibition/Fairs.html

APPENDIX

Commercial Interior Design Service Contract

ID301-2008
Small/Medium sized Commercial Interior Design
Service Agreement with Compensation Based
on a Fixed Design Fee

AGREEMENT BETWEEN
DESIGNER AND CLIENT FOR
DESIGN SERVICES
Small/Medium Commercial Contract 2008

AMERICAN SOCIETY OF
INTERIOR DESIGNERS

Fixed Design Fee
No Purchasing Services

1

AMERICAN SOCIETY OF
INTERIOR DESIGNERS, INC.

ASID DOCUMENT 301 · 2008

AGREEMENT BETWEEN
DESIGNER AND CLIENT FOR
DESIGN SERVICES
Small/Medium Commercial Contract 2008

TABLE OF CONTENTS

2

**AGREEMENT BETWEEN
DESIGNER AND CLIENT FOR
DESIGN SERVICES**

Small/Medium Commercial Contract 2008

**1. THE PARTIES AND
THE PROJECT**

**The date of this
Agreement is:**

_____

The Client is:

_____

_____

_____

_____

_____

Insert Name and Address

The Designer is:

_____

_____

_____

_____

Insert Name and Address

The Project is:

_____

_____

_____

_____

_____

_____

_____

_____

_____

_____

_____

_____

_____

3

**AGREEMENT BETWEEN
DESIGNER AND CLIENT FOR
DESIGN SERVICES**
Small/Medium Commercial Contract 2008

**2. SCOPE OF INCLUDED
DESIGN SERVICES**

2.1   Project Program

2.1.1   In this Phase of the Project, Designer will perform the following services:

A.   Meet with Client and/or Client's Designated Representative for the purpose of understanding the Project requirements, preliminary Project timeline, preliminary Project budget, design concept direction and Client's aesthetic design preferences ("Client Program").

B.   Review existing building plans, if any, of Project site.

C.   Review, for aesthetic purposes, all drawings and plans, if any submitted to Client, by Client's Third Party Professionals.

D.   Prepare and submit to Client for Client's approval a written summary of the Client Program, which shall serve as a basis to proceed with the remaining Included Design Services.

2.1.2   For the purposes of this Agreement, Client's Designated Representative shall be _____ until and unless Client designates in writing to Designer a substitute. Designer shall, at all times, be entitled to rely upon all information and approvals provided by the Client's Designated Representative.

2.2.   Interior Construction Related Design Services

2.2.1   Conceptual Design

2.2.1.1 On the basis of the approved Client Program, Designer will then prepare and present to Client recommended interior design concepts for the Project to include:

A.   Space allocation;

B.   Color palettes;

C.   Finishes;

D.   Millwork, cabinetry and fixturing;

E.   Floor coverings;

F.   Ceiling treatments;

G.   Decorative and fixed lighting treatments;

H.   Furniture layout;

I.   Interior elevations indicating suggested finishes and decorative treatments;

J.   Graphics and signage treatments;

K.   Images and illustrations to convey design intent; and

L.   Selective decorative details.

4

2.2.1.2 Designer shall submit to Client for Client's approval, a preliminary estimate of the cost of interior construction work described in this phase of the Project.

2.2.2   Design Development Documents

2.2.2.1 Upon Client's approval of the Design Concept submissions described above, Designer will prepare:

A.   Floor plans;

B.   Furniture layouts;

C.   Elevations;

D.   Ceiling and lighting design;

E.   Reflected ceiling plans; and

F.   Such other documents to illustrate and further describe the nature and character of the interior construction.

2.2.2.2 Prepare or fully develop illustrations for cabinet work, millwork and such additional drawings, illustrations, designs and specifications to more fully describe and define the conceptual Design so as to enable Designer to proceed with preparation of the Contract Documents.

2.2.2.3 Designer will seek to identify any material adjustments to the preliminary cost estimates, previously provided by Designer.

2.2.3   Contract Documents

2.2.3.1 Upon approval of the Design Development Documents, Designer will, but only to the extent permitted by applicable law, prepare plans, drawings and specifications to describe the interior construction, which may include:

A.   Interior demolition plans;

B.   Partition plans;

C.   Furniture plans showing location of furniture, furnishings and equipment.

D.   Location of outlets for power, telephone and communications;

E.   Floor and ceiling plans;

F.   Reflected ceiling plans;

G.   Finish schedules;

H.   Elevations, sections and details to describe finishing and decorative treatments;

I.   Millwork and cabinetry details;

J.   Lighting schedules and specifications; and

K.   Location and signage dimensions.

5

2.2.3.2 Designer does not under any circumstances provide architectural, engineering or construction services. Should the nature of the Project require the services of other design professionals or consultants, (including architects, engineers, lighting consultants and the like), they will be engaged directly by Client pursuant to separate agreements as may be mutually acceptable to Client and such Third Party Professionals. Designer will coordinate its Included Design Services with the work of the Third Party Professionals and Client shall have all Third Party Professionals coordinate their services with Designer.

2.2.4 Coordination of Bidding

2.2.4.1 Designer will assist Client in obtaining and evaluating bids and/or negotiated proposals from prospective contractor(s) to perform the interior construction work based upon the Contract Documents.

2.2.5 Project Administration – Interior Construction

2.2.5.1 Client understands that the nature of Project requires Client to engage the services of one or more contractors to provide work, labor, and services to implement the interior construction at the Project site (collectively the "Contractor").

2.2.5.2 Designer will make periodic visits to the Project site as Designer considers appropriate to observe the work of the Contractors to determine whether such work is proceeding in general conformity with the Project Documents. Constant observation of work at the Project site is not a part of Designer's Included Design Services. Designer is not responsible for the performance, quality, timely completion or delivery of any work, materials or equipment furnished by the Contractor.

2.2.5.3 Designer will endeavor to perform Interior Construction Design Related Services consistent with Client's Project time schedule, if any, but Client acknowledges that Designer's ability to do so is largely dependent upon: (i) Client's timely submission of all required approvals and requested information, and (ii) the timely and proper performance of Client's Third Party Professionals and other persons and entities directly or indirectly involved in the Project including, but not limited to, municipal agencies, landlords, lenders and the like.

2.2.5.4 The Client shall provide prompt written notice to Designer if the Client becomes aware of any errors, omissions or inconsistencies in the Project Documents.

2.2.5.5 Designer is not responsible for any on Project site conditions or dimensions which in any material way differ from site conditions and dimensions provided Designer by the Client, its Designated Representative or by the Client's Third Party Professionals.

6

2.3   Project Furniture, Furnishings and Equipment Selection And Specification

2.3.1   In this phase of the Project, Designer will select and/or design furniture, furnishings and equipment ("Project FF&E"). Project FF&E will be presented to Client in the format of a Project FF&E Manual.   The Project FF&E Manual will include, where appropriate, information about each item including sourcing, pricing, tear sheets, photographs, material samples, and manufacturer specifications so as to enable Client or Client's purchasing agent to place orders directly with the concerned vendors for the purchase of such Project FF&E and, where required, the installation of the Project FF&E. Designer does not provide any purchasing or installation services under this Agreement.

2.3.2   Designer will review recommended Project FF&E with Client's Designated Representative and provide Client's Designated Representative with a preliminary budget estimate for the cost of acquiring and installing the recommended Project FF&E.

2.3.3   Once Client's Designated Representative has approved the recommended Project FF&E, Designer will assist Client and/or its purchasing agent in the preparation of purchase specifications for Client's use in the purchasing and installation of Project FF&E.

2.3.4   If requested by Client's vendors, Designer will review for general conformity with Designer's overall design interest, vendor's shop drawings of custom fabricated Project FF&E.

2.3.5   During final installation of Project FF&E, Designer will, if requested by Client, visit the Project site to assist in the placement of Project FF&E.

2.3.6   At time of final installation, Designer will prepare a punch list to describe what Project FF&E remains incomplete, or non-conforming to the Designer's design concepts.

3. ADDITIONAL DESIGN SERVICES

3.1   Designer shall be compensated for any Additional Services (as defined below), on an hourly basis in accordance with the hourly rates set forth below.

3.2   Additional Services shall include any time spent by Designer performing any service not set forth in the Scope of Included Design Services, as well as any time expended by Designer if:

A.   The Client materially changes the scope of the Project.

B.   Through no fault of Designer the Included Design Services are not substantially completed by Designer within _____ (___) months of the date of signing this Agreement.

C.   More than _____ (___) revisions to the Conceptual Design and/or Design Development Plans are requested by Client.

D.   More than _____ (___) revisions to the Project FF&E Manual are requested by Client.

E.   More than _____ (_____) Project Site Visits are required.

F.   Revisions to any of the Project Documents by Designer because of inconsistencies in instructions, information or plans previously provided by Client or its Third Party Professionals.

3.3   Invoices for Additional Services will be rendered monthly by Designer and payable within _____ (_____) days of the date of invoice.

3.4   Hourly rates are billed as follows:
For the services of: Hourly Rates

_____   _____

_____   _____

_____   _____

_____   _____

_____   _____

_____   _____

8

AMERICAN SOCIETY OF
INTERIOR DESIGNERS, INC.

ASID DOCUMENT 301 · 2008

AGREEMENT BETWEEN
DESIGNER AND CLIENT FOR
DESIGN SERVICES
Small/Medium Commercial Contract 2008

4. COMPENSATION AND EXPENSES

4.1   For Designer's Included Design Services, Client agrees to compensate Designer a fixed fee in the amount of $_____ (the "Design Fee"), payable as follows.

_____

_____

_____

_____

_____

4.2   Disbursements incurred by Designer in the interest of the Project shall be reimbursed by Client to Designer upon receipt of Designer's invoices, which are rendered monthly. Reimbursable disbursements shall include, among other things, costs of local and long distance travel, long distance telephone calls, duplication of plans, drawings and specifications, messenger services, and the like.

4.3   Design Fees are subject to applicable sales taxes.

5. OWNERSHIP OF PROJECT DOCUMENTS

5.1   All concepts, plans, drawings and specifications prepared by Designer ("Project Documents") remain Designer's exclusive property at all times. The Designer shall for all purposes be deemed sole author and owner of the Project Documents and shall retain all common law, statutory and other intellectual property rights, including copyrights. Except as may be expressly set forth elsewhere in this Agreement, Project Documents may not be used by Client for the completion of this Project, unless Designer is adjudged to be in default of this Agreement. Project may not be used by the client for any other project.

5.2   Provided that Client has complied with all of Client's obligations under this Agreement, Client shall be permitted to retain copies of the Project Documents for information and reference in connection with the Client's use and occupancy of the Project.

9

6. TERMINATION RIGHTS

6.1 This Agreement may be terminated by either Client or Designer upon the other party's default in performance, provided that termination may not be effected unless written notice specifying the nature and extent of default is given to the concerned party and such party fails to cure such default in performance within_____ (____) days from the date of receipt of such notice. Termination shall be without prejudice to any and all other rights and remedies of Designer, and Client shall remain liable for all outstanding obligations owed by Client to Designer.

6.2 Client may, upon _____ (____) days written prior notice to Designer terminate this Agreement without cause. In the event of such termination, Client shall have the right to use the Project Documents provided:

A. Designer is compensated for all services performed up to and including the date of termination.

B. Client agrees to indemnify and hold Designer free and harmless from and against any and all costs, claims or expenses, including reasonable attorneys' fees and related costs, arising out of or relating in any manner to Client's subsequent use of the Project Documents.

C. Client releases Designer from any further obligations Designer may have to Client.

D. Client will not permit any other person, firm or entity to claim design credit for any work prepared by Designer prior to the date of termination.

E. Client pays Designer (whether or not Client thereafter uses any Project Documents) as additional compensation, an amount equal to _____ (____%) percent of the total amount of all fees paid and payable to Designer to the date of termination.

6.3 The Designer shall be entitled to suspend performance of its services under this Agreement upon _____ (____) days prior written notice to Client if the Client fails to make payment to the Designer in accordance with the terms of this Agreement.

10

AMERICAN SOCIETY OF
INTERIOR DESIGNERS, INC.

ASID DOCUMENT 301 · 2008

AGREEMENT BETWEEN
DESIGNER AND CLIENT FOR
DESIGN SERVICES
Small/Medium Commercial Contract 2008

7. DISPUTES

7.1   If any dispute arises out of or relates to this Agreement, or the breach thereof, and if the dispute cannot be settled through negotiation, the parties agree first to try in good faith to settle the dispute by mediation administered by the American Arbitration Association in _____ under its Construction Industry Mediation Procedures before resorting to litigation as set forth below.

7.2   Any party bringing a legal action or proceeding against any other party arising out of or relating to this Agreement or the transactions it contemplates shall bring the legal action or proceeding only in the United States District Court for the _____ District of _____ or in any court of the State of _____ sitting in the County of _____.

Each party to this Agreement submits to the exclusive jurisdiction of:

A.   The United States District Court for the _____ District of _____ and its appellate courts; and

B.   Any court of the State of _____ sitting in the County of _____ and its appellate courts, for the purposes of all legal actions and proceedings arising out of or relating to this Agreement.

8. GENERAL MATTERS

8.1   Designer's services shall not include undertaking any responsibility for the design, modification and/or re-design of any structural, heating, air-conditioning, plumbing, electrical, ventilation or other mechanical systems installed or to be installed at the Project.

8.2   Clients and/or its Third Party Professionals shall be responsible for identifying all structural, electrical, mechanical or physical elements affecting the Project and all compliance with applicable codes, rules and regulations. Client and its Third Party Professional shall be responsible for determining local building codes and/or other municipal local, city, state and/or other governmental code requirements concerning any aspect of the Project. Designer does not assume responsibility for and makes no representations that its Project Documents will meet applicable code requirements.

8.3   The Client shall provide prompt written notice to Designer if the Client becomes aware of any errors, omissions or inconsistencies in the Project Documents.

8.4   Client will provide Designer with access to the Project and all information Designer may need to complete the Project. It is Client's responsibility to obtain all approvals required by any governmental agency or otherwise in connection with this Project.

8.5   Designer shall not have control, be in charge of, nor be responsible for the means, methods, sequences or procedures of installation, fabrication,

11

AMERICAN SOCIETY OF
INTERIOR DESIGNERS, INC.

ASID DOCUMENT 301 · 2008

AGREEMENT BETWEEN
DESIGNER AND CLIENT FOR
DESIGN SERVICES
Small/Medium Commercial Contract 2008

procurement, safety precautions, the contracting of the work or the installation of the Project FF&E, or for any acts or omissions of any of the Client's contractors, subcontractors, vendors, suppliers or persons performing work or the failure of any of them to carry out the work.

8.6   Designer does not make any representations or warranties of any kind regarding the Project FF&E, it being understood that Client shall rely solely upon any and all warranties which Client may be able to obtain from the concerned vendors. Designer cannot represent that Project FF&E will be accompanied by warranties of any kind.

8.7   In light of the many contingencies which affect design projects, Designer does not make any representations that the actual price for merchandise and/or services or related Project costs will not vary from any estimates proposed, established or approved by Designer.

8.8   As Designer requires a record of Designer's design projects, Client will permit Designer or Designer's representatives to photograph and/or video the Project upon completion. Designer will be entitled to use photographs for Designer's business purposes but shall not disclose Project location or Client's name without Client's prior written consent.

8.9   To the extent that the proceeds, if any, from any insurance policy maintained by the Designer are insufficient to satisfy any claims Client has against Designer, or if the claim is not covered by insurance maintained by Designer, then in either or both of such situations, the maximum liability of Designer to Client shall not exceed the total amount of compensation paid by Client to Designer under this Agreement. Claims include, but are not limited to, Designer's breach of contract, negligence, errors, omissions, strict liability or breach of warranty. Designer shall not be responsible for consequential or special damages for any reason.

8.10   To the extent permitted by law, Client agrees to indemnify, defend and hold harmless Designer, its shareholders, officers, directors and employees from and against any claims for personal injury and/or property damage arising out of the Client's use of the Project Documents, except to the extent that Designer is adjudicated negligent.

8.11   Client and Designer, respectively, bind themselves, their partners, successors, assigns and legal representatives to the other party to this Agreement and to the partners, successors, assigns and legal representatives of such other party with respect to all covenants of this Agreement. Neither Client nor Designer shall assign or transfer any interest in this Agreement without the written consent of the other.

8.12   The contents of this Agreement may be changed only by a writing signed by the party against whom such change is sought to be enforced. No failure or delay in exercising any right or remedy under this Agreement and no act

12

AMERICAN SOCIETY OF
INTERIOR DESIGNERS, INC.

ASID DOCUMENT 301 - 2008

AGREEMENT BETWEEN
DESIGNER AND CLIENT FOR
DESIGN SERVICES
Small/Medium Commercial Contract 2008

or omission or course of dealing between the parties operates as a waiver or estoppel of any right, remedy or condition, except as is specifically provided for elsewhere in this Agreement.

8.13   If any provision of this Agreement is determined to be invalid or unenforceable, the remaining provisions of this Agreement remain in full force if the essential terms and conditions of this Agreement for each party remain valid and enforceable.

8.14   This Agreement is complete and an exclusive expression on the matters contained in this Agreement. Neither Client nor Designer has relied upon any statement, presentation, warranty or agreement of the other, except for those expressly contained in this Agreement.

8.15   The laws of the State of _____ shall govern all matters arising out of or relating to this Agreement and the transaction it contemplates including, without limitation, its interpretation, construction, performance and enforcement.

9. ADDITIONAL TERMS

[Insert such other terms to be added to the agreement]

_____

_____

_____

_____

_____

_____

_____

_____

_____

_____

_____

10. SIGNATURES

_____

[INSERT NAME OF DESIGNER]

BY: _____   DATE: _____

[INSERT NAME OF CLIENT]

BY: _____   DATE: _____

13

Glossary

evidence-based design (EBD) Approach to designing the built environment that applies the findings of research to design solutions.

globalization Conditions associated with the ease of international interactions and how an event or situation in one part of the world can have an impact throughout the planet.

licensing Legal permission that enables an individual with the appropriate credentials to practice a profession. Generally, used in a state or province when legislation is used to determine who can practice a profession. Qualifications are education, experience, and examination.

permitting State certification legislation that requires an interior designer to obtain a permit for prescribed services.

practice acts State certification legislation prescribing what an interior designer may or may not do as well as the requirements to work as a licensed interior designer.

registration Legal permission that enables an individual with the appropriate credentials to practice a profession. Associated with legislation that stipulates who may use a specific title.

self-certification State certification legislation similar to a title act except that an organization rather than a jurisdiction is responsible for administering the requirements of the law.

social responsibilities Moral obligations that help address the needs of society, such as volunteering for community projects.

title acts State certification legislation specifying requirements, such as education, experience, and examination, for using a professional title.

Chapter 2

401(k) retirement plan Self-managed retirement savings account. Employers determine when employees are eligible to participate and when employers' contributions become assets of the employees.

branding Process of creating a consistent image.

BRICs (Brazil, Russia, India, China) Identified as countries that could have a dramatic role in world markets by 2025 and beyond due to their large populations and government policies that are encouraging economic growth.

building information modeling (BIM) Software program used by the design profession to plan, design, construct, and manage a building.

commercial design (contract design) Area of the design profession that fundamentally focuses on public spaces, such as offices, retail stores, hospitals, and restaurants.

computer-aided design (CAD) Software program used by the design profession to create 2D documentation of buildings as well as 3D free-form conceptual designs.

contract design (commercial design) Area of the design profession that fundamentally focuses on public spaces, such as offices, retail stores, hospitals, and restaurants.

corporation Business structure that is a separate legal entity and is owned by its shareholders.

in-house designer Interior designer who works for a corporation and designs facilities for its internal customers as well as any external clients.

individual retirement account (IRA) Retirement savings plan that provides tax advantages by reducing an individual's taxable income.

integrated project delivery (IPD) Collaborative approach to the design process by incorporating the skills, talents, and expertise of a comprehensive team of professionals.

intellectual property rights Rights associated with creative works, such as designs, inventions, artistic endeavors, and symbols.

mixed-use building Single structure that accommodates several different functions, such as offices, condominiums, and restaurants.

mutual fund Managed accounts with a diversified composition of investments, such as stocks, bonds, Treasury bills, or cash.

post-occupancy evaluation (POE) Assessment process that occurs after people are living or working in a space or entire building.

profit sharing Corporate benefit that involves owning stock in an employer's company.

residential design Area of the design profession that focuses on designing someone's home.

Revit Software program used by the design profession to analyze concepts and coordinate processes through the design process by using automatic updates and integrated documentation.

rollover Financial term associated with transferring accounts, such as retirement plans.

sole proprietor Business structure that has a single owner.

vesting Individual's earned funds in a retirement account.

Chapter 3

career management Controlling activities associated with a professional track.

career plan Schedule of activities and timelines for a professional track.

career portfolio Collection of materials for a professional track. Items can include a career plan, résumé, cover letters, business card, promotional materials, and design portfolio.

chronological résumé Document summarizing job-related skills by featuring someone's work experience.

comp time (compensatory time) Paid time off.

compensatory time (comp time) Paid time off.

cover letter Document that accompanies a résumé to summarize a person's qualifications and skills for a job.

digital design portfolio Electronic collection of professional materials that should support the skills, knowledge, and abilities featured in a résumé and cover letter.

experience-seeking proposal Document that requests an employer to hire a person for a probationary period.

functional résumé Document summarizing job-related experiences by highlighting skills, abilities, and strengths.

human resources Department that coordinates personnel issues and processes, including screening job applicants.

informational interview Meeting in-person for the purpose of learning more about an organization.

job shadowing Following an experienced professional for the purpose of understanding job expectations, responsibilities, and tasks.

life/work balance Concept associated with creating the ideal plan for dedicating time and resources to personal and professional activities.

logo Symbol or design that represents the identity of an individual or business.

network Personal or professional groups of individuals that help each other to solve problems and provide information.

networking Building relationships in person or through virtual online experiences.

professional profile Summary of a person's professional interests and most important skills.

résumé Document that summarizes an individual's professional skills, experiences, and education.

self-assessment Process used to identify a person's abilities, skills, and values.

social networks Web-based sites, such as Facebook and LinkedIn, that enable people to connect with others around the world and build networks.

teleconferencing Meeting that uses telephones for communication.

traditional design portfolio Print collection of professional materials supporting the skills, knowledge, and abilities featured in a résumé and cover letter.

transferrable skill Abilities that can be used for various occupations.

videoconferencing A meeting that uses audio and video for communication.

visual identity system Program designed to create a unified visual appearance of professional materials, such as a résumé, cover letter, business card, and portfolio.

Chapter 4

asynchronous Activities that do not occur at the same time.

business ethics Discipline associated with the moral duty and obligations of a company.

charrette Intensive, multidisciplinary workshop structured to enable open discussions between stakeholders of a project.

communication channel Means to exchange ideas and information.

e-mail (email) Electronic message formatted as a memorandum that is used to communicate with an individual or group of people.

ethics Discipline associated with moral duties and obligations.

explicit knowledge Information that people can access via several means, such as written documents, drawings, or photographs.

feedback loop Communication system that enables the recipient to emit a response to the sender for the purpose of clarification and improving processes.

information management Means to organize and control data, such as products, vendors, manufacturers, clients, and business procedures.

instant messaging (IM) Electronic form of communication that is conducted in real time.

integrated design process (IDP) Approach to designing the built environment that involves the participation of various professionals and stakeholders.

knowledge management Means to organize and control information and skills acquired by experiences.

memorandum (memos) Brief correspondences often used for interoffice communication.

multidisciplinary collaboration Coordinated activities with several professions.

netiquette Appropriate protocols that apply to communication via the Internet, such as e-mail, instant messaging (IM), text messaging, blogs, and social media.

podcast Audio or video files that can be downloaded to a personal computer or a portable device, such as an iPod or MP3 player.

professional ethics Discipline associated with the moral duties and obligations of an occupation.

stakeholder People who have an earnest interest in a project.

synchronous Activities that occur at the same time.

tacit knowledge Information that people have in their minds.

teaming process Means to allow people who are working together to efficiently make decisions and solve problems.

teamwork Collaborative process that involves shared goals and purposes.

telepresence Type of technology that improves videoconferencing by giving people the impression that fellow attendees are actually at the meeting.

text messaging Electronic message using cell phones.

time management Means to organize and control schedules and tasks.

web-based meeting system Programs that use the Internet as the means to connect people.

virtual teamwork Electronic collaborative process that involves shared goals and purposes.

white noise system Electronic means to disguise conversations and other types of distracting noises in a space.

wikis Web pages that allow people to interact and collaboratively create and edit documents.

Chapter 5

block form letter Business letter with all parts left-justified.

collectivism Cultural dimension that is based on valuing the accomplishments of groups.

culture From a broad perspective, a concept that includes areas that affect the way people live, including housing, food, apparel, education, family, language, laws, ethics, and business practices.

egalitarian Cultural dimension that is based on the belief that people in a variety of positions can be empowered to succeed.

ethnocentrism Mindset of ethnicity superiority.

expatriate A person who is working in a foreign country for a limited period of time.

hierarchical Cultural dimension that is based on the belief that power resides with organizational positions; individuals at the top of the pyramid make decisions with or without input from others in the organization.

high context Cultural dimension based on the belief that most information is already in a person and very little is in the transmitted part of a message.

individualism Cultural dimension based on valuing the accomplishments of each person.

interpreter Person who performs verbal language translations.

low context Cultural dimension that is based on the belief that most information is vested in the transmitted part of a message.

monochronic Cultural dimension that is strict about being punctual and to be late is considered rude behavior.

namaste Common in India, a salutation or a gesture that involves a slight bow as hands are placed in the praying position.

parliamentary procedures (Roberts Rules of Order) Formal set of procedures for conducting meetings.

polycentrism Mindset that respects the values, attitudes, behavior, and customs of people throughout the world.

polychronic Cultural dimension based on the belief that tardiness is acceptable.

saving face Cultural concept associated with avoiding public humiliation.

semi-block form letter Business letter with indented first lines of paragraphs.

subculture Groups within a culture that has unique patterns and expectations.

translator Person who performs written language translations.

Chapter 6

acknowledgment (confirmation) Document sent from a vendor that indicates receipt of the order.

back order Item that will be shipped at a later date due to depletions in supplies.

billable service Expense that can be charged to a client.

billing statement Document that lists business transactions, such as fees, merchandise, and payments for a specific time period.

CFA (cutting for approval) Sample that a vendor sends to a designer for their consent.

COD (cash on delivery) Sales transaction that requires the purchaser to pay the entire bill prior to receiving goods from the vendor.

COM (customer's own material) Design term for fabrications that use textiles not supplied by the vendor.

cash flow Movement of incoming and outgoing money.

civil law system Legal structure whereby decisions are based on a nation's statutes rather than case law.

common law system Legal structure whereby rulings are reliant on case law or legal precedents.

confirmation (acknowledgment) Document sent from a vendor indicating receipt of the order.

contract law Legal system associated with agreements when two or more individuals (parties) make voluntary promises to each other. Generally, the promises are to provide goods, services, or labor in exchange for pay.

copyright law Legal system associated with "works of authorship" and creative expression.

cost Designer's charges from a manufacturer or wholesaler.

credit (cr.) Term for payments in the accounting profession.

debit (dr.) Term for charges in the accounting profession.

deposit Prepayment made to initiate a business transaction.

direct personnel expense (DPE) Costs associated with employee salaries and benefits.

discontinued Item that is no longer being produced.

drop-shipped Delivery to a client's address.

exculpatory Provisions that clear someone or an entity from a wrong or fault.

fixed fee (flat fee) Compensation method whereby the buyer is charged a specific amount for services.

flat fee (fixed fee) Compensation method whereby the buyer is charged a specific amount for services.

FOB (free/freight on board) destination Shipping provision whereby the manufacturer or seller pays the freight charges.

FOB factory Shipping provision whereby the purchaser is responsible for the charges.

gross profits Difference between what is charged to the buyer and what is the seller's cost from a manufacturer or wholesaler.

hourly fee Compensation method whereby the buyer is charged a single hourly rate.

implied warranty Inferred guarantee.

intellectual property law Legal system associated with ownership of creative expressions.

intentional tort Wrong that involves deliberate harm, such as battery, assault, false imprisonment, and trespass to land or personal property.

international law Legal system that governs the relationships between nations.

invoice Statement that includes an itemized list of services, products, and money owed to a supplier.

keystone price Designer receives a 50 percent discount on the retail price.

list price Manufacturers' suggested amount that a customer should pay for a product.

markup Amount added to the designer's cost of an item.

multiple (multiplier) Figure representing business expenses that is used to determine hourly rates.

negligence Unintentional harm caused by the failure to exercise proper care that a reasonably prudent person would have exercised in a similar situation.

net 30 Sales transaction allowing the buyer 30 days to pay a bill.

net price Designer's charges from a manufacturer or wholesaler.

net profit Money earned after expenses.

overhead Business expenses that do not vary month by month, such as rent and insurance.

patent law Legal system that regulates "new and useful" inventions.

per diem By-the-day rate charged to a client.

portal-to-portal Travel to and from a site.

pro bono Providing services for free.

pro forma Sales transaction that requires the purchaser to pay the entire bill prior to receiving goods from the vendor.

product liability Responsibility of a manufacturer or a seller of a product to provide items that are safe and free of defects.

purchase order Legal contractual agreement between a buyer and a seller for the purpose of supplying the buyer with a product.

quantity discount Special provision that enables a retailer to purchase a large number of items at a special reduced price.

restocking charge Charge levied by a manufacturer when a retailer returns merchandise.

retail price Price of an item paid by consumers.

retainer A preliminary fee paid by a client to secure the services of a designer.

sidemark (tag for) Reference to the name of a client for the purpose of identifying the client's purchase.

strict liability Wrong based on harm caused by someone's duty to ensure safe conditions.

surcharge Extra cost charged for atypical situations that can occur with a variety of situations, such as deliveries and installations.

tag for (sidemark) Reference to the name of a client for the purpose of identifying the client's purchase.

tort law Legal system based on a person or a property being injured or wronged. The injury could be caused by an act or an omission.

toxic tort Wrong that deals with extremely hazardous substances, such as asbestos exposure in buildings and hazardous waste.

trade discount Price reduction that can be provided to design professionals by a variety of businesses.

trademark law Legal system protecting words, symbols, or images that are distinctive to a company, product, or service.

tradespeople work order Document providing the detailed information that is needed to request the services of a tradesperson.

transmittal letter (form) Document used to send an item or request to a business or tradesperson.

value-oriented fee Supplemental compensation charged when a firm has considerable past experience and has attained a high level of stature.

warranty Promise or guarantee.

wholesaler Entity that purchases large quantities of merchandise from manufacturers and then sells the items to retailers.

work change order Document used to delineate alterations to a project.

work order Document used to provide instructions, measurements, and descriptions to a tradesperson or craftsperson.

client job book File created by a designer that includes all items associated with a client, such as contracts, schedules, letters, and material samples.

cold call Unexpected contact to a potential client.

cutsheet Document that includes product specifications provided by a manufacturer.

dialogue Conversation between two or more persons.

generation Group of individuals who grew up during the same time period.

house form Customized documents used by the employees of a business.

informative presentation Presentation to a client for the purpose of providing updates and disseminating facts and figures.

interim proposal Preliminary design services agreement between designers and clients.

letter of agreement (LOA) Contract for design services between designers and clients.

persuasive presentation Presentation to a client for the purpose of convincing him or her to accept concepts and plans.

prospect Potential client.

qualifications package Collection of items used to document the expertise and professional experiences of design professionals and design firms.

request for information (RFI) Document that asks a design firm to respond to inquiries.

request for proposal (RFP) Document that asks design firms to submit a proposal for a service or product.

request for qualifications (RFQ) Document that asks a design firm to document its expertise and professional experiences.

sans serif Font that does not have slight projections at the end of letters.

self-brand Image that a designer wants to portray to clients.

suspect Potential clients.

Uniform Commercial Code (UCC) Group of laws that govern commercial transactions between U.S. states and territories.

Chapter 8

actual cost (AC) Element of an earned value management system (EVMS) that represents how much money was spent.

affinity diagram Business tool used to organize large amounts of data acquired from stakeholders.

analogous estimating Cost estimate method based on actual costs expended for a similar project that ideally was recently built in the same geographic area.

arrow diagram Business tool that a design team can use to plan daily schedules and visualize interrelationships between phases, activities, schedules, and people.

baseline Planned timeline in a Gantt chart.

bid (tender) Process used to solicit price requests.

bottom-up estimate Cost analysis method that begins by examining tasks at the most simplistic level and proceeds to the most complex activities.

closed specification Descriptions that indicate an exact product or service must be provided, and that substitutes are not acceptable.

Construction Management (CMaR) at-Risk Project delivery method that involves hiring the most qualified construction manager in the earliest phases of the design process.

contingency fund Money reserved for unanticipated project expenses.

cost baseline Represents estimated costs for the project.

cost-benefit analysis (CBA) Process that involves comparisons for the purpose of identifying optimum solutions.

cost-reimbursable contract Agreement that specifies that a client is billed for merchandise at the designer's prices.

crashing Method for schedule compression by supplementing various resources to shorten the amount of construction time.

critical path Represents the series of activities that take the longest to complete in a timeline.

deliverable Item or service provided to a client.

Design-Bid-Build (DBB) Delivery method whereby a client hires a design firm to create a design and the construction documents.

Design-Build (DB) Project delivery method whereby a design team is responsible for design and construction services. One contract is awarded to the design team, which works together throughout the project.

Design Quality Indicator (DQI) Approach to quality improvement that involves evaluating the design and construction of new buildings as well as renovating existing buildings.

earned value (EV) (earned value management system—EVMS) Tool used to facilitate cost controls by measuring the project's progress.

earned value management system (EVMS) (earned value—EV) Tool used to facilitate cost controls by measuring the project's progress.

fast tracking Method to reduce the overall time required for a project by overlapping stages and tasks.

fixed-price contract Agreement that can specify a firm price for products and services throughout the life of the contract.

Gantt chart Timeline developed by Henry Gantt, used to visually review a project's activities, sequence of events, resources-per-task, and the amount of time scheduled for each activity.

matrix diagram Business tool that a design team can use to examine the interrelationships between various aspects of a project.

micromanagement Behavior that involves telling a person how to do his or her job.

milestone Represents major events in a timeline.

open specification General descriptions of a product or service; substitutes are acceptable.

padding Cost estimates with substantial price increases for the purpose of avoiding potential losses.

parallel activities Represents tasks that can be done concurrently in a work breakdown schedule (WBS).

parametric estimating Cost estimate method that utilizes statistical calculations to approximate costs.

Plan-Do-Check-Act (PDCA) cycle (Shewhart cycle) Business tool used to continuously improve a process, product, or entity. A plan is created to accomplish goals. The plan is implemented and then checked or evaluated. Actions are taken to improve the outcomes, and this information is then used to improve the next plan.

planned value (PV) Element of an earned value management system (EVMS) that represents the project's budget.

portfolio management Process for controlling several projects.

process decision program chart (PDPC) Business tool that a design team can use to identify potential problems with a project.

Program Evaluation Review Technique (PERT) Tool for developing time approximations.

progress report (project performance report) Document created to track a project.

project delivery method Type of business approach used to design, construct, operate, and maintain a built environment, such as Design-Bid-Build (DBB), Design-Build (DB), Construction Management at-Risk (CM), and Integrated Project Delivery (IPD).

project life cycle (PLC) Stages of a project from the beginning to closure.

project management Process for organizing, monitoring, and controlling all elements of a project.

project management plan (PMP) Detailed strategy for coordinating the activities required to accomplish the goals of the project.

project manager Person responsible for planning and controlling a project.

project performance report (progress report) Document created to track a project.

project scope Represents the design requirements in a project management plan (PMP).

project scope management Process that involves five basic components (PMI 2008): (1) collect the requirements of the stakeholders, (2) define the scope, (3) create a work breakdown schedule (WBS), (4) verify scope, and (5) control scope.

proposal Document that includes costs and other requirements for a project.

proprietary right Provisions associated with ownership of some entity, such as patents or copyrights.

relations diagram Business tool used to analyze the causes and effects of complex problems. Affinity themes can be used to generate the diagram. The diagram reveals the causes that have the greatest effect on the problem. Solutions focus on addressing high-impact causes.

risk category Areas of possible causes of risk, such as organizational, financial, programmatic, economic, natural environment, and technical.

risk criteria Standards used to determine the importance of a risk.

risk register Document that includes a comprehensive list of risks and their characteristics.

risk tolerance What a client is willing to lose or gain given a condition or event.

risk treatment Approaches to dealing with risks, such as avoidance/exploitation, mitigate/enhance, transfer/share, and accept/accept.

rolling wave plan Technique that involves specifying requirements for the initial phases of a project; the remaining details are determined as the project proceeds.

schedule compression Method to fulfill the project's scope while conserving time.

scope creep Additions to a project beyond the original requirements.

sequential activities Represents tasks that can be done in a logical order in a work breakdown schedule (WBS).

Shewhart cycle (Plan-Do-Check-Act [PDCA] cycle) Business tool used to continuously improve a process, product, or entity. A plan is created to accomplish goals. The plan is implemented and then checked or evaluated. Actions are taken to improve the outcomes, and this information is then used to improve the next plan.

strengths, weaknesses, opportunities, threats (SWOT) Process used to identify internal and external conditions and factors that can affect a project or organization.

systematic diagram Business tool that outlines the steps that are required to complete a task. The configuration resembles an organizational chart or the tree diagram.

tender (bid) Process used to solicit price requests.

three-point estimate Represents three approximations (optimistic, most likely, and pessimistic) used in the Program Evaluation Review Technique (PERT) formula.

time and materials (T&M) contract Agreement that includes the flexibility to adjust costs within specified limits.

time chart Diagram used to visually review a project's activities, sequence of events, resources-per-task, as well as the amount of time scheduled for each activity.

total quality management (TQM) Management philosophy that focuses on continuous improvement processes with an emphasis on the needs of the customer, leadership, collaborative relationships, education, and understanding processes from a systemic perspective.

work breakdown schedule (WBS) Systematic approach to identifying what activities must be performed for the scope of the project.

Chapter 9

alternate bid Bid with an amount added or deducted from the base bid due to some type of substitution, such as materials.

as-built drawing Architectural drawings that delineate the measurements and details of a space after construction.

bid bond Document used with a bid that guarantees a financial institution will cover all payments associated with the work in case of a default.

bid security Some type of guarantee, such as a bid bond that indicates payments will be made in case of a default.

bill of lading Document from the carrier to a shipper that lists the products shipped to the site.

certificate of occupancy Document indicating the building is in compliance with building codes and people can move in to the facilities.

certificate of payment Document used to initiate a payment to a contractor.

closed-ended survey Data collection technique using a standardized list of items with specific responses.

closeout Process of concluding a project, which should include assembling materials that a client needs for operation and maintenance, including training manuals, warranties, cleaning recommendations, and as-built drawings.

contract administration phase Last stage in the design process involving construction through post-occupancy evaluations.

contract document phase Stage in the design process prior to construction involving the development of final drawings, specifications, and schedules.

contractor's submittal Items, such as shop drawings, prepared by contractors. These items must be verified for accuracy.

cutting Small samples of a fabric supplied by a manufacturer.

design development phase Stage in the design process after the schematic design phase involving the development of initial drawings, specifications, and schedules.

focus group Facilitated discussion with approximately six to eight people for the purpose of exploring a specific issue.

formal research Research methodology involving a systematic approach to reviewing related research findings, defining a problem, and collecting and analyzing data.

freight bill Document listing shipping charges.

freight claim Document used to report lost or damaged merchandise caused while an item was shipped.

general contractor (GC) Individual or organization responsible for coordinating and overseeing a construction project.

in-depth interview Comprehensive session of questions and answers.

informal research Research methodology involving a nonsystematic approach to examining a problem by collecting and analyzing data.

jobber Entity that purchases large quantities of merchandise from the manufacturer and then sells the product in smaller quantities to designers.

just-in-time Process used to deliver goods or services approximately when needed at the site.

Leadership in Energy and Environmental Design (LEED) Green building certification program coordinated by the United States Green Building Council (USGBC).

life cycle cost analysis (LCCA) Tool used to determine the total cost of a building beginning with construction and continuing to maintenance, and disposal, when appropriate.

manufacturers' representative (sales rep) Person employed by a manufacturer who is responsible for providing service to businesses purchasing its products.

memo sample Sample of a fabric or wallcovering.

move management Process used to coordinate and schedule moves during and after construction activities.

observation study Qualitative research method that involves watching, recording, and analyzing users of a space and their activities.

open account Financial arrangement enables a designer to order and receive items, and pay the vendor within a designated period.

open-ended survey Data collection technique using a blank space for subjects to write a response; similar to a short-answer essay.

packing list Document itemizing what is in a shipped container.

programming phase Initial stage in the design process that involves gathering and collecting information.

punch list Document used at the end of construction to inventory items that must be completed or corrected.

qualitative research Research methodology involving using non-numerical data to identify meanings and interpretations.

quantitative research Research methodology involving numbers and statistical analyses of data.

redline plan Building inspection term used to identify suggested revisions to construction drawings and specifications.

refereed journal Publications using formal research methodologies and have professionals review articles to evaluate the appropriateness of the processes used to determine the results and conclusions.

request for comments (RFCs) Document asking an entity to provide a response to a fact, condition, or event.

schematic design phase Stage in the design process after the programming phase involving the initial creation of concepts and sketches.

semi-structured interview Research methodology using a combination of specific items and questions that may be tailored to a specific person.

showroom manager Person responsible for overseeing the operations of a manufacturer's exhibition facilities.

structured interview Research methodology using the same items for each participant.

subcontractor Individual hired to perform specialized services for a construction project, such as installing flooring, electrical systems, and plumbing.

subject Participant in a research study.

survey Data collection technique using a standardized list of items.

tearsheet Single sheet containing details of a manufacturers' product, including prices.

territory sales representative Person employed by a manufacturer who is responsible for providing service to the businesses purchasing its products within a specific geographical area.

triangulation Research methodology term that references using multiple research types for one study.

unstructured interview Research methodology enabling the interviewer the flexibility to change questions as an interview progresses.

upcharge Increase in a manufacturers' price due to a unique specification, such as using certain finishes.

walk-through Last major task in the contract administration phase: walking through the space with the contractor for the purpose of identifying any problems, such as missing or unfinished items.

white paper Professional reports focusing on a specific issue.

Chapter 10

accounts payable Amount owed to a creditor.

accounts receivable Amount owed to a business from clients.

advertising Placing announcements and messages in mass media for the purpose of trying to persuade a targeted market.

AIO (attitudes, interests, and opinions) Characteristics of clients that are used to understand the profile of a targeted market.

articles of incorporation Legal document that can include the purpose of a corporation, authorized shares, estimated gross amount of business for a given year, and the names of directors.

articles of organization Legal document used with a limited liability company (LLC); it can include the location of the business, the purpose for organizing the LLC, and names and addresses of managers and members.

asset Tangible item that is valuable to a business, such as furniture, equipment, computers, and merchandise.

balance sheet Accounting document that illustrates the assets, liabilities, and owner's equity (net worth) of a business for a given period.

benchmark Standard that can be used for comparison purposes.

brand A specific image associated with a person, product, service, or business.

break-even analysis Point at which a businesses' expenses and income are equal: no profits or losses.

brick-and-mortar business Business that is operated in a building.

business interruption/continuation insurance Type of insurance that covers expenses when a business must stop operations because of some specified condition in the policy, such as an earthquake or flooding.

business plan Professional document describing the major considerations associated with starting or expanding a business, such as a defining the business, determining the market, managing the business, and understanding the financials.

business profile Synopsis of the key characteristics of a business.

C corporation Based on the Internal Revenue Service (IRS) regulations, a business that is taxed as a corporation.

cash flow forecast Analysis used to project how other income sources as well as irregular expenses can affect a business on a monthly basis.

certified public accountant (CPA) Accredited accounting professional.

commercial general liability (CGL) insurance Type of insurance whereby the owner is protected if someone is injured at their place of business.

commercial property insurance Type of insurance protecting the assets of a business in the event of loss and damages due to a certain situation that is prescribed in the policy, such as vandalism, fires, high winds, and smoke.

covenant Restrictions imposed by homeowners associations.

current asset (liquid asset) Tangible item that is easily accessed, such as cash, money in savings accounts, and checking accounts.

current liability Amounts owed by a business, such as accounts payable and payroll, which must be paid within a short period.

deductible Amount an owner must pay when collecting on an insurance policy.

demographics Characteristics of a targeted market; typically includes age, gender, employment, income, and education.

depreciable asset Tangible item that decreases in value over time, such as computers and equipment.

disability insurance Type of insurance providing assistance in the event of a physical or mental condition.

Doing Business As (DBA) Term used for a business that does not use a personal name.

domain name Web address.

double tax A condition requiring a corporation to pay an additional tax.

due diligence Process of researching local zoning ordinances as well as any restrictions or covenants prescribed by homeowners associations.

Employer Identification Number (EIN) Number used by the IRS to identify a business entity.

entrepreneur Person who plans and manages a business endeavor.

escalation Term used in a lease that refers to increases in rent.

executive summary Synopsis of a report; located at the beginning of the document.

expenses Costs associated with conducting business, such as rent, travel, and utilities.

fixed asset (long-term asset) Items of value, but typically are associated with business operations, such as a building, office furniture, and equipment.

fixed cost (overhead) Business expenses that do not vary month-by-month, such as rent and insurance.

Four P's (marketing mix) Marketing strategies that focus on product, price, promotion, and place (distribution).

general market Potential clients for a design firm's services.

general partnership Ownership of a business that involves more than one person.

gross income (gross profit) The amount derived from subtracting the variable costs from the sales revenue (Sales – Variable costs = Gross profit).

gross profit (gross income) The amount derived from subtracting the variable costs from the sales revenue (Sales – Variable costs = Gross profit).

home-based business insurance Type of insurance covering a business located in a residence.

income statement (profit and loss [P&L] statement) Summary of monthly sales, cost of sales, gross profits, fixed expenses, and net profit.

insurance agent Person representing a business owner when searching for insurance policies.

insurance broker Person who is a representative from an insurance company or companies and should have a license issued by the state.

inventory Merchandise owned by a business.

key person insurance Type of insurance providing money to conduct business operations while a remaining owner attempts to hire a replacement of a founder and/or determine the fate of the business.

liability Responsibilities associated with debts, actions, and decisions associated with a business.

limited liability company (LLC) Business structure combining elements of a corporation with a partnership.

limited partnership Ownership of a business that includes a partner who is an investor of the business.

liquid asset (current asset) Tangible item that is easily accessed, such as cash, money in savings accounts, and checking accounts.

loan Money lent that must be repaid within a specific period of time.

long-term asset (fixed asset) Items of value, but typically are associated with business operations, such as a building, office furniture, and equipment.

long-term liability Business debts not due for an extended period, such as a mortgage.

market positioning Client's perception of businesses' products and services.

marketing An "organizational function and a set of processes for creating, communicating, and delivering value to customers and for managing customer relationships in ways that benefit the organization and its stakeholders" (American Marketing Association 2011).

marketing mix (Four P's) Marketing strategies that focus on product, price, promotion, and place (distribution).

mission statement Succinct statement that reflects the essence of a business.

municipal code City and county zoning ordinances stipulating land use and building practices.

net income (net profit) Amount calculated by subtracting the gross profit from a businesses' fixed costs (Gross profit – Fixed costs = Net profit).

net profit (net income) Amount calculated by subtracting the gross profit from a businesses' fixed costs (Gross profit − Fixed costs = Net profit).

net worth (owner's equity) Amount provided by a business owner, such as invested capital and retained earnings.

non-compete clause Agreement stipulating that a seller will not establish a business that could compete with the buyer's business.

non-owned vehicle liability insurance Type of insurance used by a business with employees who use their own car for business purposes.

overhead (fixed cost) Business expenses that do not vary month-by-month, such as rent and insurance.

owner's equity (net worth) Amount provided by a business owner, such as invested capital and retained earnings.

pass-through taxation Based on the rules of the IRS (Internal Revenue Service), profits or losses that are reported on personal income tax returns.

premium Payments for insurance policies.

product liability insurance Type of insurance covering the responsibility of a manufacturer or a seller of a product to provide items that are safe and free of defects.

professional liability insurance (errors and omissions) Type of insurance that can help to protect a designer from potential negligence claims.

profit and loss (P&L) statement (income statement) Summary of monthly sales, cost of sales, gross profits, fixed expenses, and net profit.

public relations Communications method used to enhance peoples' perceptions of a business.

psychographics Characteristics of people associated with lifestyles, behavioral patterns, and AIO (attitudes, interests, and opinions).

revenues Money a business receives for services and products.

rider Additional coverage on an insurance policy.

S corporation According to the IRS, entities "that elect to pass corporate income, losses, deductions and credit through to their shareholders for federal tax purposes" (IRS 2011).

search engine Website that collects and organizes items posted on the Internet.

seller's permit State certificate enabling a business to collect state and local taxes for merchandise sold to consumers.

shareholder Owner of stock in a corporation.

special use permit (zoning variance) Certificate issued by a zoning board enabling a business to operate in an area not zoned for the business.

start-up cost Initial amount required to begin a business.

stock offering Initial issuance of a corporation's stock.

stock option Benefit allowing an employee to purchase stock in his or her employer's business.

target market Potential clients interested in a specific service provided by a design firm.

tax registration certificate Document issued by a state's department of revenue enabling a business to operate and collect taxes.

unemployment insurance Business insurance required by state and federal laws that provides assistance to an employee in the event that the person is terminated.

variable cost Amounts associated with the cost of a sale, such as fees paid for a consultant on a project.

virtual business Operation of a business electronically.

web host Service enabling a business to operate a website.

workers' compensation insurance Business insurance required by state and federal laws that provides assistance to an employee in the event that the person is injured at the worksite.

zoning ordinance Local and county laws regulating building codes as well as property usages.

zoning variance (special use permit) Certificate issued by a zoning board enabling a business to operate in an area not zoned for the business.

Chapter 11

e-cycle Recycling of electronic equipment, such as computers, cell phones, monitors, and printers.

greenhouse gas (GHG) Gases that cause heat to be trapped in Earth's atmosphere and consequently increase the temperature of the planet.

greenwashing Deceptive claim that a product or service is green.

postconsumer Fibers and materials obtained from users' waste.

Processed Chlorine Free (PCF) Product made without the chlorine chemical.

Chapter 12

accountant Professional responsible for managing financial records.

accrual accounting method Accounting method whereby revenues and expenses are immediately recorded.

action plan Detailed record of activities, including timelines, resources, and the people responsible for implementing the tasks.

bookkeeper Individual responsible for recording financial transactions.

calendar accounting period Financial record-keeping time period using the calendar.

cash accounting method Accounting method whereby revenues are recorded when a business actually receives the cash and expenses are recorded when the bill is paid.

chart of accounts List of ledger account names and numbers.

collateral Tangible item used to secure a loan.

debt-equity ratio Total amount a business owes (liabilities) compared to what it totally owns (owner's equity).

debt financing Loan from a financial institution with the promise of repaying the money.

double-entry accounting system Accounting system using increases and decreases to balance two entries.

drawings Accounting term whereby a business owner takes cash withdrawals for personal uses.

D-U-N-S number Business credit classification system.

equity financing Method used to acquire funds by selling investors a percentage of ownership.

fiscal year accounting period Financial record-keeping time period using 12 months, but the ending date is not December 31. A common beginning date is July 1 and the ending date is June 30.

journal Book used to record transactions.

ledger Book with a collection of accounts.

line of credit Loan method whereby a specified amount of cash is available in a bank account for withdrawals on an as-needed basis. Interest is charged only for the amount borrowed.

net loss Amount occuring when business expenses exceed revenues.

notes payable Document specifying the amount of money someone owes a party by a specific date.

objective Specific directives for accomplishing a task that include how achievement is quantitatively measured.

posted Transactions from a journal transferred into ledger accounts.

promissory note Document for loans.

single-entry accounting system Accounting system whereby transactions are entered in only one record.

secured loan Loan that requires the borrower to provide collateral, such as a building or equipment (often required for long-term loans).

source document Documents initiating accounting transactions, such as purchase orders, sales receipts, check stubs, or invoices.

strategic plan Internal management document used to (1) assess the business' current situation, (2) determine the vision and direction of the business, and (3) identify the best approaches to successfully reach its goals.

strategy Means for accomplishing objectives with an emphasis on maximizing competitive advantages and overcoming challenges.

T-account Accounting term that depicts debit and credit entries to an account.

tactic Basic list of what must be done to accomplish a strategy.

transaction Accounting occurrence, such as paying rent, that affect the business' financial situation.

trial balance Accounting process used to verify the accuracy of ledger accounts.

unsecured loan Short-term loan without collateral that is basically granted because of a business owner's creditworthiness.

vision statement Declaration describing the highest future expectations for a business.

Chapter 13

brochure Small pamphlet a designer can use to provide an overview of his or her firm, expertise, projects, and staff.

collateral materials Various types of print communication associated with public relations, such as brochures, tearsheets, postcards, newsletters, and press releases.

digital media Digitized forms, such as audio and video, that can be transmitted electronically.

direct mail Marketing materials delivered via delivery systems, such as the U.S. Postal Service.

event management Program for the purpose of organizing and controlling activities associated with public relations.

flash animation Digitized format that creates moving objects, pictures, and text.

identity package Visual marketing strategy that involves creating distinct items, such as a firm's name, logo, color, font, stationery, and business cards.

inbound link Internet term used to describe a connection from an external website.

lead-tracking Process for contacting people a designer believes may be interested in his or her design services.

media Type of public communications tool, such as television news programs, radio, newspapers, and magazines.

media relations Process of maintaining effective connections with people responsible for communicating with the public via television news programs, radio, newspapers, and magazines.

microblogging Broadcasting medium used for short messages.

multimedia presentation Presentations using a variety of forms of communication, such as video clips, audio, and photographs.

newsletter Short document used to present current and upcoming events and announcements.

news release (press release) Short document prepared by a business or individual that targets one current or upcoming event and is distributed to the media for publication purposes.

office portfolio Collection of materials promoting a design firm, such as magazine articles, photographs of projects, and staff expertise.

online public relations Electronic communications method used to enhance perceptions of a business, such as blogs, forums, and social networks.

outbound link Internet term used to describe a connection to an external website.

pitch Marketing term describing the process of contacting the media for the purpose of trying to obtain publicity.

press release (news release) Short document prepared by a business or individual that targets one current or upcoming event and is distributed to the media for publication purposes.

public relations kit Collection of materials about a firm used to impress and inform the public.

reprints Copy of an article published in a magazine.

two- or three-fold brochure Pamphlet that can be folded into a standard business envelope.

Web 1.0 Term describing the practice of using the Internet to locate specific facts and information.

Web 2.0 Term describing the practice of using the Internet as an interactive tool.

Chapter 14

defined benefit (DB) plan Retirement vehicle determined by an employee's number of years of service and a percentage of his or her salary.

defined contribution (DC) plan Retirement vehicle whereby an employer annually allocates a certain amount for employees' individual accounts.

employee From the perspective of the IRS guidelines, "Generally, a worker who performs services for you is your employee if you have the right to control what will be done and how it will be done. This is so even when you give the employee freedom of action. What matters is that

you have the right to control the details of how the services are performed" (IRS 2011).

employee handbook Manual for employees that includes employment policies and practices.

employment-at-will doctrine Principle of law declaring that unless there is a written contract, employees can leave a place of employment for any or no reason and employers can terminate an employee for any or no reason.

extrinsic motivation Inspiration derived from awards, usually monetary.

federal income tax Government levies on the income of individuals and businesses. Employers must withhold federal income tax from their employees' wages.

Federal Unemployment Tax Act (FUTA) Government tax paid by employers.

fringe benefit Perk received from an employer, such as free vacations and discounts on services.

humanistic Set of beliefs based on human interests and values.

independent contractor According to the IRS, a person hired by an employer that is not defined under common law or under statues for certain situations. "Employers do not generally have to withhold or pay any taxes on payments to independent contractors" (IRS 2011).

intrinsic motivation Inspiration derived from work itself.

job analysis Process of determining what tasks need to be completed and what attributes a person should have to successfully perform the tasks.

leader Individual who can influence people to accomplish goals.

Medicare tax Government levy for healthcare. Employers must withhold part of Medicare taxes from their employees' wages and also pay an amount matching the employees' taxes.

paid time off (PTO) Personal leave with compensation provided by an employer.

self-employment tax Government levies that business owners must pay, including Social Security and Medicare taxes.

Social Security tax Government levy for retirement program. Employers must withhold part of social security taxes from their employees' wages, and must also pay an amount that matches the employees' taxes.

state income tax State levies on the income of individuals and businesses. Employers must withhold state income tax from their employees' wages when appropriate.

Bibliography

Abercrombie, S. *A Philosophy of Interior Design*. New York: Harper & Row, 1990.

Adam, R., and M. Hardy, ed. *Tradition Today: Continuity in Architecture and Society*. Boston: WIT Press, 2008.

Adams, D. M., and E. W. Maines. *Business Ethics for the 21st Century*. London: Mayfield Publishing Company, 1998.

Albee, A. *eMarketing Strategies for the Complex Sale*. New York: McGraw-Hill, 2010.

Albion, M. *More Than Money*. San Francisco: Berrett-Koehler Publishers, 2009.

Alderman, R. L. *How to Prosper as an Interior Designer: A Business and Legal Guide*. New York: John Wiley & Sons, 1997.

Al-Omari, J. *The Arab Way*. Oxford, UK: Howtobooks, 2005.

Andersen, E. *Being Strategic: Plan for Success; Out-think Your Competitors; Stay Ahead of Change*. New York: St. Martin's Press, 2009.

Anderzhon, J. W., I. L. Fraley, and M. Green. *Design for Aging Post-Occupancy Evaluations*. New York: John Wiley & Sons, 2007.

Anumba, C. J., C. O. Egbu, and P. M. Carrillo. *Knowledge Management in Construction*. Oxford, UK: Blackwell Publishing, 2005.

Arestis, P., R. Sobreira, and J. L. Oreiro, eds. *An Assessment of the Global Impact of the Financial Crisis*. New York: Palgrave Macmillan, 2011.

———. *The Financial Crisis: Origins and Implications*. New York: Palgrave Macmillan, 2011.

Asala, T., and K. Ozeki. *Handbook of Quality Tools*. Cambridge, MA: Productivity Press, 1990.

Asante, M. K., E. Newmark, and C. A. Blake. *Handbook of Intercultural Communication*. London; Sage Publications, 1979.

Asay, N., and M. Patton. *Careers in Interior Design*. New York: Fairchild Books, 2010.

Atkinson, T. D. *Merriam-Webster's Guide to International Business Communications*. Springfield, MA: Merriam-Webster, 1998.

Austin, J. E., and F. Hesselbein. *Meeting the Collaboration Challenge*. New York: The Drucker Foundation, 2002.

Band, W. A. *Creating Value for Customers*. New York: John Wiley & Sons, 1991.

Barnes, J. G. *Build Your Customer Strategy: A Guide to Creating Profitable Customer Relationships*. New York: John Wiley & Sons, 2006.

Barney, J. B. *Gaining and Sustaining Competitive Advantage*. New York: Prentice Hall, 2011.

Barth, J. R. *The Rise and Fall of the U.S. Mortgage and Credit Markets*. New York: John Wiley & Sons, 2009.

Bateman, T. S., and S. A. Snell. *Management: Leading & Collaborating in a Competitive World*. New York: McGraw-Hill, 2009.

Beard, J. L., M. C. Loulakis, and E. C. Wundram. *Design-Build*. New York: McGraw-Hill, 2001.

Becker, L., and C. Becker. 2001. *Encyclopedia of Ethics*. New York: Routledge.

Belk, R. W., ed. *Handbook of Qualitative Research Methods in Marketing*. Cheltenham, UK: Edward Elgar, 2006.

Bell, B., ed. *Good Deeds, Good Design: Community Service through Architecture*. New York: Princeton Architectural Press, 2004.

Bender, M. B. *A Manager's Guide to Project Management*. Upper Saddle River, NJ: Pearson Educational, 2010.

Benko, C., and A. Weisberg. *Mass Career Customization*. Boston: Harvard Business School Press, 2007.

Bennis, W., and B. Nanus. *Leaders*. New York: Harper & Row, 1985.

Berger, C. J. *Interior Design Law and Business Practices*. New York: John Wiley & Sons, 1994.

Berkun, S. *The Art of Project Management*. Sebastopol, CA: O'Reilly, 2005.

Best, K. *Design Management: Managing Design Strategy, Process and Implementation*. Lausanne, Switzerland: AVA Academia, 2006.

Blacharski, D. *The Savvy Business Traveler's Guide to Customs and Practices in Other Countries*. Ocala, FL: Atlantic Publishing Group, 2008.

Borg, W. R., and M. D. Gall. *Educational Research: An Introduction*. New York: Longman, 1983.

Bosrock, M. M. *Asian Business Customs & Manners*. New York: Meadowbrook Press, 2006.

———. *European Business Customs & Manners*. New York: Meadowbrook Press, 2006.

Botti-Salitsky, R. M. *Programming & Research Skill and Techniques for Interior Designers*. New York: Fairchild Books, 2009.

Boyer, E. "Leadership: A Clear and Vital Mission." *The College Board Review* 150 (1988–89): 6–9.

Brett, J. M. *Negotiating Globally*. 2nd ed. New York: John Wiley & Sons, 2007.

Brody, A. *Electronic Workflow for Interior Designers and Architects*. New York: Fairchild Books, 2010.

Bryan, L. L., and C. I. Joyce. *Mobilizing Minds*. New York: McGraw-Hill, 2007.

Buckley, P. J. *What Is International Business?* New York: Palgrave Macmillan, 2005.

Burnham, W. *Introduction to the Law and Legal System of the United States Fourth Edition*. St. Paul, MN: Thomson West, 2006.

Burtis, J. O., and P. D. Turman. *Group Communication Pitfalls*. Thousand Oaks, CA: Sage Publications, 2006.

Capelin, J. *Communication by Design: Marketing Professional Services*. Atlanta: Greenwood Communications, 2004.

Capon, N., D. Potter, and F. Schindler. *Managing Global Accounts*. New York: American Management Association, 2006.

Carté, P., and C. Fox. *Bridging the Culture Gap*. London: Kogan Page, 2008.

Chaney, L. H., and J. S. Martin. *The Essential Guide to Business Etiquette*. London: Praeger, 2007.

Chutani, S., J. R. Aalami, and A. Badshad. *Technology at the Margins*. New York: John Wiley & Sons, 2011.

Ciprut, J. V. *The Future of Citizenship*. Cambridge, MA: The MIT Press, 2009.

Coleman, C. *Interior Design Practice*. New York: Allworth Press, 2010.

Cooper, F. *The Customer Signs Your Paycheck.* New York: McGraw-Hill, 2010.

Cooper, G. *The Origins of Financial Crises.* New York: Vintage Books, 2008.

Crawford, T., and E. D. Bruck. *Business and Legal Forms for Interior Designers.* New York: Allworth Press, 2001.

Crenshaw, D. *The Myth of Multitasking.* San Francisco: Jossey-Bass, 2008.

Criscito, P. *E-Résumés.* 3rd ed. New York: Barron's, 2005.

Cusumano, M. A. *Staying Power.* Oxford, UK: Oxford University Press, 2010.

Dale, B. G., ed.. *Managing Quality.* 4th ed. Oxford, UK: Blackwell Publishing, 2003.

Dallago, B., and C. Guglielmetti, eds. *Local Economies and Global Competitiveness.* New York: Palgrave Macmillan, 2011.

Day, C. *Places of the Soul.* New York: Elsevier, 2004.

DeBotton, A. *The Architecture of Happiness.* New York: Pantheon Books, 2006.

DeMente, B. L. *Etiquette Guide to China.* Rutland, VT: Tuttle Publishing, 2008.

DeThomas, A. R., and S. A. Derammelaere. *Writing a Convincing Business Plan.* New York: Barron's, 2008.

Dickinson, J., and J. P. Marsden. *Informing Design.* New York: Fairchild Books, 2009.

Diran, K. M. *Doing Business in Latin America.* New York: Prentice Hall, 2009.

Doherty, N., and G. Marcelas. *The Essential Guide to Workplace Mediation and Conflict Resolution.* London: Kogan Page, 2008.

Doppelt, B. *The Power of Sustainable Thinking: How to Create a Positive Future for the Climate, the Planet, Your Organization and Your Life.* London: Earthscan, 2008.

Drucker, P. F. *Management Revised Edition.* New York: Collins, 2008.

Epping, R. C. *The 21st Century Economy.* New York: Vintage Books, 2009.

Etzel, B., and P. Thomas. *Personal Information Management.* Washington Square, NY: New York University Press, 1996.

Faimon, P. *The Designer's Guide to Business and Careers.* Cincinnati: How Books, 2009.

Farren, C. E. *Planning and Managing Interior Projects.* Kingston, MA: R. S. Means Company, 1988.

Ferraino, C. *The Complete Dictionary of Accounting and Bookkeeping Terms Explained Simply.* Ocala, FL: Atlantic Publishing Group, 2011.

Finch, B. *How to Write a Business.* 3rd ed. London: Kogan Page, 2010.

Findley, L. *Building Change: Architecture, Politics and Cultural Agency.* London: Routledge, 2005.

Fisher, T. R. *In the Scheme of Things: Alternative Thinking on the Practice of Architecture.* Minneapolis: University of Minnesota Press, 2000.

Flynn, N. *Blog Rules.* New York: American Management Association, 2006.

Friedman, G. *The Next Decade.* New York: Doubleday, 2011.

Gechev, R. *Sustainable Development: Economic Aspects.* Indianapolis: University of Indianapolis Press, 2005.

Gerzema, J., and E. Lebar. *The Brand Bubble.* San Francisco: Jossey-Bass, 2008.

Gibson, R. *Intercultural Business Communication.* Oxford, UK: Oxford University Press, 2002.

Giddens, A. *The Consequences of Modernity.* Stanford, CA: Stanford University Press, 1990.

Gillespie, R. *Manufacturing Knowledge: A History of the Hawthorne Experiments.* Cambridge, UK: Cambridge University Press, 1991.

Giroux, H. A., and G. Pollock. *The Mouse That Roared: Disney and the End of Innocence.* Lanham, MD: Rowman & Littlefield Publishers, 2010.

Gleeson, K. *The Personal Efficiency Program.* New York: John Wiley & Sons, 2000.

Goodman, A. *Winning Results with Google AdWords.* 2nd ed. New York: McGraw-Hill, 2009.

Gordon, A. *Future Savvy: Identifying Trends to Make Better Decisions, Manage Uncertainty,* and Profit from Change. New York: American Management Association, 2009.

Gordon, C. *The Business Culture in France*. Oxford, UK: Butterworth-Heinemann, 1996.

Gordon, V. N. *Career Advising*. San Francisco: Jossey-Bass, 2006.

Gordon, V. N., W. R. Habley, and T. J. Grites. *Academic Advising*. 2nd ed. San Francisco: Jossey-Bass, 2008.

Grayling, A. C. *Ideas That Matter: The Concepts that Shape the 21st Century*. New York: Basic Books, 2010.

Green, A. *Effective Personal Communication Skills for Public Relations*. London: Kogan Page, 2006.

Griffeth, R., and P. Hom, eds. *Innovative Theory and Empirical Research on Employee Turnover*. Greenwich, CT: Information Age Publishing, 2004.

Griffin. J. *Customer Loyalty: How to Earn It, How to Keep It*. New and revised ed. San Francisco: Jossey-Bass, 2002.

Grisham, T. W. *International Project Management: Leadership in Complex Environments*. New York: John Wiley & Sons, 2010.

Grootenhuis, D. A. *Practical Guide to Project Management*. New York: Writers Club Press, 2001.

Gualerzi, D. *The Coming of Age of Informational Technologies and the Path of Transformational Growth*. London: Routledge, 2010.

Guillén, M. F. *Models of Management*. Chicago: The University of Chicago Press, 1994.

Guinn, A. M. *Minding Your Own Business*. Chicago: American Bar Association, 2010.

Hall, E. T., and M. R. Hall. *Hidden Differences*. Garden City, NY: Anchor Press/Doubleday, 1969.

Hall, E. T. *Beyond Culture*. Garden City, NY: Anchor Press/Doubleday, 1976.

———. *The Dance of Life: The Other Dimension of Time*. Garden City, NY: Anchor Press/Doubleday, 1983.

———. *Handbook of Proxemic Research*. Philadelphia: Studies in the Anthropology of Visual Communication, 1973.

———. *The Hidden Dimension*. Garden City, NY: Anchor Press/Doubleday, 1969.

———. *The Silent Language*. Garden City, NY: Anchor Press/Doubleday, 1973.

Halligan. B., and D. Shah. *Inbound Marketing: Get Found Using Google, Social Media, and Blogs*. New York: John Wiley & Sons, 2010.

Harden, L., and B. Heyman. *Digital Engagement*. New York: American Management Association, 2009.

Harding, F. *Creating Rainmakers: The Manager's Guide to Training Professionals to Attract New Clients*. New York: John Wiley & Sons, 2006.

Hoffman, A. J., N. E. Parker, E. Sanchez, and J. Wallach. *Unity through Community Service Activities*. Jefferson, NC: McFarland & Company, 2009.

Hofstede, G. *Culture's Consequences: Comparing Values, Behaviors, Institutions, and Organizations across Nations*. Thousand Oaks, CA: Sage Publications, 2001.

Hoggan, J. *Do the Right Thing: PR Tips for a Skeptical Public*. Sterling, VA: Capital Books, 2009.

Hollis, N., and M. Brown. *The Global Brand: How to Create and Develop Lasting Brand Value in the World Market*. New York: Palgrave Macmillan, 2008.

Hood, J. B., B. A. Hardy, and H. S. Lewis. *Workers' Compensation and Employee Protection Laws in a Nutshell*. St. Paul, MN: Thomson West, 2005.

Howard, T. W. *Design to Thrive: Creating Social Networks and Online Communities That Last*. New York: Elsevier, 2010.

Howe, N., and W. Strauss. *Millennials Go to College: Strategies for a New Generation on Campus*. Great Falls, VA: LifeCourse Associates, 2007.

Hoyle, D. *ISO 9000 Quality Systems Handbook*. New York: Elsevier, 2009.

Hughey, K. F., D. B. Nelson, J. K. Damminger, and B. McCalla-Wriggins. *The Handbook of Career Advising*. San Francisco: Jossey-Bass, 2009.

Hugos, M. *Business Agility: Sustainable Prosperity in a Relentlessly Competitive World*. New York: John Wiley & Sons, 2009.

Husted, B. W., and D. B. Allen. *Corporate Social Strategy*. Cambridge, UK: Cambridge, University Press, 2011.

Imrie, R., and P. Hall. *Inclusive Design*. London: Spon Press, 2001.

Irving, S. *Nolo's Encyclopedia of Everyday Law*. Berkeley, CA: Nolo, 2008.

Jaffe. J. *Flip the Funnel: How to Use Existing Customers to Gain New Ones*. New York: John Wiley & Sons, 2010.

Janoff, B., and R. Cash-Smith. *The Graphic Designer's Guide to Better Business Writing*. New York: Allworth Press, 2007.

Jennings, J. *Globalizations and the Ancient World*. Cambridge, MA: Cambridge University Press, 2011.

John, S. *Strategic Learning and Leading Change: How Global Organizations are Reinventing HR*. New York: Elsevier, 2009.

Jue, A. L., J. A. Marr, and M. E. Kassotakis. *Social Media at Work: How Networking Tools Propel Organizational Performance*. San Francisco: Jossey-Bass, 2010.

Jukes, I., T. McCain, and L. Crockett. *Living on the Future Edge*. New York: Corwin, 2010.

Junco, R., and D. M. Timm. *Using Emerging Technologies to Enhance Student Engagement*. San Francisco: Jossey-Bass, 2008.

Kearns, P. *HR Strategy: Creating Business Strategy with Human Capital*. 2nd ed. New York: Elsevier, 2010.

Keidel, R. W. *The Geometry of Strategy: Concepts for Strategic Management*. New York: Routledge, 2010.

Kendall, G. T. *Designing Your Business: Strategies for Interior Design Professionals*. New York: Fairchild Books, 2005.

Kenna, P., and S. Lacy. *Business France*. Lincolnwood, IL: Passport Books, 1994.

Kennedy, P. *Local Lives and Global Transformations*. New York: Palgrave Macmillan, 2010.

Kenton, B., and S. Penn. *Change, Conflict and Community*. New York: Elsevier, 2009.

Kerzner, H., and F. Saladis. *What Functional Managers Need to Know about Project Management*. New York: John Wiley & Sons, Inc, 2009.

King, N., and C. Horrocks. *Interviews in Qualitative Research*. Los Angeles: Sage, 2010.

Kist, W. *The Socially Networked Classroom*. New York: Corwin, 2010.

Kliment, S. A. *Writing for Design Professionals*. New York: W. W. Norton, 2006.

Knackstedt, M. V. *Marketing and Client Relations*. New York: John Wiley & Sons, 2008.

Koren, D. *Architect's Essentials of Marketing*. New York: John Wiley & Sons, 2005.

Lainsbury, A. *Once Upon an American Dream*. Lawrence, KS: University of Press of Kansas, 2000.

Lancaster, L. C., and D. Stillman. *M-Factor: How the Millennial Generation Is Rocking the Workplace*. New York: HarperBusiness, 2010.

Langer, M. *Putting Your Small Business on the Web*. Berkeley, CA: Peachpit Press, 2000.

Larson, J. R. *In Search of Synergy*. New York: Psychology Press, 2010.

Lasker, R. D., and J. A. Guidry. *Engaging the Community in Decision Making*. Jefferson, NC: McFarland & Company, 2009.

Law, J. *A Dictionary of Accounting Fourth Edition*. Oxford, UK: Oxford University Press, 2010.

Leinwand, P., and C. Mainardi. *The Essential Advantage: How to Win with a Capabilities-Driven Strategy*. Boston: Harvard Business Review Press, 2011.

Leone, D. *How to Open and Operate a Financially Successful Interior Design Business*. Ocala, FL: Atlantic Publishing Group, 2010.

Lessons Learned. *Making Customers Matter*. Boston: Lessons Learned Series, 2010.

Lichtman, M., ed. *Understanding and Evaluating Qualitative Educational Research*. Los Angeles: Sage, 2011.

Liebowitz, J. *What They Didn't Tell You about Knowledge Management*. Lanham, MD: Scarecrow Press, 2006.

Lincoln, S. R. *Mastering Web 2.0*. London: Kogan Page, 2009.

Linton, H., L. Clary, and S. Rost. *Marketing for Architects and Designers*. New York: W. W. Norton & Co., 2005.

Lojeski, K. S., and R. R. Reilly. *Leading the Virtual Workforce: How Great Leaders Transform Organizations in the 21st Century*. New York: John Wiley & Sons, 2010.

Longo, N. V. *Why Community Matters*. Albany, NY: State University of New York Press, 2007.

Lovely, S., and A. G. Buffum. *Generations at School: Building an Age-Friendly Learning Community*. Thousand Oaks, CA: Corwin Press, 2007.

MacGregor, S. P., and T. Torres-Coronas. 2007. *Higher Creativity for Virtual Teams*. New York: Information Science Reference, 2007.

Macinnis, D. J., C. W. Park, and J. R. Priester, eds. *Handbook of Brand Relationships*. Armonk, NY: M. E. Sharpe, 2009.

Mackin, D. *The Team-Building Tool Kit*. New York: American Management Association, 2007.

Madeira, L. *QuickBooks 2009: Solutions Guide for Business Owners and Accountants*. Indianapolis: Que Publishing, 2009.

Magnus, G. *The Age of Aging: How Demographics Are Changing the Global Economy and Our World*. New York: John Wiley, 2009.

Martin, J. S., and L. H. Chaney. *Global Business Etiquette: A Guide to International Communications and Customs*. London: Praeger, 2006.

———. *Passport to Success*. London: Praeger, 2009.

Maurer, T. L., and K. Weeks. *Interior Design in Practice: Case Studies of Successful Business Models*. New York: John Wiley & Sons, 2010.

McCaly, R. *Fortify Your Sales Force: Leading and Training Exceptional Teams*. New York: Pfeiffer a Wiley Imprint, 2010.

McKean, J. *Managing Customers through Economic Cycles*. New York: John Wiley & Sons, 2010.

McKee, S. *When Growth Stalls*. San Francisco: Jossey-Bass, 2009.

McNeill, D. *The Global Architect*. London: Routledge, 2009.

Micek, D., and W. Whitlock. *Twitter Revolution*. Las Vegas: Xeno Press.

Michelli, D., & Straw, A. *Successful Networking*. New York: Barron's, 1997.

Miles, R. E., G. Miles, and C. C. Snow. *Collaborative Entrepreneurship*. Stanford, CA: Stanford Business Books, 2005.

Mizuno, S. *Management for Quality Improvement*. Cambridge, MA: Productivity Press, 1988.

Moeran, B. *The Business of Ethnography*. New York: Berg, 2005.

Moore, K., and D. Lewis. *The Origins of Globalization*. London: Routledge, 2009.

Morely, M. *The Global Corporate Brand Book*. New York: Palgrave Macmillan, 2009.

Morrison, T., and W. A. Conaway. *Kiss, Bow, or Shake Hands*. 2nd ed. Avon, MA: Adams Media, 2006.

Münchau, W. *The Meltdown Years: The Unfolding of the Global Economic Crisis*. New York: McGraw-Hill, 2010.

Munnell, A. H., and A. Sundén. *Coming Up Short: The Challenge of 401(k) Plans*. Washington, DC: Brookings Institution Press, 2004.

Myers, D. R. *The Graphic Designer's Guide to Portfolio Design*. New York: John Wiley & Sons, 2005.

Nabli, M. K., ed. *The Great Recession and Developing Countries*. Washington, DC: The World Bank, 2011.

Nelson, C. *TQM and ISO 9000 for Architects and Designers*. New York: McGraw-Hill, 1996.

Nester, W. R. *Globalization: A Short History of the Modern World*. New York: Palgrave Macmillan, 2010.

Nichols, R. G., and L. A. Stevens. *Are You Listening?* New York: McGraw-Hill, 1957.

Nichols, R. G., and T. R. Lewis. *Listening and Speaking*. Dubuque, IA: William C. Brown Company, 1954.

Ogden, J. R., and S. Rarick, S. *The Entrepreneur's Guide to Advertising*. Santa Barbara, CA: Praeger, 2010.

Oliver, S. *Public Relations Strategy*. London: Kogan Page, 2010.

O'Sullivan, K. *Strategic Knowledge Management in Multinational Organizations*. Hershey, NY: Information Science Reference, 2008.

Owen, G. *Architecture, Ethics and Globalization*. London; Routledge, 2009.

Pakroo, P. *The Small Business Start-Up Kit*. Berkeley, CA: Nolo, 2010.

————. *The Women's Small Business Start-Up Kit: A Step-by-Step Legal Guide*. Berkeley, CA: Nolo, 2010.

Papathanassopoulos, S., ed. *Media Perspectives for the 21st Century*. London: Routledge, 2011.

Parker, G. M. *Team Players and Teamwork*. New York: John Wiley & Sons, 2008.

Payne, R. J. *Global Issues; Politics, Economics, and Culture*. New York: Pearson Longman, 2009.

Pearce, J. A., and R. B. Robinson. *Strategic Management*. 12th ed. New York: McGraw-Hill, 2011.

Pearce, L. M.,ed. *Business Plans Handbook*. Vol. 14. New York: Gale Cengage Learning, 2008.

Peet, R. *Unholy Trinity: The IMF, World Bank and WTO*. London: Zed Books, 2009.

Pelle, S. *Understanding Emerging Markets: Building Business BRIC by Brick*. London: Response Books, 2007.

Peters, T. *Thriving on Chaos: A Passion for Excellence*. New York: Wings Books, 1987.

Phillips, D., and P. Young. *Online Public Relations: A Practical Guide to Developing an Online Strategy in the World of Social Media*. 2nd ed. London: Kogan Page, 2009.

Phillips, M., and S. Rasberry. *Marketing without Advertising*. 6th ed. Berkeley, CA: Nolo, 2008.

Pigman, G. A. *The World Economic Forum*. London: Routledge, 2007.

Piotrowski, C. *Becoming and Interior Designer*. New York: John Wiley & Sons, 2004.

————. *Professional Practice for Interior Designers*. 4th ed. New York: John Wiley & Sons, 2008.

Pittenger, D. J. *Behavioral Research Design and Analysis*. New York: McGraw-Hill, 2003.

Piven, P., and B. Perkins. *Architect's Essentials of Starting a Design Firm*. New York: John Wiley & Sons, 2003.

Plumley, G. *Website Design and Development*. New York: John Wiley & Sons, 2011.

Porter, J. *Designing for the Social Web*. Berkeley, CA: New Riders, 2008.

Prather, C. *Manager's Guide to Fostering Innovation and Creativity in Teams*. New York: McGraw-Hill, 2010.

Preddy, S. *How to Market Design Consultancy Services*. Burlington, VT: Gower Publishing Company, 2004.

Pressman, A. *Fountainheadache: The Politics of Architect-Client Relations*. New York: John Wiley & Sons, 1995.

Price Waterhouse. *Doing Business in France*. New York: Price Waterhouse, 1993.

Princeton, L. *Marketing Interior Design*. New York: Allworth Press, 2009.

Ramos, A., and S. Cota. *Search Engine Marketing*. New York: McGraw-Hill, 2009.

Rath, P. M., S. Bay, R. Petrizzi, and P. Gill. *The Why of the Buy*. New York: Fairchild Books, 2008.

Reed, S. C., and C. Marienau, eds. *Linking Adults with Community: Promoting Civic Engagement through Community Based Learning*. San Francisco: Jossey-Bass, 2008.

Reis, R. A. *The World Trade Organization*. New York: Chelsea House Publishers, 2009.

Repa, B. K. *Your Rights in the Workplace*. Berkeley, CA: Nolo, 2010.

Richards, M. D. *Setting Strategic Goals and Objectives*. New York: West Publishing Company, 1986.

Ricks, D. A. *Blunders in International Business*. Oxford, UK: Blackwell Publishing, 2006.

Rosen, B. *How to Set and Achieve Goals: The Key to Successful Management*. Englewood Cliffs, NJ: Prentice-Hall, 1981.

Rosenau, M. D., and G. D. Githens. *Successful Project Management: A Step by-Step Approach with Practical Examples.* New York: John Wiley & Sons, 2005.

Russo, M. V. *Companies on a Mission.* Stanford, CA: Stanford Business Books, 2010.

Ryan, J. D., and G. P. Hiduke. *Small Business: An Entrepreneur's Business Plan.* New York: South-Western Cengage Learning, 2009.

Sabath, A. M. *International Business Etiquette: Asia & The Pacific Rim.* New York: ASJA Press, 2002.

Sadri, H. A., and M. Flammia. *Intercultural Communication: A New Approach to International Relations and Global Challenges.* New York: Continuum, 2011.

Samara, T. *The Designer's Graphic Stew.* Beverly, MA: Rockport Publishers, 2010.

Sampson, C. A. *Estimating for Interior Designers.* New York: Whitney Library of Design, 2001.

Sanvido, V., & M. Konchar. *Selecting Project Delivery System.* Fairfax, VA: The Project Delivery Institute, 2005.

Schenkler, I., and T. Herrling. *Guide to Media Relations.* Upper Saddle River, NJ: Pearson Prentice Hall, 2004.

Schneekloth, L. H., and R .G. Shibley. *Placemaking: The Art and Practice of Building Communities.* New York: John Wiley & Sons, 1995.

Schuman, S., ed. *Creating a Culture of Collaboration.* San Francisco: Jossey-Bass, 2006.

Schwartz, H. M. *States versus Markets.* New York: Palgrave Macmillan, 2010.

Scott, D. M. *The New Rules of Marketing and PR.* New York: John Wiley & Sons, 2009.

Segal, A. *Advantage: How American Innovation Can Overcome the Asian Challenge.* New York: W.W. Norton & Company, 2011.

Seley, A., and B. Holloway. *Sales 2.0.* New York: John Wiley & Sons, 2009.

Shih, C. *The Facebook Era: Tapping Online Social Networks to Market, Sell, and Innovate.* Boston: Pearson Education, 2011.

Shneiderman, B., and C. Plaisant. *Designing the User Interface.* New York: Addison-Wesley, 2010.

Siebert, H. *Rules for the Global Economy.* Princeton: Princeton University Press, 2009.

Siegel, H. *This Business of Interior Design.* New York: Whitney Library of Design, 1976.

Siegel, J. G., and J. K. Shim. *Accounting Handbook.* 5th ed. New York: Barron's, 2010.

Sinofsky, S., and M. Iansiti. *One Strategy: Organization, Planning, and Decision Making.* New York: John Wiley & Sons, 2010.

Slotkis, S. J. *Foundations of Interior Design.* New York: Fairchild Books, 2006.

Snow, D., and T. Yanovitch. *Unleashing Excellence.* New York: John Wiley & Sons, 2010.

Society for Marketing Professional Services. *Marketing Handbook for the Design and Construction Professional.* Washington, DC: BNi Publications, 2000.

Society of Design Administration. *Handbook of Forms and Letters for Design Professionals.* New York: John Wiley & Sons, 2004.

Sokolovsky, J.,ed. *The Cultural Context of Aging Third Edition.* Westport, CT: Praeger, 2009.

Solomon, C. M., and M. S. Schell. *Managing Across Cultures.* New York: McGraw-Hill, 2009.

Snow, D., and T. Yanovitch, T. *Unleashing Excellence: The Complete Guide to Ultimate Customer Service.* New York: John Wiley & Sons, 2010.

Spiro, J. *Leading Change Step-by-Step.* San Francisco: Jossey-Bass, 2011.

Spitzeck, H., M. Pirson, W. Amann, S. Khan, and E. Von Kimakowitz, eds. *Humanism in Business.* Cambridge, UK: Cambridge University Press, 2009.

Spring, J. *Globalization of Education.* London: Routledge, 2009.

Stasch. S. E. *Creating a Successful Marketing Strategy for Your Small New Business.* Santa Barbara, CA: Praeger, 2010.

Steers, R. M., C. J. Sanchez-Runde, and L. Nardon. *Management Across Cultures.* Cambridge, UK: Cambridge University Press, 2010.

Steger, M. B. *Globalisms: The Great Ideological Struggle of the Twenty-first Century*. 3rd ed. Lanham, MD: Rowman & Littlefield Publishers, 2009.

Steingold, F. S. *Legal Forms for Starting and Running a Small Business*. Berkeley, CA: Nolo, 2008.

———. *Legal Guide for Starting and Running a Small Business*. Berkeley, CA: Nolo, 2008.

Steinhilber, S. *Strategic Alliances: Three Ways to Make Them Work*. Boston: Harvard Business Press, 2008.

Stiglitz, J. E. *Making Globalization Work*. New York: W. W. Norton & Company, 2006.

Strachan, D. *Making Questions Work*. San Francisco: Jossey-Bass, 2007.

Street, J. T. *The Secrets to Succeeding in Network Marketing Offline and Online*. Ocala, FL: Atlantic Publishing Group, 2008.

STUDIOS architecture. *Interiors: Collaboration + Technology*. Victoria, Australia: The Images Publishing Group, 2009.

Stutely, R. *The Definitive Business Plan*. 2nd ed. New York: Prentice Hall, 2002.

Sutherland, J., and D. Canwell. *Key Concepts in Strategic Management*. New York: Palgrave Macmillan, 2004.

Swanson, D. L., and D. G. Fisher. *Advancing Business Ethics Education*. Charlotte, NC: Information Age Publishing, 2008.

Swanson, R. C. *The Quality Improvement Handbook*. Delray Beach, FL: St. Lucie Press, 1995.

Tague, N. R. *The Quality Toolbox*. Milwaukee, WI: ASQC Quality Press, 1995.

Tannen, D. *Gender and Discourse*. New York: Oxford University Press, 1994.

Teten, D., and S. Allen. *The Virtual Handshake*. New York: American Management Association, 2005.

Text Development Committee, ed. *Basic Manual for the Lawyer's Assistant*. 9th ed. St. Paul, MN: Thomson West, 2007.

The Financial Crisis Inquiry Commission. *The Financial Crisis Inquiry Report*. Washington, DC: The Financial Crisis Inquiry Commission, 2011.

The Results-Driven Manager. *Business Etiquette for the New Workplace*. Boston: Harvard Business School Press, 2005.

Thomas, A., and J. Applegate. *Pay Attention! How to Listen, Respond, and Profit from Customer Feedback*. New York: John Wiley & Sons, 2010.

Thompson, J. A. A. *ASID Professional Practice Manual*. New York: Whitney Library of Design, 1992.

Thompson, M., and B. Tracy. *Now, Build a Great Business*. New York: American Management Association, 2011.

Thomsett, M. C. *The Little Black Book of Project Management*. New York: American Management Association, 2010.

Tomalin, B., and M. Nicks. *The World's Business Cultures and How to Unlock Them*. London: Thorogood, 2007.

Tuller, L. W. *Doing Business Beyond America's Borders*. New York: Entrepreneur Press – McGraw-Hill, 2008.

Turk, W. *Common Sense Project Management*. Milwaukee, WI: ASQ Quality Press, 2008.

Turner, W. *How to Work with an Interior Designer*. New York: Whitney Library of Design, 1981.

VanFossen, P. J., and M. J. Berson, eds. *The Electronic Republic?* W. Lafayette, IN: Purdue University Press, 2008.

Verstappen, S. H. *Chinese Business Etiquette*. Berkeley, CA: Stone Bridge Press, 2008.

Waymon, L., and A. Baber. *Make Your Contact Count: Networking Know-How for Business and Career Success*. New York: American Management Association, 2007.

Wendleton, K. *Navigating Your Career*. Clifton, NY: The Thomson Corporation, 2006.

Wheelan, S. A. *Creating Effective Teams*. Los Angeles: Sage, 2010.

Whitmore, J. *Business Class: Etiquette Essentials for Success at Work*. New York: St. Martin's Press, 2005.

Williams, T. L. *Interior Design Clients: The Designer's Guide to Building and Keeping a Great Clientele*. New York: Allworth Press, 2010.

Williams, T. S. *The Interior Designer's Guide to Pricing, Estimating, and Budgeting*. 2nd ed. New York: Allworth Press, 2010.

Wilshusen, F. D., ed. *Construction Checklists: A Guide to Frequently Encountered Construction Issues*. Chicago: Illinois Bar Association, 2008.

Woelfel, C. J. *Accounting, Budgeting, and Finance: A Reference for Managers*. New York: American Management Association, 1990.

Wolf, M. *Fixing Global Finance*. Baltimore: The Johns Hopkins University Press, 2008.

World Trade Organization. *Annual Report 2008*. Geneva: World Trade Organization, 2008.

Wray, D. L. *Take Control with Your 401(k): An Employee's Guide to Maximizing Your Investments*. Chicago: Dearborn Trade Publishing, 2002.

Wren, D. A. *The Evolution of Management Thought*. New York: John Wiley & Sons, 1987.

Zandi, M. *Financial Shock*. Upper Saddle River, NJ: Pearson Education, 2009.

Zeigler, K. *Organizing for Success*. New York: McGraw-Hill, 2005.

Zelinski, E. J. *Real Success without a Real Job*. Berkeley, CA: Ten Speed Press, 2007.

Zoltners, A. A., P. Sinha., and S. E. Lorimer. *Building a Winning Sales Force*. New York: American Management Association, 2009.

Image Credits

Chapter 1
1.1 Robert Day/New Yorker Magazine
1.2 Architecture for Humanity/
     Designer: Alison McCabe
1.6a Habitat for Humanity
1.6b Habitat for Humanity
1.7 © Zhang Jun/Xinhua Press/Corbis

Chapter 2
2.1 Johnson Controls
2.2 © Adam Krause
2.3 © John Miles/Getty

Chapter 3
3.2b © Condé Nast
3.3 © Joung-youn Park
3.4a © Iraissal Marrero
3.4b © Iraissal Marrero
3.6 Habitat for Humanity

Chapter 4
4.2 © Christopher Grabowski
4.3 Steve Hall © Hedrich Blessing

4.4 Southface
4.5 © rendyhimawan.com
4.6 © HO Market Wire Photos/Newscom

Chapter 5
5.1 © Lionel Cironneau/ASSOCIATED PRESS
5.4 © Purestock/Getty
5.5 © Iain Masterton / Alamy
5.6 © Payless Images, Inc. / Alamy

Chapter 6
6.1 © Gayle Babcock/Architectural
     Imageworks, LLC
6.3 Allsteel
6.4 © Getty
6.5 © Radius Images / Alamy
6.7 © Peter Geschwill / Alamy

Chapter 7
7.2 © 2Define Architecture
7.5 © Somos Images / Alamy
7.7 © Paul Doyle / Alamy

Chapter 8

8.1 Wight & Company

8.3 © Simon Feneley

8.6 © Nic Lehoux

Chapter 9

9.1 © Mark Ballogg

9.2 Southcentral Foundation

9.3 DesignIntelligence

9.4 © Farshid Assassi

9.5 © MarianneWie.net

9.6 © Steelcase

9.8 © Karl Johaentges/ageFotostock

Chapter 10

10.1 © Sam Fentress

10.2 © John Scratchley

10.3 © Beau Lark/Corbis

10.4 © Christian Richters / VIEW

10.6 © Tim Griffith

Chapter 11

11.1 Steve Hall © Hedrich Blessing

11.2 © Tom Bonaventure/Getty

Chapter 12

12.2 Intuit

Chapter 13

13.1 © Michael Weber

13.2 © Philip Durrant

13.3a Specto Design

13.3b Specto Design

13.4 Archimation

13.5 © Sandy Felsenthal/CORBIS

13.6 Contract Magazine

Chapter 14

14.1 © Science Photo Library / Alamy

14.2 © Tony Watson / Alamy

14.3 SAS

14.4 © Benjamin Benschneider

Index

Arcturis, 331f
arrow diagram, 247b
articles, as public relations tool, 419–20, 419f
articles of organization, 348
as-built drawings, 293
ASEAN (Association of Southeast Asian Nations), 131–32b, 191
ASHRAE (American Society of Heating, Refrigerating, and Air Conditioning Engineers), 14
ASID. *See* American Society for Interior Designers
asset accounts, 381
assets inventory, 351
Association of Southeast Asian Nations (ASEAN), 131–32b, 191
asynchronous communication, 116
attitudes, 137–39, 140t, 161
attitudes, interests, and opinions (AIO), 343, 407
attorneys
    contract reviews, 219–20
    international business protocols, 158
Australian Forest Certification Scheme, 374
avoidance treatment of risk, 267
awards, industry, 342, 342f
AWF (Architects Without Frontiers), 11, 101
Azure magazine, 285, 298

B
Baby Boomers, 203, 204–6t
background searches, 439
back orders, 179
balance sheets
    accounting software features, 384
    in business plan, 357–58, 357t
    purpose of, 382
Baldwin, Benjamin, 63, 64–65f
bank credit lines, 385–86
Barkow Leibinger, 342f
Bella Bella Community School, 104f
benchmarks, in financial data, 353
benefits
    compensation and, 41–42, 434–36
    fringe, 431
    maternity, 143
Berne Convention (1886), 191
Beverly Hills Supper Club fire, 105b
bidder sessions, 270
bidding procedures, 269–70, 309–14
bids, 270
Big Brothers Big Sisters, 9–10b
billable hours, 167
billing, 180
Bill & Melinda Gates Foundation Headquarters, 446f

bill of lading, 317
Biz Trade Shows, 298
BJC HealthCare buildings, 331f
blogs
    in brand communications, 417
    employee handbook policies, 442b, 443
    netiquette, 124
Blueprint magazine, 285
bookkeepers, 379
Boomer Generation, 203, 204–6t
Bosnia-Herzegovina, 43–44b, 45f
bottom-up estimates, 257
BP oil spill crisis, 418
brainstorming sessions
    etiquette, 120–21
    in risk identification, 266–67
brand communications, 147–50, 148t, 412–17
brand design services, 406, 406f
brand development, 374, 408–11
BrandDynamics Pyramid, 409, 412
branding consultants, 39
branding services, 406, 406f
brand loyalty, 409
breach of contract, 191
breach of duty, 185
break-even analysis, 353–54
BREEAM (Building Research Establishment Environmental Assessment Method), 135
Bretton Woods Agreement, 130–32b
BRICs (Brazil, Russia, India, and China), 50
brochures, 412
budgets
    in design development, 307
    determining, 258–60, 259t
    in programming phase, 295
    project cost control, 260–61
Building Research Establishment Environmental Assessment Method (BREEAM), 135
buildings
    commercial, 369, 369b
    specialized, 37b
    sustainable, 364–68
built environment
    in brand development, 410
    green certification, 135
    in programming phase, 293–94
business, defined, 326
business, virtual, 335–36
business cards, 73, 121, 151
business communications. *See also* communications plan; promotions
    digital, 413–17, 419
    direction and goals, 400
    etiquette, 119–24
    green, 372, 374
    intercultural. *See* communication styles, intercultural

interpersonal, 210–19
nonverbal, 147–50, 148t, 211, 213
project communications plan, 261–62
verbal, 120–21
in virtual teamwork, 116
written, 121–22, 123b
businesses, legal requirements, 348–50. *See also* laws, international; laws, U.S.
businesses, purchasing, 328–30
businesses, small, 330–31, 406–7. *See also* Small Business Administration
business ethics, 104–8
business etiquette. *See* etiquette, business
business financing, 385–86
business gifts, 157t, 160–61, 160f
business insurance, 350–52
business management. *See also* strategic management plans
    accounting. *See* accounting, general
    bidding procedures, 269–70, 309–14
    business insurance, 350–51
    business plans. *See* business plans
    business structures, 345–48
    contract administration. *See* contract administration
    contract documents. *See* contract documents
    design development, 301–3t, 304–8
    human resources management. *See* human resources management
    international. *See* international business practices
    legal requirements, 348–50
    post-occupancy, 318–20
    predesign. *See* predesign phase
    procurement, 268–71, 310–14, 316
    programming, 287–89t, 290–95, 300
    schematic design. *See* schematic design phase
business management, green, 363–74
    conserving resources, 367–68
    marketing and communications, 372–75
    minimizing waste, 371–72
    overview, 364
    supply chain, 368–71
    sustainable buildings, 364–68
business names, 348–49, 348f, 410
business plans, 332–58
    business description, 333–40, 337b

D

data analysis, 294
Davis-Bacon and Related Acts (DBRA), 426
Days Inn, 185–87, 186b
D&B, 342, 385
DBA (Doing Business As), 349
DBB (Design-Bid-Build) project delivery, 244
DB (defined benefit) plans, 435–36
DB (Design-Build) project delivery, 244
DBRA (Davis-Bacon and Related Acts), 426
DC (defined contribution) plans, 435–36
debits
    in client billing, 180
    in double-entry accounting, 380, 380f
debt–equity ratio, 386
debt financing, 385
decision making process
    effect on fees, 173
    international business protocols, 156–58, 157t
    in project communications plans, 262
defined benefit (DB) plans, 435–36
defined contribution (DC) plans, 435–36
deliverables
    programming phase, 290, 294
    schematic design phase, 304
    work breakdown schedule, 250
delivery methods, 177, 243–45, 244f, 317
Deming, W. Edwards
    leadership theories, 443, 444–45b, 446–47
    total quality management, 246
demographics, client, 201, 203, 204–6t
deposits, 170
depreciable assets, 358
Design-Bid-Build (DBB) project delivery, 244
DesignBuild-Network (trade publication), 285
Design Build Product & Services e-Market Express, 373
Design-Build (DB) project delivery, 244
design centers, 296
design concept, 295–96
design development, 301–3t, 304–8
design firms, 28–32, 46–49, 328
DesignIntelligence (trade publication), 285, 285f
design knowledge, assessing, 393–94
design objectives, 290

design portfolios, 73–75, 74f, 83–84. *See also* career portfolios
Design Quality Indicator (DQI), 248, 249b, 249f
Design Research News, 51
dialogue, with clients, 199, 211
Diavolo chair, 115f
digital communications, 413–17
digital design portfolios, 75, 83
digital media, 413–17
dining etiquette, 88, 118, 158–60
direct communication styles, 158
direct mail, 412
direct personnel expense (DPE), 171–72
disabilities, 436. *See also* Americans with Disabilities Act
disaster recovery search tool (D&B), 342
discounts, manufacturer, 174–75
discounts, trade, 175
discrimination, caste, 143
discrimination laws, 428–29, 439
Dockside Green, 336f
Doing Business As (DBA), 349
DOL. *See* U.S. Department of Labor (DOL)
domain names, 335, 415
double-entry accounting systems, 380, 380f
double tax, 347
DPE (direct personnel expense), 171–72
DQI (Design Quality Indicator), 248, 249b, 249f
drawings
    as-built, 293
    in brand development, 409–10
    in design development, 304
dress
    in intercultural communication, 149–50, 149f
    in job interviews, 86–87
drop-shipping, 177
Dunn & Bradstreet (D&B), 342, 385
D-U-N-S numbers, 385
dye lot variances, 179, 180f

E

earned value (EV), 260, 260t
earned value management system (EVMS), 260, 260t
EBD. *See* evidence-based design
Ecolabel Index, 374
economic analysis, 305–6, 306f
economy
    career strategies and, 32
    global, 48–51
    recession, 50f
e-cycling, 372
editors, relationships with, 419

EDRA (Environmental Design Research Association), 14
education
    career options, 39
    cultural values, 143–44
    strategic management planning, 394–95
Edward Cullinan Architects, 249b, 249f
EEOC (Equal Employment Opportunity Commission), 428
egalitarian orientations, 141
electronic payments, 384
electronic signatures, 190
Electronic Signatures in Global and National Commerce Act (2000), 190
electronic whiteboards, 117
elevator pitch, 337
Ellerbe Becket, 280b
email netiquette, 122–23
employee handbooks, 440–43, 442b
Employee Retirement Income Security Act (ERISA), 427
employees, hiring. *See* hiring practices
employees, vs. independent contractors, 430
Employer Identification Number, 349, 430
employment application forms, 436
employment-at-will doctrine, 436
employment statistics, 76, 77f
employment taxes, 349, 431
energy consumption, 368
ENERGY STAR, 367–68
entrepreneurs, defined, 326
entrepreneurship, 326–31, 327b
Entrepreneurship Theory and Practice (trade publication), 330
entry-level positions, attaining, 55–92. *See also* career opportunities
    benefits, 41–42, 434–36
    career management strategies, 56–57, 63–65
    career portfolios, 61–65, 64–65f
    cover letters, 71–73, 72b
    design portfolios, 73–75, 74f
    global economy awareness, 51
    job search plan, 75–82
    networking strategies, 65–66, 89
    professional profiles, 57–61, 62b, 87
    résumés, 66–71
    salaries, 39–41, 40t
    search strategies, 56f, 76–78
    self-assessment, 57, 58–59b, 60–61t, 89
environment, extended, 396
environment, external, 396–97
Environmental Design + Construction (trade publication), 285

scope of work, 29f
website as information resource, 286
gestures, 147
Giddens, Anthony, 45, 49
gift-giving, 157t, 160–61, 160f
GINA (Genetic Information Nondiscrimination Act), 428, 429f
global economics, 48–51
Global Enviro Team, 373
The Global Gender Gap Index (WEF), 144
globalization. *See also* international business practices
  career considerations, 46–51
  defined, 43
  effect on compensation, 39–40
  effect on generational differences, 202
  ethical issues, 107
  impact on design profession, 43–46, 43b, 128
goals, professional, 96–98, 97f
goods, sale of, 429–30
Google Docs, 117
gossip, 120, 121
government, career opportunities in, 32
Government Services Administration (GSA), 388, 388b, 389f
Green Building Certification Institute (GBCI), 19
green businesses. *See* business management, green
Green Business Handbook
  business purchase criteria, 368, 369
  hazardous waste management, 372
  marketing and communications plan, 372
  minimizing waste, 371
  policies and procedures, 366
  supply chain, 370
  sustainable building requirements, 367
green certification, 135, 364–66
GREENGUARD Indoor Air Quality, 370
Green Guides, 374
greenhouse gas emissions, reducing, 367–68
Green Paper on Copyright and the Challenge of Technology, 191
Green Seal standards, 369, 369b
Green Star, 135
greenwashing, 374
greetings, intercultural, 148t, 150–51
gross profit percentage, 354
gross profits, 170, 352

groups, vs. teamwork, 109
GSA (Government Services Administration), 388, 388b, 389f
GSA Workplace 20/20 Process, 388, 389f
Guides for the Use of Environmental Marketing Claims, 374
A Guide to the Project Management Body of Knowledge (PMI), 242

H

Habitat for Humanity International (HFHI), 21–22, 22f, 82f
Haiti School Initiative, 11, 11f
Hall, Edward, 146
Hall, Mildred, 146
handshakes, 149, 150, 156
HandsOn Network Corporate Council, 23
Hayward, Tony, 418
hazardous materials, 187, 188b, 372
healthcare coverage, 430–31, 435
healthcare interior designers, 20, 21b
hearing, defined, 211
Henriquez, Gregory, 101, 104f
Herman Miller, Inc., 22, 286, 390, 391b
HFHI (Habitat for Humanity International), 21–22, 22f, 82f
hierarchical organizational charts, 253, 254f
hierarchical orientations, 141
high context communication, 146–47
Himawan, Rendy, 115f
hiring practices, 433–40
  benefits, 41–42, 434–36
  bookkeepers, 379
  interview practices, 439–40
  job analyses, 434
  job descriptions, 436–39, 437–38b
  overview, 433–34
  policies, 436
  project management issues, 253
  recruitment, 439–40
  salaries, 39–41, 40t
  tax laws, 430
HOK
  news release, 414b
  profile, 201
  strategic planning, 388, 388b
  volunteer initiatives, 23
  website, 78
HOK Advance Strategies, 388, 388b
holidays, intercultural, 155
home-based businesses, 338, 352
Home Depot, 22
Homstvedt, Hallgeir, 296f
hourly fees, 166–69, 173, 220
hugging, 150
humanism, defined, 433

human resources management, 426–47. *See also* teams
  employee policies and practices, 440–43
  hiring practices. *See* hiring practices
  humanism in, 432–33
  laws, 426–30
  leadership, 443–47, 444–45b
  overview, 426
  strategic management planning, 394–95

I

ICANN (Internet Corporation for Assigned Names and Numbers), 335
ICSB (International Council for Small Business), 330
IDC (Interior Designers of Canada), 13t
IDEC (Interior Design Educators Council), 14–15
identity packages, 410–11, 411f
IDEP (Interior Design Experience Program), 19
IDP. *See* integrated design process
IEA (International Energy Agency), 135
IEQ (indoor environmental quality), 368
IFI (International Federation of Interior Architects/Designers), 13t, 14
IIDA (International Interior Design Association), 13t, 102–3b
IIDA Student Sustainable Design competition, 70f
iiSBE (International Initiative for a Sustainable Built Environment), 135
Illinois Interior Design Title Act, 185–87b
IMF (International Monetary Fund), 130b. *See also* World Bank
Immigration and Nationality Act (INA), 426, 427
inbound links, 416
income tax, 431, 432
independent contractors, vs. employees, 430
India, 143
indirect communication styles, 158
individualism, 139–40
individual retirement accounts (IRAs), 42, 435–36
indoor environmental quality (IEQ), 368
informal research, 281–82
informational interviews, 77
information management, 99

information technology policies, 441–43
informative presentations, 232
InformeDesign, 282, 283–84b
in-house designers, 32
ink, printer, 370
in marketing mix, 344
instant messaging netiquette, 123–24
insurance, business, 350–52
integrated design process (IDP)
    design development, 301–3t
    online resources, 298
    overview, 276–77
    predesign and programming activities, 277–81, 287–89t, 290
    role of dealers in, 299
    schematic design, 296, 301–3t, 303
integrated design process matrix
    contracts and post-occupancy, 311–14t
    predesign and programming, 287–89t
    schematic design and design development, 301–3t
Integrated Project Delivery (IPD), 244–45, 244f
intellectual property law, 183–84, 183f, 191
intercultural relationships. See also communication styles, intercultural
    business gifts, 157t, 160–61, 160f
    business protocol, 154–61
    gifts, 157t, 160–61, 160f
    hierarchical vs. egalitarian orientations, 141
    high context societies, 147
    human resource management, 254–55
    individualism vs. collectivism, 139–40
    marketing materials, 151
    meetings, 154–58, 157t
    monochronic vs. polychronic orientations, 141–42
    negotiations, 156–58, 157t
    overview, 138–39
    socializing, 158–60
    work/life orientations, 142–45
interdisciplinary design, 110f
interest rates, 385
interim proposals, 220
Interior Design Educators Council (IDEC), 14–15
interior designers
    defined, 4–5
    in-house, 32
    profiles of, 200–201
    profile survey, 341b, 342
interior designers, responsibilities, 95–126
    collaboration. See collaboration

personal management strategies, 96–100
professional ethics. See ethics, professional
virtual teamwork, 114–17
Interior Designers of Canada (IDC), 13t
Interior Design Experience Program (IDEP), 19
Interior Design magazine, 285, 299, 341
interior design profession. See also career opportunities
    data resources, 341
    defining, 4–5
    external environmental analysis, 396–97
    factors affecting, 342
    globalization and, 43–46, 48–51
    history of, 5–9, 6–8t
    knowledge of, 340–41
    misconceptions about, 4, 5f
    socially conscious organizations, 11
    value of, 5–9, 9–10b
Interiors & Sources (trade publication), 285
intermediate loans, 385
internal analysis. See SWOT analysis
Internal Revenue Service, 426, 430–32, 435
International Bank for Reconstruction and Development, 130b, 132–33
international business practices, 127–63
    business protocols, 154–61
    collaboration, 129–35
    communication. See communication styles, intercultural
    cultural dimensions, 137–38
    decision making processes, 156–58, 157t
    globalization issues, 43–46, 128
    overview, 128–29
    regulations, 135–36
    relationships. See intercultural relationships
    success factors, 46
    travel logistics, 136–37, 137b
    venture research, 129, 130–32b, 133–34b
international business ventures, 129–35, 130–32b, 133–34b
International Council for Small Business (ICSB), 330
international design firms, 46–49
International Energy Agency (IEA), 135
International Federation of Interior Architects/Designers (IFI), 13t, 14

International Initiative for a Sustainable Built Environment (iiSBE), 135
International Interior Design Association (IIDA), 13t, 102–3b
International Labour Organization, 144
international laws and standards. See laws, international
International Manufacturing Centre, 248, 249b
international monetary and trade programs, 130–32b
International Monetary Fund (IMF), 130b. See also World Bank
International Organization for Standardization (ISO)
    ISO 2010, 136
    ISO 9000, 248
    ISO 14001, 364
    risk assessment, 265, 266f
International Trade Organization (ITO), 130b
Internet Corporation for Assigned Names and Numbers (ICANN), 335
Internet use policies, 440–41
Intern LC Program, 20
internship programs, 20, 82
interrelationship diagraph, 247b
interview practices, 439–40
interviews, informational, 77, 292
interviews, job, 82–90
    interviewing skills, 87–88
    negotiations, 89–90
    post-interview activities, 88–89
    preparing for, 82–87, 84–86b
    types of, 87–88
intrinsic motivation, 447
introductions, intercultural, 121, 150
inventory records, 383–84
invoices, 180, 383
IPD (Integrated Project Delivery), 244–45, 244f
IRA (individual retirement account), 42, 435–36
IRS regulations, 378
ISO 9000 Family of Standards, 248
ISO 14001 Environmental Management Systems, 364, 370
ISO 31000:2009—Risk Management—Principles and Guidelines, 265
ITO (International Trade Organization), 130b

J

James-Hatter, Becky, 9
James R. Thompson Center, 418, 418f
job analyses, 434

search engine optimization (SEO), 419
secured loans, 386
self-assessment
    for entrepreneurship, 326–28, 327b
    in entry-level job search, 57, 58–59b, 60–61t
    in evaluating potential employers, 89
self-certification, 16f, 17
self-employment tax, 349, 431
seller's permits, 349
semi-structured interviews, 292
SEO (search engine optimization), 419
SEP (Simplified Employee Pension) plans, 436
Serve America Act (2009), 20
Service Corps of Retired Executives (SCORE), 331, 332
services, 200, 202
sexual harassment, 428
Shanghai Science and Technology Museum, 348f
Shanghai Tower, 201f
share treatment of risk, 268
Shewhart cycle, 246, 247b
shipping cartons, green, 370
short-term loans, 385
showrooms, wholesale, 296–98
signatures, electronic, 190
Silent Generation, 203, 204–6t
SIMPLE (Savings Incentive Match Plan for Employees of Small Employers) IRAs, 436
Simplified Employee Pension (SEP) plans, 436
single-entry accounting systems, 380
sites, sustainable, 367
sketches, 300
Small Business Administration (SBA)
    assistance, 331, 331f, 343
    counseling, 330–31
    employee handbook template, 440, 443
    information resources, 330
    start-up loans, 353
    statistics, 328
    training, 330–31
Small Business and Entrepreneurship (SBE) Council, 330
Small Business Development Centers (SBDCs), 331
small businesses, 330–31, 406–7
"small planet" concept, 45, 49
smiling, 150
social event etiquette, 121
socializing, intercultural, 158–59
social media
    in brand communications, 416–17
    employee handbook policies, 442b, 443
social networks
    in background checks, 439
    netiquette guidelines, 124
    as recruitment tools, 439
social responsibility, 11, 445–46
Social Security tax, 431, 432
software tools
    accounting, 378, 382–84
    data analysis, 294
    life cycle cost analysis, 305, 306
    portfolio management, 243
    project management, 243, 250
sole proprietors, 28, 345–46, 346f
SOM, 437–38b
source documents, accounting, 380–81
Southcentral Health Center, 281f
Southface Energy Institute, 112f, 113–14b
specialization, 19–20, 32–37, 37b
special use permits, 338
specifications, 269
stakeholders, 109, 262, 264
Starting a Green Business program, 331
startup cost estimates, 353
Stasch, Stanley, 406–7
State Department, 136
state income tax, 431
State of Illinois Center, 418, 418f
State of Illinois Interior Design Title Act, 185–87b
status, as cultural value, 143
Steelcase, 298–99, 299f
STEP program, 17–18
storage, 317
storming (team stage), 255
Strabala, Marshall, 201f
strategic management plans, 386–400. *See also* business management
    in business profile, 407
    components, 386–87, 387f, 400
    current assessment, 388–92
    design services and, 388
    direction and goals, 397–401
    overview, 386–87, 387f
    processes, 387–88
    SWOT external environmental analysis, 392f, 396–97
    SWOT internal analysis, 392–96, 392f
strategic marketing programs, 406–11. *See also* promotions
strict liability tort, 189–90
structured interviews, 292
subcontractors, 316
substitutions, product, 299–300
suppliers, 269, 298
supply chains, green, 369–71
support teams, 253
surrounding context, observing, 293
surveys, 292
sustainability reports, 374
sustainable design
    buildings, 364–68
    Green Business Handbook, 367
    IIDA student competition, 70f
    integrated design process, 276–77
    organizations, 135
    siting, 367
    specialization areas, 37
    as standard practice, 32–33
SWOT (strengths, weaknesses, opportunities, threats) analysis
    in business profile development, 407
    in marketing program development, 407, 408
    matrix, 399t
    in risk identification, 267
    in strategic management planning, 392–97, 392f, 399t
synchronous interaction, 115

T
T-account, 380, 380f
tacit knowledge, 100
tactics, in strategic management planning, 399
targeted market, 407–8
taxes, business
    in business plan, 353
    IRS resources, 378
    QuickBooks features, 384
    types of, 349
tax laws, 430–32
tax registration certificates, 349
Taylor, Frederick, 433–34
teaming processes, 110–11, 111t
teams
    management of, 253–57
    project communications plan, 261–65, 263b
teamwork
    in collaboration, 109–10
    virtual, 114–17
    vs. groups, 109
tearsheets, 412–13
teleconferencing, 117
telephone etiquette, 120
telephone interviews, 87
telepresence, 117, 117f
tenders, 270
territory sales representatives, 298
testimonials, client, 421
text messages, 123–24, 169
thank you notes, 88, 122, 159, 216
threats, design industry, 396–97. *See also* SWOT analysis
three-point estimates, 251
tickler systems, 217–19, 218f, 297

CPSIA information can be obtained
at www.ICGtesting.com
Printed in the USA
LVOW09s2249301117

558164LV00011B/25/P

9 781609 011383